SHELDON P. ZITNER

Grinnell College

THE PRACTICE
OF MODERN
LITERARY SCHOLARSHIP

Scott, Foresman and Company

FOREWORD

This collection is intended as a text for undergraduate or graduate courses in the practice of research in literature and as a guide to the student or general reader interested in the forms recent literary scholarship has taken. It is designed to overcome the inevitable limitations of college and university libraries—many of which do not have the range of scholarly publications, and none of which has sufficient copies of any given book or periodical for classroom use. It is also designed for the instructor or student who prefers to make his own formulations and critiques of scholarly method from specific examples rather than to modify or illustrate handbook generalizations.

The selections cover the major areas of recent scholarship, but they do not exhaust it. There are too many varieties of research for a single collection to include representative selections of all. Some areas, such as the classification of medieval manuscripts, are too specialized to be of use to most beginning students. Finally, the editor must invoke as apology Dr. Johnson's phrase: "Ignorance, Madam, pure ignorance."

The essays are presented under five rubrics: *Contexts of Scholarship, The Cycle of the Work, Toward Criticism, Newer Directions,* and *Caveats.* Essays in the first category attempt to define the nature of literary scholarship and its relation to criticism, or to present guides to those general considerations of greatest importance in literary investigation, or to prescribe the form in which scholarly writing ought to be cast. *The Cycle of the Work* comprises essays on subjects that naturally attach themselves to the "career" of a work, such as the discovery and attribution of literary documents, their composition and publication or performance, and their reception and reputation. The third category, *Toward Criticism,* includes examples of research with more immediate implications for the interpretation and evaluation of literature—that is, research which borders on the province of literary criticism. Here the reader will find essays defining literary modes; discussions of literary works in their biographical, social,

Library of Congress Catalog Card No. 66-20347
Copyright © 1966 by Scott, Foresman and Company, Glenview, Illinois 60025
All rights reserved. Printed in the United States of America.
Regional offices of Scott, Foresman and Company are located in Atlanta,
Dallas, Glenview, Palo Alto, and Oakland, N.J.

and intellectual contexts; essays in literary history; and interpretive essays that depend at least as heavily on external documentation as on esthetic discrimination. In the fourth category, *Newer Directions,* significant and novel work of the last decade is represented by essays on the relevance to literary study of the new linguistics and of statistical and computer techniques. A final category, *Caveats,* brings the collection full circle with comments on imperfect scholarly procedures. These serve to define once again the relations between scholarship and criticism. Preceding the essays is an Introduction in which each selection is discussed briefly.

In arriving at the selections themselves, I have been aided by the opinions of my Grinnell colleagues, among whom Curtis Bradford, Malcolm Nelson, and John Crossett most deserve my thanks, and by the consensus of the profession as it has emerged from bibliographies, review articles, and surveys of scholarship. Yet the selections should not be thought of as a Homeric catalogue of "names," despite the illustrious scholars represented. I have tried always to keep the pedagogical aim before me, selecting essays that were both intelligible and challenging to the not-yet-specialist student and, among these, essays that suggested typical problems and relevant procedures. This aim, needless to say, led to my reluctant exclusion of many classic or definitive articles.

The selections also reveal three biases (which require explanation rather than apology) in the large number of essays on Renaissance literature, the number on textual problems, and the number—almost all, I hope—that are in some way relevant to literary criticism. It seems to me that the least eccentric literary taste is formed on the writing of the Renaissance. Shakespeare and Spenser, Milton and Donne—these are the touchstones to which, consciously or not, we refer later and earlier efforts. The tone and diction of Shakespeare, the cadences of Donne and Milton, for better or worse, preside continually in the mind. Further, the studies relating to these periods (with the possible exception of biographical studies) are our most completely articulated scholarly achievement. Hence the number of articles dealing with these periods.

Of textual studies I think it can be said that the associates of A. W. Pollard and W. W. Greg in England and, more recently, the associates and emulators of Fredson Bowers and Charlton Hinman in America have made the most distinctive contribution to literary scholarship in our time. Not only have they illuminated Elizabethan literature, but they have fostered a standard of precision supported by ingenuity that has refreshed the scholarship on all literary periods. Biblio-textual study, though it has notable antecedents,[1] is distinctively a twentieth-century mode of inquiry, in harmony with the spirit of the age, employing rather than nostalgically rejecting its tools. One need hardly add that without a concern for authentic texts we are in the ludicrous position of practicing criticism on the habits or slips of compositors and clerks. Hence the attempt to represent—though simply and imperfectly—the variety of textual and editorial problems.

---

1. See Alice Walker, "*Edward Capell* and his Edition of Shakespeare," Proceedings of the British Academy, XLVI (1962), 131-145.

Finally, there is the question of the relation of scholarship to criticism. I have made no attempt to define either term.[2] The first essay in this collection deals with some aspects of the question. The collection as a whole is a trial definition of the practice of scholarship and, by what it points to — some of the uses of scholarship — an implied definition of criticism. Thus, in making the selections, I have tried to avoid those essays, however remarkable, that are unrelated to either an understanding or an evaluation of literary works. I am not denying the "connections among all things," the "mere scholar's" "mere fact" that in a critic's hands is later warmed to give light. But it seems to me also that — reader, scholar, or critic — one first takes up one's task for the love of literature rather than of its tangents or conditions, or even of Truth. The failure to maintain something of this initial impulse results in the pedant's learned lumber and the student's disaffection. It is platitudinous to say how much scholarly publication, divorced from this impulse, deserves Shakespeare's strictures in *Love's Labour's Lost* on the pedants who "have been at a great feast of languages, and stolen the scraps."

I should record several additional debts I have incurred in the course of preparing this book. The staff of the Burling Library at Grinnell, especially Mr. Richard Ryan, has been continually helpful, as has my student assistant, Annette Gould. Perhaps my greatest debt, though, is to my students in English 417.

S.P.Z.

---

2. But see Section III of the Introduction.

CONTENTS

Introduction   viii

I. CONTEXTS OF SCHOLARSHIP

1 The Nature and Uses of Literary Scholarship
George Whalley, Scholarship and Criticism   2

2 Literary History and Literary Theory
René Wellek, Literary Theory, Criticism and History   14

3 The History of Ideas and Literary Theory
R. S. Crane, Literature, Philosophy, and the History of Ideas   27

4 Scholarship As Argument
R. B. McKerrow, Form and Matter in the Publication of Research   39

II. THE CYCLE OF THE WORK

5 The Discovery of Works and Documents
Leslie Hotson, Literary Serendipity   46

6 Authorship and Attribution
Cyrus Hoy, The Shares of Fletcher and His Collaborators
in the Beaumont and Fletcher Canon   58

7 Dating and Chronology
W. R. Parker, F. Pyle, and J. T. Shawcross
The Dating of Milton's Last Sonnet   74

8 Composition and Revision
Curtis Bradford, "The Wild Swans at Coole"   88

9 Source and Influence
Hardin Craig, Shakespeare and Wilson's *Arte of Rhetorique,*
An Inquiry into the Criteria for Determining Sources   103

10 Conditions of Publication and Problems of Editing: An Introduction

W. W. Greg, The Function of Bibliography in Literary Criticism
Illustrated in a Study of the Text of *King Lear*   113

11 Conditions of Publication and Problems of Editing: The Printing-House and the Text

Donald F. Bond, The First Printing of the *Spectator*   136

12 Conditions of Publication and Problems of Editing: The Compositor and the Text

Philip Williams, Jr., New Approaches to Textual Problems in Shakespeare   151

13 Conditions of Publication and Problems of Editing: Emendation

John Crow, Editing and Emending   161

14 Conditions of Performance

John Russell Brown, On the Acting of Shakespeare's Plays   176

15 The Audience

Alfred Harbage, The Behavior of Shakespeare's Audience   187

16 Reception and Reputation

Joseph E. Duncan, The Revival of Metaphysical Poetry, 1872–1912   202

III. TOWARD CRITICISM

17 Definition and Terminology

Harry Levin, What Is Realism?   216

18 Literature and Biography

C. K. Hyder, Wilkie Collins and *The Woman in White*   222

19 Literature and Society

L. C. Knights, Dekker, Heywood and Citizen Morality   229

20 Literature and Ideas

A. O. Lovejoy, Optimism and Romanticism   248

21 Varieties of Literary History: Continuity of Motif

Ernst Curtius, The Muses   269

22 Varieties of Literary History: Stylistic Change

Josephine Miles, Style and Change   287

23 Varieties of Scholarly Interpretation: Explication

Leo Spitzer, Explication de Texte Applied to Walt Whitman's Poem
    "Out of the Cradle Endlessly Rocking"   300

24 Varieties of Scholarly Interpretation: Historical Interpretation

Frank Kermode, The Faerie Queene, I and V   315

25 Varieties of Scholarly Interpretation: Expertise and Cruxes

Evert Sprinchorn, The Odds on Hamlet   335

IV. NEWER DIRECTIONS

26 Linguistics and Literature

Samuel R. Levin, Suprasegmentals and the Performance of Poetry   344

27 The Use of Statistical Methods

Claude S. Brinegar, Mark Twain and the Quintus Curtius Snodgrass Letters:
    A Statistical Test of Authorship   352

28 Computer Studies

Ephim G. Fogel, Electronic Computers and Elizabethan Texts   364

V. CAVEATS

29 The Unreliability of Texts

John W. Nichol, Melville's "Soiled" Fish of the Sea   380

30 The Limitations of Transcripts

Jack Stillinger, Keats's Grecian Urn and the Evidence of Transcripts   382

31 Criticism and Scholarship Once Again

Martin C. Battestin, John Crowe Ransom and *Lycidas:* A Reappraisal   385

INTRODUCTION

I

> There mark what ills the scholar's life assail
> Toil, envy, want, the patron and the jail.

   Some assessment of the differences between the present situation of
literary scholarship and Dr. Johnson's eighteenth-century estimate
of it in this excerpt from the "Vanity of Human Wishes" is probably an
appropriate introduction to a collection of essays of modern literary scholarship. In much of the West at least, the jail is less a threat than it was in
the 1740's, though some alienation of the scholar from society is a condition
for inquiry. Patronage, which in Johnson's day came from political factions
and a few individuals, has also altered for the better. There is almost no
one to whom one would now write a letter as devastating as the one in
which Dr. Johnson asked Lord Chesterfield, "Is not a patron, my lord, one
who looks with unconcern on a man struggling for life in the water, and
when he has reached ground, encumbers him with help?" Governmental
patronage, through Fulbright and other grants, is less "political" than
the eighteenth-century pension list, and the great foundations somewhat
less quixotic. Literary scholars are, in fact, becoming their own patrons
as the teaching profession regains the real-wage status of the earlier
decades of the century and as research — significant or not — is rewarded
by conditions which scholars themselves in part determine. This should
also indicate that, here at least, the Grub Street "want" of Johnson's day
is the problem of relatively few.
   Envy is perennial and there is nothing useful to say about it, save
that scholarship and criticism are now generally more civil and less lively.
The extent and nature of the "toil" is the substance of this anthology.
Certainly Johnson's preparation of his edition of Shakespeare involved
nothing as extended or precise or laborious as would the preparation of
a similar scholarly edition today. But "we ought not compare one man's
'all' with another's." Perhaps the differences lie not in the intensity of
the work but in its variety, in its tools, and in the enormous body of information on which it is expended.
   This last should not excite pride. If we know more, we have also forgotten a great deal, and what we know, we often cannot control as well.
Intimate knowledge of classical authors, an indispensable basis for under-

standing the earlier masterpieces, is second nature to a smaller proportion of scholars now than was the case in Johnson's day. In much eighteenth-century scholarship one senses an immediate relevance of scholarly detail to critical principle and of critical principle to humane sympathy. In modern scholarship one senses perhaps more often the fragmentation, specialism, and narrow sympathies that have been so much lamented that we ignore them. And if we see further into some matters than did earlier generations, it is because the old saw is correct: we stand on their shoulders.

But such considerations cannot detract from the achievements of this century. The progress in textual studies would almost alone vindicate modern literary scholarship. If specialization has its vices, it also has its virtues. The range of possibilities for investigation has never been so fully articulated. Investigation has never been so widespread or well supported. Access to materials and findings has never been so rapid or convenient. Nor has the scholarly enterprise ever been marked by greater self-consciousness, of which this anthology is minor evidence.

II

What follows is a brief commentary on the essays in this collection. The comments on individual selections are preceded by the relevant item number. In each case I have tried to describe the substance and, where it seemed important, the tone of the selection, but without providing either a précis or a critique. I have also tried to suggest additional readings and possible directions for further study, especially in materials that present emphases different from those in the selection or that illustrate the theory and practice of a single scholar. These brief lists of additional readings are not intended as even capsule bibliographies. They are, rather — as are the essays themselves — cuttings from the materials that my students have found useful.

1. George Whalley's article on "Scholarship and Criticism" attempts to define the relations between these activities with grace and learning and with considerable sympathy for both. Among the important matters Whalley treats are the evolution of literary scholarship, the dangers of viewing criticism as "a self-enclosed activity," and the difference between criticism and scholarship as expressions of human temperament. There are useful surveys of these and related questions in André Morize, *Problems and Methods of Literary Research* (1922), pp. 1-12, and in René Wellek and Austin Warren, *Theory of Literature,* third edition (1962), Chapter One, which has an accompanying bibliography.

2 and 3. René Wellek's "Literary Theory, Criticism and History" and R. S. Crane's "Literature, Philosophy, and the History of Ideas" survey much current scholarly and critical practice. Wellek warns against historicism (often the cause or result of misapplied scholarship) in criticism, and Crane against a confusion between the role of ideas in literature and their quite different role in other kinds of writing. Together these essays provide useful contexts for the discussion of literary research. There are some stimulating observations on literary history in an essay on Thomas Warton in W. P. Ker's *Collected Essays,* I (1925), 92-108, and useful discussions in Morize, Chapter Six; Wellek and Warren, Chapter

Nineteen; and R. D. Altick's admirable *Art of Literary Research* (1963), pp. 102 ff. The relations between literature and the history of ideas are notably discussed by A. O. Lovejoy in *The Great Chain of Being* (1936), Lecture I, and by Marjorie Nicholson in "The History of Literature and the History of Thought," *English Institute Annual 1939* (1940), 56-89.

4. Some commonsensical and occasionally edgy remarks on the form and style of scholarly writing make up R. B. McKerrow's "Form and Matter in the Publication of Research." McKerrow offers eleven, rather than ten, commandments, but the analogy holds in the increasing indulgence with which we now seem to greet the breaking of the seventh (McKerrow's prohibition of humor), provided it is done with discretion. The essay provides standards for judging the composition and tone of the selections which follow it. With McKerrow's remarks in mind, it is useful to compare the tone of debate in several of the selections in this volume: the exchanges between W. R. Parker and Fitzroy Pyle, and the essays in the *Caveats* section, for example. An excellent survey of the problems of scholarly writing is the eighth chapter of Richard Altick's *The Art of Literary Research,* which has numerous relevant citations. The standard work on scholarly format, the *MLA Style Sheet,* is obtainable by mail from the Modern Language Association offices in New York and at most academic bookstores.

5. Leslie Hotson's article on "Literary Serendipity" is a gathering of charming anecdotes and information relating to literary discovery. Perhaps the foremost discovery of recent times is recorded in Hotson's own *Death of Christopher Marlowe* (1925). Good advice, though now outdated on details, is to be found in J. M. Osborn's "The Search for English Literary Documents," in *English Institute Annual 1939* (1940), 31-55. R. D. Altick's *The Scholar Adventurers* (1950) presents the story of some important literary discoveries in exciting fashion. The "moral" of all these discussions is that almost no discovery is the result of luck alone. Some of the skills needed are suggested not only by Hotson and Osborn but by the tasks accomplished by the contributors to *Shakespeare's Hand in the Play of Sir Thomas More,* edited by A. W. Pollard (1923).

6. Cyrus Hoy's first article in a series that attempts to distinguish between the work of Fletcher and that of his collaborators in the group of plays bearing his name is notable both for its thesis and for the clarity with which it presents a method and its limitations. The method is to isolate "the pattern of linguistic preferences which emerges from Fletcher's unaided plays" and then proceed on the assumption that this pattern "contrasts sufficiently with the language practices in the unaided plays of Massinger [, for example,] as to afford a basis for distinguishing the work of the two dramatists. . . ." Hoy is aware of the danger of ascribing to the author patterns that result from transcription or printing house practice. It is now possible to deal more easily and precisely with some of the problems encountered by Hoy in using linguistic patterns and other "internal evidence" of authorship. As we learn more of scribal and printing practice and their effects on the transmission of texts, we can be more nearly certain of a given author's linguistic preferences. And the development of statistical and computer techniques makes it easier to avoid subjectivity and

incompleteness in the consideration of stylistic patterns. This development has led to such research as Alvar Ellegard's definitive study of the authorship of the "Junius" papers—a series of impressive eighteenth-century political essays—in *A Statistical Method for Determining Authorship* (1962); the mathematically sophisticated study of the authorship of the *Federalist Papers* by Frederick Mosteller and David Wallace, described in their articles in the *Annals of the Computation Laboratory of Harvard University,* XXXI (1961), 163-197, and in the *Journal of the American Statistical Association,* LVIII (1963), 275-309; and Peter B. Murray's study of "The Authorship of *The Revenger's Tragedy," Publications of the Bibliographical Society of America,* LVI (1962), 195-218. An example of statistical method applied to internal evidence is Claude S. Brinegar's article in the *Newer Directions* section.

The various limitations and strengths of internal evidence are interestingly discussed in a series of articles in the *Bulletin of the New York Public Library,* LXI-LXV (1957-1961), the most important of which, by Samuel Schoenbaum, appeared in 1961, pp. 102-124. The subject is treated by Schoenbaum at greater length in *Internal Evidence and Elizabethan Dramatic Authorship* (1965). The problem of attribution as a whole is treated in Giles Dawson's "Authenticity and Attribution of Written Matter," *English Institute Annual, 1942* (1943), 77-100.

I have not included an essay that deals specifically with the use of "external" evidence—letters, diaries, records of publication, to name only a few of the many varieties—but Brinegar's article cites external evidence to corroborate his stylistic analysis and in this regard is typical of the best procedure. Extensive comments on studies of attribution are to be found in Morize, Chapter Seven, and in Altick's *Art of Literary Research,* pp. 63 ff. *Shakespeare's Hand in the Play of Sir Thomas More,* edited by A. W. Pollard (1923), is a model of several mutually corroborative lines of research, and Chauncey Sanders, *An Introduction to Research in English Literary History* (1952), pp. 142 ff., 343 ff., cites many examples.

7. The exchange between William Riley Parker and Fitzroy Pyle and the more recent comment by John T. Shawcross on the date of composition of Milton's "Methought I saw my late espoused saint" exemplify both studies of chronology and dating and the nature of academic debate. Evidence is drawn from the poem itself, from the author's life, and from intellectual history; the relevance of the question of dating to the meaning of the poem and the course of the poet's development is always in view. The general subject of chronology is discussed in Morize, Chapter Six, in Altick's *Art,* pp. 41 ff., and in Sanders, Chapter Five. A classic use of internal evidence for determining chronology involves the "metrical tests" applied to dating Shakespeare's plays. A refinement of Edmond Malone's eighteenth-century studies of the subject is to be found in E. K. Chambers, *William Shakespeare,* II (1930), 397-408. Typical of the use of external evidence is John C. Hodges' article on "The Composition of Congreve's First Play," *PMLA,* LVIII (1943), 971-976, which employs a letter and statements by both the author and a contemporary to establish a probable date for the composition of *The Old Bachelor.* An interesting and, for some at least, unsettled problem in dating concerns Milton's *Samson Agonistes.* The al-

ternatives are argued in articles by Allan Gilbert and W. R. Parker in *Philological Quarterly*, XXVIII (1949), 98-106, 145-166, and there is an excellent brief discussion of the problem in Merritt Y. Hughes' edition of Milton's *Complete Poems and Major Prose* (1957), pp. 531 ff.

8. Curtis Bradford's study of the stages in the composition of Yeats' "Wild Swans at Coole" is an example of the increasing number of studies of manuscript material whose aim is the clarification of both the poet's text and his method of work. In his commentary, Bradford attempts to explain the issues involved in Yeats' revisions and to relate the composition of the poem to the larger question of the evolution of Yeats' art. Much of the labor that went into this study is not apparent. "A typical Yeats manuscript," Bradford tells us in the Preface to *Yeats at Work* (1965), XV, "appears to be a jumble, a mere heap of confusion. The paper is of various sizes, the inks of various colors," the revisions in soft pencil and faintly made, the hand almost undecipherable, the insertions sometimes difficult to place, the cancellations seldom exact. The labor of editing such manuscripts, to say nothing of the problem of obtaining access to them, is enormous. On the problem of access J. M. Osborn's article, cited above, has several useful suggestions. John Livingston Lowes' *The Road to Xanadu,* revised (1930), is the indispensable classic among studies of composition and gives an astoundingly complete account of the making of "The Ancient Mariner" and "Kubla Khan." Among other good studies of composition is Jerome Beaty's *"Middlemarch" from Notebook to Novel* (1960). Josephine W. Bennett's *The Evolution of "The Faerie Queene"* (1942) and Allan Gilbert's *On the Composition of "Paradise Lost"* (1947) are more speculative works, based heavily on internal evidence of revision and non-*seriatim* composition. General treatments of the problems involved in studies of revision are to be found in *Poets at Work* (1948), with an introduction by C. D. Abbott and essays by the psychologist Rudolph Arnheim, the critic and scholar Donald Stauffer, and poets Karl Shapiro and W. H. Auden. The first and second essays discuss the sorts of conclusions the evidence of revision may lead to. The book itself is one of the early fruits of the important collection of manuscripts by modern poets at the University of Buffalo's Lockwood Memorial Library.

9. Hardin Craig's "Shakespeare and Wilson's *Arte of Rhetorique*" is a study of Wilson's work as a possible source for passages in Shakespeare's *Timon of Athens, Much Ado About Nothing,* and other plays and a model of procedure which clearly suggests the pitfalls such studies encounter. The subtitle of the article, "An Inquiry into the Criteria for Determining Sources," is justified. The relation between source studies and studies of the process of composition is obvious, and Lowes' *Road to Xanadu,* cited above, is a classic of both kinds of inquiry. Morize, Chapters Five and Ten, and Altick, *Art,* pp. 79-102, discuss source study and its complementary concern, the study of influences. The subject is also treated in an exchange by Kenneth Muir and F. W. Bateson in *Essays in Criticism,* IV (1954), 432-440, and by Ihab H. Hassan in "The Problem of Influence in Literary History: Notes Toward a Definition," *Journal of Aesthetics and Art Criticism,* XIV (1955), 66-76. A recent longer source study is R. W. Dent's *John Webster's Borrowing* (1960), with a general introduction to the problem. The standard consideration of the sources of Shakespeare's plays is G. Bullough's projected seven-volume *Narrative and Dramatic Sources of Shakespeare* (1957-   ), which provides ample information for student analyses of the use of sources in the plays.

10. It is impossible to suggest the range and intricacy of textual and editorial problems and of the studies treating them. I have been forced to omit entirely research dealing with relations among medieval manuscripts. The student who wants to inform himself on manuscript editing in general should turn for guidance to A. E. Housman's irascible introductions to his editions of Latin poets (to the Manilius and Juvenal introductions especially) and to his "Application of Thought to Textual Criticism," conveniently gathered in *A. E. Housman: Selected Prose,* edited by J. Carter, 1961. A cryptic survey of the principles for treating classical manuscripts is to be found in the translation by B. Flower of Paul Maas' *Textual Criticism* (1958). For those interested specifically in medieval manuscripts, perhaps the best place to begin is George A. Kane's introduction to his edition of the *Piers Plowman A-text* (1960). This introduction contains a short relevant bibliography, a lucid exposition of the problems involved in relating the A-text manuscripts, and a lengthy and closely argued classification of the manuscripts themselves.

By far the best short survey of textual and bibliographic studies is Fredson Bowers' chapter in the Modern Language Association booklet *The Aims and Methods of Scholarship in Modern Languages and Literatures,* edited by James Thorpe (1963). Other standard introductory works by Bowers are *Textual and Literary Criticism* (1959) and *Bibliography and Textual Criticism* (1964); briefer than these is *The Bibliographical Way* (1959). But they should be read in conjunction with such alternative emphases as those in Geoffrey Keynes' "Religio Bibliographici," *The Library,* 5th series, VIII (1953), 63-76, and the reviews of Bowers' work by Alice Walker in *Review of English Studies,* N.S. XI (1960), 449-451, and James G. McManaway in *Shakespeare Survey,* 14 (1961), 160-161. A standard older study, still perhaps the most useful longer guide, is R. B. McKerrow's *Introduction to Bibliography for Literary Students* (1927), whose materials are brought nearly up to date and sometimes amplified in *A Student's Manual of Bibliography,* third edition (1954), by A. Esdaile and R. Stokes. James Thorpe treats "The Aesthetics of Textual Criticism" in an article in *PMLA, LXXX* (1965), 465-482.

A good way of mastering the outlines of "biblio-textual study" (the term is Bowers') is to retrace the steps of its inventors. One can begin with J. Dover Wilson's historical account, "The New Way with Shakespeare's Texts: An Introduction for Lay Readers," beginning in *Shakespeare Survey* (1954) and continuing in the later annual volumes, and then follow the yearly reviews of the field by J. G. McManaway in the annual numbers of *Shakespeare Survey.*

A conviction of the rightness of this approach has led me to include W. W. Greg's classic presentation of "The Function of Bibliography in Literary Criticism" in this collection. Much has been learned, both about bibliography and about the text of *Lear,* since Greg delivered this address at the University of Amsterdam in 1933. But his presentation is remarkably lucid and amiable. Moreover, it can form the basis of a program of self-instruction. The textual problem of what is perhaps Shakespeare's greatest play is treated in subsequent studies such as J. Q. Adams, "The Quarto of *Lear* and Shorthand," *Modern Philology*, XXXI (1933), 135-163; A. P. Van Dam, *The Text of Shakespeare's Lear* (1935); W. W. Greg, *The Variants in the First Quarto of Lear* (1940); L. Kirschbaum, *The True Test of Lear* (1945); F. Bowers, "An Examination of the Method of Proof Correction in *Lear*," *The Library*, II (1947), 20-44; Alice Walker, *Textual Problems of the First Folio* (1953); A. S. Cairncross, "The Quartos and the Folio Text of *Lear*," *Review of English Studies*, VI (1955), 252-258; and the relevant pages of Charlton Hinman, *The Printing and Proof-reading of the First Folio of Shakespeare* (1962). Also useful are the discussions in the New Cambridge and New Arden editions of the play. But an appropriate starting point is Greg's essay, with its common-sense assertion that "at bottom all problems of transmission are concerned with material factors, . . . " and that it is "in the first place through attention to the peculiarities of these, rather than through speculation as to what we fancy may have been in an author's mind, that the attack on textual problems should be made." Greg's subsequent discussion of the source and nature of the quarto text, the source and nature of Folio texts, and the relations among them presents the intricate textual problems without prejudice to alternative solutions.

11. Studies of the relation between printing house procedures and available editions are represented by Donald F. Bond's findings on "The First Printing of the *Spectator*," which should perhaps be read in conjunction with his "Text of the *Spectator*," *Studies in Bibliography*, V (1952-1953), 109-128. This is a distinguished study, with the advantage of demonstrating that printing house practice is a problem relevant to periods other than the Elizabethan, on which the bulk of investigation has been expended so far. By a close examination of variant readings in the folio sheets of the *Spectator*, Bond is able to deduce many of the circumstances surrounding their writing and publication and to unearth clues to the authorship of individual essays. For the Elizabethan period, a brief popular account of printing methods is to be found in *Shakespeare Survey*, 17 (1964), 205-213. The monumental study by Hinman of the printing of the Folio (cited above) is the foremost achievement in this field. Representative shorter articles are Hinman, "Cast-off Copy for the First Folio of Shakespeare," *Shakespeare Quarterly*, VI (1955), 257-273, and Robert K. Turner, Jr., "Printing Methods and Textual Problems in *A Midsummer Night's Dream* QI," *Studies in Bibliography*, XV (1962), 57-69.

12. In textual studies the habits of individual compositors are as important a consideration as the practice of printing houses. More than one compositor may have set type for a given work, and the habits of compositors in spelling and punctuation varied, as did their care and skill. Attention to the effects of such variations on early printed texts enables us first to identify compositors by their characteristics and then to apply this knowledge to determining what sort of copy the compositors used in setting the printed book. Through such knowledge we can sometimes distinguish reprints from their originals or determine an author's spelling from a compositor's; in short, we can sometimes go far toward stripping off the corruptions that obscure the author's intention. Compositor determination is both difficult and fascinating. Perhaps the best introductory statement on it is Alice Walker's "Compositor Determination and Other Problems in Shakespearian Texts," *Studies in Bibliography*, VII (1955), 3-15. A clear and brief illustration of typical procedures in compositor determination is found in Philip Edwards, "An Approach to the Problem of *Pericles*," *Shakespeare Survey*, 5 (1952), 25ff., especially in the Appendix (pp. 47-49), which begins with a useful bibliography on the technique. Edwards differentiates three compositors of the *Pericles* quarto on the basis of the heaviness and kind of punctuation they use, the frequency with which they employ initial capitals for nouns, and their preference for one or another of equally acceptable current spellings. Adding to Edwards' criteria, Richard Hosley suggests that Edwards' compositor *Z* had the "unusual habit of indenting speech-headings very deeply."[1] The applications of compositor determination can be as intricate as the process itself. In addition to those suggested by Hinman's study of the Folio, there are especially useful comments and examples of such applications in Alice Walker's "Some Editorial Principles (with Special Reference to *Henry V)*," *Studies in Bibliography*, VIII (1956), 95-111, and in Fredson Bowers' textual introductions to his edition of the plays of Dekker (1953-1961). The essay on the use of information about compositors that appears in this collection is "New Approaches to Textual Problems in Shakespeare" by Philip Williams, Jr. Its revision was in progress at the time of Williams' death. But even without the additions Williams had planned, the essay treats many of the varieties of deduction possible from compositor determination and applies these to many Shakespearian texts.

13.   The final essay in this group of studies dealing with textual problems is John Crow's "Editing and Emending," which proposes "to discuss, in a most elementary manner, some of the problems of the editor and emender of English texts." Crow's astringent wit and his "tentative," "sternly ultra-conservative" attitudes toward emending and editing are salutary. The clarity of his warnings about method and his explanations of specific problems make comment superfluous. Among the more extended discussions of specific cruxes are several — useful for an understanding of the issues involved in emendation — which center on two famous instances of proposed emendations in Shakespeare: Theobald's proposal of "'a babbled" in the description of Falstaff's death in *Henry V* and the proposed reading of "sullied" in the famous soliloquy in *Hamlet*. Crow deals briefly with the latter. Fredson Bowers' article "Hamlet's 'Sullied' or 'Solid' Flesh: a Bibliographical Case-History," *Shakespeare Survey*, 9 (1956), 44-48, treats it in greater detail. But this discussion should be read in conjunction with the reply by Helge Kökeritz, "This Sullied Solid Flesh," *Studia Neophilologica*, XXX (1958), 3-10. Ephim G. Fogel's "'A Table of Green Fields': A Defense of the Folio Reading," *Shakespeare Quarterly*, IX (1958), 485-492, has a good statement of the problem involved in Theo-

1. See the New Arden *Pericles*, edited by F. D. Hoeniger (1963), p. xxvii.

bald's famous emendation of *Henry V;* earlier treatments of the emendation are conveniently grouped in Gordon Ross Smith, *A Classified Shakespeare Bibliography 1936-1958* (1963), pp. 650-651.

It should be repeated that the four selections on textual and editorial problems in this collection barely suggest the variety and intricacy of modern biblio-textual study. Several other selections provide supplementary help. Bradford's study of the Yeats manuscripts of "The Wild Swans at Coole," though it deals with a modern poet, does suggest some of the problems arising from manuscript material. The essays in explication by Frank Kermode and Evert Sprinchorn suggest what sort of historical or technical studies an editor may have to perform in order to clarify the significance of a passage. E. G. Fogel's piece on electronic computers summarizes one of the newer directions of textual studies, and the notes by John W. Nichol and Jack Stillinger in the *Caveats* section state the perils of ignoring proper procedures in treating manuscripts and editions.

14. The conditions of dramatic performance are not merely of historical importance or antiquarian interest. The dramatist's medium is not language alone but the specific qualities of the actors for whom he writes and the stages on which they perform. Gesture and spectacle are part of the significance of the play. John Russell Brown's essay "On the Acting of Shakespeare's Plays" proposes a reversal of much current opinion and advocates the view "that formalism on the stage was fast dying out in Shakespeare's age, and that a new naturalism was a kindling spirit in his theatre." This position is also taken by Alan Downer in "The Tudor Actor: A Taste of His Quality," *Theatre Notebook* (1951), with which Brown's essay should be compared. Views different from those of Brown and Downer are presented in articles cited in the notes to Brown's essay and in Henry Popkin's survey of the drama in *Contemporary Literary Scholarship,* edited by L. Leary (1958), p. 313. Other aspects of dramatic performance, such as costuming and properties, staging and stage structure, have been studied in detail. Representative of the studies dealing with the Elizabethan stage are those on *Romeo and Juliet,* among them J. C. Adams, "*Romeo and Juliet* as Played on Shakespeare's Stage," *Theatre Arts,* XX (1936), 896-904, and Richard Hosley, "The Use of the Upper Stage in *Romeo and Juliet,* III, v," *Shakespeare Quarterly,* VII (1954), 145-152. Some important works on the Elizabethan stage are George F. Reynolds, *The Staging of Elizabethan Plays at the Red Bull Theatre* (1940); C. Walter Hodges, *The Globe Restored* (1953); and the articles in *Shakespeare Survey* and elsewhere by Richard Hosley. An interesting work on Elizabethan staging is Alfred Harbage's *Theatre for Shakespeare* (1955). The standard study of Elizabethan costume is M. C. Linthicum, *Costume in the Drama of Shakespeare and His Contemporaries* (1936). Perhaps the best brief introduction to all phases of Shakespeare's stage is the book with that title by A. M. Nagler, translated by Ralph Manheim (1958). It has a short reading list. More extensive lists of recent relevant material are to be found in Gordon Ross Smith (cited above), pp. 289 ff., and in the yearly bibliographies in *Shakespeare Survey.*

Theatrical history has been the subject of exhaustive research. Allardyce Nicoll's five-volume *History of English Drama,* a standard work, is strongly oriented toward theatre history. George C. D. Odell's fifteen-volume *Annals of the New York Stage* (1927-1949) presents basic materials for theatre history, as does *The London Stage 1660-1800,* being compiled by W. Van Lennep, Emmett L. Avery, George Winchester Stone, and C. B. Hogan. Once again it must be said that theatre history is of more than antiquarian interest, for it provides considerable information on changing taste and, by reconstructing the character of dramatic performances and interpretations of specific roles, adds to the variety of critical hypotheses and often affords insights into plays that the inevitable provincialism of each age might otherwise exclude.

15. One of the most distinguished studies of the theatre audience is Alfred Harbage's *Shakespeare's Audience* (1941). The essay included here is the fourth chapter of this book. It serves as a useful corrective to such earlier attacks on the supposed depravity and violence of the Elizabethan audience as Robert Bridges' "On the Influence of the Audience" in the Shakespeare-Head Press edition of *The Works of William Shakespeare* (1904-1907), but it should be read in conjunction with H. S. Bennett's *Shakespeare's Audience* (1944). Other notable studies of the dramatic audience are Clifford Leech's essay "The Caroline Audience" in *Shakespeare's Tragedies and other Essays in Seventeenth Century Drama* (1950) and H. W. Pedicord's *The Theatrical Public in the Time of Garrick* (1954). More extensively concerned with the effect of public taste on dramatic writing is J. J. Lynch's *Box, Pit and Gallery: Stage and Society in Johnson's London* (1953).

The first major study of the English literary audience is Alexandre Beljame's *Le Public et les Hommes de Lettres en Angleterre au Dix-huitième Siècle 1660-1744,* published in 1881 and translated with modernizations in 1948. Lennox Grey's "Literary Audience" in *Contemporary Literary Scholarship* (1958), edited by L. Leary, is an introduction to developments in research on the literary audience since Beljame and provides citations of works and perceptive comments on the problems they deal with. A few major audience studies not centered on drama are Q. D. Leavis, *Fiction and the Reading Public* (1932); Dorothy Whitelock, *The Audience of Beowulf* (1951); H. S. Bennett, *English Books and Readers, 1475 to 1557* (1952); George H. Ford, *Dickens and His Readers* (1955); and R. D. Altick, *The English Common Reader* (1957), which is concerned with the nineteenth-century audience for literature. A pioneering, if sketchy, theoretical study is L. L. Schücking's *The Sociology of Literary Taste,* translated by E. W. Dickes in 1944 from the German edition of 1931. Louis B. Wright's *Middle-Class Culture in Elizabethan England* (1935) treats the audience in wider terms than do the other studies mentioned.

16. An obvious process of specification leads from audience studies to studies of reception and reputation. These again have the particular virtue of overcoming the critical provincialism of one period by reminding us of the attitudes of another. They have serious implications for literary theory as well, for any notion of the *consensus gentium* or of the relations between sociology and esthetics must depend in part on the actual history of taste. In the essay included here, "The Revival of Metaphysical Poetry, 1872-1912," Joseph E. Duncan traces the reputation of metaphysical poetry, especially the poetry of Donne, up to the point of Sir Herbert Grierson's 1912 edition of Donne's poems. Duncan suggests the reasons for Donne's appeal to certain Victorian critics of Victorianism and corrects some widely held assumptions by pointing out that "The portrait of Donne as a complex, enigmatic rebel, which has fascinated the post-First World War generations, was sketched in all its main outlines by such Victorians as Gosse, Stephen, Symons, Brooke, and others." A more speculative approach to the presentation of a writer's reputation is Bertrand H. Bronson's "The Double Tradition of Dr. Johnson," *ELH,* 18 (1951), 90-106, which, in the course of identifying aspects of Johnson's reputation as a "folk-image," illuminates the nature of the man and his work. Two quite different longer studies are Caroline Spurgeon's lapidary three-volume *Five Hundred Years of Chaucer Criticism and Allusion* (1925) and G. H. Ford's narrative *Keats and the Victorians: A Study of His Influence and Rise to Fame, 1821-95* (1944). There are some observations on "Tracing Reputation and Influence" in Altick's *Art of Literary Research,* pp. 91 ff., in Chapter Ten of Morize, and in Chapter Six of Sanders. An insight into some of the problems of method related to such studies is provided by the comments on Gerald E. Bentley's *Shakespeare and Jonson: Their Reputations in the Seventeenth Century Compared* (1945) in David Frost, "Shakespeare in the Seventeenth Century," *Shakespeare Quarterly,* XVI (1965), 81-89.

17. One of the tasks of the critic is to make "fine distinctions," among them the distinctions embodied in the terms and definitions employed in literary discussion. But when the terms and distinctions are arrived at by an extensive inductive process, as is often the case, the line between criticism and scholarship becomes blurred or irrelevant. Harry Levin's brief essay "What Is Realism?" "condenses a point of view arrived at through a continuing series of studies in the French novel." It exhibits attributes of both criticism and scholarship: the critic's sensitivity to works; the scholar's command of the thought related to them and the conditions from which they emerge. A brief bibliography of studies of literary terminology is found in F. W. Bateson's *A Guide to English Literature* (1965), pp. 247-249, and a discussion of some of the problems involved in such studies in Charles E. Whitmore's "The Validity of Literary Definitions," *PMLA,* XXXIX (1924), 722-736. Two longer studies that illustrate almost polar methods are Norman Knox' historically oriented *The Word Irony and Its Context, 1500-1755* (1961) and Edwin Honig's highly speculative *Dark Conceit: The Making of Allegory* (1959). A. O. Lovejoy's *Essays in the History of Ideas* (1948) discusses several key literary terms with an historical method quite different from Knox', and the issues surrounding alternative terminologies are suggested in W. K. Wimsatt and Cleanth Brooks, *Literary Criticism: A Short History* (1957).

18. C. K. Hyder's "Wilkie Collins and the *Woman in White*" presents the biographical origins of material transformed by Collins. Problems involved in literary biography are treated in Wellek and Warren, *Theory of Literature,* Chapter Seven, which has extensive citations and a useful bibliography; in Morize, Chapter Nine; and in Sanders, Chapter Two. Some aspects of the subject are usefully debated by C. S. Lewis and E. M. W. Tillyard in *The Personal Heresy in Criticism* (1934) and discussed from various points of view in the volume of *English Institute Essays, 1946* (1947), whose theme is the critical significance of biographical evidence. A general survey is Leon Edel's *Literary Biography* (1957). Since the writing of Wellek and Warren's chapter on literature and biography there has been increasing interest in biographical study by historians as well as literary scholars. This is due in part to the excellence of some recent literary biographies, such as Richard Ellman's study of Joyce (1959), in part to relaxation of the strictures against biographical studies once associated with the New Criticism and with the insistence, by T. S. Eliot and others, on the impersonality of great art and on the consequent divorce between "the man who suffers and the mind which creates."

19. Similar but not as thoroughgoing "new-critical" strictures were urged against the "contamination" of literary study by historical and social concerns. But L. C. Knights' essay on "Dekker, Heywood and Citizen Morality" from *Drama and Society in the Age of Jonson* (1937) is a contribution to the interpretation of these dramatists. It treats the plays as "an index of contemporary taste and opinion" and explores the relations between literature and society. But one should be aware of the critique of Knights' position briefly stated by Alfred Harbage in *Shakespeare and the Rival Traditions* (1952), pp. 267-268. The relation between a knowledge of society and the interpretation of literature is surveyed in Wellek and Warren, *Theory of Literature,* Chapter Nine, and in Morize, Chapter Eleven. The opening chapter of Knights' *Drama and Society in the Age of Jonson* on Shakespeare and the so-called profit inflation is a useful warning against the doctrinaire imposition of ideological views on works of literature, but Arnold Kettle's two-volume *Introduction to the English Novel* (1952-1953) demonstrates that a committed Marxist approach by a careful scholar does not preclude important insights into a literary text. Some essays that suggest the problems in historical and social research on literature are Lionel Trilling's "The Sense of the Past" in *The Liberal Imagination* (1950) and the section dealing, less speculatively, with "Cultivating a Sense of the Past" in R. B. Altick's *Art of Literary Research,* pp. 102-117.

20. A. O. Lovejoy's "Optimism and Romanticism" attempts to clarify the meaning and tone of eighteenth-century optimism and to treat it as promoting the acceptance of new ethical and esthetic ideas that were among the most important elements of Romantic thought and art. The essay is remarkable in its breadth of materials and exemplifies one way of writing the history of ideas as they relate to literature. It can be read usefully in conjunction with the essay by R. S. Crane in the first section of this volume and with Lovejoy's own efforts to generalize about his practice in the first lecture of *The Great Chain of Being* (1936) and in "Reflections on the History of Ideas" in *Journal of the History of Ideas,* I (1940), 3-23. Some possible limitations of Lovejoy's approach — among them its apparent reduction of literature at some points to document or illustration — are treated in Wellek and Warren, Chapter Ten, which surveys the relations between literary study and the history of ideas. Perhaps closer to centrally literary concerns are studies of ideas as they relate to the history of taste. Among these Marjorie Nicolson's *Moun-*

tain Gloom and Mountain Glory (1959) is outstanding, as are her other studies, such as *The Microscope and the English Imagination* (1935) and *Newton Demands the Muse* (1946).

21. There are so many varieties of literary history that it would be impossible to include here essays representative of all. Indeed, almost all the kinds of investigation represented in this anthology are considered by Sanders and Morize as part of "literary history," as is evident from the titles of their handbooks. Sanders deals specifically with problems of chronology in literary study in his fifth chapter, Morize in his sixth, and Morize discusses problems of literary continuity in Chapters Ten and Eleven. Perhaps the most suggestive brief statements on the nature, indeed the possibility, of literary history are by René Wellek in Chapter Nineteen of *Theory of Literature* and in his later essay, included in the first section of this book. Wellek is himself the author of the distinguished *History of Modern Criticism: 1750-1950* (1955-   ), four of whose projected five volumes have been published and permit comparison of his views and his practice.

Efforts in literary history may be classified according to method or scope. In method they range from the mosaic of entries in such guides as the *Annals of English Literature 1475-1950,* second edition, revised by R. W. Chapman (1961), which records by year the publication of important works, to "narrative" handbook histories such as the *Literary History of England* (1948) by Baugh, *et al.,* to the *Oxford History of English Literature* (1945-   ), in most of whose published volumes the emphasis is on critical and cultural analysis rather than narrative history. The polar opposite of literary annals are such essays as R. S. Crane's "English Neoclassical Criticism: An Outline Sketch," reprinted in *Critics and Criticism* (1952), which is less concerned with presenting a consecutive account than with the subtle interrelations of ideas that characterize a phase of sensibility. This essay can be read in connection with Crane's "On Writing the History of English Criticism, 1650-1800," *University of Toronto Quarterly,* XXII (1952/1953), 376-391, which surveys the major problems in writing histories of criticism.

In scope, efforts in literary history vary from the relatively few attempts at histories of world or Western literature, to the many general histories of a national literature (here the volume by Baugh, *et al.,* cited above is typical), to the histories of a genre, a period, a style, or an idea. Some examples of these are listed, together with discussion of the problem of literary history in the bibliographical appendix and the notes to Chapter Eighteen of Wellek and Warren's *Theory of Literature.*

In this collection there are excerpts from two recent distinguished volumes of literary history. Ernst Curtius surveys the altering fortunes of the Muses as a motif in European literature. His study of this "formal constant of the literary tradition" extends from Homer to Blake and illuminates both continuity and change in literary practice and sensibility.

22. The excerpt from Josephine Miles' *Eras and Modes in English Poetry* (1957) is concerned with stylistic change, specifically with the identification of a "descriptive principle of period sequence" discovered by "a closer technical look at poetic practice." This descriptive principle Miss Miles discovers not in diction or metrics alone but in "sentence structure, which does reveal a sequential pattern." Her essay contributes both conclusions and a fruitful method.

23. Scholarship moves closest to criticism in the three interpretive essays by Spitzer, Kermode, and Sprinchorn. Leo Spitzer's essay places Whitman's poem "somewhere in the cold space of world literature," rather than in a specifically American framework, and applies to the task of illuminating the poem's significance and achievement evidence drawn from several languages and the entire tradition of Western literature. The result is both good criticism and a model of the critical procedure called "explication de texte," a method quite different in the breadth of its concerns outside the poem from the "close reading" associated with the New Criticism. A short bibliography of discussions and applications of "explication" and "close reading" is found in the notes and bibliographic appendix to Chapter Twelve of Wellek and Warren, *Theory of Literature;* there are also relevant considerations of stylistics listed in the bibliographic appendix to Chapter Fourteen. Spitzer's own views are presented in his *Method of Interpreting Literature* (1949).

24. Frank Kermode's essay on two books of *The Faerie Queene* begins with a survey of scholarly discussions of Spenser's historical allegory and then goes on to employ historical information to uncover the less obvious meanings of Spenser's epic. Kermode's justification for his procedure is that "I myself find that the hidden meanings contribute to the delight of the fiction, because some of this delight arises from recognition of the writer's complex intent." The particular justification for treating the historical allegory of *The Faerie Queene* is stated at length in Kermode's earlier essay on "Spenser and the Allegorists" in *The Proceedings of the British Academy,* 48 (1962), 261-279, which discusses the interplay of Elizabethan politics with Elizabethan attitudes toward apocalyptic prophecy and with the Elizabethan's conception of his country as an "elect" nation. The virtue of both of Kermode's essays is that the historical information they present illuminates the details of the literary work rather than merely surrounding it with unrelated "background" information.

25. Evert Sprinchorn's delightful article applies a knowledge of the mathematics of probability and of gambling odds to the explanation of several passages in *Hamlet* (V, ii, 172-176; 272-281) that have been either misunderstood or ignored. More than this, the solution of these cruxes illuminates Shakespeare's construction of the whole scene: how he manages the pace and duration of the duel, increasing the tension with each pass and defining the characters involved in the duel scene. The essay illustrates the frequent need for information other than that drawn from the literary tradition or the history of ideas—areas with which students of literature assume they ought to be familiar—for understanding a literary text. A classic in the application of special knowledge to a text is William K. Wimsatt's "The Game of Ombre in *The Rape of the Lock*," *Review of English Studies,* N.S., I. (1950), 136-143.

26. Among the more important newer directions in literary scholarship are those resulting from the application of linguistics and mathematics to literary problems and from the solution of literary problems through the use of computers. Samuel R. Levin's "Suprasegmentals and the Performance of Poetry" is a contribution to the study of prosody. Literary critics often discuss the actual rhythm of a poem as the outcome of a tension between the metronomic abstractions (of iambic pentameter, say) and the prosody of ordinary language. Levin's article is one of a series of attempts by students of linguistics to put such discussions of poetic rhythm on a more "realistic" basis by showing what the prosody of ordinary language actually is. Specifically, Levin is concerned to correct what he thinks an unwarranted assumption by some previous writers—the assumption that the "performance" of a poem consists in reading it aloud. In the course of his discussion, Levin deals with ambiguity in poetry, and in particular with the type of ambiguity "occasioned by constructional homonymity, i.e., where two meanings are supported by the one construction." He is concerned to show how stress, pitch, and juncture mark subtle relations between syntactical structures and thus communicate aspects of the poem which are lost when oral performance resolves certain kinds of syntactical ambiguity. An analysis of a poem by Dylan Thomas makes clear the issues that Levin deals with and leads to his conclusion that "the assumption that oral performance of poetry is superior to visual performance" is open to question. Books and articles that deal with literature, especially with prosody, from the viewpoint of linguistics are cited in Levin's notes. Levin's own *Linguistic Structures in Poetry* (1962) is a brief overview of the contribution of linguistics to literary study. An extensive collection of relevant articles is *Style in Language* (1960), edited by T. A. Sebok.

27. Claude S. Brinegar's article on the Quintus Curtius Snodgrass letters applies a statistical test to disprove Twain's authorship of these satires on the military profession. The results of Brinegar's investigation are corroborated by external evidence on Twain's whereabouts at the time the letters were composed. Brinegar's method is to form "a frequency distribution of a great many words classified according to length" and thereby to obtain a "characteristic curve of composition" that allows the identification of the author or, more exactly, the exclusion of those authors who could not have written the work in question. The method depends on the assumption "that every author uses words which, at least in the long run," may be considered as "random drawings from a characteristic fixed frequency distribution of word lengths." It should be added that when characteristic frequency distributions closely resemble one another, it is possible to distinguish between them by further statistical tests.

Brinegar proceeds by studying the word lengths in samples of Twain's known works and by checking the consistency of Twain's style over a long time-span. He then studies the same characteristic (word lengths) in the Quintus Curtius Snodgrass letters. Resulting graphs (using number of letters per word as the base line and frequency per 1000 words as the vertical axis) permit the rejection of Twain as author of the letters on visual inspection alone. Brinegar then applies the chi-square "goodness of fit" test and the two-sample t-test to check the agreement of the various samples to the control group (Twain's known work). Both tests confirm the results of the visual inspection.

As statistical studies go, Brinegar's is relatively simple and therefore a useful introduction to its genre. It contains general remarks on statistical tests as applied to literature and cites earlier studies in its notes. More sophisticated statistical studies, such as those by Mosteller and Wallace on the *Federalist Papers,* have been cited above. G. Udny Yule's *The Statistical Study of Literary Vocabulary* (1944) states general principles and examines the authorship of *De Imitatione Christi.* Though it is a difficult book, W. W. Greg advises the literary scholar (see *MLR,* XXXIX [1944], 291) to take the mathematics "on trust," put up with "a little harmless symbolism," and follow the general argument.

28. In his essay on "Electronic Computers and Elizabethan Texts," Ephim Fogel describes applications of electronic data-processing machines in literary study. He treats some problems of harnessing the computer to do the exacting jobs of preparing concordances and bibliographies (both with or without summaries), of preparing indexes, and of carrying out studies of authorship. The citations in the footnotes form a partial bibliography of the subject, and the last pages of the essay go far to dispel the inhumane scorn and suspicion of mechanical devices that can only release the mind from drudgery. An excellent collection of general statements and specific studies on the use of computers is the *Literary Data Processing Proceedings, September 9, 10, 11 – 1964* (N.D.), edited by J. B. Bessinger, Jr., S. M. Parrish, and H. F. Arader. It is available from the Materials Center of the Modern Language Association. The pieces in this collection treat a range of computer applications to literary problems. Of special interest is V. A. Dearing's "The Use of a Computer in Analysing Dryden's Spelling," pp. 200-210, which concludes that "the first edition of *The Indian Emperour* gives us a better picture of Dryden's holograph than the Trinity College manuscript does," a conclusion with serious implications for those who see computer use as leading only to greater precision rather than to substantial revisions of opinion. There are several useful notes on computer studies in *The Shakespeare Newsletter,* XV (1965).

29, 30, and 31. The three brief pieces which end this collection require little explanatory comment. They suggest the role of the scholar as "scourge and minister" – guardian of the standards of his calling. In Nichols' brief note, one sees illustrated the dangers of working with unreliable texts; in Stillinger's note, the dangers of relying upon unchecked transcripts; in Battestin's article, the dangers of not checking alternatives to one's own critical hypothesis, especially when those alternatives can depend on available studies of the primary manuscript material under consideration. Even dependence on early documents may be unwarranted: our most important "eye-witness account" of the Elizabethan audience is actually a paraphrase of parts of Ovid's *Art of Love* (see S. P. Zitner, "Gosson, Ovid, and the Elizabethan Audience," *Shakespeare Quarterly,* IX [1958], 206-208.) Similar caveats insisting on skepticism and care with regard to texts can be found in the first chapter of Fredson Bowers' *Textual and Literary Criticism* (1959), which has numerous citations. There are some general comments on the pitfalls of unscholarly scholarship in R. B. Altick's *Art of Literary Research,* pp. 114-117.

III

In his treatise *On Sophistical Refutations,* Aristotle wrote slightingly of some teachers that "they used to suppose that they trained people by imparting to them not the art but its products." This anthology is open to such an objection. But its aim is modest: not to educate fully in the art of literary scholarship but only to describe the main features of its current practice. In a strict sense, there is no art of literary scholarship distinct from the arts of scholarship in other disciplines. There are, of course, differences in materials and procedures. But the essential scholarly aims and skills are everywhere the same, embodied in grammar, rhetoric, and logic.[2]

Without training in these, in whatever guise, one can only haphazardly pursue the discovery of the True and the Excellent, which is the goal of all scholarship and defines its art; one is largely condemned to random, though arduous, accumulation. This collection will be misused if it is taken as a guide to the latter end. It presupposes that the reader has some philosophic understanding of his own and other disciplines. Inevitably, this understanding is imperfect in all of us. Perhaps the final apology for "specialization" is that, if pursued disinterestedly, it leads us to sense our prior omissions.

2. See I. A. Richards' Introduction to *Interpretation in Teaching* (1938).

I

CONTEXTS OF SCHOLARSHIP

1

The Nature and Uses of Literary Scholarship

George Whalley

Scholarship and Criticism

Somebody has suggested that scholarship is to criticism what engineering is to architecture. At first sight this is an attractive analogy. Without some appreciation of engineering principles the architect's building may collapse. Perhaps that was the main point in making the analogy. However, the figure carries disturbing overtones, in the hint that criticism not only stands upon the shoulders of humble scholarship, but also may have something — as architecture does — to do with designing things. Without an architect's design an engineer may be expected to produce a structure useful and durable enough but probably inducing no sense of delight. But what does a critic design? and if he does produce a plan of some structure to be built to, is it as a critic that he does so? and who would be the builder? It may simply be that the apparently guileless analogy is heavy with latent clouds of glory, for Vitruvius has it that

> An Architect ought to understand Languages, to be skillful of Painting, well-instructed in Geometrie, not ignorant of Perspective, furnished with Arithmeticke, have knowledge of many histories, and diligently have heard Philosophers, have skill of Musicke, not ignorant of Physicke, know the answeres of Lawyers, and have Astronomie, and the courses Celestial, in good knowledge.

Leo Baptista Albertus, in a similar vein of transcendent rhapsody, asserts that the Architect is

> that man, who hath the skill, (by a certaine and meruailous meanes and way), both in minde and Imagination to determine ... what works so euer, by motion of weight, and cuppling and framyng together of bodyes, may most aptly be Commodious for the worthiest Uses of Man ... Wherupon he is neither Smith, nor Builder: nor,

From the *University of Toronto Quarterly*, XXIX (1959), 33-45. Copyright 1959 by George Whalley. Reprinted by permission of the author and the *University of Toronto Quarterly*.

separately, any Artificer; but the Hed, the Provost, the Directer and Judge of all Artificiall workes, and all Artificers.

So much for architects. If scholars be to such demigods mere hod-carriers, their relation to criticism may warrant examination.

The traditional and vulgar views of the scholar are—one must confess —heavily weighted with a sense of comedy, particularly on the score of his minuteness and his detachment.

> They have as much need of hellebore as others [Burton tells us]. They have a worm as well as others. You shall find a phantastical strain, a fustian, a bombast, a vain-glorious humour, an affected style ... run parallel throughout their works ... They bewray and daub a company of books and good authors with their absurd comments ... and shew their wit in censuring others, a company of foolish note-makers, humble bees, dors or beetles. ... Yet if any man dare oppose or contradict, they are mad, up in arms on a sudden, how many sheets are written in defence, how bitter invectives, what apologies?

Cervantes and Sterne give us different versions—hilarious but poignant —of the learned mind alienated from the real world; and Rabelais makes excellent use of a cumbersome grotesque erudition grown carcinomatous. Virgilius Maro, the grammarian of Toulouse, who flourished—if flourish is the correct word—round about the seventh century, tells a story of two scholars of his time who for 15 days and nights, without food or sleep, argued about the frequentative of the verb *to be*, and nearly ended the discussion at sword-point. Virgil of Toulouse might himself have been one of these: at least his choice of a name is some measure of his conceit. Yeats's lines, written when he was living in Oxford in 1914—15, shape a familiar portrait of the scholars:

> Bald heads forgetful of their sins,
> Old, learned, respectable bald heads
> Edit and annotate the lines
> That young men, tossing on their beds,
> Rhymed out in love's despair
> To flatter beauty's ignorant ear.

Yet there is something splendid about Virgil of Toulouse arguing whether there can be a vocative of *ego* while ancient empires crashed and dissolved about his ears. And we hesitate to dismiss even him out of hand as a mere pedant, recalling that it was he who first traced the transition of Latin into Provencal, and the transition of quantitative Latin verse into the accentu-

From "The Scholars," reprinted with permission of The Macmillan Company from *The Wild Swans at Coole* by W. B. Yeats. Copyright 1919, The Macmillan Company, renewed 1946 by Bertha Georgie Yeats.

al vernacular line. We may also recall that the labours of the mediaeval and humanist grammarians and editors resulted in the formation of what we now call style, evolved painfully out of the struggle between the ordered resonance of the classical tongues and the fluid recalcitrance of vulgar living speech.

The mediaeval and humanist scholar's concern — after grammar and rhetoric — was to establish a pure text when the text (if it existed) was illegible, fragmentary, or corrupt; he wished to preserve the *ipsissima verba* of texts made sacred by time, or worship, or delight. After the text, his concern was for understanding the text. This was not criticism perhaps in the present meaning of the word, but an activity of unfolding and interpreting in the light of all that was known; the cumulative shedding of light upon writings too adamantine to alter, too powerful to ignore, too fugitive in spirit to dominate. The resources of mediaeval commentary and exposition, regarded simply as pedagogic technique, were not inconsiderable. And the exploitation of contrary principles and methods provoked the wars of the schools and fostered the invention of heresies. The truculent and murderous behaviour of some scholars to some other scholars is strangely at variance with the detachment and humility that seem more proper to the recondite arts. Yet to see a learned throat slit with skill and relish, to witness the neat impaling of an opponent's absurdity on the pin of an epigram — these are among the inexhaustible delights of classical scholarship. It is like a decorous ritual of mutilation, deadly but without essential malice. For the point at issue, one feels, is not really the conflict of opinion but the integrity of knowledge, the integrity of language — the two prime concerns of the early scholar. A scholar scornfully exposes a fellow pundit's folly, it would seem, not simply because the miscreant has been ignorant, obtuse, or barbarous (though that would be reason enough), but because this man had the means of discovering something that could be set down for all time, and at the crucial moment had fumbled it. Scholarship, like watch-making, requires a good eye and a delicate touch. To see some detail of factual truth slip through the clumsy fingers of another scholar is to suffer an excruciating shock of annoyance, a surge of futile rage. For in scholarship, once a fact is caught, it is caught for good and all. But once a false fact or conclusion has been set down it may be fruitful and multiply, perpetuating itself in mis-shapen offspring.

A fully annotated classical text, in which to the unappreciative eye the notes crowd the text to death, is an impressive — even moving — performance: it brings into single compass a great store of miscellaneous relevancies drawn (it may be) from many centuries and many sources, all sifted and arranged by some final editor, who ideally is learned, urbane, and tactful. We seem here to see the noble army of scholars, their marginal squabbles at last forgotten, marching with a proud and pettifogging detachment *behind* their text. For the quarrelsomeness of scholars — the intolerable vanity in some and the total lack of discrimination in others — points in one direction: to the fact that scholarship is cumulative and co-operative, that it deals with facts to do with specific texts and contexts, and that the scholar is the accumulator and guardian of the monuments of civilization, and of all knowledge that illuminates them.

A provisional sketch may be attempted. The ideal scholar is often by habit or necessity a teacher; but he will never cease to be a learner. To a great extent he will be obliged to live in the past; but his constant aim will be to perpetuate the past for the benefit of the present and the future. His concern with fact leads him into minuteness; but it also tends to expand his interpretative attention—still in search of accurate detail and analogy —outward into custom, art, ritual, belief, philosophy, law, society, until the field of literary scholarship becomes rather like Wolf's view of philology arranged in its 24 orders to encompass the whole documentary evidence for the history and antiquities of the ancient world.

Satiric accounts of scholarship usually make fun of the scholar's minuteness; but when scholars talk about each other they tend rather to esteem comprehensiveness. Scaliger said of Casaubon that he was "the most learned of all men living today"; and Casaubon of Scaliger that "there's nothing anybody could want to learn that he couldn't teach; and there was nothing he had read—and what hadn't the man read—that he couldn't instantly recall." No scholar would happily be content to know less than everything; and this is the talk of giants about giants. Not all learned men are accomplished scholars; but any accomplished scholar may, if he decides to give time to the necessary studies, become a learned man. "It is not knowledge but a discipline, that is required," Mark Pattison said a century ago; "not science, but the scientific habit; not erudition, but scholarship."

It is refreshing to revert, if only momentarily, to a time when *science* still meant knowledge and wasn't an emotive signal to fall to secular adoration. It is curious also to remark that scientists are not commonly spoken of as scholars—for all their devotion, their withdrawal from the world, their concern with minutiae; nor have I ever heard a scientist called a pedant, though that on the face of it is surprising enough. All of which suggests that scholarship may have an irreducibly humanistic character.

Scholarly monuments of industry and erudition may seem a modern achievement. But it is well to restore to honour the assiduity and chaste industry of the early scholars—even of the pedants—who secured the make and muscle of the European languages, and preserved those monuments of imagination and thought which are the roots of our literature and civilization. One thinks not only of Petrarch and Erasmus and Scaliger and Casaubon, but also of the ingenious and affectionate searchers out of manuscripts—the papal secretary Poggio Bracciolini, and Gerardo Landriani, and Sir Robert Cotton. One would like to remember even Janus Gruter, who after prodigious labours (not all of them undistinguished) lived to see his private collection of books, and the Palatine Library of which he was curator, despoiled; and Richard Porson whose beautiful handwriting has graced most of the Greek texts printed in England for more than a century. Then there was all the devoted work done at press by Aldus Manutius and Johan Froben and by Schweighaüser and Brunck—and the long sedulous nightmare business of hunting down all the woe of reduplicative error that printing brought into the world with its blessings.

Boethius, "mightiest observer of mighty things," once went (as Helen Waddell has it) "to gather violets in a spring wood, and watched with a sore heart a bird in a cage that had caught a glimpse of waving trees and now grieved its heart out, scattering its seed with small impotent claws." The pedants are perhaps the caged birds, crazy with impotence in the blaze of a knowledge that just eludes their grasp. Scholars for their industry or an air of prodigious but futile effort are often called ants: but I think of them as bees engaged—if I may change the figure—in controlled wool-gathering. For myself, the clearest image of a scholar is set down in a little poem found in a commonplace book at the abbey of Reichenau—written it may be by one of those who, afflicted by *accidia* or the spring weather, drew mice and daffodils in the margins of the manuscript they copied, or wrote out in the secular rhythm verses to celebrate the beauty of some girl's body.

> I and Pangur Bán my cat,
> 'Tis a like task we are at:
> Hunting mice is his delight,
> Hunting words I sit all night.
>
> 'Gainst the wall he sets his eye,
> Full and fierce and sharp and sly;
> 'Gainst the wall of knowledge I
> All my little wisdom try.
>
> So in peace our task we ply,
> Pangur Bán, my cat, and I;
> In our arts we find our bliss,
> I have mine and he has his.

This is the scholar's supreme detachment. His pot-valiant conceit and exquisite touchiness may well be only a necessary protection for it. The detachment is essential. Moreover, it places the scholar on the side of the poets, marking him off from mankind at large. So minutely focused upon the task in hand are his concern and affection—his compassion even—that he seems to have none left over for the world; and so he becomes an inexhaustible subject for merriment.

Scholarship, though it requires a scientific habit, is not itself a science. Yet it is too factual, and has too large a responsibility to the past and to a cumulative future, ever to become much unlike a science. It cannot allow conjecture to go far beyond the legitimate establishment of matters of fact; whatever it interprets afresh must be based upon demonstrable evidence rather than upon the self-consistency of plausible speculation or suggestive analogy. Yet no true scholar could conduct his work without an acute critical sense, an exact sense of literary values; he needs a sense of rightness, a flair for judging what fits, what *can* fit, what belongs, what makes sense in a whole context. His criticism may tend to be fixed upon a comparatively limited field of primary material; but the very minuteness of his inquiry draws him towards the deepest and widest resources of information available, towards different kinds of judgment, a most subtle sense of the relatedness of things. Given a text he will probably assume that the author was neither an idiot nor a clown; he will trust first his eyes and his reading of the original; he will not proceed to conjectural alterations until he is forced to do so, taking due account of his own possible ignorance. In the end his labours will come ideally to rest in something definitive: in an unimpeachable text and a commentary that has grown out of the cool sifting and fitting together of all that scholarship can bring to bear in the way of cognate knowledge. "Definitive" suggests a work of such stupendous ingenuity and crushing completeness that nobody need ever in future feel impelled to make such an effort again. One thinks perhaps of the Casaubon *Persius* that Coleridge owned: "There are 616 pages in this volume, of which 22 are text; and 594 commentary and introductory matter." But not all definitive editions are quite so indiscriminately encyclopaedic. In 1912 the Oxford University Press published in two volumes H. J. C. Grierson's edition of *Donne's Poetical Works,* a book of rigorous scholarship in the traditional manner. The text is a type facsimile of the 1633 folio—long *s*'s, ampersands, ligatures, and all; and those who recognize the types will recall how John Fell's arthritic labours in the Sheldonian Theatre founded the tradition of English scholarly printing: "Whereby this Royal Island stands particularly obliged to your Generous and Publick spirits." Grierson in his commentaries speaks with plangent but unassertive authority, taking on himself no more the colour of ostentation than a mason does in setting the capstone on a wall that has been long building. Grierson sent a copy to Yeats. Yeats's reply is preserved.

> I write to thank you for your edition of Donne. . . . I have been using it constantly and find that at last I can understand Donne. Your notes tell me exactly what I want to know. Poems that I could not understand or could but understand are now clear and I notice that the more precise and learned the thought the greater the beauty, the passion; the intricacy and subtleties of his imagination are the length and depths of the furrow made by his passion. His pedantry and his obscenity—the rock and the loam of his Eden—but make me the more certain that one who is but a man like us all has seen God.

One wonders whether Grierson recognized the poetic flowering of his scholarship in the first work of Yeats's maturity when it appeared in 1914 under the title of *Responsibilities.*

The classical scholarship of the Middle Ages and Renaissance set the pattern that Western scholars in a dreamy sort of way still follow. There have been a few improvements on the fringes of scholarship—machines for collating first folios of Shakespeare, microfilm to ensure a crabbed and myopic ubiquity, stringent procedural rules that inhibit flamboyance but fail to guarantee brilliance. But the touchiness continues, the ant-like industry, the ferocious zeal for fact and accuracy. Indeed, since the invention of printing from movable types, the most ominous change to occur in the pattern of scholarship has been the sudden collapse of classical studies as the central humanistic discipline. This seems to have happened quite rapidly, about 25 years ago. Suddenly there was a painful academic vacuum, into which the study of English Language and Literature leaked —tentatively at first, and then, since there was no serious discouragement, in full spate. Previously the study of English in the great universities had been a scholarly discipline in linguistics, in grammar, in textual methods. Cultivated people read the corpus of English literature in the dog-watches, a tradition to be seen in the work of such non-professionals as Sherrington, Whitehead, Toynbee, and Trevelyan. As the study of English began to assume—almost by default—the rôle of the main humanistic discipline, professors of English had less the air of gay anti-barbarian champions of the unfettered intellect than of grave gentlemen running in an egg and spoon race. The study of English became the study of "criticism," not as an up-surge of vitality in the body of critical endeavour, but as a condition of survival, as a responsive mutation in the face of the almost impossible task it had inherited.

Dryden introduced the word *criticism;* Coleridge used it seldom; Arnold canonized it; this century has tried to deify it. Mr. I. A. Richards's early work can be seen as a first strong attempt to stake out the limits and correct dignity for the new intellectual empire, even though his impulse was more clearly psychological and scientific than scholarly and aesthetic. The New Criticism can be seen as one of the first successful attempts (based on Richards) to establish a pedagogic technique that would work in a practical way—in the lecture room. Viewed in this historical perspective, certain subtle and original critics can be seen as consolidating positions held only tentatively by raiding parties and establishing the fact that there were still wider fields to be conquered by "criticism." The advantage to literary studies has been immense, and the advantages to scholarship (as also to journalism) not inconsiderable. But criticism, like any prosperous and aggressive financial concern, has not been innocent of imperial longings. In the general hubbub of empire-building there has been, as one might expect, a certain amount of encroachment, some obliteration of borders. But a much more serious erosion occurred as criticism moved into the position of a world power—the submerging of internal boundaries. At present there is an air of stability, as though people were getting out of the practice of walking away with each other's boundary stones; but that is partly a symptom of exhaustion, and partly a sign that criticism may have forgotten what its empire was meant to do—it may, like other empires one can think of, have slipped into the habit of supposing that empire exists in order to exercise and enjoy the fruits of power. Scholarship has become fustian: criticism is cloth-of-gold. Yet to establish the just limits of a discipline is the first step in commanding that area. In this matter scholarship is the army of occupation. It remains to be seen whether the job of criticism is to provide a ruling caste. Perhaps the figure was not in the first place a happy one. Perhaps what criticism needs is a decent set of working clothes.

Between scholarship and criticism there are some obvious relations. No true scholar can lack critical acumen; and the scholar's eye is rather like the poet's—not, to be sure, "in a fine frenzy rolling," but at least looking for something as yet unknown which it knows it will find, with perceptions heightened and modified by the act of looking. For knowing is qualitative and is profoundly affected by the reason for wanting to know. Again, it is clear that no critic can afford *not* to be a scholar—even a scholar in a pretty impressive degree—if his work is to go much beyond delicate impression-ism, penumbral rhetoric, or marginal schematism. Without scholarship every synoptic view will be cursory, every attempt at a synthesis a wind-egg; without scholarship the criticism of a poem may easily become a free fantasia on a non-existent theme. Yet scholarship invading the field of criticism can hamstring and bird-lime heuristic activity, and frustrate the apprehension of literature by intellectual barbarity and emotional ped-antry. It would be a pity to regard scholarship as no more than a mounting-block for the Icarus-flights of criticism; for scholarship represents a con-trary and essential moment in the larger rhythmic process of criticism. Criticism and scholarship, though not mutually exclusive, are as different as positive and negative, fiction and fact, theory and myth.

Coleridge in one of his notebooks observed that

> In all processes of the Understanding the shortest way will be dis-covered the last, and this perhaps while it constitutes the great advantage of having a Teacher to put us on the shortest road at the first, yet sometimes occasions a difficulty in the comprehension—in as much as the longest way is more near to the existing state of the mind, nearer to what, if left to myself on starting the thought, I should have thought next.—The shortest *way* gives *the knowledge* best; the longest way makes me more *knowing*.

If the word *knowing* be taken as a noun rather than as an adjective, it forms an important contrast to *knowledge:* knowledge is terminal, know-ing is processive and continuous. If *knowledge* is taken to indicate the whole cumulus of things known, propositions formulated about events, conclusions reached, what was said *about* something, about relations actual, hypothetical, or suggestive, then *knowing* is no more like knowl-edge than thinking is like a conclusion. There is a terror and fatigue and desolation about sustained thinking that makes one understand why some societies prefer to kill the instigators of thought rather than submit to the solitary humiliation of thinking. Still, thinking can, with luck, application, and practice, be brought to a point; and then it has delights well worth the rigours of the onset. But the elation one feels at reaching a conclusion of any sort or of solving a problem should not be allowed to run over into one's judgment of the value of the conclusion. For in education—in civilization—one is constantly looking for fruitful questions and warily skirting around answers, because an answer brings everything to a halt. The value of a conclusion rests in the indications it gives of fruitful directions for further thinking.

Coleridge in another place says admirably that "there is a period of orderliness, of circumspection, of discipline, in which we purify, separate, define, select, arrange." Both these phases of heuristic thinking apply to scholarship and to criticism. Since the second phase can easily be regarded as an end, associated with knowledge, it comes to be regarded as the scholar's end. But the business of criticism is to bring the critic—and with luck others—into an initial reflective phase, and to sustain that phase until it is capable of passing over into something more orderly though still circumspect. Criticism, unlike scholarship however, does not come to a halt in the phase of knowledge; it uses each successive phase of knowledge as the beginning of a further reflective phase, a fresh activity of knowing in the presence of the poem. The end of criticism is knowing: the end of scholarship is knowledge. The unpardonable sin in scholarship is to be wrong: one could say that in criticism the unpardonable sin is to be right.

I cannot bring myself to think of criticism as a self-enclosed activity that needs literature only as something to grip its chariot-wheels. It is literature, not criticism, that is apocalyptic; and criticism cannot be driven far beyond the irreducible element of judgment that is to be found in any cognitive process. Criticism is a humble and ancillary occupation, guided, commanded, and humiliated by literature. Its character is functional. Its worth depends upon its usefulness. At the least it is a means of inducing and sustaining reflection; at best it is a mode of illumination, a means of heightening one's awareness of literature so that literature may illuminate. The critic's job is—at the mundane level—sacramental: to establish a direct contact with works of literature, to partake of the life those works encompass and disclose. The critic will talk about that contact, and about what—through that contact—he takes single works of art, and then perhaps groups of works of art, to be. Not least important is it to talk about these things in such a way as to bring others into direct contact with works of literature, with their capacity for astonishment heightened, their perceptions sharpened, their power of discovery unimpaired. I should like to keep this simple function of criticism clear by splitting off from the term at one end everything that belongs in the abstract and speculative domains of poetics and aesthetic theory, and at the other end everything that belongs to scholarship—matters of history, biography, linguistics, psychology, philosophy. So regarded, the critic's position is clearer. He will be less likely, under the pressure of professional importunity, to walk in front of the work of art with a banner flying.

In narrowing the term *criticism* in this way I am not thinking that criticism should be limited to what Professor Frye has called "public criticism"—the more or less persuasive communication of the "feel" of a poem by a perceptive reader to the public at large. I am thinking of the activity that, in the mind of a "critic," brings a work of literature into a reflective or discursive or imaginative field which is at first in some way related to the work of literature and will in the end be dominated by the work of literature. If the term criticism is allowed to expand indefinitely it comes to include the whole field of mental activity in which may occur any discussion whatsoever of anything even remotely to do with works of literature. In such a dilated and attenuated area the landmarks vanish. Yet one needs constantly to know whether what is thought or said in the name of criticism is illuminating the poem and is controlled by the poem, or whether it is part of an excursus into history, theory of semantics, metaphysics, poetics, psychoanalysis, biography, or even—as when Johnson writes a first-rate essay on a third-rate poem—into imaginative writing.

For the health of literature—and criticism—the most fruitful critical activity is reflective: throwing the mind forward, after withdrawal, refreshed and informed, upon the poem, willing to be dominated by the poem. This movement of mind is rhythmic, passing steadily in and out of resonance with the poem, the need to return to the poem becoming stronger the farther the mind moves away from the poem. The other activities—though legitimate enough, as indeed all modes of knowledge are legitimate—are refractive: they start from a poem but proceed into something else, fostering an allegiance not to the poem—and sometimes not even to literature—but to ideas which were first suggested by contact with the poem and ideas now considered worthy of exploration for their own sake without further reference to the poem. The rhythmic critical activity is capable of being continuously heuristic; it is a process of knowing perpetually destroyed and renovated by contact with the poem. The refractive critical activity terminates in knowledge which may not even be knowledge about the poem, a knowledge in which the mind gratefully comes to rest because it preferred not to come to rest in the poem.

Criticism in this narrow sense is then the functional relation between a reader and a poem; or the functional relation in the mind between the poem and another look at the poem; or the relation between the poem and some other field of interest or activity. So limited, it is a way of mind that could be clearly described both in its functional and its psychological aspects. Since it is an activity without which no recreative or discursive activity in the field of a poem can relevantly proceed, there would seem to be some advantage in defining it and giving it a name. If we call this perceptive-functional relation *criticism* we shall be at a loss for a general term to do the work now done by the generic term *critical,* and much of the present content of what is fashionably called criticism would be found to belong in the sphere of poetics. Probably it is too late to reverse a linguistic process started long ago and conveniently fortified by collusive erosion of meaning. If a new and strict meaning for an old term cannot be established, a new term may have to be found and set on course between the rock of habit and the whirlpool of jargon. The word *hapsis* might tentatively be suggested. It is not in *N.E.D.* but was not unknown to Aristotle and Plato. The verb from which the noun is formed means to touch, grasp, begin, set to work, perceive, have intercourse with, be in contact with; it can also mean to kindle, to set on fire. Unfortunately the adjective *haptic* is already used by psychiatrists to indicate a kind of distortion that occurs in drawings as an expression of a psychopathic condition; but this may only help to clarify the singular and ambiguous activity in which critics engage.

If a critic is to foster and inhabit the life of literature rather than expend his energies in founding totalitarian states, he will need to be flexible, resourceful, and modest. He might discover that criticism, like art, finds its most trenchant directness not in certainty but in obliquity. He will and must feel free to use a variety of methods, approaches, even techniques—provided he can use these with some air of appropriateness. He will need a full armoury of methods if he is in any way to transcend the limits of his own taste, sympathy, and ignorance. A critic must feel free to change his analogies, his illustrations, his images, his terms; he must even be prepared to change his mind, recalling that only a work of art has a face worth saving.

One of the few things which emerge clearly from the troublesome history of twentieth-century criticism is that any critic who approaches a work of literature with anything less than everything that might be relevant to his inquiry does so at his own peril. At this point the distinction between knowledge and knowing becomes crucial. Knowing is processive: knowledge is terminal. The intrusion of knowledge can easily obscure and arrest the activity of knowing; for it can easily distract attention from what one seeks to know and bring it to fatal rest in the null desert of things known. In the field of scholarship knowledge is paramount: knowledge factual, definitive, cumulative, fully tested on evidence. In the field of criticism, on the contrary, knowing is paramount, and ignorance assumes a positive value; and as long as ignorance does not imply complete insensibility, a positive rejection of decisive knowledge becomes a guiding principle. Since a poem is not an encyclopaedic statement of fact, but a symbolic entity, it is ringed about and even shaped by what is not said; by not-knowing, by ignorance, in the same way that the sound and rhythm of a poem is ringed about with silence. It is as important for a critic to be sure what not to know in the presence of a particular poem as it is to know what facts are critically relevant; and even the relevant facts must not, in criticism, be entertained as knowledge, but turned loose to be shaped and controlled or annihilated by the poem. A critic—like a poet—needs not only a method of bringing to bear all knowledge upon a single point but also a method for getting rid of what is not to the point.

There is correspondingly this great difference between scholarship and criticism. In scholarship anything that can be reliably said about anything is a permanent addition to the store of knowledge—even though it be centuries before anybody wants to use it. In criticism anything that can be said about a poem is tentative; and as soon as it ceases to illuminate the poem it must be thrown away or it will confuse or blind the critic. In criticism encyclopaedic knowledge may not be a virtue—it may even be the ultimate barbarity. In scholarship a little criticism goes a long way because there is a constant appeal to verifiable fact, a constant discipline and purging of fantasy in the way that value-judgments retain their essential character of directness. There is no finer training for a critic than that in scholarship, as long as it does not twist him into pedantry. Once the critic steps forth into *his* area of controlled woolgathering he can learn much from the old scholars who, with their baggy eyes and fur neckpieces, gaze quizzically at him from the engraved titlepages of the sixteenth and seventeenth centuries. There is at least this virtue in the scholar: he walks *behind* his text, processionally, knowing that the text is the only thing worth preserving. The scholar-critic needs to overcome the impulse to march like a drum-major in front of his text. A man can enjoy literature; he can by grace experience it, he can even make it his own; but try as he will he cannot devour literature, and if he plays his cards right the most he can expect is that poems will have their will of him in the end. If he is to induce knowing he will need wisdom, a light touch, nimble foot-work. The critic can learn at least this from a scholar: that he might do worse than conduct himself with the truculent evasiveness of a lover engaged in a hard courtship; for he has everything to win and only himself to lose.

2

Literary History 'and Literary Theory

René Wellek

Literary Theory, Criticism and History

In *Theory of Literature*[1] I tried to maintain the distinctions between certain main branches of literary study. "There is, first," I said, "the distinction between a view of literature as a simultaneous order and a view of literature which sees it primarily as a series of works arranged in a chronological order and as integral parts of the historical process. There is, then, the further distinction between the study of the principles and criteria of literature and the study of the concrete literary works of art, whether we study them in isolation or in chronological series." "Literary theory" is the study of the principles of literature, its categories, criteria, and the like, while the studies of concrete works of art are either "literary criticism" (primarily static in approach) or "literary history." Of course, "literary criticism" is frequently used in such a way as to include literary theory.[2] I pleaded for the necessity of a collaboration among the three disciplines. "They implicate each other so thoroughly as to make inconceivable literary theory without criticism or history, or criticism without theory or history, or history without theory and criticism," and I concluded somewhat naively that "these distinctions are fairly obvious and rather widely accepted" (pp. 30-31).

Since these pages were written many attempts have been made either to obliterate these distinctions or to make more or less totalitarian claims for some one of these disciplines: either to say, e.g., that there is only history or only criticism or only theory or, at least, to reduce the triad to a duo, to say that there is only theory and history or only criticism and history. Much of this debate is purely verbal: a further example of the incredible confusion of tongues, the veritable Tower of Babel which seems to me one of the most ominous features of our civilization. It is not worth trying to disentangle these confusions if they do not point to

From *Concepts of Criticism* (New Haven and London: Yale University Press, 1963), pp. 1-20. First printed in *The Sewanee Review*, LXVII (Winter 1960), 1-19. Reprinted by permission of *The Sewanee Review* and René Wellek. Copyright 1960 by The University of the South.

1. René Wellek and Austin Warren, *Theory of Literature* (New York, 1949).
2. I have used the term thus widely in my *History of Modern Criticism* (New Haven, 1955).

actual issues. Terminological disagreements are inevitable, especially if we take into consideration the different associations and scope of such terms in the main European languages. For instance, the German term *Literaturwissenschaft* has preserved in German its ancient meaning of systematic knowledge. But I would try to defend the English term "literary theory" as preferable to "science of literature," because "science" in English has become limited to natural science and suggests an emulation of the methods and claims of the natural sciences which seems, for literary studies, both unwise and misleading. "Literary scholarship" as a possible translation or alternative to "Literaturwissenchaft" seems also inadvisable, as it seems to exclude criticism, evaluation, speculation. A "scholar" has ceased to be so broad and wise a man as Emerson wanted the American scholar to be. Again, "literary theory" is preferable to "poetics," as in English, the term "poetry" is still usually restricted to verse and has not assumed the wide meaning of German *Dichtung*. "Poetics" seems to exclude the theory of such forms as the novel or the essay and it has also the handicap of suggesting prescriptive poetics: a set of principles obligatory for practising poets.

I do not want to trace at length the history of the term "criticism" here. . . . In English, the term criticism is often used to include literary theory and poetics. This usage is rare in German where the term *Literaturkritik* is usually understood in the very narrow sense of day-by-day reviewing. It might be interesting to show how this restriction has come about. In Germany, Lessing, certainly, and the Schlegels thought of themselves as literary critics, but apparently the overwhelming prestige of German philosophy, particularly the Hegelian system, combined with the establishment of a specialized literary historiography led to a sharp distinction between philosophical aesthetics and poetics on the one hand and scholarship on the other, while "criticism" taken over by politically oriented journalism during the thirties of the nineteenth century became degraded to something purely practical, serving temporal ends. The critic becomes a middleman, a secretary, even a servant, of the public. In Germany, the late Werner Milch, in an essay "Literaturkritik und Literaturgeschichte"[3] has tried to rescue the term by an argument in favor of "literary criticism" as a specific art-form, a literary genre. Its distinguishing characteristic is that in criticism everything must be related to *us,* while in literary history, literature is conceived as involved in a period, judged only relatively to the period. The only criterion of criticism is personal feeling, experience, the magic German word: *Erlebnis.* But Milch hardly touches on the distinction between literary criticism and theory. He rejects a general "science of literature," as all knowledge about literature has its place in history, and poetics cannot be divorced from historical relations.

I recognize that Milch's discussion raises interesting historical questions about the forms in which the insights of criticism have been conveyed, and that there is a real issue in the debate whether criticism is an art

---

3. *Germanisch-romanische Monatsschrift, 18* (1930), 1-15, reprinted in *Kleine Schriften zur Literatur- und Geistesgeschichte* (Heidelberg, 1957), pp. 9-24.

or a science (in the old, wide sense). I shall be content to say here that criticism has been conveyed in the most different art-forms, even in poems, such as those of Horace, Vida, and Pope, or in brief aphorisms, such as those by Friedrich Schlegel, or in abstractly, prosaically, even badly written treatises. The history of the "literary review" *(Rezension)* as a genre raises historical and social questions, but it seems to me a mistake to identify "criticism" with this one limited form. There still remains the problem of the relation between criticism and art. A feeling for art will enter into criticism: many critical forms require artistic skills of composition and style; imagination has its share in all knowledge and science. Still, I do not believe that the critic is an artist or that criticism is an art (in the strict modern sense). Its aim is intellectual cognition. It does not create a fictional imaginative world such as the world of music or poetry. Criticism is conceptual knowledge, or aims at such knowledge. It must ultimately aim at systematic knowledge about literature, at literary theory.

This point of view has recently been eloquently argued by Northrop Frye in the "Polemical Introduction" to his *Anatomy of Criticism*,[4] a work of literary theory which has been praised as the greatest book of criticism since Matthew Arnold. Frye, convincingly, rejects the view that literary theory and criticism are a kind of parasite on literature, that the critic is an artist *manqué*, and postulates that "criticism is a structure of thought and knowledge existing in its own right" (p. 5). I agree with his general enterprise, his belief in the necessity of a theory of literature. I want to argue here only against his attempt to erect literary theory into the uniquely worthwhile discipline and to expel criticism (in our sense of criticism of concrete works) from literary study. Frye makes a sharp distinction between, on the one hand, both "literary theory" and "genuine criticism," which progresses toward making the whole of literature intelligible, and, on the other hand, a kind of criticism which belongs only to the history of taste. Obviously Frye has little use for the "public critic" — Sainte-Beuve, Hazlitt, Arnold, etc. — who represents the reading public and merely registers its prejudices. Frye laughs at "the literary chit-chat which makes the reputations of poets boom and crash in an imaginary stock exchange. That wealthy investor, Mr. Eliot, after dumping Milton on the market, is now buying him again; Donne has probably reached his peak and will begin to taper off; Tennyson may be in for a slight flutter but the Shelley stocks are still bearish" (p. 18). Frye is obviously right in ridiculing the "whirligig of taste"; but he must be wrong in drawing the conclusion that "as the history of taste has no organic connection with criticism, it can be easily separated."

In my own *History of Modern Criticism* I have discovered that it cannot be done.[5] Frye's view that "the study of literature can never be founded on value judgments," that the theory of literature is not directly concerned with value judgments, seems to me quite mistaken. He himself

---

4. Princeton, 1957.

5. In his very generous review Mr. Frye apparently wished I had done so. Cf. *Virginia Quarterly, 32* (1956), 310-315.

concedes that the "critic will find soon, and constantly, that Milton is a more rewarding and suggestive poet to work with than Blackmore" (p. 25). Whatever his impatience with arbitrary literary opinions may be or with the game of rankings, I cannot see how such a divorce as he seems to advocate is feasible in practice. Literary theories, principles, criteria cannot be arrived at *in vacuo:* every critic in history has developed his theory in contact (as has Frye himself) with concrete works of art which he has had to select, interpret, analyze and, after all, to judge. The literary opinions, rankings, and judgments of a critic are buttressed, confirmed, developed by his theories, and the theories are drawn from, supported, illustrated, made concrete and plausible by works of art. The relegation, in Frye's *Anatomy of Criticism,* of concrete criticisms, judgments, evaluations to an arbitrary, irrational, and meaningless "history of taste" seems to me as indefensible as the recent attempts to doubt the whole enterprise of literary theory and to absorb all literary study into history.

In the forties, during the heyday of the New Criticism, historical scholarship was on the defensive. Much was done to reassert the rights of criticism and literary theory and to minimize the former overwhelming emphasis on biography and historical background. In the colleges a textbook, Brooks and Warren's *Understanding Poetry* (1938),[6] was the signal for the change. I believe my own *Theory of Literature* (1949) was widely understood as an attack on "extrinsic" methods, as a repudiation of "literary history," though the book actually contains a final chapter on "Literary History" which emphatically argues against the neglect of this discipline and provides a theory of a new, less external literary history. But in recent years the situation has become reversed, and criticism, literary theory, the whole task of interpreting and evaluating literature as a simultaneous order has been doubted and rejected. The New Criticism, and actually any criticism, is today on the defensive. One type of discussion moves on an empirical level as a wrangle about the interpretation of specific passages or poems. The theoretical issue is there put often in very sweeping and vague terms. A straw man is set up: the New Critic, who supposedly denies that a work of art can be illuminated by historical knowledge at all. It is then easy to show that poems have been misunderstood because the meaning of an obsolete word was missed or a historical or biographical alusion ignored or misread. But I do not believe that there ever was a single reputable "New" critic who has taken the position imputed to him. The New Critics, it seems to me rightly, have argued that a literary work of art is a verbal structure of a certain coherence and wholeness, and that literary study had often become completely irrelevant to this total meaning, that it had moved all too often into external information about biography, social conditions, historical backgrounds, etc. But this argument of the New Critics did not mean and could not be conceived to mean a denial of the relevance of historical information for the business of poetic interpretation. Words have their history; genres

6. Cleanth Brooks, Jr. and R. P. Warren, *Understanding Poetry; an Anthology for College Students* (New York, 1938).

and devices descend from a tradition; poems often refer to contemporary realities. Cleanth Brooks—surely a New Critic who has focussed on the close reading of poetry—has, in a whole series of essays (mainly on seventeenth-century poems) which I hear will be collected in the near future, shown very precisely some of the ways in which historical information may be necessary for the understanding of specific poems. In a discussion of Marvell's "Horatian Ode,"[7] Brooks constantly appeals to the historical situation for his interpretation, though he is rightly very careful to distinguish between the exact meaning of the poem and the presumed attitude of Marvell toward Cromwell and Charles I. He argues "that the critic needs the help of the historian—all the help he can get," but insists that "the poem has to be read as a poem—that what it 'says' is a question for the critic to answer, and that no amount of historical evidence as such can finally determine what the poem says" (p. 155). This seems a conciliatory, sensible attitude which holds firmly to the critical point of view and still admits the auxiliary value of historical information, and does not of course deny the separate enterprise of literary history.

Usually, however, the defenders of the historical point of view are dissatisfied with such a concession. They remind us loudly that a literary work can be interpreted only in the light of history and that ignorance of history distorts a reading of the work. Thus Rosemond Tuve, in three very learned books,[8] has kept up a running battle against the modern readers of the metaphysical poets and of Milton. But the issues debated by her are far from clear-cut conflicts between historical scholarship and modern criticism. For instance, in her attack on Empson's reading of Herbert's "Sacrifice,"[9] she clearly has the upper hand not because she is a historian and Empson is a critic but because Empson is an arbitrary, willful, fantastic reader of poetry who is unwilling or unable to look at his text as a whole but runs after all sorts of speculations and associations. "All the Freudian stuff," says Empson disarmingly, "what fun!" He takes the line of Christ complaining, "Man stole the fruit, but I must climb the tree," to mean that Christ is "doing the stealing, that so far from sinless he is Prometheus and the criminal," that "Christ is climbing upwards, like Jack on the Beanstalk, and taking his people with him back to Heaven." Christ is "evidently smaller than Man or at any rate than Eve, who could pluck the fruit without climbing ... the son stealing from his father's orchard is a symbol of incest," etc. (p. 294). Miss Tuve seems right in insisting that "I must climb the tree" means only "I must ascend the cross," and that "must" does not imply Christ's littleness or boyishness but refers to the command of God. Miss Tuve appeals, plausibly, to the concept of *figura*, of typology: Adam was considered as the type of Christ. Christ was the second Adam, the cross the other tree. Miss Tuve accumulates, in *A Reading of George Herbert*, a mass of learning to show that there are liturgical phrases, Middle English and

---

7. "Literary Criticism," in *English Institute Essays, 1946* (New York, 1947), pp. 127-158.
8. *Elizabethan and Metaphysical Imagery* (Chicago, 1947); *A Reading of George Herbert* (Chicago, 1952); *Images and Themes in Five Poems by Milton* (Cambridge, Mass., 1957).
9. In William Empson, *Seven Types of Ambiguity* (London, 1930), pp. 286 ff.

Latin poems, devotional treatises, etc., which anticipate the general situation of Herbert's poem, and that even many details of the complaint of Christ can be found long before Herbert in texts Herbert probably had never seen as well as in texts he might have known or knew for certain as an Anglican priest. All this is useful and even impressive as a study of sources and conventions, but it surely does not prove what she apparently hopes to prove: that Herbert's poem is somehow unoriginal, that Empson is mistaken in speaking of "Herbert's method" and its "uniqueness." Empson in his sly rejoinder[10] quite rightly argues that no amount of background study can solve the problem of poetic value. What is at issue is not a conflict between history and criticism but empirical questions about the correctness or incorrectness of certain interpretations. I think one must grant that Empson laid himself wide open to the charge of misreading, but then one must say in his defense that nobody, literally nobody, had yet commented on that poem in any detail and that Empson's method, atomistic, associative, arbitrary as it is, is at least an ingenious attempt to come to grips with the problem of meaning. "Close reading" has led to pedantries and aberrations, as have all the other methods of scholarship; but it is surely here to stay, as any branch of knowledge can advance and has advanced only by a careful, minute inspection of its objects, by putting things under the microscope even though general readers or even students and teachers may be often bored by the procedure.

But these debates, like the debate between the Chicago critics and the New Critics or between the Chicago critics and the mythographs, concern rather specific problems of interpretation than our wider debate about the relationship of theory, criticism, and history. Far greater and more difficult issues are raised by those who have genuinely embraced the creed of "historicism," which after a long career in Germany and Italy, after its theoretical formulations by Dilthey, Windelband, Rickert, Max Weber, Troeltsch, Meinecke, and Croce, has finally reached the United States and has been embraced by literary scholars almost as a new religion. To give a characteristic recent example, Roy Harvey Pearce, in an article, "Historicism Once More,"[11] — strangely enough lauded and endorsed by J. C. Ransom — preaches a new historicism and concludes by quoting a poem by Robert Penn Warren with this climactic line, "The world is real. It is there" *(Promises 2)*.

Warren, hardly an enemy of the New Criticism, is quoted as the key witness for "historicism," though his fine poem has nothing whatever to do with historicism and merely conveys, powerfully and movingly, a feeling for the reality of the past which might conceivably rather be called "existential." It asserts the kind of realization and wonder which Carlyle insisted upon in many of his later writings after he had repudiated his early adherence to German historicism. To quote Carlyle's examples: Dr. Johnson actually told a street-walker, "No, no, my girl, it won't do";

From "Promises II" in *Promises: Poems, 1954-1956* by Robert Penn Warren (New York: Random House, 1957). Reprinted by permission of Random House, Inc.

10. *Kenyon Review, 12* (1950), 735-738.

11. Ibid., *20* (1958), 554-591.

Charles I actually stayed the night in a hayloft with a peasant in 1651; King Lackland "was verily there," at St Edmundsbury, and left *"tredecim sterlingii,* if nothing more, and did live and look in one way or the other, and a whole world was living and looking at him."[12] But such wonder, appropriate to the poet or Carlyle, is only the beginning of historicism as a method or a philosophy. Pearce's historicism is a confused mixture of existentialism and historicism, a string of bombastic assertions about humanity, the possibility of literature, and so on, with the constant polemical refrain that "criticism is a form of historical study" (p. 568). It is not worth trying to disentangle the hopeless muddles of Pearce's amazing stew of existence, eschatology, history, the "creative ground of all values," the whole weird mixture of Rudolph Bultmann, Américo Castro, Kenneth Burke, and Walter J. Ong, S.J., all quoted on one page. It is better to turn to a knowledgeable and sophisticated upholder of the historic creed such as my late colleague and friend, Erich Auerbach.

In a review of my *History of Modern Criticism*[13] from which certain formulations passed, without explicit reference to my work, into the introduction of his posthumous book, *Literatursprache und Publikum in der lateinischen Spätantike und im Mittelalter,*[14] and into his English article "Vico's Contribution to Literary Criticism,"[15] Auerbach states most clearly the historistic creed:

> Our historistic way of feeling and judging is so deeply rooted in us that we have ceased to be aware of it. We enjoy the art, the poetry and the music of many different peoples and periods with equal preparedness for understanding.... The variety of periods and civilizations no longer frightens us.... It is true that perspectivistic understanding fails as soon as political interests are at stake; but otherwise, especially in aesthetic matters, our historistic capacity of adaptation to the most various forms of beauty is almost boundless.... But the tendency to forget or to ignore historical perspectivism is widespread, and it is, especially among literary critics, connected with the prevailing antipathy to philology of the 19th century type, this philology being considered as the embodiment and the result of historicism. Thus, many believe that historicism leads to antiquarian pedantry, to the overevaluation of biographical detail, to complete indifference to the values of the work of art; therefore to a complete lack of categories with which to judge, and finally to arbitrary eclecticism.... [But] it is wrong to believe that historical relativism or perspectivism makes us incapable of evaluating and judging the work of art, that it leads to arbitrary eclecticism, and that we need, for judgment, fixed and absolute categories. Historicism is not eclecticism.... Each historian (we may also call him, with

12. Carlyle, *Works,* Centenary ed. (London, 1898-99), *Essays, 3,* 54-56; *Past and Present,* p. 46.
13. *Romanische Forschungen, 62* (1956), 387-397.
14. Bern, 1958.
15. *Studia philologica et letteraria in honorem L. Spitzer,* ed. A. G. Hatcher and K. L. Selig (Bern, 1958), pp. 31-37.

Vico's terminology, "philologist") has to undertake this task for himself, since historical relativism has a twofold aspect: it concerns the understanding historian as well as the phenomena to be understood. This is an extreme relativism; but we should not fear it.... The historian does not become incapable of judging; he learns what judging means. Indeed, he will soon cease to judge by abstract and unhistorical categories; he even will cease to search for such categories of judgment. That general human quality, common to the most perfect works of the particular periods, which alone may provide for such categories, can be grasped only in its particular forms, or else as a dialectical process in history; its abstract essence cannot be expressed in exact significant terms. It is from the material itself that he will learn to extract the categories or concepts which he needs for describing and distinguishing the different phenomena. These concepts are not absolute; they are elastic and provisional, changeable with changing history. But they will be sufficient to enable us to discover what the different phenomena mean within their own period, and what they mean within the three thousand years of conscious literary human life we know of; and finally, what they mean to us, here and now. That is judgment enough; it may lead also to some understanding of what is common to all of these phenomena, but it would be difficult to express it otherwise than as a dialectical process in history....

This is an excellent statement, moderately phrased, concrete in its proposals, supported by the authority of a scholar who knew the relevant German tradition and had the experience of working within it. It contains, no doubt, a measure of truth which we all have to recognize, but still it rouses ultimate, insuperable misgivings, a final dissatisfaction with the "extreme relativism" accepted here so resignedly and even complacently. Let me try to sort out some of the problems raised and marshal some answers to this influential point of view. Let me begin at the most abstract level: the assertion of the inevitable conditioning of the historian's own point of view, the recognition of one's own limited place in space and time, the relativism elaborated and emphasized by the "sociology of knowledge," particularly by Karl Mannheim in *Ideologie und Utopie*.[16] This kind of relativism was and is extremely valuable as a method of investigating the hidden assumptions and biases of the investigator himself. But it surely can serve only as a general warning, as a kind of *momento mori*. As Isaiah Berlin observes, in a similar context:

Such charges [of subjectiveness or relativity] resemble suggestions sometimes casually advanced, that life is a dream. We protest that "everything" cannot be a dream, for then, with nothing to contrast with dreams, the notion of a "dream" loses all specific

16. Bonn, 1929, Eng. trans., London, 1936.

reference.... If everything is subjective or relative, nothing can
be judged to be more so than anything else. If words like "subjective" and "relative," "prejudiced" and "biased," are terms not
of comparison and contrast—do not imply the possibility of their
own opposites, of "objective" (or at least "less subjective") or "un-
biased" (or at least "less biased"), what meaning have they for
us?[17]

The mere recognition of what A. O. Lovejoy has called, with a barbarous word formed on the analogy of the "egocentric predicament,"
the "presenticentric predicament"[18] does not get us anywhere: it merely
raises the problem of all knowing; it leads only to universal skepticism,
to theoretical paralysis. Actually the case of knowledge and even of historical knowledge is not that desperate. There are universal propositions
in logic and mathematics such as two plus two equal four, there are universally valid ethical precepts, such, for instance, as that which con-
demns the massacre of innocent people, and there are many neutral true
propositions concerning history and human affairs. There is a difference
between the psychology of the investigator, his presumed bias, ideology,
perspective and the logical structure of his propositions. The genesis
of a theory does not necessarily invalidate its truth. Men can correct
their biases, criticize their presuppositions, rise above their temporal
and local limitations, aim at objectivity, arrive at some knowledge and
truth. The world may be dark and mysterious, but it is surely not completely unintelligible.

But the problems of literary study need not actually be approached
in terms of this very general debate about the relativity of all knowledge or even the special difficulties of all historical knowledge. Literary
study differs from historical study in having to deal not with documents
but with monuments. A historian has to reconstruct a long-past event
on the basis of eye-witness accounts; the literary student, on the other
hand, has direct access to his object: the work of art. It is open to inspection whether it was written yesterday or three thousand years ago, while
the battle of Marathon and even the battle of the Bulge have passed
irrevocably. Only peripherally, in questions which have to do with biography or, say, the reconstruction of the Elizabethan playhouse, does
the literary student have to rely on documents. He can examine his object, the work itself; he must understand, interpret, and evaluate it;
he must, in short, be a critic in order to be a historian. The political or
economic or social historian, no doubt, also selects his facts for their
interest or importance, but the literary student is confronted with a
special problem of value; his object, the work of art, is not only value-
impregnated, but is itself a structure of values. Many attempts have
been made to escape the inevitable consequences of this insight, to avoid
the necessity not only of selection but of judgment, but all have failed

17. *Historical Inevitability* (Oxford, 1954), p. 61.
18. A. O. Lovejoy, "Present Standpoints and Past History," *Journal of Philosophy, 36* (1939),
477-489.

and must, I think, fail unless we want to reduce literary study to a mere listing of books, to annals or a chronicle. There is nothing which can obviate the necessity of critical judgment, the need of aesthetic standards, just as there is nothing which can obviate the need of ethical or logical standards.

One widely used escape door leads nowhere: the assertion that we need not judge, but that we simply need adopt the criteria of the past: that we must reconstruct and apply the values of the period we are studying. I shall not merely argue that these standards cannot be reconstructed with certainty, that we are confronted with insurmountable difficulties if we want to be sure what Shakespeare intended by his plays and how he conceived them or what the Elizabethan audience understood by them. There are different schools of scholarship which try to get at this past meaning by different routes: E. E. Stoll believes in reconstructing stage conventions; Miss Tuve appeals to rhetorical training, or liturgical and iconographic traditions; others swear by the authority of the NED; still others, like J. Dover Wilson, think that "the door to Shakespeare's workshop stands ajar" when they discover inconsistencies in punctuation or line arrangement from bibliographical evidence, etc. Actually, in reconstructing the critical judgment of the past we appeal only to one criterion: that of contemporary success. But if we examine any literary history in the light of the actual opinions of the past we shall see that we do not admit and cannot admit the standards of the past. When we properly know the views of Englishmen about their contemporary literature, e.g., late in the eighteenth century, we may be in for some surprises: David Hume, for instance, thought Wilkie's *Epigoniad* comparable to Homer; Nathan Drake thought Cumberland's *Cavalry* greater than Milton's *Paradise Lost.* Obviously, accepting contemporary evaluation requires our discriminating between a welter of opinions: who valued whom and why and when? Professor Geoffrey Barraclough, in a similar argument against historians who recommend that we should study "the things that were important *then* rather than things that are important *now*," advises them to look, for instance, at thirteenth-century chronicles: "a dreary recital of miracles, tempests, comets, pestilences, calamities, and other wonderful things."[19] Clearly the standards of contemporaries cannot be binding on us, even if we could reconstruct them and find a common lowest denominator among their diversities. Nor can we simply divest ourselves of our individuality or the lessons we have learned from history. Asking us to interpret *Hamlet* only in terms of what the very hypothetical views of Shakespeare or his audience were is asking us to forget three hundred years of history. It prohibits us to use the insights of a Goethe or Coleridge, it impoverishes a work which has attracted and accumulated meanings in the course of history. But again this history itself, however instructive, cannot be binding on us: its authority is open to the same objections as the authority of the author's contemporaries. There is simply no way of avoiding judgment by us, by myself. Even the "verdict of the ages" is only the accumulated judgment of other

19. *History in a Changing World* (Norman, Oklahoma, 1956), p. 22.

readers, critics, viewers, and even professors. The only truthful and right thing to do is to make this judgment as objective as possible, to do what every scientist and scholar does: to isolate his object, in our case, the literary work of art, to contemplate it intently, to analyze, to interpret, and finally to evaluate it by criteria derived from, verified by, buttressed by, as wide a knowledge, as close an observation, as keen a sensibility, as honest a judgment as we can command.

The old absolutism is untenable: the assumption of one eternal, narrowly defined standard had to be abandoned under the impact of our experience of the wide variety of art, but on the other hand, complete relativism is equally untenable; it leads to paralyzing skepticism, to an anarchy of values, to the acceptance of the old vicious maxim: *De gustibus non est disputandum*. The kind of period relativism recommended as a solution by Auerbach is no way out: it would split up the concept of art and poetry into innumerable fragments. Relativism in the sense of a denial of all objectivity is refuted by many arguments: by the parallel to ethics and science, by recognition that there are aesthetic as well as ethical imperatives and scientific truths. Our whole society is based on the assumption that we know what is just, and our science on the assumption that we know what is true. Our teaching of literature is actually also based on aesthetic imperatives, even if we feel less definitely bound by them and seem much more hesitant to bring these assumptions out into the open. The disaster of the "humanities" as far as they are concerned with the arts and literature is due to their timidity in making the very same claims which are made in regard to law and truth. Actually we do make these claims when we teach *Hamlet* or *Paradise Lost* rather than Grace Metalious or, to name contemporaries of Shakespeare and Milton, Henry Glapthorne or Richard Blackmore. But we do so shamefacedly, apologetically, hesitatingly. There is, contrary to frequent assertions, a very wide agreement on the great classics: the main canon of literature. There is an insuperable gulf between really great art and very bad art: between, say, "Lycidas" and a poem on the leading page of the *New York Times,* between Tolstoy's *Master and Man* and a story in *True Confessions.* Relativists always shirk the issue of thoroughly bad poetry. They like to move in the region of near-great art, where disputes among critics are most frequent, as works are valued for very different reasons. The more complex a work of art, the more diverse the structure of values it embodies, and hence the more difficult its interpretation, the greater the danger of ignoring one or the other aspect. But this does not mean that all interpretations are equally right, that there is no possibility of differentiating between them. There are utterly fantastic interpretations, partial, distorted interpretations. We may argue about Bradley's or Dover Wilson's or even Ernest Jones' interpretation of Hamlet: but we know that Hamlet was no woman in disguise. The concept of adequacy of interpretation leads clearly to the concept of the correctness of judgment. Evaluation grows out of understanding; correct evaluation out of correct understanding. There is a hierarchy of viewpoints implied in the very concept of adequacy of interpretation. Just as there is correct interpretation, at least as an ideal, so there is correct judgment, good judgment. Auerbach's relativistic argument that nowadays we enjoy the art of all ages and peoples: neolithic cave-paintings, Chinese landscapes, Negro masks, Gregorian chants, etc., should and can be turned against the relativists. It shows that there is a common feature in all art which we recognize today more clearly than in earlier ages. There is a common humanity which makes every art remote in time and place, and original-ly serving functions quite different from aesthetic contemplation, acces-sible and enjoyable to us. We have risen above the limitations of traditional Western taste – the parochialism and relativism of such taste – into a realm if not of absolute then of universal art. There is such a realm, and the various historical manifestations are often far less historically limited in character than is assumed by historians interested mainly in making art serve a temporary social purpose and illuminate social history. Some Chinese or ancient Greek love lyrics on basic simple themes are hardly dateable in space or time except for their language. Even Auerbach, in spite of his radical relativism, has to admit "some under-standing of what is common to all of these phenomena" and grants that we do not adopt relativism when our political (that is ethical, vital) in-terests are at stake. Logic, ethics and, I believe, aesthetics cry aloud against a complete historicism which, one should emphasize, in men such as Auerbach, is still shored up by an inherited ideal of humanism and buttressed methodologically by an unconsciously held conceptual framework of grammatical, stylistic and *geistesgeschichtlich* categories. In such radical versions as, e.g., George Boas' *A Primer for Critics*,[20] Bernard Heyl's *New Bearings in Esthetics and Art Criticism*,[21] or Wayne Shumaker's *Elements of Critical Theory*,[22] the theory leads to a dehuman-ization of the arts, to a paralysis of criticism, to a surrender of our pri-mary concern for truth. The only way out is a carefully defined and refined absolutism, a recognition that "the Absolute is in the relative, though not finally and fully in it." This was the formula of Ernst Troeltsch, who struggled more than any other historian with the problem of historicism and came to the conclusion that "historicism" must be superseded.[23]

We must return to the task of building a literary theory, a system of principles, a theory of values which will necessarily draw on the criticism of concrete works of art and will constantly invoke the assistance of lit-erary history. But the three disciplines are and will remain distinct: history cannot absorb or replace theory, while theory should not even dream of absorbing history. André Malraux has spoken eloquently of the imaginary museum, the museum without walls, drawing on a world-wide acquaintance with the plastic arts. Surely in literature we are con-fronted with the same task as that of the art critic, or at least an analogous task: we can more directly and easily assemble our museum in a library but we are still faced with the walls and barriers of languages and his-torical forms of languages. Much of our work aims at breaking down

20. Baltimore, 1937 (renamed *Wingless Pegasus: A Handbook for Critics,* Baltimore, 1950).
21. New Haven, 1943.
22. Berkeley, 1952.
23. Cf. "Historiography," in Hastings' *Encyclopaedia of Religion and Ethics, 6* (Edinburgh, 1913), 722.

these barriers, at demolishing these walls by translations, philological study, editing, comparative literature, or simply imaginative sympathy. Ultimately literature, like the plastic arts, like Malraux's voices of silence, is a chorus of voices — articulate throughout the ages — which asserts man's defiance of time and destiny, his victory over impermanence, relativity, and history.

3

The History of Ideas and Literary Theory

R. S. Crane

Literature, Philosophy, and the History of Ideas

My subject is stated so ambiguously in my title that I must begin by saying how I intend to treat it. I propose to discuss "literary ideas," or rather ideas in literature, in the context both of ideas in philosophy and of ideas in the history of ideas; and in doing so I want to lay the final emphasis on the distinctively literary characteristics and functions of literary ideas.[1] I shall use, accordingly, what Jung calls a "constructive" as opposed to a "reductive" method of procedure. I shall look, that is, for both likenesses and differences among the three classes or embodiments of ideas I speak of; but I shall not move from differences to likenesses—as in the many attempts to interpret poetry as a kind of philosophy or philosophy as a kind of poetry or to identify the study of either poetry or philosophy with the history of ideas—but rather in the contrary direction, from the common characteristics of ideas in all three fields to the more or less sharply differentiated characteristics that distinguish ideas as they function in literature from ideas as they function in philosophy and in the history of ideas. I want, furthermore, to be as matter of fact as possible and hence to start with a minimum of commitment as to the essential natures and interrelationships of my three fields. I shall assume at the outset, therefore, only very rough discriminations of meaning among the three terms in my title—such discriminations as we all make in common discourse when we classify *Othello, Tom Jones,* and the "Ode to a Nightingale," for example, as works of literary art primarily rather than of philosophy or intellectual history; Spinoza's

From *Modern Philology,* LII (1954), 73-83. Reprinted by permission of The University of Chicago Press and R. S. Crane. Copyright 1954 by The University of Chicago Press.

1. A paper read before a conference on the history of ideas in relation to literature and the arts held at Reed College, Portland, Oregon, April 23-24, 1954, under the auspices of the Pacific Coast Council on the Humanities. The committee in charge of the conference had proposed as a theme for consideration the issues raised by Lionel Trilling's discussion (*The Liberal Imagination* [New York, 1950], pp. 281 ff.) of "the meaning of a literary idea" and especially by his criticism (*ibid.,* p. 190) of Professor Arthur O. Lovejoy's views on the relation between ideas in literature and ideas in philosophy. My assignment was primarily the literary bearings of the question; the philosophical bearings were treated in a paper by Professor Arthur E. Murphy, of the University of Washington.

Ethics, Hume's *Enquiry concerning the Principles of Morals,* and the *Critique of Judgment* as works of philosophy primarily rather than of literary art or intellectual history; and *The Great Chain of Being* and *Essays in the History of Ideas* as works of intellectual history primarily rather than of philosophy or literary art. There is no need, to begin with at least, for any greater refinement of definition than this: literature is simply what men do when they write works, whatever their special themes, that resemble more closely, in structure, method, and intent, the works in the first group than those in either of the other two; and so, similarly, for philosophy and the history of ideas.

I have singled out Lovejoy's *The Great Chain of Being* and his *Essays in the History of Ideas* for two reasons. These books embody, for one thing, a clearly defined conception of the history of ideas as an independent discipline, a distinctive way of dealing with ideas, from which much instruction can be drawn with respect to our problem. And, for another thing—and by virtue of the peculiar character of this conception—they afford as good a starting point as could well be found for discussing ideas themselves, considered apart from what happens to them when they become ingredients in the constructions of intellectual history, philosophy, and literature.

I refer here of course to Lovejoy's notion of "unit-ideas" or "individual ideas"—a notion which, so far as I am aware, he was the first, if not to entertain, at least to erect into a principle of historical method. The history of ideas, he says, is "something at once more specific and less restricted than the history of philosophy." It is less restricted in that it takes as its documents not merely the writings of accredited philosophers but any writings whatsoever in which ideas may be discerned, whether their authors be philosophers, theologians, scientists, historians, scholars, critics, essayists, preachers, orators, journalists, novelists, dramatists, or poets. And it is more specific than the history of philosophy or, presumably, of any other mode of discursive thought, in that it applies to its documents an initial procedure "somewhat analogous," as he remarks, "to that of analytic chemistry." The procedure is one of separating out from particular systems of thought, viewed as more or less unstable "compounds," the basic conceptual and methodological elements of which they are composed; and the results of this analysis—the "unit-ideas" it fixes our attention on—become the essential data of the history of ideas.[2] Examples will occur to all readers of Lovejoy's books and papers: the themes of continuity, plenitude, and gradation; the metaphor of the chain of being; the reference of values to the ambiguous norm of Nature; the antitheses of nature and art, the simple and the complex, the regular and the irregular, the uniform and the diverse; the notions of progress, decline, and cyclical change; and so on. These are all, in varying degrees of complexity, "unit-ideas."

So far, it seems to me, this is a wholly sound procedure, reflecting an insight into the nature of intellectual constructions which everyone

2. *The Great Chain of Being* (Cambridge, Mass., 1936), pp. 3 ff.

can easily verify. Considered as individual wholes, such constructions are unique things, and they are unique also, in another sense, when viewed as aggregates of particular statements about their subjects. Yet we can always discover in any work, however original, that involves thought a large number of minor forms or schemes of subject matter and reasoning which, if we are at all widely read, will have for us a familiar ring. We have met with the same things before—the same sets of general terms, the same questions, the same, or apparently the same, distinctions, the same analogies, the same bits of doctrine, the same modes or lines of proof, the same myths—in many other writers, in the same or different departments of writing, earlier or later.

The more broadly learned we are, indeed, the more correspondences of this kind, linking together parts or brief passages in writings of the most diverse sorts, we shall be likely to note in the margins of our books or in scholarly papers. And what we thus note will be "unit-ideas" in Lovejoy's meaning of the word. I should prefer to call them "commonplaces," partly to suggest their affinity with the *topoi* and places of argument of the ancient, medieval, and early modern writers on rhetoric and logic, and partly to emphasize their character as more or less crystallized and discrete conceptual materials or devices of method that are capable, as their history shows, of being put to a great variety of uses in all or many fields of discussion and literary art. Some, though by no means all, of them are *disjecta membra* of philosophic or scientific systems that have survived, independently, as parts of a common stock of usable notions and patterns of reasoning upon which all educated men can draw: for example, the divided line of Plato, the four causes of Aristotle, the atoms of Democritus, the Ciceronian division of the virtues, the moral sense of Shaftesbury, the Kantian distinction of reason and understanding, the various fragments of doctrine and method torn loose, in our day, from the psychologies of Freud and Jung. The question of origin, however, is less important here than the question of intellectual status; and of ideas in this elementary sense, including those discussed so learnedly and trenchantly by Lovejoy, I think we must say that, wherever they occur, they represent not so much what the writers in whose treatises, essays, poems, or novels we find them are thinking *about* as what they are thinking *with*. In this paper of mine, for instance, you will find the commonplaces, among others, of a "constructive" as distinct from a "reductive" method and of the difference between materials and synthesis. These enter into the paper, however, not as controlling problems in the discussion but as means of formulating and conducting it. To the extent that my paper is philosophical in form, they can doubtless be called "philosophical ideas"; but they clearly have no definite philosophical meaning or value apart from the uses, good or bad, I put them to or the uses, rather different from mine, they were put to in the philosophers who first conceived them. And the same thing would have to be said about them as literary ideas, should we encounter them, as we easily might, in works of literary art. In themselves, in short—and this is true of all ideas when isolated as unit-conceptions—they are only materials or devices and hence only potentially either philosophical or literary.

Now it is obvious that if ideas in this sense can be abstracted from the constructions of various kinds in which they have served as elements, they can be made the subject matter of historical study, and this in several different ways. One of these would involve taking as your point of departure an important philosophical or literary text and building up around it a rich body of scholarly annotation designed to show in detail the extent of its author's reliance on the commonplaces available to him in earlier writings; this has been done with notable success in such editions as Gilson's of the *Discours de la méthode,* André Morize's of *Candide,* Daniel Mornet's of the *Nouvelle Héloïse,* and Maynard Mack's of the *Essay on Man.* Another way would be that which Lovejoy himself exemplifies in *Primitivism and Related Ideas in Antiquity* and (in a more tightly organized fashion) in *The Great Chain of Being:* here you proceed by first isolating some idea or closely connected group of ideas; then bringing together from different fields and for an extended period of time as many texts expressive of it as you can find; and, finally, so correlating your materials as to exhibit the stages of its dissemination and use, in writings of all kinds, for as long as it remained current. Lastly, you might concentrate, not on a text or author or on an idea, but on a period, such as the English Renaissance or the Enlightenment, and set yourself the problem of discovering and describing the various sets of ideas that operate as recurrent commonplaces in some or all of its provinces of thought and artistic expression, and such shifts in the character of these as the texts may disclose: Lovejoy has attempted something like this in his essay on the meaning of "Romanticism" for the historian of ideas,[3] and there are approximations to it in the discussions by Hardin Craig and E. M. W. Tillyard of the so-called "world-view" of the Elizabethans. We have not made as yet, in any of these three branches of study, more than a few beginnings; but what has been done is enough to suggest the immense value of the history of ideas, as thus conceived, for philosophical interpretation and the criticism and history of literature. The things men say in philosophy and literature are conditioned, in every age, by the means available to them, in the ever changing common storehouse of intellectual materials and devices, for saying these things; and it is well to know, as fully and exactly as possible, for any of the philosophers or literary artists we may wish to study, what the means accessible to them were and from what sources – philosophical, literary, or popular – they were derived.

This is the sphere of the history of ideas in the now commonly accepted sense of that word; and its value for the interpretation of philosophical and literary works is likely to be all the greater in proportion as we recognize what it necessarily leaves out. For the history of "individual ideas" can give us at best, to use another venerable commonplace, only some of the material causes of what philosophers and literary artists think and say, abstracted from the particular forms by virtue of which the writings it investigates become significant as philosophy or literature. It is like the history of language as written by grammarians innocent of philoso-

---

3. *Journal of the History of Ideas,* II (1941), 257-78.

phy or literary criticism. It can tell us much about the conceptual vocabularies and idioms of method that philosophers and literary men at different times have used, but little or nothing about how they have used these, or why in this manner rather than in some other, or with what consequences for the vocabularies and idioms themselves. For such understanding we must look beyond the idea-materials which the history of ideas, as so defined, undertakes to study.

It must be said that Lovejoy is aware of this, with the result that the history he writes — especially, though not exclusively, in *The Great Chain of Being* — is much more than a merely descriptive account of the intellectual phenomena with which it deals. These phenomena are basically, as we have seen, unit-ideas or the distinguishable parts of idea-complexes such as the chain of being or the cluster of significations attached to the sacred word "Nature"; and concerning such elements it is sufficient for him to give descriptive definitions, as in a dictionary, in terms of their respective conceptual contents, and to apply these directly to shorter or longer passages in writings of all kinds, philosophical or literary. The ideas or idea-elements he deals with are thus, in a sense, irreducible atoms that are assumed to be constant in meaning throughout the history. The problem of the history itself, however, is what happens to the ideas, once they are, so to speak, set in motion. It is the problem, first, of showing how they coalesce to form the particular "unstable compounds" of unit-ideas — the conception is highly significant — which we call "philosophic systems" or "bodies of doctrine" in philosophy or literature and, second, and in a larger perspective, of making intelligible the major historical shifts in attitude and belief that have occurred from time to time, as when the Enlightenment gave place to Romanticism. And for these purposes Lovejoy introduces what I can only call a "philosophy" of ideas and their history.

He does this by positing, as general principles of explanation in any history of ideas, certain basic motor forces, as they may be termed, that operate as determining factors in the thought of both individual writers and ages. They appear to be of three kinds, corresponding to three levels of human thought — the semantic, the doctrinal or dialectical, and the psychological. The first force is that inherent in the ambiguity of words, and especially of those large and peculiarly multivocal catchwords, like "Nature," that have dotted the pages of philosophers, essayists, and poets in all periods. This very multivocality, he says — and illustrates in many pages — is a potent cause of confusion in our thinking and "sometimes facilitates or promotes (though it doubtless seldom or never solely causes) changes — some of them revolutionary changes — in the reigning fashions in ideas."[4] The second force is again one inherent in the materials: it is the capacity of particular unit-ideas to attract or repel one another, often without the author's being aware of what is going on. The assumption here is that ideas themselves, apart from their particular uses in philosophical or literary discourse, are connected with other ideas by logical relations of "simple congruity or mutual implication or

---

4. *Essays in the History of Ideas* (Baltimore, 1948), pp. xiv-xv.

mutual incongruity"[5] and that this fact often gives rise to latent discords or conflicts among the ideas compounded in a given system or piece of writing. The third force, which influences profoundly but never wholly dominates the operation of the other two, is the force, or rather, more often, the internally conflicting forces, of temperamental predilection. What a writer thinks is determined in considerable part by his frequently "incongruous propensities of feeling or taste," the "underlying affective factors in his personality";[6] and the history of ideas in general, Lovejoy tells us in *The Great Chain of Being*, reflects the working of two fundamental and opposing biases of temperament, which have competed with each other for domination throughout the evolution of Western thought, as "the primary antithesis in philosophical or religious tendencies." These are the two basic moods (reminiscent of William James's division of all men into the "tender-minded" and the "tough-minded") which Lovejoy calls "other-worldliness" and "this-worldliness."[7]

All the causes in Lovejoy's history can, I think, be reduced to the interplay of these three forces, each with a distinctive efficacy of its own, in the formation and exposition of thought alike by individual writers and by traditions or ages of writers. The result—unless I have missed the point entirely—is an interesting species of historical determinism, in which individual ideas are treated as solid particles, with the same thought-content wherever they appear, and in which the different syntheses they enter into are describable in terms of the never wholly harmonious impulsions, inherent in human nature, in the ideas themselves, and in the words that express them, by which writers are moved, often in spite of what they consciously intend, in one direction or another or in two directions at once. It is inevitable, on this view, that even great thinkers and literary artists should be frequently at odds with themselves and that fundamental inconsistency, in assumptions and doctrines, should be the rule rather than the exception. To see how this follows from the method, you have only to read Lovejoy's discussions of Plato, Aristotle, Aquinas, Spinoza, Milton, Pope, Rousseau, Herder, Schiller, Coleridge.

The Great Chain of Being is one of the distinguished books of our time, and it can be read in several ways: as a scholarly history, marked by fresh and impressive erudition; as a moving ironic epic of human failure in a foredoomed quest that has yet had, incidentally, some happy outcomes; finally—and this is the aspect I now want to stress—as a piece of sustained dialectic in historical guise, in which the Democritean tradition in philosophic method is given a modern and evolutionary turn.

I emphasize this last aspect because it seems to me to have a direct bearing on our central question of the nature of ideas not only in the history of ideas but in philosophy and literature. I shall leave ideas in philosophy, for the most part, to better hands, but it is necessary to say

5. *Ibid.,* pp. xv-xvii.
6. *Ibid.,* pp. xvi, 254.
7. *The Great Chain of Being,* pp. 24 ff.

one or two things, and, in the first place, to point out the inadequacy of Lovejoy's concept of "unit-ideas," taken as irreducible elements of philosophic "compounds," for the understanding even of that concept itself. If I have at all succeeded in making clear the meaning and value of the notion of "unit-ideas" in Lovejoy, it is because I have gone beyond the notion as such and inquired into the place it has, the uses it serves, and the method by which it is defined in the overall dialectic concerning ideas and their history that informs and organizes his discussion. Looked at apart from such considerations, it is merely a piece of ambiguous language that might be used in a different dialectic to signify a concept quite distinct from Lovejoy's. Its actual content and significance as a particular concept in his writings, in short, is relative to what he does with it in the construction of his argument as a whole.

And what is true of this idea of Lovejoy's is true of all the so-called "individual" concepts, distinctions, analogies, doctrines, etc., we meet with in philosophic works. They become meaningful, as ideas of the philosopher in question, only when we view them as parts of a dialectical whole that determines their peculiar contents and functions and is itself determined by the special problem the philosopher has set himself to solve, as *he* conceives it, and by his distinctive assumptions and principles of method. To talk about them in separation from the particular activity of reasoning by which they are ordered and defined in philosophic discourse is to talk about them merely as floating commonplaces or themes, as indeterminate in meaning as the hundred or so "great ideas" that Mortimer Adler has assembled, with illustrative quotations from poets and rhetoricians as well as philosophers, in his *Syntopicon.* Here, then, are necessities of a much more immediately compelling sort than the very general and, so to speak, collective necessities that alone are recognized in Lovejoy's theory; and it is these—the necessities of the particular argument as a whole—that give individual life and being to the commonplaces of human thought or of the age and that, when the argument is of one of the kinds we agree to call philosophical, confer the character of philosophical, rather than of, say, rhetorical or literary, ideas upon the various concepts and distinctions it brings into play.

The nature of literary ideas, or of ideas of literature, has to be approached in similar terms. Trilling is surely right in taking exception to Lovejoy's assertion that "the ideas in serious reflective literature are, of course, in great part philosophical ideas in dilution."[8] From one point of view and up to a certain stage of analysis, indeed, the assertion makes sense. If you concentrate on those literary productions in which the thought has an evident genetic relationship to the thought expressed in earlier works by competent philosophers, and take the kind of integration and elaboration of ideas to be found in the latter as your standard, you will almost invariably observe a falling-off in rigor of statement and connection and be tempted to view the ratio of literature to philosophy, in this aspect, as equivalent to the ratio of the "easy philosophy"

8. *Ibid.,* pp. 16-17; cf. Trilling, p. 190.

to the "abstruse philosophy" described by David Hume. In all such cases the metaphor of "dilution" is forced upon you: for example, by what has happened to the dialectic of the *Phaedrus* in the many lyrics that turn on the theme of earthly and spiritual love, or to the Aristotelian analysis of the virtues in the second book of *The Faerie Queene,* or to the psychology of Hartley in the early poems of Wordsworth. What you generally find in the poets and other literary artists who have drawn upon philosophers for ideas—when you judge them by criteria of philosophic construction—is a kind of borrowing that leaves behind the distinctive wholes philosophers have created and, in doing so, inevitably reduces the component parts of these which it seizes upon to a lower level of *philosophic* interest and value.

But not necessarily—and this is where Trilling is right—of *literary* interest and value. Would the *Divine Comedy* be better or worse, as a poem with philosophic implications, if it had more of the philosophic completeness and sophistication of the *Summa theologica?* Or is the obvious "dilution" of the "philosophical ideas" of King and Bolingbroke in the first epistle of the *Essay on Man* a merit or defect when the *Essay* is considered, as I think it must be considered if full justice is to be done to it, as a work of literary art? Or is the relative simplicity of the moral ideas that underlie *Tom Jones,* when these are viewed, abstractly, in comparison with the arguments on similar themes in (say) Hume's *Enquiry concerning the Principles of Morals,* to be counted an advantage or a disadvantage in Fielding's making of that masterpiece of comic fiction? The very fact that we can sensibly ask such questions, and not always answer them to the discredit of the poets or novelists, suggests that the problem of the uses and judgment of ideas in literature is, in some significant respects at least, quite different from the problem of the uses and judgment of ideas, even the same ideas, in philosophy. It could hardly, indeed, be otherwise. For though both philosophers and literary artists are engaged in constructing wholes, the principles that determine wholeness, completeness, integrity in philosophy and in literature are not the same—at any rate in those instances of philosophic and literary constructions that we normally regard as most typical of the two fields; and it follows that the conceptual parts in each kind of whole, however similar these may appear to be when taken as "individual ideas," will have, as parts, a different nature and significance, depending on the uses to which they are put and the relationships into which they are made to enter.

In order to talk about ideas in literature as "literary," therefore, we must consider them in the light of the literary syntheses they help to make possible and of their various functions relative to these. And here we are confronted with the fact that the principles of literary synthesis, even within what we are wont to call "poetic" literature, have been of a good many different kinds and that the line between some of these and the distinctive forms of philosophy is often hard to draw. What is the difference, if any, between the character and functioning of the ideas in Lucretius' poem and the character and functioning of the ideas, of a generally similar philosophic order, in the treatises of Gassendi and Boyle? I suppose the best answer is that, whereas the shaping of the particular thoughts is determined immediately, in both the poem and the treatises, by the exigencies of a controlling and explicitly stated line of argument, with respect to which they are logical parts, the ideas in the *De rerum natura* are also conditioned by a further set of necessities, deriving from the poet's choice of verse as his medium and, more especially, from his intention of using his argument to inculcate certain emotional states, such as freedom from superstitious fear, in his audience. It is thus a composite work, both philosophical and literary, and whether we emphasize the one or the other aspect as more essential will depend upon our scholarly preoccupations.

There are many other works of discursive or "philosophical" poetry, in all languages, for which the line separating literature from philosophy is much easier to draw. Consider, for instance, Pope's *Essay on Man* and Thomson's *Seasons*. In both poems a dialectical structure of sorts can be discerned, but this is only part of the subsuming form that determines, in each, the selection, expression, and concatenation of particular ideas and arguments, and hence their meanings and values. The ideas and arguments are not in any important sense parts of a demonstration but simply materials and devices, modified by the stylistic principles of the two authors, for achieving the predominantly rhetorical ends of the two poems: in the *Essay*, that of inducing men, as Pope said, to "look upon this life with comfort and pleasure" and of putting morality "in good humour"; in the *Seasons,* that of evoking sentiments of benevolence and deistic piety in a world which, for all its shortcomings, is yet governed by an Almighty Hand.

But let us leave discursive poetry, philosophical or rhetorical, for that large and much more central class of literary forms that is exemplified —to recur to my original instances—by *Othello, Tom Jones,* and the "Ode to a Nightingale." These may be called "representational" forms, in the sense that in them the principle of continuity—what we are invited to attend to successively and to respond to—is not the stages of an explicit argument but the moments of an imagined human activity, external or internal, long or short. They are of two main varieties, according as the depicted action is used as a means of developing, indirectly, a thesis of some sort, as in Ibsen's *Doll's House* and George Orwell's *1984*, or is invented and embodied in words for the sake of its intrinsic human and emotional interest, as is the case, I think, in my three examples. In what follows I shall have in mind chiefly forms of the second kind, in dramas, novels, and lyric poems.

What is the role of ideas—and especially of ideas that are either borrowed from, or have some analogy to, ideas in philosophy—in literary works of this type, and how are they to be judged? The answer to the first question must be as complex as are the literary structures themselves that are here in question. They are structures built out of language, and especially of language in which metaphors and analogies play an important part; and we all know how often the bases of particular metaphors or analogies involve general or even technical ideas, and this not merely in the metaphysical poets. They are structures, secondly, in which the dramatis personae are frequently made to state universal propositions or to develop generalized arguments in order that their estimates of the situation, their motives in the action, their plans and deliberations may be clear. They are structures, thirdly, that very often depend on the depiction of character and disposition as an essential source of their emotional power; and here the function of ideas and arguments is to serve as external signs or manifestations of inner moral habits and states of mind, as, for example, in Hamlet's great speeches on the nature of man. Many of them, fourthly, are structures in which the organizing activity is itself primarily an activity of thought—that is to say, of men thinking, or debating with one another, on issues of universal import as well as of personal concern, as in some of Ibsen's plays or in the innumerable lyrics in the tradition exemplified by such pieces as Milton's "Lycidas," Gray's "Elegy," Wordsworth's "Intimations" ode, Arnold's "The Scholar Gypsy," Dylan Thomas' "Altarwise by owl-light" sonnets, and so on. And, finally, there is the problem in all such structures of helping the reader or spectator to interpret, and so to feel, properly what is taking place; and here again we see an important role for ideas, whether they are given the form of discursive commentary by chorus or choral character or narrator or messenger or are signified indirectly through complex metaphors or symbols, parallel lines of action, or sequences of implicative imagery.

In all these cases the ideas we become aware of, more or less insistently, in literary works of this kind, may be regarded as functional parts or devices serving various uses, of an artistic rather than a philosophical order, in the working out of the form. But there is also something else, and it is equally important. We often speak of the "vision of life," the "world-view," the "philosophy" of particular dramatists, novelists, or lyric poets, and in doing so what we usually have in mind is some scheme of general propositions that are implied by, rather than directly asserted in, their individual works. They are what the writer has assumed, as a matter either of personal conviction or of *ad hoc* convenience, by way of more or less coherent basic presuppositions in his acts of artistic creation. There are no representational works that do not rest upon universally intelligible postulates of some kind concerning both the moral, social, political, or religious values involved in their actions and the laws of probability that operate at least within the artist's imagined world. Without them, indeed, no convincing or emotionally unified representational forms would be possible. We may say, in fact, that they are to these forms as the primary and often buried principles of a philosopher are to the particular arguments he constructs; and it is sometimes possible to trace in them the reflection of some characteristic philosophical or theological system—Stoic, Pascalian, Positivist, Kierkegaardian, Existentialist, or the like. Whether philosophic in this sense or not, they are the elements in literary works that justify us most completely in using philosophic language to talk about and discriminate what writers have thought or believed; witness such excellent recent studies as George Orwell's essays on Dickens and boys' magazines,[9] John Holloway's chap-

9. *Dickens, Dali & Others: Studies in Popular Culture* (New York, 1946), pp. 1-75, 76-114.

ters on George Eliot and Thomas Hardy in his *The Victorian Sage,*[10] Elder
Olson's analysis of the moral universe of Dylan Thomas' poems,[11] and
Eliseo Vivas' pages on Céline's *Journey to the End of the Night* in his
paper on "Literature and Knowledge."[12] This underlying and philosophically meaningful universality of literary works—though at a still broader
level of significance—is also, I think, what those modern critics have
really been getting at who have talked so much about myths and psychological "archetypes," often somewhat confusedly.

Ideas, then, are involved in literary works of the kind we are now considering in two principal ways: as moral and intellectual bases of their
forms and as parts or devices necessitated or made appropriate by their
forms. And the criteria for judging the significance and value of ideas in
literature will naturally differ according as we attend primarily to the
first or the second of these two functions. Both entail a use of ideas for
artistic rather than philosophical purposes; but the systems of moral,
physical, and psychological ideas implied by literary works appear to lend
themselves more easily than do the thoughts and reasonings such works
explicitly contain to modes of interpretation and judgment that are at
least analogous to those we use in speaking of philosophic arguments.
The difference between a tragedy or an artistically serious comedy or
novel or lyric poem and a merely sensational, melodramatic, sentimental,
or fanciful work is more than a difference in form and technique. It is a
difference we cannot very well state without bringing in distinctions
between true, comprehensive, or at least mature conceptions of things
and false, partial, arbitrary, or simple-minded conceptions; and it is in
terms of precisely such distinctions, of course, that we tend to differentiate among metaphysical, ethical, political, and aesthetic constructions in
philosophy, distinct as these are from literary constructions in method
and intent.

The peculiarly literary value of literary works, however, is a function
not of their presuppositions or of their materials of ideas and images as
such but of these as formed into fully realized and beautiful individual
wholes. We can indeed say of such wholes, with Trilling, that they give
us a kind of pleasure that is hard to distinguish psychologically from the
pleasure of "cogency" we experience in reading successfully a philosophic
argument;[13] in both cases our delight is dependent on our perception of
certain things following, necessarily or probably, from certain things
laid down. I shall not pursue this point; but it is essential to remark that
the cogency achieved in an excellent literary work is not, as in philosophy, a matter of adequate proof but rather of the sustained efficiency of
what is done in the component parts of a novel, drama, or poem relative
to the special quality of the imagined human activity that is being represented. Whatever ideas or arguments are good for this—whether as
parts of the activity itself, or as signs of character or thought and emotion, or as choral commentary, or as congruous embellishment—are good

10. (London, 1953), chaps. v, viii.
11. *The Poetry of Dylan Thomas* (Chicago, 1954), pp. 1-18.
12. *Sewanee Review,* LX (1952), 574-80.
13. *The Liberal Imagination,* pp. 289-91; cf. pp. 295-55.

ideas or arguments, regardless of what might be said of them as elements in a philosophic demonstration; and their meanings, as "literary ideas," are bound up with that fact. A merely referential or logical or "philosophical" consideration of them is never sufficient to tell us what they are, and it is likely, besides, to lead to irrelevant judgments of value. For it is clearly not true in literature, as it presumably is in philosophy, that ambiguities and *non sequiturs* are always bad; they may be, in fact, precisely what the writer requires if he is to achieve his literary ends; and it is not a weakness in "Lycidas," for example, that the final stage of the meditation is connected with the beginning by no intrinsic dialectical necessity but only by the poetic inevitability of such an outcome, in the situation depicted in the poem, for the special kind of man the lyric speaker is conceived to be.

Scholarship As Argument

R. B. McKerrow

Form and Matter in the Publication of Research

May I as one who has had occasion both as a publisher and an editor to read a very considerable number of books and articles embodying the results of research into English literary history plead for more attention to *form* in the presentation of such work?

I do not know whether advancing age has made me thicker in the head than I used to be or whether I have merely become more impatient — there is so much that one still wants to do and constantly less and less time in which to do it — but it certainly seems to me that there has been a tendency in recent years for the way in which the results of research are set out to become progressively less efficient, especially among the younger students, both in England and in America. And when I say "less efficient" I am not thinking of any high qualities of literary art, but of the simplest qualities of precision and intelligibility Indeed, I have sometimes wondered whether the fate of "English studies" will not eventually be to be smothered in a kind of woolly and impenetrable fog of wordiness that few or none will be bothered to penetrate.

It may perhaps surprise some readers of *R.E.S.* if I tell them that I have several times been compelled to refuse articles offered to me which seemed, from the evidence of the footnotes, to have been the product of real research, for no other reason than that after several readings I have completely failed to discover the point or points which the author was trying to make. In one or two cases this has perhaps been due to the author's inability to express himself in English at all, but in others the trouble has seemed to be rather due to a complete ignorance of the way in which he should present his material. Being himself fully cognizant of the point at issue and with the way in which his research corrects or supplements views currently held on his subject, the author has apparently assumed that all would become clear to his readers by the mere recital of his investigations without any commentary on the results as they appear to

From *Review of English Studies,* XVI (1940), 116-121. Reprinted by permission of The Clarendon Press, Oxford.

him. But such a mere recital of an investigation will only convey what is intended by the author to a person with the same knowledge and mental outlook as the author himself, and to anyone else may be almost meaningless.

Articles of which I have been unable to make out the point at all I have necessarily rejected, generally after trying them on a friend or two, lest I were at the time more than usually dense; but I must confess to having printed in *R.E.S.* a certain number of articles which I regarded as definitely bad work. These were some which contained good research which I was assured would be useful to those with knowledge of the subject and willing to spend time and effort in puzzling out the bearing of the new matter, but of little if any use to others. Such articles cannot, of course, be lightly rejected. The pity is they could so easily, by a writer of adequate training in presenting his facts, or with sufficient imagination to enable him to dispense with such training, have been made really interesting contributions to knowledge which would have appealed to a wide circle of readers, instead of only being absorbed with difficulty and distaste by the few.

For it is imagination which is, before all else, necessary in presenting a piece of research. It is not to be considered as, so to say, an emanation of the author's brain which has been allowed to escape into the void, a mere fragment of knowledge detached from its originator, but one which is intended to become part of the knowledge of others, and in order that it may do this it must be so shaped and adapted that it may fit with ease and certainty on to the knowledge of others, those others being of course the likely readers.

New facts, skilfully prepared for our easy assimilation, for forming part of our existing aggregate of knowledge, are invariably welcomed, even when the subject is not one in which we are normally much interested, when a badly presented bit of what should be our own special subject may completely fail to make any impression on our consciousness.

We ought, I think, at the start to realize that no readers whom we are likely to have will be nearly as much interested in our views or discoveries as we ourselves are. Most of them will be people who are a little tired, a little bored, and who read us rather out of a sense of duty and a wish to keep up with what is being done than because they have any real interest in the subject; and in return for our reader's complaisance it is our duty as well as our interest to put what we have to say before him with as little trouble to him as possible. It is our duty because we ought to be kind to our fellow creature; it is our interest because if the view that we wish to put before him is clearly and competently expressed, so that he understands without trouble what we are trying to say, he will be gratified at the smooth working of his own intelligence and will inevitably think better of our theory and of its author than if he had had to puzzle himself over what we mean and then in the end doubt whether he had really understood us, so raising in himself an uneasy doubt whether his brains are quite what they used to be!

Now I suggest that if we analyse almost any piece of research which seems to us thoroughly workmanlike and satisfactory from all points of

view, we shall almost always find that it falls into five parts in the following order.

1. The *introduction,* in which the author briefly states the present
position of research on his subject and the views currently held on it.

2. The *proposal,* in which he describes in outline what he hopes to
prove.

3. The *boost,* in which he proceeds to magnify the importance of his
discovery or argument and to explain what a revolution it will create in
the views generally held on the whole period with which he is dealing.
This is, as it were, a taste of sauce to stimulate the reader's appetite.

4. The *demonstration,* in which he sets forth his discovery or argument
in an orderly fashion.

5. The *conclusion,* or *crow,* in which he summarizes what he claims to
have shown, and points out how complete and unshakeable is his proof.

Of course I am not serious in this! It is not to be supposed necessary
that we should *formally* divide our ·research articles in this way, but it
is a real and practical division and there are few research articles which
would not be improved by the adoption of such a framework, at least
under the surface.

The following points might, I believe, be worth much more serious
consideration than seems frequently to be given to them.

1. The subject of a research article should always be a unity. The paper
should always deal either with a single subject or with a well-defined
group of subjects of the same general character. Thus a particular literary work might be dealt with in all its aspects, or any one aspect might
be dealt with, say, its origin, its date, its popularity, or what not, or its
author's life or any one period or incident of it. On the other hand it is
seldom well to mix two pieces of research on different scales, an account
of a man's works as a whole and of a particular one of his works dealt with
in much greater detail. Similarly, an article in which an attempt is made
both to give new discoveries in an author's biography and a correction in
the bibliography of one of his books will almost certainly turn out an
unreadable muddle. These various kinds of discovery may often arise as
the result of a single piece of research, but it is much better to put them
forward in quite independent articles. Opportunity may always be found
to insert a cross-reference from one to the other in order to ensure that
students do not overlook the author's other discoveries.

2. Give your book or article a name which tells at once what it is all
about. Facetious and cryptic titles should be utterly eschewed. At best
they annoy, and at worst they tend to be forgotten and to render the
work under which they are concealed untraceable. Fancy names, pastoral
and the like, should never be used, however familiar they may be to
students versed in the literature of a particular period. Thus Katherine
Philips may have been well known to students of her time as the "Match-
less Orinda," but one who writes about her by the latter name risks his
work being entered in indexes under headings where it will be missed by
scholars searching for her under her family name.

3. Remember that though the great majority of your readers are likely to have a considerable knowledge of English Literature as a whole and an expert knowledge of a certain part of it, only a minority are likely to be experts in your particular period or field. In any case very few indeed can be expected to possess the minute knowledge of it which you who have just been devoting all your time to the study of it have or ought to have. (Indeed, if you do not know *much* more than others, why are you writing about it?) Keep this in mind in the whole of your writing and *adjust what you say to the knowledge which you may reasonably expect your readers to have.* This is really the whole secret of exposition, and it is so simple that it seems incredible that writers of research articles should so often be ignorant of it. But they are, they are! If you have a young brother or sister of, say, fifteen years old or so, think that you have him or her before you and that you are trying to explain the point of your article to them and at the same time to prevent them from thinking what an ass you are to be wasting their time and yours about anything so completely futile. If in your imagination you see their eyes light up and their faces set with a desire to protest or argue, you will know that whether the thesis of your paper is sound or not its presentation is at least on the right lines!

Naturally the method of presenting an argument must depend on the persons for whom it is intended. You need not in an article in *R.E.S.* explain who Ben Jonson or John Dryden or Cynewulf or Layamon were, but it would be unwise to expect all your readers to have precise knowledge as to their dates or the details of their biography. If these are required for your argument it is easy to give them without the reader being moved to indignation by the feeling that he is being treated like a child. In this connection much offence may often be avoided by the insertion of the little phrases "of course," or "as everyone knows" — *e.g.* "Stephen Hawes, who was of course writing in the earliest years of the sixteenth century, and called Lydgate 'master'" gives information which every reader of *R.E.S.* must have known at some time, but of which a few may need to be reminded in an article concerning the poetical associations of Henry VIII's court.

In your introduction, then, take your reader metaphorically by the hand and lead him gently up to the threshold of your research, reminding him courteously and without any appearance of dogmatism, not with the gestures of a teacher but gently as a comrade in study, of what he ought to know in order to understand what you have to tell him — the object of your research. He will be far better able to appreciate your demonstration if he knows what to look for, and to know what to look for if you tell him at once just what the current views of the matter are and how your own differ from them.

4. So far as possible state your facts in chronological order. When a digression is necessary, make quite clear that it *is* a digression, and when you reach the end of it, make quite clear that you are returning to the main course of the story. And always give plenty of dates, *real* dates, not the kind of dates of which many of the historical people seem to be so fond — "about two years before the conclusion of the events which we

have described" or "later in the same year," which after reading several earlier pages turns out to be the year in which "the king" attained his majority, necessitating further research to discover what king and in what year and what part of the year he was born and what "majority" meant at the time. But enough! We have all suffered. Keep on remembering that though *you* are perhaps completely familiar with all aspects of your subject, your reader may not be.

5. State your facts as simply as possible, even boldly. No one wants flowers of eloquence or literary ornaments in a research article. On the other hand do not be slangy, and, especially if you are writing for *R.E.S.*, do not use American slang. We may be interested in it, but we may not always understand it. Only a few days ago I had to beg the author of an excellent article which I was printing to substitute some phrase more intelligible to us over in England for a statement that certain evidence — "is not quite enough to convict of actual skulduggery (and the aroma of high-binding will not down) . . ."

6. Never be cryptic nor use literary paraphrases. Needless mysteries are out of place in research articles. There are plenty of them there already. If they think that you are trying to be superior, most readers will stop reading at once.

7. Do not try to be humorous. Humour is well enough in its place, but nothing more infuriates a man who is looking for a plain statement of facts than untimely humour, especially if he does not know whether the writer is really trying to be humorous or not, a point which some would-be humorists fail to make clear.

8. Do not use ambiguous expressions. The worst of these are perhaps phrases containing the word "question." If you say "there is no question that Ben Jonson was in Edinburgh in 1618" most people, perhaps all, will take you to mean that he *was* there in that year; and the same if you say "that Jonson was in Edinburgh in 1618 is beyond question" or "does not admit of question." If, however, you say that "there is no question of Jonson having been in Edinburgh in 1618," most people, though I think not all, will take you to mean that he was *not* there in that year. But there is certainly no question that it would be better to use a phrase the meaning of which is not open to question.

Avoid also the word "doubtless," which has been defined as "a word used when making a statement for the truth of which the speaker is unaware of any evidence."

Do not overtask such expressions as "it is generally admitted that," "there can be no doubt that," "it is well known that" unless you can shift your responsibility on to at least one other person by giving a reference.

9. Always be precise and careful in references and quotations, and never fear the charge of pedantry. After all, "pedant" is merely the name which one gives to anyone whose standard of accuracy happens to be a little higher than one's own!

10. Do not treat the subjects of your research with levity. Above all avoid that hateful back-slapping "heartiness" which caused certain nineteenth-century Elizabethans to refer to "Tom Nash," "Bob Green," "Will Shakespeare" and so on, with its horrible flavour of modern gutter

journalism which refers in this way to film stars, long-distance fliers, and
the like. These Elizabethans had certain qualities which have made it
seem worth while to keep their memories green for more than 300 years,
and on this account, if for no other, they should be given the courtesy
which is their due.

11. Above all, whatever inner doubts you may have as to whether the
piece of research upon which you have been spending your time was
really worth while, you must on no account allow it to appear that you
have ever thought of it otherwise than of supreme importance to the
human race! In the first place, unless you yourself believe in what you are
doing, you will certainly not do good work, and, secondly, if your reader
suspects for a moment that you do not set the very highest value on your
work yourself he will set no value on it at all. He will on the other hand be
full of fury that you should have induced him to waste his precious time
in reading stuff that you do not believe in yourself, an attitude which will
completely prevent him from appreciating any real and evident merit
which there may be in it. After all, one can never be certain of the value
of one's own work. Often in scientific research a discovery which in itself
seemed most trivial has led to results of the utmost importance, and
though sensational occurrences of this kind may be rarer in literary
research than in science, it is still true that what is merely a side-issue
in one research may give rise, when critically examined, to results of
quite unexpected value.

As a general rule the interest and importance of a piece of research lies
either in the facts disclosed or the methods by which they have been
brought to light—or in both. To these prior considerations the manner of
presentation may indeed be subordinate. Nevertheless good presentation
may help enormously in the effective value of good research, while bad
presentation may rob it of the recognition which is its due.

II

THE CYCLE OF THE WORK

5

The Discovery of Works and Documents

Leslie Hotson

Literary Serendipity

Serendipity is my text, and Serendipity my motto. Lovers of Horace Walpole, the epistolary genius who coined this sweet and insinuating word, will recall its meaning with its fanciful derivation. In a letter of 1754 to Sir Horace Mann, Walpole makes his confession: "I once read a silly fairy tale called The Three Princes of Serendip. As their Highnesses travelled, they were always making discoveries, by accidents and sagacity, of things they were not in quest of: for instance, one of them discovered that a mule blind of the right eye had travelled the same road lately, because the grass was eaten only on the left side, where it was worse than on the right. *Now* do you understand *Serendipity?"*

From Walpole's rough sketch, we may complete the picture of the Princes of Serendip. They were more than three clever fellows spending their time, as Roark Bradford might say, "jes' projeckin'." In going out "for to admire an' for to see" they bore minds stocked with everything but prejudices, and driven by a universal and lively curiosity which sharpened their eyes.

We often appreciate a quality better by a brilliant example of the lack of it. One admirable instance of inserendipity comes from the account of a polar voyage. It is reported that when Parry was searching for the northwest passage, a boat was one day sent on shore, under charge of a petty officer, who received, besides the usual instructions to keep a look-out for anything remarkable, a printed form on which, under the heads of "Manners" and "Customs," to record what he saw among the natives. In due time the boat returned to the ship, the man delivered in his report. An extraordinary one it was for pith and brevity, running thus:

Manners.	*Customs.*
None at all.	Very beastly.

From *ELH,* IX (1942), 79-94. Reprinted by permission of The Johns Hopkins Press. Lecture before the Tudor and Stuart Club, February 6, 1942.

From our shocked and incurious petty officer, who would never get a job in the retinue of the Princes of Serendip, we turn with relief to Edgar Allan Poe. Whether Poe had encountered the term serendipity, I cannot say, but in a notable passage from the *Mystery of Marie Roget,* his Chevalier Dupin gives a luminous view of the *thing* itself, as follows. "A vast ... portion of truth arises from the seemingly irrelevant. Modern science has resolved to *calculate upon the unforeseen.* The history of human knowledge has so uninterruptedly shown that to collateral, or incidental, or accidental events we are indebted for the most numerous and most valuable discoveries, that it has at length become necessary in prospective view of improvement, to make not only large, but the largest allowance for inventions by chance, and quite out of the range of ordinary expectation." And to reassure any skeptic who may demand an authority more recent than Poe's Dupin, here is what our own Dr. Simon Flexner has to say for the Princes of Serendip: "Curiosity, not utility, is the master key to human knowledge; curiosity which may or may not result in something useful. And the less that curiosity is asked to justify itself day by day, the more likely it is not only to contribute to human welfare, but to the equally important satisfaction of the human mind." Dr. Flexner is here speaking of the scientific spirit, but the latter desideratum he mentions, the satisfaction of the human mind, is also the goal of literature.

It would be unreasonable to expect serendipity to be greatly fostered in our schools and universities. Routine is a necessity imposed by the structure of the machine, and in the large the student's curiosity is asked to justify itself day by day. Serendipity's chief enemy proudly calls himself "scientific method" when his true name is "meritorious dullness." Gradgrind will never lack pedestrian recruits.

On the other hand, a follower of the Princes of Serendip, while he runs the risk of getting nothing at all, may possibly light on a good thing; and in any event he enjoys the adventure outrageously. His apparent lack of definite direction and goal makes him seem (to Gradgrind) slightly mad. Much like the old man — as Dean Pound tells the tale — whose mental health was being tested by a Board of Insane commissioners. On being asked, "Why did you strike that boy?" he answered, "Because he was in my way." "But he was behind you," remonstrated a commissioner. "You turned round and struck him. How could he have been in your way?" "That's all right," was the reply, "I have two ways, one going and one coming." Crazy or not, the curious mind has many ways, and they lead off in unexpected directions. When all is said, the essential to bear in mind about serendipity — whether you like to call it happy accident or lucky chance — is that the Princes had to travel; and travel means labor. The searcher has to go into them thar hills, and then look about him and dig at twenty to the dozen. You don't strike devilish good luck without weevilish hard work.

The mountains of Serendip in which I have wandered prospecting are the formidable masses of documents in the Public Record Office, Chancery Lane, London. They may not be there now, but they will return when the war is won. Just what *is* the Record Office? Most of us know about the library of the British Museum. Some have an inkling of Somerset House.

But those who have more than heard of the Public Record Office are few indeed. This is all the more strange when one reflects that the Record Office houses by far the largest collection of national archives in the world. Under one roof, in times of peace, we find not only almost all the myriad files of the government departments for centuries past, but the countless records of the courts of law as well. The overwhelming mass and intricate variety of the documents stagger the mind.

Let me take you with me in imagination to this happy hunting ground, where the shades of Tudor and Stuart Englishmen await the liberators, who some day will

> set the imprison'd wranglers free,
> And give them voice and utterance once again.

We get off a Holborn bus at the top of Chancery Lane, and walk down this busy artery of Legal London. That fine old Elizabethan brick gateway on our right hand is the entrance to Lincoln's Inn, one of the four Inns of Court. In an attic ceiling over that chamber up there were discovered the State Papers of John Thurloe, Oliver Cromwell's secretary, after they had lain hidden for half a hundred years. We pass the shops of the law-stationers, booksellers, and wigmakers; and then on the left rise the great stone walls and white Gothic towers of the Record Office. Passing beneath the lofty arch of the covered gateway and under the speculative eye of the guardian bobby, we enter a spacious yard flanked by a greensward. Across the yard on the right one catches a glimpse of the buildings of old Clifford's Inn, and the windows of the bachelor chambers long occupied by Samuel Butler. Butler was the celebrated author not only of *Erewhon* but also of a sardonic attack on the female sex in this dry aphorism: "A hen is an egg's way of making another egg." I always wonder at Butler. Living right beside the Record Office, he made no attempt to mine its manuscript riches, but trudged off every morning to the library of the British Museum, to elaborate his theory that the author of the Odyssey was a woman. But it would take a great deal of that sort of thing to atone to the ladies for those contemptuous words about the hen. With a last look at Butler's windows, we turn to the steps of the Record Office. Over the portal, if I had my way, should be cut Shakespeare's phrase: "It is an office of discovery."

Once inside, we make a special plea for a tour behind the scenes through the vaults and strong-rooms, and soon find ourselves following an officer down some iron stairs leading below ground. From gloomy corridors of stone and steel we peep past heavy doors at ranks and files of bundled documents. Now a great room stacked with baled writs — scores of thousands of them — that have never been touched since they were filed away. Then our guide taps a blank wall as we pass. What is in there? Human bones, is the calm reply. That is the vault beneath the ancient Chapel of the Rolls, enclosed and incorporated in the great modern structure built at the end of the last century. What is behind this other locked door? That, we learn, is the Condemned Cell. The documents in there have been discarded as worthless, and are waiting a statutory period before they are carried out to execution. Room after room, floor after floor, acres of records. One moves as in a dream past shelves of parchment rolls laid side by side, much after the fashion of an ammunition dump—and some contain enough high explosive to blast many a pretty and well-received historical theory. At one end of the chamber of the Patent Rolls you stand with King John; and after a journey along an unbroken series of thousands of rolls, you emerge at the other end with King George the Sixth. You turn and gaze, and you are looking back from Winston Churchill to the Barons' Charter.

Evidently the millions of records, paper as well as parchment, are cared for with oriental scrupulosity. Repair work is paralleling the scholarly labor of classification, and of making indexes and calendars. The documents are as jealously guarded as if every attendant in the office had for his rule of life Chaucer's couplet:

> And if that olde bokes were aweye
> Yloren were of remembraunce the keye.

Here, in the ultimate treasure-house of England's Time Past, the mind is carried irresistibly back to the picture of the Chamber of Memory painted by the poet Spenser. Alma, you recall, is conducting Sir Guyon and the Palmer through the House of Temperance. Upstairs, in the innermost room, they come upon an ancient man.

> This man of infinite remembrance was,
> And things foregone through many ages held,
> Which he recorded still as they did pas,
> Ne suffred them to perish through long eld,
> As all things else, the which this world doth weld,
> But laid them up in his immortal scrine
> Where they for ever incorrupted dweld:
> The warres he well remembered of King Nine,
> Of old Assaracus, and Inachus divine.

> The years of Nestor nothing were to his,
> Ne yet Mathusalem, though longest liv'd;
> For he remembered both their infancies;
> Ne wonder then, if that he were depriv'd
> Of native strength now that he them surviv'd.
> His chamber all was hang'd about with rolls
> And old records from auncient times deriv'd,
> Some made in books, some in long parchment scrolls,
> That were all worm-eaten and full of canker holes.

> Amidst them all he in a chair was sett,
> Tossing and turning them withouten ende;
> But for he was unhable them to fett,
> A little boy did on him still attend
> To reach, when ever he for ought did send;

> And oft, when things were lost, or laid amis,
> That boy them sought and unto him did lend;
> Therefore he Anamnestes cleped is;
> And that old man Eumnestes, by their properties.

The little boy, yclept Anamnestes, does very well for an acolyte to the poet's fancy: but the Record Office in fact contains thousands of rolls which would stagger half a dozen of him. I have looked through scores of Coram Rege Rolls, each of which must be wheeled in on a barrow, collared by two strong adult specimens of the tribe of Anamnestes, and lifted, not without a subdued *heave-ho,* to the table.

Let us look for a moment at one of these rolls. Properly speaking it is not a roll at all, but a *file* of anywhere from 500 to 1000 skins, about a foot wide and three feet long, bound together at one end. For the Court of Queen's Bench in Elizabeth's time there are from four to six of these Leviathans for every year. We take a cloth and try to remove some of the heavy dust that the years have deposited on it. Considering its appalling size, and the legal Latin of its contents, we may be confident that in the last three centuries it has not been handled frequently. And yet on opening it we find everywhere signs that it *has* been used — finger-smudges and dog-ears are here at foot of the membranes. But these are ancient marks, and show that the records were hunted through many times by the Elizabethans.

Quite natural, you will say. These are Elizabethan lawsuits; and who should be sufficiently interested in them to make a search but Elizabethans? Yet this is a side of that many-sided age that we are all too prone to overlook. We tend to forget that the Elizabethans were far more law-minded, quarrelsome, and litigious than we; that their government was excessively paternalistic; that the courts and the business of the law, to an extent almost inconceivable today, were centralized in London and Westminster. Shakespeare's Englishmen, then, were not only forever coming to London for the Law Term, to fight cases in the courts or to enroll transfers of property, but they were incessantly running over to the Chapel of the Rolls to look up the court records. Sir Gilbert Gerrard, as Master of the Rolls in 1594, besieged by a host of importunate would-be searchers, speaks feelingly of "the infinite nombers of such as come to search."

Here then is one more typical Elizabethan activity we may add to the few that are within our power to exercise today. We can read their books and plays, sing their motets, madrigals, and catches, dance some of their country dances, attempt the recorder or (much more rarely) the lute or the virginals; and in the Record Office we can search their own thumbed parchments, catching innumerable glimpses of the seamy side, to keep our view of Shakespeare's England in perspective. Old Burton, in his delightful address of Democritus to the Reader, gives us a synopsis of the two sides: "Now come tidings of weddings, maskings, mummeries, entertainments, jubilees, embassies, tilts and tournaments, trophies, triumphs, revels, sports, plays: then again, as in a new-shifted scene, treasons, cheating tricks, robberies, enormous villanies in all kinds, funeralls, burialls, deaths of princes — now comical then tragical matters." To see Elizabethan life steadily and whole, you may not only sit an interested spectator at its holiday maskings, entertainments, revels, and plays; but must get round behind into its treasons, cheating tricks, robberies, and enormous villanies in all kinds—and this is best done in Chancery Lane.

There are people to be found who are interested only in the poetic and dramatic literature of a period. Enviable creatures, always perfectly satisfied with the finished product, and never longing to handle the raw material, the life, the fact behind the work of art. For a searcher, contrariwise, nothing is more stimulating to the imagination than the knowledge that you are looking at Elizabethan facts, most of them fresh and untouched by latter-day eyes. G. M. Trevelyan puts the strange exhilaration of the experience into words. He says, "It is the fact about the past that is poetic; just because it really happened, it gathers round it all the inscrutable mystery of life and death and time."

Now that we have had our bird's-eye view of the jungle of the records, that limitless *matto grosso* of dark and deviously tangled vegetation, perhaps we hear a warning voice that whispers

> This is the Wandering Wood, this' Error's den,
> A monster vile, whom God and man does hate.
> Therefore, I rede, beware!

But neither Drake, Ralegh, nor the Princes of Serendip will allow us to falter now, and we recklessly start off for the Search Rooms. There are two of them, the Legal and the Literary. The difference between them is that when you want to look up any document, say a title deed or a census list of a date later than 1800, you go to the Legal Room, and pay one-and-six for the privilege. This handling of money lends an official and somewhat incongruous air of commercialism to the Legal Room—an atmosphere too profane to be admitted to the Literary Room. But any document of a date before 1800 will be brought to you free in either room. I began my work in the sanctified hush of the Literary Room, but I've shifted since. I find nothing unpleasing in the sound of chinking silver coins, and, besides, the air is fresher.

The Legal Room has other attractive features. One can't spend many days in it without witnessing scenes of tragi-comedy. Most of us either know or have heard of someone who claims to have a fortune tied up in Chancery. When the rich great-uncle died, the fortune should by rights have come to him, but he was far away in America or Australia, and didn't hear of it until the trial was over and the money (because the right heir wasn't found) was put into the hands of the Lord Chancellor. Numberless persons cherish the notion that they have been diddled out of fortunes in this way, and some of the bolder or crankier spirits find their way to the Legal Room of the Record Office, and demand their imaginary millions of Mr. O'Reilly, the long-suffering Superintendent of the room. Mr. O'Reilly is large and round and good natured; and he needs all his good nature to explain very kindly to some of these determined souls that in the first place they must prove their claim; and in the second place, that the *total* sum of undistributed money in the hands of the Lord Chancellor amounts only to about £10,000.

The claimants, clinging like limpets to their golden idea, are rarely satisfied with the hard facts. Mr. O'Reilly tells of a character who pushed in and demanded a quarter of a million pounds; and when he didn't get it at once, he shouted, "You just wait! I'm going out to get a revolver, and I'll be back!" Mr. O'Reilly waited, but the revolver didn't appear. The doorman, Maddox, a retired Tommy Atkins, knew another hard case. "A queer chap come in and told Mr. O'Reilly he wanted the fortune that by rights ought to have come to him. And when Mr. O'Reilly tried to reason with him, he attacked him brutally with an umbrella." Some time ago I had a strange experience in the Legal Room. One day, while I was poring over a roll of brown parchments three hundred years old, threading my way in imagination through the disputes and quarrels of Elizabethan England, something made me look up. Conceive my amazement when I thought I saw, in conversation with Mr. O'Reilly, the man who twenty-six years ago was my music teacher in a school in Brooklyn, New York. I could hardly trust my senses, but I spoke to him. Sure enough, it *was* my music teacher, but what a difference! He had turned into another of those oddities who looked for a treasure in Chancery. He addressed me cautiously, and I gathered from what he said that there was a conspiracy against him; and even now—he threw a furtive glance over his shoulder—one of his cousins was down there in the corner of the room working to prevent him from discovering the evidence that would make him a rich man.

Such an atmosphere—of plots and counterplots, of secret missions and strange hopes and fears—such an atmosphere is obviously a perfect one to nourish a literary detective. One can't spend a day among the records without uncovering a promising clue of some sort. Fascinating trails beckon off in every direction, and one feels like a Sherlock Holmes who has scores of mysteries pouring into his lodgings in Baker Street. The problem resolves itself into one of deciding which clues, out of the mass, are most likely to lead to the lucky spot. It is necessary to select, and that selection is dubiously made. Then the excitement, impossible to describe, of finding that you have guessed right, and that the trail is growing hotter!

But even here you must arm yourself against disappointment, for in the last ditch you may lose your fox, or find that he is really only a rabbit. For example, to pick up, in some untrodden thicket, the magic name *Shakespeare;* and then, with hope running high, to trace the original document indicated by the clue, only to find that the Shakespeare named comes from a town other than Stratford, and has no connection with the dramatist!

The balanced diet for a searcher includes large portions of disappointment and a generous helping of chagrin. But digging into your iron ration of hope, you plod along through hundreds upon hundreds of documents that may hold possibilities, struggling to keep alert, to study the lie of the land, to use your scrap of acumen in casting about over the horde of ascertained details, to see if combining two of them will not flash out the spark of electric discovery. And finally the rare, the incomparable moment of realization. Before you lies what so many explorers and adventurers have desired; and you are silent like Balboa—or, if you believe Keats, like stout Cortes.

That is one side of the picture—the detective, the Sherlock Holmes side. But there is another excitement in store. Suppose you have found your treasure, your Pacific Ocean, your criminal; from that moment you must guard your find from every curious eye until you have studied it, understood it, clothed it, and are ready to claim it as your own before the world. The period of suspense is often long. For that frantic time you change from the hunter into the hunted. No longer are you the whole-hearted detective, pursuing; your apprehensions make you the criminal, pursued. Dangers hedge you in on every side. Each innocent delver among the documents becomes a potential enemy. For mind you, these records are all public. Anyone has the right to look at the parchment on which you have made your unannounced discovery.

In these days we are fed mostly with thrilling stories of detection. But some of us remember a different type of tale—the hair-raising adventures of Hornung's gentleman-criminal, Raffles, the Amateur Cracksman. For a while, Raffles, the super-criminal, vied with Sherlock Holmes, the master-detective, for the favor of the reading public. Then John Kendrick Bangs, the humorist, saw an opportunity of reconciling the rivals. He had Sherlock Holmes fall in love with the beautiful but highly moral daughter of Raffles. The lovesick detective was close on Raffles's trail at the moment, and as the price of indemnity, the Amateur Cracksman consented to the marriage of the young couple. In the course of time a son was born to them, and they called him Raffles Holmes. On growing up, this child found that he combined in his own nature the Raffles instinct for crime and the Holmes passion for detection and law-enforcement; and his criminal exploits, followed by fits of remorse, divide the interest with his amazing feats of detection. Occasionally he gets on the trail of his own crimes, and has difficulty in getting off it again before he arrests himself.

Your literary serendipitist or detective must partake of that dual nature: he must have some, at least, of the makings of a good crook. The history of Shakespearean scholarship contains at least one melancholy example of a great literary investigator who allowed the Raffles side of his nature to gain the upper hand. This unfortunate man was the famous John Payne Collier, who, after making notable discoveries in Elizabethan literature and biography, succumbed to a craving for recognition even greater than he had received. When he came to a document that he felt *should* have contained a Shakespeare discovery (but didn't), he was not content to pocket his disappointment: he would set about forging an interesting entry in an imitation of Elizabethan handwriting, and announce it as a new discovery. In the course of time he was suspected, investigated and exposed; but he never confessed his crimes. As a consequence, later scholars have been driven to a laborious untangling of the true and the false in his publications.

The terrors of a criminal cursed with an imagination, even of a man as brave as Macbeth, make one shudder. But the trepidations of the man who had discovered a treasure that may be snatched from him, are not to be envied. A friend of mine tells me of his experiences in London with the late Professor Wallace, the American who made his notable Shakespeare discoveries in the Record Office thirty years ago. Wallace's particular black beast was Mrs. Charlotte Stopes — the Scottish woman-scholar who rivalled him for energy and persistence. I am told that Mrs. Stopes was so inexorably on Dr. Wallace's mind, that even when walking along the street with you, he would unconsciously lower his voice and cast a backward glance over his shoulder to see if Mrs. Stopes were dogging his steps and listening. Mr. Giuseppi, who used to be the Superintendent of the Search Room thirty years ago, told me that Wallace would come to him with a document he had found, and implore him to hide it away so that Mrs. Stopes couldn't find it. Impossible, of course; public documents are open to the public, and Wallace had to take his chances like anybody else. I like to fancy that Wallace was driven to try what spells and incantations could do, and that he went about muttering "Mrs. Stopes, go away; come again some other day."

My own experiences have been scarcely less nerve-racking than Dr. Wallace's. The first man-hunt that excited me was tracking down the unknown killer of the dramatist Christopher Marlowe. A happy accident made me suspect that the lost man was a certain Ingram Frizer; and since I had found this man recorded as alive and not in prison several years after Marlowe's death, I at length got round to the notion that he must have secured a pardon for his homicide. Now pardons are entered on the Patent Rolls of the Chancery — one of the most obvious and frequently-searched of all the series of public records. The index to them stands in plain view on the open shelves of the Legal Search Room, and is constantly consulted. I took down the volume covering the year of Marlowe's death, 1593, and found the name of Ingram Frizer staring me in the face — with a note of a pardon for having killed in self-defense. The date fitted. When I had sent for the Patent Roll to which the index referred, I had before me a full copy of the pardon, containing the Coroner's report of the inquest on the body of the poet, lying dead and slain in the village of Deptford, near London. Here was the contemporary account of Marlowe's last hours of life, and of his tragic end at the dagger's point.

It seemed obvious that anyone might discover this priceless document at any moment. What was I to do? Dash off a panicky letter to the London *Times,* announcing the discovery, and promising to publish the full details later? Such a course would be certain to bring a raft of searchers down on the document. I took a chance, and modeled my behavior on Uncle Remus's Tar Baby. After all, if the document hadn't been discovered in three hundred years, I might risk a few months more, while I investigated the details and got the story to a publisher. If I had known then what I afterwards found out, namely that there was a keen sleuth on Marlowe's trail at that very moment, perhaps I should not have been so very brave and bold.

No doubt success and immunity here made me foolhardy; for when I attempted the same sort of thing with the lost letters of Shelley to his wife Harriet, I got a scare that will last me a long time. A pure chance led me to the copies of these long-sought and priceless letters hidden away in an obscure and almost unknown corner of the Chancery records; and by the way, it was here that I first ran into that commercial side of the Legal Room that I mentioned. For the Shelley letters date from 1816. They are therefore on the wrong side of the deadline, 1800, and are treated like any modern document which you pay for inspecting. I paid my thirty cents, and got nine hitherto unknown letters of Shelley's in return.

But now that I had the letters, I must study them, arrange them, find where they belonged in the story of Shelley's life, write the manuscript, and finally get it to the press — all of which would take time. I tried to banish care and determined not to borrow trouble, but my luck did not hold. About three months before I could hope to see the thing in print, came bad news. The secret had leaked out somehow. A certain writer, having heard through somebody's innocence where the letters had been found, was coming to the Record Office to copy them off and publish them promptly. That was a bitter moment. Fortunately my publishers were able to bring pressure to bear sufficient to deter him from his project. But all the same the *Atlantic Monthly* published my first instalment with some indications of haste. Such are some of the risks and terrors of the serendipitist in literature.

Naturally the greatest prize, and the magnetic pole which draws us all, is the life of Shakespeare. But any approach to Shakespeare the man in these latter days is so encumbered with a choking undergrowth of fanciful notions and strange theories that one is almost discouraged in the attempt to reach a fact. Confronting this troublesome vegetation, one understands the feelings of the English yokel, who, when an obstinate scrub oak resisted the best blows of his axe, muttered, "What *I* say is, gol durn t' pig that didn't eat thee when tha wast an acorn!"

The man who wishes to add to what we know about the background of Shakespeare would do better to devote his days to searching in Chancery Lane, than to emulate the homely spider in drawing gossamer out of himself to spin a web of fancy about Francis Bacon, or the Earl of Oxford, or yet a literary committee of seven noblemen. This last theory should appeal to our democratic souls, with its belief that if it takes nine tailors to make a man, it takes seven noblemen to make a Shakespeare. It has been well remarked, however, that though the wind of genius bloweth where it listeth, it never lights upon a committee.

Of all possible approaches to Shakespeare, the most diverting was related to me by a friend. He was traveling in Wales, and had come through Monmouthshire to Chepstow. Now, as Captain Fluellen tells us, "There is also moreover a river at Monmouth; it is called Wye at Monmouth." It is also moreover called Wye at Chepstow; and it was at Chepstow that my friend saw three wise men out in a rowboat, using grappling irons. On inquiry, he learned that they were dragging the bottom of Wye for a box, said to have been sunk there three centuries ago — a box believed to contain certain proof that Francis Bacon wrote Shakespeare's plays. No doubt Shakespeare had this subaqueous type of searcher in mind when he wrote, "From the banks of Wye and sandy-bottom'd Severn I have sent him bootless home."

I find something beautiful in the perfect faith shown by this trio of mudrakers, dredging for the Baconian oyster.

Our picture of Shakespeare's life is still of the fragmentary sort which must be completed by the imagination; the sort of picture full of hints which Shakespeare himself describes in his account of the painting of the Trojan Wars:

> For much imaginary work was there:
> Conceit deceitful, so compact, so kind,
> That for Achilles' image stood his spear,
> Griped in an arméd hand; himself behind
> Was left unseen, save to the eye of mind.
> A hand, a foot, a face, a leg, a head,
> Stood for the whole to be imaginéd.

More than a generation ago, Dr. Furness wrote: "To Shakespeare's friends and daily companions there was nothing mysterious in his life; on the contrary, it possibly appeared to them as unusually dull and commonplace. It certainly had no incidents so far out of the common that they thought it worth while to record them. Shakespeare never killed a man as Jonson did; his voice was never heard, like Marlowe's, in tavern brawls; nor was he ever, like Marston and Chapman, threatened with the penalty of having his ears lopped and his nose slit."

With all respect and gratitude to Dr. Furness's memory, I should like to consider this statement for a moment. Shakespeare's life, as Dr. Furness says, may have appeared usually dull and commonplace to his friends and daily companions. But we must remember that these friends and companions were Elizabethans; and that their notions of what was dull and commonplace are not ours. Our minds have been formed in an age of security, of far greater safety for health, life, and limb than anything Shakespeare knew, when he walked about London carrying a rapier and dagger to defend his life. In Elizabeth's London things occurred almost daily and passed unremarked, which if they happened today would crowd the war news. Take for instance the case of the disappearance of Henry Porter. Porter was a leading and popular playwright who collaborated with Ben Jonson. In 1599 he disappears from view. Modern scholars might suppose that he retired, became a preacher, or unobtrusively died of the plague. Some years ago, while rummaging among the criminal records of the county of Surrey, I discovered that Porter's disappearance was not so peaceful. He was stabbed to death in a fight with a rival playwright, John Day. Now before this discovery, we might have said that Porter and Day led dull and uneventful lives, for at least nothing that they did was so far out of the ordinary that men thought it worth while to record it. What would the newspapers do today with a little item mentioning that Robert Sherwood shot and killed Philip Barry?

Discoveries of this sort bring us up short; they drive home to our minds the realization that things which strike us with astonishment could happen and pass without comment in those dangerous days; and show us our mental incapacity to fill in immense gaps in Shakespeare's life with anything like probable conjecture. Shakespeare's life today is like African geography in the time of Swift:

> So geographers, in Afric maps
> With savage pictures fill their gaps,

And o'er unhabitable downs
Place elephants for want of towns.

What we need is more facts. The Record Office is a source unimaginably rich and almost untouched. I am confident that there is as much about Shakespeare still in the documents, undiscovered, as ever came out of them.

You recall Baron Munchausen's interesting experience with the toots and flourishes frozen in the postilion's horn, which, when the horn thawed out, as it hung on the inn-wall, rang out merrily. Something like that has happened to these Elizabethan words frozen into dust-covered parchment. Voices angry, appealing, threatening, sly and indignant have not only sounded over these documents, but have actually got frozen into them. The leaping, turbulent stream of Elizabethan life surged into the courts of law and the shops of the scriveners, just as it did into the playhouses. The duty of Elizabethan scholarship is not to declare a Frost Fair, and go skating on this frozen torrent, but to apply sufficient ardor to restore the waters to life.

Yet this figure of ice and freezing is at best but a cold metaphor. Let us go back to Shakespeare for a more genial figure and call the Record Office a *South Sea of discovery.* We may take the watchword from the *Merry Wives,* as follows: *"Search, seek, find out."* And the countersign from the *Taming of the Shrew:* "Tomorrow I intend to hunt again."

6

Authorship and Attribution

Cyrus Hoy

The Shares of Fletcher and His Collaborators
in the Beaumont and Fletcher Canon

The Beaumont and Fletcher canon consists traditionally of fifty-two plays, but it has long been recognized that of these only a small number represent the work of the two dramatists in collaboration.[1] The exact number has yet to be determined, but modern scholarship is agreed that less than twelve of the vast corpus of plays which are currently designated by Beaumont and Fletcher's names are indeed products of their joint authorship. Essentially, the some forty plays that remain represent the unaided work of Fletcher, or Fletcher's work in collaboration with dramatists other than Beaumont. Chief among these is Philip Massinger, whose share in the plays of the corpus can be demonstrated beyond any doubt, but there are others, and Beaumont-and-Fletcher scholarship from Fleay to Oliphant has suggested as candidates for the authorship of the non-Beaumont, non-Fletcher, non-Massinger portions of the plays in question, the names of virtually every dramatist known to have been plying his trade in Jacobean London. Among those whose names, with varying degrees of plausibility, have been advanced, are Nathan Field, William Rowley, Middleton, Shirley, Ford, Webster, Tourneur, Shakespeare, Ben Jonson, Chapman, Daborne, and Robert Davenport.

Any investigation into the authorship of the plays which comprise the Beaumont and Fletcher canon will not, in the nature of things, consist merely in separating the work of Beaumont from the work of Fletcher. Quite apart from the problem of determining which among the fifty-two plays of the corpus are indeed Beaumont and Fletcher collaborations,

From *Studies in Bibliography,* VIII (1956), 129-146. Reprinted by permission of the author. This essay is Part I of a seven-part monograph, subsequent sections of which appeared annually in the volumes of *Studies in Bibliography* from 1957 to 1962.
  1. Throughout this study, in speaking of "the Beaumont and Fletcher canon" I refer to the plays published in the second folio (1679), including Beaumont's *Masque* but excluding Shirley's *The Coronation.*

there remains the very sizeable task of distinguishing the work of Fletcher from that of his various other collaborators apart from Beaumont. To distinguish any given dramatist's share in a play of dual or doubtful authorship, one must possess some body of criteria which, derived from the unaided plays of the dramatist in question, will serve to identify his work in whatever context it may appear. On this score, the question of authorship in the Beaumont and Fletcher canon is complicated at the very outset, for with the exception of his *Masque,* there is no play that can with any certainty be regarded as the unaided work of Beaumont. And while the *Masque* may afford a good enough indication of Beaumont's metrical habits, the poetic diction in which its verse is cast tends to preclude any widespread use of the linguistic forms—especially contractions—which comprise the particular body of criteria to be used as authorial evidence in the present study. Thus, in establishing evidence that can be used in determining the respective shares of the collaborating dramatists, it is necessary to proceed from the known to the unknown, the known in this case being the unaided plays of Fletcher (which, as will be seen, can be identified) and of Massinger (about which there is no problem of identification).

My purpose in the present study is to show (1) how the unaided plays of Fletcher can be singled out from among the other plays of the canon, and (2) how the pattern of linguistic preferences which emerges from Fletcher's unaided plays contrasts sufficiently with the language practices in the unaided plays of Massinger as to afford a basis for distinguishing the work of the two dramatists one from the other. It will be noted that the tests to be applied in this and subsequent studies tend not so much to overturn the usual assignment of shares in the plays of the canon as to confirm previous attributions by a more extensive use of linguistic evidence than has hitherto been brought to bear upon the works in question. This is particularly true of Fletcher and Massinger, whose shares have been assigned within reasonably specific limits since the days of Boyle and Oliphant; though it might be argued that tests of the present kind serve to base such assignments on rather more demonstrable evidence than has sometimes been used in the past, while they tend as well to define somewhat more precisely the extent of previous attributions. In the case of such dramatists as Field, Shirley, and Ford, it will be seen in a later article that linguistic evidence provides a more certain basis for assigning their share in the plays of the canon than has yet been available.

I

The criteria which I propose to apply in investigating the plays of the Beaumont and Fletcher corpus is of a linguistic nature. By linguistic criteria I mean nothing more complicated than an author's use of such a pronominal form as *ye* for *you,* of third person singular verb forms in *-th* (such as the auxiliaries *hath* and *doth*), of contractions like *'em* for *them, i'th'* for *in the, o'th'* for *on/of the, h'as* for *he has,* and *'s* for *his* (as in *in's, on's,* and the like). There is nothing particularly new in the use of criteria of this sort, and I can claim no originality for any of the linguistic tests that I apply in the course of this study. In 1901, A. H. Thorndike drew attention to the use of the colloquial contraction *'em* as a possible test of authorship.[2] Thorndike found the form to occur frequently in Fletcher, and not at all in Massinger, but since his evidence for Massinger was based on Gifford's edition—wherein *'em* is consistently expanded to *them* —his conclusions were vitiated, as he later pointed out in an errata slip. Nonetheless, the use of *'em* as opposed to *them* can afford a significant clue to distinct linguistic preferences, and the relevance of Thorndike's evidence remains, though it does not apply in quite such a clear-cut fashion to Fletcher and Massinger as he originally believed.

In editing *The Spanish Curate* for the Variorum Beaumont and Fletcher in 1905, R. B. McKerrow noted the marked preference for the colloquial form *ye* of the pronoun *you* in Fletcher's portion of that play, and W. W. Greg, in his Variorum edition of *The Elder Brother,* made the same observation with regard to that play. The extent to which Fletcher employs the pronominal form *ye* was noted independently by Paul Elmer More, who commented upon it in an article in *The Nation* in 1912.[3] In 1916, in an article in the *Publications of the Modern Language Association of America,* W. E. Farnham considered the use of such contractions as *'t* (for *it,* as in *to't, on't, in't,* etc.), *'s* (for *his* or *us,* as in *on's in's, to's,* etc.), *i'th', o'th',* and the like, as a possible clue to authorship.[4] Most recently, in 1949, A. C. Partridge has applied linguistic evidence of this sort in his study of the authorship of *Henry VIII,* adding such additional criteria as is to be derived from the occurrence of the auxiliary *do* as a mere expletive in affirmative statements, and the use of the inflexional ending *-th* in the third person singular of notional and auxiliary verbs.[5] Linguistic tests of the sort that I have indicated have not, however, been hitherto applied to the question of authorship on any very considerable scale. The observations of both McKerrow and Greg were made incidentally in the course of editing single plays, and neither ever pursued the matter further. Paul Elmer More, after examining the occurrence of *ye* in fourteen plays, and pointing to the possible value that such evidence might have as an indication of Fletcher's share in the plays of the canon, added that work of the sort required for any detailed study of the subject was not much to his taste, and must be left to another. Farnham, who did not consider at all the occurrence of *ye,* dealt with *'t, 's* and contractions involving the (*i'th', o'th',* etc.) in only eight plays. And Partridge, to the present time, has been concerned only with *Henry VIII.* Thus the various linguistic tests that have been proposed during the past half century have yet to be applied systematically to all of the plays which comprise the Beaumont and Fletcher canon.

From an examination of the language forms present in the plays of the

2. A. H. Thorndike, *The Influence of Beaumont and Fletcher on Shakespeare,* pp. 24 ff.

3. Reprinted in *Shelburne Essays,* Tenth Series, pp. 3 ff. See also C. M. Gayley, *Francis Beaumont Dramatist* (1914), pp. 271-273.

4. W. E. Farnham, "Colloquial Contractions in Beaumont, Fletcher, Massinger, and Shakespeare as a Test of Authorship," *PMLA,* XXXI, 326 ff. Later studies of particular value are found in R. C. Bald, *Bibliographical Studies in the Beaumont and Fletcher Folio,* and in J. Gerritsen's edition of *The Honest Man's Fortune.*

5. A. C. Partridge, *The Problem of "Henry VIII" Reopened,* passim.

canon, at least one distinct pattern of linguistic preferences is evident at once. This is chiefly marked by the widespread use of the pronominal form *ye*, together with the frequent use of such contracted forms as *i'th'*, *o'th'*, *'em*, *h'as*, *'s*, for *his*, and a markedly infrequent use of third person singular verb forms in *-th*. The pattern can be traced throughout fourteen plays: *ye* is used repeatedly from the beginning to the end of each, and this is enough to set them apart from every other play in the canon. They are: *Monsieur Thomas, Rule a Wife and Have a Wife, Bonduca, The Chances, The Island Princess, The Humourous Lieutenant, The Loyal Subject, The Mad Lover, The Pilgrim, Valentinian, A Wife for a Month, Women Pleased, The Wild Goose Chase, The Woman's Prize.* In no one of these does *ye* ever occur less than 133 times (in *The Woman's Prize*), and in the remaining thirteen plays its rate of occurrence is much higher than this, as high as 543 times (in *The Wild Goose Chase*). Elsewhere in the canon, *ye* never occurs with anything approaching this frequency. In certain plays (e.g., *The Knight of the Burning Pestle, The Nice Valour, The Coxcomb, A King and no King*), *ye* appears sporadically or not at all. In certain others (e.g., *The Spanish Curate, The Prophetess, The False One, Barnavelt, The Maid in the Mill*) the form appears, but it is to be found clustered in single acts or scenes, and does not occur throughout the length of an entire play. Thus, when *ye* is found to occur regularly throughout each of fourteen plays — and this in a manner that is not paralleled in any of the other thirty-eight plays of the canon — it seems reasonable to conclude that one is here in the presence of a distinct linguistic preference that can be of use in determining the work of the dramatist whose practice it represents.

To identify the dramatist whose linguistic practice is marked by the widespread use of *ye* is not difficult. He is clearly not Beaumont. The plays of the canon with which Beaumont's name is most closely associated — plays like *Philaster, The Maid's Tragedy, A King and no King, The Knight of the Burning Pestle* — are precisely those in which *ye* seldom or never occurs. Nor is Massinger the dramatist in question. An examination of Massinger's fifteen unaided plays shows that, in all of these, *ye* occurs but twice; in all other instances, Massinger employs the pronominal form *you*. And the contracted forms (*i'th'*, *o'th'*, and the like) which are found to accompany the use of *ye* in the plays of the canon, are like *ye* itself conspicuous by their absence in the unaided work of Massinger, whose use of contractions is remarkably conservative. The assumption — a virtually inescapable one — is that the linguistic pattern characterized by a superabundance of *ye*'s must represent the pattern of Fletcher. For three of the fourteen plays in question (*The Loyal Subject, A Wife for a Month,* and *Rule a Wife*) there is external evidence for Fletcher's sole authorship,[6] and I have no hesitation in regarding them all as his unaided work.

---

6. Entries in the Office Book of Sir Henry Herbert, Master of the Revels from 1622 until the closing of the theatres, twice refer to *The Loyal Subject* as the work of Fletcher (*The Dramatic Records of Sir Henry Herbert*, edited by J. Q. Adams, pp. 22 and 53). In his record of plays licensed for acting, Herbert names Fletcher as the author of *A Wife for a Month* and *Rule a Wife* (*Ibid.*, pp. 28-29).

That they are unaided work can, I think, be demonstrated by comparing the manner in which *ye* occurs in them with its occurrence elsewhere in the canon. As I have already observed, in these fourteen plays the occurrence of *ye*, and all the linguistic phenomena that accompany its prevalence (absence of third-person verb forms in *-th*, frequency of such contractions as *i'th'*, *o'th'*, *h'as*, *'s* for *his*), is constant in its appearance through every act and virtually every scene. In plays of the type of *The Spanish Curate* and *The Prophetess,* however, the linguistic pattern established by the occurrence of *ye* is to be found only within single acts, or within individual scenes within acts, at the end of which it is abruptly broken off. In such cases, it is usually preceded or followed by a pattern of a quite different sort: one in which, first of all, the occurrence of *ye* is sharply reduced, and in which a decrease in the occurrence of other contracted forms is accompanied by an increased use of the verb form *hath.* In a very great number of cases, the linguistic pattern which accompanies the pattern established by *ye* is that of Massinger. A comparison of the first two acts of *The Spanish Curate,* the first two acts of *The Prophetess,* and the first act of *Barnavelt,* to cite but three examples, will indicate the manner in which the two linguistic patterns alternate within the same play.

It is, I think, valid to conclude that when a play, of the type represented by *The Spanish Curate,* demonstrates in consecutive acts and scenes two such sharply opposed linguistic patterns as those characterized by the prevalence and the absence of *ye*, then that play must represent the work of two separate dramatists. On the other hand, when in a play of the sort represented by *The Loyal Subject* or *Monsieur Thomas* a single linguistic pattern is found to be maintained through virtually every scene of its five acts, there is I think no real room for doubt that that play is the work of a single author. Regarding the fourteen plays of this sort in the canon, the linguistic pattern which links them together as the work of a single dramatist is far too distinct in itself, and far too evident throughout each, to admit the possibility of a second hand intervening in their authorship. When a second hand appears in a scene that has been formerly dominated by the Fletcherian linguistic pattern, its presence is noticeable at once. If the second hand is that of a collaborator, then the pattern will be immediately interrupted, and will appear but sporadically throughout the play, as it does in such plays as *The Spanish Curate* and *The Prophetess.* If the second hand is that of a reviser, then the whole pattern will be obscured: *ye*'s will, for the most part, disappear, or their number will be greatly reduced, and the whole texture of Fletcherian accidence is altered. The canon affords an illustration of this in *The Night Walker,* originally one of Fletcher's unaided plays, but revised in its extant text by Shirley.

Since the Fletcherian linguistic pattern is so pronounced and so discernible wherever his unaided work is present, I cannot consider his unaided work to be in fact represented in any play where this pattern is not evident. Thus I cannot agree with all those who have previously studied the Beaumont and Fletcher corpus in placing *Wit Without Money* among the plays of Fletcher's sole authorship. The linguistic pattern that emerges from this play resembles far more closely the pattern to be found in *The Night Walker* than the pattern which prevails in such plays as *Monsieur Thomas* or *The Wild Goose Chase.*

II

In evaluating linguistic criteria as a test of authorship, it is obvious that no linguistic form can be regarded as distinctive of a particular dramatist in any absolute sense; the extent to which he employs a given form may distinguish sharply enough his practice from that of two other dramatists, but not necessarily from that of a third. Thus emerges the necessity, in determining linguistic criteria for the work of any one dramatist, of singling out forms which are at once representative of his language preferences, while serving to differentiate his work from the maximum number of his known or supposed collaborators. The value to be attached to any piece of linguistic criteria is, in the end, completely relative: all depends upon the degree of divergence between the linguistic patterns that are to be distinguished.

With regard to the linguistic patterns which distinguish respectively the work of Fletcher and Massinger, these, as has been observed, and as will be seen readily enough from the tables at the end of this study, are composed of language preferences which are of an essentially opposite nature. From this it is to be concluded that, in distinguishing the grammatical usage of two dramatists, a given linguistic form need not be present in an author's work to afford evidence for determining his share of a collaborated play. On the contrary, when his collaborator is found to employ that form, its absence in the work of the dramatist in question affords the best possible evidence for distinguishing the work of the two. In a play of Fletcher and Massinger's joint authorship, the fact that Massinger is known to make little or no use of the pronominal form *ye* constitutes evidence just as positive for his work as Fletcher's known preference for the form constitutes for his. Evidence of this sort is of the best, precisely because here the degree of divergence between the linguistic patterns that are being distinguished is as great as it can well be. The one pattern is marked by a strong preference for *ye*, with the use of the form averaging fifty per cent; the other reflects a tendency to avoid the form altogether.

Such clearly opposed linguistic preferences are, unfortunately, rare. The extent to which the work of two such collaborators as Fletcher and Massinger can be distinguished by the presence or the absence of a single linguistic form — pronominal *ye* — is, indeed, quite exceptional in the annals of the Jacobean collaborated drama. More often, such linguistic preferences as can be shown to exist in the work of two dramatists are of a more quantitative sort, with a given linguistic form present in the work of both, but present at a higher rate of occurrence in the work of one than in that of the other. In such a case, the value to be attached to any single linguistic form as evidence for authorship must depend upon the extent to which, in their unaided work, the one dramatist will tend to employ it and the other to eschew it. The less the degree of difference in the use which two dramatists make of the same linguistic form in their unaided work, the less will be its value as evidence for distinguishing their shares in a play of divided authorship. As two dramatists tend to approximate each other in their use of a given language form, the evidential value of that form is accordingly diminished.

Fortunately for any attempt to determine authorship on the basis of linguistic preferences, a single language form may be used by both of two dramatists and yet be of value in distinguishing their work in collaboration, provided only that that form can be shown to occur at a consistently higher rate in the unaided work of one dramatist than in that of the other. The value to be attached to the verb form *hath,* as it occurs in the unaided work of Fletcher and Massinger, is a case in point. *Hath* is to be found in the unaided plays of both dramatists, yet its occurrence in any single play of Fletcher's never equals its occurrence in any one of Massinger's plays. Similarly with *ye* in the work of Fletcher and Field: *ye* occurs with some regularity in Field's unaided plays, but its occurrence there never approaches the extraordinary frequency with which Fletcher employs the form. The evidence to be derived from linguistic preferences as sharply opposed as these is second in importance only to that which is the most significant of all: the evidence that is based upon language preferences which reveal themselves in the prevalence of a given form in the work of one dramatist and its absence in that of another.

Thus far, in considering the factors that must be taken into account in evaluating linguistic criteria, I have tried to emphasize the necessity for determining the extent to which a given language form does indeed point to a clear and unequivocal linguistic preference that will serve in distinguishing the work of two dramatists. It need hardly be said that no single linguistic preference will serve equally to distinguish the work of a given dramatist from that of all others. As I have already observed, a grammatical or linguistic practice that may tend to set a particular dramatist apart from two of his fellows will not necessarily set him apart from a third. It should be obvious that no piece of linguistic criteria can be evaluated in isolation; the significance which a single form may possess for distinguishing the work of any one dramatist will derive directly from the extent to which that form is present in the work of his collaborators. The frequent use of *ye, hath, i'th'* or whatever in the plays of any dramatist is of no value in distinguishing his work from that of dramatists who employ such forms with equal or even approximate frequency. And no importance can be attached to the absence of a particular form from the work of any one dramatist unless it is known to occur in some noticeable degree in the work of another. The linguistic pattern that has been adduced for a dramatist on the basis of his unaided work will, of course, remain constant. However, the value of the evidence to be attached to the presence or absence of such linguistic forms as contribute to the distinctive nature of this over-all pattern will obviously shift in relation to the prevalence of those same forms within such other linguistic patterns as may be present with it in a single play. Or, stated in another way: if a given linguistic form is known to occur with approximately the same frequency in the work of dramatists A, B and C, but does not occur at all in the work of dramatist D, then while that particular form will have no value as evidence for distinguishing the work of A, B and C, it will have considerable value for distinguishing the work of any one of these from dramatist D. The use of the verb form *hath* in the plays of Massinger and Field will not serve to distinguish these dramatists from each other, but it may serve to distinguish both from Fletcher. And while the absence of *ye* from the plays of Massinger will have very little value in distinguishing his work from that of Beaumont, who seems to have employed the form at least as sparingly as Massinger himself, the fact that Massinger almost never uses *ye* will serve to distinguish his work not only from Fletcher's, but from that of Field as well.

Clearly, no linguistic form can be regarded as the exclusive property of a single writer. Just as clearly, however, writers can, and often do, demonstrate a preference for certain colloquial and contracted linguistic forms (a fact that is strikingly evidenced in the case of Fletcher and Massinger) and such preferences can often serve to set apart the work of one author from that of another. In a study such as this, the problem must be to distinguish what are, indeed, an author's preferential forms, and then to determine which of these can serve to differentiate his work from that of his associates. For such a purpose, the very best linguistic evidence will always consist in those forms which a given writer can be shown to have used with conspicuous frequency, but which those with whom he collaborated can be shown to have used ever so sparingly or not at all.

III

The language forms which constitute the greater part of my evidence for authorship consist, as will have been observed, of linguistic preferences which — in a great number of cases — are made manifest in only the most minute typographical features of a printed text. In dealing with such forms, and especially when one is preparing to attach any great importance to the frequency of their occurrence, the question is naturally raised as to the extent to which an author's choice of contractions is preserved in the transmission of his text. It is well known that certain seventeenth-century compositors possessed clearly defined spelling preferences which were imposed upon whatever text they might be setting, and one wonders just how far such compositorial preferences were carried. Would a compositor, for instance, venture to impose his own preferences among colloquial and contracted forms upon a text as well? If so, then any study such as the present one is the sheerest kind of folly, for the linguistic forms by means of which one is seeking to identify a given dramatist's share in a collaborated play might have been introduced into the text by any number of unknown compositors.

There is no reason, however, to believe that compositors took undue liberties with the contracted forms in the manuscript before them; there is, on the contrary, good reason for believing that they reproduced such forms with considerable fidelity. Both W. E. Farnham and Paul Elmer More have drawn attention to the extent to which the same contractions occur, with only slight variation, in the Beaumont and Fletcher quartos and folios. As Farnham has observed, it is clear from the verse that such contractions were intended by the author, and honoured by the printer, because they are a necessary part of the metrical structure. And equally to the point is his further observation that differences in the use of contractions in the parts of a collaborated play are "too orderly to be ascribed to the vagaries of a printer" (Farnham, *op. cit.*, p. 332). No one can seriously consider the two linguistic patterns present in such a play as *The Spanish Curate,* coinciding as they do with the beginning of acts and scenes, to represent the language habits of two compositors. If such linguistic patterns did in fact represent the language preferences of two compositors, their occurrence would be found to accord with the bibliographical units of the printed text, and would not in any way be related to the act and scene divisions of the play itself. Finally, the manner in which the same linguistic preferences can be shown to persist throughout the unaided plays of a given dramatist, though the extant texts of these are the work of several different printers, affords the ultimate proof that language forms of the sort which can furnish evidence for authorship originated with the author himself, and are sufficiently preserved in a printed text. Fletcher's strong preference for the pronominal form *ye* is just as evident in the 1639 quarto text of *Monsieur Thomas,* printed by Thomas Harper, or in the 1640 quarto of *Rule a Wife,* printed by Leonard Lichfield, as in the remaining twelve plays of his unaided authorship, printed for the first time by Humphrey Moseley in the 1647 folio. The unaided Massinger canon presents what is perhaps an even stronger argument for this contention, for it is the product of even more diverse compositorial hands. Of Massinger's fifteen unaided plays, thirteen were published, and these represent the work of eleven printers. Yet the linguistic preferences which emerge from these are completely consistent within themselves, and what is equally striking, they are preferences which in no way contradict what we know of Massinger's language from the manuscript — in his autograph — of one of his unpublished plays. A study of the occurrence, in some one hundred plays, of the linguistic forms that are here employed as authorial evidence, convinces me that, in the greater number of cases, the use of such forms — either in the unaided plays of a given dramatist or in plays of divided authorship — is far too systematic to admit the possibility that their presence has been affected, in any truly significant degree, by compositorial intervention.

If, however, the evidence available would tend to absolve compositors from the charge of tampering with the contractions in the manuscript which they were set to reproduce, the same cannot, apparently, be said for certain scribes in their preparation of transcripts for the use of the theatre, the printer, or a private patron. The three scribal transcripts which exist for Fletcher's unaided plays demonstrate, on the one hand, a reasonable accuracy in reproducing the linguistic preferences of the author on the part of such a scribe as Ralph Crane and, on the other, the far more erratic practice of such a scribe as Edward Knight, with the practice of the unidentified scribe of *The Woman's Prize* falling somewhere between the two.

Crane prepared a private transcript of Fletcher's *The Humourous Lieutenant* (titled in his manuscript *Demetrius and Enanthe*). Since his text contains some seventy-five lines not present in the text of the first folio, the supposition is that Crane's transcript derives from Fletcher's original manuscript, whereas the folio text represents a prompt-book containing theatrical abridgements. In his transcript, Crane introduces some thirty-four *ye*'s not present in the text of the folio, while he omits some fourteen *ye*'s which the folio text exhibits, but the difference of approximately twenty *ye*'s in the total occurrence of the form in the two texts is not great. It speaks, in fact, well for the care with which Crane reproduced his copy when it is compared with the wide divergence in the occurrence of *ye* in the two extant texts of another of Fletcher's unaided plays, *Bonduca*. (For a careful sudy of Crane's characteristics as a transcriber, see R. C. Bald, *Bibliographical Studies in the Beaumont and Fletcher Folio of 1647*, p. 95, but more especially his edition of *A Game at Chesse by Thomas Middleton,* pp. 171-173.)

The text of *Bonduca* is extant in a scribal transcript, prepared by Edward Knight, the book-keeper of the King's Company, from Fletcher's foul papers, and in the text of the 1647 folio, printed from the prompt-book. In the folio text, the pronoun *ye* is used 352 times; in Knight's transcript, the occurrence of the form has been reduced by more than half, to 147 times. The variation in the two texts in this respect is of significance because, on the basis of the first folio, the percentage of *ye*'s to *you*'s is the highest to be found in any play of Fletcher's unaided authorship. If, however, *Bonduca* survived only in Knight's manuscript, the play would present the lowest percentage of *ye*'s to *you*'s in all Fletcher, with the occurrence of the form falling markedly below its normal frequency in his unaided plays.

There is evidence of scribal intervention affecting the use of *ye* in another Fletcher play, *The Woman's Prize,* and there is good reason to suppose that the scribe responsible for the reduction in the occurrence of the form is once again Knight. Like *Bonduca, The Woman's Prize* is extant in two texts: an undated private transcript, prepared by an unidentified scribe, and the text of the 1647 folio. In the first folio text, *ye* occurs but 84 times, a number far below the usual occurrence of the form in Fletcher's unaided work. In the manuscript, *ye* is found 133 times, and while this still represents the lowest occurrence of the form in Fletcher, the increase of 49 *ye*'s makes for a rather more satisfactory basis for regarding the play as Fletcher's own.

There is external evidence which almost certainly has some bearing on the first folio text of the play and the linguistic forms which it exhibits. On 18 October 1633 the Master of the Revels, Sir Henry Herbert, suppressed a performance of *The Woman's Prize* (he refers to the play by its alternate title, *The Tamer Tamed),* which the King's Company had scheduled for that afternoon. On the following morning the prompt-book was brought to him, whereupon he proceeded to purge it of "oaths, prophaness, and ribaldrye" (*Herbert,* p. 20). The play, Herbert explains, was an old one, evidently licensed during the Mastership of one of his predecessors, which the King's Company had sought to revive, under a different title, without applying for a new license. Herbert was thereby deprived of his licensing fee, a matter about which he felt strongly, as he indicates in the entry in his Office Book, though he advances another and more public-spirited reason why old plays should not be restaged without the allowance of the Master of the Revels: "they may be full of offensive things against church and state; the rather that in former times the poetts tooke greater liberty than is allowed them by mee" (p.22).

The upshot of the whole affair was that two days later, on 21 October, Herbert returned the prompt copy, properly expurgated, to the players, accompanied by a note to Edward Knight enjoining him to "purge [the actors'] parts, as I have the booke." The players' capitulation to Herbert's demands was complete; two of their chief members apologized for "their ill manners" and asked his pardon, and the following month Fletcher's *The Loyal Subject,* which had been licensed by Sir George Buc in 1618, was submitted to Herbert for re-licensing.

Mr. R. C. Bald, in a most valuable discussion of the two texts of *The Woman's Prize* in his *Bibliographical Studies in the Beaumont and Fletcher Folio of 1647* (p. 60), points out that, while "the manuscript omits two whole scenes (II.i and IV.i), two passages of fourteen and seven lines respectively, and eight of three lines or less" that are included in the folio, the manuscript exhibits, on the other hand, "eleven passages ... varying in length from half a line to nine lines," which the folio omits. It is Mr. Bald's opinion that the manuscript gives the play, which was originally performed in 1610 or 1611, "as cut for acting before Herbert's time," while "the folio gives a fuller version of the play, but observes the cuts that were made by Herbert in 1633." To observe the cuts that Herbert demanded, it does not seem unreasonable to suppose that a new prompt-book was drawn up, and if a new prompt-book was prepared, it seems clear enough from Herbert's note of 21 October that the task would be performed by the book-keeper Knight. From Knight's transcript of *Bonduca* we know how the Fletcherian *ye* diminished under his hand (see Bald, pp. 99-100), and I can only account for the small number of *ye*'s in the folio text of *The Woman's Prize* by supposing the manuscript from which that text derives to have been prepared by him. With regard to the scribal transcript, the supposition would be that the scribe responsible for it has been somewhat more faithful in reproducing the language forms that must have stood in the original. Since the manuscript text reflects more clearly than the folio the quality of the Fletcherian original, I have used it as the basis for the statistics set forth for *The Woman's Prize* in the linguistic tables at the end of the present study.

The possibility of scribal intervention should perhaps be considered in relation to two other of the plays which can be regarded as Fletcher's unaided work, *Rule a Wife* and *A Wife for a Month.* These, apparently

Fletcher's last plays, exhibit after *The Woman's Prize* the least number of *ye*'s of all the fourteen plays that I consider to be his. The first folio text of *A Wife for a Month* gives clear indication of author's foul papers, but it is not impossible that the text has derived from a not too careful transcript of these. Two speeches are printed in alternately abridged and expanded versions, and there is a bad tangle in the second scene of the fourth act which clearly would have had to be set to rights before the manuscript in back of the first folio text could have been used as a promptbook. But if Knight's transcript of *Bonduca* is any indication of his work for a private patron, he would not have been above letting such difficulties stand in a text which he prepared, if it were not to serve as a theatrical prompt copy. And if the total number of *ye*'s still present in the text of *A Wife for a Month* (176) does indeed represent a reduction from the original number, Fletcher's favourite pronoun has here been given much the same treatment as Knight accorded it in his *Bonduca* manuscript.

The substantive text of *Rule a Wife,* that of the 1640 quarto, probably derives, as Prof. Jump has suggested, "either from a prompt-book or from a manuscript directly descended from a prompt-book."[7] The play was licensed for acting by Sir Henry Herbert on 19 October 1624, and four months later, on 8 February 1625, Herbert re-licensed *The Honest Man's Fortune,* for which Knight had prepared a new prompt-book that is extant in his autograph. It would seem likely, then, since he was actively employed by the King's Company at this time, that Knight prepared the prompt-book for *Rule a Wife* as well. There is evidence of a sort in the quarto of *Rule a Wife* that might be considered to link it with his work. The chief feature which the quarto and the *Bonduca* manuscript have in common is a frequent occurrence of the contraction *'um* (for *'em*). Since Knight employs *'em* throughout his manuscript of *The Honest Man's Fortune, 'um* is not likely to represent his own linguistic preference. And since the form is *'em* throughout the 1640 quarto of *Rollo, Duke of Normandy,* printed in the same house and in the same year as *Rule a Wife,* it seems improbable that the *'um* spelling is compositorial. I regard it rather as a Fletcherian form which Knight has reproduced forty-six times in his transcript of *Bonduca,* and – perhaps – thirty-two times in the manuscript behind the quarto of *Rule a Wife.* Seventeen times in the *Bonduca* manuscript, Knight uses the spelling *hir* for *her.* The *hir* spelling occurs twenty-nine times in the quarto of *Rule a Wife,* and it is the prevalent spelling throughout the manuscript of *The Honest Man's Fortune.* The evidence is admittedly not great, but combined with the fact that Knight was the probable person to have prepared a prompt-book for the King's Company at this period, it seems at least possible that the diminished number of *ye*'s (213) in the quarto of *Rule a Wife* may be traced to his intervention in the transmission of the text.

IV

The following tables set forth the rate of occurrence, in the unaided plays of Fletcher and Massinger, of those linguistic forms which are of value in

7. *Rollo, Duke of Normandy,* edited by J. D. Jump, intro., xiii.

distinguishing the respective shares of the two dramatists in plays of divided authorship. I have omitted *The Faithful Shepherdess* from the number of Fletcher's unaided plays, for although it is undoubtedly Fletcher's own, linguistically at least it has nothing in common with any other of his unaided works. Its language is that of pastoral poetry, uncolloquial and somewhat archaic. It abounds in linguistic forms (most notably the third person auxiliary forms *hath* and *doth*) which Fletcher seldom or never uses in his other unaided plays, while all the most distinguishing of his colloquial forms are either completely absent, or present in only a negligible degree. Nothing could be more misleading than to regard the language of *The Faithful Shepherdess* as typically Fletcherian.

Of the linguistic forms cited in the tables below, *ye* is much the most important for purposes of authorial evidence. Since Fletcher employs the form as both subject and object, direct or indirect, in either singular or plural number, the rate of its occurrence in his unaided plays is very high. In the fifteen unaided plays of Massinger, the form occurs but twice. Contractions in *y'* (*y'are, y'ave* and the like) are much less frequent in Fletcher, and are of no value in distinguishing Fletcher's work from Massinger's. The two occurrences of *y'are* in Fletcher's *Monsieur Thomas, Rule a Wife, Bonduca,* and *The Pilgrim,* for example, are matched by the two instances of the form in Massinger's *The Bondman.* The single instances of *y'ave* and *y'have* in, respectively, Fletcher's *The Chances* and *Bonduca* are paralleled by single appearances of the same forms in, respectively, Massinger's *A New Way to Pay Old Debts* and *The Guardian.* There is nothing to distinguish Massinger's use of contractions in *y'* from Fletcher's, and I have not included them among the forms cited in the following tables. Regarding the verb form *hath,* there is a distinct difference in the Fletcher-Massinger usage. In Fletcher, the form never occurs more than 6 times in a single play, and in two plays it occurs not at all. In Massinger, on the other hand, *hath* never occurs less than 8 times in any one play, and generally it is found a good deal more often than this—as often as 46 times in a single play. *Doth* comes in only one of the fourteen Fletcherian plays listed below, but since it appears but 5 times in Massinger, the distinction in the practice of the two dramatists on this point is not great. The contraction *'em* appears in all of Fletcher's unaided plays, from 23 times in *Women Pleased* to 130 times in *The Loyal Subject.* In certain of Massinger's plays, it will be noted, *'em* is to be found occurring as frequently as it does in certain of Fletcher's. But it seems significant that all of these (e.g., *The Picture, The Guardian, The City Madam*) are late plays, licensed for acting after Fletcher's death in 1625.[8] In Massinger's

---

8. The eight Massinger plays which, on the evidence that is available, can be dated after Fletcher's death are: *The Picture,* licensed 1629; *The Emperor of the East* and *Believe as you List,* 1631; *The City Madam,* 1632; *The Guardian,* 1633; *The Bashful Lover,* 1636 (licensing dates are drawn from Herbert's Office Book). The date of *The Maid of Honour* and *A New Way to Pay Old Debts* is uncertain. Malone sought to identify *The Maid of Honour* with *The Honour of Women,* licensed by Herbert on 6 May 1628. If the reference to the taking of Breda in *A New Way* (I, ii) stood in the original version of that play—and there is no reason to suppose the contrary—then the play cannot have been written before that event occurred, on 1 July 1625 (W. Gifford, *The Plays of Philip Massinger,* III, 503-4).

early plays, which would presumably reflect his language practices at the time of his collaboration with Fletcher, *'em* is used a good deal more sparingly than in the unaided plays of Fletcher or in the later work of Massinger himself: 7 times, for example, in *The Parliament of Love,* 9 times in *The Renegado,* 12 times in *The Duke of Milan.* I tabulate the occurrence of the form for whatever value it may have as a piece of corroborating evidence for distinguishing the work of the two dramatists.

The evidence to be derived from the contraction *i'th'* is, on the whole, good. Despite the fact that the 7 occurrences of the form in Fletcher's *The Island Princess* are equalled in Massinger's *The Guardian,* the form is found at least 4 times in all of Fletcher's plays, where it may appear as many as 28 times, while it is found in but 5 plays of Massinger's, and in none of these more than 7 times. It may be worth noting that the five plays in which the form occurs are late ones, and that *i'th'* appears in no play of Massinger's written before Fletcher's death. A form, however, which Massinger tends to employ occasionally, but which occurs only a single time in Fletcher, is the contraction *i'the.* The contraction *o'th'* affords evidence of a sufficiently clear-cut sort: the form occurs at least once in all fourteen of Fletcher's unaided plays; it occurs not at all in Massinger. The colloquial form *a* (for *he*) is found in six of Fletcher's plays, but appears in none of Massinger's. Of a similar nature is the contraction *'is* (for *he is*), present in five of Fletcher's unaided plays, but not present in Massinger. *H'as* (for *he has*) is found at least twice in each of the fourteen unaided plays of Fletcher, but it occurs only a single time in Massinger. The contraction *t'* (for *to,* before a following vowel or *h*) affords evidence of a sort for Massinger; it occurs at least once in ten of his fifteen unaided plays, but is found only a single time in Fletcher. Contractions involving *'s* for *his* occur chiefly in Fletcher following the prepositions *in* and *on.* There are single instances in Fletcher of enclitic *'s* for *his* with four other prepositions (*at, for, to, up*); with an adverb (*than*); with a verb (*strike*). In Massinger, *'s* for *his* occurs but three times; twice in the contraction *in's,* once in the contraction *of's.* Only the uses of *'s* for *his* with *in* and *on* have seemed worth recording in the tables that follow.

As for contractions in *'s* for *us,* these occur most commonly in Fletcher with the imperative verb form *let.* I find only two occasions in which Fletcher has used enclitic *'s* for *us* after other notional verbs (*put* and *make*); elsewhere, he uses the form only after the preposition *on* (5 times). In Massinger, *'s* for *us* is used only in the contraction *let's,* and even this quite normal form Massinger uses very sparingly. It is the only contraction in *'s* for *us* that I have recorded below. The enclitic use of *'t* for *it* with both prepositions and verbs (in contractions such as *in't, on't, for't, to't, is't*) is standard in the work of Elizabethan and Jacobean dramatists, and contractions of this sort are of no worth in distinguishing the work of Fletcher and Massinger, for their rate of occurrence in the work of each is virtually identical. In the following tables I have recorded only one form in *'t* for *it,* the contraction *of't,* and this only because the form does not appear in Fletcher, while it occurs from one to nine times in thirteen of the fifteen unaided plays of Massinger.

Table 1
LINGUISTIC TABLES FOR THE UNAIDED PLAYS
OF FLETCHER AND MASSINGER*

	ye	hath	doth	'em	i'th'	i'the	o'th'	a	'is	h'as	t'	's (his)		's (us)	of't
												in's	on's	let's	
Fletcher															
M. Thom.	343	6		27	9		6			2	3			10	
R. W.	213	2		35†	20		12		5	7	3		1	12	
Bon.	352	1		95	14		10	4		10		4	1	27	
Chan.	290	2		44	12		4	4		10		2		20	
I. P.	258			64	7		8	1	8	5		1		14	
H. L.	367	5		80	28		11	2		11		3	3	11	
L. S.	424	3		130	13		10			4		2	1	10	
M. L.	308	6		25	16	1	4	15	4	7		3		17	
Pilg.	400	3		62	15		9			9		7		18	
Valen.	412	4		71	12		8	2		4		2		16	
W. M.	176			41	4		1		1	2		5	1	17	
W. P.	288	3		23	15		16			6		4	2	3	
W. G. C.	543	1		61	8		6		1	3	1		1	15	
W. Pr.	133	4	3	58	14		21†'			3		3		10	
Massinger															
D. M.		46		12		1						8		1	3
Bond.		8	1	15								1		2	
P. L.	1	21		7										1	2
R. A.		28		14		2						3		5	1
Pict.		35		52	5	3						3		1	4
Ren.		21		9										3	2
Bel.		36		26		1									
E. E.		31	1	26								2			5
M. H.		25		31		5			•			2			4
N. W.		16		36	2	1					1	2		1	4
G. D. F.		26		15											1
U. C.		23		16										1	1
B. L.	1	41	3	21	3	2						5	2	1	5
Guard.		26		47	7	4						4		3	9
C. M.		19		46	1	1						1			3

*Abbreviations. (References to the folio, quarto, octavo, or manuscript text upon which all statistics in the present study have been based are given in parentheses after each title.) *B. L., The Bashful Lover* (O 1655); *Bel., Believe as You List* (British Museum Ms. Egerton 2828, Edited by C. J. Sisson, The Malone Society); *Bon., Bonduca* (F 1647); *Bond., The Bondman* (Q 1624); *Chan., The Chances* (F 1647); *C. M., The City Madam* (Q 1658); *D. M., The Duke of Milan* (Q 1623); *E. E., The Emperor of the East* (Q 1632); *Guard., The Guardian* (O 1655); *G. D. F., The Great Duke of Florence* (Q 1636); *H. L., The Humourous Lieutenant* (F 1647); *I. P., The Island Princess* (F 1647); *L. S., The Loyal Subject* (F 1647); *M. L., The Mad Lover* (F 1647); *M. H., The Maid of Honour* (Q 1632); *M. Thom., Monsieur Thomas* (Q 1639); *N. W., A New Way to Pay Old Debts* (Q 1633); *Pict., The Picture* (Q 1630); *Pilg., The Pilgrim* (F 1647); *P. L., The Parliament of Love* (Victoria and Albert Museum, Dyce MS. 39, Edited by K. M. Lea, The Malone Society); *Ren., The Renegado* (Q 1630); *R. A., The Roman Actor* (Q 1629); *R. W., Rule a Wife and Have a Wife* (Q 1640); *U. C., The Unnatural Combat* (Q 1639); *Valen., Valentinian* (F 1647); *W. G. C., The Wild Goose Chase* (F 1652); *W. M., A Wife for a Month* (F 1647); *W. P., Women Pleased* (F 1647); *W. Pr., The Woman's Prize* (Folger Shakespeare Library, Lambarde Ms.).

†The form occurs 32 times as *'um* in the 1640 quarto text (see above, p. 142).
‡The form occurs 10 times as *a'th* in the Lambarde Manuscript.

To summarize the chief features of the linguistic patterns of Fletcher and Massinger: the Fletcherian pattern is one which is marked above all by the constant use of *ye;* one which exhibits a strong preference for the contraction *'em* to the expanded form *them;* one which regularly employs such other contractions as *i'th', o'th', h'as,* and *'s* for *his,* and which makes sparing use of the third person singular verb forms *hath* and *doth*. Stated numerically, it is a pattern in which the average rate of occurrence for the forms in question is as follows:

Contraction	Average occurrence per play
ye	322
hath	3
'em	59
them	8
i'th'	14
o'th'	9
h'as	6
's (his)	5

The full significance of these figures can best be realized when they are compared with the average rate of occurrence for the same forms in the unaided work of Massinger. There *ye* occurs twice in fifteen plays. *Hath* occurs at an average rate of 27 times. In the seven plays of Massinger's sole authorship written before Fletcher's death, and so reflecting most nearly the author's linguistic preferences during the period of his collaboration with Fletcher, *'em* is used an average of 12 times per play, *them* an average of 23 times. The contraction *i'th'* is found 18 times in five of Massinger's unaided plays, all of which date after the death of Fletcher. *O'th'* does not appear in any of Massinger's unaided plays; *h'as* is found but once (in a post-Fletcher play); *'s* for *his* occurs twice (both times in a play written after Fletcher's death). In the linguistic pattern which emerges from the unaided plays of Massinger written during Fletcher's lifetime, it can fairly be said then that the Fletcherian *ye* has no parallel; that Massinger's average use of *hath* is nine times greater than Fletcher's; that the Fletcherian preference for *'em* to *them* is precisely reversed in Massinger; and that the contractions *i'th'*, *o'th'*, *h'as*, and *'s* for *his* are completely absent from his work at this period. The linguistic patterns of the two are as nearly opposite as they could well be.

7

Dating and Chronology

W. R. Parker, Fitzroy Pyle, and J. T. Shawcross

The Dating of Milton's Last Sonnet

I. Milton's Last Sonnet

Milton's final sonnet, 'Methought I saw my late espoused saint', is undated.
For well over two hundred years it has been assumed that the subject of
this poem is his second wife, Katherine Woodcock, whom he married on
12 November 1656, and who died on 3 February 1658. The conjecture
seems to have begun in 1725 with what Dr. Johnson called the 'honey-
suckle life' of Milton by Elijah Fenton, which states positively that the
sonnet 'does honour to her memory'. Similar flat statements without evidence or explanation, were made in rapid succession by other early writers,[1]
who seem not to have realized that Fenton's conjecture was only a conjecture. On the other hand, the first biographers — Aubrey, Wood, Phillips,
Toland, and the Anonymous Biographer — make no such statement and
are, indeed, remarkably uninformative about Milton's second marriage.
Jonathan Richardson, writing as late as 1734, ignores Fenton's statement
and declares of Katherine Woodcock: 'We know nothing of her behaviour'.

It would seem time that Fenton's guess be reconsidered, especially since
none of these early writers, including Fenton, knew anything about either
Katherine Woodcock or the date of her marriage to the poet. (Most of
them suppose that it took place two or three years after he became totally
blind.) Fenton, moreover, has no claim to be taken seriously as an authority; in fact, most modern critics, ironically enough, have been contemptuous of his biographical sketch. To argue that Katherine Woodcock was
Milton's 'best beloved' wife is no argument at all, for *apart from this*

"Milton's Last Sonnet," by W. R. Parker, reprinted from *Review of English Studies,* XXI (1945),
236-238, by permission of The Clarendon Press, Oxford; "Milton's Sonnet on His 'Late Espoused
Saint,'" by Fitzroy Pyle, reprinted from *Review of English Studies,* XXV (1949), 57-60, by permission of The Clarendon Press, Oxford; "Milton's Last Sonnet Again," by W. R. Parker, and Mr.
Pyle's letter, reprinted from *Review of English Studies,* new series, II (1951), 147-154, by permission of The Clarendon Press, Oxford; "Milton's Sonnet 23," by J. T. Shawcross, reprinted from
Notes and Queries, III (1956), 202-204, by permission of the Oxford University Press.

1. For example, Thomas Birch's *Life* (1738, p. xxxi), Francis Peck's *New Memoirs* (1740,
p. 100), Bishop Newton's *Life* (1749, p. xxvi), and so on.

sonnet we have no evidence whatsoever of the poet's attitude toward her. Richardson's statement — that 'we know nothing of her behaviour' — is still quite true; and it would be absurd to reason in a circle. The usual biographical comments on her sweetness and goodness, and Milton's deep affection for her, are all inferences from the sonnet, which may not be about her in the first place.

There is, of course, only one other person who could possibly be the subject of this poem. For so many years now we have been interpreting Mary Powell's character unsympathetically, and assuming (on little or no evidence) that Milton's married life after 1645 was unhappy, that our habits of mind rebel at considering her as the subject of this moving and poignant sonnet. But consider her we must. Few of us would have the temerity to deny that Milton loved her at the time of their marriage. The early biographers, although interpreting the later reconciliation as a great proof of Milton's generosity, are nevertheless unanimous in calling it 'an Act of Oblivion, and a firm League of Peace for the future'. These are Edward Phillips's words, and in 1645 he was living in Milton's house. The Anonymous Biographer states that husband and wife lived together 'in good accord till her death'. Toland calls it 'a perfect reconciliation', and Richardson, the sympathetic artist, thinks that the poet was probably moved by 'his unextinguished former love'. None of the early biographers suggest in any way that Milton and his first wife were unhappy after 1645. This idea is born later, and assumes the air of incontrovertible fact when stated by Masson and subsequent writers. Really incontrovertible is the fact that Mary presented her husband with four children, one of whom, their only son, died. Also beyond dispute is the fact that Mary died in May of 1652, three days after giving birth to a daughter and shortly after Milton became totally blind.

It seems that we must look to the sonnet itself for evidence of its subject, but let us first remark that if it is about Mary, it belongs in time to the period of the preceding sonnets; if about Katherine, it becomes an isolated example of its author's sonneteering, composed at least two or three years later.

The poem is clearly about a deceased wife of Milton whom, in a dream, he imagines he sees. She has been buried, for she is brought to him, as Hercules brought Alcestis in the tragedy of Euripides, back from the grave:

> Methought I saw my late espoused saint
> Brought to me like Alcestis from the grave,
> Whom Jove's great son to her glad husband gave,
> Rescued from death by force, though pale and faint . . .

The word 'late' is an indefinite time reference; it can mean four years, or one. His late wife is now a 'saint' because she is a soul in heaven. The deceased Marchioness of Winchester was a 'bright saint', a 'new welcome saint'. Leaving Alcestis, the poet returns to the description of

> Mine, as whom washed from spot of child-bed taint,
> Purification in the old law did save . . .

The syntax is difficult here, but if we pick up the verb (line 9) and re-phrase the passage, the lines read: 'Mine came vested all in white, as one whom (washed from spot of child-bed taint) purification in the old law did save.' But Milton's meaning is still not clear. Does he intend to imply that she had *actually* died in childbirth, or, on the contrary, that she had died *after* her period of purification and was thus saved? According to Leviticus, if a woman

> bear a maid child, then she shall be unclean two weeks, as in her impurity: and she shall continue in the blood of her purifying threescore and six days [XII, 5]

Katherine Woodcock, Milton's second wife, did not die in childbirth, as the early biographers and editors supposed. Pertinent to our discussion is Bishop Newton's reason for rejecting Milton's grand-daughter's assertion 'that Milton's second wife did not die in childbed ... but above three months after of a consumption'. 'In this particular', Newton declared, 'she must be mistaken ... for our author's sonnet on his deceased wife plainly implies that she did die in childbed.'[2] But Katherine's daughter was born on 19 October 1657, and the mother did not die until 3 February 1658 — a month and ten days after the 'threescore and six days' of purifi-cation. Would this circumstance, however, have reminded the poet of *Leviticus?* What is the point of the allusion? Would not Milton have been more likely to think of 'the old law' if his wife had died *before* being 'washed from spot of child-bed taint', and if he had later dreamed of her as still alive — as one who had, in other words, survived to be purified?

Mary Powell died three days after her daughter was born. If our reason-ing thus far is correct, she is a more logical subject for the sonnet than is Katherine Woodcock. The latter's child died soon after her mother; Mary's child lived. The poem says nothing about the fate of the offspring, but continues with ambiguous description:

> And such as yet once more I trust to have
> Full sight of her in heaven without restraint . . .

Blindness is, of course, the 'restraint' which the poet hopes will be removed in heaven, where he can see his wife again. In the dream, however, the poet is not blind: 'Methought I saw', he begins; to his 'fancied sight' she appears. She is 'vested all in white, pure as her mind'. Nevertheless, as in the case of Alcestis,

> Her face was veiled, yet to my fancied sight
> Love, sweetness, goodness, in her person shined
> So clear, as in no face with more delight.

Here we have an apparent contradiction. In the dream he could not see her face clearly, but could see only the virtue shining from it. On the other

---

2. *Life of Milton* (1749), p. lix.

hand, in heaven he trusts to have 'full sight' of her 'once more'. Unless one wishes to call this careless writing and assume that the poet does not mean what he says, the lines cannot refer literally to Katherine Woodcock, because there is not the slightest reason for believing that Milton ever saw his second wife before his blindness. If he never had 'full sight' of her, he could not have it 'once more'. Again the lines point to Mary Powell as a more likely subject. The evidence is not final and conclusive, but where is any evidence favouring Katherine Woodcock? Any evidence, that is, apart from the unsupported conjectures we have long been meeting in print?

The conclusion of this sonnet is as overpowering in its simplicity as the Piedmont Massacre sonnet is overpowering in majesty of sound:

> But O as to embrace me she inclined,
> I waked, she fled, and day brought back my night.

The last line, with its syntactical flurry of excitement followed by a dreary march of monosyllables, contains perhaps the most affecting ten words in all of English poetry.

Milton mentions the death of Mary Powell in only one of his prose works. Speaking of the publication of the scurrilous *Clamor* (1652), he declares in his *Defensio Pro Se* (1655):

> But at that time, in a special way, I was oppressed with concerns far different. My health was bad, I was mourning the recent loss of two members of my family, and the light had now quite vanished from my eyes.

In May of 1652 Mary had died; in June the little boy, John, had followed her. Three years later, the blind husband and father had not forgotten his grief. Is it fanciful to suppose that soon after publishing his last *Defensio,* he dreamed one day of the wife he had twice lost, and composed a sonnet of reawakened sorrow?

William Riley Parker

II. Milton's Sonnet on His 'Late Espoused Saint'

Before Professor W. R. Parker's article on 'Milton's Last Sonnet' appeared in *R.E.S.* [XXI (1945), 235-8], it had for over two centuries been assumed that the sonnet referred to the poet's second wife, Katherine Woodcock. In that article, however, Professor Parker argued that no reason at all could be adduced for relating it to her, whereas the poem itself provided evidence—weighty, if not final and conclusive—that its subject was the first wife, Mary Powell. This impressed the editor of *Notes and Queries*[1] and also Dr. F. E. Hutchinson (in *Milton and the English Mind*); but Professor T. O. Mabbott was sceptical: in the light of the nuncupative will he could not believe Milton 'likely to be sentimental about his first wife'.[2]

1. *N. &. Q.* CLXXXIX (1945), 111.
2. *Ibid.,* p. 239.

The traditional view had been put forward, as Professor Parker said, in mere 'flat statements without evidence or explanation'; and his attack upon it has shown the need for a reasoned defence. The purpose of this note is to supply that need.

First, let us have the sonnet before us.

> Methought I saw my late espoused Saint
>> Brought to me like *Alcestis* from the grave,
>> Whom *Joves* great Son to her glad Husband gave,
>> Rescu'd from death by force though pale and faint.
> Mine as whom washt from spot of child-bed taint,
>> Purification in the old Law did save,
>> And such, as yet once more I trust to have
>> Full sight of her in Heaven without restraint,
> Came vested all in white, pure as her mind:
>> Her face was vail'd, yet to my fancied sight,
>> Love, sweetness, goodness, in her person shin'd
> So clear, as in no face with more delight.
>> But O as to embrace me she enclin'd
>> I wak'd, she fled, and day brought back my night.

Professor Parker used two main arguments. The first was that since his wife appeared before the poet in his dream *as though* she had been saved from death in childbirth, the probability is that she had not in fact survived the period of purification laid down in Leviticus XII, 5. This was true of Mary Powell, who died three days after her daughter was born, but not true of Katherine Woodcock, who lived for three and a half months after the birth of her daughter. His second argument was based on ll. 7 and 8, in which Milton says that he hopes to have full sight of his wife once more in heaven. In the dream he did not see her face; and hence, Professor Parker contended, 'unless one wishes to call this careless writing and assume that the poet does not mean what he says, the lines cannot refer literally to Katherine Woodcock, because there is not the slightest reason for believing that Milton ever saw his second wife before his blindness. If he never had "full sight" of her, he could not have it "once more".'

In rebuttal, let us start by inquiring why it had for so long been assumed without question that the sonnet concerned Katherine Woodcock. Surely it was not, as Professor Parker affirmed, because Elijah Fenton said so and others echoed him parrot-fashion. It was because the poem itself appears to say so in its very first line. It is the natural thing to take 'late espoused' as meaning 'recently married', and 'Saint' as 'one of the elect', 'a saintly person', who after death becomes a saint in heaven. Milton's third wife survived him; his first had been married for ten years before she died: only the second could have been seen in a dream after her death as recently married, for she died in the fifteenth month of her married life.

It is plainly a serious flaw in Professor Parker's case that he turned a blind eye to such an obvious and easy interpretation as this (the one, surely, which springs immediately to most readers' minds), and that he gave instead a forced explanation of the opening line as though it were the only one possible. 'The word "late"', he asserted, 'is an indefinite time reference; it can mean four years, or one. His late wife is now a "saint" because she is a soul in heaven', like the Marchioness of Winchester in Milton's *Epitaph* (ll. 61 and 71). Study of a concordance shows that (leaving this place aside) adverbial 'late' = 'recently' occurs seventeen times in Milton's verse (much more often than any other use of the word) and that 'late' = 'dead' does not occur there at all. This *may* be just a matter of chance. Yet it can hardly be denied that 'late-espoused Saint' is a much more natural grouping than 'late espoused-Saint'; and it finds an exact parallel in *Paradise Lost,* X, 436-7: 'the late/Heav'n-banisht Host'.

We must conclude, therefore, that the first line establishes a strong probability in favour of identification with Katherine Woodcock; and it only remains to show that the rest of the sonnet accords with that identification. In doing so we may find it of interest to reconstruct, if we can, something of the making of the poem.

It is a dream-construction. Even in the dream Milton is aware that his wife has died; and so when he seems to see her before him he thinks of Alcestis restored to Admetus from the grave. The analogy suggests itself imperatively, for both women were supremely virtuous and loving wives. But Alcestis was brought back by the might of Hercules, and in his company: Milton's wife returns alone. What 'force', then, can have rescued her from death, 'though pale and faint'? Must the analogy break down at this point? Yet it is a good analogy: his dream-wife is silent like Alcestis in the play; like her she is veiled; and if Alcestis gave her life that her husband might live, his 'Saint' risked hers in childbirth that Milton might live in her child. So, with childbirth in mind, he persists in his effort to work out the analogy.

At the end of Euripides' tragedy we learn that, though Alcestis has been restored to her husband, subsequent purification will be necessary to release her from her consecration to the nether gods (*Alcestis,* 1144-6). The recollection of this may have helped Milton, dwelling on childbirth, to think of 'purification in the old Law' as instrumental in his wife's apparent release. Before Katherine's death the days of purification prescribed in Leviticus had been fulfilled: had she lived in Old Testament times she would have been held to be preserved from the dangers attendant upon childbirth. Under 'the old Law', then, she might indeed have returned to him from the shadow of the grave, if purification had 'force' to ward off the powers of evil. So to some extent the poet allows himself to indulge that fancy.

But cleansing from pollution was the chief effect of 'purification in the old Law'; and it is his wife's purity that Milton is most concerned to stress. If in life she had spot or blemish it could only be 'child-bed taint', and that had, as it were, been washed away. In the dream she comes in vestments so white that they are 'pure as her mind'; her very person radiates love, sweetness, and goodness. And it is this purity, he implies, that has enabled her to reach beyond the grave this once to his 'fancied sight'.

So far as we know Milton never saw his wife Katherine in the flesh. This, then, is the first time he has 'seen' her, and he entertains no hope that the seeming visit will be repeated. In heaven, however, he hopes to see her 'once more', and then to have 'full sight' of her 'without restraint', for he will not be blind and will be able to see her face. This first experience has been a foretaste of that, for her inner beauty shone in her person 'So clear, as in no face with more delight', and even in heaven itself she cannot appear more saintly. Hence he speaks of having 'full sight' of her 'once more', though then 'without restraint'.

As he had never actually seen his wife, the picture he forms of her in his dream is featureless. And when he imagines that she bends down to kiss him and so to reveal her face, his fancy cannot cheat so well as one might wish, and he is tolled back from her to his sole self. That we are reminded of the conclusion of Keats's *Ode* is not fortuitous, for both poems are examples of willing surrender to but partially directed idealizations of fancy; yet it is typical of Milton's habitual rectitude of mind that even in the dream state he will not endow the visionary figure with a face supplied by guess-work.

We can see, then, that the detail of the poem bears out the evidence of its opening line that Katherine Woodcock is its subject. Furthermore, following upon what has just been said, it can be shown in a word that Mary Powell must be ruled out of consideration altogether. The dream was caused by the poet's longing for his beloved wife's companionship, for the presence of her saintly nature, which most shines in the face. If the fancied sight of Mary Powell's face would have done anything to allay that longing, he could have conjured it up again and again—if not at will, at least in such a dream as this. The face, however, remains veiled, and he has no hope of seeing it on this side of the grave.

Katherine he had never seen; and hence in special measure the sense of miracle the poem imparts. Katherine's face he never saw, even in the dream; and hence much of the pathos the poem holds: for we know the hunger Milton felt in his blindness for the sight of 'human face divine' (*Paradise Lost,* III, 44), and whose face can he have more yearned to see than that of his 'late espoused Saint'?

Fitzroy Pyle

III. *Milton's Last Sonnet Again*

Mr. Fitzroy Pyle has truly supplied 'a reasoned defence' of the traditional assumption that Milton's second wife is the subject of his last sonnet [*R.E.S.,* XXV (1949), 57-60] and I trust that I may be allowed to answer, as well as commend, his criticism of my suggestion that the poem *might* be about Mary Powell [*R.E.S.,* XXI (1945), 235-8]. It is good to have at last an explicit argument for Katherine Woodcock. We may yet understand the sonnet.

On the other hand, whatever else Mr. Pyle or I may have demonstrated, we have surely, between us, shown that the sonnet's meaning is not so easy and obvious as might at first appear. A good many ambiguities have emerged; and if I read Mr. Pyle aright, for several parts of the sonnet he offers interpretations which had not occurred to previous commentators. After further reflection I am convinced that the key to the poem's mystery lies in the passage concerning purification and that all other doubtful passages must be referred to this and explained in terms of it. In the interests of space I assume a knowledge of our two previous articles, and in the interests of clarity I enumerate what I consider the dependent passages.

1. Milton's phrase 'my late espoused saint' can mean *(a)* 'the saint whom I recently married', or *(b)* 'the saint who was recently my wife', or *(c)* 'my recently deceased wife, now a saint'. In my first article I mistakenly *assumed* the third meaning to be the only valid one. In his reply Mr. Pyle mistakenly *argued* for the first meaning as the only valid one.[1] I must now insist that we shall not know which meaning Milton intended until we have discovered the subject of the sonnet, and that we shall not discover the subject of the sonnet by preferring one meaning and rejecting the others, since all are possible.

2. Milton's lines, 'And such, as yet once more I trust to have / Full sight of her in heaven without restraint', are also ambiguous. Simple logic would suggest that Milton could not 'once more' have full sight of anyone, anywhere, if he had not already had it; and so I argued in my first article. My mistake (for which Mr. Pyle might have chided me) was in holding Milton to strict grammatical logic here as I would not have held him elsewhere (e.g. *P.L.* IV, 323, or *P.R.* IV, 583). The lines *can* mean, as Mr. Pyle thinks they do, that Milton trusts to see her once more in heaven and then to have the full sight of her denied him in the dream. But we shall not know which meaning Milton intended until we have discovered the subject of the sonnet, and we shall not discover the subject by insisting on either logic or lack of logic here.

3. So with the veil. Of course I admit readily that the sonnet gains in pathos, and that the reference to a veil gains in appropriateness, *if* the poem is about a wife never actually seen. But this hypothesis, I trust Mr. Pyle will also admit, constitutes no evidence whatsoever; for we must not argue backwards from a pathetic 'if,' demanding one interpretation because it moves us more than another, or seems more artistic.[2] In my

---

1. He begins his rebuttal by saying that I had 'turned a blind eye' to the only 'obvious and easy interpretation, of the first line, giving instead 'a forced explanation'· of it. Blind I was, but not self-blinded, nor singularly blind if Mr. Pyle is right in saying that 'late espoused' not only means 'recently married' but also explains (by so clearly meaning *only* this) 'why it had for so long been assumed without question that the sonnet concerned Katherine Woodcock'. For while many scholars speak of the sonnet's subject as 'recently deceased', I have thus far found only one who seems to agree with Mr. Pyle that Milton emphasizes the brevity of their marriage: Laura E. Lockwood, *Lexicon to the English Poetical Works of Milton* (1907), pp. 130, 250. In a search through several dozen editions of Milton's verse I learned, as Mr. Pyle probably has, that almost no editors have thought it necessary to explain line 1 directly. An exception is Tom Peete Cross [ed. *Minor Poems* (1936), p. 94], who paraphrases: 'My wife, who died recently and is now 'sainted.' The usual prefatory comment is that 'he sees his lately dead wife'; e.g., Masson, ed. *Poetical Works* (1890), I, 239.

   Mr. Pyle rejected my assumption that 'late' = 'recently deceased' when he could not find it in a concordance of Milton's verse. But I shall probably not shake his opinion by asking him to note that the phrase 'the late King' may be found in *Iconoclastes* and elsewhere. It has also occurred to me that 'espoused saint' is possibly a nice paradox resolved by 'my late', i.e., now a saint in heaven but lately my wife.

2. Nor must we allow ourselves to be outfaced by Mr. Pyle's hypothesis that the sonnet resulted from Milton's longing for a sight of his wife's countenance. Equally strange and untenable is Mr. Pyle's preparatory interpretation of 'But O as to embrace me she inclined' as meaning 'she bends down to kiss him and so to reveal her face'. The wife's face is mentioned only in lines 10 and (possibly) 12 of the poem, and 'to embrace' means 'to clasp in the arms', not specifically to kiss, by lifting a veil or otherwise.

opinion, Milton being Milton, his dream of *any* wife returned from the grave to her husband would inevitably suggest Alcestis,[3] and remembrance of Alcestis would further suggest a veil—for the parallel, as Saintsbury remarked,[4] 'almost requires the veil'. We should notice, too, that the veil serves well Milton's purposes in characterization. In Euripides' drama Admetus *almost* recognized his veiled wife by the way her physical presence affected him—a situation which Milton seizes upon and develops, making complete and instantaneous recognition depend upon recognition of Christian virtue shining in his wife's person. It is like Milton thus to enrich a classical allusion. And, as Mr. Pyle would admit, Milton was capable of dreaming literary allusions as well as thinking them. My point, then, is that the veil constitutes no real argument for Katherine Woodcock as the subject, and does not rule Mary Powell 'out of consideration altogether'. Of course Milton could have conjured up the face of Mary at will, but not, one may surmise, in a dream which at once suggested the analogy of Alcestis. We shall know the full meaning of the veil when we have discovered the subject of the sonnet, and not until then.

This brings us to the brief passage which provides, I think, a key to unlock the several ambiguities:

> Mine as whom washed from spot of child-bed taint,
> Purification in the old law did save, . . .

Is Mr. Pyle the first to recognize Milton's true meaning: that *because* Katherine had in fact fulfilled the prescribed days of purification, and had *not* died in childbirth, the dreamer indulged the fancy that imagined purification had 'force' (paralleling the force of Hercules in bringing back Alcestis) to effect his wife's imagined release? This interpretation may be correct; but I would point out—as Mr. Pyle does not—that it runs directly counter to what generations of critics have been saying; for readers have always interpreted these lines as *implying that the subject of the sonnet had died in childbirth*. Bishop Newton was so certain of this meaning that he even corrected Milton's own grand-daughter when she protested (quite rightly, we now know) that the second wife had *not* died in childbirth. The Bishop and countless others have evidently understood Milton to say: 'my wife came back from the grave *as though* she had survived the period of purification enjoined in Leviticus—which in fact, of course, she had not; it was only a dream'. The dream-explanation was as false as the dream-appearance.

3. As Mr. Pyle says, 'the analogy suggests itself imperatively'; he elaborates by pointing out that 'his dream-wife is silent like Alcestis in the play; like her she is veiled, and if Alcestis gave her life that her husband might live, his "Saint" risked hers in childbirth that Milton might live in her child'. Perhaps the play influenced Milton still further: Admetus tells his wife that after her death he will have an effigy of her made which he can fondly embrace, and, moreover, 'Thou wilt come to me in dreams and gladden me' (*Alc.* 354-6). Incidentally, Alcestis was not 'recently married' to Admetus; there were at least two children, one of them a speaker in the play.

4. *Cambridge Hist. of Eng. Lit.* (1916), VII, 120. Miss E. G. Brown, herself blind, argued from her study of the dreams of the blind that Milton could have formed a mental picture, in his dream, of a face never actually seen; and so, while assuming Katherine to be the subject, Miss Brown nevertheless urged that the veil was a consequence of the Alcestis analogy or else thought necessary as part of the shroud. *Milton's Blindness* (1934), pp. 57-8.

I, too, think it obvious that only a wife who had died in childbirth could, seeming alive again in a dream, return 'as [one] whom . . . the old law did save' from death, for why should Milton have mentioned childbirth at all if the wife had not died in childbirth? I suspect that in these lines he is thinking about the 'churching of women' (for which 'purification' was a synonym) and remembering that his wife had not lived long enough even for this ceremony of thanksgiving. Certainly she had not, in point of fact, been 'saved' from death by any ritual, and, in point of fact, no ritual had the power to avert death. Why, then, does Milton use the word 'save'? He is probably thinking about the element of time; the old law of Leviticus is very specific about 'threescore and six days'. I submit that the dream-appearance of a wife who had in fact lived long enough to be figuratively saved from death by observance of the old law, and then had died a month and ten days later (having survived childbirth by nearly four months), would never have prompted Milton to say that she came to him as one who had been saved from death in childbirth by purification in the old law. This is not poetry; it is nonsense. Katherine died, we are told, 'of a consumption'. Why, then, should the poet explain her dream-appearance in terms of some fancied protection from the perils of childbirth? Surely the editors and critics have all been right in reading this sonnet as about a wife who died in childbirth – as Mary Powell actually did.

I repeat, Mr. Pyle's new interpretation may be the correct one; but obviously no reader should accept it merely because he is reluctant to surrender Katherine as the sonnet's subject. I must apologize for the injustice I do this interpretation by lifting it from its persuasive context, a provocative attempt to reconstruct 'something of the making of the poem' – an attempt which begins by assuming Katherine to be the subject and which therefore accomodates itself to the assumption at every point. There is only one way, really, of answering such an argument as this; little is gained by questioning details; one must show that a similar, equally persuasive reconstruction can be based on a very different assumption. This let me essay.

The sonnet is at once the record of an experience and the poet's subsequent reflections on its significance. These two factors are blended skilfully, but it is possible, at any point, to distinguish between them. In the dream, blind Milton was aware that Mary Powell had died in childbirth, but suddenly he saw her before him, and her return from the grave suggested at once, in the dream, the Alcestis story. Alcestis was in fact rescued from death by the might of Hercules. Mary's imagined return alone, in the dream, calls for explanation also; and the poet, reflecting afterwards on the total experience, tells us in the second quatrain that she appeared *as though* she had been 'saved' from death by having fulfilled the ritual of purification following her fatal childbed. We can be confident that this was afterthought and not (like the Alcestis analogy) part of the dream, because in the next two lines of the quatrain the poet clearly interrupts his narrative to exclaim, 'Yet once more I trust to have / Full sight of her in heaven without restraint'. The veil (yet to be mentioned) was a restraint; so, too, was his blindness now, when he was not dreaming. In heaven he would have 'full sight' of her again as he had enjoyed it when she was alive and he was blessed with normal vision. These reminders in the second quatrain (the word 'methought' was the only previous clue) that his wife's return was merely a dream, lend poignancy to what slight narrative remains.

In the third quatrain we are told that the dream-wife was dressed in symbolic white, 'pure as her mind'. We may be sure that this garb suggested to the poet her now saintly estate in heaven following 'great tribulation' (Rev. VII, 14; XIX, 5-8), and it is likely that it also suggested to him, in retrospect, the ritual of purification mentioned in the preceding quatrain. Not until we come to line 10 are we told that 'Her face was veiled'—a detail of the Alcestis analogy which, once the analogy was apprehended, evidently influenced a detail of the dream itself. We know that Admetus almost, but not quite, recognized Alcestis despite the veil. To Milton's 'fancied sight' in the dream, and to his fertile subconscious mind, the means of full recognition were the Christian virtues which shone clearly in the apparition's 'person'. 'As in no face with more delight', he adds, emphasizing his point that familiar features are not necessary to the recognition of a truly virtuous person. But the dream suddenly ended as Mary bent down to clasp him in loving arms.

We may notice, finally, a few matters of technique. The sonnet has its 'turn' at the end of the twelfth, not the eighth, line. Its three quatrains have a static, trance-like quality, developed by the poet's first dwelling on the classical and Judaic associations evoked by a happening which he reports in a single line, and then sustained by his expression of hope for an actual reunion in the Christian heaven. In these quatrains the dream is without sequential events, almost without circumstance. The third quatrain introduces, however, a new emphasis—on light—for which we have been prepared by the purification theme of lines 5 and 6. In the dream his silent wife is garbed in pure white, and her incandescent virtues shine 'clear'. Then, with dramatic abruptness, the last two lines of the sonnet interject four kinetic verbs—'embrace', 'inclined', 'waked', 'fled'—and conclude with the stark opposite of all bright and shining things, the endless 'night' of blindness. The poet's exclamation signals and the word 'embrace' brings the turn, dissolving at once the trance and the mood of high spirituality, telling us simply that Milton's bereavement was a very human matter. This touch, followed by the equally simple reference to blindness, gives the sonnet its almost unbearable poignancy.

I am no more confident now than I was four years ago that Milton's love for Mary Powell inspired this moving poem; I repeat that 'the evidence is not final and conclusive'.[5] But Mr. Pyle has not shaken my notion that a

---

5. I cannot take seriously T. O. Mabbott's early objection to my conjecture, namely, that the nuncupative will shows Milton unlikely 'to be sentimental about his first wife' [*N. & Q.* CLXXXIX (1945), 239]. A man may, of course, love his wife and dislike his children. Milton's oral will, moreover, reflects his attitude toward his children (*not* toward their mother) almost two decades after the composition of the sonnet.

Since the publication of my article, friends have occasionally urged against it the fact that the manuscript version of the sonnet is in the handwriting of Jeremy Picard, amanuensis of Milton in the period 1658-60. But Picard *may* have been Milton's amanuensis at an earlier date, and in any case the manuscript is obviously a fair copy, which could have been made at any later time.

key passage in the sonnet points to Mary rather than to Katherine, and other students may now judge between us. In any event it is good to have more people looking more closely at this subtle product of Milton's art.

William Riley Parker

[Mr. Pyle writes: 'My case rested on the argument that the first line of the sonnet establishes a strong probability in favour of identification with Katherine Woodcock, "late-espoused Saint" being a much more natural grouping than "late espoused-Saint". To put this more explicitly: adverbial *late,* like many other adverbs, readily forms a quasi-compound with a following participial adjective, whereas adjectival *late* is possible in that position only if the participial adjective is treated as forming a compound with the noun it precedes. The first is by far the commoner usage; but instances of ambiguity can occur (the late deposed king), or of the second sense plainly prevailing (my late honoured father). Believing "my late espoused Saint" to be such an instance, Professor Parker suggests that "espoused-Saint" is "possibly a nice paradox"; but for Milton a married saint was no paradox.

'I need not proceed, however, with the balancing of probabilities, because I now believe that the case for Katherine Woodcock is proved conclusively by the very passage which Professor Parker uses against her. When Elizabeth Foster reported that Milton's second wife did not die in childbed "but above three months after of a consumption", she was concerned primarily with dates. She was not dissociating Katherine's death from the effects of childbirth, but correcting the biographers' statement that she died (in childbed) within a year of her marriage. So she told Birch and Newton that for three months and more after her confinement she lingered on, wasting away.[1] On 19 October Katherine Woodcock's child was born. On Twelfth Night the eighty days of "purification in the old Law" were fulfilled; but, far from being "washt from spot of child-bed taint", she was then seriously ill. Twenty-seven days later came the Feast of the Purification (2 February), celebrating the best of women and her happy release from the perils of childbirth; but for Katherine — also a person of superlative "Love, sweetness, goodness" — there was no hope, unless some Hercules should be at hand to rescue her "by force though pale and faint": for the very next day she died. It seems, therefore, that Professor Parker's key-passage is indeed decisive, but that we have both misinterpreted it. The words "as whom . . . Purification in the old Law did save" refer specifically to the Virgin Mary, who, having survived "the days of her purification according to the law of Moses" (St. Luke ii. 22), was preserved. The image is a private one: if we did not know the date of Katherine Woodcock's death (3 February),

---

1. The actual cause of death is not in itself important, but it may be noted that it was, or appeared to be, connected with childbirth. The choice seems to lie between a puerperal infection on the one hand and tuberculosis on the other. 'A consumption', vague term though it is, points most probably to tuberculosis; but even so childbirth is to some extent involved. As is well known, the progress of that disease tends to be retarded during pregnancy, only to become greatly accelerated after the confinement. So if Katherine had tuberculosis, her decline must have been noticeable and rapid after the birth of her child, and so have linked her death in Milton's mind with that event.

we could not elucidate the lines with certainty. Mary Powell died "about" 5 May, and so is out of the question.

'That is the main problem: which wife the poem is about. There is another, of trifling importance in comparison: why Milton dreamed of Katherine as veiled. The explanation, I still believe, is that however often he may have touched her face and heard it described, he never clearly visualized it. The analogy of Alcestis, it will be observed, is not protracted beyond the fourth line of the sonnet. It is succeeded by that of "blest *Marie*, second *Eve*", thoughts of whom had at the time of his bereavement mingled and contrasted in Milton's mind with thoughts of his wife, deepening and exalting his emotion. That later in the poem he should return after the Virgin to the pagan pattern of wifely excellence is unthinkable. The mention of the veil, then, in line 10 arises independently of any analogy, and so, we may conclude, represents Milton's habitual manner of imagining his wife — that is, with her face blurred.[2]

'With the substance of Professor Parker's article I disagree; but I warmly appreciate his controversial skill, his technical acumen, and his courtesy.']

IV. Milton's Sonnet 23

The contention that Mary Powell is the subject of Milton's Sonnet 23, first set forth by William R. Parker in 1945, and not Katherine Woodcock as other commentators have believed, has evoked a reaffirmation of the latter assumption by Fitzroy Pyle (and others) and subsequent rebuttals from both.[1] I should like to offer readings of line 9 in conjunction with lines 5 and 6 and of lines 7 and 8 which controvert the case for Katherine and confirm the identification of Mary.

Line 9 has all but been disregarded in the present controversy. The half-line "pure as her minde" has been superfluous in all explications given; yet there must be a reason for such specification. The reason for this assertion, I believe, is that Milton wanted to contrast the purity of his wife's mind with the impurity of her body. "Pure as her minde" modifies

---

2. Miss E. G. Brown, as Professor Parker notes, argued to the contrary from the experience of Sir Arthur Pearson, shared — whether in full he did not say — by other blinded men: 'In my dreams I am never blind. Then I see as I used to; and if I dream of something bringing in people whom I have only known since I lost my sight, they are, unless I have become very intimately acquainted with them, people whose faces are indistinct, though somehow I know who they are.' Thence she inferred that as his wife Katherine was intimately known to Milton he could have formed a mental picture of her in his dream. But are the blinded any more uniform than others in their habits and powers of dreaming? Does the qualification 'unless I have become very intimately acquainted with them' hold good universally? The experience of 'people whose faces are indistinct, though somehow I know who they are' corresponds so strikingly with Milton's as recorded in his sonnet that it is reasonable to conclude that the qualification did not hold good in his case, to accept the correspondence as presumptive evidence that he had known the woman of his dream only since he lost his sight, and in short to find in it corroboration of the views here put forward.

J. S. Smart's note sums the matter up neatly: 'The allusion to a veiled face has been traced to a passage in the *Alcestis;* but in the tragedy Alcestis is not recognised by her husband when her face is covered, and is treated by him as a stranger until the veil is removed. Milton recognises his wife in spite of the veil. It is clear that he alludes to his blindness during their married life'.

1. In a lengthy footnote, omitted here, Professor Shawcross summarizes the course of previous discussion of the problems of interpreting and dating the sonnet. *Editor's note.*

her white vestment; of her body he implies that she came only *clothed* in purity. There must have been a question of purity for so much emphasis to be put on it and her vestment; the intimation is that her body was not pure. The reason for impurity was that the necessary time-lapse (the only contingency) for purification after child-birth had not been fulfilled (Leviticus xii. 5). Only Mary would be considered impure of body, not Katherine. . . . This reading is substantiated by lines 5 and 6.

As Professor Parker has argued, "as," line 5, means "as one," which implies that his wife was *not* one "washt from spot of childe-bed taint" and not saved for Heaven by purification. She was only *like* such a one; it is "as though" she were washed from taint and purified. This accords with the contrast and emphasis embodied in line 9: the whiteness of her vestment, as pure as the purity of her mind, gives her the appearance of one who is pure of body. Pyle's suggestion that Katherine's ill health and death would be associated with child-birth does not require that she be considered impure of body. It is totally inconsistent to believe in one part of the law—impurity not saving the mother—and then not to believe in the only basis for that purity or impurity—the required time for purification.

"And such," line 7, signifies "and because of the aforementioned," which in turn means, as shown above, "and because she seems like one who has been saved by purification." Upon the condition that she be washed from child-bed taint Milton is able to say, "yet once more I trust to have/Full sight of her in Heaven without restraint." It is *only* upon the basis of such purification, which, like Heracles' saving of Alcestis, is contrary to laws of God, that Milton can hope to see his wife again. Milton would not have to make the contingency "and such" if he were speaking of Katherine, who would be considered pure of body.

In view of these two readings which further substantiate Professor Parker's interpretation of lines 5 and 6 and the lack of proof to the contrary, his identification of Milton's deceased wife in Sonnet 23 should be fully accepted.

John T. Shawcross

8

Composition and Revision

Curtis Bradford

"The Wild Swans at Coole"*

Though manuscripts of many poems included in *Responsibilities* (1914) have survived, they are for the most part late drafts, and I have seen no manuscripts of some of the finest poems in the volume, such as "September 1913," and "To a Shade." *Responsibilities* is remarkable for the appearance in it of poems concerned with public issues such as the *Playboy* crisis and the controversy over Sir Hugh Lane's offer to give a collection of pictures to Dublin if a suitable gallery were supplied for them. Through the rest of his life Yeats continued to write poems on men and events; taken together they are a splendid achievement and one almost unique in our time, since few other great poets of the twentieth century have commented so directly on our tragic history as it was being made. One could hardly deduce this history from the corpus of Wallace Stevens' poetry, and Eliot has largely confined himself to one aspect of it, the loss of traditional faith and his own efforts to regain it. Pound is occasional in his special way: he becomes occasional to denounce, with the result that he often seems to beat a dead horse. Yeats's stance is different from any of these. He addresses himself in work after work to the moral question how modern man is to act in typical situations, in the process powerfully asserting custom and ceremony and extracting from the traditions of western man all that is most viable. The poems in which he does this are the cause, I think, of the continuing popularity of Yeats. Whereas for the special student Yeats's art may well seem to culminate in such cryptic poems as

From *Yeats at Work* by Curtis Bradford (Carbondale, Ill.: Southern Illinois University Press, 1965), pp. 47-63. Reprinted by permission of Miss Anne Yeats.

*"In editing I have expanded abbreviations and silently corrected obvious misspellings, but I have not added any punctuation. I have used the following devices in reproducing manuscripts of poems. An X before a line means that Yeats cancelled it; revisions within a line are printed in cancelled type.... The original reading is followed immediately by the revised reading... even when Yeats eventually abandoned the whole line.... When alternate readings occur and Yeats has allowed both of them to stand," they are separated by a slant sign. "When lines of poetry are printed without normal spacing between them, this indicates that Yeats has tried various versions of a single line but has cancelled none of them. Whenever a line of verse reaches the form in which it was first printed, I place before it the number assigned to it in the *Variorum Edition*."—from "Preface," xvi.

"Supernatural Songs," the general reader will continue to prefer "Nineteen Hundred and Nineteen."

No complete run of drafts of any of the public-speech poems in *Responsibilities* has, so far as I know, survived. There is more material available for the study of "To a Wealthy Man" than for any other poem of its kind, but even this does not reward intensive study since it begins late in the total process of composing the poem. There are two manuscripts of the whole poem written December 24 and 25, 1912, and a corrected typescript in which the poem has reached its final form. Even the first surviving manuscript is, however, a late draft during which twenty-six of the poem's thirty-six lines were finished; most of the unfinished lines are well along toward their final wording. The form has been set, the correlatives all assembled. Yeats has, that is, worked out his contrast of renaissance Italy and modern Dublin in all its detail.

The manuscripts of poems included in Yeats's next collection, *The Wild Swans at Coole* (1917), are likewise for the most part late drafts, and again there are not in Mrs. Yeats's collection any manuscripts at all of some of the finest poems, such as "In Memory of Major Robert Gregory" and "The Double Vision of Michael Robartes." This is all the more to be regretted since beginning in 1915 and 1916, in poems such as "Ego Dominus Tuus," "The Wild Swans at Coole," and "Easter 1916," Yeats experienced a breakthrough to a greater art than he had hitherto created. Fortunately the manuscripts of "The Wild Swans at Coole" do show that poem in various stages of its creation.

Yeats's general mood, his cast of mind was reminiscent and nostalgic, though an Irish event like the revolution of 1916 could, as always, arouse his interest in an occasion. He had recently finished "Reveries over Childhood and Youth" and was continuing his autobiography in the manuscript known as "First Draft" which brings the story of his life up to 1898. It is natural that Yeats while meditating on his youth should begin his questioning of old age. This theme now moves into the very center of his poetry; in October 1916 Yeats finished "The Wild Swans at Coole," one of his greatest poems on old age. In this characteristic work Yeats uses what is nearest to him and most familiar, a walk along Coole Water, to express a universal state of mind and emotion. As he does this he achieves a diction and a rhetoric that can rightly be called noble.

Three successive drafts of the poem have survived. In all of them the order of the stanzas is as in the first printing of the poem with what is now the last stanza in the middle of the poem, following line 12. Draft A must have been written very early in the process of composition, since Yeats completed only four lines of his poem in this draft; draft B is transitional, that is it grows directly out of A and moves toward draft C; here Yeats completed thirteen lines and the whole of his original last stanza; by the end of draft C Yeats had nearly finished his poem. The three drafts are printed below.

Before he began work on draft A Yeats had established his stanza form, perhaps in still earlier drafts which have not survived. In this stanza three long lines—they range in the finished poem from eight to eleven syllables—alternate with three short lines of five, six, or seven syllables.

The basic pattern seems to my ear to place four stresses against three
with a variation of five against three at each fifth line and occasionally
elsewhere. The stanza has the unusual rhyme scheme abcbdd. It has not
occurred before in Yeats's poetry and does not exactly recur, though many
years later Yeats used this rhyme scheme but not the pattern of line lengths
in "Three Songs to the Same Tune" and the related "Three Marching
Songs." The arrangement of the rhymes varies the ababcc pattern that was
a favorite scheme with Yeats. The stanza pattern described above governs
everything Yeats does in the drafts. In this A draft the last two stanzas
of the poem (in their original order) are much less far along than the first
three. The A draft was written on two sheets of paper; there is no indication
as to their order. I have arranged the stanzas as they were first printed.
In some of the drafts of "The Wild Swans at Coole" Yeats indents his short
lines. Since this was not done consistently, I have brought all the lines
out to a uniform left margin.

[A 1]
These/The woods are in their autumn colours
But the Coole Water is low
× And all the paths are dry under
And all paths dry under the foot
In the soft twilight I go

The woods are in their autumn colours
× The lake narrow and bright
But the Coole Water is low
~~And all paths dry~~ The pathways hard under the footfall
× When in the twilight
× Night after night I go
Where I at twilight go
× Indolently among the trees and the stones,
× And number the wild swans.
Indolently ~~here and there among grey stones~~ among the
        shadow of the grey stones
And number the wild swans.

[A 2]
× It is now in the 19th autumn
× Since I first made my ~~tot~~ count
8 Since I first made my count
× And now we are in the 19th year
× Since the first I counted

[At this point WBY marked "It is now in the 19th autumn" stet]

~~Should they~~ Should I go nearer to the
And when I go too near the water
Suddenly they'd mount
× And beating

Scattering, wheeling in great broken rings
On their slow clamoring wings.

25 But now they drift on the still water
× I have Coole's fifty nine
26 Mysterious, beautiful.
Among what waters low build nests/rushes laid their eggs
And by what stream or pool
Where ~~will they flee~~ they have fled when I awake some day
And find they have flown away

[A 3, the verso of A 1]

They're but an image on a lake
Why should my heart [?] be wrung
× When I first saw them I was young
The white white unwearied [?] creatures
Delighted me when young
When I first gazed upon them

× Why is [it] when I gaze upon them
× That my heart is wrung
× I found it pleasing [?] to love them
× When I

× Ah now when I do gaze on them
× My heart, my heart is wrung
× And yet the white and loving/unwearied creatures
× Delighted me when young

× And were they to clamor overhead

[A 4, the verso of A 2]

The lovely white unwearied creatures
~~Delighted~~ Always when yet young
When they flew or clamored overhead
Gave me a lighter tread

Many conquests have they
× Their hearts have not grown cold
They have not grown old
× By passion and by conquest
× By lovingness and
For wander where they will
They are attended still
Passion and conquest wander where they will
24 Attend upon them still

In draft A 1 Yeats has brought together the materials of his first stanza:
the trees in their autumn colors, the dry paths, the twilight, and contrasts

with these emblems of old age and approaching death what seems the eternal beauty of the swans. One detail, the low water twice referred to, has been significantly changed in the finished poem where Yeats departs from the reality of the observed scene and places his swans on "brimming water." He has transferred the water, always a symbol of the sensual life in Yeats's poetry, from one set to another of the contrasting images in the stanza.

In this draft and the next Yeats introduces his I-persona, that is himself, into this stanza: "I at twilight go/Indolently." Though beginning a poem in the first person is a frequent practice with Yeats, it would have been more frequent still had he not in instance after instance removed his I-persona from the onset of a poem late in the process of composing it. He will do this in the C drafts. Revisions of this sort are so common that we should ask what Yeats accomplished by them: many of Yeats's greatest poems begin with the setting of their symbolic scenes ("The Second Coming," the Byzantium poems, "Meditations in Time of Civil War," and "Vacillation" among others); then the persona arrives, so to speak, and when he does Yeats's meditative exploration of the scene begins. The result is that at the onset of these poems the scene itself and the themes it suggests have the reader's undivided attention. This does not happen when the persona is immediately present, for then we must divide our attention between the contemplator and what is being contemplated. Another way of putting this would be to say that the type of opening chosen involves the question whether Yeats wants the point of view to be controlling, or the view itself, or both equally. Yeats can accomplish marvels with all these strategems, but the marvels are of different sorts as one can see by comparing "The Wild Swans at Coole" with "The Tower." Shall Yeats begin as he eventually does here with youth/age, mortality/immortality, or with my age, my mortality, with the symbolic scene or with the masked man? Here too it seems to me that "indolently" introduces too much of Yeats's accidence, his state of being at the moment. When he cancels this in the B drafts we have a clear example of revision involving management of the persona.

The form of the stanza is set: even in these very early drafts Yeats never rhymes line 1 with line 3; he picks up his b rhyme at line 4 and goes on to his concluding couplet. In this draft four stress lines alternate with three stress lines except at line 5; in the finished poem line 3 has also five stresses. The rhyme words of the final couplet (stones, swans) are in place. Yeats has achieved very little of the diction of the finished poem: we note "autumn" and "twilight," but even that essential word "dry" has for the moment been dropped. The last line of this draft "And number the wild swans" will eventually suggest Yeats's title.

On sheet A 2 Yeats drafts his second and what was originally his third stanza. Yeats made more progress on stanza 2 than he had on stanza 1. The materials of the finished poem are all here; four rhyme words are in place (count, mount, rings, wings); line 8 is done, line 11 nearly done. Even the number of syllables in the various lines of the stanza are identical for lines 8–12 in this draft and in the finished poem: 6, 9, 5, 10, 7. The essential words are all here, though not always in their final form (scattering/scatter, clamoring/clamorous). Stanza 3 (now stanza 5) is as far along in its action, form and language. Here as in the finished poem the poet contemplates the drifting swans, "mysterious, beautiful," and fears that they will leave Coole Water. The line ends are in place for lines 25, 26, 28–30 (water, beautiful, pool, day, away); lines 25 and 26 are done; the pattern of line lengths is the same in the draft and the finished poem (9, 7, 8, 6, 10, 7). Most of the words found in the finished poem are here. The cancelled draft line "I have Coole's fifty-nine" will in the C drafts be effectively reworked to supply line 6.

The A 3 and A 4 drafts of the original fourth and fifth stanzas are not nearly so far along. Yeats uses all of A 3 and part of A 4 to work on his fourth stanza. Though the essential idea of the stanza, the poet's changing attitude toward the swans as he ages and they appear not to, is present, Yeats anticipates some of the material he will eventually use in his next stanza – the fact that the swans seem "unwearied," for example. No line is even near its final form. Three of the line ends are in place (creatures, head, tread), though "creatures" will be transposed to the first line of the stanza. Most of the essential words – brilliant, sore, twilight, bell-beat, trod – are still to be found. The first half of what was then Yeats's last stanza (lines 19–21) had still to be invented after these A drafts had been completed. Yeats does make good progress with the last three lines of the stanza; indeed by combining draft lines one can get

> Their hearts have not grown cold
> Passion and conquest wander where they will
> Attend upon them still.

In the A drafts Yeats has assembled most of his materials, he has established his stanza form, and found much of the diction of the finished poem. He has established eighteen line ends and completed lines 8, 25, 26, 24. He has brought stanzas 1, 2, and 3 much further toward completion than stanzas 4 and 5. In the B drafts which follow Yeats got very little further with his first three stanzas; he remade stanzas 4 and 5, indeed he completed stanza 5 in this draft. The B drafts are written on three sheets of punched paper; there are no page numbers. Yeats was undoubtedly working in a looseleaf notebook, and he seems to have followed his usual practice of writing first on the right hand page of an opening, reserving the left hand page for revising.

THE SWANS AT COOLE

[B 1]

The woods are in their autumn colours
But the lake waters are low
~~And all~~ The paths ~~dry~~ hard under the footfall
The pathways hard under the foot~~fall~~
~~And I when~~ In the pale twilight I [go]
× In the half dark I ~~will~~ go
× Indolently among the shadow of the grey stones

× And number the swans
× Indolently among the stones and number the swans
  Among the shadow of grey stones, and number the swans
  Floating among the stones.

  We are now at the nineteenth autumn
8 Since I first made my count.
  I make no sound for if they heard me
  Suddenly they would mount
  ~~Scattering and~~ And wheel above the waters in great broken rings
  And a slow clamor of wings.

25 But now they drift on the still water
26 Mysterious beautiful
  Among what rushes will their eggs
× Where is the stream or pool

[B 2]

× All will have flown to
× All
  Upon what stream or pool
  Shall they in beauty swim, when I come here some day
  To find them flown away

× They are but images on water
× Why should a heart be young
  I turn away from the wat
  Why do I turn from the water;
  As though my heart were wrung
× At how those
× To gaze upon
  To ~~gaze~~ look upon those brilliant creatures
  I ~~did turn~~ always, when I was young
× As they came swinging by or clamored overhead
× I did not turn with this slow tread.
× When they ~~when~~ swung by or
  When they came swinging by or clamored overhead
  I had a lighter tread.

[From the opposite page (verso of B 1). I have arranged the drafts in what seems to me their proper order.]

  ~~I looked~~ To look upon those brilliant creatures
× Gaily when I was young
  Always when I was young
  If they swung by or clamored overhead
× I'd have a
  I have trod with a lighter tread.

And yet when I was young
If they swung by, or clamored overhead
I had a lighter tread

I look upon the brilliant creatures
And am heavy and heartsore
Yet nine[teen] autumns from ~~the autumn~~ this [word undeciphered]
× I walking upon
I hearing upon this shore
17 The bell-beat of their wings above my head
18 Trod with a lighter tread

[B 3]

Many companions float around them
Their hearts have not grown cold
Their wings can carry them to where [they] please
Their bodies are not old
Passion and conquest dip in what stream they will
24 Attend upon them still

Companion by companion
× And beautiful and bold
The beautiful and the bold
Have crossed the skies and climbed the river
Their hearts have not grown cold
Passion and conquest, wander where they will
24 Attend upon them still.

[From the verso of B 2]

Ah nineteen years from now
And I am growing old
They drift there lover by lover
Their hearts have not grown cold
Passion and conquest, wander where they will
24 Attend upon them still.

[The three versions of this stanza printed just above have all been cancelled.]

I turn away — lover by lover
20 They paddle in the cold
21 Companionable stream, or climb the air
22 Their hearts have not grown old
Passion and conquest, wander where they will
24 Attend upon them still.

[Yeats returned to the bottom of sheet B 2 to write two versions of line 19, the second in final form.]

    × Ah lover by unwearied lover
   19 Unwearied still — lover by lover

STANZA 1.   After setting an intermediate title at the top of the page, "The Swans at Coole," Yeats wrote a version of stanza 1 which develops directly from the A draft. He did not finish any of his lines, he did not even establish any additional line ends. He kept the description of the lake's low level, and his "I-persona." At line 5 in the phrase "pale twilight" he fell into a characteristic cliché of the 1890's: he tried "half-dark," but cancelled that and left his difficulty unresolved. He did drop "indolently," unfortunate because it involves us too much in his own state of mind, and reversed the order of lines 5 and 6.

STANZA 2.   Here Yeats may perhaps be said to have gone backwards. He kept his finished eighth line, and the rhyme words already established for lines 10–12; but his pattern of line lengths is no longer so nearly that found in the finished poem. He did make one important change: in this draft the swans do not rise from the surface of the lake, "I make no sound for if they heard me / Suddenly they would mount." He then went on in his original third stanza to describe the swans floating on the lake: "But now they drift on the still water." Perhaps we have here the explanation of Yeats's transposition of stanza 3 to the end of the poem. The two contrary actions in the finished poem, the swans' flight up from the water and their floating on the water, come too close together in the poem as first printed.

STANZA 3.   Yeats copied the first two lines, finished in the A drafts. He made a slight change in line 3, and then went on to invent slightly new detail for the end of the stanza when he wrote

    Upon what stream or pool
    Shall they in beauty swim, when I come here some day
    To find them flown away.

Again, no additional lines have been finished, no additional rhymes set.

STANZA 4.   Yeats wrote four drafts of this stanza, and made great progress. At the outset he took over most of the language of the A draft; this he gradually cancelled as he achieved much of the splendid diction of the finished poem. For example, line 3 in the A draft ends with "unwearied creatures"; the swans now became "brilliant creatures" and their unweariable nature was reserved for stanza 5. Then in his fourth draft Yeats transferred "brilliant creatures" to line 1, where we find it still, and established his line ends. Here again Yeats makes a revision that involves management of his persona when he shifts from his state now at the imagined moment of the poem to his state when he first saw the swans. "I did not turn with this slow tread" involves us again in the accidence of the moment; Yeats cancels this and replaces it after several revisions by the statement that he, even nineteen years before, hearing

> The bell-beat of their wings above my head
> Trod with a lighter tread.

These lines are now in their final form.

STANZA 5. Yeats also made four drafts of these lines, and on his fourth try nearly finished them. These drafts provide a study in emergence. In the A drafts the swans were emblems of youth and love; they were in complete contrast with the aging man who watched them. Yeats started with these ideas, kept his b rhyme and his closing couplet, though he tried a variant of line 23 when he wrote "Passion and conquest dip in what stream they will" before re-establishing the A reading. Yeats now introduced a new idea, the fact that the swans were a company while he was alone. This led eventually to the splendid beginning of the stanza. "Many companions float around them" became "Companion by companion"; then this was dropped down to the third line and rephrased "They drift there lover by lover." Yeats then transposed "lover by lover" to line 1:

> I turn away — lover by lover
> They paddle in the cold . . .

A false start, one more change, then the lines were done:

> ✕ Ah lover by unwearied lover
> Unwearied still — lover by lover.

While working toward his finished stanza Yeats explored and abandoned many details: should he describe the swans as "beautiful and bold"? Should he explicitly state his own age and loneliness? When the poem ended with this verse it had in some ways better balance, for we end as we will begin with the "I-persona" excluded from the first — this will happen in the C drafts — and from the final stanzas. In its original form the poem moved from the objective, to the subjective, back to the objective.

The C drafts of the poem were written on four unnumbered sheets. In this draft Yeats virtually finished his poem: twenty-two of its thirty lines are done and the others nearly done.

[C 1]

> ✕ The woods are in their autumn foliage
> The trees are in their autumn foliage
> The water in the lake is low
> ✕ The paths of the wood are
> All pathways hard under the foot
> ✕ From stone to stone I go
> In the pale twilight I go
> Among the great grey stones I number the swans
> Floating among the stones.

[On a page which I believe was originally to the left of this, which I designate C 2, WBY redrafted this stanza in nearly final form.]

    The trees are in their autumn foliage
2 The woodland paths are dry
✕ The water ~~in~~   under the October twilight
3 Under the October twilight the water
4 Mirrors ~~the~~   a still sky
5 Upon the brimming water among ~~the stones~~ stones
6 Are nine and fifty swans

[Back to C 1]

    We are/I am now at the nineteenth autumn
✕ From the time of my
8 Since I first made my count
    I make no sound for if they heard me
    Suddenly/All suddenly they would mount
    Scatter and wheel in those great broken rings
    With slow clamor of their wings

25 But now they drift on the still water
26 Mysterious, beautiful
✕ Among what rushes will their eggs
✕ Upon what shore or pool
✕ Swim, when
✕ Shall five and forty dream creatures play
✕ When they have flown away
✕ Shall they disport when I awake some day
✕ To find they have fled away

[From C 2]

✕ Among what reeds
    Among what rushes do they build
28 By what lake's edge or pool
29 Delight men's eyes when I awake some day
30 To find they have flown away

    Nineteen autumns ago
    When

[C 3]
✕ In numbering the brilliant creatures
✕ I have numbered all the brilliant creatures
✕ And I am but heart sore

✕ I have counted five and forty two
✕ And I am more heart sore

I turn from all those brilliant creatures
Heavy and heart sore
× ~~And yet~~   Yet nine [teen] autumns from this evening
× I, hearing on/upon this shore
17 × The bell-beat of their wings above my head
18 × Trod with a lighter tread

13 I have looked upon those brilliant creatures
14 And now my heart is sore
15 All's changed since I hearing at twilight
16 The first time on this shore
17 The bell-beat of their wings above my head
18 Trod with a lighter tread

[On the sheet opposite, that is on the verso of C 1, WBY did another version of stanza 2.]

The nineteenth autumn has gone
Since that first time I counted
They heard when I had but half finished
And all suddenly mounted
And scattered wheeling in great broken rings
12 Upon their clamorous wings

[C 4]

19 Unwearied still — lover by lover
20 They paddle in the cold
21 Companionable streams or climb the air
22 Their hearts have not grown old
Passion and conquest wander where they will
24 Attend upon them still

STANZA 1.   The C drafts begin with two versions of this stanza. In the first, most of the detail of the B draft recurs; in the second Yeats finished the stanza except for one word. In the first form of the stanza Yeats retained the observed detail of the low lake-water, the essential word "dry" was still missing, "pale twilight" came back, and Yeats was still very much with us as poet-protagonist. Then in the second draft the miracle occurred and the "poem comes right with a click like a closing box." To make it come right Yeats abandoned his b rhyme and wrote "The woodland paths are dry"; this had the further happy effect of taking "I go" along with it by forcing Yeats to write a new form of line 4. In place of "pale twilight" Yeats definitely established the time of the poem by writing "October twilight." He now neglected what he had observed; his imagination suggested the contrast of dry land with "brimming water" on which the swans might appropriately float. Since the "I-persona" had gone, the idea of counting the swans was dropped, and Yeats speaks instead of Coole's fifty-nine swans, a detail he had tried momentarily in draft A 2, though at another place in the poem. Yeats had still to replace "Autumn foliage" with "autumn beauty," easy to do since the line end was not involved in his rhyme scheme. The stanza is now magnificently balanced, with three autumnal images (autumn beauty, dry paths, October twilight) giving way to three images of the sensual life (water, brimming water, swans); its diction is superb.

STANZA 2.   This stanza was recalcitrant, and after the C drafts were finished Yeats had still more work to do on it than on any other part of the poem. In the draft on C 1, which takes off directly from the B drafts, Yeats retains the idea of not disturbing the swans as they float on Coole Water. He made slight verbal rearrangements as when "And wheel above the waters in great broken rings" became "Scatter and wheel in those great broken rings." Then on the verso of C 1 Yeats tried another version. He dropped the idea of not disturbing the swans. Now instead of merely imagining what would happen if they were disturbed, he recalls their flight from the lake nineteen years before. For the moment he has phrased the stanza in the past tense: "heard," "mounted," "scattered." His principal revision changes these verbs to the present tense. Only line 12 is done, but lines 10 and 11 are nearly done. Line 8, the first line of the poem to be finished, has for the moment been changed.

STANZA 3.   Here, as with stanza 1, Yeats made great progress. He began by copying out his finished opening lines (25, 26), then went on to explore detail that might fill out his stanza. The progressive versions of line 29 illustrate this exploration:

> Shall five and forty dream creatures play
> Shall they disport when I awake some day
> Delight men's eyes when I awake some day.

With the invention of the line just quoted, the stanza suddenly came right; all the lines save line 27 are done; that nearly done.

STANZA 4.   Yeats began by slightly changing the action that takes place in this stanza in the B drafts, where Yeats looked at the swans. He now explored the idea of counting them again, then turning away from them, before he returned to a slight revision of B, "I have looked upon those brilliant creatures." When Yeats abandoned his second explicit reference to his condition now compared with his condition nineteen years before, the stanza came right. He has stated again the essential theme of the poem, the contrast of youth and age, but in more general terms:

> All's changed since I hearing at twilight
> The first time on this shore.

Yeats concluded the stanza with his already finished seventeenth and eighteenth lines.

STANZA 5.   This has the same form as in the B drafts.

During the course of these three drafts Yeats completed lines 2–6, 8, 12–22, 24–26, 28–30, and his unfinished lines required only slight correction before reaching the form in which they were first printed. The final word in line 1 was changed from "foliage" to "beauty"; in line 23 "and" became "or"; the verb in line 27 was changed from "do" to "will." Stanza 2 was rewritten before it was printed. I place the manuscript version above the version printed:

> The nineteenth autumn has gone
> Since that first time I counted
> They heard when I had but half finished
> And all suddenly mounted
> And scattered wheeling in great broken rings
> Upon their clamorous wings
>
> The nineteenth autumn has come upon me
> Since I first made my count;
> I saw, before I had well finished,
> All suddenly mount
> And scatter wheeling in great broken rings
> Upon their clamorous wings.

Once printed, the text of "The Wild Swans at Coole" remained unchanged except for Yeats's decision to place what was originally his final stanza in the middle of his poem. This change first appeared in the Cuala Press edition of *Wild Swans*. We have already speculated about Yeats's reasons for making this change.

The doctrine of personal utterance is clearly operative both in "Words" and in "The Wild Swans at Coole," though the great difference in dimension and quality of the poems already suggests that a personal utterance should not be too personal. In both poems Yeats is writing of his own life, but perhaps only in the second has he made of it "something intended, complete," achieved that is the ideal stated in 1937 in "The First Principle." This achievement accounts for the increasing power of his verse. The breakthrough to controlled personal utterance came with "Adam's Curse" (written 1902, see *Letters,* p. 382) and affects all the poems printed with *The Green Helmet,* poems written in the years 1908–11, among them "Words." These are not Yeats's greatest poems, though "No Second Troy," "The Fascination of What's Difficult," and "Brown Penny" are fine poems, but with them we have clearly left behind the hermetic world of *The Wind Among the Reeds*. We hear of land agitation and the Abbey Theatre, we discover in "At Galway Races" the onset of lines of speculation that will engross Yeats for many years—the ideal relation of the poet and the man of action (the horseman) which will come with the dawn of a new age.

In *Responsibilities* a breakthrough to a larger audience is achieved when in "To a Wealthy Man" and "September 1913" Yeats writes the first of his great "public speech" poems. In *The Wild Swans at Coole* Yeats's mood seems meditative—seems because Yeats reserved for his next volume the poems inspired by the Easter Rebellion, all splendid examples of public speech and all written before the content of *Swans* was set in the volume Macmillan published in 1919. "The Wild Swans at Coole" is a typical and brilliant Yeatsean meditation, clearly a personal utterance from first to last which already avoids the danger that mere accidence may intrude into and spoil such an utterance. It illustrates the enlargement of Yeats's art which took place during these middle years, an enlargement that is intellectual as well as technical. A personal utterance becomes public speech in "Easter 1916" (as yet only privately printed); this mode of poetry was more and more to prevail.

9

Source and Influence

Hardin Craig

Shakespeare and Wilson's *Arte of Rhetorique,*

An Inquiry into the Criteria for Determining Sources

When George Chalmers, provoked by what he considered the arrogancy of Malone, published *An Apology for the Believers in the Shakspeare-Papers, which were exhibited in Norfolk-Street,*[1] he did a good deal more than merely showing that the Ireland forgeries were not without much credible and even verifiable information. He took occasion to treat, from the abundance of his antiquarian knowledge, various aspects of the history of the stage, the office of the Revels, and the "studies of Shakespeare." His reply to what Steevens, Malone's enemy, called "one of the most decisive pieces of criticism that was ever produced," is of relatively small value, but the book as a whole is full of both originality and good sense. It was Chalmers who, so far as I know, was the first to advance the idea that Shakespeare was familiar with Wilson's *Arte of Rhetorique.*[2] It is desirable to quote Chalmers both because one of his parallels is perhaps the best ever adduced and because his manner of reasoning is typical; that is to say, he notes a resemblance between the book and the works of Shakespeare, shows an antecedent probability that Shakespeare knew and used the book, and then lets the case rest as satisfactorily demonstrated.

There is nothing of any importance involved either in accepting or rejecting Shakespeare's dependence on Wilson, and for that very reason it will afford us an opportunity for dispassionate inquiry into the bases of such attributions of source and, if not to arrive nearer the truth, at

From *Studies in Philology,* XXVIII (1931), 618-630.

1. London, Printed for Thomas Egerton 1797. Edmund Malone, *An Inquiry into the Authenticity of certain Miscellaneous Papers and Legal Instruments, published Dec. 24, 1795, and attributed to Shakespeare* (London, 1796).

2. Published by Richard Grafton in 1553, by J. Kyngston (Newlie sette again) in 1560, 1562, 1563, 1567, 1580, 1584, and by G. Robinson in 1585 – all editions in quarto. *Wilson's Arte of Rhetorique, 1560.* Edited by G. H. Mair. Tudor and Stuart Library (Oxford: Clarendon Press, 1909). Review by Max Förster, Sh.-Jb., XLVI (1910), 341-2. The references in the following article are to Mair's edition. For important criticism of Mair's text and information as to texts and editions of *The Arte of Rhetorique,* see Russell H. Wagner, *The Text and Editions of Wilson's "Arte of Rhetorique,"* M. L. N., XLIV, 421-428.

least to become more able to distinguish it from error. Nobody doubts, for example, the validity of Theobald's discovery that Shakespeare actually knew Samuel Harsnet's *Declaration of Egregious Popish Impostures* (1603), a most unlikely book, and derived from it the names of Edgar's fiends and other minor matters in *King Lear;* and yet there is still debate, except for the one passage in *The Tempest*[3] indicated by Capell a hundred and fifty years ago, about Shakespeare's knowledge and use of Montaigne.

"It is, indeed, more than probable," says Chalmers, "that Shakespeare had studied with great attention, Wilson's *Arte of Rhetorique,* which was published, for the *third time,* in 1585. It is sufficiently known to the readers of Shakspeare, that he had unbounded curiosity, from nature, and vigilance of observation, from habit: And, it was natural for such a poet, who early felt the ambition of authorship, to inspect, and to study, the *Arte of Rhetorique,* which was popularly known, while his inquisitive mind was on the wing. From this fountain of knowledge, both historical, and critical, such an intellect must necessarily have quaffed abundant draughts of instruction; both of ancient lore, and modern attainments: In it, he must have seen, as in a *specious mirror,* the whole mistery of writing, the good, exemplified, and the bad, exploded. In the *Arte of Rhetorique,* he also saw characters pourtrayed, which as a dramatist, he must have viewed with pleasure, and recollected with advantage: Herein, he must have seen *Tymon of Athens,*[4] and the *Pedantick Magistrate:* He, herein, discovered *the character;* but he found, in his own invention, *the constable.* He now became acquainted with *the major;* but he afterwards shook hands with Dogberry at Credenton."[5]

In a footnote to the *"Pedantick Magistrate"* Chalmers quotes from Wilson[6] as follows: "Another good fellowe of the countrey, being an *officer* and *mayor* of a toune, and desirous to speak like a fine learned man, having just occasion to rebuke a runnegate fellowe, said after this wise, in a greate heate: — Thou *yngraine* and *vacation* knave, if I take thee any more within the *circumcision* of my *dampnation;* I will so *corrupt* thee, that all other *vacation* knaves shall take *ilsample* by thee." Mair prints "yngrame" instead of "yngraine," which is obviously the original reading, especially since it presents a case of the unexpected happy hit of the wrongly used word, a feature of this type of comicality.

The possibility that Shakespeare had any debt to Wilson's brief reference to Timon of Athens is too slight to be considered. To say nothing of the accounts of Timon in Plutarch's *Life of Mark Antony,* in Lucian's dialogue *Timon the Misanthrope,* in Sir Richard Barckley's *A Discourse of the Felicitie of Man* (1598, 1603), and in Pierre Boaistuau's *Theatrum Mundi,*[7] it is to be noted that Timon the Misanthrope was a stock figure in sixteenth century literature and is frequently alluded to in just the way he

---

3. Act II, scene i, lines 147-164.
4. Footnote reference to *The Arte of Rhetorique,* edition of 1585, p. 56 (Mair's edition, p. 55), and quotation of the passage with the side-note "Tymon a deadly hater of all companie."
5. *Apology for the Believers,* pp. 558-560.
6. Edition of 1585, p. 167; Mair's edition, p. 164.
7. Englished by John Alday and published by T. Hacket, 1566? and 1574,8°, and by J. Wyght, 1581, 8°.

is in Wilson. But as regards the *"Pedantick Magistrate"* as the immediate source of Dogberry's speeches at the examination of Conrade and Borachio in *Much Ado about Nothing,* Act IV, scene ii, the case must at the outset be admitted to be a much better one, since the situations in Wilson's story and Shakespeare's play are similar, and in the severity of the magistrate there is a suggestion of Dogberry's fine burst of indignation at being called an ass. The source of the humor is also identical, and it is, moreover, a form of humor which seems to be peculiarly Shakespearean. Clowns of course always misused their words; it is impossible to think of a clown who does not do so. But in this case there is a touch of pedantry. There is a certain amount of ridicule of pedantry in Lyly, but no humor derived from a misunderstanding or misuse of learned terms. There are excellent fantastically talking clowns in Greene, Peele, and Porter; but nowhere in early comedy have I been able to find a malaprop who directly suggests Bottom, Mistress Quickly, and Dogberry. On the other hand, the pedantical misuse of fine language is not a rare form of comicality, as Wilson's story bears witness, and although it seems to have been a favorite method of Shakespeare's, it also seems to have been with him a more or less gradual growth. It is not so pronounced in Bottom as in the later characters, and there are touches of it in Launce, Launcelot Gobbo, and Jack Cade. This circumstance would indicate that Shakespeare was not immediately borrowing an idea in his creation of Dogberry. Particularly and, I think, significantly, there is no sign of the direct borrowing of names, words, or circumstances, and with reference to Chalmers's contention the findings are negative. Wilson himself possibly gives a clue to the origin of this kind of comic speech when he introduces a letter full of "ynke horne termes" with the statement that "William Sommer himselfe could not make a better for the purpose." Note also the following passage: "William Somer seeing much adoe for accomptes making, and that the Kinges Maiestie of most worthie memorie Henrie the eight wanted money, such as was due vnto him: and please your grace (quoth he) you haue so many Frauditours, so mony Conueighers, and so many Deceiuers to get vp your money, that they get all to themselues. Whether he sayd true or no, let God judge that, it was vnhappely spoken of a foole, and I thinke he had some Schoolemaster: He should haue saide Auditours, Surueighours, and Receiuers."[8]

Nathan Drake was also firmly convinced that Shakespeare knew and imitated Wilson in his *Arte of Rhetorique.*[9] He quotes Wilson's satire against the Latinizing and Italianizing of the English language to such a degree that it was scarcely intelligible to the common people, and gives as an example the "letter full of ynke horne termes," "deuised by a Lincoln-shire man, for a voyde benefice, to a gentleman that then waited vpon the Lorde Chauncellour."[10] Drake thinks it "probable, nay certain, that Shakespeare improved his limited education in the country by inspecting those treatises in philology and criticism which had acquired the popular

---

8. Mair's edition, pp. 163, 201.

9. *Shakespeare and his Times.* Two vols. London, 1817, pp. 440-441, 472-473.

10. Mair's edition, pp. 162-163. The letter begins "Pondering, expending, and reuoluting with my selfe, your ingent affabilitie."

approbation, and were adapted to the years of his manhood." He "perused with avidity" the *Arte of Rhetorique* of Wilson and the *Scholemaster* of Ascham and "availed himself professionally" of the rhetoric. This he thinks will be evident from the two passages cited above from Chalmers, which he quotes. But Shakespeare's ridicule of pedantry he need not have had suggested to him by Wilson, since it was common to Wilson, Cheke, Ascham, and perhaps a dozen other writers.[11] Halliwell-Phillipps[12] also cites the epistle of the Lincolnshire man in connection with Armado's letter to Jaquenetta in *Love's Labour's Lost,* Act IV, scene i, lines 60-89, but does not regard Armado's effusion as an imitation of Wilson. Furness,[13] who cites Halliwell-Phillipps and quotes the passage from Wilson at length, lends some color to the possibility of influence by citing the participles "illustrate" and "indubitate" from Don Armado's letter for comparison with a number of such forms from Wilson. Many Latin verbs, however, were adopted into English in the sixteenth century in the form of the passive participle, and the resemblances probably have no special significance.[14] It will be necessary for us to say something further on in the paper about a possible connection between Wilson's *Rhetorique* and *Love's Labour's Lost* in its ridicule of pedantry.

The Reverend Joseph Hunter[15] makes a more extensive use of Wilson in the elucidation of Shakespeare (usually to small purpose) than any other commentator and brings forward one of the closest and most convincing resemblances ever cited. Hunter's parallels to Beatrice's "Thus goes every one to the world but I, and I am sun-burnt" (*Much Ado,* II, i, 331), Sir Toby's "passy measures panyn" (*T. Night,* V, i, 206), Juliet's "O, swear not by the moon, the inconstant moon" (*R. & J.,* II, ii, 109), and the First Clown's protest at the privileges of "great folk" more than "their even Christian" (*Hamlet,* V, i, 32) are unimportant; but not so his parallel to the following words of Iago (*Othello,* III, iii, 155-161):

> Good name in man and woman, dear my lord,
> Is the immediate jewel of their souls:
> Who steals my purse steals trash; 'tis something, nothing;
> 'Twas mine, 'tis his, and has been slave to thousands;
> But he that filches from me my good name
> Robs me of that which not enriches him
> And makes me poor indeed.

"There are several passages," says Hunter, "in Wilson's *Rhetorique* which remind one of Shakespeare, so many that it might be affirmed to be a book which Shakespeare had at some period of his life not only read but studied. The resemblance of the lines above to the following passage found in the

11. George Phillip Krapp, *The Rise of English Literary Prose* (New York, 1915), pp. 287-306.
12. *Memoranda on Love's Labour's Lost,* London, 1879.
13. *Love's Labour's Lost,* Variorum edition, pp. 119, 120.
14. Henry Bradley, "Shakespeare's English," in *Shakespeare's England* (Oxford, 1917), Vol. II, pp. 561-563, and E. A. Abbott, *A Shakespearian Grammar,* par. 342.
15. *New Illustrations of the Life, Studies, and Writings of Shakespeare.* Two vols. (London, 1845).

chapter on Amplification is remarkable:—'The places of Logique help oft for amplification. As, where men have a wrong opinion, and think theft a greater fault than slander, one might prove the contrary as well by circumstances as by arguments. And first, he might shew that slander is theft, and every slanderer is a thief. For as well the slanderer as the thief do take away another man's possession against the owner's will. After that he might shew that a slanderer is worse than any thief, because a good name is better than all the goods in the world, and that the loss of money may be recovered, but the loss of a man's good name cannot be called back again: and a thief may restore that again which he hath taken away, but a slanderer cannot give a man his good name again which he hath taken from him. Again, he that stealeth goods or cattle robs only but one man, but an evil-tongued man infecteth all their minds unto whose ears this report shall come.'"[16]

In spite of the fact that the thought is exactly the same, namely, that slander is worse than theft, the two passages are deficient in signs which might tie them together. Wilson is not speaking in actual contempt of wealth or its transitoriness and he lacks the idea with which Shakespeare closes, that the slanderer is not himself enriched by his filchings. There are many aspects of the subject as presented by Wilson not mentioned in Shakespeare, and Wilson's chief interest in the passage as a logical demonstration is not hinted at. To Wilson it was a clever bit of unexpected argument. As used by Iago, it was a facile moral sentiment. The chances are that both Shakespeare and Wilson were doing the same thing; both were choosing an attractive bit of Renaissance learning, a well-rounded moral sentiment, to serve an immediate purpose. Wilson borrowed much from the rhetorical works of Erasmus.[17] It happens that this passage is one of his borrowings. The thought was a favorite one with Erasmus. It occurs in *Lingua* among his precepts concerning moderation in speech,[18] and is alluded to several times in his letters.[19] Wilson's actual source was, however, *De Conscribendis Epistolis*,[20] in which the following passage occurs: *Sapientis est famae suae longe diligentius, quam opibus suis, non minus vero diligenter quam vitae consulere. Minus siquidem damni, & incommodi accipit, qui pecuniam, aut etiam vitam amittit, quam qui famam. Pecunia enim amissa sarciri potest, fama semel amissa, in integrum restituitur nunquam. Et vita quidem corporis, quum certos a natura terminos acceperit, in longum tempus extendi nequit. . . . Quod si homines iis rebus maxime timere videmus, quae cum sint preciossimae, facillime tamen perduntur, ac difficillime restituuntur: sapiens existimandus non est, qui famae, quae neque restitui potest semel amissa, & qua nihil habet homo preciosius, non multo diligentius consulendum putat quam pecuniae,*

16. See Mair's edition, pp. 124-125. Wilson goes on to amplify his proposition "by the places and circumstances," showing that slander is the more heinous offence because the law does not touch it, that it is craftily committed like a poisoning, and that it is an enchantment injuring the mind rather than the body. He repeats his thought more briefly (see page 186) under the heading "Correction."

17. Russell H. Wagner, "Wilson and his Sources," *Quarterly Journal of Speech*, XV, 525-537.

18. *Opera Omnia*, Lugduni Batavorum (1703), tom. IV, 66 3 F.

19. See Ep. CCCCLXXX and DCIII.

20. Cap. xlvi; *loc. cit.*, tom. I, 407-408.

aut etiam vitae. Potest etiam tribus dumtaxat, aut quattuor partibus confici collectio: si vel confirmatio, vel expolitio, vel utraque omittitur. Erasmus then proceeds to develop the idea as a rhetorical exemplum. Wilson has apparently borrowed the idea, and condensed and adapted it to his own purposes.

Slander was not originally one of the Seven Deadly Sins, but in certain groups of treatises it found a place as one of the subheadings under Envy.[21] Slander is, therefore, usually treated under Envy in the moral treatises of the sixteenth century. I have, however, found only one in which this particular example is used. That, with the appearance in the works of Erasmus, is perhaps enough to suggest that it was a moralistic commonplace, and, for that reason, less likely to be derivable only from Wilson. La Primaudaye in his chapter "Of Envie, Hatred, and Backbiting,"[22] after inveighing against envy, declaring it like Wilson, to be sorcery (in which he is following Plutarch), and saying that it is hurtful to others "and much more noisome to him that possesseth it," makes this statement: "The occasion whereof is the ill will which naturally he beareth against all them that deserve more than himselfe, wheruppon he striveth rather to blame, or to wrest in ill part whatsoever was well meant, than to reape any profit thereby." La Primaudaye's main utterance about backbiting, which follows closely on the sentence quoted, seems to me to be, though briefer than Wilson's description, closer to the Shakesperean passage than is Wilson himself: "Of this wilde plant of envie, backbiting is a branch, which delighteth and feedeth it selfe with slandering and lying, whereupon good men commonly receive great plagues, when they over-lightly give credit to backbiters.... For seeing good fame and credit is more pretious than any treasure, a man hath no lesse an injury offered him when his good name is taken away, than when he is spoiled of his substance." Thus La Primaudaye presents all three of the ideas in the Shakespearean passage, namely, that good name is a treasure, that to be slandered is to be robbed, and that slander is without profit to the slanderer. There is of course no question of presenting La Primaudaye as a source for Shakespeare, but there is certainly removed the necessity of regarding Wilson as a source.

The tale of the relations between Wilson and Shakespeare is almost told. The late Sir Walter Raleigh of Oxford[23] made a dexterous and legitimate use of Wilson in the following passage: "Falstaff was never at the end of his resources; and if he had chosen to inveigh against his own manner of life, not without some sidelong depreciation of his companions, might he not have spoken after this fashion: 'Now, Lord! what a man is he; he was not ashamed, being a Gentleman, yea a man of good years, and much authority, and the head Officer of a Duke's house, to play at Dice in an Ale house with boys, bawds and varlets. It had been a great

21. R. Elfreda Fowler, *Une source française des poèmes de Gower* (Macon, 1905), pp. 59 ff., and "Tableau I, L'Ordre des vices et des vertus," pp. 81-96; Kate O. Petersen, *The Sources of the Pardoner's Tale* (Boston, 1901), pp. 35-81.
22. *The French Academie,* Part I. Translated by T. B. Imprinted at London by Edmund Bollifant for G. Bishop and Ralph Newbery, 1586, pp. 432-435.
23. *Shakespeare* (London, 1907), pp. 50-51.

fault to play at so vile a game among such vile persons, being no Gentleman, being no Officer, being not of such years; but being both a man of
fair lands, of an ancient house, of great authority, an Officer of a Duke,
yea, and to such a Duke, and a man of such years that his white hairs
should warn him to avoid all such folly, to play at such a game with such
Roysters and such Varlets, yea, and that in such an house as none comes
thither but Thieves, Bawds, and Ruffians; now before God, I cannot speak
shame enough on him'? This speech which is given as an example in
Thomas Wilson's *Art of Rhetoric*[24] (1553), has not Falstaff's wit, but it
has the rhetorical syntax which he borrows when he rides the high horse."
In this Sir Walter makes no claims for dependence by Shakespeare on
Wilson and yet indicates pretty clearly that Shakespeare knew the kind
of thing that Wilson's book embodies.

The last case of an actual claim of dependence is that put forward by
Mr. G. H. Mair in the introduction to his edition of *The Arte of Rhetorique*
(pp. xxxiii-xxxiv). He calls attention to Drake's suggestion (really, as we
have seen, that of George Chalmers) that the character of Dogberry was
derived from Wilson. This we have already considered. Mair finds more
certain evidence of Shakespeare's reading of Wilson in *Love's Labour's
Lost*. Holofernes remarks (Act IV, scene ii, lines 137-138), "I will look
again on the *Intellect* of the letter, for the nomination of the party writing
to the person written unto." "The word here," says Mair, "is Wilson's
Intellection, which is 'a trope, when we gather or iudge the whole by the
part, or part by the whole.'" In point of fact it is not. "Intellect" is an
Anglicization of the Latin word *intellectus*, which had and has the meaning
"sense or interpretation." It is here used as a technical term in the art
of letter-writing. Wilson's word "intellection" is for *intellectio* and means
"synecdoche." Wilson probably borrowed it from the *De Ratione dicendi
ad C. Herennium*,[25] formerly attributed to Cicero. There is thus no value
in this parellelism, which, incidentally, was first adduced by T. S. Baynes
in *Shakespeare Studies* (London, 1896, p. 192). "But," Mair continues,
"Holofernes is not the only student of *The Arte of Rhetorique* in the company
gathered in Navarre. Don Armado culled some of the splendour of his
speech from this source. His letter to Jaquenetta is modeled on one of
Wilson's examples. He is writing of King Cophetua (*Love's Labour's
Lost*, IV, i, 67-81):

> 'He it was that might rightly say, Veni, vidi, vici; which to
> annothanize the vulgar, — O base and obscure vulgar! — videlicet,
> He came, saw, and overcame: he came, one; saw, two; overcame,
> three. Who came? the king: why did he come? to see: why did he
> see? to overcome: to whom came he? to the beggar: what saw he?
> the beggar: who overcame he? the beggar. The conclusion is victory:
> on whose side? the king's. The captive is enriched: on whose side?
> the beggar's. The catastrophe is nuptial: on whose side? the king's:

---

24. Mair's edition, pp. 122-123.
25. See *Incerti Auctoris de Ratione dicendi ad C. Herennium Libri IV*, edidit Fridericus Marx
(Lipsiae, MDCCCCIV), IV, 33, 44*e*.

no, on both in one, or one in both. I am the king; for so stands the comparison: thou the beggar; for so witnesseth thy lowliness.'

"All this follows the questions appended to the Example of commending King David given below p. 21." We must see this example, for Mr. Mair adds, "A certain knowledge of it [Shakespeare's acquaintance with Wilson's work] can be proved beyond doubt." The questions referred to, given under the caption "Examining of the circumstaunces," are: i. Who did the deed? ii. What was done? iii. Wherefore did he it? iiii. What help had he to it? v. Wherefore did he it? vi. How did he it? vii. What time did he it?

Although, to begin with, I confess that with the best will in the world I cannot discover an inevitable interdependence, there is yet this behind it, that the passage from Shakespeare is making fun of just such a general rubric as Wilson gives. It is one of the most familiar of logical and rhetorical devices and rests ultimately on the "places" of logic. Aristotle himself had conceived of rhetoric as the counterpart of dialectic and had complained (*Rhet.,* I, i.) that earlier writers on rhetoric had neglected the true basis of oratory, which is persuasion through logical conviction. The *Topica* of Aristotle and of course of Cicero have to do with "places" as forms of reasoning, and both books have as intention the preparation of logical discourses. Quintilian defines a *locus* as "the seat of arguments in which they are latent and from which they are to be derived," and gives many outlines of appropriate *loci.* One of these Wilson himself repeats in this form (p. 132): i. What is done. ii. By whom. iii. Against whom. iiii. Upon what mind. v. At what time. vi. In what place. vii. After what sort. viii. How much he would have done. The particular rubric to which Mr. Mair refers in Wilson is a mere inquiry into the circumstances as they might apply to persons; and, although he gives further on (p. 112) a still more careful outline for the same inquiry, the matter is much too common to form the basis for any argument of specific reference to Wilson on Shakespeare's part. Quintilian, the Ciceronian works, and various other rhetorical writings were in wide circulation.

Indeed, the whole thing is nothing more than a form of the *methodus* of Aristotelian logic, and the pedantry of both Armado and Holofernes is, to my mind, quite as much logical as rhetorical. Had it been intentionally rhetorical one might have expected a specifically absurd use of the "figures of rhetoric" rather than of the "places" of logic. As it is (and I think this weakens the argument for Shakespeare's dependence on Wilson's *Rhetorique*), what you find ridiculed in *Love's Labour's Lost* might quite as well have come from Wilson's *Rule of Reason* (1551, 1552, 1553, 1563, 1567, 1584?, 1593) as from his *Arte of Rhetorique.* There is indeed one circumstance that connects Shakespeare with *The Rule of Reason.* Not only did Shakespeare have a considerable familiarity with the terminology of formal logic,[26] but it is just possible that he derived a suggestion from that book for the device of mis-punctuation which he uses in Peter Quince's prologue in *A Midsummer-Night's Dream,* Act V, scene i, lines

---

26. See my article, "Shakespeare and Formal Logic" in *Studies in English Philology, a Miscellany in Honor of Frederick Klaeber* (Minneapolis, 1929), pp. 380-396.

108-117. It will be remembered that a similar device appears in a letter in *Ralph Roister Doister* (III, iii, 36-70) and that this letter appears as an example in the third edition (1553) of *The Rule of Reason* and is there attributed to Nicholas Udall, thus forming the chief means of dating the play from which it was taken. Copies of *Ralph Roister Doister* were probably none too numerous, and copies of Wilson were plentiful. *The Rule of Reason* would certainly have been more available than the play, or the poem on *Women,* from Add. MS 17492, printed in Flügel's *Lesebuch* (p. 39), or that in Ebert's *Jahrbuch* (XIV, 214), or that given by Furness in the Variorum edition of *A Midsummer-Night's Dream* from a manuscript collection of short poems formerly belonging to Dr. Percy; and these are the only cases of mis-pointing for comic effect earlier than *A Midsummer-Night's Dream* which have been cited. I do not insist upon this connection, but merely state it as a possibility slightly more definite than the original contention.

The editor of *Love's Labour's Lost* in the Arden Shakespeare (Methuen, 1906) cites a number of parallels in that play to Wilson's *Arte of Rhetorique* and seems to believe that Wilson was an actual source. There is no doubt that in *Love's Labour's Lost* there is abundant satire on pedantry and that part of it is rhetorical. As the editor cites these parallels he cites others to Chapman, Harvey, and other Elizabethan writers, and I think there can be little doubt that in so doing he is pointing the way to a correct explanation of the stylistic vagaries of that play. In his introduction (pp. xxxiv-xli) the editor makes out a strong case for connecting the play with various living writers, particularly Nashe and Harvey. The idea that *Love's Labour's Lost* was intended to ridicule a particular literary coterie, a fantastic academy of advanced, if not atheistical views, has been vigorously espoused by Sir Arthur Quiller-Couch and Professor J. Dover Wilson and by various other scholars.[27] Whatever may be the value of the identification of particular persons, it is certainly a better idea that the play was meant as a satire against pedantical behavior and speech on the part of a literary coterie, than that it was a new composition made up of various pedantical bits. School learning in England had passed its infancy by the time *Love's Labour's Lost* was composed, and mere rhetoric and logic as learned in the schools had given place to the more complex forms of affectation ridiculed in that play.

We have now examined the case for Shakespeare's acquaintance with Wilson's *Arte of Rhetorique,* all the citations of parallels of importance which have ever been made. They are fairly numerous. We began by admitting that it was inherently probable that Shakespeare had read that popular and genuinely meritorious book, and we know that such books were freely read. We know that Shakespeare read widely. But there is no testimony covering the case, the argument from antecedent probability is of no value, and the argument from sign—the only one in the whole list of artificial arguments enumerated in Aristotle's *Topica* which could possibly have any weight—fails to establish itself. In every

27. *Love's Labour's Lost* (Cambridge, 1923), pp. xxviii-xxxiv; Sir E. K. Chambers, *William Shakespeare,* I, 335-337.

case we have found that the thing supposed to have been borrowed was a thing which might just as well have come from some other quarter. In the case of the borrowings from Harsnet the argument from sign is unmistakable. The names of the fiends are specific things which to any reasonable mind did actually come from *The Declaration of Egregious Popish Imposters*. They belong under the logical category of accident, not to species or proprium or any other category. It cannot be said that the large number of parallels adds to the strength of the case. A case unsupported by testimony is as strong as it can be made by the argument from sign, and in this ideational currency of sixteenth-century humanism which both Wilson and Shakespeare were using, the specific markings of the coins are not sufficient, the proper markings are themselves none too convincing, and the accidental markings are not present.

It is not my intention to imply that Shakespeare knew no formal rhetoric. He uses a number of rhetorical terms, and there is no reason to think that he may not have employed his many rhetorical figures with conscious knowledge. It is at least possible that the difference in style between the speeches of Brutus and Antony in *Julius Caesar* reflects the current rhetorical classification of oratory derived from Cicero and Quintilian. Henry V's denunciation of the traitors *(Henry V,* Act II, scene ii), particularly of Scrope, has points suggestive of the rhetorical invective.[28] I do not mean even to assert that Shakespeare did not know Wilson's *Arte of Rhetorique* but merely that there is no unmistakable evidence that he did so.

28. For a close parallel in form to the invective in *Henry V* see *An Invective ayenste the great and detestable vice, treason,* published by Berthelet in 1539, where the author, Sir Richard Morison, denounces Cardinal Pole.

10

Conditions of Publication and Problems of Editing:
An Introduction

W. W. Greg

The Function of Bibliography in Literary Criticism
Illustrated in a Study of the Text of *King Lear*

I

Gratifying as it is to be asked to speak before the Allard Pierson Institute,
I feel that so signal a distinction involves no less great a responsibility,
and when I remember the accomplished scholars who have on previous
occasions responded to the call of this generous foundation, I cannot avoid
grave misgivings at the thought of my own inadequacy. Indeed, had it
not been that there is in me somewhere, I suppose, something of missionary
fanaticism, I doubt whether I should have ventured.

But when I learned from my friend Professor Swaen that you had done
me the unexpected honour of inviting me to address you on some subject
connected with English literature, I had little difficulty in choosing my
theme. There is one field of research in which, above all, I am interested,
and it is the only one in which I am sufficiently at home to justify my
temerity in appearing before you. This is bibliography and its relation
to study of literature.

Literary criticism may, I think, be divided, conveniently if perhaps a
little arbitrarily, into three main branches. There is, to begin with, aesthetic and historical criticism, the criticism that seeks to apprize a work
of literature, to define its particular quality and value, to set it in historical
perspective, and to show, so far as can be shown from external circumstances, how it came to be, in the words of Bishop Butler, "what it is and
not another thing". No doubt, there are here two distinct lines of approach,
and many critics would insist vehemently on their being kept apart. But
I think that most of you will agree with me that they are in fact closely
bound up with one another, and that aesthetic criticism is always soundest
and most vital when brought into touch with historical environment.

From *Neophilologus*, XVIII (1933), 241-262. Reprinted by permission of the publishers.

The second branch, into which the first, I must admit, insensibly merges, is interpretation or exegetical criticism, the attempt to discover and expound an author's meaning in what he wrote, both as regards his general intention and as regards particular allusions and the sense of individual phrases.

The third branch — and again there is an obvious bridge — is textual criticism, the attempt to establish the actual words of the author, first by the collecting and sifting of documentary evidence, and afterwards by selection from the readings thus afforded, or if necessary by original emendation. It should be added that the task of textual criticism is not only to establish the true original text, but likewise to trace throughout the history of its transmission. Indeed — and this we shall see is an important point in the view I have to put before you — it is only through the second of these tasks that the first can be accomplished.

No doubt, it may be held that textual criticism is the humblest of our three branches. It is the Cinderella of literary science. But it is at the same time the most fundamental. Indeed, it must have struck you, if you pondered at all upon those transitions of which I spoke, that I have been taking the branches of criticism in what is, logically, their inverse order. A knowledge of the true text is the basis of all criticism; and textual criticism is thus the root from which all literary science grows. It expands insensibly. into interpretation, just as interpretation passes insensibly into apprizal. Criticism is indeed one and indivisible, and it is only for our convenience, and because of the needful limits imposed by an ever hardening specialization, that we divide it, as I have just done, into several fields or branches.

I suppose that every age in which criticism has been self-conscious has made its own contribution to each of these divisions. The continuity, such as it has been, of what one might call the higher faculties may be traced in such a work as Saintsbury's *History of Criticism,* that of the lower perhaps in Sandys's *History of Classical Scholarship,* without going outside the range of English writers. But undoubtedly different ages have varied much in the extent and value of their contributions, and in the manner in which these have been distributed among the different branches.

I do not know whether our own generation would claim any pre-eminence in the highest branch, though there are distinguished names that will occur to you. Confining myself to English, there is, indeed, one living writer whose work seems to me to open up new vistas of critical thought. I have in mind Professor Livingston Lowes's study entitled *The Road to Xanadu.*[1] I think that all of you who have studied that work will agree with me in recognising the brilliant qualities displayed in Professor Lowes's exciting quest, though I must admit that I am unable to follow him in some of his remoter speculations, and that I sometimes shudder to think what might be achieved by similar methods in less discriminating hands.

Exegesis has progressed soberly rather than brilliantly in our time. The labours of philologists and lexicographers have placed new and power-

1. London, Constable & Co. (pr. Cambridge, Mass.), 1927.

ful weapons in the hands of those who have the sense to use them, and gradually no doubt a new standard of interpretation will be reached, of which already some foretaste may be found in the Shakespearian labours of Professor Dover Wilson. But we are hardly, I think, likely to see any new orientation in this branch of the subject—unless, indeed, we are to include within its scope Miss Spurgeon's remarkable investigations into the imagery of Shakespeare.[2]

When, however, we pass to textual criticism the case is altered. I believe that a profound change has come over this branch of the subject, and is even affecting, in a noticeable degree, the attitude of scholars to the historical criticism of literature in general. It is a movement that began in a tentative way many years ago, but it has been gradually gathering moment, till now it is in full swing. So far as one can sum up such things in a phrase, its driving force may be said to be respect for the text. As leading motives one may discern the recognition of the fact that textual criticism is at the basis of all literary study, and the widening of textual criticism to include within its scope the whole complex problem of the transmission of literary documents. The reconstruction of the original text, while remaining perhaps the chief, has ceased to be the sole, aim of textual criticism. We have come to recognize that the history of a text is, in its own right, a study of scarcely less importance. For an author of any antiquity and standing, far from being a static datum for all time, has been and has meant something different and individual to each ensuing age, not only as this was more or less akin to his in spirit and intention, but also as it was able to draw more or less close to his actual words and meaning. Literary historians have learned that even apparently trivial corruptions of an author's text may have curious repercussions. The miswriting *celte* for *certe* in manuscripts of the Vulgate is supposed to have supplied the term "celt" to archaeological science. The fly that was a plague to the Egyptians is in the Vulgate sometimes *musca* and sometimes *coenomyia*, meaning perhaps "common fly",[3] but this is in the Septuagint κυνόμυια, which Peter Comestor duly rendered as *musca canina*. This seems to be the reason why in one of the English mystery cycles the plague of flies has become a plague of fleas ("loppis" in *Ludus Coventriae)*. Bentley knew that when Milton wrote "Hermione" he should have written "Harmonia", and he therefore condemned the passage: what he did not know was that the error occurred in the authority on which Milton relied. Did not Chaucer picture Fate as shod with partridges' wings because his manuscript of Virgil had *perdicibus* instead of *pernicibus alis?* And speaking of Chaucer, let me remind you that, while the labours of a long line of scholars have done much to settle his text and restore his metre, it is not to their works but to the corrupt sixteenth-century editions that we must go if we wish to estimate his influence on Spenser.

Now, the study that has wrought this change of critical outlook is bibliography, through the recognition of the fact that at bottom all prob-

---

2. *Leading Motives in the Imagery of Shakespeare's Tragedies* (Shakespeare Association, 1930), and *Shakespeare's Iterative Imagery* (British Academy, 1931), by Caroline F. E. Spurgeon.

3. Du Cange glosses it as *musca omnis mordax.*

lems of transmission are concerned with material factors, in the shape of
pieces of paper or parchment covered with certain written or printed
signs, and that it is in the first place through attention to the peculiarities of these, rather than through speculation as to what we fancy may
have been in an author's mind, that the attack on textual problems
should be made.

Bibliography is the study of books as tangible objects. It examines the
materials of which they are made and the manner in which those materials are put together. It traces their place and mode of origin, and the
subsequent adventures that have befallen them. It is not concerned with
their contents in a literary sense, but it certainly is concerned with the
signs and symbols they contain (apart from their significance) for the
manner in which these marks are written or impressed is a very relevant
bibliographical fact. And, starting from this fact, it is concerned with the
relation of one book to another: the question which manuscript was
copied from which, which individual copies of printed books are to be
grouped together as forming an edition, and what is the relation of edition to edition. Bibliography, in short, deals with books as more or less
organic assemblages of sheets of paper, or vellum, or whatever material
they consist of, covered with certain conventional but not arbitrary signs,
and with the relation of the signs in one book to those in another.

It is this relation of the symbols that links up bibliography most directly with textual criticism. One may press the view until bibliography
and textual criticism merge into one, and indeed I have myself argued
that essentially they are the same. But that is generally thought to be a
fanciful, and potentially dangerous, heresy of my own, and I have not
come here to advocate or to defend it. Suffice that there is a bridge, and a
pretty substantial bridge, between the two. My thesis to-day is that critical bibliography, as I sketched it a moment ago, can throw a great deal
of light on textual problems; that it has already shown by many instances
what a powerful weapon it can prove in the hands of a critic able to wield
it; and that it has established a new outlook and method of approach,
that has very considerably modified the attitude of textual critics, and
has not been without influence even upon the wider aspects of the historical study of literature.

A student of purely literary sympathies and habits of mind, when faced
with the problems of textual criticism, will in nine cases out of ten surrender to his own imaginative predilection. Now, I do not for a moment
wish to disparage the sympathetic intuition by which a subtle and sensitive mind may penetrate to the meaning and words of an author of similar intellectual and emotional outlook. Such powers are among the
greatest that a literary critic can possess. They are also the rarest. For
one critic of genuine inspiration we find a hundred shoddy pretenders.
And even the best critic is not always inspired. Nor, again, would I dis-
suade the honest work-a-day critic from using his imagination with
modesty and under due restraint. But just in so far as he is indeed honest
and modest, he will himself know only too well how needful are the
checks that objective criticism can supply, and he will accept them, not

with the impatience that the limitation of facts so often rouses, but with the welcome accorded by the true scientific spirit, the spirit of intellectual integrity. And if the critic has had a bibliographical training, he will see beside and beyond the mere accumulation of textual data as ordinarily accepted—the variational apparatus of tradition—a whole range of possibly relevant evidence in the material peculiarities of the books from which those data are drawn.

It is easy to accumulate instances of the service performed by bibliographical investigation to textual and literary studies. It was the displacement of certain quires in the manuscript of *The Testament of Love* that concealed Thomas Usk's authorship of the work, and the correction of that error that enabled Henry Bradley to read his anagram aright, and so dispose finally of the attribution to Chaucer. An alleged misplaced leaf in the archetype of *Piers Plowman* is a bone of contention among scholars, round which wages the battle of triple *versus* single authorship. A study of the watermarks in the paper gave the first indication of the false dates on a number of Shakespearian quartos, and thereby determined which was the true first edition of several of his plays. Similar examination of the wire-marks has revealed many cases of leaves cancelled before publication, and the anomalous setting of the type has drawn attention to many passages altered in the course of printing. Without the accidental preservation of the original form of pages so altered or suppressed, we should still be wondering over the genesis of the Harvey-Nashe quarrel and as to why Jonson and Chapman went to jail for writing *Eastward Ho*.

It is probable that discoveries of this kind could be cited from most ages of criticism, showing that scholars have at all times been willing to accept help from bibliography in the solution of textual problems. But what is of far greater importance is the wider change of outlook which has recently come over critics in relation to their textual and editorial duties. The traditional attitude was the not unnatural one of regarding a text primarily as a literary composition, and consequently critics were inclined to treat textual variants as a sort of literary counters in a guessing game, quite apart from the sources whence they were derived. But as soon as bibliography began to colour textual criticism—the habit, that is, of starting, not from the literary composition, but from material manuscripts and prints, and of thinking of literary problems in terms of sheets of paper or parchment bearing certain conventional signs—the question of the derivation of the variants was seen to be all-important, and attention came to be focussed less on some remote and perhaps unattainable original, than upon the more immediate sources from which the extant documents were derived. The history of the text became the first business of the critic.

So far as the criticism of manuscripts is concerned this idea appears to have been germinating for a considerable while. Its great triumph was the emergence of what is called the genealogical method in textual criticism. By this is understood the attempt to establish the relationship of extant manuscripts—their positions as it were in a family tree—with the object of determining the relative authority that their readings may possess. It is now universally accepted, and we are perhaps inclined to forget that it is after all a comparatively modern conception. I do not profess to be deeply read in the history of criticism, but I imagine that the development of the method would be covered by three generations. Its inception was perhaps due in the main to Karl Lachmann, whose most important work appeared in 1850, the year before his death. It is now half a century since Dr. Hort published his famous Introduction to the Greek New Testament, which is a classical exposition of the principles involved, and though it is evident that he was not then formulating a new system, it is equally clear that when he wrote the method was yet novel and by no means generally recognised.

The influence of the bibliographical outlook on the criticism of printed books is, curiously enough, of more recent date. Most of us, even the younger among us, have been able to follow its course, and maybe have taken a hand in its direction. It is mainly a development of the twentieth century, largely even of the post-war years. Printed books, it is true, afford little opportunity for the elaboration of anything analogous to the genealogical method. But bibliography, intent on its material pieces of paper, asked essentially the same question, and now it took the form: What was the nature of the copy that the printer had before him when he was setting up the type? This seemingly innocent question has produced something like a revolution in criticism, and has proved a curiously searching solvent to traditional modes of thought. That it only came to be asked thus late in time is perhaps not really surprising. A printed book has a certain definitive quality that is lacking in a manuscript. So soon as a contemporary work is printed, the printed book is intended to, and does in effect, supersede the manuscript; indeed in ninety-nine cases out of one hundred the manuscript is no more than a step in the production of the printed book. Thus the printed book does not invite speculation as to its origin in the same way as one published in manuscript, and critics have generally been content to leave it at that.

Not, of course, entirely. Editors have long been aware of the deficiencies of many printed texts, and only too ready to condemn the compositors who set them up. They have even been ready, at times, with assertions as to the nature of the copy used by the printer, though they have seldom based their statements on any examination of the evidence, preferring to rely on their untutored imagination. Within the present century a writer, popularly accounted the foremost Shakespearian scholar in England, enumerated, as characteristic of playhouse copies of Elizabethan plays, features that are all in contradiction to ascertainable fact.

This and similar feats of imagination set bibliographers thinking. The revolution that ensued was not, of course, the work of one man, but in the Shakespearian field at least it will always be associated with the name of Professor A. W. Pollard, that master of the art of concealing incendiary ideas under a cloak of respectable conservatism.

As soon as bibliography raised the question of the printer's copy in specific form, and forced critics to consider the actual evidence available, many interesting points came to light and the data began to sort themselves out. I am, of course, speaking mainly of the printing of the sixteenth and seventeenth centuries, the period in which research has been most active. For one thing it became evident that behind the superficially similar printed texts there must lie a great diversity of manuscript types. Approaching the question from the printer's point of view we can see various possibilities as to the copy handled. It is reasonable to suppose that many works, especially the more serious writings in prose and verse, were printed from the author's own manuscript, either holograph or prepared under his direction by a scribe and perhaps finally corrected for press. Actual examples of both types can be put in evidence.[4] At the same time many works are known to have circulated more or less widely in manuscript, being no doubt copied and recopied, and it is likely that some of them ultimately reached the printer in a form far removed from the autograph; some may even have been committed to paper from memory. At times the source of the printer's copy was even more remote. Some sermons at any rate were compiled from notes taken by a system of shorthand, though we need not suppose that this necessarily implied a piratical intention.

And when criticism starts from the other end and submits the printed texts themselves to close and unprejudiced analysis, it finds much to confirm the conclusions reached on *a priori* grounds.

So far as the great bulk of serious works is concerned the printed texts attain a very respectable level of accuracy, and in their case the abuse of the Elizabethan printer, that has been fashionable in certain editorial circles, is definitely unwarranted. We know that the author was, as a rule, given the opportunity of revising the proofs as a work went through the press, and though the facilities for doing so may not have been all that could be desired, and authors may sometimes have been negligent in making the most of them, the fact remains that, generally speaking, the better class of Elizabethan literature originally appeared in texts hardly less sound than many works of the nineteenth century.

This fact has been obscured by two or three fortuitous circumstances. For one thing, there is often a certain superficial carelessness about Elizabethan printing that tends to prejudice the modern reader. The press-work is frequently poor, while turned and wrong-fount letters and obvious literal misprints occur in a manner that would be thought discreditable to-day. But such accidents are in the main irrelevant to the soundness of the text.[5]

In the next place there are, no doubt, individual exceptions. As a rule an Elizabethan compositor was able to read his copy correctly — Elizabethan handwriting was in general more legible than modern — and to set it up, after his lights, with reasonable accuracy. But not all compositors were equally skilled, and printing houses varied in the standards they maintained. If an author wrote a really bad hand and was careless in attending

---

4. E.g. John Harington, *Orlando Furioso,* cantos XIV-XLVI, 1951, B. M., MS. Add. 18920; and Richard Hooker, *The Laws of Ecclesiastical Polity,* book V, 1957, Bodl., MS. Add. c. 165.

5. Still more irrelevant is the want of uniformity in Elizabethan spelling, for which critics like Sidney Lee have absurdly blamed the printer.

to his proofs, the result might be disastrous. It is occasionally possible to trace errors in printed works quite definitely to peculiarities of the autograph. And in some cases we know that works were printed from scribal copies in circumstances that precluded revision by the author. Greene's *Groat's Worth of Wit* was transcribed for press by Chettle after the writer's death, since his "hand was none of the best".

Lastly, prejudice has been fostered by the attempts of certain authors, in prefaces and errata, to saddle the printer with responsibility for a multitude of errors with which he manifestly can have had nothing to do. The mutual recriminations of Ralph Brooke, the herald, and William Jaggard, the stationer, are now familiar to students and can be estimated at their true worth, but there is no doubt that the former's complaints have in the past done something to blacken the typographical character of the printer responsible for the earliest collections of Shakespeare's plays.

These considerations, though they can never justify, may to some extent excuse editors who have complained of excessive inaccuracy in early prints whenever they wished to tamper with an author's text in following the dictates of their own fancy. One thing at least bibliography, in its careful enquiry into printer's copy, has already accomplished: it has largely banished the bogey of the ignorant and careless compositor, and set up the more substantial cock-shy of the ignorant and impertinent editor.

But, as Dr. McKerrow has recently argued, if modern editorial experience has tended to vindicate in general the soundness of early printed texts, there remains one special field, the drama, in which this statement needs at least serious qualification. Notoriously, many plays have come down to us in versions that can only be called perversions – what are now specifically known as "bad quartos" – and notoriously, many others are preserved in texts which, if fundamentally sound, yet contain a quite unreasonable number of seriously corrupt passages. It is, of course, true that now and again an author, like Ben Jonson, treated his plays as "works" and saw them through the press with meticulous care, while in some other cases the presence of dedications implies that plays were at least published with the author's sanction. But it is clear that playwrights as a class were rather careless of the literary fate of their offspring, and may have been impatient of the labour of proof-correcting. Massinger, we know, passed in his printed plays a number of verbal errors which he took pains to correct with his own hand in presentation copies. And once we step outside this circle of more or less authorized editions, the dramatic texts of the time, whether actually pirated and surreptitious or not, are unquestionably often very corrupt. Perhaps, when we come to consider the matter bibliographically, the reason is not very far to seek. Plays, after all, are primarily intended to be acted rather than read. The autograph is prepared for the stage; it is generally by an afterthought, and often through devious channels, that the text reaches the printing-house. Thus there is likely to be far greater diversity of copy in the case of dramatic than of non-dramatic literature. And bibliographical and textual research has already done a good deal to demonstrate this diversity. The possible fortunes of a piece written for the stage in Shakespeare's day were various in the extreme. The author might himself prepare a fair-copy of his work for the actors' use, or he might hand over his "foul papers" to a scribe skilled in the preparation of playhouse manuscripts.[6] Either the autograph fair-copy or the scribe's transcript might be submitted to the censor, and after modification become the official "book", as the prompt copy was called — and still is. From this other copies might be made, either for private collectors and patrons of the stage, or to replace a tattered original, or to supply a duplicate if a portion of the acting company went on tour in the country. In the first case, we are told, it was usual to transcribe the piece, not in the form in which the author wrote it, but in that which actors gave it in performance; in the last case the text might very likely undergo further alteration and abridgement. Sometimes a prompt-book got lost or destroyed: it might then have to be reconstituted from such "foul papers" as survived, or conceivably even from the actors' parts. Sometimes, we suspect, a down-and-out company of players, having parted with a "book", sought to vamp up some sort of acting version by an effort of communal memory. Furthermore, it has been suggested that a publisher might endeavour to obtain a version of a popular play by sending a shorthand writer to the performance, and perhaps suborning minor actors to help with their memory and fragmentary parts. When we remember that manuscripts of any of these manifold types — from the author's rough draft or the playhouse manuscript down to the memorial reconstruction or the shorthand report — might ultimately come into a printer's hands and be used as copy, we shall surely cease to wonder either at the great variety we find in the quality of dramatic texts or at the strange depravity of some among them.

The critical point which we must always keep in mind — the point that lends a wider significance to all such technical discussions — is that the form in which the text of a play has come down to us must profoundly affect our attitude towards it as a literary document, and therefore the judgement we form of it as a work of theatrical art. Admirers of Marlowe have wondered that his dramatic and poetical grasp should ever have so relaxed as in the *Massacre at Paris:* censurers of Greene have given him an extra kick for the absurdities of *Orlando Foolioso* — as Harington called it. But once we realise that the extant texts of these plays are nothing but the rehash of a very imperfect memory, we shall hardly be inclined to lay any responsibility for them to the charge of their nominal authors. And even in less extreme cases, is it altogether reasonable to blame an author for inconsistencies of plot and contradictions of character, when his plays, as preserved, may have been ruthlessly cut and botched to meet the demands of the censor and the exigencies of casting and performance? Professor Lascelles Abercrombie, in an eloquent address before the British Academy, lately invited us to accept as Shakespeare the canon of the First Folio and judge it as it stands. His plea has great force if by "Shakespeare" we are to understand no more than a certain extant body of dramatic

---

6. By "foul papers" we should understand, not a preliminary draft of a play, but the rough copy, containing what the author intended to be his final corrections, but too untidy for use as it stood.

literature; but if he means a living man to be judged as a creative artist, then I think that in his endeavour to simplify the problem he has emptied it of significance.

It is in this manner that bibliographical criticism, by enquiring into the sources and history of the text, has shifted the point of view and opened up new possibilities of literary investigation. Much of the recent work has been done in the drama, a field that offers peculiar opportunities to the critical detective, but the same principles and the same methods are applicable over the whole domain of literature, and as they become sharpened and adapted by use, we may expect to see them reshaping ever more and more the modes of thought and manner of approach alike of editors and of historical critics.

I have endeavoured in this introductory portion of my address to sketch out what I conceive to be the essence and importance of bibliography in relation to literary criticism. In my second portion I shall seek to illustrate my thesis by taking a particular case – the text of *King Lear* – and showing how at every step the problem, or rather the series of linked problems, involved depends for solution upon bibliographical principles and methods.

II

In the course of an address before the British Academy five years ago I remarked that the text of Shakespeare's play of *King Lear* still offered a problem for investigation. Criticism had, indeed, left the subject in a very unsatisfactory state. Happily my challenge met with response, and two important contributions have since appeared: one the brief but weighty pronouncement in Sir Edmund Chambers's recent work on *William Shakespeare,* the other an elaborate and able monograph by Miss Madeleine Doran.[7] The two writers take diametrically opposite views of the problem, involving very different bibliographical theories and leading to different textual conclusions. It will be my endeavour to put before you as briefly as possible the arguments with which these views are supported and the editorial consequences of their adoption.

Our authorities for the text of *King Lear* are the first collected folio of Shakespeare's *Comedies, Histories, and Tragedies* that appeared late in 1623, and the early quartos of the individual play that preceded it.

The textual study of *Lear* involves five distinct though related problems: first, the number and order of the early quartos; second, the differences of reading that exist between the several copies of the earliest of these; third, the manuscript used by the printer of the first quarto; fourth, the copy used by the printer of the first folio; fifth, the relation between the quarto and the folio texts, and the procedure a modern editor should adopt.

The Order of the Early Quartos

This problem has now reached a definite solution. A hundred years ago the number of early editions was in doubt and no serious attempt had been made to determine their order. In 1866 Clark and Wright[8] proved con-

---

7. *The Text of "King Lear",* Stanford University Press, 1931.
8. The Cambridge Shakespeare, vol. VIII, preface.

clusively that there were only two early editions, both dated 1608, which are called for convenience the "Pied Bull" and the "N. Butter" quartos respectively. They were less successful over the order. After advancing an excellent argument in favour of the "Pied Bull" as the earlier, they adopted a noncommittal attitude, concluding that "The question . . . is very difficult to decide, and at most is one rather of bibliographical curiosity than of critical importance." I know no better example of the tendency of editors to treat readings as counters in a guessing game, irrespective of the authority of their source. The question had previously been debated on quite inconclusive literary grounds; on the other hand, the evidence put forward by the Cambridge editors was bibliographical, the implication of a correction made in the course of printing. This argument was extended in 1885 by P. A. Daniel, and he reinforced it by a further appeal to bibliography, adducing the make-up of the different editions.[9] Since then no one has questioned that the "Pied Bull" quarto is the earliest, but it was naturally assumed that the two had appeared within a short space of one another in 1608. But in 1908 it was discovered that a particular group of Shakespearian plays, which included the second, or "N. Butter", quarto of *Lear,* and bore dates ranging from 1600 to 1619, far from being printed in these various years, must all have been produced within a few weeks of one another, presumably in the latest of them. The proof originally advanced was that all the plays were printed on one job lot of paper containing sheets of nearly thirty different makes, as shown by the watermarks. It is hardly surprising that so revolutionary a theory based on evidence of a character so unfamiliar should have been received in some quarters with scepticism. But confirmation was at hand, for it was shown that a single setting of type had been used for the title-pages, a common framework being left standing from play to play, while the necessary portions were altered. Thus bibliographical investigation of a purely technical character established the fact that the second quarto was printed eleven years after its fellow, and was a mere reprint of it, thus leaving the text of *Lear* dependent upon the first quarto and the first folio alone.

The Variants Between Copies of the First Quarto

Again the problem has been substantially elucidated, though some details remain obscure. The uncertainty as to the number of early editions arose from the fact that copies of the first quarto differ among themselves in a number of readings. Such variations are not uncommon in books of the time, and their origin is pretty well understood. Printing on a hand press was necessarily slow, and it sometimes happened that, while one side of a sheet (one forme as it is called) was being printed, errors were discovered in the type, work was suspended, and the mistakes corrected before any more pulls were made. But the variants in *Lear* are not quite of this simple type. From a trifling bibliographical detail[10] we know for certain as regards one

9. Introduction to the facsimile of the first quarto by C. Praetorius (*Shakespere-Quarto Facsimiles,* No. 33).

10. The alteration of the catchword on K 4 recto consequent upon the correction of the first word on the verso.

sheet, and can reasonably infer as regards others, that after a certain number of pulls had been made on both sides of the sheet, work was stopped, both formes were corrected, and then the remainder of the impressions taken. Why the sheets should have been printed in two distinct batches is at present a mystery, and so long as it is unsolved we cannot pretend to know all we need about the history of the first quarto.

But if the origin of the variants remains in some degree obscure, their nature is tolerably evident, and that matters most for the text. The important question is the degree of authority that attaches to the corrections. This certainly varies. In some cases it is evident that the compositor had merely made a slight mistake in reading his copy, and that when the press-reader altered the word to something quite different, he was merely guessing and did not trouble to consult the manuscript at all. Thus the printer's impossible "crulentious" must be a misreading of "contentious" (the corresponding word in the Folio): the corrector's "tempestuous" is his own invention.[11] But this is not always so. At times the corrector did consult the manuscript, and to good purpose. He made some true corrections in passages which are so confused that guessing would have been impossible,[12] and he restored a necessary half-line, in what no one can doubt was its original form.[13] On the other hand, there is nothing to suggest that he ever had access to any authority beyond the copy in hand. The conditions under which he worked and the limits of his ability need to be borne in mind, for some of the alterations he made are in the most difficult passages of the play[14], and our conclusions as to Shakespeare's meaning will depend in no small measure on the view we take of the activities of this erratic press corrector.

The Source of the Quarto Text

On this question opinion is sharply divided. Chambers, adopting a theory originally advanced by Alexander Schmidt, holds that the Quarto contains a reported text somehow derived from an actual performance of the play. Miss Doran, on the other hand, advances the view that it was printed from the author's own autograph, ill-written and rendered illegible by much alteration, which had been discarded in the playhouse after it had served for the preparation of the official prompt copy. Both assume that the Folio represents substantially the prompt copy, and admit that Quarto and Folio alike contain printers' errors from which the respective manuscripts were free: beyond these superficial errors Chambers accounts for the differences between the two texts by mistakes of the actors and reporter, Miss Doran by revision carried out by Shakespeare on the playhouse "book". These are the two theories we have to examine.

Some 400 lines of the text as it appears in modern editions rest on only a single authority; of these the Quarto supplies nearly 300 and the Folio 100. No doubt there are a few accidental omissions in either text. Otherwise

---

11. III. iv. 6 (all references are to the "Globe" edition).
12. E.g. I. iv. 322-3.
13. V. iii. 38.
14. Especially II. iv. 102-6, IV. ii. 25-8, 56-8.

the differences can be substantially explained by variant cutting.[15] There seems no sufficient reason to assume the extensive and elaborate revision of the prompt-book to which Miss Doran attributes them.

Apart from this question of plus and minus, the main features of the Quarto text appear to be as follows: in outward form, misrepresentation of the metrical structure, and defective and misleading punctuation; textually, constant redundancy of expression, and persistent substitution of another (and generally inferior) reading for that of the Folio.

The printing of the verse is chaotic: sometimes prose is divided as verse, more often verse is run on like prose; and when verse is recognised as such, the lines are wrongly divided with a frequency that is altogether exceptional. Of course, revision and marginal addition in a manuscript may easily lead a printer to divide the lines wrongly, but this will not account for a whole long verse-scene appearing as prose; while to suggest that Shakespeare may, for some inscrutable reason, have written it as prose, seems to me really to beg the question. Little stress can be laid on the punctuation, for some autograph manuscripts, such as the Shakespearian addition to *Sir Thomas More,* are notoriously deficient in this respect. But the general impression left by the Quarto is that the printer had before him copy that was entirely undivided metrically and altogether without punctuation. There is, indeed, some slight bibliographical evidence to this effect. Such copy would normally result from a shorthand report, and I do not know what else would produce it.

To pass to textual features: by redundancy I understand the expansion and dilution of the text, on the one hand by the introduction of exclamations, expletives, vocatives, and connective words generally, on the other hand by the use of looser and less close-knit phrasing. Such redundancy is characteristic of actors and is a marked feature of reported texts. I find it quite impossible to believe, with Miss Doran, that any writer, however familiar with the stage he might be, would in composition either deliberately or unconsciously introduce these features, which unnerve his language and destroy his verse, and then prune them away in revising the acting version.

Both forms of redundancy are united in this typical example:[16]

> *F* I am made of that selfe-mettle as my Sister,
> *Q* Sir I am made of the selfe same mettall that my sister is,....

Or, for flabby and vicious phrasing, take:[17]

> *F* Or rather a disease that's in my flesh,
> *Q* Or rather a disease that lies within my flesh,

and for the intrusion of connective phrases:[18]

---

15. This is not necessarily the whole explanation; some revision is possible, but that would be consistent with either view.
16. I. i. 70-1.
17. II. iv. 225.
18. I. iv. 332-3.

> F   *Lear.*   .... Thou shalt finde,
> That Ile resume the shape which thou dost thinke
> I haue cast off for euer [*Q* ,thou shalt I warrant thee].
>   *Gon.*   Do you marke that [*Q* my Lord]?

In all these cases the Quarto is condemned by the verse. Moreover, these connectives tend to be borrowed or repeated from other passages, such assimilation being another common trick of actors. In the first scene Lear twice admonishes Cordelia:[19]

> Nothing will come of nothing, speake againe

and later:

> How, how *Cordelia?* Mend your speech a little, ...

The Quarto borrows "How" from the second to prefix unmetrically to the first, and gives the second in the form:

> Goe to, goe to, mend your speech a little,

introducing a fretful exclamation, more in the style of Polonius than of Lear, which it employs again unmetrically later on. Similarly the Quarto makes Lear conclude two consecutive speeches with the words "goe, goe, my people", whereas in the second case the Folio has "Away, away";[20] and while in the Folio Lear cries once "Yet haue I left a daughter" and later "I haue another daughter", the Quarto uses the first phrase on both occasions.[21] There are also some traces of actors' exaggerations and bombast.

The reporter reveals his presence by a number of mistakes of hearing, such as "a dogge, so bade in office" for "a Dogg's obey'd in Office",[22] and

> striuing to better ought, we marre whats well

instead of

> striuing to better, oft we marre what's well

which is puzzling till we remember that Shakespeare rimes *oft* and *nought*.[23] That these are mishearings is not disputed: Miss Doran supposes dictation to the compositor—a rather desperate hypothesis. Further traces of the reporter are a number of speeches assigned to the wrong character, and sometimes modified to suit. For instance, where in the Folio Regan says to Edmund:[24]

---

19. I. i. 92, 96.
20. I. iv. 294, 311.
21. I. iv. 276, 327.
22. IV. iv. 163.
23. I. iv. 369.
24. V. iii. 81.

Let the Drum strike, and proue my title thine

in the Quarto it is Edmund himself who says:

Let the drum strike, and proue my title good

as if a drum could prove anything but its power of making a noise. It is also significant that inarticulate sounds and meaningless refrains indicated in the Folio, are in the Quarto either omitted[25] or quite otherwise expressed, as when "Do, de, de, de: sese" becomes "loudla doodla".[26]

But it is the verbal variants of the two texts that supply the most ample evidence of reporting. Such changes must inevitably occur on the stage, and the substituted word will be either indifferent or generally inferior. That this is what we observe in the Quarto text is agreed, but Miss Doran points out, pertinently enough, that indifferent variants may be the unconscious substitutions of a compositor or a copyist, while superior Folio readings may be due to revision. Now, theoretically this is perhaps a sufficient answer, but when we come to examine actual examples I think that it breaks down in practice. For one thing, the indifferent, or nearly indifferent, variants are rather numerous to father upon one transcriber and two compositors; for another, some superficially indifferent variants prove to be in fact due to repetition and thus suggest actors' assimilations; and lastly some are not isolated but consciously linked. When, in the line:[27]

That iustly think'st, and hast most rightly said:

the Quarto transposes the words "iustly" and "rightly", the blunder is perhaps not beyond the range of original sin latent in a copyist: but when, two lines apart, we find "Fiue dayes .... And on the sixt" consistently varied to "Foure" and "fift", this explanation becomes less satisfactory.[28] And so it is with revision. There may be cases – many cases – in which it is impossible to distinguish between corruption on the one hand or revision on the other. But I question whether this is always, or even generally, so. Where one reading is metrical and the other not; where in one the thought receives natural expression, in the other forced or inept; or where one shows a misunderstanding of the sense that is clear in the other, we have, I think, good and sufficient ground for judging.

To set forth the evidence in detail would need no less than a complete textual commentary on the play. I can do no more than select an example here and there from the cloud of witnesses. Here is a passage condemned by the metre. The Folio reads:[29]

Why brand they vs
With Base? With basenes Bastardie? Base, Base?

25. I. ii. 149, III. iv. 59, IV. vi. 207.
26. III. vi. 77.
27. I. i. 186.
28. I. i. 176, 178.
29. I. ii. 10.

The verse is correct, but the second is not an easy line to remember exactly, and it is hardly surprising to find in the Quarto no more than the unmetrical syncopation

> with base, base bastardie?

At one point Oswald says of Gloucester:[30]

> Would I could meet [him] Madam, I should shew
> What party I do follow.

The Quarto reads "What Lady I doe follow", and since the talk has been of the rivalry between Regan and Goneril this would come naturally to the lips of an actor, but it is not to that that the Steward is referring. Or consider the lines in which Lear breaks forth in true Shakespearian phrase:[31]

> Close pent-vp guilts,
> Riue your concealing Continents, and cry
> These dreadfull Summoners grace.

The Quarto's "riue your concealed centers" makes neither verse nor sense. Once more: Regan observes, shrewdly enough, of the blinded Gloucester:[32]

> Where he arriues, he moues
> All hearts against vs: *Edmund,* I thinke is gone
> In pitty of his misery, to dispatch
> His nighted life: Moreouer to descry
> The strength o'th'Enemy.

When, in place of *"Edmund"*, the Quarto reads "and now", it makes the following lines refer to Gloucester, which, remembering his attempted suicide in the next scene, might appear not unreasonable to an actor who overlooked the fact that it further credits the corpse with the purpose of spying on the French army! Failure of memory alone can account for a final example.[33] When in the first scene Lear at last turns to Cordelia, he addresses her in the tender words:

> Now our Ioy,
> Although our last and least; to whose yong loue,
> The Vines of France, the Milke of Burgundie,
> Striue to be interest.

In place of this the Quarto has only:

> but now our ioy,
> Although the last, not least in our deere loue,

30. IV. v. 40.
31. III. ii. 58.
32. IV. v. 1.
33. I. i. 85-7.

where it is surely the loss of a line and a half that has occasioned the re-construction. If anybody can see revision in this passage his conception of poetical composition must be radically different from my own.

It is contended by those who favour the report theory that the Folio constantly supplies not merely the better reading but one more natural and more consonant with the thought of the passage, in other words the more original. And even where revision is abstractly possible, we may yet question whether it was indeed thus that Shakespeare worked. While I cannot attach much weight to what Heminge and Condell tell us of the author's unblotted manuscripts, I feel even less happy at the vision of his autograph that Miss Doran conjures up. She pictures Shakespeare fumbling after his expression, and even after his meaning, with the clumsiness of a novice. That he evolved the seemingly inevitable expression of passage after passage from a welter of confused, inept, and commonplace phrases, is hard to believe. And when we are further told that the revision was carried out on the already prepared "book" of the play, we can only wonder what must have been the feelings — and the language — of the prompter who had to use it.

Miss Doran has argued that the Quarto text of *Lear* is far too good to be reported, and she is able to point with considerable force to the very different textual conditions found in admittedly reported texts, such as the earliest print of *Romeo and Juliet*. But I think that it is now agreed by most critics that these are what are called memorial reconstructions. This the quarto *Lear* emphatically is not. If it is indeed a reported text it must have been taken down by shorthand, and the question arises whether there was at the time any system in use by which the result could have been attained. That such a feat was possible with Bright's *Charactery* or Bales's *Brachygraphy,* I cannot for one moment believe. But in 1602 appeared John Willis's *Art of Stenography,* which contained what is possibly a more efficient method, and we are credibly informed that this had already been used in 1605 to produce what is at least a superficially readable text of Heywood's *Troubles of Queen Elizabeth,* a play, it is worth noting, that had been issued by the same publisher as *Lear.* Thus, whatever the difficulties involved in the assumption of a shorthand report, we have no ground to rule it out as impossible.[34]

The Source of the Folio Text

Again there are two views current. The marked difference between the Quarto and Folio texts and the general superiority of the latter are, indeed, commonplaces of criticism, and it is common ground that the main source of the Folio text is the official prompt-book of the play. But while Miss

---

34. Miss Doran also finds evidence of Shakespearian spelling and handwriting in the manuscript, behind the spelling and misprints of the Quarto. But she does not lay much stress on the argument, nor does it amount to much. As regards spelling, she herself frankly points out some serious contradictions. As regards writing, I think the most distinctive confusions in the Quarto are those of *k* with *b* and *l* with *t* (seen combined in the substitution of "bitt" for "kill" at IV. i. 39), which are exceptional in "good quartos" of Shakespeare. On the whole the evidence under this head seems to me to tell rather against than for autograph copy.

Doran believes the Folio to have been set up directly from this manuscript, Chambers follows Daniel in supposing that the printer must have used a copy of the Quarto which had been brought by collation and correction into what was intended to be, but in fact was not, complete agreement with that manuscript.

The view we take will depend a good deal upon what opinion we have formed respecting the Quarto text. If the evidence already summarized be held to prove that the Quarto offers a reported text, then I think it follows inevitably, from the community of errors and other peculiarities in the two authorities, that the Quarto played some part in the bibliographical history of the Folio. If on the other hand, we assume autograph copy for the Quarto, or indeed admit any transcriptional continuity between the two texts, most of the evidence may be capable of other explanations. In this case it will be more difficult to meet Miss Doran's contention of the Folio's direct use of the manuscript, though I think that there still remain sufficient links of a purely typographical nature to render it difficult of acceptance.

It was a consideration of the variants between different copies of the Quarto that first led Daniel to the conclusion that the Folio must have been printed from it. You will remember that when we discussed those variants it appeared that some of the alterations were genuine corrections derived from a closer inspection of the manuscript, while others were guesses of the press-reader which might sometimes be right, but were certainly sometimes wrong. If, therefore, we find the Folio agreeing with one of the original readings of the Quarto the correction of which we are entitled to believe true, we shall reasonably conclude that the Folio was printed from a copy of the Quarto which contained that sheet in question in the uncorrected state. Similarly, if we find the Folio agreeing with one of the altered readings that we have reason to suppose is not a true correction but an erroneous guess of the press-reader, we shall conclude that the Folio was printed from a copy of the Quarto which contained the sheet in question in the corrected state. Both cases, I believe occur.

There is a passage that runs in the Folio thus:

> This milky gentlenesse, and course of yours
> Though I condemne not, yet vnder pardon
> [You] are much more at task for want of wisedome,
> Then prais'd for harmefull mildnesse.

Now, the third line[35] was originally set up in the Quarto as:

> y'are much more alapt want of wisedome,

of which the corrector made sense by reading:

> y'are much more attaskt for want of wisedome, ...

---

35. I. iv. 366.

Here "for" must have been accidentally omitted by the compositor, but "attaskt" cannot possibly have been the reading of the copy. Behind "alapt" must, on recognized graphic grounds, have been the word "ataxt"; and *atax'd,* i. e. taxed, is even better in the context than *attask'd,* i. e. taken to task, though as a matter of fact neither word is otherwise recorded. Thus "attaskt" is a ghost word invented by the press-reader,[36] and when the folio editor or compositor further emended it to "at task", he proved that he had before him a corrected sheet of the Quarto, since the word had no other existence.

So far as I know this example has hitherto escaped notice, but there is another, and well-known, passage which equally proves the dependence of the Folio elsewhere upon an uncorrected sheet of the Quarto. The lines should read:

> Sir, I thought it fit,
> To send the old and miserable King
> To some retention and appointed guard,
> Whose age had Charmes in it, whose Title more,
> To pluck the common bosome on his side, ...

In this the half-line "and appointed guard",[37] necessary to the metre and unquestionably original, was supplied by the press-reader in the corrected state of the Quarto; it is absent in the original state, and is again absent in the Folio, and both alike print the previous line and a half as a single verse.[38]

To explain this away Miss Doran is forced to suppose that the passage had been much altered in the autograph, with the result that the three words in question, presumably written in the margin, were illegible to the compositor; that the corrector managed to decipher them; but that they baffled the scribe who prepared the prompt copy. This seems to involve several improbabilities. We have to suppose that the Quarto corrector, whose abilities in the way of deciphering were certainly not conspicuous, was able to make out the words, though to do so had proved beyond the

---

36. The press-reader presumably read the manuscript "ataxt" correctly, but assumed that *tax* was only another and inferior spelling of *task.* The two verbs were used synonymously at the time, and in III. ii. 16 the Quarto again substitutes "taske" for "taxe". The doubling of the *t* in "attaskt" seems due to analogy with such words as *attain.*

37. V. iii. 47.

38. The three versions are exactly as follows:
> *QA* *Bast.* Sir I thought it fit,
>> To saue the old and miserable King to some retention,
>> Whose age has charmes in it, whose title more
>> To pluck the coren bossom of his side, ...
>
> *QB* *Bast,* Sir I thought it fit,
>> To send the old and miserable King to some retention, and ap-
>> Whose age has charmes in it, whose title more, (pointed guard,
>> To pluck the common bossome of his side, ...
>
> *F*   *Bast.* Sir, I thought it fit,
>> To send the old and miserable King to some retention,
>> Whose age had Charmes in it, whose Title more,
>> To plucke the common bosome on his side, ...

The argument is that *F* is based on *QA* imperfectly corrected by comparison with the playhouse manuscript.

power of the playhouse scribe, who must have been well used to dramatic "foul papers" and was probably familiar with Shakespeare's handwriting; further that this trained scribe was content to leave the previous line in its impossible state; lastly that the author himself, making an extensive and careful revision of the prompt-book, never observed or troubled to correct so glaring a defect. *Credo quia impossibile* may be good theology: *credo quia non impossibile* is certainly bad criticism.

A few words must be said respecting the confirmatory evidence to be found in errors and peculiarities common to the Quarto and Folio texts in passages unaffected by the variants in the former, and particularly in such features of the Folio as can be explained by the typographical arrangement of the Quarto. Chambers speaks of "a general orthographic resemblance" between the two, and it is certainly possible to draw up a long list of correspondences which, if individually of little weight, are collectively suggestive. Still more so are many agreements in punctuation, since the two texts generally follow very different systems in this respect. As I have already remarked, the pointing of the Quarto is light and even defective; there are seldom any points except commas within a speech. On the other hand, the Folio pointing is notoriously heavy. When, therefore, we find several passages in which the Folio not only reproduces exactly the deficient punctuation of the Quarto, but even retains definite and obvious errors which make nonsense of the text, we can hardly fail to suspect the cause.[39] And we are confirmed in our suspicion when we find the Folio here and there following the Quarto exactly in printing as verse passages that are really prose, or *vice versa;* retaining unnatural line-divisions, the original reason for which has disappeared; and omitting short speeches that are easily overlooked through being abnormally placed.

There is much evidence of this kind to be gathered in a minute comparison of texts, but it is hardly possible to explain it without ocular demonstration, and I am therefore obliged to pass it over on this occasion.

There is no dispute, and no possibility of disputing, that the agreements between the two texts are significant. Miss Doran writes.[40] "If there were no adverse evidence, these correspondences . . . would have to be accepted as proof that a printed copy of Q^1 was altered in accordance with the playhouse manuscript". From this I conclude that she would prefer Daniel's view to her own, were it not for certain difficulties she finds in accepting it. Her chief objection is of an *a priori* character. If, she argues, the prompt-book was available, it would have been far less trouble to hand it over to the printer than to prepare a copy of the Quarto for press by collation with it; moreover, to have attempted the latter task would have been to produce illegible copy, so great and so numerous are the corrections that would have had to be made. That it would have been simpler to hand over the manuscript is obvious; equally obvious that there may have been good reasons for not doing so. The prompt-book was presumably still in use and bore the Master of the Revels' official licence for the performance of the

39. See particularly I. i. 128-9, II. i. 59-60, II. iv. 259-62.
40. On p. 89 of her study.

play. To send it to press would be at any rate to run a serious risk.[41] The choice may well have lain between making a transcript for the purpose, or correcting a copy of the Quarto, and I have no doubt that the latter would be, and still more would be thought to be, the less laborious. As to the objection of illegibility, it is simply a matter of experiment, and I am confident that I could correct any page of the Quarto so as to serve as copy for the Folio without making it in the least illegible or even difficult for the printer.

Miss Doran further produces one very ingenious argument in favour of her hypothesis that the Folio was set up directly from the manuscript, by pointing out that it apparently contains a number of what are called graphic errors. Now, if the compositor of the Folio made mistakes through the misreading of handwriting, he must obviously have set it up from manuscript, and therefore not from the Quarto. Miss Doran adduces in support a large number of errors peculiar to the Folio, many of which I venture to think cannot possibly be of this type. But some there certainly are which one would naturally assume to be graphic. The most striking is the word "Reuenge" in a passage[42] where the Quarto is unquestionably right in printing "Reneag", for in some hands the misreading would be a very easy one. Now, let me say at once, that while I entirely agree that many errors in Shakespeare's text are graphic errors, like "alapt" for "ataxt", I think the graphic theory is in danger of being, and in fact has been, overworked by Leon Kellner, Dover Wilson, and their followers. There are many errors which cannot be explained on graphic grounds, and it follows that apparently graphic errors must sometimes be in fact due to other causes. For instance, in the present case, suppose that the Folio compositor, intending to set "Reneag", accidentally through foul-case substituted a u for the $n;$ he would produce the word "Reueag", which the proof reader would inevitably "correct" to "Reuenge". Thus there may be nothing graphic about the error at all. And even if it is a misreading, it may still be due to the editor and not to the compositor. For "Reneag" is not a very common word and may not have been understood. The editor may have consulted the manuscript and actually misread it "Reueng", which, though certainly wrong, makes sense of a sort.[43] Thus I cannot think that the dependence of the Folio on manuscript copy is

---

41. That the bulk of the copy for the 1623 folio came from the playhouse seems probable, but I doubt whether there is any evidence of the sacrifice of actual prompt-books. The trend of opinion seems to be in the opposite direction. Both Professor Dover Wilson and Signor Ramello have recently come to the conclusion that a transcript of the prompt-book was made in the case of *Hamlet*.

42. II. ii. 84.

43. Kent is arguing that obsequious servants obey every whim of their masters, and the prosecution of a vendetta might well be one of their activities.

There are other errors in the same passage in the Folio, which Miss Doran also treats as graphic, relying on Kellner for one very improbable misreading. I wholly disagree with her analysis. Elsewhere I think "crying" for "coyning" (IV. vi. 83) an unlikely misreading in any but the very worst hands of the period: more probably the compositor accidentally set "coying" and the proof-reader guessed "crying". I believe that "latch'd" for "làncht" (II. i. 54) is correct: if not, it is a literal error, not a misreading. Similarly I am not convinced that "spirits" for "spurres" (II. i. 78) is wrong: anyhow it is not an easy graphic error. Still less is "strangenesse" for "strange newes" (II. i. 89): it is a compositor's blunder of the memorial type.

proved, and I conclude that the difficulties Miss Doran experiences in accepting Daniel's inference are of her own making.[44]

The Relation of the Texts

We have now concluded our bibliographical discussion of the Quarto variants and the copy that must be supposed to lie behind the two textual authorities, and it remains to consider what bearing these matters should have on an editor's procedure.

On Miss Doran's theory special authority might be supposed to attach to the Quarto, seeing that it was printed from the author's own manuscript. But the text of the Quarto is depreciated, in her view, first by being printed with quite remarkable incompetence from a confused and illegible original, and secondly by the rather extensive revision to which the author subsequently submitted it. Nevertheless, her theory affords what is probably the best defence of the large extent to which modern editors have relied on the Quarto for their readings. What, so far as I am aware, no theory can justify is the extent to which they have used the second quarto: it is an evil legacy from the days when the order of the editions was in doubt.

On the rival theory all authority rests with the Folio. Unless there is some serious reason to suspect corruption, we are bound to prefer its readings to those of the Quarto. But we must remember that, on this theory, the Folio was not printed directly from the manuscript, but from a copy of the Quarto which had been brought into general agreement with it. Some errors of the Quarto are, however, certain to have remained uncorrected. Thus it is only when the readings of the two differ that there is any strong ground for supposing that the Folio preserves that of the prompt-book; the negative inference, that where the two agree the prompt-book had the same reading, is much weaker. And so we reach the remarkable conclusion that the testimony of the Quarto and Folio together is of appreciably less authority than that of the Folio alone.

The editorial consequences of this are obvious, and the effect on the received text would be considerable in two ways. In the first place there would be a general restoration of Folio readings which editors have displaced in favour of the Quarto. The "Globe" text must contain nearly four hundred Quarto readings (apart from passages only preserved in the Quarto) of which perhaps three hundred would go. This would involve some loss of polish, both because the Quarto text, having passed through the mouths of actors, has sometimes been worn smooth in a way the Folio text has not, and further because a long line of editors have pleased their fancy by adopting whatever reading appeared the more elegant to

---

44. I ought to mention that Miss Doran has collected a number of instances in which the Folio agrees with the second quarto against the first, whence she concludes that the compositor of the Folio sometimes consulted a copy of the second quarto when in difficulty over the manuscript. Her examples include some rather striking coincidences, but they do not convince me of any actual dependence. Moreover, the second quarto of *Lear* is one of the 1619 collection, and it must not be forgotten that the reprints in the same series of the "bad quartos" of the *Contention* and *Henry V* contain some curious anticipations of the texts in the first folio.

Augustan and Victorian taste. But this loss would, to my thinking, be more than offset by a considerable gain in pregnancy and vigour. The second effect might be even more considerable. For, by depriving the agreement of Quarto and Folio of some of its supposed authority, it would open the way to much greater freedom of emendation than would otherwise be proper. What use editors might make of this, and whether the final result would be good or bad, is perhaps better only guessing, but it would undoubtedly alter to an appreciable extent the play of *King Lear* as we know it.

Between the rival theories I do not claim to pronounce. I have not attempted to conceal the direction in which, after six months' patient work, I personally incline; but at the same time I can see here and there sufficient contradictions in the evidence to make me cautious, and I am inclined to think to-day what I thought five years ago, that there still remains a problem for investigation. Which shows that even bibliography is not yet able to answer all questions.

11

Conditions of Publication and Problems of Editing:
The Printing-House and the Text

Donald F. Bond

The First Printing of the *Spectator*

The original 555 numbers of the *Spectator* of Addison and Steele, printed on both sides of a folio half-sheet, were published daily, except Sunday, from March 1, 1711, to December 6, 1712. The earliest numbers bear the imprint, "*LONDON:* Printed for *Sam. Buckley,* at the *Dolphin* in *Little Britain;* and Sold by *A. Baldwin* in *Warwick-Lane;* where Advertisements are taken in." Beginning with No. 16 (March 19, 1711), the words "as also by *Charles Lillie,* Perfumer, at the Corner of *Beauford-Buildings* in the *Strand,*" are added.[1] The three names of Buckley, Baldwin, and Lillie appear on the imprint for the greater part of the original run; but, beginning with No. 499 (October 2, 1712), Lillie's name is dropped and that of Jacob Tonson (the younger) is added, so that the imprint for the last fifty-seven numbers reads: "*LONDON:* Printed for *S. Buckley,* and *J. Tonson;* And Sold by *A. Baldwin* in *Warwick-Lane.*" A notice in No. 499, however, informs readers that advertisements continue to be taken in by S. Buckley, J. Tonson, C. Lillie, and A. Baldwin, information which is repeated ("Advertisements and Letters continue to be taken in") in Nos. 500, 505, 506, 507, 511, and 512. Buckley and the younger Tonson were joint publishers of the *Spectator* when the numbers were reprinted, both in octavo and in duodecimo, in 1712 and 1713; and all subsequent editions of the essays, including those of Henry Morley, G. A. Aitken, and G. Gregory Smith, have been based on the octavo reprint. The three editors just mentioned include occasional variant readings from the folio sheets, but none seem to have studied the original numbers very carefully for the light that they might throw upon the composition of the *Spectator.* An examination of these sheets should give us more knowledge than we have hitherto had of the circumstances surrounding the writing and

From *Modern Philology,* XLVII (1950), 164-177. Reprinted by permission of The University of Chicago Press and Donald F. Bond. Copyright 1950 by The University of Chicago Press.
1. These words fail to be added, however, in No. 17, for reasons which will be evident later.

publication of the *Spectator* and should offer some clues toward further study of the authorship of the essays.

I

Samuel Buckley, Jacob Tonson the Younger, and Mrs. Ann Baldwin were all well-known booksellers, i.e., publishers, of the early eighteenth century. Buckley, originally a bookseller, was, as early as 1705, better known as a printer, according to John Dunton,[2] and at the time when the *Spectator* was appearing was also printer of the first daily newspaper, the *Daily courant*. Tonson, nephew of the first Jacob Tonson, was the second member of the great firm which published for Dryden, Addison, Steele, Pope, and many others and which had but recently removed to the Shakespeare's Head, "over-against Catherine-street in the Strand."[3] Mrs. Baldwin, the widow of Richard Baldwin, is listed by Plomer as in business from 1698 to 1711, but she continues to advertise books in the *Spectator* through 1712, and Nichols' *Literary anecdotes*[4] affords evidence that she was still active in 1713. Her bookselling business was conducted at the Oxford Arms in Warwick Lane, between Newgate Street and Ludgate Hill, and not far from Buckley's shop in Little Britain. Charles Lillie, "Perfumer," was not, of course, a professional bookseller, but he had assisted in the publication of the *Tatler*,[5] and he was later to edit and publish the *Original and genuine letters sent to the Tatler and Spectator, during the time those works were publishing: none of which have been before printed*,[6] with a prefatory note by Steele authorizing their publication. In the first numbers of the *Spectator* letters were directed "to be left with Mr. Buckley at the Dolphin in Little-Britain,"[7] but in No. 16 (March 19, 1711) the essay for the day concludes with a letter from Lillie asking for the appointment "to take in Letters and Advertisements for the City of *Westminster* and the Dutchy of *Lancaster*." From this date to No. 499 (October 2, 1712) the imprint includes Lillie as one authorized to take in advertisements, and even after this date, as we have seen, a separate notice apprised readers that he continued to take in letters and advertisements.[8]

In addition to Lillie and Mrs. Baldwin, there were ten other distributing agents for the *Spectator*, whose names are to be found in the advertisements for monthly sets, beginning in No. 29 (April 3, 1711) and

---

2. *Life and errors*, ed. John Nichols (London, 1818), I. 324.

3. Plomer, *Dictionary*, pp. 291-92.

4. I, 62.

5. The imprint of the first collected octavo edition of the *Lucubrations of Isaac Bickerstaff* reads: "LONDON, Printed: And to be deliver'd to Subscribers, by *Charles Lillie*, Perfumer, at the Corner of *Beauford-Buildings* in the *Strand*; and *John Morphew* near *Stationers-Hall*.

6. "London: Printed by R. Harbin, for Charles Lillie, Perfumer, at the Corner of Beaufort-Buildings in the Strand, 1725." 2 volumes.

7. See the notices in Nos. 7 and 13.

8. Lillie's friendship with the authors of the *Spectator* may be seen in various allusions. A mock advertisement for instruction in "the exercise of the snuff-box" at Charles Lillie's appears in No. 138. He is referred to in Nos. 140, 258, and 310 (all by Steele), and his engraving of a mosaic design "lately discovered at Stunsfeild near Woodstock" is given free publicity by Steele at the beginning of No. 358. This engraving, "Imprinted on a large Elephant Sheet of Paper," is advertised by Lillie in Nos. 355, 361, and 365.

running intermittently through No. 223 (November 15, 1711), with new agents added from time to time.[9]

Though the name of Tonson is not included among these agents, we know that he fairly early acquired an interest in the paper. The elder Tonson had long known Addison and had published, among other things, *The campaign, Remarks on...Italy,* and *Rosamond.* Jacob Tonson, Jr., had apparently taken over the publishing of the *Tatler* volumes by the middle of 1711,[10] and his name was added, we have seen, to the imprint of the original numbers of the *Spectator* in October, 1712. Addison and Steele assigned their rights to the seven collected volumes of the paper to Tonson and Buckley, for which each paid £575, on November 10, 1712. Though both the octavo and the duodecimo volumes bear the names of Buckley and Tonson in the imprint, the wording of the advertisements inviting subscriptions to the octavo edition suggests that Tonson took a leading part in the publication. The first advertisement appears in No. 227 (November 20, 1711):

> There is now Printing by Subscription two Volumes of the SPECTATORS on a large Character in Octavo; the Price of the two Vols. well Bound and Gilt two Guineas. Those who are inclined to Subscribe, are desired to make their first Payments to Jacob Tonson, Bookseller in the Strand; the Books being so near finished, that they will be ready for the Subscribers at or before Christmas next.

This advertisement is repeated intermittently through No. 248 (December 14) and then ceases. In No. 269 (January 8, 1712) readers are informed that *"The First and Second Volumes of the* SPECTATOR *in 8vo are now ready to be delivered to the Subscribers, by* J. Tonson *at* Shakespear's Head over-against Catherine-street *in the* Strand."

It seems clear, then, that in the publication of the *Spectator* Buckley and the younger Tonson were chiefly concerned; in taking in letters and advertisements, Mrs. Ann Baldwin and Charles Lillie; and in the general distribution of the original numbers a dozen agents, including such well-known booksellers as James Knapton and Egbert Sanger. But on such

---

9. Before the first month was out, readers were advised that "Compleat Setts of this Paper, for the Month of March, are to be sold by Mr. [Thomas] Graves in St. James's Street; Mr. Lillie, Perfumer, at the Corner of Beaufort-Buildings; Mr. [Egbert] Sanger at the Temple Gate, Mr. [James] Knapton in St. Paul's Church-Yard, Mr. [James] Round in Exchange Ally, and Mrs. Baldwin in Warwick-Lane" (No. 29, April 3, 1711). This advertisement, which is repeated in later numbers (31, 35, 37, 39, 41, 43, 45, 47, 49, and 53), is followed by similar notices of sets cumulatively for succeeding months, through May, June, July, August, September, and October, with an increasing number of distributing agents. "Mr. [William] Lewis under Tom's Coffee House [Covent Garden]" is added in No. 39; "Mr. [O.] Lloyd near the Church in the Temple" in No. 69; "Mrs. Boulter next the Rose Tavern at Temple Bar" in No. 125; "Mrs. Treganey, near Essex-Street" in No. 135; "Mrs. Bond at the Old Vine at Charing-Cross" in No. 145; and "Mrs. Dodd at the Peacock without Temple Bar" in No. 221 — a total of twelve agents by the end of October. With the exception of Mrs. Bond, Mrs. Boulter, Mrs. Treganey, and Lillie, none of whom is listed by Plomer, these were all well-known booksellers, and Lillie and Mrs. Baldwin took, as we have seen, an active part in the promotion of the *Spectator.* Plomer's only entry under Dodd is "A. Dodd, bookseller in London, Peacock without Temple Bar, 1714-31."

10. See the letter in Steele's *Correspondence,* ed. Rae Blanchard (Oxford, 1941), p. 50 and note.

matters as the circulation figures for the original numbers, the identity of the printers, and the arrangements made for seeing the essays through the press we have very little external evidence. The correspondence of Addison and that of Steele tell us almost nothing beyond the fact that Addison liked one of the essays well enough to send a copy to his friend Edward Wortley Montagu.[11] Pope told Spence that "Many of his Spectators [Addison] wrote very fast; and sent them to the press as soon as they were written. It seems to have been best for him not to have had too much time to correct."[12] A certain amount of speculation and traditional legend is to be found in the columns of the *Gentleman's magazine* toward the end of the century and in the early editions of Percy, Calder, and Bisset,[13] but this is not very satisfactory.

II

The circulation figures for the original numbers have been variously estimated, but we are on surer ground if we look at the statements in the *Spectator* itself. At the beginning of No. 10 (March 12, 1711) Addison records his satisfaction in hearing "this great City inquiring Day by Day after these my Papers, and receiving my Morning Lectures with a becoming Seriousness and Attention. My Publisher tells me, that there are already Three Thousand of them distributed every Day...." Four months later (No. 124, July 23, 1711) "my Bookseller tells me," he says, "the Demand for these my Papers increases daily"; and in retrospective mood at the end of the year (No. 262, December 31, 1711) he finds gratification in the thought that "notwithstanding I have rejected every thing that savours of Party, every thing that is loose and immoral, and every thing that might create Uneasiness in the Minds of particular Persons, I find that the Demand for my Papers has encreased every Month since their first Appearance in the World." The growth in number of distributing agents for the monthly sets is also indicative of the increasing popularity of the paper. The stamp tax imposed in August, 1712, certainly decreased the sale of the *Spectator:* "it at first reduced it to less than half the number that was usually Printed before this Tax was laid," writes Steele in the final number (No. 555, December 6, 1712); but, even so, "the Tax on each half Sheet has brought into the Stamp-Office one Week with another above 20 *l.* a Week arising from this single Paper." If Steele's statement is correct, this would mean a printing of between sixteen and seventeen hundred after the imposition of the tax. "I once heard it observed," wrote Johnson in 1781, "that the sale may be calculated by the product of the tax, related in the last number to produce more than twenty pounds a week, and therefore stated at one and twenty pounds, or three pounds ten shillings a day; this, at a halfpenny a paper, will give sixteen hundred and eighty for the daily number."[14] If this is "less than half the number" of those printed before August 1, 1712, the

11. *Letters of Joseph Addison*, ed. Walter Graham (Oxford, 1941), p. 263.

12. Spence, *Anecdotes*, ed. Singer (2d ed.; London, 1858), p. 38.

13. Best summed up in Nathan Drake's *Essays, biographical, critical, and historical, illustrative of the Tatler, Spectator, and Guardian* (3 vols.; London, 1805).

14. "Life of Addison," *Lives of the poets* ("World's Classics" ed.). I, 426.

circulation would be between three and four thousand in the second year of publication.[15] Moreover, if the stamp duty were evaded, as it certainly was by other newspapers, the circulation figures would be even greater; and there is evidence that this was the case with the *Spectator*.[16]

A circulation of upward of even three thousand was very large for a daily paper. The official *Gazette* seems to have attained a circulation of six thousand and the *Post-boy* three thousand, but these were published only twice and thrice a week, respectively.[17] We need not perhaps take too seriously the estimate of the Bishop of St. Asaph[18] that the circulation of No. 384 rose "above 14,000" or the statement in the *Biographia Britannica*,[19] repeated by Thomas Tyers[20] and the author of *Addisoniana*,[21] that twenty thousand were sometimes sold in a day. Later scholars have been skeptical of such figures because of the physical difficulties of printing so many copies of a daily paper. Professor Nichol Smith shows, from the rate of working estimated in Timperley's *Printer's manual,* that eight hours of steady work would be required to print two thousand sheets, and that "if the circulation rose to 3,000, twelve hours' printing at top speed would be required."[22] "These figures have only to be stated," he continues, "to show that in the printing-house of a popular paper at least four presses had to be used — two for each side of the sheet, and that, in these days before stereotyping, the whole paper had therefore to be set at least twice."

We should be forced, to the conclusion, therefore, that if the circulation of the *Spectator* rose to three thousand and if the original numbers were set up in one printing-house from day to day, there would have to be duplicate printings. If, however, Buckley — already busy with the printing of the *Daily courant* — shared the work with another printing-house, Buckley doing the work on one day and the other printer on the alternate day, the time available for preparing three thousand copies would be

15. Aitken (*Life of Steele,* I, 319-20) makes much the same computation. "A payment of over £20 a week for stamp duty represents a daily circulation of more than 1600 copies, or 10,000 a week, from the 1st August to the 6th December 1712, and the daily circulation before the 1st August would therefore be, according to Steele's statement, nearly 4000."

16. James R. Sutherland, "The circulation of newspapers and literary periodicals, 1700-30." *Library,* 4th ser.; XV (1934), 121. "It would be interesting to learn if unstamped copies of the *Spectator* — after the stamp duty came into force — are in existence. If so, an estimate based on Steele's statement would have to be revised." I have a copy of Nos. 535 and 555 without the stamp, and two copies of No. 530, one with the stamp and one without.

17. *Ibid.,* p. 111.

18. William Fleetwood, letter dated June 17, 1712, printed in *Mr. Pope's literary correspondence* (London: Curll, 1736), IV, 107.

19. (2d ed., 1778), I, 49. Kippis gives Tickell as authority for this figure, but Tickell actually says nothing of the circulation of the *Spectator.*

20. *An historical essay on Mr. Addison* (London, 1783), p. 42.

21. *Addisoniana* (London, 1803), II, 52.

22. D. Nichol Smith. "The newspaper," *Johnson's England* (Oxford, 1933), II, 334. Professor Nichol Smith's figures may need some revision if we assume, as would certainly seem to have been normal printing practice, that the folio half-sheets of the *Spectator* were printed by half-sheet imposition, i.e., by laying both type-pages in one form to be printed and perfected. If whole sheets were thus printed at one time (the recto and verso of a *Spectator*), perfected on the same press, and then cut in two, it would be possible to turn out four thousand completed *Spectators* in eight hours. For this point, and other suggestions, I am indebted to Professor Fredson T. Bowers, who very kindly read this paper in manuscript.

exactly doubled. In such a case there would be two days, not one, for setting up type and running off the copies, and the difficulty of issuing three thousand copies a day would be obviated. If a popular number, such as No. 159, had to be reprinted, there might, of course, be variants, but a system of printing on alternate days would relieve us from the necessity of assuming duplicate printings for all the numbers.

An examination of the original sheets[23] shows that this was, in fact, the procedure followed in the printing of the *Spectator,* that not one print-ing-house but two were employed and that these two — for the greater part of the original run of 555 numbers — worked in exact alternation. For the first 132 numbers (March 1-August 1, 1711) Printer A is respon-sible for all the odd-numbered papers — 1, 3, 5, 7, etc. — and Printer B for all the even-numbered — 2, 4, 6, 8, etc. There is a break in the alterna-tion in Nos. 133-62, with Nos. 133-47 all done by Printer A, and Nos. 148-62 by Printer B. The exact alternation is resumed with No. 163 (September 6, 1711) and continues as far as No. 410 (June 20, 1712). Another break occurs in Nos. 411-21 (the series by Addison on "the pleas-ures of the imagination"), which are all done by Printer A, followed by Nos. 422-32 by Printer B. From this point to the conclusion of the series there is a different pattern of printing — not alternately, but in groups of three, Nos. 433, 434, 435 by Printer A; Nos. 436, 437, 438 by Printer B; and so on to the end, with Nos. 553, 554, and 555 done by Printer A.

Evidence for two distinct printings can be readily seen in the recurring features which were kept standing in type — the letters forming the head-ing "THE SPECTATOR," the rules separating the date from the body of the paper, the broken or bent rules recurring in papers printed by one or the other of the shops,[24] and the various misprints in the "colophon" which occur only in alternate issues.[25] It is also observable if one compares the width of the type-line, the size of type,[26] and the physical characteristics of certain letters in the text, notably capital Q and the italic capital M.[27]

The advertisements provide additional confirmation. One of the patent medicines most frequently advertised in the *Spectator* is the "famous Elixir" for "Consumptions of all sorts," sold at 3*s*. 6*d*. a bottle "only at Mr. Osborn's Toyshop at the Rose and Crown under St. Dunstan's Church,

---

23. This examination is based on four sets of the original sheets — two in the University of Chicago Library, one in the Newberry Library, and one in my possession.

24. Compare, for example, the rule separating the body of the paper from the imprint in Nos. 198, 200, 202, etc., and so on, alternately through No. 252, with that in the odd-numbered papers through the same series.

25. For example, in the imprint for No. 350, there is a new setting of type, with *Buildings* misspelled *Buildsngs* and *Strand* misspelled *Serand.* These misspellings do not occur in No. 349 or No. 351. In No. 352, the next number by Printer B, they are corrected, but *Dolphin* is misspelled *Dhiolpn.* This misspelling is absent in No. 353 (by Printer A) but recurs in No. 354 (by Printer B). Similarly, Lillie's name is misspelled *Lille* in Nos. 41, 43, 45, and 47 (all by Printer A) but not in Nos. 42, 44, 46, and 48 (by Printer B). Note also the misspelling ADVERTEIS-MENTS in Nos. 356, 358, 360, and 362 (by Printer B) but not in the odd-numbered issues of the same period.

26. In the work of Printer A twenty lines measure 71mm.; in that of Printer B they measure 74.

27. Even the position of the halfpenny-stamp mark in the issues after August 1, 1712, shows a distinction between the papers done by Printer A and those by Printer B. In the former it is always, in the copies I have examined, on the reverse of the paper; in the latter, on the face.

in Fleetstreet." This rather long advertisement first appears in No. 118, set in italic type, and is repeated in Nos. 160, 176, 186, 200, and 212 of the B series. It does not appear again in the B series until No. 248, exactly as before, except for the last line (the final line ·of type having dropped out and been reset in the interval?): the comma after *Church* is omitted and the last word misspelled *Fleesttreet*. This variation in the final line appears in the advertisement each time it is reproduced in numbers by Printer B—Nos. 266, 272, 286, 294, and so on, at intervals through No. 490, a total of twenty-four appearances. If we look at the same advertisement in the numbers done by Printer A, we find that it is set in roman type and that the misprint in the final line never occurs.[28]

Some of the advertisements, moreover, appear only in papers done by Printer A or in those by Printer B. "Sir Theodore Maynern's . . . Opiate for the Teeth," for example, is to be found only in numbers for which Printer B is responsible.[29] When an identical advertisement occurs in papers by Printer A and by Printer B, a different setting of type is clearly observable. This is true for the advertisements of "Angelick Snuff,"[30] "the famous Bavarian Red Liquor,"[31] "Holman's London Ink Powder,"[32] and Payne's electuary for loss of memory,[33] to cite only a few. Occasionally, if there is a long interval between appearances, there will be a new setting of type, but always distinct from the setting used by the other printing-house.[34]

The advertisements for books show the same practice, and these are more interesting because in many cases they are for books published or sold by three of the persons intimately connected with the *Spectator,* namely, Samuel Buckley, Jacob Tonson, and Mrs. Baldwin. Advertisements of books printed or published by Buckley are to be found almost exclusively in numbers done by Printer B. Thus Bysshe's *Art of English poetry*[35] is advertised only in numbers by Printer B, and the same is true of [Sir Richard Blackmore's] *The nature of man,*[36] [Vertot's] *History of the revolutions in Portugal,*[37] *The Bishop of St. Asaph's charge to the clergy . . . in 1710,*[38] and the second edition of *A sermon on the fast-day,*

28. There are eight occurrences of the advertisement in papers by Printer A: Nos. 144, 229, 420 (with a new setting of type), 439, 445, 452, 464, and 500.

29. Numbers 48, 104, 116, 130, 152, 270, 354, and 378.

30. Compare Nos. 92, 102, 110, 120, 154, 160, 182, 204, 294, 366, 386, and 442 (by Printer B) with Nos. 136, 146, 193, 239, 273, 311, 421, 501, and 511 (by Printer A).

31. Compare Nos. 124, 162, 176, 202, 250, 296, 318, 358, 398, 428, 438, and (with a resetting of type) 461 and 545 (by Printer B) with Nos. 143, 197, and 233 (by Printer A).

32. Compare Nos. 330 and 400 (by Printer B) with No. 377 (a different notice, by Printer A).

33. Compare Nos. 134, 147, 173, 229, 269, 420, 441, 482, 513, and 549 (by Printer A) with Nos. 200, 212, 244, 298, 322, 356, and 404 (by Printer B).

34. Lawrence Lewis, in *The Advertisements of the Spectator* (London, 1909), reprints a number of the advertisements from the original sheets but does not notice the differences in printing.

35. "Printed for Sam. Buckley at the Dolphin in Little-Britain, and Sold by the Booksellers," advertised in Nos. 4, 12, 16, 20, 26, 56, 64, 68, 72, 76, 84, 86, 98, 104, 108, 112, 122, 128, and 162.

36. "Printed for Sam. Buckley; and sold by D. Midwinter, Jacob Tonson, and A. Baldwin," advertised in Nos. 32, 34, 36, 38, 42, 50, 56, 64, 68, 72, 78, 84, 92, 98, 102, 108, 112, 118, 122, 126, 128, 132, 166, 178, 188, 190, 194, 198, and 200.

37. "Printed by Sam. Buckley in Little-Britain: Sold by S. Crouch and R. Smith, E. Sanger, D. Browne, and J. Graves," advertised in Nos. 332, 350, 352, 354, 356, and 358.

38. "Printed by Sam. Buckley, and sold by D. Midwinter . . .," advertised in Nos. 423, 424, 426, 427, 428, 431, and 437.

January 16, 1711-12, against such as delight in war. By a divine of the Church of England [William Fleetwood, Bishop of St. Asaph].[39]

Books "printed for J. Tonson," on the other hand, are advertised generally, though not uniformly, in *Spectators* done by Printer A. This is true, for instance, of the one book advertised most frequently in the *Spectator—The retir'd gardner*, "Being a Translation of Le Jardinier Solitaire, or Dialogues between a Gentleman and a Gard'ner [of Louis Liger], . . . Revis'd, with several Alterations and Additions, which render it proper for our English Culture, By George London and Henry Wise." The advertisement for this book, first appearing in No. 31, is repeated at intervals nearly fifty times throughout the run of the *Spectator—*from No. 457 merged with an omnibus advertisement of books printed for Tonson—and always in papers done by Printer A.[40] It cannot be by mere chance that the advertisements for a book publicized so widely in the *Spectator* should appear regularly and solely in the numbers done by Printer A.

It is in *Spectators* issued by this Printer A that we find the great majority of advertisements by Tonson, including those for the duodecimo edition of *Paradise lost;*[41] *A letter to the Right Honourable Mr. Harley, wounded by Guiscard;*[42] the first volume of Temple Stanyan's *Grecian history;*[43] a Life of *Pythagoras;*[44] the octavo edition of Beaumont and Fletcher, in seven volumes;[45] Prior's *Poems on several occasions;*[46] the second edition of *Le Diable boiteux;*[47] "Mr. Steele's two Comedies, *The funeral* and *The tender husband*";[48] *Antiochus,* an opera;[49] "A print of Lord Sommers, by George Vertue";[50] *Hamlet,* an opera;[51] Ovid's *Art of love;*[52] [John Weaver's] *Essay towards a history of dancing;*[53] Echard's *General ecclesiastical history;*[54] the sixth edition of Steele's *Christian hero;*[55] the third edition of Cibber's *Careless husband;*[56] and an omnibus advertisement of several books.[57]

---

39. "Printed by Sam. Buckley, and sold by A. Baldwin," advertised in Nos. 388, 390, 394, 396, 406, 410, 427, and 437. The first edition, however, published on January 19, 1712, is advertised in Nos. 279 and 291 (by Printer A) and Nos. 284, 286, and 290 (by Printer B).

40. Numbers 31, 47, 49, 57, 95, 99, 105, 119, 131, 133, 134, 135, 138, 145, 167, 169, 173, 201, 259, 261, 265, 275, 359, 367, 371, 373, 377, 379, 397, 399, 401, 405, 407, 419, 420, 433, 434, 435, 441, 446, 457, 458, 469, 471, 475, 481, 529, 530, and 531.

41. Numbers 29, 31, 35, 37, 39, 47, 73, 79, 85, 91, 95, 285, 359, 361, 373, and 379.

42. Numbers 35 and 37.

43. Numbers 35, 37, 47, 49, and 73.

44. Numbers 57 and 71.

45. Numbers 85, 87, 89, 91, 95, 97, 99, 105, 107, 111, 119, 127, and 129.

46. Numbers 105, 107, and 111.

47. Numbers 103, 119, 144, 167, and 201.

48. "Printed for J. Tonson, and Sold by Owen Lloyd," advertised in Nos. 181, 183, 185, 199, 203, 217, 219, 221, 229, 249, 259, and 261.

49. Number 245.

50. Numbers 281, 283, 285, 287, 289, 291, 293, 295, 299, 301, and 305.

51. Number 311.

52. "Printed for J. Tonson, and Sold by W. Taylor," advertised in Nos. 329 and 331.

53. Numbers 476, 477, 481, and 483.

54. Number 512.

55. Number 517.

56. Number 523.

57. Numbers 134, 138, 139, 141, 145, 167, 169, 173, 191, 201, 247, 249, 257, 259, 275, 355, 359, 371, 373, 379, 399, 401, 403, 405, 407, 411, 415, 417, 419, 420, 433, 434, 435, 441, 446, 457, 458, 469, 471, 475, 481, 529, 530, and 531. As noted above, from No. 457 this advertisement is combined with that for *The retir'd gardner.*

On the other hand, there are four advertisements for books by Tonson which appear only in numbers done by Printer B: *A course of chirurgical operations,*[58] *Several orations of Demosthenes,*[59] Fontenelle's *Dialogues of the dead,*[60] and *Hercules,* an opera;[61] but these appear in a relatively few numbers of the *Spectator,* fourteen in all, and mainly within the months of September and October, 1711.

Tonson also advertises a few works in both series of papers: Le Vassor's *Account of Germany;*[62] Charles Johnson's comedy, *The wife's relief;*[63] the duodecimo edition of Otway's *Works,* in two volumes;[64] Lord Landsdowne's *Poems upon several occasions;*[65] Tickell's *Poem on the prospect of peace;*[66] and the *Ode to the Creator of the world, occasion'd by the fragments of Orpheus* [by John Hughes].[67]

As for advertisements of books printed for or sold by Mrs. Baldwin, these are mainly of Whig pamphlets and are not repeated with much frequency. It is possible to find some in papers done by only one or the other of the printers, but the advertisements are too sporadic for any general conclusions to be drawn. The same differences in settings of type are, of course, to be found in these advertisements when the same book is advertised in papers printed by Printer A and in those done by Printer B.

The advertisement for the first two volumes of the duodecimo edition of the *Spectator,* which was published jointly by Buckley and Tonson, is to be found, as might be expected, in both series of papers,[68] but each has a distinctive setting of type.

The evidence of these advertisements, both for patent medicines and for books, points conclusively to separate printing-shops. Do they afford any clues as to who the printers were? Tonson, we have seen, advertises for the most part in *Spectators* done by Printer A, and Buckley almost exclusively in those by Printer B. One is tempted to guess that the A series was done in Tonson's shop and that the B series was printed by Buckley himself. We have, fortunately, additional evidence from another daily paper, which was being printed at the same time—the *Daily courant,* "Printed by Sam. Buckley, at the Dolphin in Little-Britain." If we look at the issues of this paper which were being printed by Buckley during 1711 and 1712, we can compare these with advertisements for the same products appearing in the A and B series of the *Spectator.*

Taking, first, the advertisement of the elixir for "consumptions of all sorts" sold at Osborn's toyshop, which shows such marked differences in

58. Numbers 158, 162, 166, 178, 182, 184, 188, 196, 200, and 212.
59. Numbers 160, 166, 178, 182, and 188.
60. Numbers 160, 166, 178, 182, 188, 196, 204, and 212.
61. Numbers 368 and 396.
62. Numbers 68, 72, 76, 80, 84, 94, 98, 102, 110, and 128 (by Printer B); Nos. 69, 77, 79, 81, 83, 85, 87, 91, 95, 111, 125, 131, 134, 138, 141, 144, 146, 163, 167, 169, and 259 (by Printer A).
63. Numbers 231 and 233 (by Printer A); Nos. 232, 234, 248, 270, 274, 276, 278, 286, 292, and 298 (by Printer B).
64. Numbers 385, 393, 399, 401, 405, 407, and 517 (by Printer A); Nos. 394, 396, 402, 410, 520, 521, and 522 (by Printer B).
65. Numbers 495 and 501 (by Printer A); Nos. 497 and 498 (by Printer B).
66. Numbers 521, 522, 528, 532, and 552 (by Printer B); Nos. 523 and 529 (by Printer A).
67. Numbers 540, 546, and 552 (by Printer B); Nos. 541, 553, and 554 (by Printer A).
68. Numbers 278, 280, 290, 292, 296, 322, and 324 (by Printer B); Nos. 283, 285, 287, 289, 291, 293, 295, 299, 301, 305, and 307 (by Printer A).

the papers produced by Printer A and those by Printer B, we find the advertisement in the *Daily courant* of October 15 and 23, 1711, exactly as it appears in the B issues of the *Spectator* of July 16, September 3 and 21, October 3 and 19, and November 2, 1711.[69] It next appears in the B issues on December 14, 1711 (No. 248), this time with the variation in the final line (the comma omitted and the misspelling *Fleesttreet*). In the *Daily courant* of December 24, 1711, and in a number of issues thereafter we find the advertisement with the same variation in the final line.[70] Nowhere do we find it as it appears in the A printing of the *Spectator*. It seems clear that the type for this advertisement was left standing in Buckley's shop, to be used when needed for the *Spectators* printed by Buckley or for the *Daily courant.*

Confirming evidence is supplied abundantly by other advertisements in the *Daily courant.* Without citing all, we may note that the advertisement for Holman's London Ink Powder in *Spectator,* Nos. 330 (March 19, 1712) and 400 (June 9, 1712) is to be found with the same setting of type in the *Daily courant* of October 13, 1711, and February 8, March 1, and May 9, 1712. Similarly, the advertisement for "Angelick Snuff" as printed in the B issue of the *Spectator* for February 6, April 30, May 23, and July 28, 1712,[71] is identical with the advertisement in the *Daily courant* of January 3, February 19 and 26, April 8, May 9, June 5, and July 4, 1712. Typographical errors will again be found to coincide. For example, in the advertisement of "Famous Drops for Hypocondriack Melancholly," to be sold "only at Mr. Bell's Bookseller at the Cross-Keys and Bible in Cornhill near the Royal-Exchange," as it appears in *Spectator,* No. 196 (October 15, 1711), the last words are printed "near he Royal-Exchange," an error which is duplicated in the same advertisement in the *Daily courant* of October 13, 1711. When it again appears, in *Spectator,* No. 218 (November 9, 1711), the error is corrected, as it is in the *Daily courant* of November 6, 1711, December 31, 1711, and so on. The same observation applies to the advertisement of the electuary for loss of memory, sold at Mr. Payne's at the Angel and Crown in St. Paul's Church-Yard. This is to be found in both the A series of the *Spectator*[72] and in the B series, but the latter contains the misspelling *strenthens* in the appearances of October 19, November 2, December 10, 1711, etc.[73] The same misprint occurs in the advertisement in the *Daily courant* of October 24, 1711, and later.

Coincidence cannot account for all these identical readings in the B series of the *Spectator* and the *Daily courant.* They never appear in the advertisements printed in the A series, as they almost certainly would have done had the A and B series emanated from the same printing-shop. The evidence points unmistakably to Samuel Buckley, the printer of the *Daily courant,* as the printer of the B papers of the *Spectator.*

Turning, now, to Printer A, we may note, in the first place, that he was

---

69. Numbers 118, 160, 176, 186, 200, and 212.
70. *Daily courant,* January 7 and 25, 1712; February 4 and 20; March 12, 21, and 31; April 11, 23, and 30; May 7; June 2, 13, and 25; and July 1, 5, and 17, 1712.
71. Numbers 294, 366, 386, and 442.
72. Numbers 134, 147, 173, 229, 269, 420, 441, 482, 513, and 549.
73. Numbers 200, 212, 244, 298, 322, 356, and 404.

someone very close to the authors of the *Spectator*. The first number is printed by him, as are also the final three numbers. The more or less "official" or editorial notices in the *Spectator* appear uniformly in numbers done by Printer A. It is in those printed by him that we find the earliest editorial notice;[74] and much later, when a change was made in the imprint, the notification that advertisements and letters were still to be received by Buckley, Tonson, Lillie, and Mrs. Baldwin, appears only in numbers done by Printer A.[75] Without exception, the announcements informing readers where complete monthly sets of the *Spectator* are to be found occur only in papers done by Printer A.[76] All this suggests a person experienced in the publishing world and in close connection with Addison and Steele.

The name that most obviously fits this description is that of Jacob Tonson. What printing-house other than Tonson's would be most likely to share with Buckley the printing of the *Spectator?* It is in *Spectators* produced by Printer A, we have seen, that the bulk of Tonson's advertisements for books appear; and the Tonsons were connected both by business and by personal friendship with both Addison and Steele. It is not difficult to conjecture that, in launching the *Spectator,* Addison and Steele would naturally turn to Tonson as publisher and that, in order to produce a paper which was to appear every day, an arrangement would be made with Buckley for a share of the printing. Just why, if this is true, Tonson's name does not appear in the imprint from the start is not immediately clear. There may have been some reason, not now apparent, for Tonson's not revealing his connection with the *Spectator* at the beginning, perhaps a reason involved in his taking over the remaining *Tatler* business. If Buckley had been the sole printer, the imprint might well have read "Printed by Sam. Buckley"; if Tonson had been in sole charge, it would certainly have read "Printed for J. Tonson." Parenthetically, it may be pointed out that when the additional series of the *Spectator* came to be written (Nos. 556 – 635) by Addison, without the help of Steele, from June 18 to December 20, 1714, the imprint of the original sheets read: "LONDON: Printed by S. Buckley in Amen-Corner, and J. Tonson in the Strand; where Advertisements are taken in." Buckley was chiefly a printer and known as a printer of periodicals, whereas the Tonsons were publishers, and mainly of books. While absolute proof cannot be offered here to identify Printer A with Tonson, it seems at any rate a reasonable hypothesis that it was Tonson's shop which shared with Buckley the labor of the alternate daily printing of the *Spectator.*

Such an arrangement, with two printing-houses responsible for alternate numbers, might be awkward for a paper of news, where daily supervision would be necessary, but for a series of periodical essays like the *Spectator* it would offer a very convenient method of working. It explains

---

74. Numbers 7, 13, and 27.

75. Numbers 499, 500, 505, 506, 507, 511, and 512.

76. For March, Nos. 29, 31, 35, 37, 39, 41, 43, 45, 47, 49, and 53; for March and April, Nos. 65, 69, 71, 73, and 75; For March – May, Nos. 83, 85, 87, 91, 93, 95, 97, 99, 101, 103, 105, and 107; for March – June, Nos. 109, 111, 115, 117, 119, 125, 127, 129, 131, 133, and 134; for March – July, Nos. 135, 137, 138, 139, 141, 143, 144, 145, 146, and 147; for March – August, Nos. 163, 165, 167, 169, 173, and 179; for March – September, No. 205; for March – October, Nos. 215, 217, 221, and 223.

how three thousand copies and more could be produced every day, since each printer had two days instead of one for his work. And when enough material had accumulated, there was nothing to prevent the papers being run off in advance and properly dated ahead.

The first break in the regular alternation of papers occurs in August, 1711, with numbers from August 2 to August 18 (Nos. 133-47) done by Printer A, and numbers from August 20 to September 5 (Nos. 148-62) done by Printer B. With the exception of six papers,[77] these thirty numbers are all by Steele. We know that Addison was at Bath during the greater part of August, 1711,[78] and Steele may have found it more convenient to have these papers done in two large consecutive batches. The only other break in the alternating series occurs from June 21 to July 16, 1712, with numbers from June 21 to July 3 (Nos. 411-21, the series on the pleasures of the imagination) done by Printer A, and numbers from July 4 to July 16 (Nos. 422-32) done by Printer B. The tradition that the essays on the pleasures of the imagination had been written earlier and were adapted to the *Spectator* is confirmed by this explanation of the printing. It would be much simpler for Addison at this point to turn over the whole manuscript to one printer than to divide it between two. While Printer A was occupied with these eleven papers, Printer B would be intrusted with the material for Nos. 422-32, which would then follow with proper dates. The rest of the papers (Nos. 433-555) were done, as we have seen, alternately in groups of three. It seems reasonable to assume that, by this time, Addison and Steele were a little weary of daily concern over a paper which had occupied their energies for some sixteen months and that they found it easier to prepare material at once for three numbers, each group of three to be turned over to the appropriate printer. Moreover, by this time a great deal of material, in the form of letters and contributed essays, had accumulated, which could be rapidly prepared for the printer. Many of these later numbers, it will be remembered, consist mainly or entirely of letters from a great variety of correspondents.

III

We may consider, finally, whether there is any connection observable between the authors of the *Spectators* and the printers responsible for the two series of papers — Printer A and Printer B, as we shall continue to call them. Out of a total of 238 papers attributable to Steele, 29 are issued by Printer A and 209 by Printer B. Out of a total of 252 for which Addison is responsible, 203 are issued by Printer A and 49 by Printer B.[79] The close

77. Numbers 135, 159, 160, and 162 by Addison, and Nos. 150 and 161 by Budgell.

78. This is revealed by the letter of Addison to Joshua Dawson, dated from Bath, August 18, 1711, and first printed by Graham (p.264). The preponderance of essays by Steele at this point puzzled G. Gregory Smith, who wrote: "Was Addison on holiday, or indisposed, or was he in Ireland looking after his threatened interests?" (Note to No. 132.)

79. The total number of attributions to Steele and Addison can be only approximate. Aitken (*Life of Steele*, I, 312) assigned 236 to Steele and 274 to Addison; and various other estimates have been made. In assigning 238 to Steele and 252 to Addison, I have followed, of course, the signatures R and T of Steele, and C, L, I, and O of Addison. I exclude the following papers by John Hughes: No. 210, signed T in the Original sheets and in the 12mo edition, and Z in the 8vo edition; No. 224, signed Z in the original sheets, and unsigned in 8vo and 12mo; No. 375, unsigned throughout; and Nos. 525, 537, 541, and 554, each of which is unsigned throughout;

connection of Steele with Printer B and Addison with Printer A is even more considerable if we take into account the essays which were published beginning with No. 163 (September 6, 1711), when the regular alternation of printings resumes after the interruption of Nos. 133-62. Here, out of a total of 179 numbers by Steele, only 8 are by Printer A and 171 by Printer B. Of a total of 169 by Addison, on the other hand, 160 are by Printer A and only 9 by Printer B. Table 1 illustrates the proportions of essays by Steele and Addison issued by the two printers.

Table 1

Printer	Steele	Addison
Nos. 1-80 (Vol. I)		
A	14	24
B	19	21
Nos. 81-169 (Vol. II)		
A	22	22
B	20	21
Nos. 170-251 (Vol. III)		
A	3	34
B	33	3
Nos. 252-321 (Vol. IV)		
A	2	27
B	29	2
Nos. 322-94 (Vol. V)		
A	0	23
B	36	0
Nos. 395-473 (Vol. VI)		
A	0	38
B	34	0
Nos. 474-555 (Vol. VII)		
A	2	35
B	38	2

In the papers beginning with No. 433, when the printing is done in groups of three, the numbers issued by Printer A are almost uniformly written by Addison and those by Printer B written by Steele. In this latter series, when a given number consists entirely of letters or a contributed essay and there is no signature, it would seem safe to assume that Addison is responsible for such a number if it is printed by A, and Steele if the number is printed by B. Number 518, for example, which consists of (1) a short introductory paragraph, (2) a letter on epitaphs inspired by the news of the death of Sir Roger de Coverley, and (3) a letter on physiognomy signed "Tom Tweer," has generally been assigned by the editors to Steele. But the paper (which has no signature) comes in the group of three (Nos. 517, 518, and 519) printed by A, the first and third of which have Addison's signature, and should almost certainly be reassigned to Addison. In this case Addison would be the author of the introductory paragraph and responsible for the entire paper. The letter from "Tom Tweer" is probably contributed, but the letter on epitaphs may well be by Addison. The account of Sir Roger's death had appeared only in the preceding number (for Thursday, October 23), which would allow very little time for a genuine letter to be written and sent to the

No. 232, sometimes attributed to Henry Martyn, signed X in the original sheets, Z in the 8vo edition, and unsigned in the 12mo; No. 237, reprinted as Addison's by Tickell in 1721, but sometimes attributed to Hughes, and unsigned throughout; No. 302, often attributed to Hughes, though signed T throughout; No. 338, unsigned throughout; and No. 410, often attributed to Tickell, though signed T throughout. In this computation I have assigned to Steele or to Addison papers which are mainly by another writer if there is a prefatory or concluding note by Steele or Addison. Thus I have given credit to Steele for No. 378, though it mainly consists of Pope's *Messiah*, since it is introduced by Steele. The same is true for the two allegories by Thomas Parnell (Nos. 460 and 501): the first is introduced by Steele and the second by Addison and they are here assigned to Steele and Addison, respectively.

Spectator, particularly if the copy for Nos. 517, 518, and 519 had been turned over to Printer A at one time.

If these conclusions are valid, it should be possible in the future to investigate the problems of authorship of other doubtful papers with more precision. We have Steele's authority (in No. 555) for assigning the twenty-seven papers signed X to Eustace Budgell, the cousin and intimate associate of Addison. It is not surprising to find almost all of them in the group of *Spectators* done by Printer A. The two exceptions (Nos. 116 and 150) occur before September 6, 1711, when the more regular association of Addison with Printer A begins.[80] Since Budgell's essays are, as a rule, to be found in numbers issued by Printer A, any future attributions to Budgell are to be looked for, it would seem, among the A series. Budgell has been suggested, by Morley and Aitken, as the author of Nos. 408 and 425. Since these numbers are both issued by Printer B and since both lack the signature X, there would seem to be no valid grounds for assigning them to Budgell.

The papers with the signature Z present a more difficult problem. There are ten papers[81] so marked in one or another of the editions, and these have been attributed to a variety of authors, including John Hughes, Henry Martyn, Budgell, Henry Carey, and Pope. Aitken is probably correct in believing that they are not by any one person. Only one, No. 210, can with certainty be assigned to Hughes: it is in the list of Hughes's contributions to the *Spectator* drawn up by his brother-in-law, William Duncombe, in 1735,[82] and it is also assigned to him in a concluding note in *Spectator,* No. 537. Hughes is credited with Nos. 224 and 316 by the latest editor of the *Spectator,* G. Gregory Smith; Henry Morley suggested him as the author of No. 467; and Aitken thought he might be the author of Nos. 286, 292, 316, and 467. If we look, however, at the papers which we know to be by Hughes,[83] namely, Nos. 210, 375, 525, 537, 541, and 554, we see that, with the exception of No. 210, all are issued by Printer A.[84] But the ten papers signed Z are all, without exception, issued by Printer B, and it seems unlikely, in the absence of positive evidence, that they should be by Hughes. They may be by Martyn, Carey, or Pope, as has frequently been suggested, though the evidence is slight.[85] At any rate, since

80. The papers signed X are Nos. 67 (signed R in the original sheets, but X in the 8vo and 12mo editions), 77, 116, 150, 175, 197, 217, 277, 283, 307, 313, 319, 325, 331, 337, 341, 347, 353, 359, 365, 373, 379, 385, 389, 395, 401, and 506. Number 232 is excluded here: it is signed X in the original sheets, Z in the 8vo edition, and is without signature in the 12mo.

81. Number 210, signed T in the original sheets, Z in the 8vo edition, and T in the 12mo; No. 224, signed Z in the original sheets, and left unsigned in the 8vo and 12mo editions; No. 232, signed X in the original sheets, Z in the 8vo edition, and unsigned in the 12mo; No. 286, signed Z throughout; No. 292, signed Z in the original sheets and the 12mo edition, and unsigned in the 8vo; and Nos. 316, 404, 408, 425, and 467, signed Z throughout.

82. Preface to Hughes's *Poems on several occasions, with some select essays in prose,* I, xxxiv-xxxv.

83. On the evidence of the statements in *Spectator,* Nos. 537 and 554.

84. This is also true of No. 237, which Duncombe assigns to Hughes but which is not mentioned in *Spectator,* Nos. 537 and 554 and is reprinted as Addison's by Tickell in 1721.

85. In the first volume of *The prose works of Alexander Pope* (Oxford, 1936) Mr. Norman Ault assigns, on the basis of internal evidence, seven *Spectator* essays to Pope from this group signed Z — Nos. 224, 292, 316, 404, 408, 425, and 467. I have discussed his evidence in "Pope's contributions to the *Spectator,*" *MLQ,* V (1944), 69-78.

the papers are all in the group issued by Printer B, any future investigation might look to persons more closely associated with Steele for clues to their authorship. The same can be said for the one *Spectator* with the signature Q (No. 250), which is issued by Printer B and for which no author has been proposed.

There are, finally, sixteen numbers without signature whatever, in the original sheets, the octavo edition, and the duodecimo.[86] Setting aside Nos. 237 and 538 (which were reprinted by Tickell in the collected works of Addison in 1721), No. 555 (which contains a long prefatory letter by Steele and may therefore be assigned to him), Nos. 375, 525, 537, 541, and 554 (already discussed and certainly by Hughes), and No. 518 (which, we have seen, may with some certainty be assigned to Addison), we are left with seven doubtful papers—five issued by Printer B (Nos. 338, 396, 527, 539, and 551) and two by Printer A (Nos. 524 and 548). Without attempting to examine all these papers here—they are largely made up of letters and contributed essays—we should be justified in assuming that Steele is responsible for the group of five issued by Printer B and that he at least selected the letters which make up their content. One of them (No. 527) contains a letter and some verses by Pope,[87] and the attribution of this number to Steele is consistent with what we know of the relationship between Steele and Pope. Of the two papers issued by Printer A (Nos. 524 and 548), we may likewise believe that the material in them was selected by Addison and that his was the responsibility for their publication. The allegory in No. 524, on heavenly and worldly wisdom, is exactly—whoever the author or authors were—the kind of "dream vision" which he would approve. It is quite possible that the other paper, on poetical justice, was actually written by Addison. Although not reprinted by Tickell, it has often been attributed to Addison on internal evidence; the fact that it was issued by Printer A gives some further probability for adding it to the list of his essays.

With the evidence afforded us by a study of the first printing of the *Spectator* we should be better able to investigate not only these whole papers whose authorship has been in doubt but also the letters and contributed essays which comprise parts of many of the other numbers. Textual problems and annotation of allusions may be approached, too, with more hope of success. Although a beginning was made by Henry Morley in 1868, there is still no authoritative, or even reliable, text. Many of the obscure points of annotation have been solved by Morley, Aitken, and Gregory Smith, but much remains to be done before the *Spectator* can be read in an edition as satisfactory as those now available for many other eighteenth-century classics. It seems clear that the long-neglected original sheets provide the best clue to an understanding of the problems surrounding the famous collaboration of Addison and Steele.

86. Numbers 237, 338, 375, 396, 518, 524, 525, 527, 537, 538, 539, 541, 548, 551, 554, and 555. Number 553, which was issued without signature in the original sheets, consists of an introduction and a letter; in the 8vo and 12mo editions the signature O of Addison has been added at the end of the introduction. This paper is issued by Printer A.

87. Lines on Cephalus and Procris, from Ovid, reprinted in Pope's *Works* (1717) under the title, "On a fan."

12

Conditions of Publication and Problems of Editing:
The Compositor and the Text

Philip Williams, Jr.

New Approaches to Textual Problems in Shakespeare

One of the most promising approaches to the textual problems in Shakespeare is the study of those compositors who from manuscript copy first set the plays in type. In the transmission of the texts, these type-setters played a role the importance of which can hardly be overemphasized: if they were literal and painstaking, they reproduced relatively accurately the manuscript from which they worked; if they were inept, careless, or intent on improving their copy, the printed texts differed considerably from their manuscript copy. Thus in a given text we may find what a printing house employee *thought* Shakespeare wrote, or what he thought Shakespeare *might* have written, or — more disastrous still — what a printing house employee thought Shakespeare *should* have written, rather than what he actually wrote. In what follows I shall not discuss the methods by which compositors can be identified, but assuming that identification is possible, I should like to examine some of the implications of compositor analysis and related bibliographical techniques for the texts of Shakespeare. I shall here be concerned with those plays in the 1623 folio that were set from manuscript rather than printed copy. For purposes of illustration, I shall rely mainly on the histories, although the comedies or tragedies would serve equally well: the same or related textual problems are encountered in all three sections of the first folio.

One of the weaknesses in editing Shakespeare has been a tendency to specialize: a single editor does one play. While such a procedure has much in its favor, it sometimes seems to prevent the editor's bringing to bear on the problems of his text a detailed knowledge of other related textual problems. Those editors who, like Dover Wilson and Peter Alexander,

From *Studies in Bibliography,* VIII (1956), 3-14. Reprinted by permission of The University Press of Virginia. Read before the English Institute on 15 September 1954. At the time of his death Dr. Williams was engaged on investigations designed to supplement and revise this paper. However, since these were left only as jottings, it has seemed best to reproduce here the original paper as read, without addition or alteration. *Note from the Editor of* Studies in Bibliography.

have worked their way through the texts of many plays have each been able to make important contributions that might have been beyond the scope of the editor of a single play. The texts of the twenty-four plays that, according to Sir Walter Greg, were set from manuscript copy in the First Folio should be studied collectively as well as singly, just as those plays set from annotated quartos must be studied as a group as well as individually. Only when studied in this way can we obtain reliable information about the hypothetical editor of the folio, for example, and the character of his work. To make deductions about his editorial practices on the basis of the study of a single play is almost useless. The value of this broader approach is amply demonstrated by Dr. Alice Walker's *Textual Problems of the First Folio.*

For our purposes, it is unfortunate that William Jaggard printed so few plays. Unlike Okes, Simmes, and Eld, for example, the Jaggards did not specialize in drama. In the ten years from 1617 to 1627, no plays (except those in the First Folio) were printed from manuscript copy in their shop. In 1619, however, William Jaggard had printed ten plays for Thomas Pavier, but the so-called Pavier collection consists entirely of reprints of quartos that had appeared earlier. If instead of turning out rather pompous heraldries, histories, and books on theology, Jaggard had printed first editions of plays, these texts would serve as useful checks and controls for conclusions about how his compositors handled manuscript dramatic copy.

The study of these compositors in Jaggard's shop has had a brief yet significant history. In 1920, Mr. Thomas Satchell published in *The Times Literary Supplement* some observations on the spellings in the folio text of *Macbeth,* noting that some words consistently spelled in one way in the first part of the play were consistently spelled differently in the latter part. Satchell's deductions from these observations were modest: he simply raised the question whether the variant spellings were to be explained by a change in the manuscript copy or by a change in the compositors who set the type. Dr. Willoughby, in 1928, supplied the answer: the different spellings in *Macbeth* were to be explained by the habits of two compositors whom he distinguished as A and B, and some (but not all) of the spelling differences in *Macbeth* could be used to identify their work in other parts of the folio. Dr. Willoughby found these two compositors at work in *The Tempest,* with which the folio opens, and in *Troilus and Cressida,* the last of the plays to be printed. Although the importance of Willoughby's discovery should have been immediately recognized, compositor determination and analysis was almost completely neglected until an important article by Professor Hinman in 1940 stimulated interest in the subject. Since then, the study of the folio compositors has received considerable attention both here and in England.

The unfortunate neglect of the subject following the publication of Dr. Willoughby's monograph resulted in serious defects in several important editions of Shakespeare. Professor Shaaber, for example, in his almost model *Variorum* edition of *2 Henry IV,* did not make use of compositor determination and analysis. Had he done so, the vexing problem of the exact relationship of the quarto and folio texts might have been solved then and there. Since the publication of the *Variorum* edition in

1940, Dr. Walker has argued that the folio text was set from an annotated quarto; Professor Shaaber has re-affirmed his earlier position that the folio text was set from a manuscript having independent authority. The implications of this controversy for the editor are of course considerable. In view of the basic disagreement between two outstanding authorities, the relationship of the quarto and folio texts will have to be re-examined. There are indications that neither Dr. Walker nor Professor Shaaber is wholly correct. As Professor Bowers has observed, the quarto and folio texts are clearly not independent as Professor Shaaber believed, and yet an annotated quarto can hardly have served directly as copy for the folio text. The abnormal spellings of both compositors A and B are not consistent with such a theory. Printed copy exerted a greater influence on the compositors than did manuscript and caused them to deviate from their normal practices, but the abnormal spellings in *2 Henry IV* cannot be accounted for by the quarto text. The most likely explanation now seems to be that the copy for the folio text of *2 Henry IV* was neither an independent manuscript nor an annotated quarto but rather a manuscript transcript of a quarto annotated for use in the theater. But until the work of the two compositors has been competently analyzed, the answer to this puzzling question must remain in doubt. Whatever the answer may be, I am confident that it will not be achieved without the use of compositor analysis.

But deductions based on even the most detailed study of a single text are at best hazardous and at worst dangerously misleading and wrong. After his remarkably thorough study of the *Hamlet* texts, Professor Dover Wilson concluded that the good second quarto had been set from Shakespeare's foul papers by a hurried compositor — perhaps a dishonest Welshman — who could not work quickly because he had not mastered his craft. On this theory, Wilson constructed his complex textual and critical structure. Professor Wilson's single harried compositor now turns out to have been two men, both regular compositors in Roberts's shop, and both competent workmen at that. I once made an outrageous generalization about a minor point in the folio text of *Troilus and Cressida*. In the *Troilus* quarto the spelling of the exclamation *oh* varies, apparently indiscriminately, between *o* and *oh*. The folio text reproduces this variation with remarkable fidelity. I used this evidence, validly I think, to support my theory that the folio text had been set directly from a corrected copy of the quarto, but I added that the usual spelling of both folio compositors seemed to be *o* on the basis of my analysis of their work in *Julius Caesar*. It is true that the spelling in *Julius Caesar* is *o*, but it is likewise true that in *The Comedy of Errors,* another play set by the same two compositors, the spelling is *oh*. For reasons that I now do not pretend to understand, the folio compositors generally reproduced the copy spellings of this form. I can not seriously believe that two compositors mutually decided to use one spelling for one play, another for a second, and to mix the two spellings in a third. These *o* and *oh* spellings must then represent the spellings found in the copy, and because they do, they shed some light on the underlying manuscripts. It would be useful to know what Shakespeare's own usage was. Unfortunately the Hand D of *Sir Thomas More* (which I accept as

Shakespeare's) is not much help, for the form appears only once, spelled *o.* But I would suggest that the answer is not beyond the reach of the analytical bibliographer. The good second quarto of *Romeo and Juliet* was almost certainly set from Shakespeare's foul papers. A study of Thomas Creede's compositors (not in this text alone but of their total output) might reveal that they generally reproduced the copy spelling without imposing personal idiosyncracies. If so, we might establish that Shakespeare, in his early career at least, used one spelling or the other, or both indiscriminately. We could then apply this evidence to the folio text of *King John,* which Sir Walter Greg believes was printed partly from Shakespeare's foul papers and partly from prompt copy. In the first three acts (which may have been set from foul papers) the spelling is *o;* in the last two acts, the spelling is predominantly *oh.* Knowing how conservatively Compositors A and B treated this form, we should have a neat, and I think rather convincing, bit of evidence to support Greg's theory about the copy for *King John.* For the later period, a like study of the second quarto of *Hamlet* might be applied to *Timon of Athens* to support Greg's belief that *Timon* was set from unfinished foul papers, or my belief that it was set from a fair transcript made by the same scribe who prepared the manuscript from which the folio text of *Coriolanus* was set. The trivia of analytical bibliography can sometimes be put to good use.

The text of *King John* will serve to illustrate another use which compositor analysis can serve. Although he found it "difficult to envisage a composite manuscript actually made up partly of foul papers and partly of a section of the prompt-book," Sir Walter discovered what seemed to be confirmation of sorts when he noted that "in the first three acts the directions tend to appear a line or two late, in the others a line or two early." The fact that some pages of *King John* were set by Compositor A and others by Compositor B raises some question as to the significance of Greg's evidence. There are, at the very most, twelve stage directions (of which two are very doubtful) that can be described as being either early or late. The ten certain ones occur on pages set by Compositor A; the two doubtful ones on pages set by Compositor B. Judging from his work throughout the folio, Compositor A tended to reproduce the copy position of directions, whereas B tended to normalize and was reluctant to interrupt a speech to insert even a needed stage direction. Greg's theory therefore receives very little support from the positions of these stage directions, for the variation is better explained by the typographical practices of the two compositors who set the folio text.

If indeed there was a change in the character of the manuscript copy from which the folio text of *King John* was set, the evidence to establish the fact will be found by an analysis of the eight pages in Acts I, II, and III set by Compositor A as compared with the four pages in Acts IV and V set by the same compositor. Because Compositor B reproduced the accidentals of his copy less faithfully, the pages set by him are less likely to produce helpful evidence, but compositor analysis can certainly help to elucidate the textual problems of this play.

My discussion so far has been based on the assumption that in the transmission of the text from manuscript copy to type, some characteristics of the manuscript were preserved, perhaps quite inadvertently. This palimpsest of the underlying manuscript is fainter in the work of Compositor B, stronger in the work of Compositor A. The folio text of *Titus Andronicus* furnishes a useful illustration to support the validity of the basic assumption. *Titus Andronicus* was not, of course, set from manuscript in the First Folio: the folio text was set from a copy of the third quarto of 1611. But one scene in the folio text (III.2) does not appear in any of the preceding quartos and must therefore have been set from manuscript copy. Had no copy of the three earlier quartos survived, it would nevertheless have been possible to show that the copy for Act III, scene 2, differed from the copy for the rest of the play. In this scene the name *Tamora* is spelled with an *i;* in a speech-heading *Andronicus* is used rather than *Titus,* and — more interesting — the word *upon* which appears four times in this short scene is each time spelled with a double *p* — a spelling that is extremely rare elsewhere in the First Folio. Because of the weight that I would have the textual scholar attach to such apparently trivial evidence, it is reassuring to have this one example that has the unquestioned check of external evidence. One would like to see what compositor analysis can reveal about the troublesome Hecate scenes in *Macbeth* or the Fool's distasteful prophecy in *Lear.* Unfortunately, both were set by Compositor B who may well have obscured any traces of a change in copy.

The three parts of *Henry VI* present problems that may be insoluble; certainly at present they are far from solution. All three parts were set from manuscript in the First Folio, but for parts 2 and 3, some use was made of the earlier corrupt quartos which the folio texts supersede. No version of Part 1 — whether memorial reconstruction or early draft — had previously appeared in print. It is Part 1 that I wish briefly to consider for what compositor analysis can and what it can not contribute to the study of this text.

Of the folio text, Sir Walter Greg writes: "Many directions are elaborate and descriptive; most noticeably so in the first two acts, but 'Enter in skirmish with bloody pates' is a nice example from the third, and the closely following 'Begin again' also suggests the author. Several . . . [directions] begin with 'Here': this has an archaic appearance and may be a personal peculiarity. . . . Instances are confined to the first act, except for one in the third. . . . As in other early plays we seem to have an authorial manuscript used with little modification as prompt copy. Either composite authorship or revision would explain certain contradictions and inconsistencies in the text. Whether the copy itself was 'heterogeneous' is uncertain. . . ."

We now know that the text of *1 Henry VI* was set by Compositors A and B. The former set all of Acts I, II, and III save for the first 46 lines of Act II; Compositor B set all of Acts IV and V save for page 113 which is the work of A. The unusual features of the text (including the 'Here' directions) that Greg comments on are all found on pages set by Compositor A. Such directions may, as Greg suggests, be a personal peculiarity of one of the disputed hands in the play, and one wonders if the absence of the unusual directions in Acts IV and V is not to be explained by Compositor B's revamping the directions of his copy. He was, as we know from his work elsewhere, quite capable of doing so.

But the most striking textual anomaly of *1 Henry VI* can not be attributed to the two compositors and their differing practices. The act division is very imperfect and irregular: only Acts III and IV are divided into scenes, and Act V consists of a single 108-line scene. Credit for the introduction of scene division can not be given Compositor B, nor can the absence of division be blamed on Compositor A, for having set Acts I and II without division, Compositor A set all of Act III, which is divided into four scenes. It is incredible that having set two acts without scene division, Compositor A should have introduced the convention with the third act. We are therefore left with the puzzle of manuscript copy with scene division in Acts III and IV only.

If this anomaly does indicate a change in the manuscript copy for *1 Henry VI,* analysis of Compositor A's work in Acts I and II compared with his work in Act III should disclose it. The evidence may be slight, but because of the literalness with which he followed copy, a change, if there was one, should be demonstrable. I cite the following as examples of the kind of evidence that should be brought forward to support such a theory. In Acts I and II, *Burgundy* is invariably spelled with a *d,* but when the name appears in Act III (coinciding with the introduction of scene division) Compositor A consistently uses the spelling *Burgonie.* Even more striking is the treatment of the name of Joan of Arc. In undivided Act I, Compositor A consistently spells the name *Puzel* for the eighteen times that it occurs in directions, speech-headings, and text. But in divided Act III, in which the name appears twenty-six times, he invariably spells it *Pucell.* In short, the name appears spelled with a *z* in the pages before scene division, and spelled with a *c* (by both compositors) in the pages after scene division is introduced. Because the change is not due to a shift in compositors, and because Compositor A was literal in such matters, it is safe to conclude that the change represents a spelling change in the manuscript. Coinciding as it does with the introduction of scene division, the obvious conclusion is that there was some change in the manuscript at the beginning of Act III. When corroborated by additional evidence of this kind, it will be possible to refine Greg's statement "Whether the copy itself was 'heterogeneous' is uncertain." The copy for *1 Henry VI* was almost certainly heterogeneous.

But evidence of this kind can be very tricky and must be handled judiciously. In this same play, for example, two spellings for the name Joan are used: *Joane* and *Jone.* At first sight it might appear that this variation is as significant as the *Puzel—Pucell* variation, but such is not the case. The *o* spellings all appear on pages set by Compositor B; the *oa* spellings on pages set by A. Without the check of compositor analysis, a naive scholar might well fall into the error of attempting further to disintegrate the text on the basis of these variant spellings.

Henry VIII, the last of the histories, offers an even better illustration of the curb that compositor analysis can put on unbridled and injudicious speculation. If the bibliographer cannot solve the principal problem of this play, he can at least lay solid foundations upon which other disciplines can build. The problem here, of course, is divided authorship.

When Alfred Lord Tennyson remarked to his friend James Spedding that "many passages in *Henry VIII* were very much in the manner of Fletcher," he set up a puzzle that has fascinated Shakespearians ever since. Spedding — who was a scholar — took the poet's hint and made a 'stylistic' analysis, publishing his findings in *The Gentlemen's Magazine* for August, 1850. To Shakespeare he assigned Act I, scenes 1 and 2; Act II, scenes 3 and 4; Act III, scene 2, lines 1-203; and Act V, scene 1. This division, corroborated by many subsequent studies, has been generally accepted. To distinguish the hands of Shakespeare and Fletcher, Professor Thorndike later developed and applied the *'em* vs. *them* test; Dr. Partridge analyzed other contracted forms; and Professor Oras, in a study published only last year, found confirmation for the traditional assignments to Shakespeare and Fletcher. Among recognized authorities, only Professor Alexander has held out for single and Shakespearian authorship. His argument, however, is far from convincing: the 'stylistic' differences that have so often been reduced to statistics do exist; they are in the printed text to be counted, analyzed, and interpreted as one sees fit.

In all the counting and tabulating that has been done, not one of the investigators has been aware that the folio text of *Henry VIII* was set in type by two compositors with very different working habits and very different ways of treating some of the data that have been subjected to statistical study.

Henry VIII occupies about twenty-seven pages in the folio. Of the twelve pages attributed to Shakespeare, Compositor B set seven and Compositor A set five; of the fifteen non-Shakespearian pages, B set six and Compositor A set nine. It is therefore significant, in the vocabulary of statistics, that of the sixty-six *'em's* found in the text, fifty-five appear on pages set by Compositor A, and only eleven on pages set by Compositor B. The conclusion is, I think, inescapable: Compositor A reproduced his copy more literally than did B who, taking expected liberties, normalized many of his copy spellings to *them.* If the paucity of *'em's* in the pages set by Compositor B represents the compositor's sophistication of copy rather than a Shakespearian characteristic in the copy from which he worked, I am afraid that in a text worked on by Compositor B any division between Shakespeare and Fletcher on the basis of this test is of questionable value and may be dangerously misleading.

Another characteristic that has been used to distinguish the hands of Shakespeare and Fletcher is Fletcher's well established fondness for the pronoun *ye.* On the pages set by Compositor B, we find that the ratio is 208 *you's* to 25 *ye's,* or eight to one. On the pages set by Compositor A, the ratio is 191 to 48, or four to one. In other words, the ratio between *you* and *ye* is almost exactly twice as great on A pages as it is on B pages. John Fletcher may have had a preference for *'em* and *ye,* but we can be sure that the anonymous Compositor B of Jaggard's shop was not William Shakespeare.

I do not mean to suggest that the differences between what are generally called the Shakespearian parts of *Henry VIII* and the non-Shakespearian parts are all to be explained away by the practices of the two folio compositors. The differences in the play are most striking, and Tennyson's ear was a good one. But I would insist that no stylistic analysis of *Henry VIII* can be satisfactory that is not based on a knowledge of the two compositors, the pages they set, and their practices, not only in this play but throughout the folio.

I have illustrated some of the many uses that compositor analysis can serve in solving problems in the text of Shakespeare. The most important use (from the editor's point of view) has not been mentioned: the number and kinds of errors that the different compositors were likely to make. The uses to which this relatively new approach can be put are so varied that there has been no need for me to poach on what has become Dr. Walker's particular territory. But almost as important for the editor is the information that compositor analysis can supply about the character of the manuscripts from which the folio texts were set.

When we find a compositor consistently tending to mix his spellings of words for which he has an established preferential spelling, it is safe to conclude that the aberrant forms represent copy spellings. If, in a single play, Compositor A consistently gives up his characteristic *deare-deuel-young* spellings while retaining other characteristic spellings of his own, he presumably did so because of the influence exerted by his copy. When Compositor B intersperses frequent *deuell-young-Weele* spellings, the same conclusion seems inescapable. After compositor spellings have been isolated and the copy spellings established, the manuscripts from which the folio texts were set can be grouped according to common spelling characteristics. We may find one group of manuscripts characterized by the chain of *doe-heere-honour-Wee'll* (and so on) spellings; another group by *do-here-honor-Wee'l*. A third group will, I suspect, be related by short spellings of *wil, shal, tel* and the like, a marked preference for final *ie* instead of *y*, and the long spelling of pronouns ending in *e*. When we find Compositor A spelling *to the* as *toth'* (one word) in *Macbeth* and *Coriolanus,* and nowhere else in the folio, we have strong evidence linking the manuscripts from which these two plays were set. And when we find the pages set by Compositor A in *Henry VIII* and *Hamlet* characterized by a phenomenally great number of semi-colons, quite in excess of his usual usage, we have a link between the manuscripts which is supported by his aberrant spelling *Wee'l* etc. in both texts.

When the varnish of the folio compositors has been removed, the grain of the underlying manuscripts will be revealed in its true color. Then, and not until then, shall we have exhausted the evidence possible about the kinds of copy from which these plays were set. I may be too optimistic, but I venture to hope that when the job is done, we shall be able to distinguish those plays which were set from Shakespeare's holograph from those set from scribal transcripts, and to assign with some certainty the transcripts to the scribes who made them. A good place to start will be with the five plays which are now thought to have been set from transcripts made by Ralph Crane. The extant manuscripts in his hand will first have to be studied not only to isolate his personal idiosyncracies that may show through in the folio texts, but also to establish the latitude of variation that can be expected in his work. In spite of similarities, there are marked differences in his work as exemplified, for example, by the manuscript of *Barnavelt* and the Bodleian manuscript of *A Game at Chess*. When the spade work has been done, we may find absolutely convincing evidence to support Greg's hypothesis that *The Tempest, The Two Gentlemen of Verona, The Merry Wives of Windsor, Measure for Measure,* and *The Winter's Tale* were set from Crane manuscripts—or we may find something else. Until the possibilities of compositor analysis are fully exploited, we can not be sure.

Having spoken at such length about the importance of compositor analysis, it is embarrassing to own up to some of its deficiencies and to point out difficulties that, in the case of the Jaggard compositors, have yet to be overcome. Neither Dr. Walker nor I have yet been able satisfactorily to identify the compositor who set the folio texts of *Titus Andronicus* and *Romeo and Juliet* and whose work we suspect in other plays.[1] While Compositor B remained remarkably stable and changed very little from 1619, when he worked on the Pavier collection, through 1623 and the last play printed in the folio, Compositor A, who was more sensitive to copy, is more difficult to isolate. There are long stretches in the folio that may have been set by Compositor A or that may have been set by a third compositor whose work, either because of copy influence or because of his own A-type characteristics, closely resembles Compositor A's work. The deficiencies in spelling tests based on a few words only have been well demonstrated. On some pages the key words simply do not appear, or appear so infrequently as to be of little use. What is wanted is a fuller list of preferential spellings, supplemented for Compositor A by a list of copy spellings that he would tolerate and that B would not. Neither compositor was willing to reproduce Crane's habitual spelling *theis* for *these,* but there are many spellings that A might reproduce but which B would balk at. Although a great deal of work remains to be done before we shall have perfected the techniques by which Jaggard's compositors can be pin-pointed, there is every reason to believe that the effort will be successful, especially so if supported by other investigations that the analytical bibliographer can make.[2]

An analysis of the press work of the First Folio is urgently needed. If Dr. Walker is correct in her assumption that Compositors A and B followed their copy more closely when working rapidly, it follows that we should like to know when the compositors were hurried by the press or presses. I should like to see corroborative mechanical evidence to explain the almost literatim faithfulness with which the folio reproduces the quarto texts of *Much Ado About Nothing* and *Titus Andronicus,* if hurried composition is indeed the answer. Or, from many important examples that come to mind, to cite a minor one: the use of white-space in the folio should be investigated. It is surprising how often act or scene division coincides with the top of a column. In *King John,* six of the sixteen divisions are found in this position. In addition to other ways of conserving or wast-

---

1. Acting on a hint from Dr. Hinman, the editor [of *Studies in Bibliography*] is at present engaged on an investigation of these two Folio texts and their compositors.

2. Dr. Hinman's most recent discoveries about the compositors and the printing of the Folio fully bear out this prophecy and help to answer some of the queries in the next paragraph. *Note from the Editor of* Studies in Bibliography.

ing space, the compositor could leave white-space above and below stage directions. Sometimes he left space above and below, sometimes above only, and sometimes none at all. This practice explains the loose appearance of Compositor B's page 305 in *Lear* and the tighter appearance of the same compositor's page 135 in *Macbeth*. The subject has never been investigated, but a study might reveal that some of the copy for the folio was looked over and roughly counted off before it reached the compositors. Unless it was known by pre-arrangement that Compositor A was to take over in *Hamlet* at II.2.219, it is difficult to explain why Compositor B stretched out the prose speeches of Polonius and Hamlet into irregular lines of verse at the bottom of 003. If copy for the folio was first read over by the printer for this purpose, perhaps other indications to guide the compositors were made at the same time. Sir Walter Greg suggested long ago that it may have been the printer rather than the illusive folio editor who removed some of the profanity from certain of the 1623 texts.

The more closely compositor analysis is related to other approaches, the more productive it will be. It can support the paleographer who attempts to recover manuscript spellings by analysis of errors caused by misreading Elizabethan handwriting. The linguist who brings order out of the seeming chaos of Elizabethan spelling can be of great help. Is the quarto spelling *arre* (*Troilus and Cressida*, I.3.392) a compositor's error and therefore to be emended, or is it an acceptable spelling of a 17th-century variant form of the folio's *tarre?* Is there any real significance in the folio's alternation between *does* and *do's,* or is it just chance that in *Hamlet* the contracted form is used in unstressed syllables and the full form in stressed? Anyone interested in Shakespeare's prosody would like to know.

Much of the bibliographical work that remains to be done for the text of Shakespeare may seem terribly time-consuming and unrewarding. Much of it certainly is. The collation of the extant copies of the 1609 *Troilus and Cressida* quarto revealed only the most trivial and uninteresting variants. But until the job was done, the editor of this play—if he had a conscience—had qualms when he spoke of "the quarto reading," for he could not be sure. All of this tedious collation and analysis must be done. The task is not more overwhelming (although it may be more complex) than that presented by the text of Chaucer. The *Chicago Chaucer* was undertaken, and the Chaucer scholar has a text for which he need not apologize—as we must today for the antiquated Old Cambridge edition of Shakespeare, reproduced substantially in recent years by Kittredge, Neilson, Harrison, Craig, and others. Inexpensive old-spelling editions of Milton are readily available, and few of us would care to read *Paradise Lost* in a modernized text. When an old-spelling edition of Shakespeare finally does appear, the study of the compositors in the dozen shops where substantive editions of Shakespeare were printed, will have contributed to the excellence of this badly needed edition.

13

Conditions of Publication and Problems of Editing: Emendation

John Crow

Editing and Emending

"The Science of Criticism, as far as it affects an Editor, seems to be reduced to these three Classes; the Emendation of corrupt Passages; the Explanation of obscure and difficult ones; and an Inquiry into the Beauties and Defects of Composition". So Lewis Theobald. But he was writing before the textual critic began to call himself a bibliographer. Have we, in connection with the Emendation of corrupt Passages, changed all that?

The painter may represent the charge of the Light Brigade, an arrangement of geraniums, the wreck of the *Hesperus,* or what he will. The maker of teapots knows no such liberty; he may indulge his genius by making teapots which in shape resemble Sir Winston Churchill or a giant panda or a motor-car; but he never forgets that he is working to produce something which will contain tea. The bibliographer is like the teapot-maker. Whatever fun he may have on the way, the end he has ever in view is Theobald's end—the establishment of correct texts.

I desire to discuss, in a most elementary manner, some of the problems of the editor and emender of English texts. I do not hope to glean more than an occasional lean ear from fields already reaped by notable textual critics. I offer no startling emendations to resolve famous Shakespearean *cruces.* Some points have become visible to me in various texts which I have studied. I shall exhibit some conjectures; but my attitude towards emending is tentative, towards editing sternly ultra-conservative.

The editor of a text desires, I take it, to come as close as he can to what the author wrote—not what he should have written. When Shakespeare in his classical plays writes of hats, we shall not, though we know that Greeks and Romans wore no hats, emulate Pope in emending to "caps". We shall not be worried by the Bohemian *plage,* nor by Hector's reference to Aristotle. When in Henry Smith's sermon, "The Magistrate's Scripture"

From *Essays and Studies 1955,* ed. D. M. Low, published by John Murray Ltd. for The English Association (London, 1955), pp. 1-20. Reprinted by permission of the author.

(1590), we find a reference to "the king of the Bees", our superior knowledge will not impel us to alter "king" to "queen". A recent Shakespearean editor, however, having explained that his play was printed from Shakespeare's own manuscript, said of one reading that it "was probably in the manuscript" — and then permitted an emendation in his text.

I have nothing to say about, and precious little for, the editor who wishes to improve Shakespeare by making him fit for family reading. I found a sort of "The Bard for the Tots" edition of *Romeo and Juliet,* whose editor obligingly provided in an introduction (Heaven help us) "character-studies" of all the people in the play. He had much to say about the frank, earthy, vulgar (I don't think he said "bawdy") talk of the Nurse. When I turned to the text, I found that he had sliced out so much of the poor woman's part that only about a dozen lines were left her and not one of those could bring a blush to the cheek of the most modest G.C.E. candidate. Where the First Folio reads, "And Fortune on his damned Quarry smiling, Shew'd like a Rebells Whore", a For-the-Tots *Macbeth* read (with no warning word) ". . . on his wretched quarrel smiling, Show'd like a rebel's lass". Why it did not later, read "Out wretched spot", I cannot guess.

The first hope of the editor is that he will not have to emend. The ideal laborious collator will try to resist the temptation to frolick in conjecture. He will try first to justify the reading which he finds in his "copy-text". Only when he has decided that the reading is impossible will he seek to alter what lies before him. He will not be happy merely to substitute a good reading for a bad; he will wish also to explain to himself how the "bad" reading came into the text.

An editor faced with a number of different printed editions will first set out to arrange those editions in order of authority. He will, almost invariably, find that the earliest edition is the best, that it derives from the author's manuscript and that subsequent editions are inferior, diverging unauthoritatively from it. Of the seventeenth-century folio collections of Shakespeare's plays, as Johnson found, none has independent authority but the first. The later ones may exhibit attempts to emend obscurities, to modernize archaisms, to clean up in general; there is no shred of evidence that any one of them introduces a new reading for which someone went back to a manuscript. Occasionally, however, a corrupt text, like the 1597 quarto of *Romeo and Juliet,* is the first in the field, to be replaced later by an authoritative text. The second (1599) quarto of the play claims to be (and is) "Newly corrected, augmented, and amended" — which does *not* mean that Shakespeare sat down and added pieces to it between 1597 and 1599.

Having established the authoritative edition, the editor will try to decide what was the manuscript from which the compositor set type for that edition. He will, in fact, want to know, for every edition which he studies, what was the nature of the "copy" underlying it — was it the author's rough draft, his fair copy, a theatrical prompt-copy, a corrected printed text, an uncorrected printed text, or some mixture of these things? He will not set before himself all the "old editions" and pick his readings now from one, now from another. He will strive to follow the most authoritative. If his personal taste inclines to a reading in the 1632 Folio of Shakespeare rather than one in the 1623 Folio, he will be well aware that the later reading has no more actual authority than has a conjecture by Lewis Theobald.

The production of an "explanation" of the status of any old text is not a matter of proof. It is not strictly demonstrable that a given early printed text has been set by a compositor who had Shakespeare's own manuscript before him. We are presented with some facts; we are called upon to produce some work of the imagination, to compose a fiction which will account for as many as possible of those facts. It has been suggested that certain symptoms found fairly often in concatenation indicate certain kinds of "copy". Investigators have worked out theories about how we can recognize "foul papers" ("author's manuscript in its last stage before the making of a fair copy", to quote a recent definition), what are the symptoms of prompt-copy, what idiosyncrasies were displayed by Ralph Crane, a man employed early in the seventeenth century as a manuscript copier of plays. Such things are theories; those who use them know that they are theories, which may, when new facts are unveiled, have to be discarded.

We may demand of the theories offered that they fit the unyielding facts and that they be, in themselves, not too improbable. A recent *Penguin* book has a note on its back about the American novelist, Scott Fitzgerald. The note states that Fitzgerald "gave a name to an age—the 1933 Age—lived through that age, and saw it burn itself out". I am surely entitled to emend "the 1933 Age" to "the Jazz Age", to go beyond that to the deduction that the copy for the publisher's note was manuscript, not typewritten, and even make further guesses about the handwriting of the writer of the copy.

The fictions of Z. Jackson, in his *Shakespeare's Genius Justified* (1819), may be thought to lapse into improbability. Prince Hal, in the first part of Henry IV, says (1623 text):

> Didst thou neuer see Titan kisse a dish of Butter, pitifull hearted Titan that melted at the sweete Tale of the Sunne?

And thus Jackson writes upon the passage:

> This passage being corrupt, has been totally misunderstood, and the story of Phaëton introduced as an elucidation; but the idea of the passage having relation to the Heathen Mythology is absurd! The picture is drawn from terrestrial nature; and was, I am confident, so perfectly familiar to our Author, that he scrupled not in making it equally familiar to the Prince.
>
> In former days, more than the present, fools were encouraged about taverns, for the purpose of amusing the company; they were lusty and lazy, like our Author's *Caliban,* and willingly degraded nature by doing whatever wit and wickedness could devise.
>
> We see the Prince associating with characters of a very inferior order: and frequently in taverns: even Hotspur was aware that he resorted to ale-houses; for, knowing that the Prince was partial to good ale, he says, "I'd have him poison'd with a pot of ale".
>
> Now, let us suppose the Prince and his merry companions at the *Sun Tavern;* and at which tavern there is retained an unfortun-

ate idiot, named Titan, and who is known in the neighbourhood as *Titan of the Sun.* This tavern is celebrated for *sweet ale.* The Prince and his companions drink freely; Titan makes sport for them, as Francis frequently did, at Dame Quickley's: A dish of *butter* is introduced for *Titan to kiss;* perhaps Poins, to make the scene more ludicrous, pops poor Titan's head into the dish of butter, who, crying at his greasy disgrace, is promised a pot of *sweet ale* to restore him to good humour. He dries his eyes; the ale is presented, but, to tantalize him withdrawn; he then *melts* again; the tears run down his greasy cheeks; and, finally, a pot of *sweet ale of the Sun Tavern* is given to Titan, which reconciles all matters. Now, let us read with the corrected word:

Didst thou never see Titan kiss a dish of melted butter? pitiful hearted Titan, that melted at the *sweet ale* of the *Sun.*

To this figure the Prince compares Falstaff,—who, after gaining and losing a booty; after a hard ride to and from Rochester; after fretting like a *gumm'd velvet,* enters, in a violent heat, *"larding the earth"* as he moves along, and—with *"a plague of all cowards",* vents his spleen at the Prince.

The transcriber wrote—*sweet tale*—the person who recited to him, not pronouncing *sweet ale* sufficiently distinct, carried the 't in *sweet* to the word—*ale.*

The Judean Apella may believe. My view is that a few clean strokes of Occam's razor would have helped Mr. Jackson no end.

It is generally held that the "corruption" of certain texts of Shakespeare —such as the early quartos of *Romeo, Merry Wives, Henry V, Hamlet* and others—is due to the fact that the earliest editions derive from manuscripts which represent something put together from memory by one or more actors. Few would be ready to reject this theory of origin for these plays, which were superseded by later, authoritative texts—*Hamlet* and *Romeo* in later quartos, *Merry Wives* and *Henry V* not until the publication of the 1623 Folio. It is indisputable that some of the sermons of Henry Smith were printed not from the author's manuscript but from shorthand ("charactery") versions taken down by hearers. The editor of Smith's sermons would consider this fact. The 1591 text of Smith's "Trumpet of the Soul", for instance, contains the sentence:

I wold giue all the goods in the world, that I might escape this dredfull day of wrath and iudgement, and that I might not stand among the goe.

The editor hardly needs to consult the New Testament to recognize that the shorthand expert has erred either in his hearing or in his transcribing, and that for "goe" we should read "goats".

Anyone, however, who sets much pen to paper knows that errors of this kind, "auditory errors", can be made by any not-necessarily-fatigued writer of longhand. However good a speller you be, you may by sheer carelessness write "I enclose a receit". You may go further and, because, while writing, you silently say the words to yourself, write an entirely wrong near-homophone: "I have pains in my insight".

The editor who finds such an error in an Elizabethan play will first think of memorial reconstruction by actors. He must not entirely rule out the possibility that the author has committed a nonsense. A compositor, hand-setting the play in type, will not set letter by letter but will memorize (almost invariably by ear) a convenient number of words and then pick out and put in his stick the type that may produce the wrong near-homophone. In *The Rambler,* number 87, 1751 edition, Johnson seems to have written that very few men who pass their lives among books "try their own Manners by Actions of Justice". The 1752 edition reads "axioms of justice". Again the "before their Approaches perceived" of 1751 (number 89) is corrected to "before their approach is perceived" in 1752. Here we need not blame actors, nor assume that Johnson dictated to an amanuensis. That he wrote the wrong words or that the compositor memorized and blundered is a more probable explanation.

When the First Folio compositor who was setting *Romeo and Juliet* found in his copy "For twas your heauen she should be aduanst" and himself set the words ". . . she shouldst be aduan'st", he obviously made a bungle because he memorized by ear. An undergraduate reading me an essay said something about "Macbeth's moving line, 'Wake Duncan with thy knocking; I would'st thou could'st' ". Another undergraduate, in an essay, referred to "sixteenth-century court-poets, Wyatt and Surrey, Sidney and Sussex" — another kind of error and, presumably, not relevant in this context.

Various knowledges are required of the editor of a text. The editor of Homer must know Greek. The editor of an Elizabethan play or sermon must know Elizabethan English. When an editor finds, in the play *A Looking-glass for London,*

> She that basht the Sun-god with her eyes,
> Faire Semele,

he will realize that the word *basht* does not describe an act of violence. Semele abashed the Sun-god and emendation is not demanded.

When Rosaline plans a revenge on Berowne, she says,

> So perttaunt like would I ore'sway his state,
> That he should be my foole, and I his fate.

Ignorance of a meaning for the word *pertaunt* has led editors to make what Dr. Onions, in his *Shakespeare Glossary,* calls "many conj."; but Dr. Percy Simpson, fairly recently, found the explanation of the word, a term from a sixteenth-century card game. Still more recently, however, an editor has permitted the *conj.* "planet-like" to stand in his text.

The well-bred editor will not, finding "Swits and spurs, swits and spurres" in *Romeo,* follow a recent writer in putting it among what he calls "a considerable number of misreadings", because the editor will know the spelling to be perfectly tolerable in 1599, and, even later, in 1607, when you may find, in Dekker and Webster's *Northward Hoe,* "Come Switts and Spurres! lets mount our Cheualls". When we read Mercutio's words,

> Crie but ay me, prouaunt, but loue and day,

we shall almost certainly be right to emend the line to

> Crie but ay me, pronounce but loue and doue,

but, having looked in the New English Dictionary, we shall not follow a recent textual critic in calling the word *provant* "nonexistent". When we find Romeo saying, in the "good" (1599) quarto, to Tybalt,

> I do protest I neuer iniuried thee,

we shall remember that "to injury" was a good Elizabethan verb and we shall not, perhaps, gallop too much apace to accept the reading *iniur'd* from the modernizing 1623 Folio, or *iniured* from the "stolne and surreptitious" 1597 quarto.

Again, and likewise in *Romeo,* Benvolio tells Lady Capulet,

> A troubled minde driue me to walke abroad.

There is no need to accept the modernized 1623 reading,

> A troubled mind draue me to walke abroad,

nor the corrupt 1597 line,

> A troubled thought drew me from companie.

The word *drive* (pronounced to rhyme with *give,* I suppose) can be paralleled in Spenser's

> The whilest at him so dreadfully he driue,

and again to emend is unnecessary.

There must sometimes be a doubt about a usage. In Dekker's *Patient Grissel* (1603), Walter says, after describing to the rest of the hunting party the beauties of the morning before they go out,

> Then sally not this morning with foule lookes.

The run of the whole passage suggests that we want the word *sully* rather than *sally,* and it is easy to imagine the compositor misreading a *u* as an *a,* or merely picking the wrong letter from his case. But when the Princess in *Love's Labour's Lost* (1598) says

> Now by my maiden honour yet as pure,
> As the vnsallied Lilly I protest,

and Hamlet (in the "good" 1604-05 quarto) says

> O that this too too sallied flesh would melt,

and Polonius later speaks of

> laying these slight sallies on my sonne,

it is hard to believe that we are not in the presence of an alternative spelling rather than a succession of errors.

If he believes that the first quarto of *Romeo* is the result of memorial reconstruction and that the second quarto represents Shakespeare's own manuscript (and, according to current theories, the matter is not as simple as that), how will he decide what kind of a blow Gregorie was to remember? The "bad" quarto reads *swashing,* the "good" one *washing.* There being strong sixteenth-century evidence for the existence of the word *washing* as a kind of blow, I should accuse of frivolity an editor who elected to receive the (easier) reading from the less authoritative text.

Old Capulet says (in the "good" quarto),

> euen such delight
> Among fresh fennell buds shall you this night
> Inherit at my house,

where the "bad" quarto offers *female buds.* Two recent conservative editors have differed from all their predecessors in accepting the word *fennel* and saying that it was regarded as an aphrodisiac. For myself I should feel inclined with extreme reluctance to read *fennel* and explain that the case for it was highly unconvincing, but that I didn't really think that the case for *female* was a particularly strong one.

Some of the errors of printed texts will arise from the compositor's failure to read his manuscript correctly. The emending editor will be unable to handle such a situation without a knowledge of the scripts used in the time of his text. When Titania speaks of the vileness of the weather and explains that

> The humane mortals want their winter heere,

the similarity of the *g* and the *h* in an Elizabethan hand makes the emendation of *geere* for *heere* not improbable. Many errors in an "old text" will doubtless arise from this inadequacy of the compositor. It is, obviously, absurd to edit one's text on the assumption that all, or even most, of the errors will have this provenance. When a sixteenth-century compositor sets a remark about the soul being *putrified* (for *purified*), it is unlikely that he misread the word in the manuscript. The editor will familiarize himself with all the obstacles which can be erected between his author's manuscript and the printed text which represents it. Many of these obstacles will be the result of the ordinary happenings of the printing-house of other days.

J. Cottrel appended to a book which he printed in 1659, "Parnassi Puerperium, or Some Well-wishes to Ingenuity ... By ... Tho. Pecke of the Inner Temple, Gent.", some verses:

THE PRINTER TO THE READER

> If you demand what kinde of fate there's in't,
> That Printers cann't be faultless when they print:
> One cause why this misfortune to them comes,
> Is by the multitude of *Individuums*
> Vs'd in Composing. What faults are slipt here,
> To curious Readers obviously appear.
> For which I pardon crave ...

It is not always as obvious, however curious the reader be, as Cottrel would suggest; I think also that one may be led astray if one is ready to lay the blame on the *Individuums* rather than on the printer himself. The curious reader should always remember that, when there is a book, Men have been At Work. If there is an error, it is because a compositor has made an error.

A character, Rooksby, in one play appears at one point as *Kookesbie,* and, in the same play, the words *vnterous, burdering, fortte, geust, forrh,* and *Lutheraus* come in place of *venterous, murdering, fortie, guest, forth,* and *Lutherans*. It is legitimate here to deduce carelessness in the compositor and inadequacy in the proof-reader, rather than a necessary illegibility in the author or tiresome behaviour among the individuums.

A small book of essays printed in 1579 asks, "Why shoulld Pate be vnpauned and the owner lyke to be imprisoned?" It is not difficult to guess here that the compositor wrongly set "Why should Pate", that the proof-reader spotted that it ought to be "Why should Plate" and marked the insertion of an *l* — and that the unlucky compositor inserted it in the wrong word.

The Kookesbie and other errors come from *When You See Me, You Know Me,* a hideously printed play of 1605 by Samuel Rowley about Henry VIII. A passage in the play runs:

> Why this is easie enough, heres passage at pleasure,
> What wretch so wicked, would not giue faire words
> After the foulest fact of Villainie?
> That may escape vnseene so easily,
> Or what should let him that is so resolu'd
> To murder, rapine, theft, or sacriledge?
> I see the Citie are the sleepie heads,
> To do it, and passe thus vnexamined.
> Fond heedlesse men, . . .

Henry is commenting to himself on the ease with which the men of the watch allow anyone to pass inadequately examined. There seems to be, as elsewhere in the play, no reasonable way of making sense of the punctuation. But, whatever the punctuation, the passage is nonsense. Sense can, however, be restored, I think, if we switch the two lines beginning "I see the Citie" and "To do it". Editors have been far too ready to transpose single lines in Elizabethan plays; but here the "I see the Citie" line comes at the bottom of one page and the other at the top of the next. I think that the error can easily have arisen from a muddle when the forme was being made up.

Many books provide examples of errors by their own lists of *errata*. I have been unable to trace an alleged example from a modern text-book of logic, "For *carnal connexion* read *causal connexion*" — but the preface to a recent collection of poems refers to "casual connexion" when the word desired is patently "causal". Romeo's father says that his son is

> So farre from sounding and discouerie,
> As is the bud bit with an enuious worme,
> Ere he can spread his sweete leaues to the ayre,
> Or dedicate his beautie to the same.

Many editors dislike the word *same* and accept Theobald's emendation, *sun*. The emendation is not strictly necessary and the ultimately conservative editor would be able to adduce many examples of the Elizabethan use of the word *same* without the unpleasant suggestion of twentieth-century commercialese ("Your favour of the 16th inst. to hand. With ref. to the same, we wish to inform your good self...."). But the emender could encourage himself with clear evidence that the mistake could be made, and was made, in Shakespeare's time. Gervase Markham's poem, *Devoreux* (1597), contains the lines

> Thou reasonlesse desire that makes men seeke
> To kisse the sunne, whilest fire doth them imbrace.

The lines are quoted (obviously with a manuscript copy having been made intermediately) in the 1600 anthology *Englands Parnassus* — but with a difference. The second line is altered to

> To kiss the same, whilest fire doth thee imbrace.

The fact that the two lines have been made totally meaningless is, one must suppose, irrelevant. Again, the list of *errata* at the end of John Sprint's *Cassander Anglicanus* (1618) indicates that on page 97 the words "afterwards the same" must be corrected to "afterwards the Sunne". Mr. Sprint, it may be said, informs the "good Christian Reader" that "there is great neede of thy patience in respect of the many slippes escaped in the Printing, and other alterations thereof, yet without the Printers fault or mine". He adds that he has corrected "the chiefe whereof" and offers a list of 119, four columns of them (read *salt* for *foote, purity* for *paritie, begge* for *begin, reuoke* for *reuolue, mutually* for *mystically,* and so on). The author and the printer both being faultless, one may wonder whose was the guilt. *Individuums* may, perhaps, be blamed.

Sir Walter Greg, it may be added, examining a presentation copy of Massinger's *The Emperor of the East* (1632), found that the author had made some manuscript corrections in the text. One of the errors corrected was the word "Constantinople", which the compositor had somehow contrived to set in place of "Courte".

The careful reader of the works of Shakespeare soon recognizes a number of his author's habits of mind. If he doesn't do it for himself, he may be guided by a multitude of counsellors. He can learn from the writings of Walter Whiter, Caroline Spurgeon and Mr. E. A. Armstrong that Shakespeare has a mental quirk which impels him to link together spaniels and sweetmeats and flattery and melting and other matters. When he reads, in Antony and Cleopatra,

> The hearts
> That pannelled me at heeles, to whom I gaue
> Their wishes, do dis-Candie, melt their sweets
> On blossoming *Cæsar,*

he will feel little hesitation in accepting the emendation of Hanmer's edition and reading the fourth word of the quotation as *spaniell'd.*

The curious emender will remember odd turns of phrase in his author. His brain will pigeonhole the fact that Boyet says

> This *Armado* is a *Spaniard* that keepes here in court,
> A Phantasime a Monarcho, and one that makes sport
> To the Prince and his Booke-mates

and that Holofernes, "the Pedant", says, also of Don Armado,

> I abhorre such phanatticall phantasims, such insociable and
> poynt deuise companions.

When, therefore, he finds Mercutio saying in the authoritative quarto,

> The Pox of such antique lisping affecting phantacies, these new
> tuners of accent,

he will remember that both Holofernes and Mercutio are talking of affected modes of pronunciation. It is likely, then, that he will, rather than go to the "bad" quarto for the reading *fantasticoes,* prefer to think that the compositor found in his manuscript "phantasīe" as a contracted form of *phantasime.* A probable parallel may be found in *When You See Me,* where Wolsey relates that his plans are going agley,

> Our trustie friend, the king of *France* is dead,
> And in his death, our hopes are hindred:
> The Emperour too, mislikes his praises,
> But we shall crosse him fort I doubt it not.

I imagine that Rowley's "foul-paper" manuscript contained the word "prōises" [=promises], misread as "praises". The manuscript of John Day's *Law-Trickes* (1608) must have contained the words īgrose [=ingrose, i.e. engross] and payting [=paynting]; but the compositor set them as "igrese" and "paȳting". The word "kisman" found for "kinsman" more than once in the 1599 *Romeo* would be similarly explicable.

A character in Nathan Field's *A Woman is a Weathercocke* (1612) says,

> Good Morrow to your honour, and all ioy
> Spring from this match, and the first yeare a Boy,
> I commend these two verses a purpose to salute your Honour.

I should guess that Field wrote, not "I commend" but "I conned", which the compositor misread as "comēd". As the reading "commend" can have a case (though it is a weak one) made for it, the safe editor would read "commend" in his text and discreetly offer his emendation in his *apparatus* or notes.

Shakespeare, we know, often uses a word only once in his writings; he may well prove often to be the coiner of a word. An editor should not be surprised to find words from other languages taken into Shakespeare's English.

When Boult says of Marina that "shee'le disfurnish vs of all our Caualereea, and make our swearers priests", most editors before Professor Peter Alexander have emended to "cavaliers". Professor Alexander recognizes the Italian word *cavalleria;* both he and Shakespeare knew better than most opera-goers and do not pronounce the word to rhyme with "drearier".

Juliet's father (in the "good" quarto) says that the County Paris is

> A Gentleman of noble parentage,
> Of faire demeanes, youthfull and nobly liand.

Someone was worried by the last word and the 1623 Folio reads "... Youthfull, and Nobly Allied", while the corrupt 1597 quarto reads

> a Gentleman,
> Of Princely parentage, youthfull, and nobly trainde.

There are other conjectures and Mr. Richard Hosley's recent and admirable "Yale" edition reads "nobly limb'd". I find it difficult to doubt that Shakespeare meant that the County was well connected, had noble *"liens de famille"*, was *nobly lien'd*.

Shakespeare could surprise editors in other ways. He would be ready, for instance, to use a word in a satirical manner. When Sampson says, in *Romeo,*

> Tis all one, I will shew my selfe a tyrant, when I haue fought with the men, I will be ciuil with the maides, I will cut off their heads,

the editor ought surely to be ready to accept that good-quarto reading
and not turn, literal-mindedly, to the reading *cruel* for *ciuil,* a reading
first found in a later (undated) quarto.

Shakespeare (like other Elizabethan authors) was happy to use the word
haviour — as, apparently, a normal word, not a conscious contraction.
Onions quotes five examples; Hamlet, for instance, speaks of

> the deiected hauior of the visage,

and when, in the 1599 quarto, Juliet says

> And therefore thou maiest think my behauior light,

most editors (with, I fancy, better excuse than most of them would offer)
improve the metre of the line by reading with the "bad" quarto, *hauiour.*
I, therefore, do not find it hard to believe that the odd word "mishaued"
has the right to stand in Friar Lawrence's

> But like a mishaued and sullen wench.

Here most editors seem to follow the "bad" 1597 reading *misbehaude*
=misbehav'd: baffled, apparently, by *mishaved,* the 1623 Folio compositor
made either an unhappy guess or an unhappy literal and set *mishaped.*

It might be thought that an editor could, by close study of the plays
believed to be set from an author's own manuscript, make many valid
deductions about the author's idiosyncrasies of spelling. The attempt
would, however, seem to be hazardous. The British Museum manuscript
of the play *Sir Thomas More* has in a page believed to be in the handwriting of Shakespeare,

> *Linc.* Shreiff moor speakes shall we heare shreef moor speake
> *Doll* Letts heare him a keepes a plentyfull shrevalty, and a made
>   my Brother Arther watchins Seriant Safes yeoman lets
>   heare shreeve moore
> *All* Shreiue moor moor more Shreue moore.

If an author will spell the word "sheriff" or "shreeve" in five different
ways in five lines, and the name "More" three different ways in one line,
can we draw deductions about his idiosyncrasies? In the same (? Shakespeare) section are the words "peace peace scilens peace" and much has
been made of the fact that the spelling "scilens" is found in a printed
Shakespeare text. But as thirty lines lower down, still in the ? Shakespeare
section, "silenced" is spelt "sylenct", and as the word "scilens" is found
also in a printed play by John Marston, deducers should proceed cautiously.

Recent (and cautious) investigations by Miss Alice Walker into the
spelling habits of some sixteenth-century and seventeenth-century compositors have shown that compositors are far more likely than authors
to allow after-ages to see their spelling idiosyncrasies, and that it is
highly dangerous to make statements about Shakespeare's spelling. Again,

another Museum manuscript, part of Sir John Harington's translation of
Ariosto, was actually used as printer's copy for the edition of 1591. Harington's spellings are almost totally submerged by those of the compositor.

Most modern editors of Elizabethan texts are aware (and a recent one
who seemed to take leave to doubt, has since cried *Peccavi)* that earlier
printers made corrections during the printing of an edition and would
cheerfully bind and sell sheets in all stages of correction. I once examined
(if I must renew the unspeakable dolour) twenty copies of a single edition
of a gloomy sixty-page pamphlet, *The Dolefull Euen-Song,* by Thomas
Goad, printed in 1623. Ten of the twenty copies were entirely different
from any other copy — each of those ten copies, I mean, was unique. What
is more, one solitary copy showed no fewer than 22 readings which appeared
nowhere else. The "correction" during printing was often not a single
act but a progressive process. Examination of a number of copies of Day's
Law-Trickes showed one "forme" in four progressive stages of correction.
The outer forme of the first sheet of the authoritative 1599 quarto of *Love's
Labour's Lost* seems to be found in three states. There are at least five
variant formes demonstrable in the first edition of *Pericles.*

Professor Charlton Hinman has perfected an amazing machine for the
collation of printed texts. He is engaged in the gruesome task of working
through the ninety-odd copies of the 1623 Shakespeare Folio in the Folger
Library in Washington, D.C. He expects to find no two copies identical.
(It may not be generally known, by the way, that Hinman has, with the aid
of his machine, spotted in the tragedies section of the Folio, examples of
corrected proof-sheets bound normally into three Folger copies. In other
copies the proof-reader's corrections have been carried out. Five proof-
sheets of the Folio are known; all are in Folger.)

Hinman is working on the Folio. Sir Walter Greg examined all extant
copies of the first quarto of *King Lear.* It is strange to find that, apparently,
no scholar, by eye or by machine, has attempted to collate *all copies* of
any other Shakespeare quarto. It is true that the corrections in Elizabethan plays seem to be almost always due to a press-reader without
reference to the author's manuscript. Thomas Dekker seems to have been
responsible for corrections in one of his plays; and I suspect that Day had
a personal hand in the correction of *Law-Trickes.* But, whoever was responsible, it is evident that until full collation of all known copies has been
made, an editor cannot know all he ought to know about his play. To
collate *all* seems to be necessary. If you omit one, it may turn out to be as
widely variant as the odd example of *The Dolefull Euen-Song.* The Cambridge University Library copy of the 1623 quarto of John Webster's *The
Deuil's Law-case* seems to differ, in one particular forme, from all other
examples; it displays the wildest variations and type has been moved
from one page to another in order to correct an apparently minor error.

An editor, when he has reason to believe that "correction" is due to no
greater authority than a proof-reader who has not consulted copy, may
sometimes be right in preferring an uncorrected reading to a "corrected"
one. The First Fisherman in *Pericles* (1609) says,

Why do'e take it: and the Gods giue thee good an't

(in other words, "Well, take it and good luck to you with it"), but in the un-corrected state the text is "di'e take it". The editor who wished to come as near as possible to the manuscript would feel fairly certain that the manu-script read *d'ye,* a strict monosyllable, not *do 'e,* two syllables. But the point is hardly worth pursuit.

The conservative editor will, I fancy, be cautious about permitting emendations which are necessary only for the reforming of the metre. The 1597 (authoritative) quarto of *Titus Andronicus,* for instance, prints, on one page, three lines thus:

> Are singled forth to trie thy experimens, . . .
> Beleeue me Queene your swartie Cymerion, . . .
> The King my brother shall haue notice of this,

and editors are accustomed to emend the lines to,

> Are singled forth to try experiments, . . .
> Believe me, Queen, your swart Cymmerian, . . .
> The King my brother shall have note of this.

Were I editing *Titus,* I should shrink from any of these emendations. We have all, I suspect, been brought up on a Shakespeare as metric-ally smoothed by Pope and other eighteenth-century editors, and we imagine, quite possibly, a greater regularity than we can confidently demonstrate from reliable early texts. We do not yet know the last thing about Elizabethan prosody (nor, I fancy, about Elizabethan punctuation).

Even though an editor might well think that Shakespeare in an early play like *Titus* may have indulged in occasional slightly irregular lines, he might be inclined to boggle at two consecutive ones. Old Capulet says ("good"-quarto text),

> And too soone mard are those so early made.
> Earth hath swallowed all my hopes but she,
> Shees the hopefull Lady of my earth.

Some would regard both the second and third lines as metrically deficient and the editor who does care to frolick in conjecture might fairly con-vincingly suggest that the manuscript from which the compositor was setting had a deficiency in the left-hand margin which had lopped off the first syllable of each line.

There is no attainment of perfection for an editor. Modern bibliograph-ical methods can tell him part of a story but not the whole story. We can have a collating machine; we shall never have an editing machine. Some *cruces* will always defy the ingenious emender. When a daily paper tells us of a painting of "a soldier with an automatic gun at the ready", any schoolboy can emend.* When the same paper tells in an obituary notice of

---

*But someone has obviously emended Professor Crow's example. "Gun" should read "gin."
Editor's note.

the head of an Oxford college that (I quote from memory) "he played little part in university politics, preferring to devote himself to his own particular brandies", I can be fairly sure that emendation is necessary. But, had I not been told by the writer of the article, I could surely never have known that I must emend "brandies" to "branch of studies".

•   •   •   •   •

I have deliberately abstained from footnotes and proper references in this paper, which attempts to be popular and occasionally frivolous. Those who desire to trace my quotations will not be hampered by my lack of precision. I have done no more than to point a finger at one corner of a very large map. I should have said much about the shining labours of such textual experts of this century as McKerrow, Pollard, Sir Walter Greg, Dr. Dover Wilson and Dr. E. E. Willoughby, Professors Peter Alexander, F. P. Wilson, Fredson Bowers and Charlton Hinman, Mr. Herbert Davis and Miss Alice Walker. I offer them all my apologies (but not, I trust, for misinterpretation). I offer them also my thanks for the light that they continue to shed.

As I must most thank Sir Walter Greg, so to him must I most apologize. His superlative *Principles of Emendation in Shakespeare* and *The Editorial Problem in Shakespeare* deserve to be followed by something better than this poor, ill-organized compilation.

Much of the material of this paper was gathered when, with a Smith-Mundt grant, I was working in the Folger Library, Washington, D.C. For the friendliness, assistance and hospitality I received from staff and fellow-readers in that, for me, best of all libraries, I can never adequately express my gratitude.

14

Conditions of Performance

John Russell Brown

On the Acting of Shakespeare's Plays

It used to be possible to quote Hamlet's advice to the players, point out that no extravagancies were to be used, and leave the rest to the actor to interpret in the tradition of his art, but today we are told that a completely new technique of acting is needed in order to present Shakespeare's plays in the spirit in which they were written. It is true that not all scholars are agreed on these matters, but even temperate opinion would say that the acting of Shakespeare's contemporaries was "fundamentally formal" and only "shaded by naturalism from time to time."[1] "Formal acting" has not been properly defined but it is generally assumed to be the opposite of "natural," and to make no attempt to give an impression of real life. "Poetry and its decent delivery" are considered "the only real essentials of Elizabethan drama."[2]

The study of Elizabethan acting is comparatively new, and although one book has already been published on the subject,[3] the time is hardly ripe for an authoritative and balanced treatise. But in the meantime, what guidance can scholarship give to actors and producers of Shakespeare's plays? It seems to me that the subject has been approached from an unfortunate angle and that, in consequence, the evidence has been distorted and misapplied. Briefly, I believe that formalism on the stage was fast dying out in Shakespeare's age, and that a new naturalism was a kindling spirit in his theatre. This naturalism was not what we understand by the word today, but, in contrast to formalism, it did aim at an illusion of real life. I want to reverse the statement which I have quoted above, and to say that Elizabethan acting aimed at an illusion of life, although some vestiges of an old formalism remained. If this is the case, our modern actors stand a better chance of interpreting Shakespeare than those who were his contemporaries, for the modern tradition is

From *Quarterly Journal of Speech*, XXXIX (1953), 477-484. Reprinted by permission of the Speech Association of America and John Russell Brown.

1. S. L. Bethell, "Shakespeare's Actors," *R.E.S.*, new series, I (1950), 205.
2. *Ibid.*
3. B. L. Joseph, *Elizabethan Acting* (1951).

based on a thorough-going naturalism unknown to Elizabethans. If the relics of formalism are properly respected, we can realize the illusion of life with a new delicacy and completeness.

To prove my point, I would have to examine in detail, and in chronological sequence, the whole *corpus* of Elizabethan drama.[4] All I can do here is to counter some of the arguments which might be brought against my statement, and present some evidence which I do not think has been sufficiently discussed.

The earliest advocates of formal acting base their statements on Elizabethan stage conditions; for example, after describing the circled audience and the gallants sitting on the stage, Mr. S. L. Bethell maintains that

> ... even with the abundance of make-up, scenery, and properties in use to-day, it would have been impossible for actors so closely beset with audience, to create and sustain an illusion of actual life, especially as they performed in broad daylight.[5]

Obviously these conditions made it difficult to sustain an illusion of real life, but nevertheless it was certainly attempted and achieved. Thomas Heywood in his *An Apology for Actors* (1612) writes,

> ... turne to our domesticke hystories: what English blood, seeing the person of any bold Englishman presented, and doth not hugge his fame, and hunnye at his valor, pursuing him in his enterprise with his best wishes, and as beeing wrapt in contemplation, offers to him in his hart all prosperous performance, *as if the personator were the man personated?*[6]

John Webster, the probable author of the Character of "An Excellent Actor" (1615), uses almost the same words; "what we see him personate, we thinke truely done before us."[7] John Fletcher was praised for giving opportunity for a similar illusion;

> How didst thou sway the Theatre! make us feele
> The Players wounds were true, and their swords, steele!
> Nay, stranger yet, how often did I know
> When the Spectators ran to save the blow?
> Frozen with griefe we could not stir away
> Vntill the Epilogue told us 'twas a Play.[8]

4. Previous work on dramatic technique has generally ignored the question of changing or developing methods; e.g., M. C. Bradbrook's pioneering *Themes and Conventions of Elizabethan Tragedy* (1935) explicitly states that "the development of the conventions has been only slightly indicated" because the subject was too large (p. 1).

5. *Shakespeare and the Popular Dramatic Tradition* (1944), p. 31. See also M. C. Bradbrook, *Themes and Conventions of Elizabethan Tragedy* (1935), pp. 20-21.

6. Sig. B4; the italics are mine.

7. John Webster, *Works*, ed. F. L. Lucas (1927), IV, 43.

8. F. Beaumont and J. Fletcher, *Comedies and Tragedies* (1647), Sig. f2v.

Prolonged death speeches must have made the simulation of real life very difficult – *The Knight of the Burning Pestle* ridicules their excesses – but Burbage evidently could achieve it; not only did the audience think he died indeed, but the dramatic illusion extended to the other actors in the scene with him:

> Oft haue I seene him play this part in ieast,
> Soe, liuely, that spectators, and the rest
> Of his sad crew, whilst he but seem'd to bleed,
> Amazed, thought euen then hee dyed in deed.[9]

From such descriptions, we must assume that Elizabethan actors aimed at an illusion of real life and that the best of them achieved it.

Even when it is accepted that the Elizabethan actors aimed at an illusion of real life, it is still possible to write down their acting as "formal." So Professor Harbage maintains that

> we are told *what* the actor did (in the estimation of the spectator), but not *how* he did it. Since the conventions of formal acting will be accepted as just while formal acting prevails, testimony like the above is nugatory.[10]

But this argument only "explains" the evidence if, on other grounds, the acting is known to be "formal." Even if this could be shown, it does not imply that our actors today should attempt formalism; the fact remains that an illusion of life was attempted. If our actors are more thorough in this respect, may they not be interpreting the plays in the spirit in which they were written?

The arguments for formal acting which are based on the plays themselves are difficult to answer directly; a detailed, chronological study is required. But one may point out, in general, that much of the evidence is taken from early plays, the famous Towton scene in *III Henry VI* (II.v) being always to the fore.[11] The formal, didactic arrangement of such scenes died out as the Morality plays, on which they seem to be based, disappeared also; it is not representative of the first decade of the seventeenth century. Direct address to the audience is another feature of Elizabethan plays which has been adduced in support of formal acting; such speeches have been thought to shatter "all possibility of dramatic illusion."[12] In this case, it is admitted that Shakespeare's plays do not provide any strikingly clear example,[13] yet even if such were found it would not be an unsurmountable obstacle to the simulation of real life on the stage. There was no gap between the audience and the stage in the Elizabethan

---

9. Quoted from Sir E. K. Chambers, *The Elizabethan Stage* (1923), II, 309.
10. A. Harbage, "Elizabethan Acting," *PMLA*, LIV (1939), 692; the evidence he quotes includes the verses on Burbage quoted above.
11. For instance, see B. L. Joseph, *op. cit.*, pp. 116-122.
12. S. L. Bethell, *op. cit.*, p. 86.
13. *Ibid.*, pp. 84-85.

theatre, and the actors did not address the audience as if it were in another world. There was a reciprocal relationship; the audience could participate in the drama as easily as the actors could share a joke or enlist sympathy. The very fact that it is difficult to distinguish direct address from soliloquy, and soliloquy from true dialogue, shows that the contact with the audience was quite unembarrassed. They shared the illusion of life.

The use of verse in Elizabethan drama has also been taken for a sign that acting was formal; for instance, of the sonnet embedded in the dialogue of *Romeo and Juliet* (I.v.95ff.) it has been said,

> Shakespeare's purpose can only be achieved if his audience is allowed to respond to the figures, the images, and the metrical pattern of these fourteen lines. There is no need to imitate dialogue realistically.[14]

But once more the development of new styles in writing and acting must be taken into account. When Jonson wrote *Timber,* the style of Marlowe already belonged to another age:

> The true Artificer will not run away from nature, as hee were afraid of her; or depart from life, and the likenesse of Truth; but speake to the capacity of his hearers. And though his language differ from the vulgar somewhat; it shall not fly from all humanity, with the *Tamerlanes,* and *Tamer-Chams* of the late Age.[15]

Once the idea of development is accepted, the question about Elizabethan acting ceases to be "Was it formal or natural?"; it is rather, "Which was the new, dominant style, the fashionable mode in which they would strive to produce even old plays or recalcitrant material?" I believe that the comparison between the style of Jonson's age and that of Marlowe's points in one direction only. It had become possible to speak the verse as if it were meant — as if, at that instant, it sprang from the mind of the speaker. Shakespeare's mature style has the best of two worlds; there is the eloquence, precision, and melody of verse, but there is also the immediacy and movement of actual speech. The dramatist has achieved the ideal which Puttenham sought in the courtly poet; he is now

> a dissembler only in the subtilties of his arte, that is, when he is most artificial, so to disguise and cloake it as it may not appeare, nor seeme to proceede from him by any studie or trade of rules, but to be his naturall.[16]

14. B. L. Joseph, *op. cit.,* p.129.

15. *Works,* ed. C. H. Herford and P. and E. Simpson, VIII (1947), 587. Jonson's editors date *Timber* between 1623 and 1635, XI (1952), 213, but Professor C. J. Sisson has shown that the work was probably composed as lecture notes while Jonson was acting as deputy for Henry Croke, the Professor of Rhetoric at Gresham College, in 1619, *TLS* (September 21, 1951).

16. *The Art of English Poesie* (1589); G. Gregory Smith, *Elizabethan Critical Essays* (1904), II, 186-187.

For such dialogue, a formal, rhetorical delivery would destroy the very quality which the poet had striven to attain. The new dialogue needed a new style of acting, and as the verse became less formal and declamatory, so did the acting. Both aimed at an illusion of life.

The internal evidence of the plays has only been hurriedly considered, for its proper treatment would need a greater scope than this present article provides.[17] I would like to turn, therefore, to one piece of external evidence which has been generally accepted as an indication of formal acting. This is the Elizabethan comparison between the actor and the orator. The *locus classicus* is the Character of "An Excellent Actor":

> Whatsoever is commendable in the grave Orator, is most exquisitly perfect in him; for by a full and significant action of body, he charmes our attention.[18]

A later statement is in Richard Flecknoe's *A Short Discourse of the English Stage* (1664) where it is said that Richard Burbage

> had all the parts of an excellent Orator (animating his words with speaking, and Speech with Action).[19]

The comparison between orator and actor is further testified by the use of the word *action* to describe the bodily movements of both artists. From this comparison several deductions might be made; first, the actor used a declamatory voice as distinct from a conversational; secondly, he observed the phrasing, figures, and literary quality of his lines in the manner laid down for the orator; and thirdly, he used "action" to enforce the meaning of his lines rather than to represent the emotion of a character. It has been suggested that John Bulwer's *Chirologia* and *Chironomia,* two books of manual signs for the use of orators, published in 1644, and written by a specialist in the teaching of the deaf, might represent the "actions" used on the Elizabethan stage.[20] But the deductions can go further, and the actor is sometimes endowed with the intentions of the orator; it is thought that he excited the emotions of his audience rather than expressed those of the character he was representing. Under such conditions a play would be a number of speeches, or, at best, a ritual, rather than an image of actual life. It has even been suggested that, in Johnson's words, an Elizabethan went to the theatre in order to

17. Asides, the arrangement of exits, entries, and other stage movement, the use of type costume and characterization are some of the more obvious details which need chronological analysis.

18. Cf. A. Harbage, *op. cit.,* pp. 701-702; B. L. Joseph, *op. cit., passim;* and S. L. Bethell, "Shakespeare's Actors," *op. cit.,* p. 202.

19. Quoted from E. K. Chambers, *op. cit.,* IV, 370. There has been some argument about the validity of this evidence; see A. Harbage, *op. cit.,* p. 695 and S. L. Bethell, "Shakespeare's Actors," *op. cit.,* pp. 200-201.

20. So B. L. Joseph, *op. cit.* Even as an indication of an orator's art the books are suspect, for Bulwer himself confesses that "I never met with any Rhetorician or other, that had pictur'd out one of these Rhetoricall expressions of the Hands and fingers; or met with any Philologer that could exactly satisfie me in the ancient Rhetoricall postures of *Quintilian."* (*Chironomia,* p. 26; quoted from Joseph, *ibid.,* pp. 45-47).

hear a certain number of lines recited with just gesture and elegant modulation.[21]

Obviously one cannot deny the comparison between actor and orator,
but this does not imply that the comparison held at all points; both artists
spoke before the people and used gestures—and there the comparison
might rest. Distinctions between the two were clearly recognized by
Elizabethans. So Abraham Fraunce, speaking of the orator, says that the
gesture should change with the voice,

> yet not parasiticallie as stage plaiers vse, but grauelie and de-
> centlie as becommeth men of greater calling.[22]

The distinction may not be flattering to the actor but that there is one is
plain enough. Thomas Wright's *The Passions of the Mind* (1604) makes
another distinction; the orator is said to act "really" to "stirre vp all sorts
of passions according to the exigencie of the matter," whereas the player
acts "fainedly" in the performance of a fiction "onely to delight" (p.179).
These distinctions are quoted by Joseph in his book *Elizabethan Acting*,[23]
but he does not seem to accept their implications.

Rhetoric was taught in Elizabethan schools and universities and "pronunciation," or delivery, received its due attention. Indeed, Heywood in
his *Apology* shows that acting was used as a means of training the young
orator (Sig's. C3ᵛ-4). If the arts of acting and oratory were truly similar,
here was an excellent "school" for actors. But the evidence clearly shows
that it was not; the scholars learned a style of acting which was suitable
for oratory but condemned on the public stage. So in *II The Return from
Parnassus* (c. 1602), Kemp, the professional actor, criticizes the scholar-
players as those who

> neuer speake in their walke, but at the end of the stage, iust as
> though in walking . . . we should neuer speake but at a stile, a gate,
> or a ditch, where a man can go no further. (IV. iii)

Kemp criticizes them because they did not act as men do in real life.
Richard Brome makes a similar distinction against scholar-players in
The Antipodes (1640):

> Let me not see you act now,
> In your Scholasticke way, you brought to towne wi' yee,
> . . . Ile none of these, absurdities in my house. (II.ii)

The gestures described in Bulwer's books for orators might well be among
the scholastic absurdities which Brome inveighs against. In Campion's
A Book of Airs (1601) the criticism is more precise:

21. B. L. Joseph, *op. cit.,* p. 141.
22. *The Arcadian Rhetoric* (1588), Sig. 17ᵛ
23. Pp. 54 and 58.

> But there are some, who to appeare the more deepe, and singular
> in their iudgement, will admit no Musicke but that which is long,
> intricate, bated with fuge, chaind with sincopation, and where
> the nature of euerie word is precisely exprest in the Note, like the
> old exploided action in Comedies, when if they did pronounce
> *Memeni,* they would point to the hinder part of their heads, if
> *Video* put their finger in their eye.[24]

Here, the orator's gestures are considered both scholastic ("deepe and
singular") and old-fashioned; clearly Campion thought they were not in
use in the up-to-date theatres in London.

Perhaps the distinction between actor and orator is most clearly stated
in Flecknoe's praise of Burbage which has already been quoted:

> He had all the parts of an excellent Orator...., yet even then,
> he was an excellent Actor still, never falling in his Part when he
> had done speaking; but with his looks and gesture, maintaining
> it still unto the heighth....

Flecknoe says, in effect, that though Burbage had the graces of an orator,
yet even then he was an excellent actor — in spite of some likeness of his
art to that of oratory.

Earlier in the same passage, Flecknoe had claimed that Burbage

> was a delightful Proteus, so wholly transforming himself into his
> Part, and putting off himself with his Cloathes, as he never (not
> so much as in the Tyring-house) assum'd himself again until the
> Play was done.

Such absorption in one's part has nothing to do with oratory; it is closer
to the acting techniques of Stanislavsky. It suggests that an Elizabethan
actor sunk himself in his part and did not merely declaim his lines with
formal effectiveness. A similar impression is given by the Prologue to
Antonio and Mellida (first performed in 1599) where actors are shown
preparing for their parts and speaking in the appropriate "veins." An
incidental image in *Coriolanus* implies a similar technique:

> You have put me now to such a part which never
> I shall discharge to the life. (III.ii. 105-106.)

In the event, Coriolanus was unable to do as Burbage did and wholly
transform himself into his part.

There are many extant descriptions of Elizabethan acting but the value
of this evidence is commonly belittled because it is written in the same
technical language as the criticism of rhetoric and oratory. So Hamlet's
advice to the players is dismissed as "a cliché from classical criticism,
equally applicable to all the arts."[25] Or again, it is claimed that

---

24. To the Reader; *Works,* ed. P. Vivian (1909).
25. A. Harbage, *op. cit.,* p. 690.

the poet has put into the mouth of his Prince nothing that conflicts with the directions normally provided by the teachers of rhetorical delivery.[26]

But the fact that the same language was used for acting and oratory does not mean that the same effect was being described. The language of criticism for all the arts was in its infancy and it was perhaps inevitable that acting should be dependent on the technical vocabulary of a more systematic art.

In attempts to interpret descriptions of acting, words and phrases from the criticism of rhetoric and oratory are frequently noted. But their use in another art may give an entirely different interpretation and may be equally pertinent. The phrase *imitation of life* is an example. It is basic to the conception of poetry as an art of imitation, a conception which was not generally understood by Elizabethans—except for Sidney—as referring to the poet's revelation of ideal and universal truth. The usual interpretation is seen in Sir Thomas Elyot's description of comedy as "a picture or as it were a mirrour of man's life"[27] or in Ascham's idea that drama was a "perfite *imitation,* or faire liuelie painted picture of the life of euerie degree of man."[28] The phrase is constantly repeated; Lodge, Jonson, and Heywood all claimed on Cicero's authority that Comedy was "*imitatio vitae, speculum consuetudinis, et imago veritatis.*"[29]

The idea of drama as a picture of life suggests a parallel in the art of painting, and here the meaning of imitation is much clearer. For instance it is implicit throughout the description of the pictures offered to Christopher Sly in the Induction of *The Taming of the Shrew:*

> —Dost thou love pictures? we will fetch thee straight
> Adonis painted by a running brook,
> And Cytherea all in sedges hid,
> Which seem to move and wanton with her breath,
> Even as the waving sedges play with wind.
> —We'll show thee Io as she was a maid,
> And how she was beguiled and surprised,
> As lively painted as the deed was done.
> —Or Daphne roaming through a thorny wood,
> Scratching her legs that one shall swear she bleeds,
> And at that sight shall sad Apollo weep,
> So workmanly the blood and tears are drawn. (ii. 51-62.)

"As lively painted as the deed was done" is the key to the whole of this description, and "life-likeness" or the "imitation of life" were constantly used in the criticism of the visual arts. So Bassanio exclaims when he finds

---

26. B. L. Joseph, *op. cit.,* p. 146.
27. *The Governor* (1531), ed. H. H. S. Croft (1880), I, 124.
28. *The Schoolmaster* (1570), *English Works,* ed. W. A. Wright (1904), p. 266.
29. *A Defence of Poetry* (1579), ed. G. Gregory Smith, *Elizabethan Critical Essays* (1904), I, 81; *Every Man Out of His Humour* (1600) III, vi, 206-207; and *An Apology for Actors* (1612), Sig. F1v.

Portia's picture in the leaden casket, "What demi-god Hath come so near creation?" (*The Merchant of Venice* III.ii. 116-117), or Paulina claims that her "statue" can show life "lively mock'd" (*The Winter's Tale* V.iii. 19). For an example outside Shakespeare, we may take Thomas Nashe's description of the floor of an Italian summer house; it was

> painted with the beautifullest flouers that euer mans eie admired; which so linealy were delineated that he that viewd them a farre off, and had not directly stood poaringly ouer them, would haue sworne they had liued in deede.[30]

The imitation of life was not the whole concern of renaissance artists, but their experiments in perspective and light were at first designed to deceive the external eye; their paintings were meant to look like real life.

When the phrase is used of acting, of performing in the "picture" that was the drama, it seems to carry the same implications of deception and the appearance of reality. So Webster praises the Queen's Men at the Red Bull for the acting of *The White Devil* in 1612 or 1613:

> For the action of the play, twas generally well, and I dare affirme, with the Ioint testimony of some of their owne quality, (for the true imitation of life, without striuing to make nature a monster) the best that euer became them.

So also, the imitation of life is praised in *The Second Maiden's Tragedy,* performed in 1611:

> thow shalt see my ladie
> plaie her part naturallie, more to the life
> then shees aware on.[31]

Shakespeare implies the same standards in the *The Two Gentlemen of Verona:*

> For I did play a lamentable part: ...
> Which I so lively acted with my tears
> That my poor mistress, moved therewithal,
> Wept bitterly. (IV.iv. 171-176.)

The idea of a play as a "lively" picture may be seen in Rowley's verses on *The Duchess of Malfy* (1623):

> I Neuer saw thy Dutchesse, till the day,
> That She was liuely body'd in thy Play.

Perhaps most important, the "imitation of life" is implicit in Hamlet's advice to the players: he says that the end of playing is

---

30. *The Unfortunate Traveller* (1594); *Works,* ed. R. B. McKerrow, II (1904), p. 283.
31. Malone Society Reprint (1909), II, 2015-17.

> to hold, as 'twere, the mirror up to nature; to show virtue her own
> feature, scorn her own image, and the very age and body of the time
> his form and pressure. (III.ii. 25-29.)

When he criticizes strutting and bellowing, he invokes the same standard:

> I have thought some of nature's journeymen had made men and
> had not made them well, they imitated humanity so abominably.
> (ll. 39-41.)

Hamlet is applying the same criterion to acting that Bassanio did to
Portia's picture—how near is it to creation?

The conception of acting as an imitation of life agrees with the other
evidence I have quoted, and suggests that Elizabethan actors aimed at an
illusion of real life. It does not explain *all* in the best renaissance painting
or the best Elizabethan acting, but it has an important place in the artists'
intentions. To describe the resultant art as formal is to deny this intention;
natural seems a more appropriate word.

There is probably some reluctance among scholars to admit that naturalism was a keynote of Elizabethan acting. Some critics would obviously
wish the plays to be acted in a formal manner. For instance, it is said
that a person in a play may be

> first a symbol, second a human being; .... [and the play itself
> can be] primarily an argument or parable, only secondarily forced,
> as it best may, to assume some correspondence with the forms
> and events of human affairs.[32]

This is an extreme case, but there are other hints of a fear that naturalism
would make Shakespeare's plays "smaller," that they would lose the
meaning and richness that had been found in the study. Formal acting,
on the other hand, seems to offer a declamation in which technical accomplishment could be appreciated and the argument or pattern of the
drama could stand revealed. But there is more than one kind of naturalism;
there is one for plays set in a drawing-room, and another for plays dealing
with kings and soldiers, inspired prophets, and accomplished courtiers.
A true naturalism would not disguise the high themes of Elizabethan
tragedy or the idealism of their comedy.

We have said that Elizabethan dramatists and actors imitated life, but
this does not mean that they tried to make their plays exactly the same
as real life; they did not labor, in Marston's words, to "relate any thing as
an historian but to inlarge every thing as a Poet."[33] Their plays were more
exciting and colorful, more full of meaning, than real life; indeed, compared
with them, "Nature never set foorth ... so rich [a] Tapistry."[34] Yet we may
say that they aimed at an imitation of life and the audience was encouraged

32. Written of *Timon of Athens;* G. Wilson Knight,*The Wheel of Fire* (1930), p. 274.
33. "To the General Reader," *Sophonisba* (1606): *Plays,* ed. H. H. Wood (1938), II, 5.
34. Philip Sidney, *The Defence of Poesie* (1595);*Works,* ed. A. Feuillerat (1923), III, 8.

to take all this as real while the performance was in progress. Within the charmed circle of the theatre, a new world might be accepted as real, and what they saw personated could be accepted as truly done before them.

George Chapman once wrote a preface to a play of his which had never been performed, and in it he tried to analyze what this play had missed. Unlike some critics, he believed that

> scenical representation is so far from giving just cause of any least diminution, that the personal and exact life it gives to any history, or other such delineation of human actions, adds to them lustre, spirit, and apprehension.[35]

A "personal and exact life" was what Chapman expected the actors to give to his play, and these words may serve to describe the naturalism which I believe to be the new power of Elizabethan acting. If actors in today's theatre wish to present Shakespeare's plays in the spirit in which they were written, they should respect and enjoy the magniloquence and music of the language, enter into the greatness of conception, and play all the time for an illusion of real life. They must constantly expect a miracle — that the verse shall be enfranchised as the natural idiom of human beings and that all of Shakespeare's strange creation shall become real and "lively" on the stage. Because the Elizabethan actor was capable of working for this miracle, Shakespeare, like other of his contemporaries, dared to "repose eternitie in the mouth of a Player."[36]

---

35. Dedication, *Caesar and Pompey* (1631); *Tragedies*, ed. T. M. Parrott (1910), p. 341.
36. Thomas Nashe, Preface to Robert Greene, *Menaphon* (1589); *Works*, ed. R. B. McKerrow (1905), III, 312.

15

The Audience

Alfred Harbage

The Behavior of Shakespeare's Audience

Modern American audiences are prodigiously well behaved; in public, at the theatre as at the dinner table, relish must wait upon refinement. We sit in decorous rows, scrupulously ignoring our neighbors, applauding generously and in cautious unison whatever is tolerable and well meant, suffering in docile silence whatever is feeble, dull, or foolish. The hiss, the catcall, and the boo profane no more the hallowed air. Whether such behavior amounts to an unwholesome supineness might be profitably debated; certainly it sets up a false standard for judging the Elizabethans.

Shakespeare's audience did not behave so well. Nevertheless, the boisterousness at the Globe has been overestimated. Sometimes such rowdiness and riot are envisioned that the performance of the play seems an irrelevance, a pitiable intrusion, while playgoing seems a hazardous occupation uninsurable at Lloyds, if Lloyds had then existed. Reminders are necessary. Pickpockets and prostitutes in an audience do not mean an audience of pickpockets and prostitutes—there is a law of diminishing returns. What we have really to decide is whether the criminal and unruly element in the audience was large enough and active enough to create a sinister atmosphere; whether the theatres were associated in the minds of Londoners with immorality, danger, and disorder. Initially, it seems improbable. Seeing a play is, after all, one of the more meditative pursuits and, considered *in vacuo,* neither an allurement to criminals nor an incitement to crime. Plays were the only unique attraction in the theatres. Theatregoing was voluntary; theatregoing was an expense. Elsewhere in London one could mingle with crowds and perpetrate grave crimes and minor misdemeanors without paying an admission charge.

In substantiation of the statement that "intrigues and other nefarious transactions" were carried on at the theatres and that "law-court and other records preserve the memory of both grave crimes and minor mis-

From *Shakespeare's Audience* (New York: Columbia University Press, 1957), pp. 92-116. Reprinted by permission of the Columbia University Press.

demeanours of which they were the scenes,"[1] Sir Edmund Chambers offers evidence like the following:

> The Middlesex justices had to deal with cases of stealing a purse at the Curtain in 1600, of a "notable outrage" at the Red Bull in 1610, or stealing a purse at the Red Bull in 1613, and of stabbing at the Fortune in 1613 (*Middlesex County Records,* I, 205, 217, 259; II, xlvii, 64, 71, 86, 88).[2]

Recognizing though I do that the above forms only a part of Chambers's list of offenses and that the effect of such a list is cumulative, I still submit it as my judgment that "so far as the external abuses of theatres go, the complaints of their bitterest enemies" are not "fairly well supported by independent evidence."[3] That legal offenses were committed at the theatres is in no need of proof — it might be taken for granted. That such offenses were committed at the theatres commonly, more commonly there than elsewhere, has not been proved.

We must remember two things: first, that the justices were allied in interest with those who denounced the theatres in general terms and were solicitous that every playhouse offense should be a *cause célèbre;* and, second, that court records by their very nature are memorials of the abnormal and apt to warp the view. In the law-abiding communities where most of us live, crimes are committed every day. Shakespeare and his theatre have been objects of such keen interest that court records have been ransacked. Cause for reflection is given us by the editor's preface to those same *Middlesex County Records* of which Chambers makes use:

> XIV. Choice of Documents. — It will be for the reader's satisfaction that I should indicate the various considerations that have determined my choice of documents for especial notice in the ensuing calendar. Throughout my labours I have been controlled by the opinion that I ought to call attention to those writings, which afford particulars, however minute, of new or otherwise peculiar information, likely to be in any way or degree serviceable to historians, biographers, students in any department of literary research, or artists in form and colour.[4]

Obviously, by the modern recorder as by the Elizabethan, although from a purer motive, playhouse crimes are not to be missed.

At least some attempt at statistical method should precede generalization. In the limited degree to which statistical method is possible in the present case, it argues for the law-abiding nature of Elizabethan audiences. If it is fair to remark that the Middlesex justices dealt with a crime at the Curtain in 1600, it is also fair to add that they dealt, so far as we know,

---

1. See p. 5.
2. Chambers, *Elizabethan Stage,* I, 264, note 5. Citation of these crimes at the Fortune is repeated in *ibid.,* II, 441.
3. See p. 5.
4. *Middlesex County Records,* ed. Jeaffreson, I, xlix.

with only one, whereas there were hundreds of acting days in the year with throngs of spectators in attendance each day. If we hear of a second crime in 1610, we should pause in breathless admiration at the stainless interval from 1600 to 1610. The least we can do is to view playhouse disorders against the general background. In 1600 a recognizance was taken for the cutting of a purse at the Curtain. If a true bill were found, this would be a capital felony. In the year 1600 the Middlesex justices must have taken many recognizances because 118 true bills were found, all for offenses committed elsewhere than in playhouses.[5] In 1610 a purse was cut at the Red Bull. In this year, in the jurisdiction of the Middlesex justices, true bills were found for 15 larcenies from the person besides 47 other larcenies (none committed in playhouses), not to mention housebreakings, burglaries, and horse-stealings.[6] In 1613 there was a stabbing at the Fortune, but elsewhere than at the Fortune there were 11 murders, 12 cases of manslaughter, 28 cases of assault and battery, 3 assaults with a sword, and 7 attacks upon officers. Seventy-two males and four females were sentenced to be hanged.[7] Evidently the playhouses were relatively safe.

The centers of criminality in Elizabethan London were not the playhouses but, as we might expect, the alehouses and taverns.[8] Such crimes as were committed at plays were the concomitant of crowds and bear no relation to theatres as such or to the mood of audiences or the type of people composing them. Wherever there were crowds there were pickpockets: "their gains lies by all places of resort and assemblies, therefore their chief walks is Paul's, Westminster, the Exchange, plays, beargarden, running at tilt, the Lord Mayor's day, and festival meetings, frays, shootings, or great fairs."[9] In the favor of pickpockets, the plays, we observe, share place with the Exchange, Paul's, and Westminster — the centers respectively of commerce, religion, and the law. In Dekker's *The Bel-Man of London,* churches, markets, and law courts are revealed to have been as popular with the fraternity as the theatres, while the parade of civic virtues in the Lord Mayor's pageants furnished a field day for the vicious.[10]

The number of prostitutes who attended the theatres and the amount of solicitation carried on there cannot now be determined. From the very nature of the case some doubt in the matter must have existed among the more scientific minds of Shakespeare's own day. However, a calm contemplation of the problem of sin, especially sexual sin, is not to be looked for among those who share that attitude of mind which we term puritanical: Elizabethan censors were prone to believe the worst. Encouragement to evil-thinking resided in the fact that the theatres did actually bring men and women informally together, in a sociable and even flirtatious mood. At a country performance we hear that "The people which

5. *Ibid.,* II, 282.
6. *Ibid.,* p. 296.
7. *Ibid.,* p. 297-98.
8. Judges, ed., *Elizabethan Underworld, passim.*
9. Greene, *Second and Last Part of Connycatching* (1591), in *ibid.,* p. 162.
10. In Grosart, ed., *Non-Dramatic Works,* III, 157-59.

were in the Roome were exceeding Joviall, and merry before the Play began, Young men and Maides dancing together, and so merry and frolick were many of the Spectators, that the Players could hardly get Liberty that they themselves might Act."[11]

London audiences would have been less buoyant—but not repressed. Gosson and Stubbes provide us with an interesting sequence. First, the arrivals:

> In the playhouses at London, it is the fashion of youthes to go first into the yarde, and to carry theire eye through euery gallery, then like vnto rauens where they spye the carion thither they flye, and presse as nere to ye fairest as they can.[12]

Then the assembled audience:

> you shall see suche heauing, and shoouing, suche ytching and shouldring, too sitte by women; Suche care for their garments, that they bee not trode on: Such eyes to their lappes, that no chippes light in them: Such pillowes to ther backes, that they take no hurte: Such masking in their eares, I knowe not what: Such giuing them Pippins to passe the time: Suche playing at foote Saunt without Cardes: Such ticking, such toying, such smiling, such winking ... that it is a right Comedie.[13]

And finally the departures:

> Than, these goodly pageants being done, euery mate sorts to his mate, euery one bringes another homeward of their way verye freendly, and in their secret conclaues (couertly) they play the Sodomits, or worse.[14]

Observe in the last line where description ends and conjecture begins.

To an observer like Thomas Nashe, playhouse flirtation seemed not only innocent but educational. In a pamphlet which sincerely flagellates lechery, Nashe approves of the young gallant who

> haunts Plaies, & sharpens his wits with frequenting the company of Poets: he emboldens his blushing face by courting faire women on the sodaine, and lookes into all Estates by conuersing with them in publike places.[15]

But beauty is in the eye of the beholder; compare with the following:

---

11. John Rowe, *Tragi-Comoedia: Being a Brief Relation of the Strange, and Wonderfull Hand of God Discovered at Witney* (1653), signature*.

12. Gosson, *Playes Confuted in Fiue Actions* (1582), in Hazlitt, ed., *English Drama and Stage,* p. 215.

13. Gosson, *Schoole of Abuse* (1579), ed. Arber, English Reprints, No. III, p. 35.

14. Stubbes, *Anatomie of Abuses* (1583), ed. Furnivall, New Shakspere Society Publications, Ser. VI, No. VI, p. 145.

15. *Pierce Penilesse, His Supplication to the Divell* (1592), in McKerrow, ed., *Works,* I, 210.

> Whosoeuer shal visit the chappel of Satan, I meane the Theater,
> shal finde there no want of yong ruffins, nor lacke of harlots,
> vtterlie past al shame: who presse to the fore-frunt of the scaf-
> foldes, to the end to showe their impudencie, and to be an obiect
> to al mens eies. Yea, such is their open shameles behauior, as
> euerie man maie perceaue by their wanton gestures, wherevnto
> they are giuen; yea, they seeme there to be like brothels of the
> stewes. For often without respect of the place, and company
> which behold them, they commit that filthines openlie, which
> is horrible to be done in secret; as if whatsoeuer they did, were
> warranted.[16]

That the writer, in his enthusiasm, is applying the word "filthiness" to
what is now called "petting" is apparent from an admission by a member
of his own party, who used the term in the more usual sense. "Not that
any filthynesse in deede," said Gosson, "is committed within the com-
passe of that grounde";[17] the bitterest critics of the theatres stop with
the charge that they are the scene of "privy and unmete contracts." A
modern writer seems to go further. Commenting on Dekker's statement
that the lords' room "by the iniquity of custome, conspiracy of waiting
women and Gentlemen-Ushers, are contemptibly thrust into the reare,
and much new Satten is there dambd, by being smothred to death in
darknesse," W. J. Lawrence says that since the lords' room is called the
"stages Suburbs" and since "Suburbs" must have been used in "a sinister
metaphorical sense," the cupidity of the players had induced them to turn
the lords' room into "a licentious rendezvous for the lower middle classes."[18]
But my dear Sir!

The English courtesan was not, as in several continental nations,
distinguishable by her attire. Thomas Cranley's *Amanda,* although belonging to 1635, describes a practice that probably prevailed throughout
our period:

> Like to a chamber-maid thou com'st to-day:
> The next day after thou dost change thy note;
> Then like a country wench thou com'st in grey,
> And sittest like a stranger at the play:
>   Tomorrow after that, thou comest then
>   In the neat habit of a citizen.
> The next time rushing in thy silken weeds
> Embroider'd, lac'd, perfum'd, in glittering show;
> So that thy look an admiration breeds,
> Rich like a lady and attended so:
> As brave as any countess dost thou go.[19]

---

16. *Second and Third Blast of Retrait from Plaies and Theaters* (1580), in Hazlitt, ed., *English Drama and Stage,* p. 139.

17. *Schoole of Abuse* (1579), ed. Arber, English Reprints, No. III, p. 35.

18. *Elizabethan Playhouse and Other Studies,* I, 30-31.

19. Quoted in Collier, *History of English Dramatic Poetry,* III, 411.

It is in the last of the above metamorphoses that we have our most detailed picture of a courtesan in an Elizabethan playhouse. Chaplain Busino of the Venetian embassy was accosted during a visit to the Fortune in 1617-18:

> Scarcely was I seated ere a very elegant dame, but in a mask, came and placed herself beside me.... She asked me for my address both in French and English; and, on my turning a deaf ear, she determined to honour me by showing me some fine diamonds on her fingers, repeatedly taking off no fewer than three gloves, which were worn one over the other.... This lady's bodice was of yellow satin richly embroidered, her petticoat of gold tissue with stripes, her robe of red velvet with a raised pile, lined with yellow muslin with broad stripes of pure gold. She wore an apron of point lace of various patterns: her head-tire was highly perfumed, and the collar of white satin beneath the delicately-wrought ruff struck me as extremely pretty.[20]

That this "elegant dame" was a courtesan seems likely, although Busino does not say so and it is impossible to know. If so, she was literally a bona roba such as would have added "tone" to the gathering. If courtesans assumed the attire of chambermaids and ladies, the neat habits of citizens and of country wenches in grey, they must have had a regard for the proprieties. We cannot take too seriously the tendency of the Elizabethan satirist to identify as a "punk" any young woman seen conversing with a man.[21] An amusing contradiction exists in the writings of those who called the theatres "An appointed place for Bauderie," for whereas they imply that all the women in the audience are abandoned, they also insist that "the most honest wife is the soonest assalted"[22] and seem quite concerned for the virtue of women who presumably have none to lose. We may safely conclude that solicitation in the playhouses would have been no more open than in London assemblies generally and that the disinterested spectator would have been either unconscious of it or accustomed to it. There is a great deal of justice in a retrospective defense of the theatres written after they were closed:

> though some have taxed our Houses unjustly for being the receptacles of Harlots, the exchanges where they meet and make their bargaines with their franck chapmen of the Country and City, yet we may justly excuse our selves of either knowledge or consent in these lewd practices, we having no propheticke soules to know womens honesty by instinct, nor commission to examine them.[23]

20. "Diaries and Despatches of the Venetian Embassy at the Court of King James I, in the Years 1617, 1618," *Quarterly Review,* CII (1857), 416.

21. See Dekker, *Newes from Hell* (1606), *Iests to Make you Merrie* (1607), and *Lanthorne and Candle-Light* (1609), in Grosart, ed., *Non-Dramatic Works,* II, 96, 292; III, 269.

22. *Second and Third Blast of Retrait from Plaies and Theaters* (1580), in Hazlitt, ed., *English Drama and Stage,* pp. 125-26.

23. *Actors Remonstrance or Complaint* (1643), in Hazlitt, ed., *English Drama and Stage,* pp. 261-62.

The afflictions most commonly associated with Elizabethan audiences are frays and riotousness. Two friends of the stage may be permitted to testify first:

> Whereas some Petitioners of the Counsaile against them obiect, they corrupt the youth of the Cittie, and withdrawe Prentises from theyr worke; they heartily wishe they might bee troubled with none of their youth nor their prentises; for some of them (I meane the ruder handicrafts seruants) neuer come abroade, but they are in danger of vndoing: and as for corrupting them when they come, thats false; for no Play they haue, encourageth any man to tumults or rebellion, but layes before such the halter and the gallowes.[24]

Nashe's sentiments are echoed by Henry Chettle:

> And lette [the ghost of] Tarleton intreate the yoong people of the Cittie, either to abstaine altogether from playes, or at their comming thither to vse themselues after a more quiet order.
>
> In a place so ciuill as this Cittie is esteemed, it is more than barbarously rude, to see the shamefull disorder and routes that sometime in such publike meetings are vsed.
>
> The beginners are neither gentlemen, nor citizens, nor any of both their seruants, but some lewd mates that long for innouation; & when they see aduantage, that either Seruingmen or Apprentises are most in number, they will be of either side, though indeed they are of no side, but men beside all honestie, willing to make boote of cloakes, hats, purses, or what euer they can lay holde on in a hurley burley. These are the common causers of discord in publike places. If otherwise it happen (as it seldome doth) that any quarrell be betweene man and man, it is far from manhood to make so publike a place their field to fight in: no men will doe it, but cowardes that would faine be parted, or haue hope to haue manie partakers.[25]

Chettle here affirms that personal quarrels are infrequent in the theatres, but he deplores with Nashe a type of disorder fresh in the minds of both because it had resulted in the closing down of the theatres shortly before their pamphlets were written.

The situation was as follows. Between the apprentices (who felt that London was theirs) and the young gentlemen placed out in service (who were insistent upon their social superiority) there existed a natural antagonism. At places where these factions met in numbers, trouble was apt to brew, especially in the presence of setters-on who would profit by a

24. *Pierce Penilesse, His Supplication to the Divell* (1592), in McKerrow, ed., *Works,* I, 213-14.
25. *Kind-Harts Dreame* (1592), in Ingleby, ed., *Shakspere Allusion-Books,* New Shakspere Society Publications, Ser. IV, No. 1, Part I, pp. 65-66.

melee. Chettle is an accurate observer, and a case of precisely the sort of thing he had in mind occurred in June of 1584. William Fleetwood, Recorder of London, reported that "nere the Theatre or Curten at the tyme of the Playes there laye a prentice sleeping vpon the Grasse and one Challes at Grostock dyd turne vpon the too vpon the belly of the same prentice."[26] Understandably, a fight ensued, and Challes with his mates, who "were litell better than roogs that took vpon theym the name of gentilmen," proclaimed that "prentizes were but the skomme of the worlde." On the following days the apprentices, already in a mood for "mutines and assembles," were whipped on by one Browne, "a shifting fellowe having a perrelous witt of his owne entending a spoil if he cold have brought it to passe." Browne's methods lacked subtlety: he bullied "certen poor boyes handicraft prentises" standing at the door of The Theatre and wounded one of them in the hand. Crowds milled about, the growing ill-feeling creating disturbances in various parts of London. Fleetwood's underlying sympathies must have been with the apprentices — a note of pride creeps into his report of the next episode: "my lo ffitzgerrold with a nosmber of gentilmen with hym at moor gatt met a tall yong fellowe being a pretize and strooke hym vpon the face with his hatt wherevpon my lo and his compane were glad to take a howse." All of this, be it noted, has to do with the theatres only in that it began in the fields nearby, where the belly of the sleeping apprentice tempted the toe of a shoddy young gentleman. The logical conclusion of the Lord Mayor and Aldermen was that The Theatre and Curtain should be pulled down.

In June, 1592, a feud flared up between the fellmongers of Southwark and the officers of the knight marshal. The officers had a warrant to serve upon a workman and, according to the depositions in the case, "entred the house, whear the warrant was to bee served with a dagger drawen affreyting the goodwyfe who satt by the fire with a young infant in hir armes." A touching scene! with the sanctity of hearthside and motherhood violated. The fellmongers must be avenged! Unfortunately for the drama, in attempting to rescue the arrested workman from the Marshalsea, the crusaders "assembled themselues by occasion, & pretence of their meeting at a play, which bysides the breach of ye Sabboth day giveth opportunitie of committing these & such lyke disorders."[27] The theatres in consequence were closed from June 23 to the following Michaelmas.

The disturbances just described are the only ones of the kind recorded in any detail; in both cases the theatres seem to have functioned as scapegoats. Chambers speaks of a document of 1595, wherein "the origin of yet another prentice riot was traced to the obnoxious performances."[28] But the document in question reads that plays and theatres

> wee verely think to bee the cheif cause, aswell of many other
> disorders & lewd demeanours which appear of late in young people
> of all degrees, as of the late stirr & mutinous attempt of those

<hr />

26. "Dramatic Records from the Lansdowne Manuscripts," in *Malone Society Collections*, I, Part II, 164-66.

27. *Ibid.,* p. 188.

28. *Elizabethan Stage*, I, 297.

fiew apprentices and other seruantes, who wee doubt not driew
their infection from these & like places.[29]

The traces are pretty faint, existing it appears chiefly in the interpretive
minds of the civic officials. We can take no more seriously a similar document of 1597, in which certain unspecified culprits arrested for unspecified
crimes are alleged to have said that the theatres were the meeting place
for their "mutinous attempts."[30]

It is little wonder that the Lord Mayor and aldermen made all that they
could of even the slenderest relationship between theatres and riots. They
could be certain that, in this matter at least, the Privy Council, ever on
the alert for rebellions, would lend an attentive ear. Assemblies were
dangerous, and audiences were assemblies: here was solid ground. But
after 1592 the enemy failed them, and in the absence of anything definite
the city fathers resorted to vague mutterings and reminders. They have
little meaning. Real disorders would have resulted in specific charges and
in real penalties. The evidence for habitual riotousness in Shakespeare's
audience becomes tenuous upon examination. It resembles the evidence
for rebelliousness in Elizabethan England generally. The popular upris-
ings of the time seem pathetically feeble and inadequate in view of the
seriousness with which they were taken and the cruelty with which they
were suppressed. If our two instances of riots about the theatres prove
anything, they prove, in their denouements, that audiences were normally
peaceful; otherwise the theatres would have been clamped permanently
shut.

On one score the Elizabethan audience comes off better than would any
modern audience under similar circumstances. Three disasters occurred
in the theatres with the spectators assembled. Each is described by an
inimical writer, yet in no case is there evidence of panic. On April 6, 1580,
an earthquake rocked The Theatre and the Curtain. Stubbes writes of
the spectators maiming themselves by leaping from "the turrets, pinacles,
and towres, wher they stood,"[31] but the fact appears to be that the only
casualties of the day were two children attending a sermon in Christ
Church.[32] On January 13, 1583, the galleries of the Bear Garden collapsed.
With a terrible zest, Stubbes describes how seven spectators were "killed
dead," some with their "heads all to squasht,"[33] but the injuries appear
to have been the result of the collapse itself. The spectators extricated each
other and bore the injured home. On June 29, 1613, the Globe burned to
the ground in a single hour, "and yt was a great marvayle and fayre grace
of God, that the people had so litle harme, having but two narrow doores
to get out."[34] It was a fair grace of God manifested in the self-control of

29. "Dramatic Records of the City of London: the Remembrancia," in *Malone Society Collections,* I, Part I, 76.
30. *Ibid.,* p. 78.
31. *Anatomie of Abuses* (1583), ed. Furnivall, New Shakspere Society Publications, Ser.
VI, No. VI, p. 180.
32. Chambers, *Elizabethan Stage,* IV, 208.
33. *Anatomie of Abuses* (1583), ed. Furnivall, New Shakspere Society Publications, Ser.
VI, No. VI, p. 179.
34. *Letters of John Chamberlain,* ed. McClure, I, 467.

Shakespeare's audience. The theatre was a deathtrap, filled to capacity for the spectacular first performance of *Henry VIII.*

No "frays" originating actually within the theatres are on record for Shakespeare's own period, but there are two earlier examples. In April, 1580, there was "a certaine fraye betwene the servauntes of th'erle of Oxforde and the gentlemen of the Innes of the Courtes."[35] We cannot expect much impartiality among the authorities when law students come in conflict with such "superfluous sort of men" as actors, and we are not surprised to hear of two of the actors being sent to Marshalsea "for committing of disorders and frayes appon the gentlemen of the Innes of the Courte."[36] In July, 1581, there was a similar quarrel between the Gentlemen of Gray's Inn and the some of Lord Berkeley's Men.[37] No detailed information about these conflicts survives, not enough even to prove that they originated in the theatres, although they probably did; but if similar records were plentiful, we might justly conclude that a potential enmity existed between actors and audience. Such records, however, begin and end with these two early examples.

Theatres were sometimes molested as part of the Shrove Tuesday bacchanalia of the apprentices, once quite seriously in 1617 when the new Phoenix was badly damaged; but these outbursts have no especial significance in dramatic history. Theatres, brothels, and similar places — conspicuous and public — attracted revelers in a suggestible mood. Churches and citizens' houses were naturally immune, and something had to be destroyed. Riotous collegians now detrolley street cars and destroy goal posts, expressing thus no general pique against public transit or the game of football. Only twice are we confronted with Elizabethan audiences in a vengeful mood, and each time the provocation was great. Having paid premium prices, the spectators were defrauded of their entertainment. In 1614 at the Hope, after John Taylor had advertised a contest of extemporal wit, his rival failed to appear.[38] In 1602 Richard Vennor, having promised a magnificent operatic display to be performed by gentlemen and gentlewomen at the Swan, exacted eighteenpence and two-shilling admission charges and then decamped with the proceeds — whereupon "the common people when they saw themselves deluded, revenged themselves upon the hangings, curtaines, stooles, walles, and whatsoever came in theyre way very outragiously and made great spoyle: there was great store of good companie and many noble men."[39] The ingenuous reader will confess that in the circumstances he might have gone into action himself; such episodes belong to no one age and obliterate the distinctions between "common people" and "good companie."

The onepenny patrons are apt to be particular sufferers from our preconceptions of Elizabethan theatrical behavior. W. J. Lawrence writes that "Attendants must have been placed at frequent intervals to keep

35. Minutes of the Privy Council, April-July, 1580, quoted in Chambers, *Elizabethan Stage,* IV, 280.
36. *Ibid.*
37. *Ibid.,* p. 282.
38. Adams, *Shakespearean Playhouses,* p. 333.
39. *Letters of John Chamberlain,* ed. McClure, I, 172.

each portion of the audience in its place during the performance, otherwise the Groundlings would have been unceasing in their invasion of the higher regions."[40] As doors have locks, so the lower gallery of Elizabethan theatres had spiked railings; otherwise there is no evidence whatever for Lawrence's supposition. The acting companies seem to have got along admirably without the aid of civil officers within the houses, and we hear of no employee functioning as "bouncer." The gatherers were sometimes, in fact, elderly widows holding their positions as a company obligation. A disposition to interrupt the performance, by the Gentlemen in Day's *Isle of Gulls* and by the Grocer's family in Beaumont's *Knight of the Burning Pestle,* is combated by the child actors with appeals for coöperation or capitulation to the demands. The adult actors were able men, but without power over an audience unless it was self-policed. A hint of such policing occurs in Dekker's *Guls Horne-Booke* (1609), and it comes from the groundlings. Twice while the gallant is making a nuisance of himself comes the cry "Away with the fool!"—once from the "rabble" and again from "all the garlike-mouthed stinkards."[41]

The gentry were no paragons of deportment. At court banquets following masks, the food was apt to be so "rapaciously swept away" as to send the tables crashing; and when the Knights of the Bath were entertained by the Lord Mayor at Drapers Hall in 1616, "some of them were so rude and unruly and caried themselves so insolently divers wayes but specially in putting citizens wives to the squeake"[42] that the party broke up without the serving of the dinner. Jonson's bitterest complaints are not at groundlings but at "caprichious gallants" such as "haue taken such a habit of dislike in all things, that they will approue nothing, be it neuer so conceited or elaborate, but sit disperst, making faces, and spitting, wagging their vpright eares, and cry filthy, filthy."[43] Dekker's Gull does not confine himself to a display of ennui; he exhausts human ingenuity in becoming an active pest: he arrives late, sits on the stage, laughs aloud during tragic scenes, tickles the ear of his neighbor with a straw, and makes a noisy exit at the climax of the play. Showing off on such a scale could not have been common even among capricious gallants; indeed Dekker himself clearly implies that to tarry too long before the anger of the "opposed rascality" was not safe. It is probable that both the upper and lower classes behaved best when each was under the surveillance of the other, before the audience was split in two by the system of high-priced and low-priced theatres. It is to the post-Shakespearean years that the complaints, never very numerous, about bad conduct in the audience mostly belong. It is then that plebeian audiences interrupted the players to demand the performance of old favorites instead of the play originally billed[44] and that the gallants in the private theatres displayed the contempt that enraged

40. *Elizabethan Playhouse and Other Studies,* II, 98.
41. In Grosart, ed., *Non-Dramatic Works,* II, 203, 250.
42. *Letters of John Chamberlain,* ed. McClure, II, 34.
43. *The Case Is Altered* (before 1609), Act II, Scene vii, in Herford and Simpson, eds., *Ben Jonson.*
44. Edmund Gayton, *Festivous Notes on Don Quixote* (1654), quoted in Collier, *History of English Dramatic Poetry,* III, 417. See also Chambers, "Elizabethan Stage Gleanings," *Review of English Studies,* I (1925), 186.

Ben Jonson. Yet even the audiences of these years were looked back upon as models of decorum in Restoration times.[45]

Considerable good feeling evidently existed between the acting companies and the public. We must not be deceived by the manner in which officialdom clung to the antique terms classifying actors as masterless men and vagabonds. Actors "walked gentlemen," and their prestige was great with the rank and file. An appropriate symbolism exists in the Elizabethan playhouse with its stage in the heart of the audience. The great actors like Tarleton, Alleyn, Burbage, and Kempe were respected and loved. Young gentlemen became hero-worshipers. Among the reforms claimed for the Caroline theatre was:

> the inveigling in young Gentlemen, Merchants Factors, and Prentizes to spend their patrimonies and Masters estates upon us and our Harlots in Tavernes [has ceased]; we have cleane and quite given over the borrowing money at first sight of punie gallants or praising their swords, belts and beavers, so to invite them to bestow them upon us.[46]

We cannot take too literally a statement like the following of 1638, but there is no evidence to refute it:

> they, he swears, to th' Theatre would come
> Ere they had din'd to take up the best room;
> Then sit on benches, not adorn'd with mats
> And graciously did vail their high-crowned hats
> To every half dress'd Player, as he still
> Through th' hangings peep'd to see how th' house did fill.[47]

A tendency to visit the sins of the children upon the parents has existed in stage chronicles, to note the behavior in theatres in the mid-eighteenth century and to conclude that if audiences could be thus one hundred and fifty years ago, then three hundred years ago they must have been twice as bad. But new times generate new abuses, and, for certain abuses of the Restoration and later theatres, there is no evidence whatever in the Elizabethan. The actors apparently were not pilloried for personal or political reasons, and the companies were not forced to view their forestage as a first line of defense against an embattled multitude.

If Shakespeare's audience was noisy before the play, silence prevailed when the play began. Prologues occasionally prayed for silence just as epilogues prayed for applause.[48] The only complaints that occur in number

45. James Wright, *Historia Histrionica* (1699), in Dodsley, *Select Collection of Old English Plays*, ed. Hazlitt, Vol XV: "Then the prices were small (there being no scenes), and better order kept among the company that came."

46. *Actors Remonstrance or Complaint,* in Hazlitt, ed., *English Drama and Stage,* pp. 260-61.

47. Davenant, Prologue, *The Unfortunate Lovers* (1638), in Maidment and Logan, eds., *Dramatic Works.*

48. See the prologues to *Alarum for London* (c. 1599); *Merry Devil of Edmonton* (c. 1602); and *Whore of Babylon* (c. 1606).

about disturbing sounds during performances refer to nutcracking.[49] If such sounds as this could provide the major annoyance (like coughing and paper-rustling now), a standard of silence may be inferred little inferior to ours. C. J. Sisson has remarked with unimpeachable logic: "Il n'est donc pas inutile de redire que les pièces de Shakespeare ont été écrites pour l'auditorie du Globe ... et que le populaire y'a payé le prix d'entrée pour les écouter et non pour se refuser à les écouter."[50] What indeed would have been the point of noisiness and inattention? The spectators who could afford to do so smoked during the performance and drank bottled ale during the intermissions. These ministrations to the body argue no deficiency of soul.

The satirical pamphleteers of Shakespeare's day have a buoyant and witty style. They hold no steel glass up to nature. Consider the following:

> What swearing is there, yea, what swaggering, what facing and out-facing? what shuffling, what shouldering, what Iustling, what Ieering, what byting of Thumbs to beget quarrels, what holding vppe of fingers to remember drunken meetings, what brauing with Feathers, what bearding with Mustachios, what casting open of cloakes to publish new clothes, what muffling in cloakes to hyde broken Elbows.[51]

This, as it happens, is a description not of a playhouse audience but of Londoners strolling in the walks of St. Paul's Cathedral. The playhouses stimulated the author to even more colorful efforts, and his junketing Gull has sometimes been taken to exemplify typical audience behavior. Not a single one of the foreign visitors, who have given us our most objective and trustworthy view of the Elizabethan theatre, has anything to say about disorder in the audience. On the contrary, "the best treat was to see such a crowd of nobility so very well arrayed that they looked like so many princes listening as silently and soberly as possible."[52] The playhouse was only the Fortune, but to Busino the audience seemed "a crowd of nobility." If his eyes descended to the pit, he must have seen nothing to deface the picture.

Shakespeare's audience gathered to enjoy an experience dearly bought with time and money. They wore their finest clothes.

> For few of either sex come thither, but in theyr holy-dayes appareil, and so set forth, so trimmed, so adorned, so decked, so per-

49. Collected in W. J. Lawrence, *Those Nut-Cracking Elizabethans,* pp. 1-9.

50. *Le Goût public et le théâtre élisabéthain,* pp. 52-53. The author has also pointed out (pp. 53-54) that a sympathetic hearing is given to poetic drama in modern English theatres where Elizabethan manners are paralleled: "Les galeries sont bruyantes encore, mais le silence descend devant le génie de l'actrice à la voix d'or, devant les beaux vers et les belles émotions d'une tragédie lointaine."

51. Dekker, *The Dead Tearme* (1608), in Grosart, ed., *Non-Dramatic Works,* IV, 50-51.

52. "Diaries and Despatches of the Venetian Embassy at the Court of King James I, in the Years 1617, 1618," *Quarterly Review,* CII (1857), 416.

fumed, as if they made the place the market of wantonnesse, and by consequence to unfit for a Priest to frequent.[53]

They enjoyed the opportunity to mingle with each other, and some of the men and women who had come singly flirted and made friends. The atmosphere was gay. But they had come to see a play, and the criminal or quarrelsome or persistently noisy were a threat to their enjoyment. Usually their enjoyment was unimpaired. A pleasing passage inspired by the audience of the Fortune gives us an idea of what Shakespeare saw in the Globe when *As You Like It* was performed and he peered outward through the misty eyes of old Adam:

> Nay, when you look into my galleries,
> How bravely they're trimmed up, you all shall swear
> You're highly pleas'd to see what's set down there:
> Stories of men and women, mix'd together,
> Fair ones with foul, like sunshine in wet weather;
> Within one square a thousand heads are·laid,
> So close that all of heads the room seems made;
> As 'many faces there, fill'd with blithe looks
> Shew like the promising titles of new books
> Writ merrily, the readers being their own eyes,
> Which seem to move and to give plaudities;
> And here and there, whilst with obsequious ears
> Throng'd heaps do listen, a cut-purse thrusts and leers
> With hawk's eyes for his prey; I need not shew him;
> By a hanging, villainous look yourselves may know him,
> The face is drawn so rarely: then, sir, below,
> The very floor, as 't were, waves to and fro,
> And, like a floating island, seems to move
> Upon a sea bound in with shores above.
> ALL.   These sights are excellent![54]

Little has been said thus far of the behavior of the audience as an audience—of the visible signs of its attitude toward the plays. The general topic of responsiveness will be treated in the following chapter, but a word about its external manifestations may be added here. The poet could read the fate of his play in the faces of the multitude. If fortunate, he could

> giue an Actor, Sorrow, Rage, Ioy, Passion,
> Whilst hee againe (by selfe-same Agitation)
> Commands the Hearers, sometimes drawing out Teares,
> Then Smiles, and fills them both with Hopes & Feares.[55]

---

53. Prohibition of William Harison, Archpriest, wherein English secular priests are forbidden to attend the theatres, March 9, 1617, f.25r. Manuscript in the Folger Shakespeare Library.

54. *The Roaring Girl* (1604-10), Act I, Scene i. Quoted in Adams, *Shakespearean Playhouses*, p. 279. The audience is similarly pointed out, though more briefly, in the Epilogue to *Eastward Hoe* (1605).

55. Dekker, Prologue, *If It Be Not Good the Devil Is in It* (1610-12), in Shepherd, ed., *Dramatic Works*.

Notwithstanding the huge mixed company and the daylighted theatres, spectators literally wept. Nashe speaks of the "teares of ten thousand spectators" evoked by the fate of brave Talbot,[56] and such allusions are not uncommon. When a bit of comedy struck home, the audience laughed in mighty volume: "in the Theatres they generally take vp a wonderfull laughter, and shout altogether with one voyce, when they see some notable cosenedge practised."[57] Concerning the general opinion upon their offering the actors were never kept in doubt. No mechanical aids to noisemaking appear to have been utilized by the audience, as in the eighteenth century, but if the play failed to please, it was uncompromisingly mewed and hissed. No worse affliction for playwrights could occur to their enemies:

> When they haue writ a sceene in which their brains
> Haue dropt there deerest sweetes, and their swoln vains
> Emptied their Cundits of their purest spirit;
> As they stand gaping to recieue their merrit,
> Instead of plaudits, their chiefest blisses,
> Let their desarts be crowned with mewes and hisses.[58]

But applause, expressed by hand clapping and cries of approval, was correspondingly hearty. "Player is much out of countenance, if fooles doe not laugh at them, boyes clappe their hands, pesants ope their throates, and the rude raskal rabble cry excellent, excellent."[59] "Excellent" is a fine word on the lips of a rabble. That Elizabethan applause was loud and enthusiastic is affirmed by many an angry moralist and many a sneering aspirant whose dramatic offering had failed to evoke it. Whatever may be said of the crimes and misdemeanors of Shakespeare's audience, it was never guilty of that final affront to art and artists—an attitude of apathy and indifference.

---

56. See p. 49.
57. Gosson, *Playes Confuted in Fiue Actions* (1582), in Hazlitt, ed., *English Drama and Stage,* p. 184.
58. Day, *Isle of Gulls* (1606), Act IV, Scene iv, in Bullen, ed., *Works.*
59. T. G.[ainsford?], *The Rich Cabinet Furnished with Varietie of Descriptions* (1616), in Hazlitt, ed., *English Drama and Stage*, p. 230.

16

Reception and Reputation

Joseph E. Duncan

The Revival of Metaphysical Poetry, 1872–1912

A great deal of attention has been given to the surge of critical interest in metaphysical poetry that followed the publication of Herbert Grierson's edition of John Donne's poems in 1912. Theodore Spencer and Mark Van Doren, for instance, have examined the revival of the seventeenth-century metaphysical poets from 1912 to 1938.[1] The achievement of these and of other recent critics has tended to obscure the earlier phase of the metaphysical revival. It has been assumed frequently that the revival began with Grierson's edition and that current theories about the sensibility reflected in metaphysical poetry were first presented in some essays by T. S. Eliot that appeared in the early 1920's. In reality, however, Grierson's edition and the reviews that acclaimed it marked the end of the first stage of the metaphysical revival. His edition was no doubt in part the cause of the enthusiasm about Donne that reached a scholarly climax in 1931 with the observance of the tercentenary of the poet's death. It was also the result of the increased interest in Donne's poetry and personality that began during the later decades of the nineteenth century. Similarly, Eliot's essays were not so much a new note as a sensitive formulation of ideas that had become familiar by 1912.[2]

During the earlier nineteenth century there was a gradually broadening acceptance of the metaphysicals both in Great Britain and in the United States. Then from the 1870's until 1912 there was a steady quickening in

From *PMLA*, LXVIII (September 1953), 658-671. Reprinted by permission of the Modern Language Association.

1. See their *Studies in Metaphysical Poetry* (New York, 1939). The work includes a bibliography of books and articles about the metaphysical poets for the years 1912-38. Spencer wrote that he believed that the list of 540 titles was "at least twice as long as a similar list would be for the whole nineteenth century" (p. 3). My investigation of the 19th-century criticism of the metaphysicals substantiates Spencer's surmise. More books and articles of a popular nature, however, appeared in the 19th century—when the metaphysicals were often regarded as quaint—than have appeared since 1912.

2. Some reviews of the Grierson edition appeared after 1912. I shall refer to these when they illuminate the whole earlier stage of the metaphysical revival and seem to belong logically to this earlier movement. It will also be necessary to quote frequently from Eliot's essays in order to show in what ways his ideas were anticipated during the first stage of the revival.

the tempo of the revival. This first phase of the revival may be dated from the appearance of Alexander Grosart's edition of Donne's poems in 1872, despite the editor's timid praise and apologetic assertion that "those whom these volumes may be assumed to reach are 'strong' enough to use them for literary purposes unhurt."[3] During the 1870's and 1880's Grosart also published editions of the poems of George Herbert, Crashaw, Marvell, and Cowley. In spite of his formidable "memorial introductions" and his wayward scholarship, his successful efforts — sometimes at his own expense — to "get these glorious old fellows into appreciative hands and hearts"[4] were a significant contribution to the metaphysical revival. He was the first of the three G's — Grosart, Gosse, and Grierson — who dominated this stage of the revival. Edmund Gosse's biography of Donne, published in 1899, climaxed a decade of excitement about the poet-preacher. During the 1890's there appeared editions of his poems by the Grolier Club and the Muses' Library, Augustus Jessop's biography of Donne as a religious leader, and numerous articles. Frank L. Babbott edited a bowdlerized American edition of Donne's poems in 1905. Wightman Fletcher Melton announced in 1906 that he was preparing a new edition of Donne's poems, but the work was never completed.[5]

During the late nineteenth century Francis Thompson and several American critics noted the increased interest in Donne and the other metaphysicals.[6] Grierson has recalled that he was interested in the textual problems of Donne's poetry as early as the 1890's.[7] Shortly after the turn of the century W. J. Courthope explained that "the revival of mediaeval sentiment, which has coloured English taste during the last three generations, has naturally awakened fresh interest in the poems of Donne, and there is perhaps in our own day a tendency to exaggerate his merits."[8]

Almost all the reviews of the Grierson edition referred to the Donne revival as a *fait accompli*. E. K. Chambers remarked that Donne's reputation "stands now higher than ever it did since a new manner of writing first displaced his." He credited the revival to "men of letters, caught by the essential poetry in Donne, and literary historians, discerning his unique influence upon the fashioning of Caroline verse." In a similar vein the *Spectator* critic asserted that "for the last fifteen years there has probably been more genuine interest taken in his poetry by lovers of

---

3. *The Complete Poems of John Donne, D. D.* (London, 1872), I, x.

4. "Intimate Glimpses from Browning's Letter File," ed. A. J. Armstrong, *Baylor Bull.,* XXXVII (Sept. 1934), 58, 61.

5. See his *The Rhetoric of John Donne's Verse* (Baltimore, 1906), p. 206.

6. See *Literary Criticisms by Francis Thompson,* ed. Terence L. Connolly (New York, 1948), p. 149; John Chadwick, "Poet and Preacher," *New World,* IX (March 1900), 48; Truman J. Backus, *Shaw's New History of English Literature,* rev. ed. (New York, 1884), pp. 143-144.

7. In a letter to the author on 31 Jan. 1951, Professor Grierson wrote that it had occurred to him during the 1890's that Donne's poems needed textual study similar to that he had recently given Aristotle's *Nicomachean Ethics* while studying at Oxford. He recalled that criticisms of Donne by Edward Dowden and William Minto had stimulated his interest in the poet and that he had first read Donne with real interest in E. K. Chambers' edition of 1896. He explained that he had been asked to write the article on Donne in *The Cambridge History of English Literature* because of his treatment of the poet in his *The First Half of the Seventeenth Century,* published in 1906. While occupied on these two studies, he said, he realized that both the canon and text of Donne's poems needed careful re-examination.

8. *A History of English Poetry* (London, 1911), III, 167-168.

English literature than during the whole preceding period since the days of Dryden." In another review Rupert Brooke rejoiced that "Donne's glory is ever increasing." Apparently already weighing the effect of the long-awaited Grierson edition, another critic announced that Donne had "suddenly become to many readers and lecturers the most exciting poet of his century."[9]

The increased interest in Donne was due not only to an awakened appreciation of his work but also to a growing concern with his personality. William Minto even maintained that "the admiration which Donne's contemporaries expressed for him as a writer was doubtless largely influenced by the impression which he made upon them as a man."[10] Most of the current conceptions of Donne are rooted in later nineteenth-century criticism. From the mass of Donne criticism there emerged three closely related conceptions of the man: Donne the rebel, Donne the mystery, and Donne the unique individual. These conceptions of the man are basic to the recent critical accent on the originality, complexity, and psychological realism of his work.

To regard Donne as a rebel was not unreasonable. Thomas Carew in his elegy on Donne had credited him with purging the muses' garden and with planting "fresh invention." Most of the earlier writers associated with the metaphysical revival failed to notice, however, that Donne's distinctive qualities were well grounded in Renaissance tradition. They pictured him as an isolated, morose hero, coldly and deliberately attempting to change the course of English poetry. Frederic Carpenter portrayed Donne as a "thoroughly original spirit and a great innovator . . . thoughtful, indirect, and strange," who "nurses his fancies, lives with them, and broods over them so much that they are still modern in all their distinction and ardour in spite of the strangeness of their apparel."[11]

Gosse's conception of Donne the rebel was both the most extreme and the most influential. Gosse attributed to Donne "the scornful indifference of the innovator, the temperament of the man born to inaugurate a new order of taste." He referred to "his austere and contemptuous silence" in regard to the other poets of the Countess of Bedford's circle and to the attraction of "the severe and repellent Donne" for Jonson. He also elaborated upon the idea that Donne "intentionally essayed to introduce a revolution into English versification." Reviewers of Gosse's biography embroidered the growing myth of Donne the tortured, tragic literary rebel. Arthur Symons, dwelling on Donne's "morbid state of body and brain and nerves" and the neurotic "preying upon itself of the brain," concluded that his strange personality led Donne to seek to "correct" English poetry and to "make a clean sweep of tradition." H. M. Sanders characterized Donne as an "intentional innovator" with an "iconoclastic impulse." Grierson helped to perpetuate the idea by pointing out Donne's scoffing challenge

9. Chambers, "The Poems of John Donne," *MLR,* IX (1914), 269; "The Poetry of John Donne," *Spectator,* CX (1913), 102; Brooke, "John Donne the Elizabethan," *Nation* (London), XII (1913), 826, and "The Poems of John Donne," *TLS,* 30 Jan. 1913, p. 13.

10. "John Donne," *Nineteenth Century,* VII (1880), 848.

11. *English Lyric Poetry, 1500–1700* (London, 1897), pp. lvii–lviii.

of the style of Petrarch and his emancipated and critical attitude toward religious problems.[12] American critics pictured Donne as a great rebel, but as a less romantic one. Paul Elmer More declared that Donne was like Socrates in arousing men from their apathy and that his originality was responsible for "one of the few real turning points in our literature." Melton investigated Donne's innovations in the use of the same words and sounds in arsis and in thesis and concluded that "while the verses of other poets rime in the middle or at the end, Donne's rime everywhere." John Chadwick alluded to Donne's "stiff-necked individuality" and William Vaughn Moody and Robert Morss Lovett stressed his strong new note.[13]

Donne's contemporaries did not regard him as a mystery. They fitted him into the ready-made Augustinian mold of the convert, as Izaak Walton's biography and many of the elegies show. But the later nineteenth century was fascinated by the seeming paradox between Jack Donne the gay libertine and Dr. John Donne, the somber dean of St. Paul's. Francis Palgrave expressed a common attitude in asserting that Donne was "almost equally fascinating and repellent." Another critic wondered whether Donne did not leave his own character as one of the riddles which he wished posterity to solve. Gosse described the poet as "this enigmatical and subterranean master, this veiled Isis whose utterances outweigh the oracles of all the visible gods." Symons referred to Donne as "a fascinating and puzzling creature whom each of us may try to understand after his own fashion."[14] Leslie Stephen mourned that "the real Donne . . . has disappeared, and just enough is revealed to make us ask for more." American critics were similarly enchanted with Donne the mystery. Chadwick characterized Donne himself as "the one riddle surpassing all those connected with his life," and another writer declared that "Donne drew around him a cloudy something which keeps him forever to himself."[15]

The emphasis upon the unfathomable mystery of Donne's personality led almost inevitably to a comparison with Hamlet. As early as 1880 Minto compared Donne, weak-willed, contemplative, and despondent, to Shakespeare's puzzling hero. Sanders declared that as W. E. Henley had written of Robert Louis Stevenson, there was in Donne "much Antony, of Hamlet most of all." Brooke later observed that "Hamlet, with his bitter flashes, his humor, his metaphysical inquisitiveness, and his passion, continually has the very accent of the secular Donne, but that he is an avenger, not a lover. To Ophelia he must have been Donne himself."[16]

12. Edmund Gosse, *The Life and Letters of John Donne* (New York, 1899), II, 330–334; Symons, "John Donne," *Fortnightly Rev.*, n.s. LXVI (1899), 735–740; Sanders, "Dr. Donne," *Temple Bar*, CXXI (1900), 624; Grierson, ed. *The Poems of John Donne* (London, 1912), II, xi-xvii, and "John Donne," *CHEL* (New York, 1910), IV, 226, 254.

13. More, "George Herbert," *Shelburne Essays*, 4th Ser. (New York, 1905), pp. 74–75; Melton, pp. 166, 206; Chadwick, p. 35; Moody and Lovett, *A History of English Literature* (New York, 1906), p. 144.

14. Palgrave, ed. *The Treasury of Sacred Song* (Oxford, 1889), p. 333; "John Donne and His Contemporaries," *Quart. Rev.*, CXCII (1900), 231; Gosse, *The Jacobean Poets* (London, 1899), pp. 47-48; Symons, *Fort. Rev.*, n.s. LXVI, 735.

15. Stephen, "John Donne," *National Rev.*, XLV (1899), 595–596; Chadwick, p. 33, and "Briefs on New Books," *The Dial*, XX (1 May 1896), 280.

16. Minto, p. 848; Sanders, p. 615; Brooke, *Nation*, XX, 825.

The conception of a mysterious Donne was closely bound up with the idea of Donne the unique individual. This idea involved a questionable faith in the confessional character and psychological realism of his writings. The seventeenth century did not share the nineteenth and twentieth centuries' high regard for uniqueness *per se,* and even the most flattering elegies on Donne did not represent him as a unique personality. Grosart, however, insisted that Donne was "an absolute and unique genius." Edward Dowden asserted that Donne's poetry could be understood most readily "through an interest in his life as an individual." He characterized Donne as "one who communed with lust and with death," who alternated between restless wandering and sullen brooding. One reviewer complained that in Clyde Furst's discussion of Donne in *A Group of Old Authors* "one misses those picturesque details with regard to Donne's personal peculiarities," indicating that no treatment of the poet was complete without the familiar emphasis upon his marked individuality. Stephen referred to Donne as a "strange complex human being" who had "extraordinary talents at the service of a most peculiar idiosyncrasy." Brooke helped to bridge the gap between the romantic criticism which dramatized Donne's eccentricities and the more recent tendency to distinguish sharply between the ordinary man and the man with a unified sensibility. In the United States F. E. Schelling contended that Donne "glowed with a strange light all his own" and interpreted his rugged metrics in terms of his "strange personality." Martin G. Brumbaugh considered Donne's personality "immeasurably precious."[17]

While earlier critics were dramatizing the personality of Donne, they were also engaged — although less consciously — in another important phase of the revival. They were forging new instruments for evaluating, interpreting, and enjoying metaphysical poetry, especially Donne's. These ideas, which were to attain their most significant formulation in some of Eliot's essays of the 1920's, were gradually developed and refined. The criticism of the late nineteenth and early twentieth centuries reveals the development of the conceptions of the merging of thought and feeling, psychological realism, and the modernity of the metaphysical poets. These ideas had become familiar before the publication of Grierson's edition of Donne's poems; since its appearance they have become increasingly popular. They were crystallized in Eliot's "The Metaphysical Poets," "Andrew Marvell," and "John Donne." In these essays Eliot held that much seventeenth-century metaphysical poetry reflected a unified sensibility that could relate disparate experience. He also explained that metaphysical poetry often expressed the truth of human experience in all its flux, complexity, and ambiguity, and declared that this earlier poetry was similar to much modern poetry.

17. Grosart, *Poems of John Donne,* II, xlvii; Dowden, *New Studies in Literature* (London, 1895), pp. 92–95; Clarence Child, "A Group of Old Authors," *MLN,* XV (1900), 62; Stephen, pp. 595–596; Schelling, ed. *A Book of Elizabethan Lyrics* (Boston, 1895), pp. xxii, lxviii; Brumbaugh, "A Study of the Poetry of John Donne," unpubl. diss. (Univ. of Pennsylvania, 1893), p. 98. See also Grierson, *CHEL,* IV, 244, and *The First Half of the Seventeenth Century* (Edinburgh, 1906), p. 160, and *The Poems of John Donne,* ed. James Russell Lowell and Charles Eliot Norton (New York: The Grolier Club, 1895), I, xxi.

The development of the idea of the close relationship between hard thinking and deep feeling in metaphysical poetry was possible only because during the nineteenth century critics gradually dismissed the notion that conceits and other displays of intellect were inimical to feeling. Criticism made a complete right-about-face and held that intellectual devices could play a significant role in the expression of sincere personal feeling. Conceits and wit were regarded with increasing favor during the first stage of the metaphysical revival. Grosart maintained that Marvell's conceits "sprung out of a vital thought or emotion or fancy." George Herbert Palmer defended Herbert's conceits as "cases of condensed imagination," and another early twentieth-century American critic asserted that the "cunning of the intellect is as necessary in verse as the display of emotions or sensibility."[18]

Grosart was one of the first critics to stress the quick transitions between thought and feeling in the work of the metaphysicals. To illustrate the thought-feeling relationship in Crashaw's poetry, he turned to Donne's familiar description of Elizabeth Drury:

> her pure and eloquent blood
> Spoke in her cheekes, and so distinctly wrought,
> That one might almost say, her body thought. . . .

"I have much the same conception of Crashaw's thinking," Grosart wrote. "It was so emotional as almost always to tremble into feeling." He pointed out that in Donne's poetry "the light of his imagination lies goldenly over his thinking." Praising Cowley's combination of "high thought" with "high imagination," he asserted that in his poetry "the thought is not only illumined with imagination, but made to pulsate with feeling, whenever and wherever the emotional is touched."[19] Grosart discovered in metaphysical poetry a dynamic process in which thought and feeling were merging into one another. He denied the contention of many earlier critics that thought clogged the flow of feeling and began to investigate the way in which thought and feeling fused and formed a new whole.

The idea of a vital interaction between thought and feeling in metaphysical poetry was gradually developed and defined. Symons wrote of Donne: "This lover loves with his whole nature, and so collectedly because reason in him is not in conflict with passion, but passion's ally."

---

18. Grosart, ed. *The Complete Works in Verse and Prose of Andrew Marvell* (London, 1872–75), I, lxvi; Palmer, ed. *The English Works of George Herbert* (Boston, 1905), I, 163, and "The Cloister Library," *The Independent*, LV² (1903), 1211.

19. Grosart, ed. *The Complete Works of Richard Crashaw* (London, 1872–73), II, lxx, *Poems of John Donne*, II, xxxix, and ed. *The Complete Works in Verse and Prose of Abraham Cowley* (Edinburgh, 1881), I, xcv–xcvii. During the 19th century the passage from Donne's "The Second Anniversary" about Elizabeth Drury's speaking soul and almost thinking body was quoted much more than any other lines from Donne, and it apparently came to be regarded as Donne's expression of a psychological and aesthetic theory. In the 19th century the concept of the union of thought and feeling throve in an intellectual climate particularly sympathetic to the 17th century. Thoreau, referring to Donne's words, "one might almost say, her body thought," affirmed: "I quite say it." Quoted from F. O. Matthiessen, *American Renaissance* (London, 1941), p. 98.

He added that in Donne's elegies "his senses speak with unparalleled directness." These observations anticipated Eliot's remarks about the desirability of a poet's looking into the cerebral cortex and nervous system before writing. Stephen believed that metaphysical poetry took its peculiar flavor from its "odd combination of syllogism and sentiment" resulting from the cramming of passionate outbursts into logical frameworks. Grierson similarly referred to the "intimate wedding of passion and argument which is the essential quality of the metaphysical lyric."[20] Meanwhile American critics were thinking along similar lines. Lowell praised Donne's ability to "open vistas for the imagination through the blind wall of the senses." In the 1890's Schelling called attention to Donne's contributions to the development of "intellectualized emotion" in the English lyric, and later Edward Bliss Reed supposed that Donne's mind, when deeply moved, transformed thoughts and feelings into apt conceits which were arrived at instinctively.[21] Thompson anticipated recent custom in finding this metaphysical blend of thought and feeling in the poets of his own time. Even in his own psyche he perceived a "sensoriness instinct with mind" and a "blended twilight of intellect and sensation." He asserted that Coventry Patmore was "like Crashaw for his power of fusing translucent abstractions by a white flame of passion" and that the essence of Alice Meynell's poetry was "feeling oozed through the pores of thought."[22]

Some of Brooke's critical essays strikingly suggest those of Eliot in their sensitive insight, style, and treatment of similar ideas. In his "John Donne" and "John Donne the Elizabethan," both inspired by the Grierson edition, he gave a preliminary formulation to ideas which Eliot was to treat more definitively. Like Eliot, Brooke stressed the relationship of the metaphysicals to the sensibility that pervaded much English Renaissance drama. He declared that "Donne applied the same spirit the dramatists applied to the whole world, almost solely to love."[23] Eliot later discovered the same kind of sensuous thought in both Chapman's plays and Donne's lyrics. Both poet-critics distinguished sharply between the ordinary man and the man with a particular kind of sensibility. Brooke wrote of Donne:

> The whole composition of the man was made up of brain, soul, and heart in a different proportion from the ordinary prescription. This does not mean that he felt less keenly than others; but when passion shook him, and his being ached for utterance, to relieve the stress, expression came through the intellect. Under the storm of emotion, it is common to seek for relief by twisting some strong stuff. Donne, as Coleridge said, turns intellectual pokers into love-

20. Symons, *Fort. Rev.*, n.s. LXVI, 741; Eliot, *Essays*, pp. 249–250; Stephen, p. 601; and Grierson, *CHEL*, IV, 245.

21. *The Writings of James Russell Lowell* (Cambridge, Mass., 1890), III, 171; Schelling, p. xxii; Reed, *English Lyrical Poetry* (New Haven, 1912), p. 241.

22. Everard Meynell, *The Life of Francis Thompson* (New York, 1913), p. 298, and Thompson, pp. 555, 188.

23. *Nation*, XII, 825.

knots. An ordinary poet, whose feelings find far stronger expression than a common man's, but an expression according to the same prescription, praises his mistress with some idea, intensely felt. . . . Donne, equally moved and equally sincere, would compare her to a perfect equilateral triangle, or the solar system. His intellect must find satisfaction.[24]

Eliot similarly explained that while "the ordinary man's experience is chaotic, irregular, fragmentary," the poet with a unified sensibility is always forming new wholes, even from such disparate experiences as falling in love, reading Spinoza, hearing the typewriter, and smelling the cooking.[25]

Both Brooke and Eliot pointed out that the metaphysicals were frequently able to view an experience both emotionally and intellectually at the same time. Brooke wrote: "And as Donne saw everything through his intellect, it follows in some degree that he could see everything humorously. He could see it the other way, too. . . . But while his passion enabled him to see the face of love, his humor allowed him to look at it from the other side. So we behold his affairs in the round." Eliot, discussing seventeenth-century wit as an "intellectual quality" often confused with erudition and cynicism, declared that it involved "a recognition, implicit in the expression of every experience, of other kinds of experience which are possible." Brooke's statement that Donne "could combine either the light or grave aspects of love with this lack of solemnity that does but heighten the sharpness of the seriousness" resembles Eliot's allusion to an "alliance of levity and seriousness (by which the seriousness is intensified)." Brooke also said of Donne that "it must not appear that his humor, or his wit, and his passion alternated." In other words, he was the exact opposite of some of the post-metaphysical poets of whom Eliot wrote: "They thought and felt by fits, unbalanced; they reflected."[26]

Brooke's and Eliot's conceptions of a metaphysical sensibility involve important similarities and differences. Both considered Donne as an intellectual poet because of the quality of his view, not because of intellectual subject matter. Both also devoted considerable attention to the interaction of the intellectual and emotional elements in his poetry. Although Brooke's theories were never completely defined, he apparently perceived in Donne's poetry a conversion of the emotional into the intellectual. "The pageant of the outer world of matter and the mid-region of the passions came to Donne through the brain," he explained. Eliot, however, found in metaphysical poetry primarily a conversion of the intellectual into the emotional.[27]

Very closely associated with the idea of a dynamic thought-feeling relationship was an increased emphasis upon the metaphysical poets'

24. "John Donne," *Poetry and Drama,* I (June 1913), 186.
25. *Essays,* p. 247.
26. Brooke, *Poetry and Drama,* I, 186-187, and Eliot, *Essays,* pp. 247, 248, 255, 262.
27. Eliot praised poets who had the "essential quality of transmuting ideas into sensations, of transforming an observation into a state of mind." He found in Chapman and Donne a changing of thought into feeling (*Essays,* pp. 246–249).

psychological realism, their fidelity to psychological process and to the flux and flow of complex experience. This conception of the expression of the whole truth of human experience, only dimly envisioned in the seventeenth century, grew out of the confessional temper of the romantic era; it later received one of its most significant formulations in Eliot's criticism.[28] During the later nineteenth and early twentieth centuries this growing interest in psychological realism was accompanied by an increased sympathy for a mixture of wit and seriousness. Grosart assured readers that there was nothing irreverent in Herbert's "serious punning" nor in the alleged "levity" of Crashaw's "The Weeper." Minto defended Donne's "quick shifting between jest and earnest," but regarded his wit as unconscious and sincere rather than as deliberate and playful.[29]

A full-blown theory of psychological realism in poetry, however, did not appear until the 1890's. It was concerned chiefly with the poetry of Donne and was closely bound up with the fabulous interpretations of Donne the man. Pointing out the particularity, complexity, and "abundance of mental movement" in Donne's poetry, Gosse asserted that the poet was, "in a totally new and unprecedented sense, a realist," and concluded that he was the "forerunner of modern Naturalism in English poetry." Similarly, Carpenter found in Shakespeare and Donne a "self-consuming subjectivity" and "passionate introspection" that did not again appear until the contemporary period.[30]

Several critics noted Donne's faithful expression of the flow of experience. George Saintsbury held that "for those who have experienced, or who at least understand, the ups-and-downs, the ins-and-outs of human temperament, . . . there is no poet and hardly any writer like Donne." Symons maintained that no one else "has ever rendered so exactly and with such elaborate subtlety every mood of the actual passion." He explained that Donne "forgot beauty, preferring to it every form of truth." Grierson developed more fully this contrast between a poetry of static beauty, which records an ideal passion recalled in tranquillity, and Donne's "strain of vivid realism," which "utters the very movement and moment of passion itself."[31] Brooke further stressed Donne's psychological realism, his faithful recording of "all the pitched battles, alarms, treaties, sieges, and fanfares of that extraordinary triangular warfare" of the body, the soul, and the mind. "Donne," he wrote, "was true to the reality of his own heart." Chadwick found that Donne's poems "give an impression of profound reality."[32]

Critical opinion slowly reversed itself. During the earlier nineteenth century critics had often held that complexity, obscurity, and harshness

28. Eliot wrote that the structure of metaphysical poetry is "sometimes far from simple — but that is not a vice (it is a fidelity to thought and feeling)." He referred to Donne's faithful expression of "emotion as he finds it, his recognition of the complexity of feeling and its rapid alterations ‛and antitheses," *Essays,* p. 245, and "John Donne," *The Nation and the Athenaeum,* XXXIII (1923), 332.

29. Grosart, ed. *The Complete Works in Verse and Prose of George Herbert* (London, 1847), II, lxvii, lxix, and *Works of Richard Crashaw,* II, lxiv, lxxvii, and Minto, p. 856.

30. Gosse, *John Donne,* II, 339–340, and Carpenter, p. lx.

31. Saintsbury, Introd., *The Poems of John Donne,* ed. E. K. Chambers (London, 1896), I, xxxii; Symons, *Fort. Rev.,* n.s. LXVI, 742–744; Grierson, *Poems of John Donne,* II, xxxiv–xxxv.

32. Brooke, *Nation,* XII, 826, and *Poetry and Drama,* I, 187; Chadwick, p. 46.

prevented sincere personal expression. By the first decade of the twentieth century, however, it was granted that these qualities reflected a fidelity to the truth of experience. With a penetrating insight into the change that was taking place at the turn of the century, Palmer wrote: "Indeed, I believe it will be found that the most lucid poets of our language are the least sincere, and that writers peculiarly intricate are often at the same time peculiarly sweet, tender, and veracious. What startling insights into reality has Donne! And how inevitably we distrust the lucidity of Pope! These metaphysical poets often seem artificial because they observe profoundly and speak individually." Defending Donne's knotty structure as evidence of his sincerity, Barrett Wendell declared that his lack of conventional grace made his poems seem astonishingly genuine. He observed that "they seem to express not fancy, but fact, and in a temper very like that of the art which modern cant calls realistic."[33]

While seventeenth-century metaphysical poetry was being interpreted in the light of new aesthetic ideas, Donne and his followers were coming more and more to be considered as among the foremost representatives of the modern temper. Turning back to the seventeenth-century poets with whom they had an affinity, poets and critics of the late nineteenth and early twentieth centuries insisted that the metaphysical poets were moderns — much more "modern" than most nineteenth-century poets. This movement began with the comparison of John Keble with Herbert and of Keats and Shelley with Crashaw, and it was given impetus by the persistent comparison of Browning with Donne. In 1900 one critic perceived significant similarities between literary movements at the beginning of the Jacobean period and at the beginning of the twentieth century. This tendency to compare seventeenth-century and modern poetry was later climaxed by Eliot's consideration of metaphysical poetry as closely akin to French symbolist poetry and as a desirable influence on contemporary English writers.[34]

Among the first recent poets to be compared with the metaphysicals was Thompson. Patmore credited him with qualities that would put him "in the permanent ranks of fame with Cowley and Crashaw." Geoffrey Bliss elaborated on the similarities in the work of Thompson and Crashaw, and Mrs. Meynell noted that Thompson enthusiastically responded to the cry to his time from the seventeenth century. Symons later emphasized Thompson's relation to Donne and to Crashaw and regarded Marvell's ode on Cromwell as a model for Thompson's "To the Dead Cardinal of Westminster."[35]

The chief stress was on Donne's modernity. Stephen, for instance, wrote:

33. Palmer, I, 155, and Wendell, *The Temper of the Seventeenth Century in English Literature* (New York, 1904), pp. 120–125.

34. *Quart. Rev.,* CXCII, 239-240, and Eliot, *Essays,* p. 250.

35. R. L. Mégroz, *Francis Thompson: The Poet of Heaven in Earth* (London, 1927), p. 113; Bliss, "Francis Thompson and Richard Crashaw," *The Month,* CXI (1908), 1-12; Alice Meynell, "Some Memories of Francis Thompson," *Dublin Rev.,* CXLII (1908), 172; Symons, *Dramatis Personae* (Indianapolis, 1923), p. 162.

In one way he has partly become obsolete because he belongs so completely to the dying age. But on the other side, Donne's depth of feeling, whether tortured into short lyrics or expanding into voluble rhetoric, has a charm which perhaps gains a new charm from modern sentimentalists. His morbid or neurotic constitution has a real affinity for latter-day pessimists. If they talk philosophy where he had to be content with scholastic theology, the substance is pretty much the same. He has the characteristic love for getting pungency at any price; for dwelling upon the horrible till we cannot say whether it attracts or repels him; and he can love the "intense" and supersublimated as much as if he were skilled in all the latest aesthetic canons. (p. 613)

Another impetus to this tendency to associate Donne with contemporary poets was given by members of a little group of Georgian poet-critics, including Brooke and Walter De la Mare. Brooke remarked that it was fitting that Donne "should be read in an age when poetry is beginning to go back from nature, romance, the great world, and other fine hunting places of the Romantics, by devious ways and *ambages,* to that wider home which Donne knew better than any of the great English poets, the human heart."[36]

De la Mare pictured Brooke himself as a kind of twentieth-century John Donne. He compared his own era with the Jacobean period and elaborated upon Donne's influence on Brooke's poetry. He considered Brooke, like Donne, to be "more self-centered than the rest, more analytical, and intellectual," more defiant of tradition, and closer to actual experience. After Brooke's death he said that "in his metaphysical turns, he reminds us not less — he reminded even himself (in a moment of exultation) — of the younger Donne."[37]

A few other poets were compared with Donne. Gosse suggested that Robert Bridges' "irregular lyrics" and Donne's new poetic forms were the products of similar aesthetic attitudes. Another critic declared that Bridges was the hierophant of "a tendency, which reminds us of Donne, to vary metrics, to study balance, and the use of resolved feet." As the interpretation of Donne continued, it was to be expected that an American critic would compare him to a distinctly American poet. Citing his "riot of the senses," Chadwick regarded Donne as "a Whitman born in Shakespeare's time."[38]

Before 1912 there was also the beginning of a tendency to compare the seventeenth-century metaphysicals with the nineteenth-century French symbolist poets. Gosse suggested that the symbolists' "endless experiments" would shed light on Donne's aesthetic aims, and Grierson maintained that both Donne and Baudelaire were "naturally artificial; for them simplicity would be affectation." No great emphasis was given to the resemblance until the 1920's, when Eliot found in the symbolists

36. *Poetry and Drama,* I, 188.
37. Walter De la Mare, "An Elizabethan Poet and Modern Poetry," *Edinburgh Rev.,* CCXVII (1913), 385, and *Rupert Brooke and the Intellectual Imagination* (London, 1919), p. 27.
38. Gosse, *John Donne,* II, 339; *Quart. Rev.,* CXCII, 240; Chadwick, p. 36.

"a method curiously similar to that of the metaphysical poets."[39] Although the relationship was dimly perceived and inadequately defined, several critics were interested in both metaphysical and symbolist poetry. The two styles tended to stimulate interest in each other. This fertilization was natural since there were basic similarities between the metaphysical and symbolist aesthetics.[40]

The forty years that preceded the Grierson edition were as important a part of the metaphysical revival as the forty that have passed since its publication. The portrait of Donne as a complex, enigmatic rebel, which has fascinated the post-First World War generations, was sketched in all its main outlines by Gosse, Stephen, Symons, Brooke, and others. In their own complex revolt against strict Victorianism these critics probably identified themselves in some measure with the Donne of their own creation. Moreover, the ideas about the thought-feeling relationships, the psychological realism, and the modernity of metaphysical poetry — ideas that have been spun fine by the "new" critics and other recent writers — were first developed during this earlier phase of the revival. The continuity in the revival of Donne and the metaphysicals gives added stature and perspective to this movement that Douglas Bush has called "the main single factor in effecting the modern revolution in taste."[41]

39. Gosse, *John Donne*, II, 339; Grierson, *CHEL*, IV, 249; Eliot, *Essays*, pp. 248-249, 255. For Eliot's comparison of the sensibility of Donne and Malarmé see "Note sur Mallarmé et Poe," *La Nouvelle Revue Française*, XXVII (1926), 524-526.

40. Both metaphysical and symbolist poets believed in a system of underlying analogies and in the relationship between man as microcosm and the universe as macrocosm. Both Baudelaire and Thompson, for example, were influenced by Swedenborg. However, metaphysical poetry is more closely related to symbolist theory than to symbolist practice. Even when the symbolists practiced what they preached, their techniques differed in several ways from those of the metaphysicals. The metaphysicals' approach to analogy was primarily intellectual and logical; that of the symbolists was primarily anti-intellectual and intuitive. The symbolists were chiefly interested in the secret affinities of all things with an individual soul, while the metaphysicals were more concerned with the relations of things to each other and to God. Nevertheless, some of the symbolists, particularly Corbière and Laforgue, employed metaphors, puns, neologisms, and other devices similar to those in metaphysical poetry.

41. *English Literature in the Earlier Seventeenth Century* (Oxford, 1945), p. 125.

III

TOWARD CRITICISM

17

Definition and Terminology

Harry Levin

What Is Realism?

In stating an issue which others will be called upon to face, propounding very sketchily the terms to which example must lend concrete significance, perhaps I should invoke the special protection of jesting Pilate—that patron saint of profound inquiries superficially pursued. For the problem that I have undertaken to pose brings up a number of incidental and ultimate questions which we could not stop for, even if we knew the answers, here. The most we can hope for is to focus, upon the main tendency of modern literature, the same sort of analytic and evaluative discussion that has already been concentrated upon the topic of romanticism. At the outset we can answer Pilate's question, positivistically and tautologically, by defining truth as the accurate correspondence between reality itself and a given account of reality. We are thereupon confronted by the question, "What is reality?" Since it cannot bear precisely the same significance for any two human beings, Carlyle declared that "reality escapes us." Let us concede the point; let it stand as *x*, the unknown element in whatever formulation we may reach. We come closer by approaching the problem from the other side—by sorting out the testimony that various witnesses have deposed, charting the general direction they seem to indicate, and tentatively calling this process of approximation *realism*.

But here another difficulty arises, insofar as some of them lead in opposite directions. For instance, the trend of modern thought toward empiricism, materialism, pragmatism, naturalism came to a head a

Reprinted by permission of the publishers from *Contexts of Criticism* by Harry Levin (Cambridge, Mass.: Harvard University Press, 1957). Copyright 1957 by the President and Fellows of Harvard College.

A paper presented at the Modern Language Association, December 30, 1948, under the title "The Definition of Realism." Published as the introductory article in *Comparative Literature*, III, 3 (Spring 1951), under the present title. From an appended paragraph, here omitted, the following sentences may be relevant: "In reducing our theme to a handful of historical and critical generalizations, I am aware that these preliminary comments do much less than justice to its large diversity and striking particularity; and, for this reason and others, I have greater confidence in the major part of our collective undertaking, which is embodied in the five essays that follow.... Our task ... is not conclusive but introductory; we merely wish to open a discussion which, we sincerely hope, others will broaden and deepen."

generation ago when two schools of philosophers all but agreed: the so-called "New Realists" and the so-called "Critical Realists." V. L. Parrington broadened the area of agreement by applying the term "critical realism" to the recent period in American literature. More recently, however, there have been accumulating signs of reversion to an older kind of realism, the scholastic kind that proceeded from the doctrine of *universalia ante rem*. Shunted between two extreme positions which claim the same title, we may turn from epistemology to etymology, and take the Latin root word *res* as our starting point. It is well to remember that the word contains, as it were, the thing. It is not altogether far-fetched to observe that, semantically speaking, *realism* is distantly connected with *real estate*. That quasi-legal connection is tangibly supported by the bonds of interest that tie so many novelists to the realistic tradition: by Balzac's sense of property, Dickens' inventories and Tolstoy's estates, Henry James' preoccupation with "things."

We lose little by confining our attention to that terrain of experience which philosophical sophistication would label "naïve realism." Its classic gesture occurred when Dr. Johnson kicked the stone. Characteristically it manifests itself by repudiating some manifestation of idealism. When publicists tell us to look at a situation realistically, we can be fairly certain that we are about to be asked to condone some piece of moral skulduggery. Instead of an appeal to principle, we are presented with a repudiation of principle. Thus the realistic attitude derives its meaning from the conditions of its application. Like the concept of liberty, it cannot exist in a vacuum; in the abstract it means virtually nothing. History defines our liberties in terms of the specific constraints they sought to overcome; free speech and free trade presuppose unjust imprisonment and arbitrary taxation, the *lettre de cachet* and the *gabelle*. The purport of President Roosevelt's Four Freedoms lay in their counterattack against four tyrannies. In this respect as in others, realism closely parallels the development of liberalism – another protean phenomenon which can only be pinned down by firmly grasping its varied responses to particular issues.

So much is clear, as Karl Mannheim has said: "Realism means different things in different contexts." Its would-be historians may well be deterred by the object-lesson of Lord Acton's uncompleted *History of Liberty*. But students of literature have the measurable advantage of working from texts as well as contexts, and Erich Auerbach's *Mimesis* has lately shown what stylistic analysis can do, when trained upon the descriptive techniques of selected authors from Homer to Virginia Woolf. When Professor Auerbach finds no formula for the presentation of actuality (*dargestellte Wirklichkeit*) in different languages at different epochs, he impressively documents our need for assuming a relativistic point of view. Possibly an absolute standard could be set up in the plastic arts, where the actual object can be directly compared with its artistic treatment. Yet even there the realism seems to be a matter of degree, varying with choice of subject and emphasis on detail. Even when we speak of "photographic reproduction," we cannot take for granted its objectivity. The very phrase *trompe-l'oeil* gives it away. The camera's eye is relatively less subjective than the eye of the beholder; yet it was photography which opened the way for impressionistic painting, which in turn has angled and composed and highlighted the art of the photographer.

Perhaps, like students of the diverging "romanticisms," we should pluralize our subject; but we should not, like some of them, allow divergences to obscure a fundamental impetus. Art has continually adapted itself to man's changing conceptions of reality—that is to say, his successive adjustments to society and nature. In a static culture, where his position is fixed and his worldview unchanging, expression is likely to be conventionalized. But occidental culture has been dynamic, and its arts have endeavored to keep pace with its accelerating changes. This distinction, which is broadly exemplified in the contrast between East and West, sharply emerged from the Iconoclastic Controversy, when Eastern orthodoxy prescribed a rigid convention while Western artists were free to move toward secularization, individuality, realism—from the symbolic, in short, to the representational. Now if, as Aristotle maintains, art springs from the interplay of two complementary instincts, μίμησις and ἁρμονία, there are times when the imitation of nature predominates and other times when it is subordinated to the imposition of a pattern. When Plato condemned poetry for its unreality, in the most idealistic and paradoxical sense of that term, Aristotle proposed a compromise in the name of poetic truth and higher reality, and thence handed on the doctrine of verisimilitude to the neoclassical critics.

Meanwhile the sphere of the probable expanded, while much that the ancients regarded as universal was seen by the moderns to be more limited. Against such limitations romanticism protested, when Wordsworth and Coleridge set out to write about lower ranks of society and stranger wonders of nature than classicism seemed willing to recognize. Not that the classicists excluded realism, but they relegated it to the comic stage; comedy was the *imago veritatis,* and the common man was no hero but a figure of fun. The medium that most completely mirrors the increasing stature of the middle class has been, of course, the major vehicle of literary realism, the novel. The novel originated, with a characteristic gesture, by repudiating its medieval predecessor; the picaresque tale overtook the knightly romance; and Cervantes, by pitting the daily realities of the developing city against the chivalric ideals of the declining castle, provided an archetype for all novelists and future realists. *"La rivalité du monde réel et de la représentation que nous nous en faisons"* —this might be a French critic's description of *Don Quixote.* It happens to be André Gide's description of what his novelist is attempting in *Les Faux-monnayeurs.*

Conversely, looking backward from Gide, we can see how every great novel has attempted—*mutatis mutandis*—to distinguish what is real from what is counterfeit. Defoe's narrations, he invariably assured his readers, are not fiction but fact; and Diderot pointedly entitled one of his stories *Ceci n'est pas un conte.* To convince us of his essential veracity, the novelist must always be disclaiming the fictitious and breaking through the encrustations of the literary. *"La vraie éloquence se moque de l'éloquence."* It is no coincidence that, from Rabelais to Jane Austen, so many realists have begun as parodists; it has even been argued, by Viktor Shklovsky, that parody is the basis of the novelistic form. We must not assume that, because it is polymorphous, the novel is formless; nor that writers very easily or spontaneously express themselves in a realistic mode. "No more literary school than the realists has ever existed," as George Moore, their leading British apologist, allowed. But we must first go — as Moore did — to France, where most of the problems of modern literature have been formulated, if we would track the critical usage down to its historical context. If we would trace it to its metaphysical chrysalis, we should have to look even farther back to Germany, to Schiller's *Über naive und sentimentalische Dichtung*, where antique *Realismus* is contrasted with the idealistic outlook of the romantics.

The earliest applications of the term that we encounter in the *New English Dictionary* are cited from Emerson in 1856 and Ruskin in 1857: the first is roughly synonymous with "materialism," the second with "grotesquerie," and both are decidedly pejorative. In France, on the other hand, the latter year marks the trial and vindication of *Madame Bovary* — a date as important for realism as the *première* of *Hernani* is for romanticism. The relationship between the two movements, as we acknowledge more and more, is continuous rather than antithetical. The realism of the romanticists has its dialectical counterpart in the romanticism of the realists, and it would be hard to say under which category we should classify *La Chartreuse de Parme* or *Les Misérables*. As early as 1826, investigation has shown, *le romantisme* and *le réalisme* echoed interchangeably through contemporary periodicals. But in the phrase of its journalistic fugleman, Champfleury, realism was one of "those religions in *-ism*" which came into the world in 1848. Its preparation had been technical as well as ideological; it profited from Daguerre's epoch-making invention, which entered the public domain in 1839, as well as from Houssaye's history of Flemish painting published in 1846. It reached its artistic climax when Courbet, whose paintings were rejected by the Salon of 1855, set up his own exhibition of these solidly executed studies in humble life, which he called his *Pavillon du Réalisme*.

The critic Duranty summed up objectives when he called for "the exact, complete, and sincere reproduction of the social milieu in which we live." His little magazine, *Réalisme*, coincided with a collection of essays under the same title, brought out by Champfleury in 1857. By then the catchword was becoming popular; even M. Prudhomme, the bourgeois incarnate, could sign his letters with assurances of his "distinguished consideration and realism." However, Duranty believed that the realists were too individualistic to establish a school, while Champfleury considered them transitional and expected them to give way before another movement in thirty years. Within half that time, in the eighteen-seventies, Zola was putting out manifestoes for naturalism. Where the older group had posthumously venerated Balzac, the naturalists paid homage to Flaubert; but he remained indifferent to schools and slogans. When Zola amiably admitted that these were devices to gain publicity for younger writers, he scarcely did justice to the grimmer implications of the newer term — the boundless distance between Robinson Crusoe's easy control over his environment and the crushed victims of Hardy's cosmic irony or Dreiser's chemical determinism.

Naturalism found its inspiration in science rather than art, its exemplar in Darwin rather than Courbet. In contrast to the accumulation of things, the jumbled catalogues of realism, its objects were meticulously selected and related through the chain of cause and effect. Seeking to complete the process of identification between literature and life, it conceived a book as a *document humain* and a play as a *tranche de vie*. But Zola's novels were experimental in quite a different sense from the physiological experimentation of Claude Bernard. Their twofold aim is reflected in their subtitle: *Histoire naturelle et sociale d'une famille sous le Second Empire*. As natural history, they demonstrate nothing; they simply illustrate the obsolescent theories of Zola's scientific contemporaries. Their social story is something else again, combining the exposure of bureaucracy with a plea for the underdog, each volume covering another field of documentation. Zola, writing in retrospect, gave voice to the political opposition that the Second Empire had tried to silence. Similarly in Russia, under the czars, in spite of censorship, suppression, and regimentation, writers were able to lodge their protest against an even more autocratic regime. Perhaps because Russians had to live a lie, as Turgenev suggested, their novels were so intensely devoted to truth.

Into the second half of the nineteenth century, realists and naturalists carried augmenting burdens of social criticism and humanitarian sympathy. The brothers Goncourt, for all their aristocratic tastes, furthered the advance of proletarian fiction; they urged, in the preface to *Germinie Lacerteux,* the right of the lower class to a novel of its own. The spread of democracy, the rise in the standard of living, the exploitation of typography and literacy brought pressure for further extensions of the literary franchise. Hence Harriet Beecher Stowe announced that *Uncle Tom's Cabin (or Life among the Lowly)* would treat a theme "hitherto ignored by the associations of polite and refined society." Politeness and refinement inevitably hold a vested interest in the *status quo,* which is loudly outraged by the depiction of uncomfortable facts and ignoble existences, and would outlaw them by invoking the ambiguous sanction of universality. Official and academic sponsorship, reducing the dynamic to the static, produce what William Dean Howells termed "a petrification of taste." Resistance is no less inevitable than movement, and repeats itself over the years. Just as Brunetière deprecated the naturalistic school, just as the disillusioned novels of the First World War were attacked by propagandists for the Second, so the hired moralists of *Life* magazine have latterly been editorializing against *From Here to Eternity* and *The Naked and the Dead.*

Nonetheless realism, heralded by romanticism and continued by naturalism, has been the animating current of nineteenth-century literature. Today it no longer operates as an *avant-garde;* it has acquired tradition and even academies. Watchwords continue to become outmoded, and novelties must be rediscovered again and again; the naturists supersede the naturalists and the verists yield to self-proclaimed veritists; and yet the real thing seems even more remote than before. Can it be that this

progression, which has moved on so rapidly from generation to generation, is slowing down to an impasse? The next step, to judge from *sur-
réalisme* (or super-realism), seems to be less a new projection of the old
realism than a sharp reaction against it—against representation in favor
of symbolism. Such landmarks as Joyce's *Ulysses,* pointing in two directions, lead forward—or is it backward?—via psychology toward fantasy
and myth. The technological obsolescence of the novel itself is predictable
in an era when fiction can hardly keep up with fact, when the reporter
turns novelist and the novelist turns reporter, when the instinct for
imitation is more efficiently satisfied by journalism, radio, film, and
above all television. Within the abstracted realm now left to the purer
arts, it may be that the instinct for harmony—for order, degree, and
arrangement—will again prevail.

Whatever happens is bound to register the adaptation to change, but the
quality of change may prove so far-reaching as to undermine the tendencies upon which realism has been grounded: a democratic attitude
toward society, an experimental attitude toward nature. The forces that
work against social mobility and scientific inquiry are those that steer
writers back into the province of convention. Much of the writing that
confronts us, at this midpoint of the twentieth century, seems transitional in character: conventional in pattern, realistic in detail. Yet an
art which must submit itself, either to production codes or party lines,
is basically unrealistic. Witness, on the one hand, the Hollywood cinema.
And, on the other, the neo-Marxist slogan of "socialist realism" is, in the
light of historical definition, a contradiction in terms. The role of the
great realists—as who but Gorky pointed out?—has been to transcend
their own class, to criticize the bourgeoisie. It does not necessarily follow
that their successors ought to panegyrize the proletariat. Middle-class
culture, with all its faults, has had its virtue—the redeeming virtue of
self-criticism. *"Kunst wird Kritik,"* Thomas Mann has lately remarked, and
the bourgeois novel is nothing if not critical. It may have told the whole
truth very rarely, and included many other things than the truth; but
it has kept open the question "What is truth?" in the teeth of dogmas and
systems that strive to close it.

18

Literature and Biography

C. K. Hyder

Wilkie Collins and *The Woman in White*

Inscribed on a tombstone in Kensal Green Cemetery are the following words: "In memory of Wilkie Collins, author of 'The Woman in White' and other works of fiction." This inscription, written (as his will shows) by Collins himself, pays tribute to the book which probably stands highest among his works in the esteem of his readers.

No other name is marked on that stone, but with Collins lies buried Caroline Elizabeth Graves,[1] who died in June, 1895, at 24 Newman Street, aged sixty-one, apparently the widow of a George Robert Graves.[2] After Mrs. Graves's death Collins's grave was for a time under the care of Martha Rudd.[3] These two women, Mrs. Graves and Martha Rudd, had shared Collins's bequest. To Mrs. Graves, Collins left his "gold studs and gold sleeve links" and some furniture, £200, and one moiety of the income from his estate; to Martha Rudd his watch and chain, £200, and a moiety of the income from his estate.[4] After the death of Mrs. Graves, her share of the income was to pass to "her daughter," Elizabeth Harriet. In the record of her marriage (dated early in 1878) Elizabeth Harriet, called "Harriette Elizabeth Laura Graves," gave her age as 24, so that obviously she was born about 1854. The heroine of *The Woman in White* may, therefore, have been named after her. One cannot be entirely certain about her exact relationship to Collins: was she more than a foster daughter?[5] After the death of Martha Rudd, her moiety of the estate was to go to the three children whom Collins acknowledges as his own: Marian, born at

From *PMLA*, LIV (March 1939), 297-303. Reprinted by permission of the Modern Language Association.

1. Private information.
2. Entry of death at Somerset House.
3. Private information.
4. Wilkie Collins's will.
5. Unpublished portions of Dickens's letters to Collins (written in 1861) apparently refer to the "Dutter" and "the Dutter's mama." A distant relative of the family into which Elizabeth Harriet (incidentally, Harriet was the name of Collins's mother) married mentions "Wilkie Collins's daughter." An unpublished letter written by Collins in 1880 appears to mention "Mama." Hall Caine, on the other hand, *My Story* (New York, 1909), p. 333, speaks of Collins's "affectionate adopted daughter."

33 Balsover Street, Portland Place, July 4, 1869; Harriet Constance, born in the same place on May 14, 1871; William Charles, born at 10 Taunton Place, on December 25, 1874. Martha Rudd and her children, at least for some time after Collins's death, passed under the name of Dawson.[6]

In a biography of his father, the artist Millais, who was a friend of Wilkie Collins, John G. Millais declares that a scene in *The Woman in White* — the scene which Charles Dickens considered one of the two most dramatic descriptions he could recall[7] — was based on experience.[8] According to Millais, as his father and Wilkie and Charles Collins were walking one night, they saw a beautiful young woman dressed in white approach, hesitate as if in distress, and walk on, to be followed by Wilkie Collins. Collins later told his companions that the young woman, from a good family, had fallen into the power of an unscrupulous man who had subjected her to threats and "mesmeric influences" of an alarming nature. Kate Dickens, who married Charles Collins, Wilkie's brother, is said to have believed that it was the fugitive in white who afterwards lived with Collins.[9] If this belief was correct, the young woman was Caroline Elizabeth Graves, whose name is listed in London directories under the same address as Collins's. It is noteworthy, if not especially significant, that *The Fallen Leaves,* one of Collins's most daring books (and one which incurred considerable censure because of the Socialist hero's befriending and finally marrying a girl of the streets), was dedicated "To Caroline."[10]

Though Millais's attempt to connect fact and fiction should be regarded with some skepticism, Collins's emotional experience may have affected his writing. More than once he introduces a character whose allegiance in love is divided.[11] The facts about his private life, hardly more than hinted at in print, must have been known in some circles. Not long after his death, when some friends proposed a memorial in his honor, in St. Paul's, the Dean and the Chapter reported adversely, stating that other than literary considerations had to be taken into account.[12]

It is no secret that Collins was fond of reading records of criminal cases,[13] especially those written in French, and more than one commentator has

6. The entry of the son's birth gives his name as William Charles Collins Dawson, the mother's name as Martha Dawson, formerly Rudd, the father's name as William Dawson, and the father's profession as Barrister at Law (Collins had received legal training at Lincoln's Inn). "Martha Dawson" was the informant.

7. *The Recollections of Sir Henry Dickens, K. C.* (London, 1934), p. 54.

8. The passage by Millais is quoted in S. M. Ellis's *Wilkie Collins, Le Fanu and Others* (London, 1931), p. 27.

9. S. M. Ellis, *op. cit.,* p. 28.

10. In a letter to Louise Chandler Moulton, dated June 22, 1880, Collins speaks of his plan for continuing the story begun in *The Fallen Leaves* — a plan never to be carried out: "The Married life — in the second part — will be essentially a happy life, in itself. But the outer influence of the world which surrounds this husband and wife — the world whose unchristian prejudices they have set at defiance — will slowly undermine their happiness and will, I fear, make the close of the story a sad one."

11. As in *The Evil Genius* and "Brother Griffith's Story of a Plot in Private Life," in *The Queen of Hearts.*

12. *The Critic,* April 12, 1890, p. 182.

13. Some of the "Cases Worth Looking at," in *My Miscellanies,* were drawn from J. Peuchet's *Mémoires tirés des Archives de la Police de Paris* (Paris, 1838).

mentioned casually that Collins derived from such a source suggestions for *The Woman in White*.[14] The exact source, which seemingly has not been pointed out, was the celebrated case of Madame de Douhault, which Collins found discussed fully in Maurice Méjan's *Recueil des Causes Celebres* ... (second edition, Paris, 1808, etc.),[15] a book in his own library.

The relevant parts of this famous case may be briefly outlined: Adéläide-Marie-Rogres-Lusignan de Champignelles (1741-1817) was married in 1764 to the Marquis de Douhault, and became a widow in 1787. Her father died in 1784. Madame de Douhault's brother, M. de Champignelles, obtained as much of his father's estate as he could, including some of the inheritance rightfully belonging to his mother and his sister. Of the mother's hardships under altered circumstances, another sister, abbess of Montargis, had some knowledge, and urged her sister Madame de Douhault to recover for their mother some share of the paternal bequest. Madame de Douhault thereupon planned a trip to Paris and announced her plan both to her sister and to Madame de Polignac, a correspondent. During a visit to some friends she expressed misgivings about the proposed journey, but her friends succeeded in calming her temporarily. Near the end of December, 1787, she left Chazelet, accompanied by a coachman, a chambermaid, and a servant. She stopped at Orléans, where she usually lodged at the house of M. Dulude (or du Lude), a nephew and an heir. On this occasion Dulude refused to receive her and induced her to go to the house of M. de la Roncière, a relative, whose mother had died suddenly eight days before at her son's house, about four leagues distant from Orléans. On January 15, 1788, on the eve of departing for Paris, Madame de la Roncière invited Madame de Douhault to go for a drive along the banks of the Loire. Soon after taking a pinch of snuff given her by Madame de la Roncière, Madame de Douhault suffered a violent headache which obliged her to return. Directly she fell into a deep slumber and was put to bed.

Madame de Douhault remembered all these events clearly, but what happened subsequently at Orléans was as indistinct as the events in an evil dream. She believed that she slept for several days; she woke to find herself in the Salpêtrière, under the name of Blainville. The supposed Madame de Douhault being dead, her estate was liquidated by M. de Champignelles and her heirs.

The correspondence of Madame de Douhault was for a time intercepted, but in June, 1789, by means of a woman whose favor she had won she succeeded in sending a letter to Madame de Polignac, and through Madame de Polignac's agency regained her liberty.

> Une surveillante reçut l'ordre de lui remettre ses habits, dont l'indication était écrite sur un papier, et Madame de Douhault reprit son déshabillé blanc, le linge et les poches qu'elle avait en entrant à la Salpêtrière.

14. See, for example, Hall Caine's *My Story* (New York, 1909), p. 329.
15. The chief details may be found in III, 5 ff., "Affaire de Madame de Douhault"; VI, 5-92, "Suite de L'Affaire de Madame de Douhault."

Madame de Polignac and her friends recognized Madame de Douhault; in fact, nobody at Versailles questioned her identity. When she went to the château at Champignelles, she was recognized by her own former domestics as well as by other people. The elaborate system of intrigue and defamation and the ingenious machinations by which Madame de Douhault's brother sought to discredit her attempt to regain her rightful status need not be reviewed here.[16] The case dragged on for years. To her cause the son of a former member of her household, an advocate named Delorme, with whom Madame de Douhault lived for a time, in vain devoted his talent and his fortune.[17]

Obviously Collins took from the story of Madame de Douhault the idea for Count Fosco's plot, to rob Laura of her property by destroying her identity. Fosco and Sir Percival carry out the plan by burying Anne Catherick, Laura's half-sister, as Laura, and substituting Laura for Anne at the asylum from which Anne had escaped—details which Collins added to make his narrative more logical. Laura's instinctive dread of spending a night at her aunt's house in London, on her journey towards Cumberland, may correspond to Madame de Douhault's misgivings, though a novelist's foreshadowing needs no such explanation. Laura's imperfect memory of the events which preceded her trip to the asylum is possibly a bit more reminiscent of the French case. Finally, one wonders whether Madame de Douhault's "déshabillé blanc" did not suggest the detail from which the novel derives its title,[18] in spite of Millais's story. To be sure, women in white are strangers neither to fiction nor to legend.[19]

The use of a legal case may have influenced the form of the narrative.[20] In the first chapter of *The Woman in White* Collins explains: "The story here presented will be told by more than one pen, as the story of an offence against the laws is told in Court by more than one person...." Thus a section of the story is related by the character whose testimony seems most pertinent; at the same time this character, like the speakers in *The Ring and the Book*, reveals a good deal of himself. An early reviewer pointed out that since each witness tells only what he knows, his ignorance piques the reader's curiosity.[21]

16. A brief resumé of the case may be found in Larousse's *Grand Dictionnaire universel du XIXe Siècle* (Paris, 1870), VI, 1157.

17. In an address to the Emperor in later years, Madame de Douhault is made to say: "J'ai soixante-six ans, j'existe au milieu de trente millions d'individus; et tous les rapports qui meliaient à la société sont brisés! Je ne suis civilement ni fille, ni épouse, ni Française, ni étrangère!" She finally died in wretched circumstances.

18. The choice of title was difficult. Collins explains that he smoked an entire case of cigars before finding a suitable title. Chewing the end of his last cigar, he looked at the North Foreland Lighthouse and thus addressed the building: "You are ugly and stiff and awkward ... as stiff and as weird as my white woman. White woman!—woman in white! The title, by Jove!" The story is told in an article in *The World*, Dec. 26, 1877, pp. 4-6.

19. For a discussion of the White Lady of Avenel, a character in Scott's *Monastery*, and several legendary white ladies, see Coleman O. Parsons, "Association of the White Lady with Wells," *Folk-Lore*, XLIV (September, 1933), 295-305.

20. According to *The World (loc. cit.)*, Collins had been asked to take up a case of wrongful imprisonment in an asylum. His short story "Fatal Fortune" deals with such a theme, which also interested Charles Reade. See *Readiana* (London, 1883), pp. 113-126.

21. *The Times*, October 30, 1860, p. 6.

In his introductory remarks to *Basil* Collins called the novel and the play "twin-sisters in the family of Fiction," the one "a drama narrated" and the other "a drama acted." In a dramatic novel like *The Woman in White* every incident is necessarily planned with care. One inconsistency of time in the first edition, subsequently corrected, did escape the author.[22] In a dramatic novel, too, fatalism is often prominent. Dreams, a favorite subject with an author himself susceptible to weird dreams, foreshadow important events: The letter warning Laura against marriage with Sir Percival (Chapter XI of the first part) contains an account of an ominous dream. Before departing on the journey that ended at the asylum, Laura has bad dreams. More important is the dream of Marian Halcombe (Chapter VI in the second epoch) in which she sees Walter Hartright escaping pestilence, shipwreck, and other perils; the dream ends with the prophetic vision of Hartright at a tomb—as events are to prove, the tomb of Anne Catherick. And Anne Catherick herself enters the story like a figure in a vision:

> There, in the middle of the broad, bright highroad—there, as if it had that moment sprung out of the earth or dropped from the heaven—stood the figure of a solitary Woman, dressed from head to foot in white garments, her face bent in grave inquiry on mine, her hand pointing to the dark cloud over London, as I faced her.

And thus she disappears:

> So the ghostly figure which has haunted these pages, as it haunted my life, goes down into the impenetrable gloom. Like a shadow she first came to me in the loneliness of the night. Like a shadow she passes away in the loneliness of the dead.

The plot having been conceived, certain characters were essential. As Collins once explained,[23] a victim can hardly exist without a villain, and because the crime was too ingenious for an English villain, the author chose a foreigner. Since Collins had visited Italy in his boyhood, his choice of an Italian was natural. Moreover, Italy was the home of such organizations as "The Brotherhood." Fosco's tool, Sir Percival, was necessarily a "weak shabby villain."

To Count Fosco, justly regarded as Collins's greatest achievement in characterization, Collins gave a Falstaffian physique, because, he said, of the popular notion that a fat man could hardly be villainous. He accounted for Fosco's pets thus: "I knew a man who loved canaries, and I

22. *The Times, loc. cit.,* pointed out that Collins was "a whole fortnight out of his reckoning. ... We could easily show that Lady Glyde could not have left Blackwater Park before the 9th or 10th of August." The fact that Dickens and the readers of *All the Year Around* did not observe the error, *The Times* adds, is a tribute to Collins's narrative skill. Collins acknowledged the error in a letter to his publisher, commenting, however, that "Shakespeare has made worse mistakes—that is one comfort, and readers are not critics who test an emotional book by ... rules of arithmetic, which is a second consolation. Nevertheless we will set it right the first opportunity...." The letter is quoted in Edward Marston's *After Work* (London, 1904), p. 85.
23. *The World, loc. cit.*

had known boys who loved white mice, and I thought the mice running about Fosco while he meditated on his schemes would have a fine effect." Fosco's devotion to his pets, like Long John Silver's fondness for his parrot, is a humanizing touch. To be sure, there are harsher qualities behind the Count's kindness: "The Count lit a cigarette, went back to the flowers in the window, and puffed little jets of smoke at the leaves, in a state of the deepest anxiety about killing the insects." Collins attributed to Fosco some of his own tastes and interests—for example, knowledge of the arts, fondness for Italian opera and good cooking, cosmopolitanism, criticism of English ways. His kind of humor is an apt vehicle for Fosco's egoistic gusto and self-assertive banter. Collins's admiration for Napoleon led him to attribute to Fosco the physical appearance of that dramatic character. There is something grandiose, too, in Fosco's *savoir-faire,* his skill in intrigue, his virtuosity in deception, his knowledge of human nature. So convincing is the portrait that one foreigner considered himself the pattern for Fosco, as Collins relates:

> He naturally insisted on receiving satisfaction for this insult, leaving the choice of swords or pistols to me as the challenged person. Information, on which he could rely, had assured him that I meditated a journey to Paris early in the ensuing week. A hostile meeting might, under such circumstances, be easily arranged. His letter ended with these terrible words: "J'attendrai Monsieur Vilkie [*sic*] avec deux temoins à la gare." Arriving at Paris, I looked for my honorable opponent. But one formidable person presented himself whom I could have wounded with pleasure—the despot who insisted on examining my luggage.[24]

Marian Halcombe writes of Fosco: "The one weak point in that man's iron character is the horrible admiration he feels for *me.*" Fosco says of Marian:

> With that woman for my friend I would snap these fingers of mine at the world. ... This grand creature—I drink her health in my sugar-and-water—this grand creature, who stands in the strength of her love and her courage, firm as a rock, between us two and that poor, flimsy, pretty blonde wife of yours—this magnificent woman, whom I admire with all my soul. ...

Readers have always shared Fosco's admiration. *The Woman in White* inspired several letters from bachelors who expressed their wish to marry the original of Marian.[25] Next to Fosco she is Collins's most memorable character.

In comparison with Fosco and Marian, Laura and Walter do seem rather colorless—virtuous enough but less interesting than some minor figures: Professor Pesca, Italian teacher of languages, as eccentric as Gabriele

24. From "Reminiscences of a Story-Teller," *The Universal Review,* I, 182-192.
25. *The World, loc. cit.*

Rossetti (at one time perhaps the best-known teacher of Italian in London; and, by the way, a member of the *Carbonari* in his youth, as Pesca was of "The Brotherhood"), important at the beginning and towards the end of the novel; Mr. Gilmore, whose professional and individual oddities are well sketched; Philip Fairlie, a delightfully self-centered hypochondriac (doubtless partly inspired by the author's occasional irritations and drawn *con amore*)—"nothing but a bundle of nerves dressed up to look like a man." Nor can one forget Mrs. Catherick, atoning for an unconventional past by a respectability which rejoices at the clergyman's bow. The Dickensian touch, slight in most of these characters, is more marked in one or two of the servants.

When all is said, it is as a story that *The Woman in White* has most interest. It was the story-tellers—Scott and Cooper and Dumas—that Collins cared for most among novelists; and he usually chose to write in an unadorned style, relishing most such prose as that of Byron's letters. Since Collins himself belongs among the great story-tellers rather than among the great novelists, *The Woman in White* well opens with this thrilling sentence: "This is the *story*[26] of what a Woman's patience can endure, and what a Man's resolution can achieve."

26. The italics are mine.

19

Literature and Society

L. C. Knights

Dekker, Heywood and Citizen Morality

To turn from Jonson to Dekker is to be jolted into recognition of the gulf between the higher and the lower ranges of Jacobean dramatic literature. With a few exceptions Dekker's plays are uniformly dull, and the effort of attention they require — the sheer effort to keep one's eyes on the page — is out of all proportion to the reward. They were, however, 'best sellers' — most of them were acted 'with great applause' by the Admiral's (afterwards the Prince's) Men, the Queen's Men or the Children of Paul's — and as an index of contemporary taste and opinion they provide some information that is relevant to this study.

Dekker was one of the neediest of the journeymen of letters at a time when authorship was one of the most precarious trades.[1] He had neither a share in a fellowship of players, nor aristocratic patronage, and he was forced to follow the taste of the moment as closely and as quickly as possible, either in play or pamphlet. It is usual to think of him as primarily a playwright, but his essentially journalistic talent is best brought out if we approach him through his non-dramatic works; many of his plays are little more than dramatized versions of these.

As a journalist Dekker addressed the lower levels of the London reading public. His journalism was not, of course, the newsmongering of a Nathaniel Butter. A representative pamphlet such as *The Wonderful Year* (1603) consists of desultory gossip together with rhetorical accounts of events that were known to everybody, larded with 'tales cut out in sundry fashions, of purpose to shorten the lives of long winter nights'.[2] His accounts

From *Drama and Society in the Age of Jonson* (New York: Barnes & Noble, Inc., 1937), pp. 228-255. Reprinted by permission of the publisher.
  1. He began by hack-writing for Henslowe, and between 1598 and 1602 he is said to have had a hand in thirty-nine plays for the Admiral's Men. — Chambers, *Elizabethan Stage*, III, pp. 302-304. And Henslowe 'made money by shrewd dealing, by an often slavish following of the popular taste of the moment, and by the active competition of authors in an age when nearly anybody could write an acceptable play' (Schelling, *Elizabethan Drama*, I, p. 318).
  2. For the gossip and its significance see Appendix A, 'Elizabethan Prose', p. 305. A representative example of his rhetoric is the account of the plague quoted below, p. 322.

of wonders and marvels are all homely and commonplace,[3] and the descriptions are matched by the moralizing. Dekker's purpose was not solely to amuse. The majority of the pamphlets contain accounts of 'an Army of insufferable abuses, detestable vices, most damnable villainies, abominable pollutions, inexplicable mischiefs, sordid iniquinations, horrible and hellhound-like perpetrated flagitious enormities',[4] so 'that thou and all the world shall see their ugliness, for by seeing them, thou mayst avoid them'.[5] There is no need to doubt Dekker's moral purpose in his description of damnable villainies, but the quality of the description is fairly indicated by the tautological introduction that I have quoted. In the pamphlets mainly designed to show up abuses we learn little of the peculiar quality of contemporary social life; or rather, such evidence as they present is incidental.

In *The Seven Deadly Sins of London* (1606) the seven sins are 'Politick Bankruptism', Lying, 'The Nocturnal Triumph', Sloth, Apishness, 'Shaving' and Cruelty. There are the usual puns and forced rhetoric, but what distinguishes the pamphlet is its humanitarianism. In the section on cruelty Dekker denounces parents who drive their children into unwilling marriages, cruel creditors, and unconscionable masters, and he pleads for the provision of hospitals and decent burial grounds. The approach to economic problems is entirely moralistic. In his denunciation of the 'politic bankrupt' he appeals to the Commandments, and shows the sin as a combination of covetousness and theft,[6] whilst the practice of imprisonment for debt is described as both useless and inhuman: 'We are most like to God that made us when we show love one to another, and do most look like the Devil that would destroy us, when we are one another's tormentors'.[7] So too he complains of the members of the London Companies who try to limit their numbers, and who will not allow apprentices, their seven years expired, to become masters,

> as if Trades, that were ordained to be communities, had lost their first privileges, and were now turned Monopolies. . . . Remember, O you rich men, that your servants are your adopted children; they are naturalized into your blood, and if you hurt theirs, you are guilty of letting out your own, than which, what cruelty can be greater?[8]

Dekker, in short, is following the traditions of the Church in regarding 'buying and selling, lending and borrowing, as a simple case of neighbourly or unneighbourly conduct'.[9] It is on these grounds that he judges landlords who rack rents, cheating tradesmen, brewers and bakers who give false measure, fraudulent executors, and usurers,

---

3. E.g. the history of Charing Cross, or the account of the kings buried at Westminster, *The Dead Term, Non-Dramatic Works*, IV, pp. 11, 39-40, 152 ff. And cf. his frequent accounts of gipsies, thieves, etc.
4. *The Belman of London*, ibid., III, p. 168.
5. *The Seven Deadly Sins of London*, ibid., II, pp. 14-15.
6. *The Seven Deadly Sins of London*, ibid., II, p. 17 ff.
7. *Ibid.*, II, p. 72.
8. *Ibid.*, II, p. 74.
9. Tawney, *Religion and the Rise of Capitalism*, p. 54.

who for a little money and a great deal of trash (as fire-shovels, brown paper, motley cloak-bags, etc.) bring young novices into a fool's paradise till they have sealed the mortgage of their lands, and then like pedlars go they (or some familiar spirit for them, raised by the usurer) up and down to cry *Commodities,* which scarce yield the third part of the sum for which they take them up.[10]

A summary of the admirably humane proposals scattered throughout Dekker's pamphlets would suggest that I had done him an injustice. But what I am complaining of is the lack of something that can only be called the artistic conscience. Dekker is never sure of what he wants to do. The moral drive is dissipated by the constant striving after obvious 'effects', by the recurring introduction of irrelevancies, by the failure to maintain a consistent tone, so that although Dekker is never guilty of tickling his readers' palates with descriptions of vice, one often suspects the journalistic intention. One thing at least is proved by the blemishes themselves: Dekker was completely at one with his London audience.[11] He does not draw on popular thought and refine it, like Jonson; his thoughts *are* the thoughts of the average Londoner.

Dekker's social morality is a morality that the average decent citizen would find acceptable. He does not despise or distrust riches so long as they are used conscionably. Virtue itself is rewarded by earthly prosperity —

> England shall ne'er be poor, if England strive
> Rather by virtue than by wealth to thrive.[12]

The rich should be fair and charitable; the poor should aim at content; the honest workman should maintain himself decently in his calling, and if he rises it must only be within the limits of his own order. One cannot classify this morality as either 'medieval' or 'modern'. Dekker accepts the traditional social ethic, but his Protestant Christianity is that of the seventeenth-century middle class.[13] It is significant that in *A Strange Horse Race* (1613) the first virtue that he mentions is Humility, the second, Thrift. Thrift, running a race with Prodigality, is 'vigilant in his course, subtle in laying his wager, provident in not venturing too much, honest to pay his losses, industrious to get more (twenty sundry ways) if he should

10. *The Seven Deadly Sins of London, Non-Dramatic Works,* II, p. 64. Cf. *ibid.,* II, p. 135 ff. (usury), III, p. 367 (monopolies). Miss Gregg points out that 'The intimate relationship between personal sin and national calamity had a first place in all of Dekker's muck-raking pamphlets, and probably had a considerable part in making him one of the popular writers of his day'. He was, she adds, as thoroughgoing a conservative as Spenser, Shakespeare, Bacon, or Jonson. — *Thomas Dekker, A Study in Economic and Social Backgrounds,* pp. 96-97.

11. Cf. The address to the City in the Induction to *The Seven Deadly Sins of London:* 'From thy womb received I my being, from thy breasts my nourishment' (*ibid.,* II, p. 10 ff.; and *The Dead Term* (1608), *ibid.,* IV, pp. 9-10).

12. *Old Fortunatus,* V, ii.

13. Decidedly anti-Catholic. See *The Double PP* (1606), directed against the Catholics after the Gunpowder Plot, and *The Whore of Babylon* (1605-1607).

happen to be cheated of all'.[14] It is a citizen morality, but it is neither entirely individualistic nor out of touch with tradition.

The plays, like the pamphlets, gave the public — Alleyn's public — what it wanted and what it could digest easily: amusement, naïvely 'dramatic' situations, moral 'sentences' and pictures of contemporary virtues and vices, eked out occasionally by fireworks.[15] Shakespeare took popular elements and transformed them to his own purposes; Dekker gives us an amalgam of all that popular taste demanded. His dramatic satire is usually directed against fairly obvious abuses:

> *1st Devil.* I have with this fist beat upon rich men's hearts,
> To make 'em harder: and these two thumbs thrust, ˙
> (In open churches) into brave dames' ears,
> Damming up attention; whilst the loose eye peers
> For fashions of gown-wings, laces, purles, ruffs,
> Falls, cauls, tires, wires, caps, hats, and muffs and puffs.
> For so the face be smug, and carcase gay,
> That's all their pride.[16]

His satire, that is, either deals in generalities, or else it presents particulars drawn from the life of the time without grasping their full significance and implications. It does not penetrate far below the surface.

It is for this reason that Dekker's comedies, although far less 'universal' than Jonson's, tell us comparatively little about the economic and social changes that can be discerned behind *The Alchemist*. There are, of course, scattered references. *Westward Ho!* (1604), in particular, gives some interesting thumbnail sketches. There are needy courtiers[17] and luxurious citizens;[18] there is satire on the buying of knighthoods,[19] and on monop-

---

14. *Ibid.,* III, p. 334. Cf. 'London ... being ravished with unutterable joys ... puts off her formal habit of Trade and Commerce, treading *even Thrift itself* underfoot' (*The Magnificent Entertainment given to King James* (1603), *Dramatic Works,* I, p. 303).

15. *Old Fortunatus* (1599) — generally considered one of Dekker's best plays — is chiefly remarkable for the number of popular elements which he has contrived to work in. There is a morality framework containing a romantic story and a satirical sub-plot; there is music, song and dance, together with pageantry, jewels and fine dresses; there is a quibbling clown, and there are scraps of foreign languages and broken English, such as might be heard on the quay side or at the Exchange; but there really isn't much else.

16. *If it be not Good, the Devil is in It* (1610-1612) (III, 328-329). (Unless otherwise stated the references in brackets are to the volume and page of Dekker's Plays, edited by R. H. Shepherd, in the Pearson Reprints.)

17. *Monopoly* (the courtier). 'O no sir. I must disburse instantly: we that be courtiers have more places to send money to, than the devil hath to send his spirits' (I, i (II, 289)).

18. *Merchant's Wife* (to her husband). 'Your prodigality, your dicing, your riding abroad, your consorting yourself with noblemen, your building a summer house hath undone us' (I, i (II, 287)).

19. *Clare* (a merchant's wife). 'Fabian Scarecrow us'd to frequent me and my husband divers times. And at last comes he out one morning to my husband, and says, master Tenterhook, says he, I must trouble you to lend me 200 pound about a commodity which I am to deal in, and what was that commodity but his knighthood' (V, i (II, 342)).

olies;[20] and farmers are described as 'grinding the jaw-bones of the poor'.[21] But in this play Dekker collaborated with Webster, and I think that it is to Webster that the most effective satire belongs. In *If It be not Good, the Devil is in It* (1610-1612), it is true, there is a straightforward attack on commercial wiles. Pluto sends to earth three devils, one to corrupt a court, another a monastery, and a third is given these instructions:

> Be thou a city-devil. Make thy hands
> Of Harpy's claws, which being on courtiers' lands
> Once fasten'd, ne'er let loose. The Merchant play,
> And on the Burse, see thou thy flag display,
> Of politic bankruptism: train up as many
> To fight under it, as thou canst, for now's not any
> That break, (They'll break their necks first). If beside,
> Thou canst not through the whole city meet with pride,
> Riot, lechery, envy, avarice, and such stuff,
> Bring 'em all in coach'd, the gates are wide enough.
> The spirit of gold instruct thee.[22]

Bartervile, the merchant with whom the city-devil takes service, does not need much instruction. He gets the lands of a gentleman who owes him money by pretending that the hour for repayment is passed;[23] he loses the farm of some royal imposts, but obtains it again because the King needs to borrow money ('Who bids most, he buys it').[24] He devises a variation on 'Politic bankruptism',[25] and boasts that he has the royal protection:

> *Bartervile.* A merchant, and yet know'st not
>   What a protection is? I'll tell thee. . . .
>   It is a buckler of a large fair compass,
>   Quilted with fox-skins; in the midst
>   A pike sticks out, (sometimes of two years long,
>   And sometimes longer). And this pike keeps off
>   Sergeants and bailiffs, actions, and arrests:
>   'Tis a strong charm 'gainst all the noisome smells
>   Of Counters, Jailors, garnishes, and such hells;
>   By this, a debtor craz'd, so lusty grows,

---

20. *Monopoly* (promising to reward Birdlime, a bawd). '. . . I'll stick wool upon thy back.' *Birdlime,* 'Thanks sir, I know you will, for all the kindred of the Monopolies are held to be great fleecers' (II, ii (II, 309)). Cf. *Match me in London,* Act I (IV, 149): 'A flat-cap, pish! If he storm, give him a court-loaf, stop's mouth with a monopoly.'

21. *Justiniano.* 'Why there's no minute, no thought of time passes, but some villainy or other is brewing: why, even now, now, at holding up of this finger, and before the turning down of this, some are murdering, some lying with their maids, some picking of pockets, some cutting purses, some cheating, some weighing out bribes. In this city some wives are cuckolding some husbands. In yonder village some farmers are now-now grinding the jaw-bones of the poor' (II, i (II, 299)). I have quoted the passage to show how unlike Dekker a good deal of the satire is.

22. (III, 270.)

23. (III, 296-301.)

24. (III, 297, 317, 320-321.)

25. (III, 323.) Compare *The Seven Deadly Sins of London, Non-Dramatic Works,* II, p. 17 ff.

He may walk by, and play with his creditor's nose.
Under this buckler, here I'll lie and fence.[26]

Above all, he lives solely for his immediate gain:

Lurchall. But pray sir, what is't turns you into a Turk?
Bartervile. That, for which many their Religion,
   Most men their Faith, all change their honesty,
   Profit, (that gilded god) Commodity,
   He that would grow damn'd rich, yet live secure,
   Must keep a case of faces. . . .[27]

Dekker, however, is not often so consistently explicit. Generally he is content to denounce gold, 'the world's saint',[28] in general terms. Old Fortunatus, given the choice of wisdom, strength, health, beauty, long life, and riches, chooses riches:

My choice is store of gold; the rich are wise.
He that upon his back rich garments wears,
Is wise, though on his head grow Midas' ears.
Gold is the strength, the sinews of the world,
The health, the soul, the beauty most divine,
A mask of gold hides all deformities;
Gold is Heaven's physic, life's restorative,
Oh therefore make me rich.[29]

But it is obvious that Dekker's acceptance of citizen thrift and industry is severely qualified by the traditional distrust.

'Twas never merry world with us, since purses and bags were invented, for now men set lime-twigs to catch wealth: and gold, which riseth like the sun out of the East Indies, to shine upon everyone, is like a cony taken napping in a purse-net, and suffers his glistering yellow-face deity to be lapped up in lambskins, as if the innocency of those leather prisons should dispense with the cheveril consciences of the iron-hearted gaolers.[30]

Dekker never manages to work up this theme into an effective play (the effect of a single play is very different from the effect of these assembled extracts); but what we have to notice is that even in giving the public what it wanted, even in praising the citizen virtues, he is far nearer to the medieval moralists than to the new economic rationalists.

26. (III, 324.) The play also shows Church revenues farmed out to a courtier. (III, 319.)
27. (III, 322.)
28. (III, 271.)
29. *Old Fortunatus* (1599), I, i (Mermaid Edition, 303).
30. *Ibid.,* I, ii (Mermaid Edition, 307).

Dekker's best known play – a favourite with his contemporary audience – is *The Shoemaker's Holiday*.[31] There is no doubt that its success was largely due to the way in which it appealed to the pride of the citizen-craftsman in his craft and status.[32] It called for no effort of readjustment or reorganization, but – like the long line of patriotic chronicle plays[33] – simply reinforced a prevalent social attitude. In the first place, the citizens had the pleasure of familiar recognition. Simon Eyre, celebrated by Stow as well as by Deloney, was a figure of traditional legend, and the account of the building and naming of the Leadenhall[34] appealed to the taste which produced such things as *If You Know not Me You Know Nobody, With the Building of the Royal Exchange*. Eyre's progress from master craftsman to Sheriff and finally Lord Mayor of London (not, significantly, to a house in the country) represented a dream which a good many apprentices must have cherished.[35] And Eyre's relations with his workmen are presented in the most attractive light. He drinks and jests with them, listens to their advice, and protects them from the tongue of his wife; 'By the Lord of Ludgate', he swears, 'I love my men as my life'. The relationship, although obviously idealized, had, as we have seen, a basis in fact, and its presentation would be particularly appreciated since it depicted a state of affairs that was rapidly vanishing as business became more impersonal. Moreover, the pride, the ambition, the prejudices of Eyre and his men are limited by the city. Not only does the Earl of Lincoln oppose the marriage of Lacy, his nephew, to Rose, a citizen's daughter; her father the Lord Mayor 'scorns to call Lacy son-in-law',[36] and Eyre advises her:

> A courtier, wash, go by, stand not upon pishery-pashery: those silken fellows are but painted images, outsides, outsides, Rose; their inner linings are torn. No, my fine mouse, marry me with a gentleman grocer like my lord mayor, your father; a grocer is a sweet trade: plums, plums. Had I a son or daughter should marry out of the generation and blood of the shoemakers, he should pack; what, the gentle trade is a living for a man through Europe, through the world.[37]

Rose, it is true, marries Lacy in the end, but Lacy has proved himself a good fellow and has not scorned the gentle craft; besides, romance de-

31. Acted by the Admiral's Men in 1599 at the Fortune and at Court. There are extant editions dated 1600, 1610, 1618, 1624, 1631, 1657.

32. Like Deloney's *Gentle Craft* (1598), on which the play is based.

33. See below, pp. 243 ff.

34. (V, ii.)

35. Dr Robertson points out that Eyre made his fortune 'by a sharp practice of which the modern equivalent would be obtaining credit by false trade references' (*Economic Individualism*, pp. 190-191). Certainly the bargain by which Eyre gains 'full three thousand pound' (III, i, iii) is not very reputable, but there is no need to make much of it, or to connect it, as Dr Robertson does, with 'the wave of speculation' which was then affecting all classes. Dekker merely intends to show that fortune is on the side of the good-hearted tradesman; it is characteristic that he slurs over the issues without thinking very hard about them.

36. I, i (Mermaid Edition, 8).

37. III, v (Mermaid Edition, 47).

manded it. It is the citizen's independence, however, that is most applauded. Even the surly attitude of the shoemakers when they demand the journeyman's wife, Jane, from the wealthy and inoffensive Hammon (V,ii) is presented for approval; and Eyre, though proud of his civic dignities, has none of those ambitions to step outside the limits of his order which were already providing material for the comic dramatists.

> Am I not Simon Eyre? Are not these my brave men, brave shoemakers, all gentlemen of the gentle craft? Prince am I none, yet am I nobly born.[38]

It is impossible, however, merely to dismiss Dekker by saying that *The Shoemaker's Holiday* is an appeal to prejudice (in any case its appeal was wider than my account may suggest) or that his work in general is a mere reflection of popular taste. What we have to ask ourselves, with the twentieth-century reading public in mind, is what that taste demanded besides easy amusement. For in spite of Dekker's feeble grasp of tradition, his narrow moral scope, his work does embody, or reflect, however fragmentarily, a decent traditional morality. I am not thinking of the stilted moralism of *The Honest Whore* but of the shrewd, caustic comments on social ambition, wealth and luxury that are scattered throughout his plays. His approval of Eyre does not prevent him from laughing at the naïve assumption of dignity by Eyre's wife,[39] and I have shown something of his attitude towards mere acquisition. But the point is best made by a comparison with a modern novel. There is no need to draw on the fiction that caters for the needs of a class corresponding to 'the original civility of the Red Bull'. The standards behind Arnold Bennett's popular *Imperial Palace* are fairly indicated by extracts such as these:

> And he liked her expensive stylishness. The sight of a really smart woman always gave him pleasure. In his restaurant, when he occasionally inspected it as a spy from a corner behind a screen, he always looked first for the fashionable, costly frocks, and the more there were the better he was pleased. . . . Only half an hour ago she had probably been steering a big car at a mile a minute on a dark curving road. And here with delicate hands she was finishing the minute renewal of her delicate face.[40]

38. III, i (Mermaid Edition, 30). Cf. Candido's defence of the flat cap in *The Honest Whore, Part II*, I, iii (Mermaid Edition, 208):
> It is a citizen's badge, and first was worn
> By th' Romans. . . .
> Flat caps as proper are to city gowns,
> As to armours helmets, or to king's their crowns.
> Let then the city-cap by none be scorned,
> Since with it princes' heads have been adorned.

39. III, iv (Mermaid Edition, 40 ff.). *Margery.* 'Art thou acquainted with never a farthingale-maker, nor a French hood-maker? I must enlarge my bum, ha, ha! How shall I look in a hood, I wonder? . . . It is very hot, I must get me a fan or else a mask. . . . But, Ralph, get thee in, call for some meat and drink, thou shalt find me worshipful towards thee,' etc.

40. *The Imperial Palace*, p. 9.

Gracie, stared at by a hundred eyes until she sat down, was just as much at her ease as a bride at a wedding. Created by heaven to be a cynosure, rightly convinced that she was the best-dressed woman in the great, glittering, humming room, her spirit floated on waves of admiration as naturally as a goldfish in water. Evelyn, impressed, watched her surreptitiously as she dropped on to the table an inlaid vanity-case which had cost her father a couple of pounds. . . . Surely in the wide world that night there could not be anything to beat her! Idle, luxurious rich, but a master-piece! Maintained in splendour by the highly skilled and expensive labour of others, materially useless to society, she yet justified herself by her mere appearance. And she knew it, and her conscience was clear.[41]

Throughout the book — there is a little, uneasy, irony — the reader is invited to admire, or to accept with complacence, the monstrous material standards symbolized by a modern luxury hotel. Dekker and his audience had another set of values.

Lord, Lord, to see what good raiment doth. . . . O sweet wares! Prunes, almonds, sugar-candy, carrot-roots, turnips, O brave fatting meat![42]

Whenever Dekker dwells on luxury there is no doubt of the expected response: here, for example:

Birdlime. O the entertainment my Lord will make you. Sweet wines, lusty diet, perfumed linen, soft beds, O most fortunate gentlewoman![43]

Or here, where the devil, disguised as a novice, is told to say grace:

Prior. Stand forth, and render thanks.
Rush. Hum, hum:
  For our bread, wine, ale and beer,
  For the piping hot meats here:
  For broths of sundry tastes and sort,
  For beef, veal, mutton, lamb, and pork:
  Green-sauce with calve's head and bacon,
  Pig and goose, and cramm'd-up capon:
  For pastries rais'd stiff with curious art,
  Pie, custard, florentine and tart.
  Bak'd rumps, fried kidneys, and lamb-stones,
  Fat sweet-breads, luscious marrowbones,

41. *The Imperial Palace*, p. 81. For comment, see Q. D. Leavis, *Fiction and the Reading Public*, p. 199.
42. *Shoemaker's Holiday*, III, i.
43. *Westward Ho!* I, i (II, 285).

> Artichoke, and oyster pies,
> Butter'd crab, prawns, lobsters' thighs,
> Thanks be given for flesh and fishes,
> With this choice of tempting dishes:
> To which preface, with blithe looks sit ye,
> Rush bids this Convent, much good do't ye.[44]

It is not merely that Dekker, without Jonson's poise, is nevertheless insistent on 'the rotten strength of proud mortality'[45] –

> And though mine arm should conquer twenty worlds,
> There's a lean fellow beats all conquerors[46] –

he had been taught by religion, by the traditional morality, that there were other standards than those implied by 'the high standard of living' of the Imperial Palace.

And finally, Dekker's conception of the ordered state is, in general, the traditional conception that lies behind Ulysses' speech on 'Degree',[47] on the one hand, and the acts of the Elizabethan Privy Council on the other. So far as one can piece together a coherent social attitude behind the plays, it is approval of a scheme in which each man has his proper place, the whole being bound together by justice. The King in *If It be not a Good Play*, planning his reign, gives first place to equity.

> That day, from morn till night, I'll execute
> The office of a judge, and weigh out laws
> With even scales. . . .
> The poor and rich man's cause
> I'll poise alike: it shall be my chief care
> That bribes and wrangling be pitch'd o'er the bar. . . .
> Tuesdays we'll sit to hear the poor man's cries,
> Orphans and widows: our own princely eyes
> Shall their petitions read: our progress then
> Shall be to hospitals which good minded men

---

44. *If It be not Good, the Devil is in It* (III, 281).
45. *Old Fortunatus*, II, ii.
46. *Ibid.*, I, i.
47. *Troilus and Cressida*, I, iii. It is perhaps worth noticing that Dekker imitates this speech in *The Double PP, Non-Dramatic Works,* II, p. 185, on the Judge:
> The fourth that stands this quarrel, is more strong
> In scarlet than in steel: look how the moon
> Between the day, so he twixt right and wrong
> Sits equal umpire: like the orbed moon
> Empires by him swell high, or fall as soon;
> For when Law alights, uproars on foot-cloths ride . . .
> The regal chair would down be thrown: religion
> Take sanctuary: no man durst be good,
> Nor could be safe being bad: confusion
> Would be held order: and (as in the Flood
> The world was covered) so would all in blood
> If Justice eyes were closed: No man sleeps, speaks,
> Nor eats but by her.

Have built to pious use, for lame, sick, and poor.
We'll see what's given, what spent, and what flows o'er.
Churls (with God's money) shall not feast, swill wine,
And fat their rank guts whilst poor wretches pine.[48]

Dekker praises thrift, industry, and the citizen virtues, but his description of the artisan is significant:

The rear-ward last advanced up, being led
By the industrious, thriving Artisan:
The ways of science needs he well must tread,
For seven years go to make him up a man.
And then by all the lawful steps he can,
Climbs he to wealth. Enough is his he vaunts,
If though he hoard not much, he feels not wants.[49]

The 'lawful steps' are insisted upon, and Dekker sets his face against the 'doctrineless individualism' represented by the merchant, Bartervile:

Nature sent man into the world, alone,
Without all company, but to care for one,
And that I'll do.[50]

It is the devil who insists that this is 'True City doctrine, sir'.

The Knight of the Burning Pestle was first acted in 1607. Most of its genial ridicule was directed against the absurdities of Heywood's *Four Prentices of London,* and similar plays, which made London citizens the heroes of romantic adventures in exotic settings. But Beaumont's Citizen stands for popular taste in general:

Why could you not be contented (he asks the speaker of the Prologue) . . . with 'The Legend of Whittington', or 'The Life and Death of Sir Thomas Gresham, with The Building of the Royal Exchange', or 'The Story of Queen Eleanor, with the rearing of London Bridge upon Woolsacks'.[51]

The class of plays indicated here was large, varied and extremely popular. It included histories, biographies, plays of adventure and of domestic life, the common element being that they all presented 'something notable in honour of the commons of the city'[52]—or of the countryside. They appealed to local, as well as to national, patriotism, and they exalted familiar types and familiar virtues. Since they formed a natural development of the chronicle plays they are best approached through these.

48. (III, 274.)
49. *The Double PP, Non-Dramatic Works,* II, p. 190.
50. *If It be not Good, the Devil is in It* (III, 324).
51. Induction to *The Knight of the Burning Pestle.*
52. *Ibid.*

The increased intensity of national feeling, particularly in the years immediately before and after 1588, was accompanied by a new interest in England's past. But although the chronicle play, as such, dates from about 1580, it sprang, as Schelling points out, from a deep-rooted popular interest — something attested by the historical and familiar elements in the mystery and morality plays, the plays and ballads about Robin Hood and St. George, as well as by the chronicles of Hall, Stow, Fox, and Holinshed, and versified chronicles such as Warner's *Albion's England*.[53] The popularity of the chronicle plays reached its height in the last decade of the sixteenth century, when political circumstances made it inevitable that they should not be disinterested dramatic accounts of past times, but direct incitements to patriotic feeling, propaganda designed to make one Englishman feel that he really was as good as three Spaniards.[54]

In these plays the effects are simple and obvious. There is, said Puttenham, 'no one thing in the world with more delectation reviving our spirits than to behold as it were in a glass the lively image of our dear forefathers',[55] and it did not matter whether the 'dear forefathers' were the mythical sons of Brutus, King of Britain, popular figures from history such as Henry V or Sir Thomas More, or semihistorical worthies like Robin Hood, Earl of Huntingdon. The truly *Lamentable Tragedy of Locrine* (c. 1591, by Peele?) may, as Schelling thinks, have contained 'a take-off of the Senecan excesses of the moment',[56] but it is unlikely that the patriotic speeches were received as parody. The overthrow of a barbarian invading force must have been received with cheers,[57] and the proof that God is on the side of his Englishmen would certainly be acceptable.[58] 'What a glorious thing it is', said Nashe, ironically, 'to have Henry the Fifth represented on the stage leading the French king prisoner, and forcing both him and the Dauphin swear fealty'.[59] We can at least imagine the thrill

---

53. F. L. Schelling, *The English Chronicle Play,* chaps. i and ii. Schelling shows the popularity of the chronicles; Stow's *Summary,* for example, went into a tenth edition in 1604.

54. Between 1562 *(Gorboduc)* and 1642 there is record of more than 150 chronicle plays, about half of which are extant; some eighty of them were produced in the years 1590 to 1600. *Ibid.,* p. 51. Cf. Schelling, *Elizabethan Drama,* I, pp. 251-252. Schelling refers to the 'Mystères Patriotiques', 'which the misfortunes of the Hundred Years' War caused to flourish in France', *e.g. La Mystère du siège d'Orléans, La Déconfiture de Talbot advenu en Bordelais* (1453). See G. Bapst, *Essai sur l'histoire du théâtre,* chap. iii:

'Le jour même de la délivrance de l'Orléans, le 8 mai 1429, les habitants encore tout émus de la lutte acharnée de la journée, organisèrent spontanément une grande procession, qui parcourut les principales voies de la ville, en "faisant pose" sur les places. ... Au milieu de la procession, marchaient la Pucelle, le Bâtard, d'Orléans, plus connu sous le nom de Dunois, Gilles de Raiz et d'autres capitaines. Tous les ans, à la même date, la même cérémonie se renouvelle. ...La municipalité fait construire sur son parcours des tréteaux, sur lesquels on représente des pantomimes relatives aux événements du siège'.

55. *The Art of English Poesy* (1589), *Elizabethan Critical Essays* (ed. Gregory Smith), II, p. 41.

56. *Elizabethan Drama,* I, p. 256.

57. Lo, here the harms that wait upon all those
        That do intrude themselves in other lands
        Which are not under their dominions. (II, ii.)
The Britons defy Troglodytes, Æthiopians, Amazons and 'all the hosts of Barbarian lands', if these 'should dare to enter in our little world' (IV, i).

58. Mighty Jove the supreme king of heaven,
        That guides the concourse of the meteors
        And rules the motions of the azure sky,
        Fights always for the Briton's safety. (IV, i.)

59. *Pierce Penilesse* (1592).

with which, in the year of the Armada, the audience received the more resounding lines from *The Famous Victories of Henry the Fifth*,[60] or even, later, those from Shakespeare's histories.[61]

But I am not concerned with the cruder forms of patriotic propaganda, the point to notice is that the chronicle play was one of the earliest forms of drama drawing upon and reinforcing group sanctions. The historical plays were recognized as containing direct topical references, and they led naturally to such plays as *George a Greene, The Pinner of Wakefield* (1588-1592), *The Shoemaker's Holiday* (1599) and Haughton's *Englishmen for my Money* (1598), pseudohistories and biographies such as *Thomas, Lord Cromwell* (1592) and *Sir Thomas More* (c. 1596) — the plays, in short, of the kind that Beaumont's citizen demanded.

In plays of this kind the dramatist is concerned to stabilize or invigorate a mode of feeling that is generally considered desirable amongst the group addressed: to provide his audience with a sense of well-being that comes from seeing slightly idealized copies of themselves upon the stage. The historical and biographical plays, and the plays that had for subject national or local types, appealed in various ways. They provided information (more or less reliable), they showed picaresque adventures, and they gave opportunity for miscellaneous pageantry, devices and clowning; but all of them fostered, in some way, what Schelling calls the 'sense of community'.[62] Often the method consists of crudely derogatory remarks about foreigners and foreign countries:

> Pigs and Frenchmen speak one language, *awee, awee,*[63]

or

> My Lord, no court with England may compare
> Neither for state nor civil government:
> Lust dwells in France, in Italy, and Spain,
> From the poor peasant to the Prince's train.
> In Germany and Holland riot serves,
> And he that most can drink, most he deserves:
> England I praise not, for I here was born,
> But that she laugheth the others unto scorn.[64]

60.   Tell the French King
       That Harry of England hath sent for the crown,
       And Harry of England will have it. (*Famous Victories,* Scene ix.)
61.   This is the English, not the Turkish court;
       Not Amurath an Amurath succeeds,
       But Harry Harry.   (*2 Henry IV,* V, ii.)
   Cf. Gaunt's eulogy of 'This happy breed of men, this little world'; the defiance of the Pope and the Bastard's final speech in *King John;* and Cranmer's prophecy in *Henry VIII.*
62. *The English Chronicle Play,* p. 5.
63. *Englishmen for my Money* (1598, Admiral's Men), I, i. In this play Pisario, a usurer, wishes to marry his three daughters to a Frenchman, a Dutchman and an Italian, respectively. These, however, love three Englishmen, who have mortgaged their lands to Pisario. These flout the foreigners, outwit them and Pisario, and finally marry the daughters.
64. *Thomas, Lord Cromwell* (not later than 1602, Chamberlain's Men), III, iii. Cromwell, says Schelling, 'stands for the glorification, the very apotheosis of citizen virtue. It is Cromwell's honourable thrift and capacity in trade, his temperance, piety and staunch Protestantism which are dwelt on and extolled. He befriends the broken debtor and outwits the wrong-doer. He is mindful of others' favours to him, forgetful of his own' (*English Chronicle Play,* p. 217). That is as good a summary as one can make of a very bad play.

But other effects were possible. Sometimes historical plays provided moral instances,[65] and the plays on various worthies held up examples of the accepted virtues of the different classes. George a Greene, the Pinner of Wakefield, for example, stands for the yeoman class 'that in times past made all France afraid',[66] and the play makes much the same kind of appeal as Deloney's *Jack of Newbery*.[67]

But it is not enough to say that 'community' plays stabilized accepted social attitudes; so does *Punch*. Most of the popular plays representing English types are bad enough as poetry and as drama; an attempt at evaluation can only be an attempt to answer the question, What sanctions are appealed to, what kind of prejudices are played upon? With this question in mind, a short study of those of Heywood's plays that fall within the category will do more than suggest a profitable approach to the class in general.

Heywood, like Dekker, was 'a typical literary Jack-of-all-trades of the epoch'.[68] Unlike Dekker he wrote at least two plays that have some life in them and do not consist of assembled parts, and the best of his verse is at least dramatically effective. But he was no poet; and to say this is to say that he was incapable of exploring, modifying or making effectively his own the morality of the age: 'his sensibility is merely that of ordinary people in ordinary life'.[69] It is this indeed that gives him his significance

65. The general approach to history was moral, as can be seen from the school text-books in use at the time. Reusner's *Symbola Heroica,* for instance, was 'a collection of character sketches ... treated symbolically "so as to portray from the concrete instance some instruction, by way of example or warning, helpful towards the inculcation of prudence, wisdom and morality"' (Foster Watson, *English Grammar Schools to 1660,* chap. xxvi). And the plays were explicit: *Gorboduc*
>   A mirror shall become to princes all
>   To learn to shun the cause of such a fall.
66. Harrison, *Description of England,* Book II (ed. Furnivall), p. 133.
67. See the Dedication 'To all the famous clothworkers of England': '... those for whose sake I took pains to compile it, that is, for the well minded clothiers; that herein they may behold the great worship and credit which men of this trade have in former times come unto'. In *George a Greene* (before 1593) the hero, after repulsing the Scots invaders, refuses knighthood at the hands of the king:
>   Then let me live and die a yeoman still.
>   So was my father, so must live his son.
68. T. S. Eliot, *Elizabethan Essays,* p. 102.
69. *Ibid.,* p. 107. Since the literary judgement is relevant to one's opinion of Heywood as a representative of popular taste it may be reinforced here. Consider the imagery of *A Woman Killed with Kindness,* for example:
>   *(a)* My God! what have I done? what have I done?
>   My rage hath plunged into a sea of blood,
>   In which my soul lies drowned. (I, iii.)
>   *(b)* A song! ha, ha: a song! as if, fond man,
>   Thy eyes could swim in laughter, when thy soul
>   Lies drenched and drowned in red tears of blood. (II, iii.)
>   *(c)* Drops of cold sweat sit dangling on my hairs
>   Like morning's dew upon the golden flowers. (III, ii.)
Where the imagery is not inept, as in *(c)*, it is commonplace, as in *(a)* and *(b)*; there is nothing highly charged or potently evocative. In Heywood's general dramatic technique statement takes the place of evocation: Mrs Frankford is *stated* to be the model wife, and the moral of the play is stated, not implicit; in other words Heywood's drama is sentimental rather than ethical. And sentimental drama is made by exploiting situations provided by conventional morality rather than by exploring the full significance of those situations.

here. Just as *A Woman Killed with Kindness* is based on conventional ethics, so his plays of London life reflect prevailing attitudes and sentiments.

The immensely popular *Edward IV* and *If You Know Not Me, You Know Nobody* are the most interesting in this connexion.[70] Each of them appeals to national and local pride.

The early part of *Edward IV* shows the siege of London by the rebel Falconbridge and his repulse by the citizens. The events are acted in familiar places:

> The Mint is ours, Cheap, Lombard Street our own[71] —

and the Lord Mayor and Aldermen with their 'Velvet coats and gorgets, and leading staves', the citizens in their flat caps, 'the whole companies of Mercers, Grocers, Drapers, and the rest' are represented on the stage.[72] The rebels are finally beaten off by the true citizens and 'the prentices do great service'[73] —

> Nay, scorn us not that we are prentices.
> The Chronicles of England can report
> What memorable actions we have done,
> To which this day's achievements shall be knit,
> To make the volume larger than it is.[74]

The second part of *If You Know Not Me* makes a similar appeal to London pride, and provides the pleasure which comes from a recognition of the familiar. We see the planning, building and naming of the Royal Exchange, which is declared peerless:

> *1 Lord.* Trust me, it is the goodliest thing I have seen:
>   England affords none such.
> *2 Lord.* Nor Christendom;
>   I might say all the world has not his fellow.[75]

Heywood's quality as moralist and journalist is brought out by his *Gynaikeion, or Nine Books of Various History Concerning Women* (1624), in which one forgets the essential purpose in working through the mixture of anecdotal, historical and moralistic fiction ('For variety of history, intermixt with discourse of times, makes the argument less tedious to the reader', as he remarks in *A Curtain Lecture* (1637), p. 49).

70. The two parts of *Edward IV* were probably acted towards the end of the sixteenth century, and were published in editions dated 1600, 1605, 1613, 1619 and 1626. There is some dispute about the authorship, but I cannot doubt that the greater part of the play is by Heywood. *If You Know Not Me, You Know Nobody* was produced in 1605. Part I, or *The Troubles of Queen Elizabeth,* was published in 1605 (it was pirated), and reprinted in 1606, 1608, 1610, 1613, 1623, 1632 and 1639. Part II, *With the Building of the Royal Exchange: And the Famous Victory of Queen Elizabeth, in the Year 1588,* was published in editions dated 1606, 1609, 1623 (?) and 1632. According to *Eastward Ho!* (III, ii) the actors called it 'their get-penny'.

71. I, 26. (The references are to the volume and page of Heywood's *Dramatic Works* in the Pearson Reprints.)

72. I, 11-13.

73. I, 20.

74. I, 18.

75. I, 295. Gresham also speaks of Gresham College: 'my school of the seven learned liberal sciences' (I, 301).

But Heywood demands the sympathy of his audience in more important ways than these. In the first place, we notice the faithful representation of homely wisdom.

> *King* (in disguise). Prithee tell me, how love they King Edward?
> *Hobs* (the Tanner of Tamworth). Faith, as poor folks love holidays, glad to have them now and then; but to have them come too often will undo them. So, to see the king now and then 'tis comfort; but every day would beggar us; and I may say to thee, we fear we shall be troubled to lend him money; for we doubt he's but needy.[76]

> *King.* King Henry is dead... How will the Commons take it?
> *Hobs.* Well, God be with good King Henry.
> Faith, the Commons will take it as a common thing.
> Death's an honest man; for he spares not the King.
> For as one comes, another's ta'en away;
> And seldom comes the better, that's all we say.[77]

The homeliness is significant. Heywood may appeal to prejudice, he may occasionally reinforce undesirable attitudes (as in the scene of vulgar ostentation where Gresham boasts of his wealth and drinks a priceless pearl[78]), but neither he nor any of his fellows encouraged the audience to indulge in enervating fantasy. The plays of romantic adventure, such as *The Four Prentices* and *The Fair Maid of the West,* are frankly romantic and extravagant, — fairy tales, although their characters are taken from everyday life. In Heywood's realistic plays, as in Dekker's, there is the usual insistence on the happiness of humble life:

> *King.* Farewell, John Hobs, the honest true tanner!
> I see plain men, by observation
> Of things that alter in the change of times,
> Do gather knowledge; and the meanest life
> Proportion'd with content sufficiency,
> Is merrier than the mighty state of kings.[79]

And although citizen advancement to wealth and dignity is frequently represented[80] it is almost always shown as advancement within one's order, a result of honest dealing; and it involves corresponding duties. In *Edward IV* the Lord Mayor, Sir John Crosbie, 'in his scarlet gown', tells how as a castaway he was found by a shoemaker, and later apprenticed to the Grocer's trade:

---

76. *Edward IV,* Part I; I, 45.
77. *Ibid.,* I, 51.
78. The Second Part of *If You Know Not Me,* I, 301.
79. *Edward IV,* Part I; I, 47.
80. *Lord Mayor.* And, prentices, stick to your officers,
     For you may come to be as we are now. (*Edward IV,* Part I; I, 17.)

Wherein God pleased to bless my poor endeavours,
That, by his blessing, I am come to this.
The man that found me I have well requited,
And to the Hospital, my fostering place,
An hundred pound a year I give for ever.
Likewise, in memory of me, John Crosbie,
In Bishopsgate Street, a poor-house have I built,
And as my name have called it Crosbie House.[81]

Honest thrift is, of course, applauded; thus one of Gresham's factors describes his master:

He is a merchant of good estimate:
Care how to get, and forecast to increase,
(If so they be accounted) be his faults.
Merchant. They are especial virtues, being clear
From avarice and base extortion.[82]

But descriptions of advancement are usually made the occasion for moral homilies. When the Dean of St. Paul's has reconciled the merchants, Gresham and Ramsie, he shows them portraits of London worthies and their wives, and recounts their civic fame:

This, Ave Gibson, who in her husband's life,
Being a Grocer, and a Sheriff of London,
Founded a Free School at Ratcliff,
There to instruct three score poor children;
Built fourteen alms-houses for fourteen poor,
Leaving for Tutors 50 pound a year,
And quarterly for every one a noble.[83]

The merchants are moved to emulation:

Gresham. And we may be ashamed,
For in their deeds we see our own disgrace.
We that are citizens, are rich as they were,
Behold their charity in every street,
Churches for prayer, alms-houses for the poor,
Conduits which brings us water; all which good
We do see, and are relieved withal,

---

81. I, 57. Compare the 'increase of wealth and advancement' brought by 'honest and orderly industry' to the goldsmith's apprentice Goulding, in *Eastward Ho!* (1605). There is an obvious element of parody in this play, written by Jonson, Chapman and Marston, acted at the Blackfriars, and dedicated 'to the City'—but it shows what the citizens liked. At the Blackfriars Touchstone's tags—'Keep thy shop and thy shop will keep thee', etc.—the sudden rise of the honest apprentice and the equally sudden repentance of the prodigal were probably not received in the same spirit as they would have been at the Fortune.
82. The Second Part of *If You Know Not Me*, I, 251.
83. *Ibid.*, I, 278.

And yet we live like beasts, spend time and die,
Leaving no good to be remembered by.[84]

The Dean replies with a little sermon obviously addressed to the audience:

If you will follow the religious path
That these have beat before you, you shall win Heaven.
Even in the mid-day walks you shall not walk the street,
But widows' orisons, lazars' prayers, orphans' thanks,
Will fly into your ears, and with a joyful blush
Make you thank God that you have done for them;
When, otherwise, they'll fill your ears with curses,
Crying, We feed on woe, you are our nurses,
O is't not better than young couples say,
You rais'd us up, than, You were our decay?[85]

The charitable ideal expressed here was not, of course, by itself sufficient to meet the new economic problems of the age, of which Heywood,
like Dekker, was imperfectly aware. But it represents the medieval
tradition of neighbourliness, and on the few occasions that Heywood
mentions specific economic diseases of the time he treats them in the
same spirit. Enclosers of commons are 'greedy cormorants'[86]— the usual
phrase—and usurers' claws are more cruel than those of the devil.[87]
An interesting passage occurs where Edward IV offers the Tanner of
Tamworth a boon:

King. Hast thou no suit touching thy trade, to transport hides or
sell leather only in a certain circuit; or about bark, or such like,
to have letters patent?
Hobs. By the mass and the matins, I like not those patents. Sirrah,
they that have them do as the priests did in old time, buy and
sell the sins of the people. So they make the King believe they
mend what's amiss, and for money they make the thing worse
than it is. There's another thing in too, the more is the pity . . .
that one subject should have in his hand that might do good
throughout the land.[88]

84. I, 277.
85. I. 278.
86. *Edward IV*, Part I; I, 9.
87. Thou wretch, thou miser, thou vile slave
    And drudge to money, bondman to thy wealth,
    Apprentice to a penny, thou that hoards up
    The fry of silver pence and half-pennies,
    With show of charity to give the poor,
    But put'st them to increase. . . .
    Thou that invent'st new clauses for a bond
    To cozen simple plainness: O not a dragon
    No, nor the devil's fangs are half so cruel
    As are thy claws. (*The Fair Maid of the Exchange*, II, 29.)
88. I, 46.

Economic individualism is met by arguments based on considerations of the common good. One of the petitioners of Jane Shore complains that she has forgotten his suit:

> *Jane.* Oh, 'tis for a licence to transport corn
> From this land, and lead, to foreign realms.
> I had your bill; but I have torn your bill;
> And 'twere no shame, I think, to tear your ears,
> That care not how you wound the commonwealth.
> The poor must starve for food, to fill your purse,
> And the enemy bandy bullets of our lead!
> No, Master Rufford, I'll not speak for you,
> Except it be to have you punished.[89]

It is not, however, in isolated instances of this kind that we find the main social significance of these plays, but in the kind of conduct that they extol. Most of them contain examples of neighbourly dealing; debts are forgiven, the poor and unfortunate are relieved.[90] 'Impersonal' economic processes, that is, are not accepted with complacency; they are seen in terms of human suffering and happiness. However bad the plays of the category we have been discussing may be, most of them fostered that 'sense of community' that was a legacy from the Middle Ages, and helped to stabilize decent social attitudes on which the greater dramatists could build.

89. *Edward IV*, Part I; I, 83.
90. Cf. *The Life and Death of Thomas, Lord Cromwell*, II, i, IV, ii, and IV, iv, and The Second Part of *If You Know Not Me*, I, 304-307.

20

Literature and Ideas

A. O. Lovejoy

Optimism and Romanticism

The purpose of this paper is, first, to attempt to correct a still rather widely prevalent error concerning the logical import and the usual emotional temper of eighteenth-century optimism, and, second, to point out that the significance in the history of ideas of the multiplication and the popularity of theodicies in the first half of that century consisted less in the tendency of these arguments to diffuse optimistic views of the nature of reality than in their tendency to procure acceptance for certain new ideas of the nature of the good, which the logical exigencies of the optimistic argument involved — ideas pregnant with important consequences for both ethics and aesthetics, since they were to be among the most distinctive elements in what perhaps best deserves to be named "Romanticism."

I

The common thesis of eighteenth-century optimists was, as every school-boy knows, the proposition that this is the best of possible worlds; and this fact, together with the connotation which the term "optimism" has come to assume in popular usage, has given rise to the belief that the adherents of this doctrine must have been exuberantly cheerful persons, fatuously blind to the realities of human experience and of human nature, or insensible to all the pain and frustration and conflict which are manifest through the entire range of sentient life. Yet there was in fact nothing in the optimist's creed which logically required him either to blink or to belittle the facts which we ordinarily call evil. So far from asserting the unreality of evils, the philosophical optimist in the eighteenth century was chiefly occupied in demonstrating their necessity. To assert that this is the best of possible worlds implies nothing as to the absolute goodness of this world; it implies only that any other world which is metaphysically capable of existence would be worse. The reasoning of the optimist was directed less to showing how much of what men commonly reckon good

From *PMLA*, XLII (December 1927), 921-945. Reprinted by permission of the Modern Language Association.

there is in the world of reality than to showing how little of it there is in the world of possibility—in that eternal logical order which contains the Ideal of all things possible and compossible, which the mind of God was conceived to have contemplated "before the creation," and by the necessities of which, ineluctable even to Omnipotence, his creative power was restricted.

At bottom, indeed, optimism had much in common with that Manichean dualism, against Bayle's defense of which so many of the theodicies were directed. Optimism too, as Leibniz acknowledged, had its two antagonistic "principles." The rôle of the "evil principle" was simply assigned to the divine reason, which imposed singular impediments upon the benevolent intentions of the divine will. The very ills which Bayle had argued must be attributed to the interference of a species of extraneous Anti-God, for whose existence and hostility to the good no rational explanation could be given, were by the optimist attributed to a necessity inhering in the nature of things; and it was questionable whether this was not the less cheerful view of the two. For it was possible to hope that in the fullness of time the Devil might be put under foot, and believers in revealed religion were assured that he would be; but logical necessities are eternal, and the evils which arise from them must therefore be perpetual. Thus eighteenth-century optimism not only had affinities with the dualism to which it was supposed to be antithetic, but the arguments of its advocates at times sounded strangely like those of the pessimist—a type by no means unknown in the period.[1] The moral was different, but the view of the concrete facts of experience was sometimes very much the same; since it was the optimist's contention that evil—and a great deal of it—is involved in the general constitution of things, he found it to his purpose to dilate, on occasion, upon the magnitude of the sum of evil and upon the depth and breadth of its penetration into life. It is thus, for example, that Soame Jenyns, in one of the typical theodicies of the middle of the century, seeks to persuade us of the admirable rationality of the cosmic plan:

> I am persuaded that there is something in the abstract nature of pain conducive to pleasure; that the sufferings of individuals are absolutely necessary to universal happiness. . . . Scarce one instance, I believe, can be produced of the acquisition of pleasure or convenience by any creatures, which is not purchased by the previous or consequential sufferings of themselves or others. Over what mountains of slain is every empire rolled up to the summit of prosperity and luxury, and what new scenes of desolation attend its fall. To what infinite toil of men, and other animals, is every flourishing city indebted for all the conveniences and enjoyments of life, and what vice and misery do those very equipments introduce. . . . The pleasures annexed to the preservation of ourselves

1. See, for an example, the writer's paper "Rousseau's Pessimist," *Mod. Lang. Notes,* XXXVIII (1924), 449; and for an earlier one, Prior's *Solomon* (1718), a poetical elaboration of the thesis that "the pleasures of life do not compensate our miseries; age steals upon us unawares; and death, as the only cure of our ills, ought to be expected, not feared."

are both preceded and followed by numberless sufferings; preceded
by massacres and tortures of various animals preparatory to a
feast, and followed by as many diseases lying wait in every dish
to pour forth vengeance on their destroyers.[2]

This gloomy rhetoric was perfectly consistent in principle with optimism,
and it manifested at least one natural tendency of the champions of that
doctrine; for the more numerous and monstrous the evils to be explained,
the greater was the triumph when the author of a theodicy explained
them.

The argument, indeed, in some of its more naïve expressions tends to
beget in the reader a certain pity for an embarrassed Creator, infinitely
well-meaning, but tragically hampered by "necessities in the nature of
things" in his efforts to make a good world. What could be more pathetic
than the position in which—as Soame Jenyns authoritatively informs
us—Omnipotence found itself when contemplating the creation of mankind?

> Our difficulties arise from our forgetting how many difficulties
> Omnipotence has to contend with: in the present instance it is
> obliged either to afflict innocence or be the cause of wickedness;
> it has no other option.[3]

In short the writings of the optimists afforded abundant ground for
Voltaire's exclamation:

> Vous criez "Tout est bien" d'une voix lamentable!

Voltaire's chief complaint of these philosophers in the *Poem on the Lisbon
Disaster* was not, as has often been supposed, that they were too indecently
cheerful, that their view of the reality of evil was superficial; his complaint was that they were too depressing, that they made the actual evils
we experience appear worse by representing them as inevitable and
inherent in the permanent structure of the universe.[4]

> Non, ne présentez plus à mon coeur agité
> Ces immuables lois de la nécessité!

2. *A Free Inquiry into the Nature and Origin of Evil* (1757), 60-2. Jenyns for the most part
merely puts into clear and concise form the arguments of King, Leibniz and Pope; but he differs
from these in unequivocally and emphatically rejecting the freedomist solution of the problem
of moral evil. His book had a considerable vogue, went into numerous editions, and was translated into French.
3. *Ibid.*, 104, where the curious reader may, if he will, find why this option was "necessary,"
and how "Infinite Wisdom" made the best of it.
4. Voltaire, however, is arguing in the poem against two distinct and essentially opposed
types of theodicy: the philosophical and necessitarian type, which endeavored to explain such
a thing as the Lisbon earthquake as
  l'effet des éternelles lois
 Qui d'un Dieu libre et bón nécessitent le choix,
and the theological and indeterminist type, which saw in such catastrophes special interposi-
tions of deity in punishment of men's free choice of moral evil. The reasonings aimed at these
two opposite objectives Voltaire confusingly runs together.

An evil unexplained seemed to Voltaire more endurable than the same evil explained, when the explanation consisted in showing that from all eternity the avoidance of just that evil had been, and through all eternity the avoidance of others like it would be, logically inconceivable. In this his own feeling, and his assumption about the psychology of the emotions in other men, was precisely opposite to that of Spinoza, who believed that everything becomes endurable when we once see clearly that it could never have been otherwise, that it is truly rooted in the eternal world of Ideas: *quatenus mens res omnes ut necessarias intelligit, eatenus minus ab affectibus patitur.*[5] Though most of the optimistic writers of the eighteenth century were less thorough-going or less frank in their cosmical determinism than Spinoza, such philosophic consolation as they offered was at bottom the same as his. It was an essentially intellectual consolation; the mood that it was usually designed to produce was that of reasoned acquiescence in the inevitable, based upon a conviction that its inevitableness was of the nature of *logical* necessity, and was due to no arbitrary caprice; or, at a higher pitch, a devout willingness to be damned — that is, to be as much damned as one was — for the better demonstration of the reasonableness of the scheme of things. Whether confronted with physical or moral evils, wrote Pope, "to reason well is to submit"; and again:

> Know thy own point; this kind, this due degree,
> Of blindness, weakness, Heaven bestows on thee.
> Submit!

It is, of course, true that the optimistic writers were eager to show how good comes out of evil; but the point which it was indispensable for them to establish was that it could come in no other way. It is true, also, that they were wont, when they reached the height of their argument, to discourse with eloquence on the perfection of the Universal System as a whole; but that perfection in no way implied either the happiness or the excellence of the finite parts of the system. On the contrary, the fundamental and characteristic premise of the usual proof of optimism was the proposition that the perfection of the whole depends upon, indeed, consists in, the existence of every possible degree of imperfection in the parts. Voltaire, once more, summarized the argument not altogether unjustly when he wrote:

> Vous composerez dans ce chaos fatal
> Des malheurs de chaque être un bonheur général.

The essence of the optimist's enterprise was to find the evidence of the "goodness" of the universe, not in the paucity but rather in the multiplicity of what to the unphilosophic mind appeared to be evils. And it was also from this central paradox of optimism that those ulterior implications followed which were to help to generate the "Romantic" view of life and of art.

5. *Ethica,* V., Prop. 6.

II

All this can best be shown by an analysis of the argument in its logical sequence, as it is set forth in the earliest and, perhaps, when its indirect influence is also considered, the most influential, of eighteenth-century theodicies—the *De origine mali* (1702) of William King, then Bishop of Derry, afterwards Archbishop of Dublin. The original Latin work does not appear to have had wide currency; but in 1731 an English version appeared,[6] with copious additions, partly extracts from King's posthumous papers, partly original notes "tending to vindicate the author's principles against the objections of Bayle, Leibnitz, the author of a Philosophical Inquiry concerning Human Liberty, and others," by the translator, Edmund Law, subsequently bishop of Carlisle. The translation went through five editions during Law's lifetime,[7] and it seems to have been much read and discussed. Law was a figure of importance in his day, being the spokesman of "the most latitudinarian position" in the Anglican theology of the time;[8] and his academic dignities as Master of Peterhouse and Knightbridge Professor of Moral Philosophy at Cambridge in the 1750's and 60's doubtless increased the range of his influence. There can hardly be much doubt that it was largely from the original work of King that Pope derived, directly or through Bolingbroke, the conceptions which, re-arranged with curious incoherency, served for his vindication of optimism in the First Epistle of the *Essay on Man*.[9]

It can by no means be said that King begins his reflection on the subject by putting on rose-tinted spectacles. He recognizes from the outset all

6. *An Essay on the Origin of Evil by Dr. William King, translated from the Latin with Notes and a Dissertation concerning the Principle and Criterion of Virtue and of the Passions; By Edmund Law, M. A., Fellow of Christ College in Cambridge*. I quote from the second edition, Lond., 1732, here referred to as "Essay."

7. The dates are 1731, 1732, 1739, 1758, 1781.

8. Stephen, *English Thought*, p. 406.

9. Bolingbroke in the *Fragments* quotes King frequently and with respect; he recognizes in him the one theologian who "saw plainly" the truth of the thesis which Bolingbroke devotes scores of pages to developing and defending, viz., that man is not the final cause of the creation; and his own argument for optimism, though less methodically stated, follows in great part the same line as King's (see references below). I can see no reason for doubting that in the *Fragments* as printed we have, as Bolingbroke asserted, in a somewhat expanded form "the notes which were communicated to Mr. Pope in scraps, as they were written," and utilized by the latter in writing the *Essay on Man;* the numerous and exact verbal parallels between passages in the *Fragments* and the *Essay* are not susceptible of any other probable explanation. (See Bolingbroke's *Works*, 1809 ed., VII, 278 and VIII, 356). Law wrote in the preface to the 1781 edition of the *Essay on the Origin of Evil:* "I had the satisfaction of seeing that those very principles which had been maintained by Archbishop King were adopted by Mr. Pope in the *Essay on Man*." When this was challenged by a brother-bishop, Pope's truculent theological champion Warburton, Law replied by referring to the testimony of Lord Bathurst, "who saw the very same system in Lord Bolingbroke's own hand, lying before Mr. Pope while he composed his *Essay*"; and added: "The point may also be cleared effectually whenever any reader shall think it worth his while to compare the two pieces together, and observe how exactly they tally with one another" (*op. cit.,* p. xvii). Such a comparison seems to me to give reason to believe that Pope made use of King's work directly, as well as of Bolingbroke's adaptation of a part of it. Since it was in 1730 that Pope and Bolingbroke were "deep in metaphysics," and since by 1731 the first three Epistles seem to have been completed (*cf.* Courthope, V, 242), it must have been from the Latin original, not Law's translation, that the poet and his philosophic mentor drew. Thus essentially the same theodicy appeared almost simultaneously in Law's English prose rendering and in Pope's verse. On the relation of King's work to Haller's *Ueber den Ursprung des Uebels* (1734) *cf.* L. M. Price in *PMLA*, XLI (1926), 945-8.

the facts which seem most incompatible with an optimistic view: the "perpetual war between the elements, between animals, between men"; "the errors, miseries and vices" which are "the constant companions of human life from its infancy"; the prosperity of the wicked and the suffering of the righteous. There are "troops of miseries marching through human life." And King is innocent of the amazing superficiality of Milton's theodicy; while he, too, assumes the freedom of the will, he sees clearly that this assumption can touch only a fraction of the problem. Not all evils are "external, or acquired by our choice"; many of them "proceed from the constitution of Nature itself."[10] The dualistic doctrine of Bayle, while it, too, has the advantage of "acquitting God of all manner of blame," is philosophically an "absurd hypothesis." King, in short, is to attribute evil, not—at least not primarily nor chiefly—either to the mysterious perversity of man's will or to the machinations of the Devil; he is to show its *necessity* from a consideration of the nature of deity itself. His undertaking is nothing less than that of facing all the evils of existence and showing them to be "not only consistent with infinite wisdom, goodness and power, but necessarily resulting from them."[11]

The traditional division of evils into three classes—evils of limitation or imperfection, "natural" evils, and moral evils—provides the general scheme of the argument, which is, in brief, that there could not conceivably have been any creation at all without the first sort of evil; and that all of the second sort, at least, follow with strict logical necessity from the first. Even Omnipotence could not create its own double; if any beings other than God were to exist they must in the nature of the case be differentiated from him through the "evil of defect"—and, as is assumed, be differentiated from one another by the diversity of their defects. Evil, in short, is primarily privation; and privation is involved in the very concept of all beings except one. This Law puts in the terms of Aristotelian and Scholastic philosophy in his summary of King's "scheme":

> All creatures are necessarily imperfect, and at an infinite distance from the perfection of the Deity, and if a negative principle were admitted, such as the Privation of the Peripatetics, it might be said that every created being consists of existence and non-existence; for it is nothing in respect both of those perfections which it wants, and of those which others have. And this... mixture of non-entity in the constitution of created beings is the necessary principle of all natural evils, and of a possibility of moral ones.[12]

In other words, in King's own phrase, "a creature is descended from God, a most perfect Father; but from Nothing as its Mother, which is Imper-

10. *Essay,* I, 103
11. *Ibid.,* 109-113
12. *Ibid.,* XIX. This argument remained as the usual starting point of a numerous series of subsequent theodicies, some of which have a place in literature: *e.g.,* Victor Hugo still thought it needful to devote a number of lines to the exposition of it in *Les Contemplations* ("Ce que dit la Bouche d'Ombre," 350 *ff.*)

fection." And the virtually dualistic character of this conception is shown by the fact that the inferior parent, in spite of the purely negative rôle which appeared to be implied by her name, was conceived to be responsible for many seemingly highly positive peculiarities of the offspring. This, however, was felt to be an unobjectionable dualism, partly because the second or evil principle was *called* "Nothing," and partly because its existence as a factor in the world, and the effects of it, could be regarded as logically necessary and not as a mysterious accident.

But the significant issue did not lie in this simple, almost tautological piece of reasoning. Doubtless, if the Absolute Being was not to remain forever in the solitude of his own perfection, the prime evil of limitation or imperfection must characterize whatever other beings he brought forth. But that evil was not thereby justified unless it were shown, or assumed, that the creation of such other, necessarily defective beings is itself a good. This crucial assumption King unhesitatingly makes, as well as a further assumption which seems far from self-evident. Even if it were granted that it is good that *some* beings other than God, some finite and imperfect natures, should exist, would it not (some might ask) have been less irrational that only the highest grade of imperfection should be generated — as had, indeed, been originally the case, according to an account of the creation supported by a considerable weight of authority in the theological tradition of Christianity, and comparatively recently revived by Milton.[13] If God could be supposed to need company — which it seemed philosophically a paradox and was theologically a heresy to admit — should it not at least have been good company, a *civitas dei* composed wholly of pure spirits? King saw no way of achieving a satisfactory theodicy unless this latter question were answered (again with the support of many ancient and medieval writers) in the negative. It was requisite to show that not only imperfection in general, but every one of the observable concrete imperfections of the actual world, ought to have been created; and this could not be shown unless it were laid down as a premise that it is inherently and absolutely good that *every* kind of thing (however far down in the scale of possibles) should actually be, so far as its existence is logically conceivable, *i.e.*, involves no contradiction.

This proposition then — expressed in theological terminology — was the essential thesis in the argument for optimism propounded by King and Law. There is inherent in the divine essence as an element in God's perfection a special attribute of "goodness," which makes it necessary that all other and less excellent essences down to the very lowest — so far as they are severally and jointly possible — shall have actual existence after their kind.

> God might, indeed, have refrained from creating, and continued alone, self-sufficient and perfect to all eternity; but his infinite Goodness would by no means allow it; this obliged him to produce

---

13. See the patristic authorities cited by Sumner in his tr. of Milton's *Christian Doctrine*, 187, n. 4. The view adopted by Milton, however, was of doubious orthodoxy. It had been rejected by Thomas Aquinas, *Summa Theol.*, I, q. 61, a. 3; and by Dante, *Paradiso* XXIX, 37.

external things; which things, since they could not possibly be perfect, the Divine Goodness preferred imperfect ones to none at all. Imperfection, then, arose from the infinity of Divine Goodness.[14]

And, thus committed by his own nature to the impartation of actual being to *some* imperfect essences, God could not refuse the boon of existence to any:

> If you say, God might have omitted the more imperfect beings, I grant it, and if that had been best, he would undoubtedly have done it. But it is the part of infinite Goodness to choose the very best; from thence it proceeds, therefore, that the more imperfect beings have existence; for it was agreeable to that, not to omit the very least good that could be produced. Finite goodness might possibly have been exhausted in creating the greater beings, but infinite extends to all. . . . There must then be many, perhaps infinite, degrees of perfection in the divine works. . . . It was better not to give some so great a degree of happiness as their natures might receive, than that a whole species of being should be wanting to the world.[15]

Not only must all possible *species* enjoy existence, but, adds King's editor, "from the observation that there is no manner of chasm or void, no link deficient in this great Chain of Being, and the reason of it, it will appear extremely probable also that every distinct order, every class or species, is as full as the nature of it would permit, or [Law devoutly but, upon his own principles, tautologically adds] as God saw proper."

The foundation, then, of the argument for optimism was a very old conception, than which few, I think, have affected Western thought more profoundly or at more diverse points—but which has been so little recognized or connectedly studied by historians that it has received no appropriate name. I shall call it the principle of plenitude. It is the assumption that a good or rational universe must be a *plenum formarum,* that every Platonic Idea has—subject only to the law of contradiction, to the limitations of logical impossibility and incompossibility—a valid claim to existence, that if a single such claim remained avoidably unrealized the world would be *eo ipso* shown to be, not merely incomplete, but irrational and therefore evil, and that the entire series of other essences whose necessary actualization is thus implied by the assumption of the perfection of the divine essence must constitute a minutely graded hierarchy, a *continuum* of forms from highest to lowest, of which any two adjacent members differ only infinitesimally. The conception takes its

14. King, *op. cit.,* I, 116 f. For the same conception of the Scale of Being and its necessary completeness in a well-ordered universe, *cf.* Bolingbroke, *Fragments (Works,* 1809, VIII, 173, 183, 186, 192, 218 f., 232, 363, 364-5).

15. *Op. cit.,* 137 f., 129-131 f., 156. Both King and Law fell into curious waverings, and in the end into self-contradiction, when the question was raised whether the number of degrees in the scale of being is actually infinite. Into this it is unnecessary to enter here.

start in a famous passage of the *Timæus;*[16] it is the essential principle of the dialectic of Neoplatonic emanationism;[17] it had been used by Abelard in the twelfth century as the basis at once for a proof of cosmical determinism similar to Spinoza's, and of optimism similar to that of King and his eighteenth-century successors;[18] it had played a great part in the system of Thomas Aquinas, though accompanied by ingenious distinctions and elusive modifications designed to rid it of its heterodox consequences;[19] and in the seventeenth century it had been a favorite theme of some of the English Platonists. On the other hand it, or the rationalistic premises on which it rested, had been rejected, as inconsistent with the freedom of the divine will, by a slightly less long line of philosophers and theologians, notably by Peter Lombard in the famous compend which was for centuries the chief textbook of students of theology,[20] and by Duns Scotus and his followers; and it had been not only conspicuously absent from, but plainly contradicted by, the cosmogony and theodicy of Milton, who in this matter is a continuer rather of the Scotist than the Thomist tradition. Since the principle of plenitude had received expression from hundreds of writers before King, its utilization by later optimists is no evidence that they derived it from him. Nevertheless, for reasons already indicated, the probability remains that it was because of the reiteration and elaboration of the principle in the *De origine mali* that Pope gave the fundamental place, in his own argument for the thesis that whatever is, is right, to the premise that, in the "best of systems possible,"

> All must full or not coherent be,
> And all that rises, rise in due degree.

For the purposes of a theodicy, the principle of plenitude served most directly and obviously as an "explanation" of the "evil of defect." The limitations of each species of creature, which define its place in the scale, are indispensable to that infinite differentiation of things in which the "fullness" of the universe consists, and are therefore necessary to the realization of the greatest of goods. Man, therefore, cannot rationally complain because he lacks many endowments and means of enjoyment which might conceivably have been granted him. In Law's words:

> From the supposition of a Scale of Being, gradually descending from perfection to non-entity, and complete in every intermediate rank and degree, we shall soon see the absurdity of such questions as these, Why was not man made more perfect? Why are not his faculties equal to those of angels? Since this is only asking why

16. *Timæus,* 29.
17. Cf., *e.g.,* Plotinus, *Enn.* V, 4, 1; IV, 86.
18. *Introd. ad Theologiam,* III; in Migne, *Patrol. Lat.,* CLXXVIII, cols. 1093-1101.
19. *Summa contra Gentiles,* I, 75; II, 45; II, 68; II, 71.
20. *Liber Sent.,* I, 442.

he was not placed in a different class of beings, when at the same time all other classes are supposed to be full.[21]

It was, in short, "necessary that the creature should fill the station wherein it was, or none at all." If he were anywhere else, he would not be the same entity; and if he did not exist at all, there would be a gap in the series, and the perfection of the creation would thereby be destroyed. Undeniably these distinguishing deficiencies "bring many inconveniences on the persons whose lot it is to fill that part of the universe which requires a creature of such an imperfect nature." For example, a man has no wings, a perfection granted to birds.

> 'Tis plain that in his present circumstances he cannot have them, and that the use of them would be very mischievous to society; and yet the want of them necessarily exposes us to many inconveniences. . . . A thousand instances may be given where the evil of imperfection necessarily subjects us to disappointment of appetite, and several other natural evils, which yet are all necessary for the common good.[22]

To this particular form of purely logical consolation Pope recurs repeatedly, with fairly evident dependence upon King. In a "full" system "there must be, somewhere, such a rank as Man"; and the occupant of that rank cannot rationally desire the distinctive attributes of those below or those above him in the scale.[23]

> Why has not man a microscopic eye?
> For this plain reason, man is not a fly.

And

> On superior powers
> Were we to press, inferior might on ours;
> Or in the full creation leave a void,
> Where, one step broken, the great scale's destroyed.[24]

But if the principle of plenitude had been applicable only for the explanation of the "metaphysical" evil of limitation or particularity, it would not have carried the optimist far towards his goal. Most of the things we call evil hardly appear to be adequately describable as mere deficiencies. Even a Platonistic philosopher with a toothache will probably find it difficult to persuade himself that his pain is a wholly negative thing, a metaphysical vacuum consisting merely in the absence of some conceivable positive good. King was therefore forced to use some ingenuity

21. *Essay* I, 131. The argument may already be found in Plotinus, *Enn.* III, 2, 11.
22. *Op. cit.*, 137.
23. For the same argument in Bolingbroke, see *Fragments (Works,* 1809 ed., VIII, 233, 287, 363, 364-5).
24. *Essay on Man,* Ep. I, 48, 193-4, 241-4.

—or rather to utilize the ingenuity of his many precursors—in order to exhibit the numerous train of "natural" evils as equally necessary implications of the same fundamental principle. He seeks to do this, in the first place, on the ground that in a really "full" universe there must be opposition. Creatures necessarily crowd upon, restrict, and therefore come into conflict with, one another. This necessity appears in its primary form in the motion of matter. It was theoretically possible for God to have so disposed matter that it would move "uniformly and all together, either in a direct line or in a circle and the contrariety of motions by that means be prevented." But a material system so simple and harmonious must also, we are assured, have been barren and useless.

> Such a motion therefore was to be excited in it as would separate it into parts, make it fluid, and render it an habitation for animals. But that could not be without contrariety of motion, as any one that thinks of it at all will perceive. And if this be once admitted in matter, there necessarily follows a division and disparity of parts, clashing and opposition, comminution, concretion and repulsion, and all those evils which we behold in generation and corruption. ... The mutual clashing of these concretions could therefore not be avoided, and as they strike upon one another a concussion of the parts and a separation from each other would be necessarily produced, . . . [*i.e.*] corruption.[25]

And since man's place in the Scale of Being is that of a creature partly material, partly spiritual, he is necessarily involved in, and unhappily affected by, these collisions of matter. The preoccupation of the optimists with the notion of the "fullness" of the organic world sometimes led them (by a natural confusion of ideas) to draw an almost Darwinian or Malthusian picture of a Nature over-crowded with aspirants for life and consequently given over to a ubiquitous struggle for existence. King assures us that there is something like a housing-problem even in Heaven.

> If you ask why God does not immediately transplant men into heaven, since 'tis plain they are capable of that happier state; or why he confines them so long . . . on the earth as in a darksome prison, . . . I answer, Because the Heavens are already furnished with inhabitants, and cannot with convenience admit of new ones, till some of the present possessors depart to a better state, or make room some other way for these to change their condition.[26]

Into the further naïve reasonings by which King seeks to deduce the genesis of "pain, uneasiness and dread of death," and indirectly of the

25. *Essay,* I, 147-8; *cf. Essay on Man,* I: 169:
    But all subsists by elemental Strife,
    And passions are the elements of life.
26. *Ibid,* I, 134.

other emotions by which man is tormented, we need not enter. It suffices to quote the concise genealogy of woes in which he sums up his reasons for holding this to be the best of possible worlds:

> Behold how evils spring from and multiply upon each other, while infinite Goodness still urges the Deity to do the very best. This moved him to give existence to creatures, which cannot exist without imperfections and inequality. This excited him to create matter, and to put it in motion, which is necessarily attended with separation and dissolution, generation and corruption. This persuaded him to couple souls with bodies, and to give them mutual affections, whence proceeded pain and sorrow, hatred and fear, with the rest of the passions. Yet all of them are necessary.[27]

Such an argument for optimism closely resembles, and might easily be substituted for, some of the formulas in which primitive Buddhism summed up the creed of pessimism.

The author of the most popular English theodicy of the mid-nineteenth century found, as everyone remembers, peculiar difficulty in the spectacle of "Nature red in tooth and claw with ravin" — in the universal conflict, the daily and hourly cruelties and little, dumb tragedies, which are hidden behind the surface-beauty of every field and wood. But to the typical eighteenth-century writer of a theodicy, even these aspects of Nature gave little trouble. He was no more blind to them than Tennyson; but his universal solvent, the principle of plenitude, served him here as elsewhere. Doubtless, King granted, God could have made a world free from these horrors, simply by refraining from creating carnivorous and predacious animals. But this, again, would have meant a world less full of life.

> A being that has life is *(caeteris paribus)* preferable to one that has not; God, therefore, animated that machine which furnishes out provision for the more perfect animals; which was both graciously and providently done: for by this means he gained so much life to the world as there is in those animals which are food for others; for by this means they themselves enjoy some kind of life, and are of service also to the rest.... Matter, which is fit for the nourishment of man, is also capable of life; if therefore God had denied it life, he had omitted a degree of good which might have been produced without any impediment to his principal design, which does not seem very agreeable to infinite goodness. 'Tis better, therefore, that it should be endowed with life for a time, though 'tis to be devoured afterwards, than to continue totally stupid and unactive.... Let us not be surprised,

---

27. *Ibid*, I, 176. The argument for the necessity of natural evils based upon the principle of plenitude is supplemented by that drawn from the indispensability of uniform general laws; *e.g.* I, 150-3, 196-7, *cf. Essay on Man*, I, 145 ff. This part of King's reasoning does not fall within the theme of the present paper.

then, at the universal war as it were among animals,... or that the strong devour the weaker.[28]

The application of this to the special case of domesticated animals reared for slaughter, which furnished Pope with the theme for some characteristic and detestable lines, was also made by King. Man

> Feasts the animal he dooms his feast,
> And, till he ends the being, makes it blest.

Undeniably the carnivora were among the antecedently possible kinds of creatures; and if the excellence of Nature or its Author consists quite simply in having as many kinds as possible, nothing more need be said in justification of the existence of such animals; in the words of another contemporary divine, quoted with admiration by Law, "it is evident that by this means there is room for more whole species of creatures than there otherwise would be, and that the variety of the creation is thereby very much enlarged and the goodness of its Author displayed."[29] The tendency of the theodicies to promote belief in the blessedness of sheer multitude, the all-importance of having an abundance of "different natures" in the world, at whatever cost, could hardly be better illustrated.

But even if the criterion of the goodness of the universe were assumed to consist, not solely in the diversity of creatures, but in the quantity of the *joie de vivre* it contains, the creation of beasts of prey could still, according to a further argument of King's, be justified. "Animals are of such a nature as to delight in action, or in the exercise of their faculties, nor can we have any other notion of happiness even in God himself." But among the pleasurable activities conceivable before the creation were those which might attach to the procuring of food by predatory creatures. Why, then, should these intense and positive pleasures be lacking, merely that feebler kinds might be spared the transitory pains of being pursued and eaten? Clearly, since "the infinite Power of God was able to produce animals of such capacities," his "infinite Goodness" may "be conceived to have almost compelled him not to refuse or envy (them) the benefit of life." "If you insist," says the archbishop genially to a supposititious critic, "that a lion might have been made without teeth or claws, a viper without venom; I grant it, as a knife without an edge; but then they would have been of quite another species [*i.e.,* there would have been a missing link in the Chain of Being], and have had neither the nature, nor use, nor genius, which they now enjoy." As for the lion's victim, if it were a rational animal it doubtless would, or at all events should, rejoice as does its Maker in the thought of the agreeable exercise which it is affording the "genius" of the lion. If the victim be not endowed with reason, or be too mean-spirited to take a large philosophical view of the matter, the consoling insight into the higher meaning of its sufferings is still, through

---

28. *Ibid,* I, 184-5.

29. J. Clarke, *Discourse concerning Natural Evil,* 1719; the same argument in Plotinus, *Enn.* III, 211. Goldsmith, among others, was still repeating it later in the eighteenth century; v. his *Essays* (1767), 132.

the happy ordering of things, left to be enjoyed vicariously by optimistic archbishops.[30]

Plainly this amiable and devout ecclesiastic had, in the course of his endeavor to justify God's ways to men, been driven not only to a conception of God but also to a conception of ultimate values which came somewhat strangely from a Christian teacher. Though King would, of course, have said that his God was a God of love, the term must necessarily have had for him an unusual sense. The God of the *De origine mali* loved abundance and variety of life more than he loved peace and concord among his creatures and more than he desired their exemption from pain. He loved lions, in short, as well as lambs; and loving lions, he wished them to behave in accordance with the "nature," or Platonic Idea, of a lion, which implies devouring lambs and not lying down with them. And in these preferences the "goodness" of God was assumed to be most clearly manifested—"goodness" thus coming to mean a delight in fullness and diversity of finite being, rather than in harmony and happiness. King and his editor seem only occasionally and confusedly aware how deeply their argument has involved them in such a radical transvaluation of values; they waver between this and the more conventional conception of "divine goodness," and for the most part touch but lightly upon the more paradoxical implications of their premises. Yet they at times betray some uneasy feeling of the incongruity between these premises and certain traditional elements of Christian belief. It was, for example, a part of that belief that in the earthly paradise before the Fall, and also in the celestial paradise which awaits the elect, most of the evils which these theologians were zealously proving to be "necessary," because required by the "divine goodness," were in fact absent. It seemed, therefore, difficult to avoid the awkward dilemma that either the paradisaical state is not good, or else a good "system" does not, after all, require quite so much evil and so many degrees of imperfection as the authors of the theodicies conceived. King meets this difficulty but lamely; he is, in fact, driven to suggest that the felicity of our first parents in Eden has probably been somewhat exaggerated: "it doth not appear that Adam in Paradise was altogether without pain or passion," but rather "that he was only secured from such pains as might cause his death, and that for a time, till removed to a better place."[31]

The outcome of King's reasoning (so far as it was consistently carried through) is not, of course, surprising. He who attempts a theodicy with-

---

30. It is only fair to add that King is equally ready to view as "necessary," and consequently to approve and justify, specific evils less remote from archiepiscopal experience, such as "gout, one of the most tormenting diseases that attend us"—by which, in fact, this resolute optimist was cruelly harassed for nearly half a century, and from an attack of which, according to his biographer, he died. (See Sir C. S. King's volume, 1906, p. 14 and *passim*). Gout, the archbishop observes, in a sportsmanlike if not wholly edifying vein, has compensations which, on the whole, outweigh its pains: "Who would not rather endure it than lose the pleasure of feeling? Most men are sensible that eating certain meats, and indulging ourselves in the use of several drinks, will bring it; and yet we see this doth not deter us from them, and we think it more tolerable to endure the gout, than lose the pleasure that plentiful eating and drinking yields us." (I., 177). Why it was "necessary" *a priori* that these pleasures should be purchasable only at that price remains, in the end, somewhat obscure.

31. *Essay*, I, 176; *cf.* also 148-9.

out first shutting his eyes to a large range of the facts of experience, must necessarily take for the object of his piety the God of Things as They Are; and since things as they are include the whole countless troop of natural ills, it became necessary so to transform the conception of the good as to make it possible to argue that these ills are—not, indeed, goods, considered by themselves—but implicates of some supreme good, in the realization of which the essential nature of deity is most truly manifested. The principle of plenitude, taken as a species of value-theory, was a natural, if not the necessary, result of this enforced revision of the notion of good. Certainly that which the Author of Nature as it is chiefly values could not, on empirical grounds, be supposed to be identical with those things which men have commonly set their hearts upon and have pictured to themselves in their dreams of paradise. Stated in its most general terms, the paradox underlying all these singular implications of the optimist's reasoning is the assumption which is of the essence of the principle of plenitude itself—that *the desirability of a thing's existence bears no relation to its excellence.*

King's further reflections upon the problem of evil do not concern us here, since the conception of the Chain of Being does not much figure in them. It might, indeed, and with more consistency, have done so. For the sort of evil not dealt with by King upon the principles already indicated, namely, moral evil, might naturally have been regarded as a special case of the "evil of defect." A creature having the specific degree of blindness and weakness appropriate to man's place in the scale, and at the same time subject to the passions which King had represented as necessarily inseparable from our psychophysical constitution, could hardly fail, it would seem, to make frequent "wrong elections." So much, indeed, King is constrained to admit; there are many errors of conduct which are due to our ignorance and necessary imperfection, and these are to be classed among the "natural evils" and explained in the same manner as others of that class. But there remains a residuum of "moral evil" not so explicable, but due to a "depraved will." On this theme King for the most part repeats the familiar arguments. Bolingbroke did not follow the archbishop in this, but derived the necessity of moral evil directly from the principle of plenitude. If men had been so constituted as to follow always the ethical "law of nature,... the moral state of mankind would have been paradisaical, but it would not have been human. We should not have been the creatures we were designed to be, and a gap would have been left in the order of created intelligences."[32] In this application of the principle, the antinomian implications of which are sufficiently obvious, Bolingbroke had been anticipated by so saintly a philosopher as Spinoza:

> To those who ask, Why has not God created all men such as to be directed solely by the guidance of reason, I reply only that it is because he had no lack of material wherewith to create all things, from the very highest to the very lowest grade of perfec-

32. *Fragments or Minutes of Essays,* Sec. XVI.

tion, or, more properly speaking, because the laws of his nature were so ample as to suffice for the production of everything that can be conceived by an infinite intellect.[33]

This was carrying a step farther the argument which Pope was to versify: since the best of systems must be as "full" as possible,

> Then in the scale of reasoning life, 'tis plain,
> There must be somewhere such a rank as—

not man only, but also, among men, the fool and the evil-doer.

III

The theodicy of Leibniz was in most essentials the same as that of his English precursor;[34] and in summarizing with approval the main argument of the archbishop's *bel ouvrage, plein de savoir et d'élégance,* Leibniz significantly accentuated the theological paradox contained in it:

> Why, someone asks, did not God refrain from creating things altogether. The author well replies that the abundance of God's goodness is the reason. He wished to communicate himself, even at the expense of that delicacy which our imaginations ascribe to him, when we assume that imperfections shock him. Thus he preferred that the imperfect should exist, rather than nothing.[35]

This emphasis upon the implication that the Creator of the actual world cannot be supposed to be a "delicate" or squeamish God, caring only for perfection—and that, in fact, he would, if more nicely selective in his act of creation, have thereby shown himself the less divine—illustrates clearly the tendency of the optimistic argument to generate a new conception of that in which the goodness of things in general consists. And in developing the theory of value thus implicit in optimism, the German philosopher is franker, more ardent, and more cheerful, than the Anglican theologian. Some analogies in human life to the standards of valuation which the optimists had applied in explaining the supposed purpose of the deity in the creation are not obscurely suggested by Leibniz.

> Wisdom requires variety *(la sagesse doit varier).* To multiply exclusively the same thing, however noble it be, would be a super-

33. *Ethics,* I, *ad. fin.*
34. There is no question of any influence of King upon Leibniz or of Leibniz upon King. Though the *Théodicée* was not published until 1710, eight years after the *De origine mali,* the greater part of it was written between 1697 and the beginning of 1705; and the ideas it contains had long been familiar to Leibniz. Cf. Gerhardt's preface to Leibniz's *Philosophische Schriften,* vol. VI, 3-10.
35. "Remarques sur le livre sur l'origine du mal publié depuis peu en Angleterre," appended to the *Théodicée; Philos. Schriften,* VI, 400 ff. Leibniz observes that he is in agreement with King "only in respect to half of the subject"; the disagreement relates chiefly to King's chapter on liberty and necessity, which (quite inconsistently with the implications of his argument for optimism) asserts that God exercised a *liberum arbitrium indifferentiae* in creating the world.

fluity; it would be a kind of poverty. To have a thousand well-bound copies of Vergil in your library; to sing only airs from the opera of Cadmus and Hermione; to break all your porcelain in order to have only golden cups; to have all your buttons made of diamonds; to eat only partridges and to drink only the wine of Hungary or of Shiraz—could any one call this reasonable?[36]

Something very similar to this had, in point of fact, been regarded as the essence of reasonableness both by neo-classical æsthetic theorists and by a multitude of influential moralists. It would scarcely have seemed evident to the former that two copies of Vergil are of less value than one copy *plus* a copy of the worst epic ever written—still less that a reading of the first followed by a reading of the second is preferable to two readings of Vergil. And the apparent object of the endeavor of most ethical teaching had been to produce a close approach to uniformity in human character and behavior, and in men's political and social institutions. The desire for variety—or for change, the temporal form of it—had rather commonly been conceived to be a nonrational, indeed a pathological, idiosyncrasy of human creatures. But Leibniz not only gave it a sort of cosmic dignity by attributing it to God himself, but also represented it as the very summit of rationality.

The ethically significant consequence which is most plainly drawn from this by Leibniz is that neither what is commonly called moral goodness, nor pleasure, is the most important thing in the world. Both hedonism, in short, and an abstract moralism (such, for example, as Kant and Fichte were afterwards to express) were equally contrary to the value-theory implicit in the principle of plenitude. Virtue and happiness both, of course, have their place in the scale of values; but if it were the highest place, it is inconceivable that God would have made the kind of a world he has made.

> The moral or physical good or evil of rational creatures does not infinitely transcend the good or evil which is purely metaphysical, that is to say, the good which consists in the perfection of the other creatures. . . . No substance is either absolutely precious or absolutely contemptible in the sight of God. It is certain that God attaches more importance to a man than to a lion, but I do not know that we can be sure that he prefers one man to the entire species of lions.[37]

To this thesis Leibniz reverts again and again throughout the *Theodicy:*

> (It is) a false maxim that the happiness of rational creatures is the sole purpose of God. If that had been so, there would, perhaps, have been neither sin nor unhappiness, not even as concomitants. God would have chosen a set of possibles from which all evils were excluded. But he would in that case have fallen short of what is due to the universe, that is, what is due to himself. . . . It is true that one can imagine possible worlds without sin and without suffering,

36. *Théodicée,* § 124.
37. *Théodicée,* § 118.

just as one can invent romances about Utopias or the Sévarambes; but these worlds would be much inferior to ours. I cannot show this in detail; you must infer it, as I do, *ab effectu,* since this world, as it is, is the world God chose.... Virtue is the noblest quality of created things, but it is not the only good quality of creatures. There is an infinite number of others that attract the inclination of God; it is from all these inclinations together that the greatest possible sum of good results; and there would be less good than there is if there were nothing but virtue, if only rational creatures existed.... Midas was less rich when he possessed only gold.[38]

To this is added the trite æsthetic argument for the indispensability of contrast in the production of beauty in a work of art, and, indeed, in the mere physical pleasure of the gustatory sense:

Sweet things become insipid if we eat nothing else; sharp, tart and even bitter things must be combined with them so as to stimulate the taste. He who has not tasted bitter things does not deserve sweet, and, indeed, will not appreciate them.

Thus the argument for optimism represented the Cosmic Artist as cramming his canvas with diversified detail to the last infinitesimal fraction of an inch; as caring far more for fullness and variety of content than for simplicity and perfection of form; and as seeking this richness of coloring and abundance of contrast even at the cost of disharmony, irregularity, and what to us appears confusion. For there is much truth, says Leibniz, in "the fine principle of St. Bernard: *ordinatissimum est, minus interdum ordinate fieri aliquid.*"

IV

The word "Romanticism," I have suggested in an earlier paper, ought to be used in the plural or with the indefinite article; there is a formidably large collection of distinct, seemingly unrelated, and even opposed, ideas or tendencies to which the name has been applied by different writers, and since none has taken the precaution of obtaining copyright for the term, it can hardly be said that one of the current uses is more authorized than another.[39] Nevertheless, if one were to select from among these meanings that one which would do most to clarify the history of ideas, the criteria to be applied are not difficult to formulate. It is usually agreed that "Romanticism" should designate a thing which, if it did not originate, at all events became far more explicit and potent, in the later eighteenth century, and was essentially antithetic to the tendencies of thought and taste dominant in the earlier part of that century and in the preceding one. "Romanticism" *par excellence,* then, should be that change in ruling presuppositions, occurring in the period in question, which is at once the most profound, the most completely and significantly opposed to the

38. *Ibid.,* §§120, 10, 124; *cf.* also 213.
39. On the ambiguities of the term, *cf.* the writer's "The Discrimination of Romanticisms," *PMLA,* XXXIX (1924), 299 ff.

preconceptions alike of the ruling philosophy of the Enlightenment and of the neo-classical æsthetics, the most fruitful of revolutionary consequences, and from which the greatest number of other "Romanticisms" can be seen to derive. If the same innovation can be shown to have been fundamental in the program of those German writers who first introduced the term "romantic" into the vocabulary of philosophy and literary criticism, it would be still better entitled to be considered the prime Romanticism.

There is one manifest change in fundamental conceptions which meets all these criteria. For two centuries the thought of the Western world and, above all, the efforts made during those centuries for improvement and correction in beliefs, in institutions, and in art, had been, in the main, dominated by the assumption that, in each phase of human activity, excellence consists in conforming as nearly as possible to a standard conceived as universal, static, uncomplicated, uniform for every rational being. Rationality and uniformity were, indeed, commonly assumed to be inseparable notions, and there was a marked tendency to define the rational simply as that which is found to be actually universal in the human mind. "Nature" was the word oftenest used to designate such a standard of excellence; and the amazing proposition endlessly reiterated by seventeenth- and early eighteenth-century writers was that nature "is everywhere the same." The norm, then, whether of truth or of beauty, was simple and invariant. In religion the champions of deism, the religion of nature, sought to bring men back to the simple creed which could be supposed (in Leslie Stephen's phrase) to be literally catholic, *i.e.,* to have been understood and accepted *semper, ubique et ab omnibus.* Ethics was summed up in the law of nature, of which universality was the distinguishing mark:

La morale uniforme en tout temps, en tout lieu.

Political philosophy, in so far as it rested upon the notion of natural rights, was concerned only with that which is generic in man; and it tended on the whole, though not without important exceptions, to set up a uniform scheme of government as the ideal for all peoples. In the æsthetics of literature the high neo-classical dogma demanded that the subject-matter and emotional content of a drama or epic should be limited to that which is universal in human experience and capable of appealing equally to all men in all times and all lands. It was their supposed greater universality, both in content and in appeal, which constituted the essence of the superiority attributed to the classical models. In every domain, in short, the program of improvement or reform was one of simplification, standardization, the avoidance of the particular, the elimination of local variations and individual diversities supposed to have arisen through some strange and unhappy aberration from the uniformity of the "natural" order.[40]

There has, in the entire history of thought, been hardly any change in standards of value more profound and more momentous than that which

---

40. A part of Milton's argument in the *Areopagitica* is perhaps the most remarkable seventeenth-century exception to this universalism.

came when the contrary principle began widely to prevail – when it came to be believed that in many, if not all, phases of human activity, not only are there diverse excellences, but that diversity itself is of the essence of excellence; and that of art, in particular, the objective is neither the attainment of some ideal perfection of form in a small number of fixed *genres,* nor, on the other hand, the gratification of that least common denominator of æsthetic susceptibility which is shared by mankind in all ages, but rather the fullest possible expression of the abundance of differentness that there is, actually or potentially, in nature and human nature, and – for the function of the artist in relation to his public – the evocation of capacities for understanding, sympathy, and enjoyment, which are latent in most men, and perhaps never capable of universalization. These assumptions, though assuredly not the only important, are plainly the one *common,* factor in a score of otherwise diverse tendencies which, by one or another critic or historian, have been termed "Romantic": the immense multiplication of *genres* and of verse-forms; the admission of the æsthetic legitimacy of the *genre mixte;* the *goût de la nuance;* the naturalization in art of the "grotesque"; the quest for local color; the endeavor to reconstruct in imagination the *distinctive* inner life of peoples remote in space or in cultural condition; the *étalage du moi;* the demand for particularized fidelity in landscape-description; the revulsion against simplicity; the distrust of universal formulas in politics; the æsthetic antipathy to standardization; the apotheosis of the "concrete universal" in metaphysics; sentimentalism about "the glory of the imperfect"; the cultivation of personal, national and racial idiosyncrasy; the general high valuation (wholly foreign to most earlier periods) of originality, and the usually futile and absurd self-conscious pursuit of that attribute. It is, however, of no great consequence whether or not we apply to this transformation of current assumptions about value the name of "Romanticism"; what it is essential to remember is that the transformation has taken place and that it, perhaps, more than any other one thing distinguishes, both for better and worse, the prevailing assumptions of the thought of the nineteenth and of our own century from those of the preceding period in the intellectual history of the West.

Now the historical thesis which I here suggest – space is not available for the full proof of it[41] – is that the general transition from universalism

41. The rôle of the principle of plenitude, as it had been presented by the optimistic writers, in bringing about this transition may most clearly be seen in Schiller's *Philosophische Briefe,* especially the *Theosophie des Julius* and the concluding letter; in the passages in the *Athenaeum* in which Friedrich Schlegel developed the conception of *romantische Poesie* (on which see the writer's papers, *Mod. Lang. Notes,* 1916 and 1917); and in Schleiermacher's *Reden* (especially II and V) and *Monologen.* I cite only the following: "So ist mir aufgegangen, was jetzt meine höchste Anschauung ist, es ist mir klar geworden, dass jeder Mensch auf eigne Art die Menschheit darstellen soll. in einer eignen Mischung ihrer Elemente, damit auf jede Weise sie sich offenbare, und wirklich werde in der Fülle der Unendlichkeit alles, was aus ihrem Schosse hervorgehen kann.... Allein nur schwer und spät gelangt der Mensch zum vollen Bewusstein seiner Eigentümlichkeit; nicht immer wagt er's drauf hinzusehn, und richtet lieber das Auge auf den Gemeinbesitz der Menschheit, den er so liebend und so dankbar festhält; er zweifelt oft, ob er sich als ein eignes Wesen wieder aus ihm ausscheiden soll.... Das eigenste Bestreben der Natur wird oftmals nicht bemerkt, und wenn am deutlichsten sich ihre Schranken offenbaren, gleitet an der scharfen Ecke das Auge allzuleicht vorbei, und hält nur das Allgemeine fest, wo eben in der Verneinung sich das Eigne zeigt." (*Monologen,* ed. Schiele, 1914, p. 30).

to what may be called diversitarianism in the normative provinces of thought was promoted — by no means solely, but perhaps chiefly — by the emphasis and reiteration given to the principle of plenitude in the arguments of the eighteenth-century defenders of optimism, in the course of the controversy in which so considerable a part of the religious interest and intellectual energy of that age was absorbed. These subtle philosophers and grave divines, and poets like Pope and Haller who popularized their reasonings, rested their assertion of the goodness of the universe ultimately upon the same ground as Stevenson's child in the nursery:

> The world is so full of a number of things.

This did not, it is true, necessarily make them "as happy as kings." That was a matter of individual temperament; and in point of fact most of them had not the child's robust delight in the sheer diversity and multiplicity of things. They were often men whose natural taste or training would have inclined them rather to prefer a somewhat thin, simple and exclusive universe. The philosophers of optimism were not, in short, as a rule of a Romantic disposition; and what they were desirous of proving was that reality is rational through and through, that every fact of existence, however unpleasant, is grounded in some reason as clear and evident as an axiom of mathematics. But in the exigencies of their argument to this ambitious conclusion, they found themselves constrained to attribute to the Divine Reason a conception of the good extremely different from that which had been most current among men, and especially among philosophers; and they were thus led, often against their original temper and intention, to impress upon the minds of their generation a revolutionary and paradoxical theory of the criterion of all value, which may be summed up in the words of a highly Romantic and optimistic lover of paradox in our own day:

> One thing alone is needful: Everything.   •
> The rest is vanity of vanities.

21

Varieties of Literary History: Continuity of Motif

Ernst Curtius

The Muses

The starting point of our inquiry was the historical fact that the Mediterranean-Nordic West was culturally one. Our goal was to demonstrate the same unity in its literature. We had, therefore, to make manifest certain continuities which had hitherto been overlooked. A technique of philological microscopy permitted us to find identical structural elements in texts of the most various origins—elements which we were justified in regarding as expressional constants of European literature. They indicated a general and generally disseminated theory and practice of literary expression. One of these common denominators was rhetoric. We found that poetry frequently entered into combination with rhetoric, as it also did with philosophy and theology. All these complexes had to be examined and clarified. An intricate skein had carefully to be disentangled. In each chapter a different aspect of the same historical material was investigated. In each, as it were, a new net was cast. Our hauls of fish brought to light many individual historical facts—a welcome subsidiary result. But our principal object was to obtain a more accurate knowledge of the structure of our literary material by the use of precision methods which were sound both empirically and systematically. From the most general concepts we descended, by the road of analysis, to particular concepts: from rhetoric to topics, from topics to the topics of eulogy, and so on. The further one proceeds along this line, the more one may hope to approach the historical concrete. One finds it in the "fruitful bathos of experience"...

Among the "concrete" formal constants of the literary tradition are the Muses. In the view of Antiquity, they belonged not only to poetry but to all higher forms of intellectual life besides. To live with the Muses means to live humanistically, as Cicero puts it ("cum Musis, id est, cum humanitate et doctrina": *Tusc.*, V, 23, 66). For us the Muses are shadowy figures of a tradition that has long since had its day. But once they were vital forces.

From *European Literature and the Latin Middle Ages,* tr. W. Trask (New York: Bollingen Foundation, 1953), pp. 228-246. Reprinted by permission of the Bollingen Foundation.

They had their priests, their servants, their promise — and their enemies. Every page in the history of European literature speaks of them.[1]

The history of religion considers the Muses to be deities of springs and connected with the cult of Zeus. In the Pierian sanctuary of the Muses, it is conjectured, there was cultivated a poetry dedicated to the victory of Zeus over the gods of the primal world. This would account for the connection of the Muses with poetry.[2] Homer, to be sure, gives us no hint of such an origin. His Muses are Olympians. Their function in epic is to infuse into the poet the things he is to say. At the beginning of the *Iliad* Homer asks the goddess to sing the wrath of Achilles; at the beginning of the *Odyssey* he asks the Muse to tell him of the man who.... A more elaborate development of the invocation to the Muses is found in the *Iliad* at the beginning of the Catalogue of the Ships (II, 484 ff.). Here Homer needs the Muses not only because they bestow inspiration but also because they know all things. For our purposes it is immaterial whether the Catalogue of the Ships is an interpolation by a Homerid or not. We should read Homer only as he was read for two thousand years. The Catalogue of the Ships is the model for innumerable poetical catalogues even down to our own period. The originator of didactic poetry, Hesiod, also feels bound to the Muses. In him and in Pindar the invocation of the Muses must serve to prove the poet's pedagogical vocation.

Unlike the Olympians, the Muses had no well-marked personalities. No one knew much about them. They incarnate a purely intellectual principle, which could be dissociated from the Greco-Roman pantheon. The only figure in Homer's world of gods with whom they were regularly associated was Apollo. Their image was vague even in ancient Greece. From the earliest times there were conflicting traditions as to their number, lineage, dwelling-place, and function. Hesiod's Muses are different from Homer's, those of Empedocles from those of Theocritus. But from of old the Muses had been patronesses not only of poetry but also of philosophy and music. The schools of both Pythagoras and Plato were connected with the cult of the Muses from their beginnings. But the consensus also placed all higher intellectual pursuits under the sign of the Muses. We have already seen this

1. I published a survey of the Muses from the Augustan Age to *ca.* 1100 in *ZRPh,* LIX (1939), 129-88. Some 25 pagan and 70 Christian authors were treated in it. I added to it in *ZRPh,* LXIII (1943), 256-268. The text of the present chapter is based on these two studies, but uses only a part of them. Those who may wish to familiarize themselves with the evidence or to obtain further details on the subject of the Muses in the Middle Ages are referred to these two essays. For philological readers I add the following: In Walter of Speyer's *Scolasticus (Poetae,* V, 19, 81) Apollo appears, then "Pales Hinnidum plebe secuta," which the editor, Karl Strecker, found incomprehensible. I conjectured (*ZRPh,* LVIII [1938], 139 n.) that the reading should be *Hymnidum*="Muses." Later I came upon an essay by H. Chamard, "Une Divinité de la Renaissance: les Hymnides" (*Mélanges Laumonier* [1935], 163). According to this, the Hymnids are a class of nymphs who are frequently mentioned together with Dryads and Oreads in French texts of the first half of the sixteenth century. They come from Boccaccio's *De genealogia deorum,* where, in Bk. VII, c. 14, he treats "De nymphis in generali." There he says: "Aliae Hymnides appellantur, ut placet Theodontio, quas dixit pratorum atque florum Nymphas existere." Who Boccaccio's "Theodontius" is, no one knows. Cf. Jean Seznec, *The Survival of the Pagan Gods* (Bollingen Series XXXVIII; New York, 1953), pp. 221 f. Boccaccio's Hymnids, then, were already known to Walter of Speyer. But even in Antiquity the Muses were occasionally equated with nymphs (Virgil, *Ecl.,* 7, 21). And later in Isidore, *Et.,* VIII, 9, 96. The Hymnids appear neither in Roscher's *Lexikon der Mythologie* nor in *RE* under *Nymphai.*

2. Otto Kern, *Die Religion der Griechen,* I (1926), 208.

concept in Cicero. He is a cultured writer who feels at ease in the possession of his culture. Virgil's profound, soulful, and passionate love of the Muses is a very different thing. He has expressed it in but one passage in his works, in his poem on husbandry (*Georgics,* II, 475 ff.). He has praised the happy life of the countryman, and now he contrasts with it his own aim in life:

> *Me vero primum dulces ante omnia Musae,*
> *Quarum sacra fero ingenti percussus amore,*
> *Accipiant, caelique vias et sidera monstrent,*
> *Defectus solis varios, lunaeque labores,*
> *Unde tremor terris, qua vi maria alta tumescant*
> *Obicibus ruptis, rursusque in se ipsa residant,*
> *Quid tantum Oceano properent se tinguere soles*
> *Hiberni, vel quae tardis mora noctibus obstet.*
> *Sin, has ne possim naturae accedere partis,*
> *Frigidus obstiterit circum praecordia sanguis,*
> *Rura mihi et rigui placeant in vallibus amnes;*
> *Flumina amen silvasque inglorius . . .*
> *Felix qui potuit rerum cognoscere causas,*
> *Atque metus omnis et inexorabile fatum*
> *Subjecit pedibus strepitumque Acherontis avari!*

(Me indeed first and before all things may the sweet Muses, whose priest I am and whose great love hath smitten me, take to themselves and show me the pathways of the sky, the stars, and the diverse eclipses of the sun and the moon's travails; whence is the earthquake; by what force the seas swell high over their burst barriers and sink back into themselves again; why winter suns so hasten to dip in Ocean, or what hindrance keeps back the lingering nights. But if I may not so attain to this side of nature for the clog of chilly blood about my heart,[3] may the country and the streams that water the valleys content me, and lost to fame let me love stream and woodland. . . . Happy he who hath availed to know the causes of things, and hath laid all fears and immitigable Fate and the roar of hungry Acheron under his feet!) *

It is not the gifts of poetry that Virgil begs from the Muses, but knowledge of cosmic laws. He moves in a circle of ideas in which some scholars have wished to see the eclectic stoicism of Posidonius. The Muses are here the patronesses of philosophy. They bestow the knowledge which conquers the fear of death and the underworld. In the *Aeneid* Virgil again brings in a poet who recites a didactic poem on natural philosophy (I, 740).

In the concluding lines of the *Georgics* (IV, 559-566) the poet turns to contemplate Augustus, contrasts his military exploits with the life of the poet, signs the work with his own name, and connects it with the bucolic poetry of his youth by quoting from himself:

---

3. According to Empedocles the seat of the intellectual faculty is the blood. Virgil, then, is using a dignified periphrasis for "poor intellectual capacity."

[* J. W. Mackail's translation (replacing R. A. Schröder's).]

> *Haec super arvorum cultu pecorumque canebam*
> *Et super arboribus, Caesar dum magnus ad altum*
> *Fulminat Euphraten bello, victorque volentis*
> *Per populos dat iura, viamque adfectat Olympo.*
> *Illo Virgilium me tempore dulcis alebat*
> *Parthenope, studiis florentem ignobilis oti,*
> *Carmina qui lusi pastorum, audaxque iuventa*
> *Tityre, te patulae cecini sub tegmine fagi.*

(Thus I sang of the tending of fields and flocks and trees, while great Caesar hurled war's lightnings by high Euphrates and gave statutes among the nations in welcome supremacy, and scaled the path to heaven. Even in that season I Virgil, nurtured in sweet Parthenope, went in the flowery way of lowly Quiet: I who once played with shepherds' songs, and in youth's hardihood sang thee, O Tityrus, under the covert of spreading beech.)*

Some introductory verses to the *Aeneid* have come down to us (their authenticity is doubted—rightly, it would seem):

> *Ille ego qui quondam gracili modulatus avena*
> *Carmen, et egressus silvis vicina coegi,*
> *Ut quamvis avido parerent arva colono,*
> *Gratum opus agricolis: at nunc horrentia Martis...*

(I who once piped a song on a slender reed; who, quitting the woods, then caused the nearby fields to obey the ever greedy tiller of the soil—a work pleasing to farmers; I now sing the dread weapons of Mars.)

Here Virgil's epic is linked with his bucolic and didactic poetry. This biographical sequence of Virgil's works was regarded by the Middle Ages as a hierarchy grounded in the nature of things—a hierarchy not only of three poetical genres, but also of three social ranks (shepherd, farmer, soldier) and of three kinds of style. It extended to the corresponding trees (beech—fruit-tree—laurel and cedar), locales (pasture—field—castle or town), implements (crook—plow—sword), animals (sheep—cow—horse). These correspondences were reduced to a graphic schema of concentric circles, known as *rota Virgilii* (Virgil's wheel).[4] In Renaissance England bucolic is still regarded as preparatory to epic (Spenser, Milton).

The Muses could not be fitted into this schema. Pastoral poetry, however (in honor of Theocritus), kept its connection with the Sicilian Muses. In Virgil, as we have seen, the Muses of didactic poetry are the patronesses of science and philosophy. The Muses of epic, on the other hand, are close to the Homeric Muses. They impart the mythological prehistory of Aeneas' sufferings (I, 8), give information concerning ancient Latium (VII, 37) and are invoked in connection with the catalogues of troops[5] (VII, 641;

[*Idem.]
4. Faral, 87.
5. The historian Gibbon (1737-94) could still make a study of the question whether the catalogue of troops is a necessary element of an epic.

X, 163). Though the *Aeneid,* the Muses were once again confirmed as stylistic elements of the Western epic. The epic invocation of the Muses, which could be repeated before particularly important or particularly "difficult" passages,[6] serves in Virgil and his followers to decorate the narrative and to emphasize its high points.

Horace devoted to the Muses a poem (*Carm.,* III, 4) by which he sought to further the ethico-religious restoration desired by Augustus. It is not among his happiest productions. More convincing is the high-pitched eloquence with which he celebrates his lyrical activity as a service of the Muses which makes him fellow of the gods (*Carm.,* I, 1, 30):

> *Me doctarum hederae praemia frontium*
> *Dis miscent superis, me gelidum nemus*
> *Nympharumque leves cum satyris chori*
> *Secernunt populo, si neque tibias*
> *Euterpe cohibet, nec Polyhymnia*
> *Lesboum refugit tendere barbiton.*

(Me the ivy, prize of learned brows, makes to mingle with the gods above; me the cool grove and the light-footed companies of nymphs and satyrs set apart from the people: if Euterpe withhold not her flute and Polyhymnia refuse not to tune the Lesbian lyre.)

Declining esteem for the invocation of the Muses is evidenced in Horace in the form of parody (*Sat.,* I, 5, 51); instead of the Muse, Tibullus invokes his friend (II, 1, 35), Propertius his beloved (II, 1, 3). Ovid treats the Muses ironically (*Ars,* II, 704). His own Muse is called "wanton" by his censors (*Rem.,* 362), "playful" by himself (*Rem.,* 387). This Ovidian *musa iocosa* is often invoked by the hedonistically-minded poets of the twelfth century.

Even during the reigns of Augustus' first successors we find a conscious turning away from mythology and heroic poetry: typical examples are Manilius and the poet of the *Aetna.* People had wearied of material which had been thrashed over countless times. A further cause lay in the moralistic criticism of the heroic epic, developed by the Stoic-Cynic philosophy and reproduced by Cicero (*De natura deorum,* III, 69 ff.). While the myths of Hellas paled, the Imperial Age brought a new cult: the apotheosis of the Caesars. Invocation of the ruler could now replace that of the Muses. The first example of this innovation is in Virgil (*Georgics,* I, 24 ff.); and he was followed by Manilius, Ovid, Seneca, and others. Statius clings to the Muses in epic, but in his occasional poems he takes pains to find substitutes for the invocation of the Muses. He becomes a mannered specialist in these substitute forms.

Persius (34-62), by rejecting the Muses, influenced later times. He had cultivated philosophy. His first satire is an attack on the degenerate poetry and rhetoric of his time from the standpoint of Stoic ethics. Hence,

---

6. Hence the "second" or even multiple *invocatio.* The *locus classicus* for it is Quintilian, IV, *prooemium,* S4.

in the brief prologue to his book, he represents himself as an "outsider" of poetry who has never drunk at the spring of Hippocrene. He is "half a layman" — "semipaganus": that is, he has no proper place in the village festival ("paganalia") of the professional poets or at least he but half shares in it:

> *Nec fonte labra prolui caballino*
> *Nec in bicipiti somniasse Parnaso*
> *Memini, ut repente sic poeta prodirem.*
> *Heliconidasque pallidamque Pirenen*
> *Illis remitto, quorum imagines lambunt*
> *Hederae sequaces: ipse semipaganus*
> *Ad sacra vatum carmen adfero nostrum.*[7]

How must a medieval clerk have read these lines? He could hardly translate *semipaganus* otherwise than as "only half a pagan." So — he must have thought to himself — this Persius, this contemporary of Paul and the half-Christian Seneca, must have abjured his erroneous faith in the pagan gods! That was why he would have no more converse with the Muses!

In addition to invoking the Muses, antique poetry also invoked Zeus.[8] Christian poetry was able to establish contact here too: Paradise was equated with Olympus, God with Jupiter (Dante still writes: "sommo Giove"). Finally late Antiquity developed the poet's apostrophe to his own soul. The preparatory stages are found in early Greek poetry. The Homeric Ulysses speaks "with himself in his stout heart" (*Od.,* V, 298). Pindar calls upon his soul.[9] In the first line of the *Metamorphoses,* Ovid tells us that his soul ("animus") urges him to write poetry. Lucan (I, 67) borrowed this formula. In addition to *animus,* we find more emphatic expressions for the poet's creative urge.[10] Prudentius addresses his soul (ed. Bergmann, 54, 82):

> *Solve vocem, mens sonora, solve linguam nobilem*
> *Dic tropaeum passionis.*[11]

Here the poet's soul has entered the *invocatio* as a substitute for the Muse.

It is characteristic of the poetry of the Imperial Age that the Muses lose ground, are devalued or replaced. But the same period sees the accomplishment of a change in thought which takes the Roman world from

---

7. "I have never wet my lips at the fountain of the horse [Hippocrene] nor do I remember that I ever dreamed on two-peaked Parnassus in order that I should thereby suddenly come forth a poet. The Muses of Helicon and the pale [or pallor-inducing] fountain of the Muses Pirene [near Corinth], I leave to those whose statues supple ivy caresses; I myself bring my verses to the sacred festival of the poets only as an outsider."

8. Pindar, *Nem.,* 2; Theocritus, XVII, 1; Aratus; Virgil, *Bucolica,* II, 60; Ovid, *Met.,* X, 148.

9. *Nem.,* 3, 26; *Ol.,* 2, 89; *Pyth.,* 3, 61.

10. Statius: "Pierius calor," "Pierium oestrum" (*Thebais,* I, 3 and 32); Claudian: "mens congesta" (*De raptu Pros.,* I, 4).

11. "Loose thy voice, sonorous mind, loose thy noble tongue, tell the triumph of the Passion."

scepticism to belief in the survival of the soul after death. Franz Cumont
has given us an insight into this change, which he was the first to infer
from the sarcophagi of the first to fourth centuries.[12] The sculptural
decorations of these precious marbles represent scenes from mythology
and the heroic age, but understood in accordance with the philosophical
principles of Homeric and mythological allegoresis. Pythagorean speculation interpreted the Muses as divinities of the celestial sphere. Their song
produced the harmony of the spheres. Thus they were included in the
eschatology of late pagan Antiquity and became bestowers of immortality
—not for all men but for those who had dedicated themselves to their
service as poets, musicians, scholars, or thinkers. Virgil admits not only
pious priests and bards into Elysium but also the introducers of higher
culture (*Aen.*, VI, 663). The search for knowledge—either profane or
religious—is a road to immortality and is connected with the cult of the
Muses.[13] It is in this light that we are to understand the Muses of the
late Roman sarcophagi. Until recently they were supposed to have been
the graves of poets. Cumont refuted this view. He summarizes his conclusions as follows: "The sister goddesses, who govern the harmony of the
spheres, awaken in the human heart through music a passionate longing
for that divine melody and a nostalgia for heaven. At the same time the
daughters of Mnemosyne cause the reason to remember the truths which
it had known in a previous life. They impart to it wisdom, a pledge of
immortality. By their favor thought mounts toward the ether, is initiated
into the secrets of nature, and comprehends the evolutions of the choir
of stars. It is delivered from the cares of this world, transported to the
world of the ideas and of beauty, and purified from material passions.
And after death the divine virgins summon to themselves in the starry
spheres the soul which has sanctified itself in their service, and cause it
to share in the blessed life of the Immortals." Cumont was the first to
answer the question which Bachofen raised in his *Gräbersymbolik* (1859)
and which he confused by fantastic theories; he has made it possible for
us to see a new side of the religion of late antique paganism.

The religious significance of the Muses during the decline of paganism
is in all likelihood the fundamental reason for their express rejection by
early Christian poetry. This rejection then becomes a poetic topos itself,
the history of which can be traced from the fourth to the seventeenth
century. It is an index of the rise and fall of ethical and dogmatic rigorism.
It is frequently connected with the attempt to find a Christian substitute
for the antique Muses. This opened the way to more or less intelligent
innovations. The entire development is important for the history of literature because it reveals continuities; but it also reflects the religious
atmosphere of the several periods.

The earliest Christian epic poet, Juvencus, turns for assistance to the
Holy Ghost, imploring him to sprinkle him with the water of Jordan—

---

12. *Recherches sur le symbolisme funéraire des Romains* (Paris, 1942). In the discussion above
I follow this great work of the eminent scholar.

13. Among the many examples that Cumont publishes, the following are particularly noteworthy: Themistius, 234 a; Maximum of Tyre, X; Proclus, *Hymn to the Muses* (ed. Ludwich,
143).—The funeral epigram for Vettius Agorius belongs here too (*supra*, p. 210).

which thus takes the place of the Muses' spring. Sedulius, in his verse preface to his work, explains it as a Passover meal at which nothing is served but vegetables in vessels of red clay.[14] Toward the beginning of the poem (I, 60 ff.) he invokes God. He says nothing about the Muses, but he inveighs against the pagan poets (I, 1 ff.). This appears to be the first seed of the topos "Contrast between Pagan and Christian Poetry," which we shall frequently encounter hereafter. Prudentius bids the Muse exchange her wonted ivy crown for "mystical crowns," for the glory of God (*Cath.*, 3, 26). Paulinus of Nola (d. 431) rejects the Muses (X, 21):

> *Negant Camenis nec patent Apollini*
> *Dicata Christo pectora.*[15]

Instead of the Muses and Apollo, Christ shall be the choregus and inspirer of his song (XV, 30). The pagan poets have set forth false fictions; this a servant of Christ cannot do (XX, 32 ff.). In addition to his protest against the pagan Muses, Paulinus has a christological theory of inspiration and a concept of Christ as the cosmic musician which suggests Alexandrian speculations upon Christ as Orpheus (see *infra,* p. 244).

The hagiographic epic naturally affords particular occasion for the protest against the Muses. About 470 Bishop Paulinus of Périgueux composes his metrical paraphrase of Sulpicius Severus' *Life of St. Martin.* In Book IV, 245 ff., he introduces an original invocation. It is addressed to his personal Muse, to whom he ascribes the dignity of a priestess, and to his powers of mind. Then follows the rejection of the antique Muses:

> *. . . Vesana loquentes*
> *Dementes rapiant furiosa ad pectora Musas:*
> *Nos Martinus agat. Talis mutatio sensus*
> *Grata mihi est, talem sitiunt mea viscera fontem.*
> *Castalias poscant lymfatica pectora lymfas:*
> *Altera pocla decent homines Jordane*[16] *renatos.*[17]

The Italian Fortunatus also had a particular devotion to St. Martin. He, after all, had been cured of an ophthalmic disease by anointing his eyes with oil from a lamp on the altar of St. Martin in a church at Ravenna. In gratitude he visited the saint's grave at Tours; then remained in France. He too wrote a metrical life of St. Martin. But in his secular poems he has no objection to the. Muses. In the preface to his collected poems he describes how, when he was on a laborious journey through the countries along the Danube, Germany, and Gaul, a Muse—albeit more frigid than intoxicated, it would seem—inspired him to sing to the woods as a new

---

14. This image was a favorite in the Middle Ages, e.g., in Marbod of Rennes (*PL*, CCXXI, 1548 C). It stems from II Cor. 4:7.

15. "Hearts dedicated to Christ are closed to the Muses and Apollo."

16. Here, then, the Jordan has the same function as in Juvencus.

17. "Let those madmen who discourse folly clasp the Muses to their raging breasts. Our guide be Martin. Such a frenzy of the mind I welcome, for such a fount my vitals thirst. Let frantic hearts demand Castalian dews; other drink is fit for men reborn in Jordan."

Orpheus (ed. Leo, p. 2, 8). In his case secular and Church poetry go side by side. There can be no doubt that his convictions are genuinely Christian. But he has a warm sympathy for antique poetry too. He describes for us (ed. Leo. p. 161 f.) how, in summer, a traveler finds a seat in the shade and then recites verses to himself: Whether he chooses Virgil and Homer or the Psalmist, each bewitches the birds by his own Muses.

Patristic allegoresis[18] makes the Muses harmless through euhemeristic explanations and reinterprets them as concepts in musical theory (this reappears later in the sequences).

In the seventh century and the Germanic North, we again find a rigoristic rejection of the pagan Muses: in Aldhelm. But it is of a very different caste from Paulinus of Nola's. It is not to Christ that the Anglo-Saxon turns in the prologue to his collection of riddles, but to the almighty Creator who formed behemoth (Job 40:10 ff.). He rejects the "Castalian Nymphs" and Apollo. Like Persius, he "has not dreamed on Parnassus." God will vouchsafe him a song—did He not inspire Moses to "metrical poems"? Aldhelm, then, combines the rejection of the Muses with patristic "Biblical poetics." Balaam's ass (Num. 22:27) is cited as proof that Jehovah can bestow eloquence—a motif which had already appeared in Sedulius (*Carmen paschale,* I, 160 ff.) and which became very popular later.[19] It is one of the aberrations of Biblical or Jehovistic poetics.

Linking poetic theory with the Old Testament, one of the results of patristic Biblical exegesis, struck deeper roots in England than in any other country. It exhibits a continuity from which the conclusion may be drawn that England, and even Saxon England, was especially receptive to the poetry of the Old Testament. We shall still find it in Milton. John Bunyan, in his prologue ("The Author's Apology") to *Pilgrim's Progress,* takes his stand on Biblical poetics. It was also influential in English Pre-Romanticism, which was the prelude to the European literary revolution of the eighteenth century. Robert Lowth (1710-87) who held the chair of poetry at Oxford from 1741 to 1751 and died Bishop of London, caused a sensation with his treatise on Hebrew poetry.[20]

One may see an expression of Carolingian Humanism in the fact that it restored the Muses to honor. The Anglo-Saxon Alcuin felt himself out of place in a court life which found heightened expression in a secular poetry of eulogy and friendship. He granted the Muses a place in this realm, but banned them from spiritual poetry. We find the same separation in Angilbert, Theodulf, Raban Maur, and Modoin. Only a strict churchman like Florus of Lyons, known for his orthodox writings and his

18. Clement, *Protreptikos,* II, c. 31; Augustine, *De doctrina christiana,* II, c. 17 after Varro.

19. Cf., e.g., Orientius, *Commonitorium* I, 29 ff. — Bede, *Vita Cuthberti metrice,* ed. Jaager, p. 63, 74. — *Poetae,* III, 308, 18; 509, 37. — In *Poetae,* III, 7, 34 ff., there are references not only to Balaam's ass but also to the verse "Dilata os tuum, et implebo illud" (Ps. 80:11) and to Christ who, since he is "verbum" (logos) can also bestow "munera linguae." — Odo of Cluny, *Occupatio,* p. 2, 25 and p. 68, 18. — Bede (*Vita Cuthberti,* 35) prays to the Holy Ghost for "munera verbi."

20. *De Sacra Poesi Hebraeorum* (Oxford, 1753). According to Lowth the Greek view of poetry as a sacred gift from heaven is a memory of the primitive concept of poetry which was once common to all mankind. The Greeks lost it in practice, the Old Testament has preserved it to us. — The treatise produced such an effect at the time because everyone was looking for primitive poetry. Lowth stimulated Herder. See Goethe, *Dichtung und Wahrheit,* Book 2, ch. 10. — Paul Van Tieghem, *Le Préromantisme,* I (1924), 39.

persecution of heretics, represents rigorism: if poets need mountains for inspiration, let them take Sinai, Carmel, Horeb, Zion. The Humanism of the period was also of advantage to the schools and to school poetry. A teacher in a monastery school like Mico of St. Riquier bids the Muse sing Christian festivals. As her reward she asks a tankard of beer, but of wine at Christmas. The Irishman Sedulius Scottus (in Liége from 848) pays homage to the Muses in a cult of hedonistic enjoyment, delight in life, and praise; he is not afraid to ask a kiss from the lips of the bucolic Muse that he may worthily celebrate a bishop. His Muse is Greek and gives him ambrosia to drink. But he too occasionally borrows something from the Old Testament. He knows a dark-skinned Muse, whom he calls "the Aethiopian woman" after Moses' wife (Num. 12:1), and who provides a charming conclusion to a request for a roast of mutton. Here Anglo-Saxon Biblical poetics is parodied by a Celt.

Of great significance is the appearance of the Muses in the sequence poetry which is cultivated in southern France and whose centers are St. Martial in Limoges and Moissac. According to recent research,[21] we must accept the view that the rise of the sequence is explained by the combined action of two processes: the penetration of secular music into the services of the church and the importation of Byzantine hymns into France after 800. Accordingly, it is precisely in the earliest sequence poetry that we find secular materials too—"extravagances" which the process of development swept into the discard "as soon as the sequence gained official recognition and thus passed into the hands of church musicians and church poets." Now, that the Muses were invoked in the liturgical sequences of the earliest period is explained by the musical origin of the sequence. The Muses are here to be regarded as representing the art of music, not the art of poetry; and this the Fathers had sanctioned. From the sequence arose the new lyrical poetry of the West (*supra,* p. 150). The Muses, then, stand at its cradle too. In the Renaissance of the twelfth century, the antique concept of the Muses lived again in a great variety of forms. We will pass this over and come to Dante.

Carlyle said of Dante that in him "ten silent centuries found a voice." And it is true that, in the garb of poetry, the *Commedia* provides a "summa" of the Middle Ages. But Dante attained to a freedom and breadth which the Middle Ages did not know. Yet his freedom is not to be regarded as heralding the Renaissance or the Reformation. Boccaccio and Petrarch immediately sink back into medieval bondage. Dante's freedom is the unique freedom of his great and lonely soul. It allows him to pass judgment upon popes and emperors; to reject Augustine's interpretation of history no less than the total claims of Scholasticism; to present his personal view of history as messianic prophecy. Dante's uniqueness lies in the fact that he takes such freedom to himself *within* the hierarchical Christian historical cosmos. It is the last time that the aristocratic-heroic

21. I refer especially to the work of Hans Spanke. For a summary, see his *Beziehungen zwischen romainischer und mittelalterlicher Lyrik* (Berlin, 1936). *Idem,* "Aus der Formengeschichte des mittelalterlichen Liedes" (in the journal *Geistige Arbeit* [Sept. 5, 1938]). On the question of priority (southern France or St. Gall?), cf. *idem in HVjft,* XXVII, 381 *and ZfdA* (1934), 1.

man who had formed the West[22] is able to do this. The "ten silent centuries" had bridged over the strained relationship between Antiquity and
Christianity partly by a cautious harmonizing, partly by a questionable
syncretism, or else had found an answer to it in rigorism and ascetic
denial of the world. The majority, to be sure, were not even capable of
realizing the acuteness of the dilemma. Dante, the greatest poet of the
Christian world, took the liberty of assigning an Elysian precinct in the
other world to the poets and heroes of Antiquity. He had them accept him
into their circle, had Virgil guide him as far as the earthly paradise.
Such a minor scruple as the question—may the Christian poet mention
the Muses?—could not affect him. The *Commedia* is not an epic in the
antique sense, yet it took over the epic invocation of the Muses. For Dante
as for Virgil they are "our nurses" *(Purg.,* XXII, 105), the "most holy
virgins" *(Purg.,* XXIX, 37), the "Castalian Sisters" of his last poetical
work *(Ecl.,* I, 54). They nourish poets with their sweet milk *(Par.,* XXIII,
56). They are invoked—in strict accordance with classical practice—at
every important turning-point: *Inferno,* II, 7 and XXXII, 10; *Purg.,* I, 8
("O sante Muse poi che vostro sono") and XXIX, 37-42. Even at the beginning of the *Paradiso* (II, 8) they must impart inspiration, together with
Minerva and Apollo; they reappear once more before the description of the
Heaven of Jupiter (XVIII, 82). Elsewhere too they are frequently mentioned, especially Calliope, Clio, Polyhymnia, and Urania. A generic
designation is *(Par.,* XVIII, 82) "diva Pegasea" (the name also appears
in Walter of Châtillon). Dante calls one of his sonnets a "sermo Calliopeus"
(Letter 3, *S* 4). Apollo is invoked alone in *Par.,* I, 13-27; the Greek God
must help the Christian poet to describe the realm of the blessed. Dante
himself gave a detailed explanation of this *invocatio* in his letter to Can
Grande, *S* 86 ff. There too he discusses the prologue and its varieties
(*S* 45 ff.), distinguishing between the rhetorical and the poetical *exordium.*
Poets need the *invocatio* because they must ask a "divine gift" from the
"higher substances." Among these higher powers Dante counts not only
Apollo and the Muses but also the constellations *(Par.,* XXII, 121). Dante
also knows the address to his own mind *(Inf.,* II, 8). In his prose he chooses
Christian forms of the *invocatio.* In the *Monarchia* (I, 1, *S* 6) he leans upon
Augustine's preface to the *Civitas Dei,* at the same time continuing the
invocation of God which was so cherished by the Middle Ages. He puts
an *invocatio* at the beginning of the *De vulgari eloquentia* too: "Verbo
aspirante de coelis." The invocation of Christ as the Word was already
current in the early Middle Ages.[23] It was one of the most obvious Christian substitutes for the antique *invocatio.*

Boccaccio already considers it necessary to explain the invocation of
the Muses in *Inf.,* II, 7 by lengthy antiquarian considerations.[24] He cites
the authority of Isidore, who was a man of such sanctity ("christiano e
santissimo uomo e pontefice"), of Macrobius and Fulgentius. The Muses

---

22. Alfred Weber, *Kulturgeschichte als Kultursoziologie* (Leiden, 1935), 389.
23. Cf. *supra,* p. 237, n. 19.—Further examples: Smaragdus *(Poetae,* I, 619) and Arnulf in his
Delicie cleri (RF, II, 217).—What Marigo says in his commentary on the passage is misleading.
24. *Il Commento alla Divina Commedia,* ed. D. Guerri, I (1918), 198 ff.

are daughters of Zeus and Mnemosyne, that is, of God the Father and Memory; for God shows the reasonable truths of all things, and his "demonstrations," stored in the memory, bring forth knowledge in men. Boccaccio, then, has relapsed into the venerable practice of interpreting the Muses allegorically for purposes of edification. This tendency is even more obvious in four hexameters that he composed as a conclusion to the *Commedia*.[25] God and the Virgin Mary are invoked: May they grant Paradise to suffering mortals after death. Boccaccio composed his commentary on Dante during a painful illness, not long before his death. In a letter of the same period he regrets having written the *Decameron*. Between his conception of the Muses[26] and Dante's there lies an abyss. From the first, the rejection of the Muses by Christian poets is scarcely anything but a badge of conventionally correct ecclesiastical thought. The more vehemently it is expressed, the less does it carry conviction. It is very seldom more than an obligatory topos. But this is perfectly consistent with the general character of medieval poetry, in so far as it is metrical literary composition. The force of religious feeling is seldom to be found in it. Didacticism and a liturgically objectified devotion predominate. It is not until the twelfth and thirteenth centuries that the tone for the *mysterium fascinosum* is found. The question of the forms and degrees of religious fervor in the Latin poetry of the Middle Ages still awaits investigation. But even the outworn topos of rejection of the Muses can become alive in the mouth of a true poet. It found its finest expression in Jorge Manrique's (1440?-1478) stanzas on the death of his father, the most celebrated poem in Spanish literature:

> *Dexo las invocaciones*
> *De los famosos poetas*
> *Y oradores;*
> *No curo de sus ficciones,*
> *Que traen yervas secretas*
> *Sus sabores.*

> *Aquel solo me encomiendo,*
> *Aquel solo invoco yo*
> *De verdad,*
> *Que en este mundo biviendo,*
> *El mundo no conoscio*
> *Su deidad.*

(I will not here invoke the throng
Of orators and sons of song,

---

25. *Opere latine minori,* ed A. F. Massèra (1928), 99.

26. In his introduction to the 4th *Giornata* of the *Decameron* Boccaccio defensively points out that his book of tales is compatible with the service of the Muses. "The Muses too are women," one of his arguments runs. In the vicious satire of the *Corbaccio* the tables are turned: Certainly the Muses are women, "ma non pisciano" (ed. Bruscoli [1940], 218). Here devotion to the Muses is placed at the service of medieval misogyny (222 f.). Boccaccio's relation to the Muses is not flawless. The medieval clerk's resentment has a place in it.

The deathless few;
Fiction entices and deceives,
And, sprinkled o'er her fragrant leaves,
Lies poisonous dew.

To One alone my thoughts arise,
The Eternal Truth, the Good and Wise,
To Him I cry,
Who shared on earth our common lot,
But the world comprehended not
His deity.)*

That in every century the Muses continued to trouble Christian poets may seem strange. Would it not have been more natural simply to say nothing about the Muses, instead of attacking them or finding ingenious substitutes for them (which after all was a way of recognizing their existence)? Had not Christianity conquered? Certainly it had—but the tradition of Antiquity *had conquered too.* The dominion of the Church was uncontested; with the Inquisition, by the persecution of heretics, it could stamp out all resistance—save one, the "famosos poetas y oradores," to use Jorge Manrique's phrase. The Muses alone could have been successfully dealt with. But they were not alone: since the times of Homer and Virgil they had been indissolubly connected with the epic form. The West was able to get along without the drama for over a thousand years, but before 1800 there is not a single century without epic. The Christian Biblical epic is older than the Christian hymn. It is succeeded by the metrical saint's-life; Virgil, as W. P. Ker and Heusler point out, provides the model for the heroic poetry of the Germanic-Romance Middle Ages. In the twelfth, thirteenth, and fourteenth centuries it flowers anew in Latin; in the sixteenth and seventeenth centuries, in Italy, Portugal, and England, it produces masterpieces of world literature, sanctioned as to theory by the authority of Aristotle, whose *Poetics* had begun to triumph about 1550 as his theoretical and practical philosophy had triumphed since 1200. Even in the eighteenth century, Biblical epic and historical epic produce a belated succession in Klopstock and Voltaire. But already the first waves of the literary revolution are running. Like the industrial revolution, it starts from England about 1750. It breaks the spell of the antique tradition; the "voices of the peoples" can ring out. There is no longer a problem of the Muses.... To be sure, the Christian tradition too entered upon a crisis at the same time. The philosophical Enlightenment reaches its peak in Rationalism, the social Enlightenment in Rousseauism.

The French and the German epic of the Middle Ages produced important works. But not one of them has remained alive in our cultural heritage. Why not? Not one of them could even distantly approach the perfection and beauty of the *Aeneid.* Dante's *Commedia* first scaled those heights —but in form and content that cosmic poem has no connection with the

[*Trans. Longfellow.]

vernacular heroic epic. Lines of Virgil and lines of Dante are of the living
present to all those to whom great poetry means something great. But
who—aside from specialists—quotes *Beowulf,* the *Song of Roland,* the
Nibelungen, or *Parzival?* This poetry has always to be artificially revived,
has always to be re-created in a new medium, to produce an effect upon
modern men. For some of this material Richard Wagner accomplished a
re-creation in the form of the opera, though it already seems very dated
today and, in any case, is more significant musically than textually. But
long before that, the "matter of Arthur" and the "matter of Roland" had
been given a brilliant new life in poetry: in Ariosto's *Orlando Furioso*
(1516).

By its perfection of form, its variety, its music, its mood, the *Orlando
Furioso* puts the epics of Petrarch and Boccaccio in the shade. It is the one
work of Italian poetry which can be set beside the great painting of the
cinquecento. But, aside from its beauty, it is also important historically,
for it is wholly indifferent to antique epic theory—just as indifferent as
it is to the intellectual problems of the age. Ariosto knows and loves
Latin poetry, and borrows a great many themes from it. But he has no
wish to produce a Virgilian epic with invocations of the Muses and mythological machinery. He continues Boiardo's *Orlando Innamorato,* and
takes over his predecessor's form—the minstrel's romance of chivalry
elevated to the tone of the court. In this form there was a mixture of
contradictory tendencies: the religious earnestness of militant faith;
the chivalric ideal (which, however, the noble pagan too could fulfill);
love in both its higher and lower forms; delight in festive amusements.
Ariosto was able to resolve these tensions in the medium which was the
gift of his poetic personality: the magic of irony. But in an inharmonious
personality they could be sounding boards augmenting ethical and religious conflicts—both such as resulted from the realm of problems suddenly
opened up by Luther and those inherent in the antinomy between the old
pagan and the old Christian traditions. This is illustrated in Ariosto's
contemporary Teofilo Folengo. His inner discord is reflected in the linguistic form which he chose for his epic parody *Baldus* (first published
in 1517)—macaronic Latin.[27] His Muses feed him on macaroni and polenta:

> *Non mihi Melpomene, mihi non menchiona Thalia,*
> *Non Phoebus grattans chitarrinum carmina dictent;*
> *Panzae namque meae quando ventralia penso,*
> *Non facit ad nostram Parnassi chiacchiara pivam.*
> *Pancificae tantum Musae doctaeque sorellae,*
> *Gosa, Comina, Striax, Mafelinaque, Tona, Pedrala*
> *Imboccare suum veniant macarone poetam*
> *Dentque polentarum vel quinque vel octo cadinos.*

The macaronic epic remained a thing apart, an episode. But it illuminates
the intellectual crisis of the period, as the intellectual crisis of our day

27. On antique forerunners of macaronic poetry cf. W. Heraeus, *Kleine Schriften* (1937), 244 f.

is illuminated by our contemporary macaronic prose epic, James Joyce's *Finnegans Wake.*

The elevation of the three great Tuscans to the position of models of language and Trissino's program for a "Hellenization" of Italian literature now acted in conjunction with poetic Aristotelianism. Though Aristotle saw tragedy as the highest genre of poetry, Trissino, who had produced a tragedy based on Greek models in 1515 and who in 1548, after twenty years of work, completed the first classicistic epic in unrhymed Italian verse *(L'Italia liberata dai Goti)* brought up the point that the general consensus held Virgil and Homer to be greater than any of the tragedians. He could not but disapprove of the *Orlando Furioso;* it was a romance ("romanzo"), not an epic. The answer was made that the rhymed romance of chivalry was a new genre; Aristotle could not know it, hence his rules were inapplicable to it.[28] Was it possible to reconcile the "romantic" and the Aristotelian epic? Tasso sought a solution to the problem. In subject matter and versification (the faith militant, in ottava rima) his *Gerusalemme liberata* starts from the romance of chivalry, but it obeys the schema of the classicistic epic. He begins by rejecting the antique Muse and the fading laurels of Helicon and invoking instead the heavenly Muse whose dwelling is in Paradise with the choirs of the blessed. On the other hand, he also has the *invocatio* of Memory (I, 36), and charges the Muse (who here has no Christian elements) to enumerate the embattled peoples (XVII, 3). Tasso's poetic theory corresponds to the moralizing Aristotelianism of the Counter Reformation.

In the England of Elizabeth there were neither Aristotelian nor Tridentine scruples to hamper poets. Edmund Spenser can take up the thread of Chaucer and medieval allegory and at the same time situate his *Faerie Queene* in the succession of Homer, Virgil, Ariosto, and Tasso. The artfully wrought prologue comprises four stanzas: The first states the theme in a formula which combines elements from Virgil and Ariosto, the second and third are the *invocatio,* the fourth the dedication of the poem to Queen Elizabeth. In the *invocatio* Spenser addresses a Muse whom he calls "holy virgin chief of nine" and who has been variously interpreted. He also asks the aid of Venus, Cupid, and Mars. Later he has invocations to Clio, daughter of Phoebus and Mnemosyne (III, 3, 4), to the sacred child of Zeus (hence one of the nine Muses) who knows the names of all the ocean and water deities (IV, 11, 10). Book VI opens with a "second *invocatio*" of the Muses, because the poet feels that his powers are failing.

The seventeenth century in England brings us Milton's protestant Muse. The artistic yet artificial prologue of *Paradise Lost* comprises: 1. statement of the theme; 2. invocation of the Christian (Davidian) Muse; 3. promise of a theme never yet attempted; 4. invocation of the Holy Spirit. The "heavenly Muse" is here (1, 6 ff.) derived from the Old Testament, which was a spiritual power in Puritanism. This Hebraic Muse inspired Moses on Horeb and Sinai. She is to raise Milton above Helicon. In the "second *invocatio*" (7, 1 ff.) she is addressed as Urania. But she is

---

28. Giraldi Cintio, *Discorso intorno al comporre dei Romanzi* (1549).

not one of the nine Muses, she does not dwell on Olympus, she is older
than the earth. Before creation she played with her sister, Wisdom, in
the presence of the Almighty (Proverbs 8). She drives off Bacchus and the
Maenads. She is a heavenly being, the antique Muse but an empty dream.
Thus Milton goes back to the rigorism of an Aldhelm. But he is as un-
successful as Tasso or Prudentius in filling the Christian Urania with
life. She remains the product of an embarrassing predicament. Milton
and Tasso both came to grief over the deceptive phantom of "Christian
epic." The Christian cosmos could become poetry in Dante's journey to
the otherworld, and after that only in Calderón's sacred plays.

Calderón produced a Christian solution to the problem of the Muses.
An apologistic tradition of the early Church which the patristic studies
of the sixteenth century had revived taught that pagan mythology contained a proto-revelation — in more or less distorted form — and that it
told of many things which were also related in the Bible. This harmo-
nistics is developed in Calderón's work. He accepts both the entire Christian tradition and the antique tradition and reconciles them in the sense
of the Christian Gnosticism of Clement of Alexandria, for whom Greek
wisdom was a "second" Old Testament. We find this view clearly expressed in Calderón (*Autos sacramentales* [1717], II, 172):

> ... *la voz de la Escritura*
> *Divina en los Profetas*
> *Y humana en los poetas.*

It pervades the entire system of concordances in which Calderón raises
all arts to God. In Calderón the divine Logos is musician, poet, painter,
architect.[29] The "Logos as poet" inspired his sacred play *El Divino Orfeo.*
There the system of concordances is expounded more thoroughly *(Autos,*
VI, 249 b). Holy Scripture *(divinas letras)* and the wisdom of Antiquity
(humanas letras) are related by "consonance," even though they are
severed in religion. How often prophets and poets agree when hidden
truths are touched upon! The text of the Eternal Wisdom and the harmony
of the world are linked by proportion and number. God is the musician
who plays on the "instrument of the world." Christ is the divine Orpheus.[30]
His lyre is the wood of the Cross. By his singing he draws human nature
to himself. This is the "Christus musicus" of Sedulius, and behind both
stands the Orphic Christ of Clement. In the *Sacro Parnaso* the concordance is carried further. Faith bids Pagandom and Jewry read something
from their books. The latter finds the Psalm verse, "Praevenerunt principes
conjuncti psallentibus, in medio juvencularum tympanistriarum" (Ps.
67:26). A.V. (68:25): "The singers went before, the players on instruments
followed after; among them were the damsels playing with timbrels." For
Calderón these timbrel-playing damsels correspond to the Muses. But

---

29. Cf. Excursus XXIII, *infra.*
30. Orpheus as witness to Christianity: Clement of Alexandria, *Ausgewählte Schriften,*
trans. O. Stählin, I (1934), 150 f.

the Musagetes is Christ, "el verdadero Apolo" (V, 35 a). To the earthly
Parnassus, Paradise corresponds as "sacro Parnaso."

Spain needed no Counter Reformation because it had had no Reformation—even as it had had no Renaissance Paganism. It also remained
almost untouched by the tyranny of Aristotelianism. Hence the Catholic
poetry of Spanish "Baroque" exhibits, in form and in philosophic content,
a freedom which Italy, cramped by classicistic preoccupations, and France,
infected with Jansenism, could not know. The timid scrupulosity in literary theory, religion, and ethics, which darkened the mind of a Tasso,
which made a Racine forsake the stage, had no place in Spain. The Spanish
drama produced no classic tragedy, but it caught the color and variety
of the stage of the world, as in a magic mirror.

From Ariosto's poetic *romanzo* to the modern novel runs a broad and
winding road which we need not follow here. The first great modern novel
which we can still read today with pleasure is Fielding's *Tom Jones* (1749).
The author is writing a "history" and does not want the word "romance"
applied to it (I, ch. 1). In the introductory chapters to the eighteen books
there are leisurely reflections upon literary subjects. Classicistic literary
theory is at once the point of reference and the object of attack throughout
(a parody of a battle "in the Homerican style" appears in IV, ch. 4). One
chapter (VIII, 1) is devoted to a discussion of "the Marvellous." As an
enlightened man of reason Fielding must reject Homer's mythology, unless
the illustrious poet intended to mock at the superstitions of his age. In any
case a Christian poet makes himself ridiculous when he troubles pagan
deities who have long since been dethroned. Nothing is more chilling and
absurd than for a modern to invoke the Muses. Better—as Samuel Butler
did in his *Hudibras* (1663)—to invoke a jug of beer, which perhaps has
inspired more poetry and prose than all the waters of Hippocrene and
Helicon. (We remember that even in Carolingian times the Muses had
a fondness for beer.) The year Fielding died (1754) Thomas Gray (1716-
71) composed a "Pindaric ode" on "the Progress of Poesy." It is a rehabili-
tation of the antique Muse. Her realm is far wider than had been supposed.
In the icy North she cheers the shivering native. In Chile's odorous forests
too she lends her ear to the young savage. These are ideas in which the
spirit of English Pre-Romanticism is perceptible. But the attempt to save
the Muses by transplanting them to the Arctic or the Tropics shows only
that they have been retired. Their music, which once was the harmony of
the spheres, has ceased to sound. It was left for the great William Blake
to bid them farewell in a heart-rending lament:

> *Whether on Ida's shady brow*
>   *Or in the chamber of the East,*
> *The chambers of the Sun, that now*
>   *From ancient melody have ceased;*
>
> *Whether in heaven ye wander fair,*
>   *Or the green corners of the earth,*
> *Or the blue regions of the air*
>   *Where the melodious winds have birth;*

Whether on crystal rocks ye rove,
  Beneath the bosom of the sea,
Wandering in many a coral grove,
  Fair Nine, forsaking Poetry:

How have you left the ancient love
  That bards of old enjoy'd in you!
The languid strings do scarcely move,
  The sound is forced, the notes are few.

22

Varieties of Literary History: Stylistic Change

Josephine Miles

Style and Change

Conventionally, we have distinguished the boundary lines of centuries as significant to the history of poetry and of literature in general. We speak with a sense of unities when we speak of sixteenth, seventeenth, eighteenth, or nineteenth-century poetry. Then also we have tended to divide each century in two, speaking of pre-Elizabethan and Elizabethan, divided at the Restoration, of neoclassical and preromantic, divided by the death of Pope in 1744; of romantic and Victorian, divided by Scott's death in 1832 or the crowning of Queen Victoria. Often the divisions waver all across the mid-century: from 1640 to 1660, for example, or from 1744 to 1770, as if we had a sense of a middle period as well as of a beginning and end to each century. I have used such vague words as "sense" and "tend" for our divisions, because I do not think we have an actual philosophy for them, any taxonomical principle of temporal classification. We feel that a literary period begins and ends when a certain kind of writing, or spirit of writing, begins and ends; we set and reset these boundary lines as we redistinguish kinds; yet all the while the century marks seem to preserve their significance, as if writers were apt to end one kind and begin another with the changing of the numerals. Perhaps these divisions are merely "arbitrary," merely "convenient"? Then would they be convenient if they seemed to run counter to the facts as we felt them to be?

Wondering whether a closer technical look at poetic practice might not discover some descriptive principle of period sequence, I have found that neither diction nor metrics alone seems to provide a pattern regular enough to mark change; but that, on the other hand, both are closely involved with sentence structure, which does reveal a sequential pattern. Both serve by certain emphases to support the pattern of basic sentence form.

From *PMLA*, LXX (September 1955), 853-875. Reprinted by permission of the Modern Language Association.

The distinction which I have found pertinent in kinds of sentence structure is between the sort which emphasizes substantival elements—the phrasal and coördinative modifications of the whole statement—and the sort which emphasizes clausal coördination and complication of the statement. The first or phrasal type employs an abundance of adjectives and nouns, in heavy modifications and compounding of subjects, in a variety of phrasal constructions, including verbs turned to participles; it is a cumulative way of speaking. The second or clausal type emphasizes compound or serial predicates, subordinate verbs in relative and adverbial clauses, action, and rational subordination; it is a discursive way of speaking. The first might say, "Rising and soaring, the golden bird flies into the stormy night of the east"; the second if given the same terms would say, "The golden bird rises and soars; it flies into the night which storms in the east." The motion and concept both differ; and, indeed, the discursive type is less apt to be speaking of "golden birds" at all than to be dealing with abstractions or complex events.

Theoretically, there might be a third type between these two: not merely a scale of degrees between extremes, but a mode of statement characterized by a balance between clausal and phrasal elements. And actually, just as we do in fact find kinds of poetry which are dominantly phrasal or dominantly clausal, so we find a kind of poetry in which sentence structure is balanced between the two. We have, then, three modes technically describable in terms of dominant sentence structure and emphasized by usage in meter and vocabulary; these I call provisionally the adjectival, predicative, and balanced modes of poetic statement.

Classifying the poetry written from 1500 to 1900 in accordance with this distinction, we discover a sequence which runs as follows: predicative, then balanced; predicative, then balanced; adjectival, then balanced; predicative, then balanced. In other words, there are four groups, one in each century, each begun by an extreme and terminated by a balance. No periods of extreme come immediately together, because each is followed by moderation in a balanced form.

These four groupings appear to coincide closely with the four centuries. The Skeltonic satiric poets of 1500 wrote an extremely clausal poetry, as did Wyatt and Surrey and their followers in mid-century; then the final thirty years were the golden Elizabethan years of a relatively balanced mode. The seventeenth century began with the clausal verse of Jonson, Donne, and Herbert, and continued with that of Cowley and Vaughan; after 1670 came again the balance of the neoclassicists. The eighteenth century began with Prior and Thomson and continued with Collins and the Wartons the opposite extreme of phrasal emphasis, countered slightly by the classicism of Pope and Johnson, until finally in 1770 the new balance began to be achieved with Goldsmith, Crabbe, Rogers, even finally Wordsworth. The nineteenth century then began with the active clausal balladry of Coleridge, Byron, Moore, Landor, proceeded with that of the Brownings and the Pre-Raphaelites, and ended again, after 1870, with the balanced modes of Swinburne, Bridges, Thompson, Phillips, Hopkins—to begin again in the twentieth century the clausal revival of the Donne tradition, in Housman, Hardy, Cummings, Frost, Auden.

That there can be felt some poetic sense of century seems undeniable. Over and over the pattern recurs, of a new mode for a new era, and then of a balanced moderation at the end. Unless the structure of sentence, sound, and reference is utterly impertinent to poetry, which does not seem possible, the slightest suggestion of developing pattern is significant for poetic history; and a pattern as regularly recurrent as this one is especially so, since it coincides with many commonly accepted patterns. We may learn technically not only how structural patterns coincide with centuries, but also why internal divisions have conventionally suggested a span of middle years: the modes at beginning and end are clear, but the middle years represent modification and transition from the one to the other.

One may ask the Why of this discoverable pattern, but I have no idea of the Why, and am indeed still much concerned with the details of the How. It may be simply that artists, like others, are intensely aware of living and working in a beginning or ending century, and so suit their tones and structures. It may be some repetition we have been caught up in, as many cyclical theorists suggest. Curt Sachs in *The Commonwealth of Art,* François Mentré in *Les Générations sociales,* and Max Förster in "The Psychological Basis of Literary Periods" (*Studies for Wm. A. Read*) are three, for example, who suggest pendular swings. Agnes Young in *Recurring Cycles of Fashion* finds three eras of dress fashion in each sequence. Dialectics, whether idealist or materialist, suggest a clash of opposites and then a resolution. But the poetic pattern seems rather a matter of mediation between opposites, a pendular swing but not a smooth one, in stages, not in a continuous arc. Perhaps the stages are a matter of generations, as Mentré suggests, with epochs of rebellion, transition, and reconciliation; at least, the consciousness of era seems part of the problem.

More needs to be known before we can fairly speculate. The pattern is present in the language of poetry: could we find it in prosaic language also, in which case it would seem to be a part of social history? Or could we find it analogically in the material structures of other arts, in which case it would seem more specifically aesthetic? Or could we find it in both, as part of a more sweeping human pattern? We do not know, because we have not looked. At least we do know that it is close enough to conventional divisions in English literary history, confirming most of them, to offer alternative suggestions for a few.

We have long accepted, for example, the fact that the last thirty years of the sixteenth century brought a new richness and smoothness to English poetry. Now we may note that technically this meant, among other things, an increased balancing of typically English clausal structures by Latin participial constructions, accompanied by, as cause or consequence, a fuller and smoother pentameter line and a more aesthetic and appreciative vocabulary. Shakespeare's sonnets are representative of the new possibilities. Since it moves toward Latin and away from Saxon structure, this poetry of balance may justly be called classical, just as its kind will be a century later, from 1670 to 1700, when Waller and Dryden even more effectively succeeded in drawing away from the roughly intellectual and clausal poetry of the metaphysicals toward Rome again. Granting these two familiar end-century stages of poise, we may then recognize that they also recur in the eighteenth and nineteenth centuries, in the group of Goldsmith and Crabbe, and then again in the "decadence" of Swinburne and Bridges, a leveling, composing, classicizing of what had gone before, an enriching by sensuous and presentative vocabulary, a filling in and loading of metrical line, a stabilizing of action for the sake of reception. In each of these four end-century periods we find a strong express interest in Latin and Greek poetical style, as a necessary model perhaps for the counterbalancing of preceding native or Biblical extremes. The interests are relative, not wholly repetitive; Crabbe does not necessarily echo Dryden; nor Bridges, Crabbe; but each acts as the same sort of modifier for his immediate predecessors. In the pattern of the whole, their relative positions become clear.

So also in relation to the early and mid-century extreme of the native English clausal structure which we have conventionally recognized in Skelton and Wyatt, in Donne and Cowley, in Byron and Browning, and their respective eras, we may more clearly recognize the opposite extreme extending through most of the eighteenth century, the phrasal structure of the poetry from Blackmore through the Wartons, too excessive to be "classical" as it is often called, too vigorously opposite to the active romantic mode meaningfully to be called "preromantic" as it often is. While classical poetic usage is characterized by regularity of meter and richness of reference along with its structural balance, and while metaphysical and romantic clausal usages are characterized by conceptual vocabulary and stanzaic verse forms, the eighteenth-century phrasal extreme—for which we may supply the label "sublime," because it combines qualities of the Gothic, the Greek Pindaric, and the Biblical—is characterized by blank verse or irregular ode forms and a vocabulary of lofty ceremony and enthusiasm.

The forward motion of usages never allows a mode exactly to recur, but progessively alters materials even while it is recalling structures. Therefore historians have tended to name the periods of poetic practice seriatim, without labels of significant renewal which would indicate the pattern of tradition as well as of development. Actually our Tudor and metaphysical, our romantic and modern, all share along with a dominantly clausal structure a language of sound and reference which keeps them in close bond. They are early- and mid-century forms, and in strongest contrast to the early and middle eighteenth-century form of the sublime, which swung to an opposite extreme of language. Late-century forms, on the other hand, are persistently balanced, in grammatical structure as well as in sound and sense, and may as well be called classical for all four centuries as for the first two.

We could read the pattern of recurrence, then, as follows, generation by generation: sixteenth-century English clausal, English clausal, classical balanced; seventeenth-century metaphysical clausal, metaphysical clausal, classical balanced; eighteenth-century sublime phrasal, sublime phrasal, classical balanced; nineteenth-century romantic clausal, romantic clausal, classical balanced. This is too heavy a terminology, but it may merely indicate the close relation between what we have felt and what we may learn technically about periods of poetic development. For while subject matter and sound pattern move progressively and selectively forward in one direction, with a few significant renewals, structure moves rather periodically back and forth, in stages from extreme through balance to extreme, conditioning and altering always, as it is altered by, the developing materials of sound and sense it works with. The simple line of motion is something as follows:

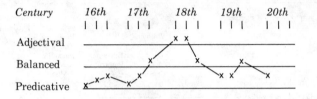

The apparent symmetry of the pattern is interesting and troubling. Does our language so regularly move, even in poetry? Are periods meaningfully marked by the sentence structures of poets? With ten poets for each X, the pattern appears as shown in the table on pages 292 and 293.

Many interesting details may be noted. Chaucer and his colloquial tradition, for example; and the early participation of the aureate poets in the classical tradition which reaches to Yeats and Stevens. Or the ascending line from Spenser and Waller to Milton and Thomson; it is interesting that Denham, often grouped with Waller by his contemporaries, here seems far apart. Denham and Cowley are true transitional figures: most of their work was traditionally clausal, but they were interested in trying a few new forms. Marvell is listed late, for his classically formed satire; note how the more colloquial satire of Creech and Oldham, and then of Gay, with whom Swift could be grouped, is the last of the English clausal mode to fade, until it is revived again at 1800 by Coleridge's and Byron's narrative techniques. Blake's *Songs* should be linked with Coleridge; but it is rather his phrasal prophetic poetry which predominates, and which is here listed. By the mid-nineteenth century, poets as important as Morris, Bridges, Patmore have to be omitted for lack of space, but do not affect the pattern, as their works vary widely within the range of possibilities. Inclusion of Phillips in the late nineteenth-century list is based on Jerome Buckley's stress, in *The Victorian Temper,* on his importance. Other well-known modern poets would further support the full variety of possibility, with characteristic emphasis on balance. At least I think the main outlines of the pattern will remain clear through the many changes that are possible. Most readily acceptable to the reader will probably be that part of the pattern which represents the early clausal emphases of Wyatt and the metaphysicals, along with the clearly opposing mode of the eighteenth century. Least acceptable will seem the partly romantic emphasis on balance; I think we may learn a good deal more, however, about the specific nature of nineteenth-century classicism. The discrimination of modes simply fails to make many pertinent

TYPES OF PROPORTIONS FOR 200 POETS

England

PHRASAL (Most adjectives per verbs)

Pre-1470	1470	1500	1530	1570	1600	1630	1670	1700	1730
							Thomson		
							Somerville		
								T. Warton	
							Philips	Armstrong	
				Fletcher			Dyer	J. Warton	
					Milton				Bowles
								Collins	Cowper
								Mason	Blake
						Prior		Akenside	
			Sylvester		More	Blackmore	Blair	Gray	

BALANCED --

Pre-1470	1470	1500	1530	1570	1600	1630	1670	1700	1730
			Spenser					Shenstone	Rogers
	Hawes							Lyttelton	Crabbe
	Dunbar				Waller		Pope		Goldsmith
			Shakespeare				Young		Burns
			Fairfax			Dryden	Parnell		Churchill
							Pomfret		Wordsworth
					Crashaw		Addison		
	Douglas	Sackville		Sandys				Johnson	Chatterton

CLAUSAL (Fewest adjectives per verbs) --------------------------

Pre-1470	1470	1500	1530	1570	1600	1630	1670	1700	1730
Henryson			Chapman		Lovelace	Roscommon			
Gawain P.		Gascoigne		Quarles	Marvell	Vaughan			
James I	Lindsay	Breton	Sidney	Carew	Denham	Garth	Gay		
Lydgate	Skelton	Wyatt	Drayton	Herrick	Cleveland	Walsh			
Chaucer	Barclay	Googe	Marlowe	Shirley	Cowley	Oldham			
Pearl P.	Coverdale	Baldwin	Campion	Donne		Creech			
Minot	Sternhold	Turberville	Daniel	Herbert					
Gower	Ballads	Surrey		Wither					
Hoccleve	Heywood	Crowley		Jonson	Suckling				
Langland		Churchyard							

TYPES OF MEASURES FOR 200 POETS

England

LINES

Pre-1470	1470	1500	1530	1570	1600	1630	1670	1700	1730
							Thomson		
							Blair		
							Young		
Langland							Philips	J. Warton	Burns
Minot		Gascoigne	Chapman		Milton		Somerville	Akenside	Blake
									Cowper

COUPLETS --

Pre-1470	1470	1500	1530	1570	1600	1630	1670	1700	1730
						Pomfret			
						Prior			
						Garth			
						Creech	Dyer		
						Blackmore	Pope		
									Rogers
								T. Warton	Crabbe
Chaucer	Lindsay			Carew	Marvell	Oldham	Gay	Johnson	Chatterton
Gower	Barclay		Marlowe	Quarles	Denham	Roscommon	Parnell	Lyttelton	Churchill
Lydgate	Skelton		Sylvester	Sandys	Waller	Dryden	Addison	Armstrong	Goldsmith

STANZAS ---

Pre-1470	1470	1500	1530	1570	1600	1630	1670	1700	1730
		Breton							
		Turberville							
	Heywood	Googe							
	Coverdale	Sackville	Fairfax	Shirley					
Henryson	Sternhold	Baldwin	Campion	Herbert	Lovelace				
James I	Douglas	Crowley	Shakespeare	Herrick	Cowley				
Hoccleve	Hawes	Churchyard	Drayton	Wither	More				
Gawain P.	Dunbar	Surrey	Daniel	Fletcher	Cleveland			Mason	
Pearl P.	Ballads	Wyatt	Sidney	Donne	Crashaw	Walsh		Collins	
			Spenser	Jonson	Suckling	Vaughan		Gray	Wordsworth
								Shenstone	Bowles

TYPES OF PROPORTIONS FOR 200 POETS

England (continued)					America				
1770	1800	1830	1870	1900	1770	1800	1830	1870	1900

PHRASAL (Most adjectives per verbs)

England 1770	1800	1830	1870	1900	America 1770	1800	1830	1870	1900
Hemans Keats	Tennyson Hood Horne	Henley Wilde Swinburne	Blunden Aldington de la Mare	D. Thomas Spender	Barlow	Whittier Chivers Whitman	Guiney	Moore Crane	Hecht

BALANCED —————

England 1770	1800	1830	1870	1900	America 1770	1800	1830	1870	1900
Shelley Southey Hunt	Clough Arnold	Phillips Thompson Bridges Hopkins Yeats	Sitwell Graves Masefield Lawrence Owen	Barker MacNeice Nicholson Ridler Raine	Dwight Trumbull Bryant Drake Sigourney Freneau Pinkney Halleck	Lowell Poe Timrod Longfellow Emerson	Moody Lanier Sterling Sill Miller	Pound Williams Jeffers Stevens Eliot Cummings	Shapiro Rukeyser Bishop Wilbur Roethke Scott Eberhart

CLAUSAL (Fewest adjectives per verbs) ——————

England 1770	1800	1830	1870	1900	America 1770	1800	1830	1870	1900
Campbell Moore Byron Coleridge Landor	E. Browning Tupper Meredith Rossetti R. Browning	Hardy Housman	Muir E. Thomas	Auden Gunn Jennings	Percival	Holmes Very	Wilcox Robinson Field Dickinson	Millay Frost	Warren Lowell

TYPES OF MEASURES FOR 200 POETS

England (continued)					America				
1770	1800	1830	1870	1900	1770	1800	1830	1870	1900

LINES

England 1770	1800	1830	1870	1900	America 1770	1800	1830	1870	1900
Keats Landor	Tupper Horne	Phillips Henley	Lawrence Aldington	Barker	Dwight Barlow	Whitman Timrod Lowell	Moody Sill	Crane Jeffers Eliot Moore Pound Williams Stevens	Lowell Rukeyser Bishop Roethke Warren

COUPLETS ————

England 1770	1800	1830	1870	1900	America 1770	1800	1830	1870	1900
Campbell Hunt									

STANZAS —————

England 1770	1800	1830	1870	1900	America 1770	1800	1830	1870	1900
Hemans Shelley Byron Moore Southey Coleridge	Rossetti Meredith Arnold Clough R. Browning Tennyson E. Browning Hood	Yeats Thompson Housman Wilde Hopkins Bridges Hardy Swinburne	Blunden Graves Owen Sitwell Muir E. Thomas Masefield de la Mare	Gunn Jennings D. Thomas Nicholson Ridler Spender Raine MacNeice Auden	Pinkney Percival Drake Bryant Sigourney Halleck Freneau Trumbull	Very Poe Holmes Chivers Whittier Longfellow Emerson	Sterling Robinson Guiney Wilcox Field Lanier Miller Dickinson	Cummings Millay Frost	Hecht Wilbur Shapiro Scott Eberhart

distinctions, as between Hopkins', Bridges', and Swinburne's styles, for example; on the other hand, it indicates underlying likenesses which may be worth further study.

The tendency of one sort of sentence structure to predominate in the poetry of a generation, and the tendency in the past four hundred years to move from one extreme of structure, the native clausal, through classical balance, to an extreme of elaborated phrasal structure, and then back again, is borne out by other characteristics of language such as sound structure and vocabulary. Clausal poems, we find, tend to be stanzaic and active poems, working out an argument or narrative in clearly defined stages and formal external order. Phrasal poems, and phrasal eras, on the other hand, emphasize line-by-line progression, and cumulative participial modification in description and invocation without stress on external rhyming or grouping. So the strongly stanzaic verse of the sixteenth century became moderated in the more skillful blank verse and couplet of its last generation, just as in the next century the metaphysical stanza narrowed to the neoclassical couplet, carrying its linear organization partly inward by caesural balances. Then the eighteenth century aimed for the other extreme, not only a blank verse freer from end-stop emphasis, but even the irregular lines and motions of the ode forms, settling again into such couplet moderations as Goldsmith's and Crabbe's, before turning back in the nineteenth century to the clausal ballad stanza and in the twentieth to the more metaphysical involutions of Cummings, Frost, and Auden.

In the same way, the major vocabulary, the nouns, adjectives, and verbs most used and most agreed upon in each generation, follow the periodic pattern, though their main line of development is in one direction. Certain primary words thus drop out of poetic usage not to return; others persist through all four centuries; but some come and go in periodic fashion. The persisting ones name the basic human concerns that we should expect: *God, heart, life, love,* and *man,* modified by value in *good,* by magnitude in *great,* by time in *old,* active in *coming, going, giving, taking, making, seeing.* The lost words, on the other hand, are those most closely reflecting the limitations of interest in a period: the early *cruel fortune, pain, king, lady,* and *lord,* for example; the *blood* and *fire* of the metaphysicals; or, at the extreme opposite to these socially analytic and conceptual terms of clausal poetry, the equally limited ceremonious ones of the phrasal eighteenth century: *soft, breast, maid, muse, scene, song, youth, virtue, rising,* and *falling.*

Most significantly, the terms which neither persist nor vanish but recur do so along with recurring sentence and verse forms. So, for example, the early Tudor vocabulary of concept, in words like *mind* and *thought, word* and *thing, time* and *world,* recurred strongly again in the clausal poetry of the nineteenth century. So also each century in its last generation, in its classical mode, contributed a special sort of recurring term, sensory and observational, like *sweet, heaven, night, sun* for the Elizabethans, with their corresponding verbs of *lie, love, look;* then the neoclassicists' *happy, mighty, art, fate, nature, grow;* the late eighteenth century's *little, sad, tear, woe, weep;* and the late nineteenth's *young, child, dream, foot, summer, woman:* always a vocabulary of human dimension and feeling in the natural world.

As of structural continuity, we may say of this referential continuity that it begins in the sixteenth and seventeenth centuries with emphasis on social and relational terms, moves through the descriptive vocabulary of the classical generations to the sublime and ceremonious world of the eighteenth, and then back to more abstract relational terms again, though never in conceptual vocabulary so strong as at first, and with a late classicism in which direct natural and human image seems partly to have turned to symbol.

One is not surprised to learn that reference and sound work closely with sentence; that the language of poetry is integral in its characteristics. Which moves first: which new sound makes for new sense, or new structure for new sound, is a question needing more than the evidence available. At least, in generational stages, we can see that the three phases move together, though not with equal force, vocabulary the least likely, structure the most, to return to old stages. All work as one poetic unit: the relational pattern of clausal sentence with stanzaic sound and with conceptual vocabulary; or the cumulative pattern of phrasal sentence with internal and onomatopoetic sound and with sublime vocabulary; or the distinct, not merely transitional, balanced pattern of structure, line, and human nature in nature which we call classical. Here, in this nucleus of language properties, we may find some of the basis for a definition of modes; and in modes, of styles; and in styles, of eras.

Perhaps it would be useful to see each mode at work in a single poem, not as widely different as possible, but as close together in one century. Here is first, the active, Wyatt's sonnet "Against His Tongue":

> Because I still kept thee fro' lies and blame,
> And to my power always thee honoured,
> Unkind tongue! to ill hast thou me rend'red,
> For such desert to do me wreke and shame.
> In need of succour most when that I am,
> To ask reward, thou stand'st like one afraid:
> Always most cold, and if one word be said,
> As in a dream, unperfect is the same.
> And ye salt tears, against my will each night
> That are with me, when I would be alone;
> Then are ye gone when I should make my moan:
> And ye so ready sighs to make me shright,
>> Then are ye slack when that ye should outstart;
>> And only doth my look declare my heart.

The conceptual terms are typical; the metaphors, functional; the difficulty of speech, thematic. The sonnet structure is tightly woven and enclosed. The sentences are active and clausally constructed; there are seventeen verbs to ten adjectives in the fourteen lines. In general, the proportioning in the poetry of Chaucer, Wyatt, Donne, Herrick, Cowley, and later Byron, Housman, Browning, Frost, and others, is about seven adjectives to fourteen nouns to eleven verbs in an average ten lines; and this single poem by Wyatt is fairly representative of it, using just that sort of colloquial language with its *becauses, ifs, whichs,* and *whens,* which makes for an active complexity of thought and structure.

What are the simple signs of that classically balanced poetry for which some of the late Elizabethans then strove? A thoroughly symmetrical proportioning, an inner onomatopoeia and harmony of sound along with the tight outward rhyme, a sensory, normative, and emotional vocabulary. This was the less active, more responsive world of the Shakespearean sonnet, clauses balanced by modifying phrases, and some of the need for connectives smoothed away, in a proportioning of ten adjectives to twenty nouns to ten verbs in ten lines. For example, Shakespeare's sonnet I is near the pattern:

> From fairest creatures we desire increase,
> That thereby beauty's rose might never die,
> But as the riper should by time decease,
> His tender heir might bear his memory:
> But thou, contracted to thine own bright eyes,
> Feed'st thy light's flame with self-substantial fuel,
> Making a famine where abundance lies,
> Thyself thy foe, to thy sweet self too cruel.
> Thou that art now the world's fresh ornament
> And only herald to the gaudy spring,
> Within thine own bud buriest thy content
> And, tender churl, mak'st waste in niggarding.
>> Pity the world, or else this glutton be,
>> To eat the world's due, by the grave and thee.

Adjectives and verbs are nearly balanced here, because many clausal constructions have been made phrasal, in the classical fashion. *But thou, contracted,* and *self-substantial,* and *making a famine,* and *And, tender churl,* all, by participial, appositional, or compounding construction, turn verbs to adjectives, smooth the transitions, integrate the sound.

Each late-century generation called itself classical, and strove consciously for what it thought to be a Roman mode of language. Sidney's age and Dryden's, and later Wordsworth's and Bridges', wrote of their pleasure in what they called classical proportions. Wordsworth withdrew to the simplicities of classicism under the early influence of Goldsmith, away from the eighteenth-century "gaudy and inane"; and Bridges and Hopkins in turn tried to win back some of that gaudiness, to make a balance against the stringencies of the ballad tradition. Furthermore, the great Latin poets themselves wrote the sort of syntax in the sort of line which we, following Dryden, have been calling classical. That is, the proportioning of language by Ovid, Virgil, and Horace was just that balanced one adjective to two nouns to one verb which Dryden together with his poetic colleagues achieved and which he praised in his preface "On Translation" as the "golden" line of classical literature. It suited the rhymed pentameter as it had suited unrhymed hexameter, and it dealt explicitly with emotion and sense of the natural world for Shakespeare and Marvell and Dryden as for Virgil. *Laetus, magnus, amicus, caelum, nox, video* were among the major terms for Roman classicism as for English. The mode was one literally worked for and achieved in England, and was renewed again and again as extremes of English experiment outwore themselves.

The outstanding classical poets to offer the model of a different mode were Pindar and Lucretius. Their cosmic and ceremonious overload of sublime epithets and phrasal constructions indicated a kind of extreme which English poetry did not reach until the eighteenth century. But Biblical richness and the Platonic tradition early offered to such poets as Spenser and Sylvester, and then Milton, the idea of a poetic language as free as possible from clausal complication, as resilient as possible in richly descriptive participial suspension. The signs of such a mode are more adjectives than verbs, some free variation in line length as in the ode, much inner harmony and less rhyme, and a vocabulary of physical presence, ceremony, and pleasure. The proportioning of statement ranges from about twelve adjectives, sixteen nouns, ten verbs in ten lines for Milton and Collins and Keats to fifteen adjectives, eighteen nouns, eight verbs for Thomson and the Wartons in the height of the mode. Even so early as Spenser, to say nothing of the aureate poets, the mode of speech is visible; in Spenser's *Amoretti,* sonnet I:

> Happy ye leaves when as those lilly hands,
>> which hold my life in their dead doing might,
>> shall handle you and hold in love's soft bands,
>> lyke captives trembling at the victors sight.
> And happy lines, on which with starry light,
>> those lamping eyes will deigne sometimes to look
>> and reade the sorrowes of my dying spright,
>> written with teares in harts close bleeding book.
> And happy rymes bath'd in the sacred brooke,
>> of *Helicon* whence she derived is,
>> when ye behold that Angels blessed looke,
>> my soules long lacked foode, my heavens blis.
> Leaves, lines, and rymes, seeke her to please alone,
>> whom if ye please, I care for other none.

The poem is an exclamation, not an argument. It rests in its adjectives, *happy, trembling, starry, lamping, bleeding, blessed,* in the physical sense of bodily images which are also symbols. *Handle, look, behold,* and *please* are the few significant actions, and they are subordinate to the substance. Connections are provided by participles, and these together with the descriptive adjectives are half again as many as the verbs.

This is the mode which would give us the heavens and earth of *Paradise Lost,* the cosmological reaches of Akenside, the rich details of Thomson, the personifications of Collins, the great aesthetic and social divine wars of Blake, the figure of Keats's Autumn, the vigor of symbol and celebration in Whitman and Henley. In our own day, such poets as Dylan Thomas may lead us back to it. The style of which this mode is an enduring part has been given no name by the literary historians, though the eighteenth-century poets themselves often called it "sublime." It is an extreme we have not met in our language strongly for almost two centuries, but an extreme that some of the Imagists, under Pound's guidance, may have been aiming at, and may aim at again.

The examples of the three modes, representing as they do the range within one century and within one genre, do not represent the full reach of variation from century to century, particularly in patterning of sound. The Elizabethan classicism did manage to free itself somewhat from the tight stanzaic forms of the clausal mode, into more straightaway couplets and blank verse, but the height of the couplet form for classicism did not come until the next century, and the height of blank verse and freer odal forms not until Milton and his eighteenth-century followers. What I have tried to illustrate in the quotation of the three sonnets is, first, the power of the three modes to work within one genre; and, second, the temporal concurrence of modes, the latent potentiality of all, while one may dominate.

Neither genre nor era seems to control mode, though of the two era seems the stronger. Perhaps individual aptitude may be the controlling force, though I suppose it might be strongly conditioned by era or by genre models. At any rate, we find sonnets, epics, pastorals, satires written in any of the modes, apparently depending largely upon period; and we find some versions of each mode, however scant, in every period. The sense of language complex, the core of fitting-together structure, sound, and reference, seems to be the basic force for choice and emphasis. Some poets experiment with one and another, as Blake for example tried the clausal mode in his *Songs of Innocence and of Experience,* and then turned back to elaborate in his prophetic poems the phrasal pattern with which he had begun. But many poets, Donne, Dryden, Thomson, Keats, for example, stay by one identifying mode for their work, sometimes even when they are translating others of a different sort. Sometimes, within an era, the idea of a certain suitability of mode to genre or topic does occur, perhaps even is debated; then we see, for example, Pope modifying his structure, to suit what he considers the satiric tradition. As a whole, we may surmise from present evidence, first, that a poet has an aptitude for a mode as basis for development of his individual style; second, that his own and his era's general concept of the importance of distinct genres may condition his adaptation of modes; and third, that much agreement of usage in any one era seems to suggest some temporal conditioning force in the language itself, or at least in the poets' attitude toward it.

At any rate we may testify to the persisting use of all the modes in English poetry, with some correlation in Latin and Greek backgrounds, and we may even surmise that the traditional high, middle, and low styles had some basis in language structure. At least in English we may see a simple correspondence. The phrasal mode of Sylvester, Milton, and the eighteenth century, with its lofty phrases and cadences, its figures larger than life, and its high passions, was a clear part of what the century itself called the high or sublime style, not so much heroic as cosmic, not so much active as receptive and "passionate," in Pindar's richly ceremonious sense. The balanced and medial mode has been traditionally recognized as classical, the golden mean in the golden line of an adjective, two nouns, and a verb, as Dryden described it, the sharing of ethos with pathos in human heroism in moderated language. The relation of clausal mode to low style is somewhat less clear in tradition, perhaps because the mode was not so strong in Latin as in English, and the English put it, like the iambic, to uses not all simple, common, and low. Nevertheless, there was some recognition. Elizabethans were troubled that the clausal English was low, as Richard Foster Jones has shown us; the long critical argument against monosyllables in poetry was also an argument against English clausal construction and connection; Donne's rough "masculine" style was recognized as low and English, not classical enough; and Wordsworth, when the style was renewed two centuries later in the balladry of Coleridge, had come round to praising the low and common, as Emerson did and as Frost did, not only for the ethos of social tradition, but for the pathos which nature had drawn down to man from the Bible and the sublime. In other words, though there was a shift in meanings by the nineteenth century, a new notion of the low as natural, and a new use of natural vocabulary and colloquialism in clausal construction, the structure itself had persisted and seemed steadily to be recognized as part of the tradition of common or lowly style. The scholarly work of Ernst Robert Curtius, of J. V. Cunningham, Klaus Dockhorn, Sister Miriam Joseph, Erich Auerbach, F. W. Bateson, and Samuel Monk has interesting bearing on the problems of spirit and intention behind the modes we have here distinguished.

The study of modes should lead to the study of the styles of which they are a part. The question of complexes of usage in language should lead to questions of the ideas and attitudes that are conveyed through these complexes, and of the power of stylistic indirections like figurative speech, like metaphor, symbol, hyperbole, and irony, to alter the quality and effect of the medium. But my present concern is the modes themselves, to try to distinguish them clearly so that they may be recognizable, to suggest their usefulness as characteristic of poets and of eras in poetic history. How strong was the Chaucerian tradition of speech in English, how close were Donne and Jonson as opposed to Spenser, how different was Jonson's classicism from Dryden's, how different was Keats's romanticism from Byron's, how vividly new was the renewal of an old mode by the ballad makers of the nineteenth century – these are the sorts of questions which discrimination of modes may help to answer.

23

Varieties of Scholarly Interpretation:
Explication

Leo Spitzer

Explication de Texte Applied to Walt Whitman's Poem
"Out of the Cradle Endlessly Rocking"

I may state first that our poem treats the age-old theme of world harmony within which the bird is one voice, the sea another, and the poet the third. The classical and Christian ideas of world harmony have been treated by me in *Traditio* (II and III, 1945-6) and it may be apposite for me to extract from this article a brief survey: Pythagoras and Plato had defined music as an art practiced not only by human musicians, but also by the cosmos. According to Plato's *Timaeus,* the music of the spheres is produced by Sirens each of whom, in her particular sphere, sings notes whose pitch is conditioned by the velocity of the revolution of her sphere. The totality of these notes produces that world harmony, or symphony inspired by loving rivalry, ἔρις καὶ φιλία, which is inaccessible to human ears, and which is willed by the demiurge, the world spirit. It was not difficult for the Christians to replace the pagan world spirit by the Christian God of Love and thus to associate the music of the spheres with Christian *Caritas.* In Dante, the Pythagorean world harmony will be sung, not by the Sirens of the *Timaeus* but by the pure intelligences, the angels vying with each other in the different revolving heavens through the physical and spiritual attraction of that Divine Love "che muove il sole e le altre stelle." Already Augustine had seen the world as a "magnum (musicum) carmen creatoris et moder-

From *ELH,* XVI (1949), 229-249. Reprinted by permission of The Johns Hopkins Press.

Since I have no thorough acquaintance with Walt Whitman's sources, I am forced to place him, not within the framework of his American *ambiente,* but somewhere in the cold space of world literature (as far as I know it), to treat the poem "Out of the Cradle Endlessly Rocking" as one among other poetic monuments belonging to the Western tradition, apart from the question of Whitman's familiarity or non-familiarity with these monuments. My ignorance, however, may in the end be redeemed to some degree: for I feel that the direct, concrete sources which may be established for a particular work of art, are generally somewhat petty and trivial in comparison with the parallels to be found in international art, together with which the particular work combines in an eternal pattern. I have used Stovall's *Walt Whitman,* N.Y. 1934. *Author's note.* .

atoris." The theme that the music of nature blends with human voices in praise of the Lord is first developed in an exegetic text of Saint Ambrose, intended to interpret the line of *Genesis* in which God is presented as satisfied with his creation of the sea. In surging prose Ambrose offered a powerful acoustic description of the harmony *(concentus = συμφωνία)* in which are fused the song of the waves and the choirs of the devout congregation in an island sanctuary: the voices of men, women, children chanting psalms. "Quam dulcis sonus, quam jucundus fragor ('refraction'), quam grata et consona resultatio (='harmonious echo')!" With Ambrose we find for the first time in our occidental literatures the fusion of nature and humanity into one *Stimmung,* into a unity of tone and atmosphere prompted by Christian feelings. It is this transcendental unity which permits the single objects to lose their matter-of-fact identity and to melt into the general atmosphere of piety; whereas in the pantheism of the ancients, though the single phenomenon may even change into another form (as in the metamorphoses of Philomela or Echo), clear-cut forms still continue to exist individually, not fused into an all-embracing atmosphere.

After Ambrose we find birds presented in Latin medieval poetry as psalmists of God, Nature's singers introduced into the more sophisticated company of human singers. Among these birds the nightingale figures predominantly. The classical Philomela, the ravished, mutilated, sorrowing woman-become-songbird (in accord with the ancient tendency to explain the healing effect of music by tragic suffering overcome), becomes in Christian poetry the singer, naturally endowed with divine Grace, who sings to testify to Grace. In a tenth-century Latin poem the nightingale sings at Eastertime, inviting all believers to join with her in praise of the resurrected Christ. From now on medieval love songs reflecting the theological theme begin with a picture of nature revived in spring, with the birds and the poet vying in grateful song (the *Natureingang* of the Minnesingers and troubadours). The word *refrain* (lit. 'refraction'), which in Old French was applied to the twittering of birds as well as to the musical or verbal *refrain,* must be explained by the concept of the echo which is represented in the response of the birds to the music of the world. Similarly, the modern word *concert* (lit.'musical contest'), and the Elisabethan word *consort* ('concert')= *consortium* ('association'), are late derivatives from this same idea of peaceful strife, of musically harmonious emulation in the praise of God. The thirteenth-century Spanish poet Gonzalo de Berceo goes so far as to portray learned birds that serve as preachers of religious orthodoxy. Church-fathers and prophets of the Old Testament, Augustine, Saint Gregory, and Isaiah, are presented as nightingales in an earthly paradise competing under the dictation of the Virgin Mary. A one-man concert is Saint Francis' famous canticle: "Altissimo onnipotente bon signore,/tue so le laude, la gloria e l'onore e onne benedizione." This minstrel of God, feeling that one human being alone would not be worthy of praising the Lord, brings into his poem all creatures which may testify with him to the greatness of the Creator: "Messer lu frate Sole" (the Lord my brother Sun), my brother the wind, my sister the water, my sister the earth – and my sister Death. According to legend, the last stanza was added by Saint Francis on the day of his death. The Saint does not mention his brother the bird, but we remember the painting of Giotto in which Francis is depicted as preaching to the birds.

In the Renaissance, the original classical concept of Pythagorean and Platonic World Harmony was revived by poets and scholars: Marsilio Ficino, Kepler *(Harmonices mundi)*, and others. The Christian implications, however, which had come to be associated in the Middle Ages with that ancient theory, were not disregarded by the Platonists whether Catholic or Protestant. This we see in the *Musurgia* of the Jesuit Athanasius Kircher and in the writings of the Protestant Leibnitz. Thus when Shakespeare stresses the unmusical in Shylock or Cassius, he means that these characters are untouched by Christian grace. The Renaissance painter *par excellence,* Raphael, shows us Saint Cecilia, surrounded by such figures as Saint Augustine and Saint Mary Magdalen (the Christian theoretician of music and the representative of love rewarded by grace), in a moment of ecstasy when she, an earthly being, gifted for music, or endowed with grace, is privileged to hear the music of heaven. Dryden's "Song for St. Cecilia's Day" and Milton's "At a Solemn Music" celebrate the reunion in heaven with God's music from which we earthly singers have been estranged through original sin.

> Disproportioned sin
> Jarr'd against nature's chime, and with harsh din
> Broke the fair *music that all creatures made*
> To their great Lord.
> O may we soon again renew that song,
> And keep in tune with Heav'n till God ere long
> To his celestial consort us unite,
> To live with him, and sing in endless morn of light.

To die with the expectance of heavenly, Pythagorean-Christian music is sweet. Not only the sweetness of musical reunion with Christ, but the sweetness of a musical death for Christ is expressed by a seventeenth-century German mystic Friedrich von Spee who, in a language that has the simplicity of the folksong, gives a baroque twist to the classical motif of the tragic death of Philomela. He combines this motif with that of the Echo that we found in Ambrose, although the scenery here is not the all-embracing ocean, but a German forest. A nightingale exultantly sings out the name of Christ to which the echo responds with equal enthusiasm:

> Da recht, du fromme Nachtigal,
> Du jenem Schall nit weiche,
> Da recht, du treuer Widerschall,
> Du stets dich ihr vergleiche,
>   Zur schönen Wett'
>   Nun beide trett,
> Mein Jesum lasst erklingen.

Then the 'risings and fallings' of the two voices that descend in order to ascend to ever-higher pitch suddenly cease. The nightingale has died in the praise of "mein Jesum,"—a martyr of love and strife for God.

The English Romantics introduce into poetry their selves and their problems of disenchantment, caused by the waning of faith in the eighteenth century. Now the poet is isolated from the musical birds; no concert materializes. Shelley is startled to hear a lone nightingale "answering him with soothing song" when he sits "pale with grief beneath the tower." Or else he will address the skylark: "*Teach* us, Sprite or Bird, What sweet thoughts are thine . . . Teach me half the gladness / That thy brain must know." The bird is here a teacher as in medieval poetry, but not a teacher of a firmly established orthodoxy which is shared by bird and poet alike, nor a brother in the love of God. The teaching which the poet requests of the strange visitor ("sprite or bird") from another world is apparently concerned with the knowledge of ultimate things inaccessible to the poet. Keats who apostrophizes the Nightingale ("Thou wert not born for death, immortal bird") feels himself to be immediately thrown back "from thee to my sole self," and as the bird's voice fades away, the poet is left, unlike his medieval confrère, in "forelorn" uncertainty. Was this a vision or a dream?

The German pre-Romantics and Romantics do not express the feeling of basic isolation from nature. On the contrary, the Germans wished to recognize themselves in articulate nature. Along with the discovery of folk poetry and of Ossian there went the resurrection of those elemental spirits or sprites, those degraded demi-gods of antiquity who, in spite of the ban of the Church, had been able to survive in popular superstition and in whom were incarnated the irrational cosmic fears of man and the daemoniac magic by which man may be seduced at any moment. Whereas Plato's Sirens sang their symphonic chorus in accord with a Pythagorean mathematical order, now the sirens of the folklore, the daemoniac daughters of the *Erlkönig* in Herder and Goethe sing to lure innocent children away from their parents. The mermaid by her singing and pleading attracts the fisherman toward the abyss (Goethe, *Der Fischer:* "Sie sang zu ihm, sie sprach zu ihm, da war's um ihn geschehn"), and Heine's *Loreley,* by dint of singing and combing her fair German hair, sends the boatsman down to the deep. Thus, as man, gradually dechristianized, realizes his own daemoniac nature — we may remember Goethe's belief in his (and Napoleon's) *daimonion* —, an ambiguous folkloristic religion of underworld Gods tends to replace the truly religious world of order and clarity that had produced the concept of musical world harmony. But though the orderly picture of the world has faded by the eighteenth century, the original desire of the individual to fuse somehow with nature has survived, particularly with the Germans, who always feel their own individuality to be somehow incomplete. This desire may assume two forms: the pantheistic and the religious. Werther, so much torn in his feelings, is never shaken in his craving for pantheistic union with nature; in fact, to integrate with the whole of nature is the purpose of his suicide. The religious variant is represented by Eichendorff. This Catholic poet is not a narcissistic intellectual mirroring himself in nature, but an unproblematic, gaily bird-like being, somewhat puerile perhaps, but living in unison with the aimless beauty of the world. No German poet has identified himself so thoroughly with the German forest and its denizens. He speaks in the first person in the name of the skylark which sings bathed in sunlight, feeling its breast bursting with song. His nightingale is called upon to announce the meaning of his poetic universe:

> ... in der Einsamkeit verkünde
> was sie alle, alle meinen:
> dieses Rauschen in den Bäumen
> und der Mensch in dunkeln Träumen.

The rustling of the dusky leaves of the forest as well as the dark confused dreams of man carry the same message: the affirmation of the aimlessness of nature (human and non-human), whose inexplicability should be respected. It remained for the French Romantics, the seraphic Lamartine and the gigantic Victor Hugo, to celebrate pantheistic world harmony with their French articulateness, with the rhetorical grandiloquence and sonority of their voices. One was the flute, the other the organ. Victor Hugo's Satyr *(Le satyre)* dethrones the serene Gods of the Olympus and reveals himself with a stentorian voice as Pan, before whom Jove must abdicate. There is no doubt that Hugo saw himself as that animal-God, as the incarnation of a strange Gallo-Greek earthiness which owes more to Rabelais than to Theocritus. Never since the time of the early Christian hymns had one heard such powerful songs of world-harmony nor since the time of Horace such strong affirmation of the rôle of the poet as *vates,* as Bard. In 1830 Victor Hugo writes:

> C'est que l'amour, la tombe, et la gloire, et la vie,
> L'onde qui fuit par l'onde incessamment suivie,
> Tout souffle, tout rayon, ou propice ou fatal,
> Fait reluire et vibrer mon âme de cristal,
> Mon âme aux mille voix, que le Dieu que j'adore
> Mit au centre de tout comme un écho sonore.

The poet himself is both the echo and the crystal placed in the center of the universe by a God whom he, so to speak, crowds out. Victor Hugo is the almighty sensorium that unites, reflects, and speaks for the whole of creation. Obviously the tiny voice of a bird would be superfluous in the concert of thousand voices, or in the pandemonium set in motion by the Bard alone. For, unlike Saint Francis, Hugo believes that the poet may give voice to the world concert. Less optimistically and more modestly, de Musset saw in the poet the voice of suffering incarnate; he offers humanity his bleeding heart for food as the pelican does to her young. "Les plus désespérés sont les chants les plus beaux, / Et j'en sais d'immortels qui sont de purs sanglots." For Baudelaire the poet is the albatross, an exile from heaven plodding clumsily on this earth. Similarly for Matthew Arnold Philomela is a "wanderer from a Grecian shore" and her song is, as in Greek times, "eternal passion, eternal pain." The function of the Hugoian "sonorous world-echo" was taken over in the second half of the nineteenth century by the greatest sorcerer-artist of all times, the musi-

cian Richard Wagner. With him operatic art is used to express the will
to love and death, which, according to Schopenhauerian philosophy,
animates all of creation, man and nature alike. The opera which had been
created in the Baroque period as a demonstration of the soothing power of
music on all creatures — it is not chance that Orpheus, the tamer of animals
and the conqueror of hell, was its original main protagonist — is called
upon by Wagner to express the religion of the nineteenth century: pantheism, the voice of the forest in *Siegfried,* of fire in the *Walküre* and of
the individual striving for dissolution in death in *Tristan and Isolde.*
Wagner gave to his concept of world harmony an orchestration which
interpreted the togetherness of voices in the world, each singing its own
unendliche Melodie, in a novel density of design and compactness of
texture which has overpowered millions of listeners on a scale never
attained by any artist working with the medium of sound.

After this rapid and over-simplified survey it should have become clear
that in the poem "Out of the Cradle" Whitman has offered a powerful
original synthesis of motifs which have been elaborated through a period
of 1500 years of Occidental poetry. The poems I have mentioned are not
necessarily his immediate material sources; but I am convinced that his
"bird or demon" is a descendant of Shelley's "Sprite bird," that the brother
mocking-bird is one of Saint Francis' brother creatures, that his "feathered guest from Alabama" is a derivate from Arnold's "wanderer from a
Grecian shore," that the conception of "a thousand singers, a thousand
songs . . . a thousand echoes" all present in the poet is a reëlaboration of
Victor Hugo's "âme aux mille voix" and "écho sonore." Be this as it may,
the basic motifs in which the idea of world harmony has taken shape in
Europe must be in our mind when we read Whitman's poem, which becomes greater to the degree that it can be shown as ranking with, and
sometimes excelling, the great parallel poems of world literature.

Our poem is organized in three parts: a *prooemium* (l. 1-22), the tale of
the bird (l. 23-143), and the conclusion in which the influence of the bird
on the "outsetting bard" is stated (l. 144 — to the end). Parts one and three
correspond to each other and occasionally offer parallel wording.

The proem, composed in the epic style of *arma virumque cano,* not only
defines the theme of the whole poem clearly but translates this definition
into poetry. The proem consists of one long, "oceanic" sentence which
symbolizes by its structure the poetic victory achieved by the poet: "Out
of the Cradle . . . down . . . up . . . out . . . from . . . I, chanter of pains and
joys, uniter of here and hereafter . . . A reminiscence sing." Out of the
maze of the world, symbolized by those numerous parallel phrases, introduced by contrasting prepositions, which invite the inner eye of the
reader to look in manifold directions, though *out of* and *from* predominate
— out of the maze of the world emerges the powerful Ego, the "I" of the
poet, who has extricated himself from the labyrinth (his victory being as
it were sealed by the clipped last line "a reminiscence sing").

The longer the sentence, the longer the reader must wait for its subject,
the more we sense the feeling of triumph once this subject is reached: the
Ego of the poet that dominates the cosmos. It is well known that this is

the basic attitude of Walt Whitman toward the world. "Walt Whitman, a kosmos, of Manhattan the son, turbulent, fleshy, sensual...", he says in the "Song of Myself." He felt himself to be a microcosm reflecting the macrocosm. He shares with Dante the conviction that the Here and Hereafter collaborate toward his poetry, and as with Dante this attitude is not one of boastfulness. Dante felt impelled to include his own human self (with all his faults) because in his poem his Ego is necessary as a representative of Christendom on its voyage to the Beyond.[1] Walt Whitman felt impelled to include in his poetry his own self (with all his faults) as the representative of American democracy undertaking this worldly voyage of exploration. "And I say to mankind, Be not curious about God ... I see God each hour of the twenty-four, ... In the faces of men and women I see God, and in my own face in the glass." "I am of old and young, of the foolish as much as the wise, one of the Nation of many nations ... A Southerner soon as a Northerner ... Of every hue and caste am I, of every rank and religion."[2] But in contrast to Dante who knew of an eternal order in this world as in the Beyond, Whitman finds himself faced with an earthly reality whose increasing complexity made correspondingly more difficult his achievement of poetic mastery. Therefore Whitman must emphasize more his personal triumph. The complexity of the modern world finds its usual expression with Whitman in the endless catalogues, so rarely understood by commentators, in what I have called his "chaotic enumeration" ("La enumeración caótica en las literaturas modernas," Buenos Aires 1945), a device, much imitated after him by Rubén Darío, Claudel, and Werfel. This poetic device consists of lumping together things spiritual and physical, as the raw material of our rich, but unordered modern civilization which is made to resemble an oriental bazaar. In this poem it is only one specific situation whose material and spiritual ingredients Whitman enumerates: the natural scene (Paumanok beach at night), the birds, the sea, the thousand responses of the heart of the boy-poet, and his "myriad thence-arous'd words,"—they are all on one plane in this poem, no one subordinated to another, because this arrangement corresponds to Whitman's chaotic experience. Similarly the two temporal planes, the moment when the boy felt the "myriad words" aroused in him on Paumanok beach, and the other when the mature poet feels the rise of "the words such as now start the scene revisiting," are made to coincide because, at the time of the composition of the poem, they are felt as one

---

1. Cf. my "Note on the poetic and empirical 'I' in medieval authors" in *Traditio* IV, 414.
2. Whitman has expressed the necessity of his Ego for his poetry in the following prose lines of his "Backward glance o'er travel'd roads": "I saw, from the time my enterprise and questionings positively shaped themselves (how best can I express my own distinctive era and surroundings, America, Democracy?) that the trunk and centre ... must be an identical body and soul, a personality—which personality, after many considerations and ponderings, I deliberately settled should be myself—indeed could not be any other ... 'Leaves of Grass,' indeed ... has mainly been ... an attempt, from first to last, to put *a person,* a human being (myself in the latter half of the Nineteenth Century, in America,) freely, fully and truly on record." Whitman could not realize that he was repeating Dante's procedure, that the poet of democracy must impersonate this sublime abstraction with the same consistency that made Dante impersonate the universal Christian quest for the Beyond. The sea must whisper its oracle 'privately' to Whitman just as Beatrice in the Beyond calls Dante by his personal name.

chaotic but finally mastered experience: the boy who observed the birds now has become the poet. When defining his creative rôle here in the poem, Whitman does not indulge in chaotic enumeration of his qualities as he does in the passage from the "Song of Myself" in which he appears as a Protean demigod. Now he presents himself simply and succinctly as: "I, chanter of pains and joys, uniter of here and hereafter." Out of hydra-like anarchy he has created unity; and, as we see, he has gained not only an emotional, but an intellectual triumph; he represents himself as "taking all hints, but swiftly leaping beyond them" like a master phil-ologian or medieval glossator (later he will insist on his rôle as cautious "translator of the birds' cry," 31 and 69). Whitman takes care to impress upon us the intellectual side of the synthesis he has achieved; a claim that is not unjustified and an aspect that should be stressed more in a poet in whose work generally only the sensuous and chaotic aspect is empha-sized.

His "uniting" powers have been revealed to us in his first stanza; in fact in the first line of the poem which gives it its title. With its rocking rhythm, the line suggests the cradle of the infinite sea from which later, at the end of the poem, *death* will emerge. At this stage, however, death is already a part of the situation. It is present in the phrase "From a word stronger and more delicious than any," which the reader is not yet able to understand. Now we can visualize only the ocean, the main instru-ment in the concert of world harmony with which the song of the bird and the thousand responses of the poet fuse. Whitman restores the Ambrosian fullness and the unity of *Stimmung* of the world concert of love, music, and ocean (but obviously without Ambrose's theism). There will be no dainty *Vogelkonzert* in a German romantic nook, no dolorous dialogue between a soul estranged from nature and a bird-sprite in an English countryside; the American ocean, "the savage old mother," will provide the background and the undertone to the whole poem. In this Ambrosian concert of world harmony we may distinguish also the Hugoian voice of the poet consisting of a thousand voices; but the insistent repetitions "a thousand singers, a thousand echoes" give rather the effect of a strug-gle on the poet's part, a struggle with the infinite, than that of a com-placent equation ("I am the universe!") such as we find in Hugo.[3]

After the organ- and tuba-notes that resound in the proem, the tone changes entirely in the main part, which is devoted to the reminiscence proper, to the singing of the mocking-birds and the listening of the boy. Here we find a straightforward narrative interrupted by the lyrical songs or "arias" of the birds. Given the setting of nature within which the boy and the bird meet, the term *aria* (130, 138) with its operatic, theatrical connotation as well as the musicological term *trio* (140) that immediately follows (applied to the ears, the tears, and the soul of the boy), may seem too *précieux*. In *Song of Myself*, we recall, Whitman speaks of the tree-toad

3. But we should keep in mind that Whitman's pantheistic unification of the cosmos, as is true of all similar modern attempts, is informed by a pantheism that comes *after* Christianity, a pantheism-that-has-absorbed-Christianity. The Christian feeling for the unity of the world in God can never be lost in modern times, not even when God Himself is lost.

as "a *chef-d'œuvre* for the highest." But we must also remember that Whitman's world-embracing vision is able to contain in itself opposite aspects of the world at once together. In this vision the man-made or artificial has its genuine place near the product of nature and may even be only another aspect of the natural. The song of the mocking-bird, so naturally sweet, is an artefact of nature that teaches the human artist Whitman.

To return to our narrative, this offers us a development in time of the theme that had been compressed to one plane in the proem: the boy become poet. In such a development, we would expect, according to conventional syntax, to find the historical flow of events expressed by verbs. But to the contrary, this narrative section offers throughout an almost exclusively nominal style, that is, the coupling of nouns with adjectives or participles, without benefit of finite verbs or copulas. This is an impressionistic device known in French as "écriture artiste," which was introduced by the Goncourts in their diary in the 1850's; for example, "Dans la rue. Tête de femme aux cheveux retroussés en arrière, dégageant le bossuage d'un front étroit. les sourcils remontés vers les tempes...; un type physique curieux de l'énergie et de la volonté féminines" (*Journal des Goncourt,* [1856], I 134). This we call impressionistic because with the suppression of the verb the concatenation and development of happenings gives way to the listing of unconnected ingredients, or, in pictorial terms, to touches of color irrespective of the units to which the colored objects belong. Accordingly, we find with Whitman: "Once Paumanok...two feathered guests ... and their nest ... and every day the he-bird to and fro ... and every day ... I cautiously peering ...", a procedure that is brought to a high point of perfection in that masterpiece of the last stanza of the second part: "The aria sinking, all else continuing, the stars shining ... The boy ecstatic ... The love in the heart long pent ..." I see in these participles nervous notations of the moment which serve not to reënact actions, but to perpetuate the momentary impressions which these have made on the boy when he was perceiving them. When the boy sensed that the melancholy song was subsiding, he jotted down in the book of memory the words: "Aria sinking," and we the readers may still perceive that first nervous reaction. The development of the boy is then given the style appropriate to a "reminiscence." The style here chosen is such as to impress upon us the fragmentary nature of the naked "reminiscence." Because of the non-finite form of the participles, single moments are forever arrested, but, owing to the verbal nature of these forms, the moment is one of movement, of movement crystallized. Of course, such vivid rendering of a reminiscence is possible only in languages, such as English or Spanish, that possess the progressive form, of which the simple participle may represent the elliptical variant.[4]

---

4. One will notice that in the sentence quoted above from the *Journal des Goncourt* the style of the diary is applied to a static picture, not to an action in the making. *Dégageant le bossuage* stands in attributive relationship to *tête de femme* whereas *sinking* offers a predication about *the aria* (in other words, *the aria sinking* contains a double beat). Moreover, the participles of the Goncourts are all grouped under one heading *tête de femme* finally summed up as *un type physique...*, whereas in Whitman's stanza we have a list of different actions, all of equal

Now, from line 138 on, while the initial rhythm of the stanza seems to continue, there appear strange inversions such as "The aria's meaning, the ears, the soul, swiftly depositing" (for "the ears, the soul swiftly depositing the aria's meaning" and similarly in 140 and 141), inversions quite unusual in English, even jarring upon the English *Sprachgefühl*. We must evidently suppose that the "extasis" (l. 136) of the boy is working in an effort comparable to travail toward an intellectual achievement. It is "the aria's *meaning*" that is now being found by him and the jarring construction is the "impressionistic" rendering of the difficulty with which this inner event is made to happen. It has already been noted that the activities here reflected by the sequence of participles and other modifiers are all of equal weight. We have not yet stressed the extent to which the "enumerative" procedure has been carried out in our stanza, which indeed consists only of detached phrases of the type "the .... -ing (-ed)." The chaotic enumeration offered us here is intended to show the collaboration of the whole world ("all else," "the stars," "the winds," "the fierce old mother," "the yellow half-moon," "the boy extatic," "the love," "the ears, the soul," "the strange tears," "the colloquy, the trio," and "the undertone of the sea") toward that unique event—the birth of a poet out of a child who has grasped the meaning of the world. The nervous, impressionistic enumeration is symbolic of the travail of this birth. On the other hand, the repetition in this whole stanza of the atonic rhyme -*ing,* an ending that appeared already in the first line with the suggestion of *rocking,* evokes the all-embracing rhythm and permanent undertone or counterpoint of the sea, whether fiercely howling or softly rocking, as it comes to drown out the chamber-music, the *trio* of ears, soul, and tears in the boy. The rhyme in -*ing* is a *leitmotif* that orchestrates the arias of boy and bird and gives the poem a Wagnerian musical density of texture.

As for the songs of the birds, let us note first that Whitman has chosen to replace the hackneyed literary nightingale by a domestic bird of America, the mocking-bird, compared to which, Jefferson once declared, the European nightingale is a third-rate singer. The manner in which Whitman has "translated," to use his modest expression, the song of the mocking-bird into words deserves boundless admiration. I know of no other poem in which we find such a heart-rending impersonation of a bird by a poet, such a welding of bird's voice and human word, such an empathy for the joy and pain expressed by nature's singers. The European poets we have listed above have accurately defined or admiringly praised the musical tone of the bird-notes issuing from tiny throats, but no one attempted to choose just those human articulate words[5] which would cor-

weight. Accordingly, the Goncourt passage offers a tighter sentence structure. This quality was evidently perceived by Lanson who, in his *Art de la prose,* p. 265, discussing this passage, remarks of the *Journal* in general: "Ce Journal est très *écrit;* on n'y sent jamais l'abandon, la furie de la notation improvisée." There is then a pose of diary-writing in the Goncourts. With Whitman, on the contrary, the sequence of nominal sentences gives the effect of genuinely improvised notation, such as the boy himself might actually have made at the moment in *his* 'note-book,' the book of memory.

5. Onomatopoeias (for example *tweet-tweet*) such as occur in folk-poetry would be stylized phonetic approximations, neither human nor bird-like, of the inarticulate sounds of the birds.

respond to birds' song if these creatures had possessed the faculty of speech (Eichendorff had the bird sing in the first person, but it sang conventional Romantic lines): the simple, over and over repeated exclamations of a helpless being haunted by pain, which, while monotonously repeating the same *oh!* or giving in to the automatism that is characteristic of overwhelming emotion ("my love, my love"), call upon all elements to bring back the mate. Thus in one common purpose the whole creation is united by the bird in the manner of Saint Francis, but this time in a dirge that associates the creation ("Oh night,"—"Low-hanging moon," "Land, land, land," "Oh rising stars," "Oh darkness") with the mourner, with his elemental body and his elemental desires "Oh throat,"..."Oh throbbing heart,"..."Oh past," "Oh happy life," "O songs of joy."[6] The mournful bird shakes out "reckless despairing carols," songs of *world disharmony* in which love and death are felt as irreconcilable enemies ("carols of lonesome love,"—"death's carols"). The long outdrawn refrains of despair ("soothe soothe soothe," "land land land," "loved loved loved ...") alternate with everyday speech whose minimum of expressivity becomes a maximum in a moment of tribulation that is beyond words ("so faint, I must be still, be still to listen, but not altogether still, for then she might not come immediately to me," or "O darkness, O in vain! O I am very sick and sorrowful"). The most dynamic American poet has here become the gentlest. We remember Musset's lines quoted above; Whitman's bird's song is a *pur sanglot.*

We may surmise that this lyric section (within a lyric poem) has been somewhat influenced by Matthew Arnold's "Forsaken Merman," ("Come dear children, let us away; down and away below. /Come dear children, come away down;/Call no more!..."). But Arnold's merman is one of the last offsprings of that futile masquerade of elementary spirits revived by the Romantics, a pagan demon who is presented as *defeated* by Christianity instead of a figure dangerously seductive to Christians. But Whitman's mocking-bird, the spirit become human, who symbolizes all earthly loveliness subject to grief and death, will live forever. It is one of those historical miracles we can not explain that in the age of machines and capitalism there should arise a poet who feels himself to be a brother to nature as naturally as did Saint Francis, but who at the same time was enough of an intellectual to know the uniqueness of his gift. To *him* the bird poured forth the "meanings which I of all men know, Yes, my brother, I know, the rest might not." This is again no boasting; this is the simple truth, a perspicacious self-definition of one who has a primeval genius of empathy for nature.

Now let us turn to the last part of the poem which begins with the words "demon *or* bird" (143), an expression followed later (175) by my "dusky demon *and* brother." The Shelleyan ambiguity disappears here. This marks the end of the parabola that began with "the two feathered guests from Alabama" (26) and was continued sadly with "the solitary guest from Alabama" (51) and "the lone singer wonderful" (58). While

---

6. On this point, cf. Hermann Pongs, *Das Bild in der Dichtung* I, pp. 223 *seq.*

the mood of the birds develops from careless rapture to 'dusky' melancholy, a contrary change takes place in the sea. "The fierce old mother incessantly mourning" (134), the "savage old mother incessantly crying" (141) becomes the "old crone rocking the cradle,"[7] "hissing melodious," "laving me all over." The two opposite developments must be seen in connection. To the degree that the bird is crushed by fate, the sea develops its soothing qualities; to the degree that beauty fades away, wisdom becomes manifest. The sea represents the sweet wisdom of death. The forces of nature are thus ambivalent, Janus-like. Nature wills sorrow and joy, life and death, and it may be that death will become or foster life. "Out of the cradle endlessly rocking," that is (we understand it now), out of the cradle of *death,* the poet will sing life. By presenting, in the beginning, the sea only as a cradle gently rocking, there was suggested the idea of birth and life; but now, the gently rocking cradle is seen as the symbol of recurring death and re-birth. A poet is born by the death of the bird who is a brother and a demon. A brother because he teaches the boy love; a demon, because he "projects"[8] the poet, anticipates, and heralds him, stirs up in him those creative faculties which must partake of the frightening and of the daemoniac. But while the bird was destined to teach the boy love ("death" being a reality the bird was not able to reconcile with love), the sea, wiser than the bird and the "aroused child's heart," has another message to bring to the boy: "Death, death, death, death, death" (173). This line is the counterpart of the mocking-bird's "loved loved loved loved loved!", and it is couched in the same exclamational style, as though it were the organic continuation thereof. The word *death* is "the word final, superior to all," "the key," "the clew" which awakes in the boy the thousand responses, songs, echoes, and the myriad of words; and once he has discovered this *meaning* of life, which is death, he is no longer the boy of the beginning ("never again leave me to be the peaceful boy I was before") . He has become the poet, the "uniter[9] of here and hereafter," able to fuse the voices of the *musica mundana* into one symphony, and we the readers can now understand his words in their full

7. Professor Anderson has drawn my attention to the fact that the parenthetic mention of the "old crone" is not contained in the first versions of the poem. In fact, the whole inversely parallel development of the bird and the sea is missing in them: The 'Shelleyan' expression *demon or bird!* occurs only from 1867 on, the 1860 edition having only *bird!* in the passage in question, although this is followed by two allusions to *(dusky) demon.* Similarly the expression "dusky demon and brother" appears in final form only after several rewordings and owes its form to a meticulous carefulness on the part of that supposedly rather careless stylist Whitman, comparable indeed to that of the French classicist Malherbe who changed his first draft: "Et ne pouvait Rosette être mieux que les roses qui ne vivent qu'un jour" into the exquisite lines: "Rose, elle a vécu ce que vivent les roses, L'espace d'un matin" (cf. my *Stilstudien* II [1928], p. 18).

8. This term must be understood in the light of what Christian theologians call 'prefiguration' or 'adumbration' (e.g. David, by his existence, announces or anticipates Christ who will be the *final king).* The bird in its song of grief attempts to unite the whole universe and thereby anticipates the poet who, having absorbed the teaching of the sea (he is not land-bound like the bird), will be able *truly* to 'unite' the cosmos in his poem.

9. The "will to unite" in Whitman is reflected by his habit of leaping from the particular to a comprehensive *all* as in "the word of the sweetest songs, and all songs" or in a discarded version of our poem: "O how joys, dreads, convolutions, human shapes, and all shapes, spring as from graves around me!" One feels here the impatience of the 'uniter.'

depth. In the conclusion we recognize certain lines of the proem textually repeated but now clarified and deepened by the keyword; we understand at last the symphonic[10] value of "that strong and delicious word" alluded to in the proem. The liquid fusion suggested by the sea of death is symbolized by the fluid syntax of the last three stanzas; the relative constructions which we find in l. 163 "Whereto answering the sea..." and l. 174 "Which I do not forget" weld the three stanzas together into one stream or chain which comprehends the question of the boy, the answer of the sea and his choice of avocation, into one melody in which inspiration flows uninterruptedly from the watery element to the poet. The bird and the poet have been given their respective solos in the symphony. The bird's solo is the *aria* and boy's the *trio* of ears, soul, and tears; the endless counterpoint and contrabasso of the sea has accompanied their detached musical pieces. Now all voices blend in an *"unendliche Melodie,"* an infinite melody, the unfixed form of nineteenth-century pantheism, with Wagnerian orchestration. "But fuse the song of my dusky demon and brother... with the thousand responsive songs, at random, my own songs... and with them the key, the word up from the waves." The last word in the poem, however, is the personal pronoun *me*. Though placed inconspicuously in an unstressed position in the short line "the sea whispered to me," this personal word nevertheless represents a modest climax. It is to Whitman that has been revealed the musical meaning of the world, the chord formed by Eros and Thanatos, the infinite cosmos created from infinite chaos, and, finally, his own microcosmic rôle in the creation. It is the knowledge of death that will make him the poet of life, of this world, *not* of the Hereafter. The promise in the beginning to sing of the Here and Hereafter can be said to have been fulfilled only if the Hereafter is understood as comprised in the Here.[11] We will note that no reference is made in Whitman's poem to the world harmony of the Christian Beyond in the manner of Milton. The fullness of life of which Whitman sings can come to an end only in the sealike, endlessly rocking embrace of nothingness, an end that is sweet and sensuous ("delicious" is Whitman's epithet), and, indeed, he appears sensuously to enjoy the sound of the word *death* that he so often repeats. We may pause at this point to remember that in 1860, one year after our lyric was written, Whitman gives expression to the same feeling in the poem "Scented herbage of my breast":

10. It must be noted that the "symphonic fusion" in our poem was achieved by Whitman only in the process of time (cf. also note 7): The title of the poem in the first versions, 1860 and 1867, was "A Word Out of the Sea"; the oracular word *Death!* appeared in two passages, repeated five times in each, and the climactic line: 'the word final, superior to all' was preceded by a passage of six lines, in which was repeated several times the exclamation: "oh, a word!" The original versions show then the orchestra of the world concert dominated by the monody of the oracle; the fierce old mother "out of" whom "the word" was to come, was in the exalted position of the Delphian Pythia. It may be added that Whitman showed himself then also more conscious of the new "chaos" opening up before him as a consequence of his new awareness of his destination: "O a word! O what is my destination? (I fear it is henceforth chaos)." This line is deleted in the final draft, because it would have jarred with the rôle of the 'uniter' assumed by Whitman in the beginning, but its original presence confirms our view that the poet has felt it indeed to be his task to create cosmos out of chaos.

11. Cf. the line in "Walt Whitman," 48: "No array of terms can say how much I am at peace about God, and about death?"

You [the leaves] make me think of death,
Death is beautiful from you (what indeed is finally
   beautiful except death and love?)
Oh I think it is not for life I am chanting here
   my chant of lovers,
I think it must be for death...
Death or life I am then indifferent, my soul
   declines to prefer
(I am not sure but the high soul of lovers welcomes
   death most).

The same feeling for the voluptuousness of death and the death-like quality of love we find not only in Wagner's *Tristan und Isolde* (1857), in which we hear the same words applied to the love-scene and to the death-scene, *unbewusst—höchste (Liebes-) Lust*. There is also the same motif in Baudelaire's *Invitation* of 1857, in which the 'invitation' is the lure of death, described as voluptuous hashish and scented lotus. Perhaps powerful personalities crave death as a liberation from the burden of their own individuality, and sensuous poets wish to have a sensuous death. Perhaps also the concurrence in one motif of three poets not in direct contact with each other means that their subtle sensitivity instinctively anticipated the death-germs implanted in a luxuriant, sensuous, worldly civilization of "Enrichissez-vous," of Victorianism, and the Second Empire. This was long before the *fin de siècle* generation of D'Annunzio, Barrès, Hofmannsthal, and Thomas Mann, when the theme of love-death, inherited from Baudelaire and Wagner, finally became the theme *par excellence*. But Whitman, unlike his two sickly European contemporary confrères will remain for us not the poet of death (although the idea of death may have perturbed him more than once), but the unique poet of American *optimism* and love of life, who has been able, naturally and naively, to unite what in other contemporary poets tends to fall apart, the life of man and that of nature.[12]

A last question arises. To what sub-genre does our lyrical poem belong? It is obviously an *ode,* the genre made famous by Pindar, Horace, Milton, and Hölderlin, if the ode may be defined as a solemn, lengthy, lyric-epic poem that celebrates an event significant for the community, such as, with Pindar, the victory of a champion in the Olympic games. Ancient poems belonging to this very aristocratic genre are filled with erudite mythological allusions since the origin of the heroes must be traced back to gods or demigods. These odes are also written in a difficult language that can not easily be sung, for they are replete with whimsical breaks and changes of rhythm and tone that reflect the fragmentary nature of the inspiration of the poet, carried away as he is by his divine enthusiasm or θεία μανία. Of course, as is true of all ancient poetry, the ode had no rhymes. In the period of the Renaissance this ancient genre was revived,

---

12. ... And in addition to all that—though this peculiarity is not represented in our poem—the vitality of the machine.

but enjoyed only a precarious existence in modern literatures because
the social set-up of Pindar's Greece was missing in our civilization, filled
as it is with social resentment, and because the travesty involved in presenting contemporary figures as ancient heroes could only be sadly dis-
appointing. The genre fared relatively better in Germanic than in Romance literatures because the Romance languages are not free enough
in word-formation to offer coinages worthy of Pindar and because Romance
needs the rhyme as a constitutive element of verse. Ronsard's Pindaric
odes were signal failures. Whitman has acclimated the ode on American
soil and democratized it. The lyric-epic texture, the solemn basic tone
and the stylistic variation, the whimsical word-coinages and the chaotic
fragmentariness are preserved. The latter feature has even found a modern
justification in the complexity of the modern world. For the rhymeless
Greek verse, Whitman by a bold intuition found an equivalent in the
Bible verset, but he used this meter in order to express a creed diametrically opposed to that of the Bible. Theoretically, he could have borrowed
expressions of his pantheistic beliefs from the mythology of the Greeks,
but in reality, he did away with *all* mythology, pagan as well as Christian.
He replaces the pagan Pantheon by the deified eternal forces of nature to
which any American of today may feel close. The Ocean is the old savage
mother, not Neptune with the trident (a mother, a primeval chtonic
goddess) and the bird is not Philomela, but the mocking-bird who is a
demon of fertility (only in the phrase "feathered guests of Alabama"
do we find a faint reminiscence of Homeric expression, the *epitheton
constans).*[13] The Neo-Catholic poet Paul Claudel who, as recently as the
last decades, gave the French for the first time a true ode and was able
to do so only by a detour through America, by imitating Whitman (even
the metric form of his free verse), found it necessary to discard Whitman's
pantheistic naturalism and to replace it by the *merveilleux chrétien* which
a hundred years ago Chateaubriand had introduced into French prose.[14]
But it can not be denied that Whitman's ode can reach a wider range of
modern readers than can Claudel's orthodox Catholic *grande ode.* As for
the solemn event significant for the community which the ode must by
its nature celebrate—this we have in the consecration of Walt Whitman
as a poet, the glorification, not of a Greek aristocratic athlete born of
Gods, but of a nameless American boy, a solitary listener and singer on
a little-known Long Island shore who, having met with nature and with
his own heart, becomes the American national poet, the democratic and
priestly *vates Americanus.*

13. It may be noted that even this is no pure case of an 'epitheton constans' since it does not
reappear in later situations; on the contrary, as we have said, the gay epithet 'feather'd guests
from Alabama' will lead us to the melancholy 'loneful singer wonderful.' In the case of 'the
savage old mother incessantly crying' there is from the start no indication of 'constancy' of
attribution; *crying* is not an attribute, but a predicate. But that Whitman had the Homeric
epithet in mind is shown by the line quoted above from 'Song to myself': 'Walt Whitman . . . of
Manhattan the son' which is a travesty of the ancient type 'Ajax the Telamonian son.'

14. Cf. my interpretation of an ode by Paul Claudel in *Linguistics and Literary History* (Princeton 1948, pp. 193 *seq.).* This ode, one of five intended "pour saluer le siècle nouveau," and reminiscent of Horace's *Carmen saeculare,* also glorifies the achievements of modern industry and
in this manner replaces the *fin de siècle* pessimism of the poetic schools that preceded Claudel
by a "siècle nouveau" optimism which harks back to Whitman.

24

Varieties of Scholarly Interpretation:
Historical Interpretation

Frank Kermode

The Faerie Queene, I and V

To speak of the "world" of a particular poet is to use a figure no one will find unfamiliar. It is a question of the natural uniformity, cohesion and interrelation of a body of work, however various, however divided into continents and elements. It is to assert that in Wordsworth, for example, there is a force universally at work, like gravity. And indeed the study of such worlds has sometimes been held to be analogous to physics. It would seem, on the face of it, that to make such a world (and poets have not scrupled to claim that they imitated God in doing so) is the labour of a major poet. For one thing, there is a requirement of size; a world has bulk before it has this kind of complexity. There is also a requirement of order and continuity, qualities one senses in a Shakespeare as well as in a Dante or a Milton, in the artist who seems to have no explicit philosophical or theological programme as well as in the poet whom we think of as in some way "committed".

Literate persons bring to such worlds certain expectations. These are the product of civilized conversation, of allusions encountered in literary comment. But the first thing that happens when they reach the new world is that these expectations are falsified and have to be dismantled. It is something like the experience Keats describes in his sonnet on Homer. The unaffected reader of Milton has a similar experience; he approaches Eden with certain expectations of severity and is disarmed by pleasure and human beauty, two features often omitted from maps of Milton. This dismantling process tends to be more violent with Spenser than with almost anybody else, partly because his poem is less well known than *Paradise Lost* or *Hamlet,* even to people who admire it. It is long, unfinished, and darkly related to the learning and images of an age fundamentally strange to us. It is true that there is an abundance of scholarly guidance

Reprinted, by permission of the Librarian, from the *Bulletin of the John Rylands Library,* XLVII (1964/1965), 123-150. A lecture delivered in the Library series of public lectures.

to be had; but in the end that also creates, as guides to public monuments usually do, expectations not always to be exactly realized. Furthermore, the guide one employs will always omit to mention what to the unconditioned eye may seem very striking features, so that there are not only unattained but unexpected experiences.

What I have now to say takes issue with some learned and acute modern guides to Spenser; but I say it not in a spirit of contention, but with proper gratitude for the help I have accepted from them. Spenser is very diverse, and lends support to many generalizations which seem flatly counter to one another. Thus, as everybody knows, *The Faerie Queene* fluctuates from a philosophical extreme — as in the Garden of Adonis, and the Mutability Cantos — to relatively naîve allegory such as the House of Alma.[1] It contains passages — such as Guyon's stay in the Cave of Mammon, or Britomart's in the Church of Isis — which seem to deal with high matters, but deliberately conceal their full meaning; yet it also contains transparent historical allusions to the trial of Mary Queen of Scots and the campaigns in the Netherlands. Its mood varies from the apocalyptic in Book I to the pastoral in Book VI. Sometimes, as with Florimel, one senses the need to complete Spenser's allegory for him, and sometimes one feels that he has for the time being almost forgotten about it; yet there are other times when one wonders at the density of meanings the fiction is made to bear. Readers of Spenser's own epoch seem to have enjoyed the allusions to great men of the age as well as the moral allegories; but later there was some danger of his sinking under the explanations of scholars, and in recent years there has been a noticeable trend towards simplicity of interpretation.

Obviously, we should not cumber his world with our own planetary ingenuities; but I think this process has gone too far. I shall now briefly characterize some of these simplifications, and then examine some aspects of the poem which seem to me to remain stubbornly what the simplifiers do not wish them to be.

At the beginning of this century it was assumed by all who considered Spenser's more philosophical passages that he knew Plato's dialogues, and that he may have interested himself in Renaissance Neo-Platonism. Later there came a different understanding; philosophical sources were found in Lucretius, in Empedocles, in "old religious cults". And it became a commonplace of scholarship that Spenser could be illuminated by reference to the learning of Ficino, Benivieni, or Bruno.[2]

The picture of Spenser as a very learned man is not in itself absurd, since he understood that the heroic poet should be a "curious and universal scholar". But perhaps only an unfamiliarity with the conditions of Renaissance scholarship could have permitted anyone to imagine him to be systematically acquisitive of learning. Also there was prevalent an oversimple view of the Renaissance as a clean new start, which implied a failure to understand the extent to which medieval syntheses — including much

---

1. See A. D. S. Fowler, "Oxford and London Marginalia to *The Faerie Queene*", *Notes and Queries,* CCVI (1961), 416-19.
2. Robert Ellrodt, *Neoplatonism in Spenser* (1961) — a book which argues admirably for a Spenser simplified philosophically by the elimination of Renaissance Neoplatonism from *The Faerie Queene* — opens with an account of this development.

Aristotle and Plato which scholars have misguidedly traced back to the original – persisted in the learning of Spenser's time. Thus the Garden of Adonis, which has attracted much speculation, possibly contains little philosophy that would have surprised an educated reader in any age between that of Spenser and that of Boethius. Not surprisingly there has been a reaction, and such influential books as those of W. L. Renwick (1925) and C. S. Lewis (1936) presented a more credible philosopher-poet, Lewis even labelling him, in a famous passage, "homely" and "churchwardenly".[3] Whether or no we accept this provocative formula, it remains true that Spenser used compendia, handbooks of iconography and so on; that he learnt from popular festivals; and that it would have been harder than used to be supposed to catch him working with an ancient classic open before him.

Yet we should not make the mistake of thinking that what seems exotic or far-fetched to us necessarily seemed so to Spenser. It is enough, perhaps, to remind ourselves of the great differences between his map of knowledge and ours – to remember, for instance, the continuing importance of astrology; the over-riding authority of theology; and a view of classical antiquity which seems to us simply fantastic. Spenser's mind was trained in forms of knowledge alien to us, and habituated to large symbolic systems of a kind which, when we read of them in Huizinga's *The Waning of the Middle Ages,* are likely to strike us as almost absurdly frivolous. Yet he was very serious in his wish to "make it new" – "it" being the sum of knowledge as it appeared to an Englishman at what seemed to be a great crisis of world history. It is hard for us to remember that Spenser served a queen whom he regarded as technically an empress, and whose accession was regularly thought of as the sounding of the seventh trumpet in the Book of Revelation.[4] Spenser saw this world as a vast infolded, mutually relevant structure, as inclusive as the Freudian dream; but he also saw it as disconnected, decaying, mutable, disorderly. We should expect to find his mind, especially when he deals with systematic ideas of order, very strange to us; and we should not easily allow this strangeness to be lost in learned simplifications.

I turn now to a second device for reducing the proportion of relatively inaccessible meaning in *The Faerie Queene.* This is to minimize the importance of a characteristic which had certainly appealed to Spenser's contemporaries, namely the element of historical allegory. Dryden thought that each of Spenser's knights represented an Elizabethan courtier; even Upton, who in his way knew so much more about *The Faerie Queene* than we do, stressed the historical allegory and elaborately explained allusions to Elizabethan history. This way of reading Spenser persisted and, perhaps,

---

3. *The Allegory of Love* (1936; references to edition of 1958). "Popular, homely, patriotic" (p. 311) is Lewis's description of the allegory of Book I. "We have long looked", he says, "for the origins of *The Faerie Queene* in Renaissance palaces and Platonic Academies, and forgotten that it has humbler origins in the Lord Mayor's Show, the chap-book, the bedtime story, the family Bible, and the village church" (p. 312). "Churchwardenly", "honest", "domestic", belong to a provocative list of epithets on p. 321.
4. This apocalyptic strain persisted into the next reign in the posthumous portraits of Elizabeth; see Roy C. Strong, *Portraits of Queen Elizabeth I* (1963). And see T. Brightman, *The Revelation of S. John Illustrated* (1616), pp. 490 f.

reached its climax in the work of Lilian Winstanley half a century ago. But it was dealt a blow from which it has not recovered at the hands of the great American Spenserian, Edwin Greenlaw, in his book *Studies in Spenser's Historical Allegory* (1932).

Greenlaw's object is, broadly, to subordinate historical to ethical allegory. Historical allegory, he says, has reference principally to general topics; it refers to specific persons only momentarily and with no high degree of organization. This is now, I think, the received opinion, and it certainly makes sense to relieve Spenser of barrenly ingenious commentary relating his poem to obscure, forgotten, political intrigues. But if we apply Greenlaw's criteria indiscriminately we are likely to be left with a Spenser drained of that historical urgency which seems to be one of his most remarkable characteristics; it is the adhesive which binds the dream image to immediate reality. And certainly one consequence of the modern simplification of Spenser has been to loosen the bond between his great First Book and an actual world by denying the complexity of his historical allegory.

Finally, there is a third and very sophisticated mode of simplification, and this we can represent by reference to two critics, Mr. A. C. Hamilton in his *The Structure of Allegory in The Faerie Queene* (1951) and Mr. Graham Hough in his *Preface to The Faerie Queene* (1962). Mr. Hamilton is an enemy of "hidden allegorical significance", at any rate in Spenser, though of course he knows how much Renaissance critical theory has to say about "dark conceits". He suggests that we have now established "a fatal dichotomy" between poet and thinker, and that the despised old romantic habit of reading the poem for the beauties of its surface was no more harmful than the modern way of looking straight through to the emblematical puzzles beneath. We have, he argues, made the poem a kind of Duessa "whose borrowed beauty disguises her reality". Or, ignoring the fiction, we seek historical allusion, treating Book I, for example, as a concealed history of the English Reformation; or we devise some "moral reading yielding platitudes which the poet need never have laboured to conceal". Offering some instances of this, he asks, "Is this the morality which More found divine? . . . The 'conceit as passing all conceit'?" And he proposes his "radical reorientation": by concentrating upon the fiction – the image – he will show that the poem is not like Duessa but like Una, who "did seem such, as she was". He finds support for his policy of subordinating all allegorical meanings to the literal in some remarks of Sidney, and asks us to see the moral senses not as kernels of which the fiction is the shell, but as the expanding petals of a multifoliate rose – the meaning "expanding from a clear centre".[5]

Mr. Hamilton shows much skill and sensibility in developing a reading along these lines. But the method, attractive as it sounds, will not serve. We lose too much. Not that I deny the pre-eminence of the literal meaning, which Aquinas himself would have accepted; only it does not mean quite what Mr. Hamilton thinks. The praise of Henry More, for example, which was not in the least extravagant, depended upon a well established view that images could combine old truths to make a new one; the whole was greater than its parts, and if you broke down the "icon" into its original

5. A. C. Hamilton, *The Structure of Allegory in The Faerie Queene* (1961), pp. 5, 7, 10, 11, 17.

constituents the parts together would have less meaning than the whole icon. The pleasure and instruction, you may say, is double: it is the intellectual delight of breaking down the icon and the intuitive benefit of perceiving its global meaning. In short, although we may welcome the figure of the multifoliate rose, we still need the idea of the kernel and the shell, or of the fiction as a means of concealment: it will not, in Spenser, be as perversely opaque as it is in Chapman, but it may well be as elaborate as the sixth book of Aeneid, as read by Renaissance mythographers.

What you find under the surface depends upon your learning and penetration. Behind the Garden of Adonis are philosophic constituents, behind the First Book, constituents of world history; behind the Fifth Book and especially the elaborate dream of Britomart, high matters of imperial and national legal theory. I want, so far as it is possible to have the best of both worlds, to enjoy the fiction much as Mr. Hamilton does, but also to deny his contention that the "universal reference prevents our translating events into historical terms". Thus I am sure that Book V is impoverished if the Church of Isis passage is treated simply as a figurative rendering of the love-relationship of Artegall and Britomart; and this is how Mr. Hamilton, following a note in A. S. P. Woodhouse's famous essay, would have us read it.[6]

Mr. Hough tries, in his very agreeable book, to satisfy the contestants in this kind of quarrel by arguing that there are intermediate stages in literature between complete "realism" and naïve allegory; Shakespeare is equidistant between these extremes, his magic fully absorbing his theme so that one might speak of an "incarnation". Nobody, I suppose, using Mr. Hough's chart, would care to put Spenser — so far as the epic poem is concerned — anywhere save where he puts him, between Shakespeare and "naïve" allegory, as a maker of "poetic structures with various degrees of allegorical explicitness". And Mr. Hough's insistence that the allegory is "relaxed and intermittent" ought to remind us of the constantly varying "thickness" of Spenser's thematic meanings. But I do not think he serves us so well in asking us to depend in our reading upon our "general sense" of how "mythical poetry" works".[7] *The Faerie Queene* is an epic and so historical; we simply do not have an instinct which enables us to participate in historical myths relating to the religious, political and dynastic situations of Spenser's day. And our feeling for "mythical poetry" tells us nothing relevant to the juristic imperialism of his Church of Isis.

I have respect for both of these books; each in its way says that Spenser is a great poet who can mean much to modern readers; and I have given only a very partial account of them. But I quarrel with them, as with the others, because they habitually ignore what I think may be the peculiar strength of Spenser. Probably no other English poet has ever achieved so remarkable a *summa* as his. And it seems to me that we must not modernize him at the cost of forgetting this. "Poetry is the scholar's art". We should be glad to find in *The Faerie Queene* not only the significances of dream, but that fantastic cobweb of conscious correspondences, running

---

6. "Nature and Grace in *The Faerie Queene*", *E.L.H.*, XVI (1949), 216, n. 42.
7. Graham Hough, *A Preface to The Faerie Queene* (1962), p. 107.

over all the interlinked systems of knowledge, which a scholar-poet and a courtier might be expected to produce. Leaving out of account the philosophical simplification I began with, I intend now to speak of two parts of the poem: the historical allegory of Book I, and the allegory of justice in two parts of Book V. In each case, I myself find that the hidden meanings contribute to the delight of the fiction, because some of this delight arises from recognition of the writer's complex intent. And I do not think it does the dreamlike narrative any harm to include in it elements recognizable by conscious analysis.

The First Book of *The Faerie Queene* is well known to be apocalyptic, in the sense that it presents a version of world history founded rather closely upon the English Protestant interpretation of the Book of Revelation. I have elsewhere[8] tried to explain how the force of the book – as I see it – stems from a peculiarly subtle and active interplay of actual history with apocalyptic-sibylline prophecy. In its more political aspect, Book I is a celebration of the part of Elizabeth Tudor, the Protestant Empress, in the workings of providence. This a writer sufficiently sympathetic to Spenser – Milton, for example – would take in at a glance; and nothing in Milton is more Spenserian than the apocalyptic exhortations to England in the pamphlets *On Reformation* and *Areopagitica,* with their emphasis on God's manner of dealing with the nations, and the special role chosen for his Englishmen in the overthrow of antichrist. The Puritan commentators on Revelation, especially Bullinger and Bale, had long insisted upon the degree to which the text foretold the history of the Church, now reaching a climax; and for the better part of a century English opinion accepted Foxe's reading of ecclesiastical history as prefigured in the flight of the woman clothed with the sun – the true catholic church – into a wilderness from which, after forty-two months, she returns to her own as the Church of England. Discussing elsewhere the profusion of references to Revelation in Spenser's text, I expressed some surprise that the very scholars who, by the citation of patristic and Reformist commentaries, have made these identifications so sure, should, under the inhibition of Greenlaw, have forborne to study them in their obvious historical dimension. The text of *The Faerie Queene,* Book I is admittedly studded with the prophetic emblems of Revelation; it admittedly suggests that the Elizabethan settlement – the *renovatio mundi* brought by the Phoenix, the Astraean Elizabeth – fulfils the plan of history laid down in the Bible. Would it not seem likely that the narrative should allude to the history of the Church in the wilderness – that the story of Una and Duessa should, like Foxe's history of the Church, demonstrate the culmination of the divine plan in Elizabeth's accession?

It is clear that the limited series of allusions admitted by most editors to the course of English Reform under Henry VIII and Edward VI would not be enough for the apocalyptic-historical purpose Spenser announces with his imagery from Revelation. If you once identify the English with the primitive Catholic Church, you begin its history, as Jewel said, "after the first creation of the world".[9] After that, Joseph of Arimathaea brought

---

8. *Spenser and the Allegorists* (1963).
9. John Jewel, *Works* (Parker Society, 1848), III, 79.

Eastern Christianity to England; later there was a Christian king, Lucius; hence the early splendours and purity of the English Church, and the historic English independence of Rome and the "ten-horned beast" or Latin Empire, impaired only by the treachery of Hildebrand and his successors.[10] The imperial claims of Elizabeth, however, defied the papal power and were traced back to Constantine.

Now the celebration in image and allegory of the Foxian version of history is not a remote and learned fancy; just as *The Faerie Queene* had her "yearly solemne feaste", so had Elizabeth. Her Accession Day (17 November) was celebrated with increasing fervour, especially after the Armada, so that the Papists called it blasphemous and a parody of the adoration of the Virgin. Mr. Roy C. Strong has well surveyed the main themes of sermon, tract, ballad and entertainment relating to this feast.[11] Elizabeth is *rarissima Phoenix, ultima Astraea,* the renewer of the Church and faithful true opponent of antichrist. She has undone the work of the wicked popes who usurped the emperor's power and rights; she inherits both Lucius' recognized position as God's vicar, and the imperial power of Constantine and Justinian. Antichrist, the murderous sorcerers of the see of Rome, stands finally exposed. The queen is the defender of the true Church in an evil world. In a sense she *is* that Church. When Mr. Strong's preacher speaks of her as the sun shedding beams of religion, he is remembering "the woman clothed with the sun", who turns into the Una of whose sunshiny face Spenser speaks, "glistening euery way about with the light of the euerlasting Gospel".[12] As Mr. Strong observes, "the complexities of eschatological and imperial theory are never far away from the Accession Day themes".[13] Foxe's book, available with the Bible in every church, had become part of the body of patriotic thought, a textbook of English imperialism.

Now "homely Spenser" made, in the First Book of his poem, an epic of these very Accession Day themes, and he too chains up Foxe beside the Bible. An appeal to history was a prerequisite not only of the claims of the Catholic Church of England to antiquity and purity, but also of the queen's claim to possess imperial power over the bishops. *The Faerie Queene* may be mythical poetry; but its myths are the myths of English polity in the fifteen-eighties and nineties. Greenlaw himself observed that the use of Arthurian legend was for the Elizabethans not a Tennysonian archaism, but an argument from antiquity. The Elizabethans in fact saw Arthur's not as Malory's world, but as a unified Britain, and Arthur himself as king of the whole island, which, under the diadem of Constantine, was an empire according to *Leges Anglorum*.[14] Greenlaw observed also that it was commonplace in popular pageants to present the queen as True Religion; and that Spenser's poem reflects the view that her greatest service was the es-

10. John Napier, *A Plaine Discovery of the Whole Revelation* (1593), p. 36.

11. "The Popular Celebration of the Accession Day of Queen Elizabeth I", *Journal of the Warburg and Courtauld Institutes,* XXI (1958), 86-103.

12. M. Augustine Marlorat, *A catholike exposition upon the Revelation of Saint John* (1574), p. 167 verso.

13. Strong, "Accession Day", 101.

14. See E. Kantorowicz, *The King's Two Bodies* (1957), p. 346.

tablishment of true religion in England.[15] We are speaking of an age that venerated Foxe — the age of Archbishop Parker, of Sandys, of a queen who herself insisted upon her role as head of a church founded by Joseph of Arimathaea and a State that inherited the powers of the Constantinian Empire. Indeed she had, the claim ran, reunited the two.[16] Spenser could not avoid allusion to the whole of church history according to Foxe in describing the struggle between Una and antichrist.

Earlier interpretations of this kind — such as those of Scott and Keightley — have been ignored or coldly dismissed by Spenser's modern editors.[17] I think Scott and Keightley were wrong in detail, since they did not look at the history of the church through the medium of Elizabethan propaganda; but they had the right instinct. Any apologist of the Elizabethan settlement was obliged to produce historical arguments, and Spenser, as an allegorical poet, did so by means of hidden meanings in his fiction.

No one is in much doubt about the relationship of Una and Duessa. Una is pure religion, which came to England direct from the East: she is descended from "ancient Kings and Queenes, that had of yore/Their scepters stretcht from East to Westerne shore" (I. i. 5). Duessa, on the other hand, claims descent only from an Emperor "that the wide West under his rule has/And high hath set his throne, where *Tiberis* doth pas" (I. ii. 22). Her false description of her father as emperor alludes to papal usurpations on the imperial power, a constant source of Protestant complaint. As Miss Frances Yates rightly says, Duessa and Una "symbolize the story of impure papal religion and pure imperial religion".[18] The success of the Tudors against the papacy is a restoration of Una, of imperial rights over the *sacerdotium*. The emperor, or empress, is, as Jewel says,[19] the Pope's lord and master; Rome is not directly descended, he adds, from the primitive Eastern church, whereas the reformed Church of England can make exactly this claim. Duessa is in fact a representative of a religion not only antichristian but also anti-imperialist, anti-universalist. Duessa's very name accuses her of schism.

The Red Cross Knight has dealings with both ladies, appearing first with Una in his capacity of defender of the true faith. It is part of the dreamshift technique of the poem that he begins thus, and as *miles Christi*, to end as the knight *fidelis et verax* or Christ himself (whose bride Una is the Church) — after a career of error typical of the human pilgrimage and also of the history of England. In confronting him with Error in the opening Canto, Spenser fulfils a multiple purpose, having in mind not only Christ's victory over sin in the wilderness, but Una's great enemy, heresy, against which the early English Church protected her. Scott thought Error stood for Arianism; it probably corresponds more generally to that

---

15. E. Greenlaw, *Studies in Spenser's Historical Allegory* (1932), cap. I.

16. Thus the queen is shown in portraits not only as wearing the imperial diadem and trampling on the Pope (so revenging the indignity of Frederick Barbarossa) but also as the woman clothed with the sun, or True Church. See Roy C. Strong (p. 26, n. 1 *supra*).

17. See *The Works of Spenser: a Variorum Edition*, ed. E. Greenlaw, C. G. Osgood, F. M. Padelford, and R. Heffner, I (1932), 450.

18. "Queen Elizabeth as Astraea", *Journal of the Warburg and Courtauld Institutes*, X (1948), 68.

19. Jewel, *Works*, III, 76, 85-86.

series of heresies which Bale associates with the opening of the second
and third apocalyptic seals: Sabellianism, Nestorianism, Manichaeism,
as well as Arianism.[20] Modern heresy, for which Jewel firmly places the
responsibility on Rome, is the brood of these earlier errors. The locusts
of stanza xiv derive, as Upton pointed out, from Revelation ix. 7, and were
traditionally associated with heretical teaching — a point made by that
herald of reform, Matthew of Paris, whom Foxe quotes approvingly.[21] The
association is also remembered by Bale.[22] The enemies of Una had existed
as long as there had been a Roman antichrist; Red Cross is her champion,
since God had entrusted her, as Milton thought it natural, to "his Englishmen". The victory of Constantine, which made possible the Christian
Empire, was achieved, according to Foxe, with the aid of British troops;
he thought it represented the end of 294 years since the Passion, and the
binding of Satan for a thousand years. Constantine was himself of course
British, born of St. Helena at York.

Archimago, as is generally agreed, corresponds to the false prophet and
the beast from the land, and so to antichrist. But it is worth observing
that Spenser gives him a name which suggests that he is a magician; and
this is a charge incessantly made against popes by Foxe and many others.
Marlorat's compendious commentary on Revelation, published in 1574,
says, on Rev. xiii. 15 (where the dragon seeks by supernatural means to
destroy the woman clothed with the sun), that popes were often "nigro-
mancers". He cites Cardinal Buno, who, in a life of Gregory vii, "writeth
that many obtained the Popedom by divelish arts", especially Sylvester ii,
John xviii, John xx, Benedict viii, and Benedict ix. Gregory vii himself,
"erst called Hildebrand", was a "notable nigromancer, who with the shaking
of his sleeues woulde make as it were sparks of fire to flye abroad as often
as he liked".[23] Boniface vii and viii, and most of the sixteenth-century
popes, are also on the list. Napier the mathematician, in his commentary
of 1593, finds allusion to popish necromancy in the Sibylline books, and
says on the evidence of "Platina, the Popes own secretarie", that there
have been twenty-two "Necromantick Popes and . . . eight Atheists".[24]

Sylvester ii, who is frequently said to have sold his soul to the devil,
was in fact a man of learning, a mathematician, and one who had a good
try at reconciling papacy with empire; but doubtless the special odium
reserved to him may be accounted for by his having been Pope in A.D. 1000,
when according to some accounts (not Foxe's) Satan was loosed after a
thousand years of bondage. The other Pope most persistently charged with
necromancy is Gregory vii, who was specially detested because, having
gained authority in England through the Conqueror, he began that interference with English government which disfigured so many subsequent
reigns, notably those of Henry ii (who claimed judicial authority over the
clergy) and John. Foxe singles him out as the Pope who started the en-

---

20. John Bale, *The Image of Both Churches, Select Works,* ed. Christmas (Parker Society,
1849) pp. 322 ff.
21. *Acts and Monuments of the Church,* ed. M. H. Seymour (1838), p. 221.
22. Bale, *Image of Both Churches,* p. 352.
23. Marlorat, op. cit., p. 199 recto.
24. Napier, *Plaine Discovery,* Appendix (unpaginated). See also Jewel, *Works,* II, 85.

croachment on the rights of the temporal governor "whereby the Pope was brought to his full pride and perfection of power in the fourteenth century".[25] I have little doubt that Spenser was thinking chiefly of Hildebrand when he made Archimago a master of magic arts and described his plots against Red Cross.

We hear of Archimago's arts in xxxvi, and in xlviii he produces a succubus, a false church "most like that virgin true" until her real nature is revealed. She deceives Red Cross with her claim to be *una sancta ecclesia,* and makes outrageous demands on his body. Spenser may not have been thinking only of the troubles of the eleventh to the fourteenth century; the Synod of Whitby, where, according to Foxe,[26] Wilfrid first led England into the power of Rome, may also have been in his mind. But Gregory VII, who first claimed control of both the swords, ecclesiastical and temporal,[27] and so usurped the power of the emperor (Foxe has a woodcut illustrating the incident of Henry IV waiting Hildebrand's pleasure in the snow), was the greatest papal villain. The powers resigned by Henry IV and later by Barbarossa, upon whose neck Alexander III set his foot, were recovered and refurbished by Spenser's empress, a point upon which Jewel is explicit.[28] So Spenser allows Archimago to conjure up the demonic church which tried to rule the world, and which the British Tudors were to exorcise. But the disgrace of Red Cross, which begins here, represents the long misery of the English Church from the time of Gregory VII until the first stirrings of reformation with Wyclif.

Other crucial events in the Anglican version of church history are reflected in Spenser's narrative. The presumptions of Boniface III coincided with the rise of Islam, and a monk called Sergius gave aid and comfort to these new enemies. The Turks were part of antichrist, said Foxe,[29] taking the contemporary threat from this quarter to be the loosing of the angels of the river Euphrates (Rev. xvi. 12); it reached its present form and strength at the end of the thirteenth century, just when papal power was greatest. Now Spenser has this, or something very like it, in mind when he makes Sansfoy an ally of Archimago. Red Cross first meets Duessa in the company of the infidel Sansfoy (ii. 13). She is adorned with a Persian mitre which, together with the bells and flounces of her "wanton palfry", signify the union of popish flummery and oriental presumption.[30] Sansfoy is the pagan antichrist, defeated by Red Cross as Arthur defeated the pagan Saxons and the crusades the Saracens. I do not say he does not, with his brothers, make a triad opposed to that of the Theological Virtues; the readings are perfectly consistent with one another. Sansloy and Sansjoy are also aspects of antichrist and paganism. It all goes back to Boniface and the Turks — even, perhaps, Duessa's lie about her past when she claims[31]

25. *Acts and Monuments*, p. 112.
26. Ibid. p. 663.
27. *Acts and Monuments*, p. 112.
28. *Works*, III, 75, 76, 99, 116.
29. *Acts and Monuments*, p. 391. Foxe does not name Sergius, but see Wyclif, *De pontificium Romanorum Schismate, Select Works*, ed. Arnold (1869-71), III, 245, and E. L. Tuveson, *Millennium and Utopia* (1949), p. 23.
30. *Works*, III, 104.
31. *F. Q.*, II, II, 23.

to have been betrothed to a great prince who was murdered, which might be an allusion to the establishment by Boniface III of the puppet emperor Phocas.

There is surely reason to suppose that Spenser would think along these lines. Let me, to avoid tedium, spare analysis of the Fraelissa and Fradubio episode, clearly another allegory of the wrong choice of faith, and pass on to the story of Kirkrapine, Abessa and Corceca. Corceca is obviously blind devotion. Abessa, as Sr. Mary R. Falls established,[32] is not an abbess but absenteeism, from *abesse*. The main difficulty is with Kirkrapine. I agree with Sr. Mary Falls that he cannot refer to the evils of monasticism; she argues, with some force, that the reference to church-robbing is more likely to apply to the behaviour of English bishops and courtiers after the Reformation. She cites much evidence, and more could be adduced. Sandys, for example (though himself not innocent of the charges he brings against others), asked the queen to end the abuses of the "surveyors"[33] "that trot from one diocese to another, prying into churches. The pretence is reformation; but the practice is deformation. They reform not offences, but for money grant licences to offend". And he asks the queen – "our most mild Moses" – to stay the hand of these "church-robbers". But he also calls this a perpetuation of a characteristic antichristian practice; and this is really our clue. Spenser is not thinking exclusively of a topical issue; what he has in mind is the duty of the newly restored church to abolish a practice typical of popery, that of using the goods of the church for personal and temporal purposes. Luther gloomily foresaw that church-robbers would not be checked till Armageddon.[34] Long afterwards Milton echoed him in *Of Reformation*,[35] speaking fiercely of prelates: "How can these men not be corrupt, whose very cause is the bribe of their own pleading, whose mouths cannot open without the strong breath and loud stench of avarice, simony and sacrilege, embezzling the treasury of the church on painted and gilded walls of temples, wherein God hath testified to have no delight, warming their palace kitchens, and from thence their unctuous and epicurean paunches, with the alms of the blind, the lame, the impotent, the aged, the orphan, the widow?" Milton accuses the prelates of theft in several kinds; Jewel specifically calls the Roman hierarchy *sacrilegos,* which is in the contemporary translation "church-robbers", for refusing the laity the wine at communion. Clearly any act which impoverished the church could be called church-robbing; there were contemporary instances, but Spenser has in mind the long record of antichrist and his misdeeds. In *The Shepheardes Calender* "September"[36] he is more specifically attacking contemporary misappropriations; but when he speaks of the foxes replacing the wolves in England he is thinking of the clergy as having taken over the role of thieves from the pagans. To compare the antichristian clergy to foxes is an old device stemming from Christ's description of Herod as a fox, and from a gloss on Cant. ii. 14; Sandys

32. "Spenser's Kirkrapine and the Elizabethans," *Studies in Philology,* I (1953), 457-75.
33. *Sermons,* ed. John Ayre (Parker Society, 1842), p. 122.
34. *Preface to the Revelation of Saint John,* 1545; in *Works* (1932), VI, 479-88.
35. *Prose Works* (Bohn edition, 1895), ed. J. A. St. John, II, 415.
36. See Paul E. Maclane, *Spenser's Shepheardes Calender* (1961), p. 127.

uses it[37] and so does Spenser when he gives Duessa, revealed in all her ugliness, a fox's tail (I. vii. 48). What is scandalous is that this ancient wrong should have survived in the reformed church. Kirkrapine, incidentally, lives in concubinage with Abessa. This certainly suggests the unholy relation between simony and absenteeism in Spenser's time, but also suggests that it is a leftover from an earlier period; for Abessa reproaches Una with unchastity, which hints at the Romanist distaste for the married priesthood of the reformed church,[38] and again associates Kirkrapine with the bad religion before reform.

Archimago, disguised as Red Cross and having Una in his charge, represents a bogus English church betraying true religion. That Sansloy should bring Archimago near to death suggests the self-destructive follies of Urban vi (1318-89, Pope from 1378), who seems in fact to have been more or less insane; Wyclif said that he destroyed the authority of the papacy; after him "there is none to be received for the pope, but every man is to live after the manner of the Greeks, under his own law".[39] This lawless folly, and the contemporary inroads of the Turks, probably account for the episode. The rescue of Una from Sansloy by satyrs, as Upton noticed,[40] means the succour of Christianity by primitivist movements such as the Waldensian and Albigensian; some primitives fall into idolatry (hence the follies of some puritan heretics) but the true Reformation line is represented by the well-born primitive Satyrane, who instantly knows the truth and opposes Sansloy.

The subjection of Red Cross to Orgoglio is the popish captivity of England from Gregory vii to Wyclif (about 300 years, the three months of viii. 38). The *miles Christi*, disarmed, drinks of the enervating fountain of corrupt gospel and submits to Rome. He is rescued by Arthur, doing duty for Elizabeth as Emperor of the Last Days, saviour of the English Church. The viciously acquired. wealth of Duessa is confiscated. In ix.17 Red Cross places Una under the charge of Gloriana, head of the Church. In this warp of allegory the capitulation to Despair must mean the Marian lapse; after that Red Cross is assured of his Englishness, and shown the New Jerusalem, of which Cleopolis or London, capital of the Earthly Paradise,[41] seat of the empress, is the earthly counterpart. Only then does he assume the role of the warrior *fidelis et verax* and, with the aid of the two sacraments of the true church, enact the slaying of the beast, the harrowing of hell, the restoration of Eden and the binding of Archimago. The English settlement—to which, as Revelation proved, all history tended, is a type of that final pacification at the end of time. Spenser makes it clear that it is *only* typical; but the boldness with which he conflates history and the archetype in Revelation proves how fully he accepted Foxe's bold formula, "the whole church of Christ, namely . . . the church of England".[42]

---

37. *Sermons,* p. 64.

38. It must be admitted that Spenser himself, like the queen, felt some distaste for married priests, at any rate in the *Shepheardes Calender*.

39. Quoted in Foxe, *Acts and Monuments,* p. 227.

40. *Variorum.*

41. See J. W. Bennett, "Britain among the Fortunate Isles," *Studies in Philology,* LIII (1956), 114 ff.

42. *Acts and Monuments,* p. 998.

I have tried, in making this sketch of the allegory of ecclesiastical history in Book I, not to forget that Spenser's historical view was that of Anglican church historians. This, after all, is rather to be expected than not, in view of the apocalyptic and protestant-imperialist nature of Spenser's poem. What I suggest, in short, is that given the apocalyptic character of Book I — which cannot be denied — allegories of the kind I propose *must* be present in the poem; consequently the historical allegory is not the flickering, limited affair it is sometimes said to be; nor can we pick it up in all its depth by a learnedly ignorant contemplation of the surface of the fiction.

I now turn to a different aspect of Spenser's allegory, the episodes of Mercilla and the Church of Isis in Book V. I take it that the allegory is both juristic and imperialist. Obviously Justitia is here presented as superior to the private virtue treated by Aristotle, and of course also to *ius,* which is one of its servants. Thus it is in the great fourteenth-century fresco at Siena, and thus it is in the commonplaces of Roman law.

There is no longer any need to prove the existence of Spenser's imperial theme; Miss Yates has clearly established it. Elizabeth claimed imperial status, adapting with the Emperor Charles v and others a view of empire that goes back to the Ghibellines. She was the world-leader who maintained the imperial peace, and renewed the time, preparing her people for the coming of Christ. This was the official role of Spenser's Virgin, the Empress-Astraea.[43] And this Protestant and nationalist imperialism denies what even Frederick II admitted, that the Pope has a complementary task. In the empress the *potestates distinctae — imperium* and *sacerdotium —* of medieval law are united.

The opening lines of Book V describe how very far we have got from the age of gold. Spenser's poem throughout maintains a tension between the ideal and the actual, and he knows that the return of the Imperial Virgin, first prophesied for Constantine, has occurred only in a figurative and restricted sense. Yet he is prepared to maintain this tension, and to present his Elizabeth as Iustitia or Astraea.[44]

He speaks thus of Justice:

> Most sacred virtue she of all the rest
> Resembling God in his *imperiall* might:

And thus of Elizabeth:

> Dread Souerayne Goddesse, that doeth highest sit
> in seate of judgement, in th'Almighties stead . . .

43. F. A. Yates, "Queen Elizabeth as Astraea", see note 2, p. 133, *supra;* and "Fêtes et Cérémonies au temps de Charles Quint", *Les Fêtes de la Renaissance,* n.d., pp. 57-97.

44. For Astraea as Justice (in a temple) see the lines addressed by Sir Robert Whittington to Sir Thomas More: they allude to *Astraeae criticae mystica chrismata/et Aeris fixa tholo verba minantia.* See R. S. Sylvester's transcription of the lines in *Huntington Library Quarterly,* XXVI (1963), 147 ff.

First we hear of the agents of justice, of Arthegall as pupil of Astraea and disciple of Bacchus and Hercules, dispensing justice with the aid of Talus. The allegory proceeds simply enough until Arthegall falls victim, Hercules-like, to Radigund; and although there is much of political interest in these cantos, and we see instances of Injustice, we have not yet encountered the formal Iustitia. This we do when Britomart, at the beginning of Canto vii, enters the Church of Isis to prepare for the liberation of Arthegall.

We shall understand neither the Church of Isis nor the Court of Mercilla unless we have some notion of the contemporary connotations of the word "Equity", and its relation to Justice. Spenser, though in translating Plutarch's "Iseion" he probably borrowed the expression "Isis Church" from Adlington's Apuleius,[45] obviously intended in this part of the Fifth Book to make a formal *Templum Justitiae*.[46] In doing so he is remembering a tradition at least as old as Augustus, whom Ovid congratulated on raising a temple to Justitia. Ulpian called judges the priests of Justice; Justinian speaks of the "most holy temple of Justice" and of "the temple of the Roman Justice". Statues were made showing governors, as Justice embodied, with Dike, Eunomia and Themis beside them.[47] The twelfth-century glossator Placentinus elaborately describes an allegorical Temple of Justice: Justitia is a dignified figure with Ratio over her head, many Virtues about her, and Equity in her embrace.[48]

This figuration developed along with the Roman law. The Neapolitan lawyer Lucas de Penna held that Iustitia, properly conceived, is identical with Equity.[49] Equity is indeed the source of law, that which makes Justice just; for *summa ius, summa iniuria* is an old saying. Penna's jurisprudence was influential in sixteenth-century France,[50] and the allegorical representations of Justice and Equity were modified accordingly. Thus Delbene shows Equity controlling Justice with a rod (*obtemperatio quasi virgula*).[51] Equity is the mother of law, the mediator between natural and human law; and this point was given cosmological significance by the equation between *mater* and *materia* in the dicta of late medieval jurisprudence.[52] In this way the justification of cosmic inequalities and of human law — perhaps even of human salvation, since the *Billigkeit* of Luther is related to these conceptions of Equity[53] — are all related, and Spenser's choice of

45. *Variorum*, V, 216.

46. As in Bartolomeo Delbene, *Civitas Veri* 1609 (written in the fifteen-eighties). There are Temples of Justice and of Injustice in this book, which was dedicated to Henry III and reflects the mode of the philosophical discussions held in the Palace Academy (see F. A. Yates, *The French Academies of the Sixteenth Century* (1947), pp. 111 ff.)

47. See E. Kantorowicz, "ΣΥΝΘΡΟΝΟΣ ΔΙΚΗΙ", *American Journal of Archaeology*, LVII (1953), 65 ff.

48. H. Kantorowicz, *Studies in Glossators of the Roman Law* (1938), pp. 183 ff.

49. W. Ullmann, *The Medieval Idea of Law* (1946), p. 43, quoting de Penna: *Ius simpliciter sumptum est aequitas.*

50. Ullmann, *Medieval Idea of Law*, pp. 183 ff.

51. *Civitas Veri*, pp. 168 and 174 (illustration).

52. Ullmann, p. 50.

53. This large suggestion I make in the hope that someone may pursue it. It was put to me by Professor Gordon Rupp after my lecture. It does not seem improbable that Luther should apply to theology doctrine associated with the emperor.

the Plutarchan myth of Isis begins to have the look of a very rich allegorical invention.

Imagery of this kind formed a part of that juristic myth which, as Kantorowicz showed, replaced earlier liturgical conceptions of the emperor after the death of Frederick II.[54] It is therefore intimately associated with the imperial mythology cultivated at the court of Elizabeth I. The emperor, as a fount of equity, directly mediates divine law, without the intervention of the Pope. But even if it is allowed (as it must be) that the Elizabethan propaganda borrowed freely from European imperialist mythology, it is also evident that the imagery so far spoken of is related to Roman law, and not to English. This calls for a word on the contacts between the two systems.

The prospect of a Reception of Roman law in England seems to have existed but briefly during the reign of Henry VIII. More, Elyot and Starkey admired Roman law, largely because of its superior equity; the king's cousin Cardinal Pole was its advocate. The king himself, when he abolished the study of canon law in England, set up Chairs of Civil Law at Oxford and Cambridge, and Gentile at Oxford, an Italian refugee, was a learned Roman civilian. Maitland, who at one time held the view (now disputed) that a Reception came very near to occurring, notes that Roman law "made pleasant reading for a King who wished to be a monarch in church as well as state: pleasanter reading than could be found in our ancient English law-books".[55] But the common lawyers prevailed. How then could the king's daughter develop her imperial mythology in terms of the Roman law? Admittedly, the close relationship between English and French courts in the fifteen-eighties, when there were high hopes of a *politique* agreement, might alone have ensured that the French mystique of *imperium* should affect English practice. Of course it was possible to maintain that even "by the common law of England, a Prince can do no wrong", as Bacon put it to the Council during the examination of Essex in 1600.[56] And the Tudors had always founded their rights in the common law. But they were certainly not unwilling to improve their security by reference to another system (appropriate, after all, to the re-embodiment of Augustus and Constantine) in which the Prince was not merely *legibus solutus* but also *lex animata* and a god on earth.

That Elizabethan England was conscious of a double standard in law is suggested by the contemporary debate on English equity. Formerly it had been considered an aspect of the common law, and since 1873 it has returned to the common law; but in the time of Elizabeth it was the province of the queen. The prerogative courts, especially those of Chancery and Star Chamber, represented the queen's justice independent of the common law courts. The Chancellor in Chancery was not bound by common law precedent but by equity and conscience; Hatton called himself the queen's conscience, and when Hamlet speaks of "the conscience of the

54. E. Kantorowicz, *The King's Two Bodies,* cap. IV.
55. F. W. Maitland, "English Law and the Renaissance", in *Historical Essays* (1957), p. 140.
56. See G. B. Harrison, *Robert Devereux, Earl of Essex* (1937), pp. 263-4.

King" he is presumably remembering a familiar expression, "the conscience of the Queen", which was the motive of Chancery. The positive function of the Court was to remedy injustices that had no remedy in common law. This might be for many reasons, and not only because the common lawyers were bound by rule and precedent, and the common law incompetent in certain causes, such as those relating to uses and trusts. The plaintiff might be a poor man, or the defendant a magnate with power to bribe, threaten or persuade a jury. (One remembers that the earl of Leicester was surprised to be told that it was an offence to influence a juryman.)[57] The increased use of this court brought many protests from Elizabethan lawyers, who saw in the growing activity of the courts of equity a usurpation of their authority.[58] Already, in fact, Chancery was building up the colossal backlog of business and the concern for precedent that made it, for Dickens, not so much a court of equity as a death-trap for innocent litigants. But in Spenser's time it was still the court of the queen's conscience; and inevitably the judgements of the chancellor, which were unrelated to the common law, touched the older tradition of the Roman law at many points.

So did the Court of Star Chamber. This court grew out of the Council, and dealt equity in criminal cases, notably those touching the security of the queen. Thus it punished scandals, seditions, riots, and, in this reign, recusancy; for which reason, and because of its brutal examinations and punishments, it was hated by Puritans and abolished when the Long Parliament came to power in 1641. Chancery had its enemies also. Star Chamber was a court in which the monarch was present, either symbolically (as in Elizabeth's reign) or in person, as at least twice in the reign of James I.[59] The association of this court with absolutism was strong in the minds of its enemies, and absolutist doctrine was in turn associated with the Roman law.[60] In 1610 Cowell, a Cambridge law professor, argued that Roman law and absolute monarchy went hand in hand; and Bacon on the other side assured James I that the Court of Chancery was the court of his absolute power, as well as the conscience of the realm.[61] It is hardly surprising, then, that when Parliament triumphed so did the common law; when Star Chamber was put down Chancery narrowly escaped. In the reign of Elizabeth a Roman absolutism would affect not only the imagery of a poet but the speculations of jurists. Raleigh argued that the capacity of Parliament was merely advisory;[62] and later Lord Ellesmere, known as the great enemy of the common law, could declare that the judges had no rights of equity since these belonged to the chancellor in his capacity as the king's conscience.[63]

---

57. W. S. Holdsworth, *A History of English Law* (1924), I, 505.
58. Evidence for this in Holdsworth, I, 508-9, and in George Spence, *The Equitable Jurisdiction of the Court of Chancery* (1846), I, Part 2, Book I. For a useful recent summary see John W. Dickinson, "Renaissance Equity and *Measure for Measure*", *Shakespeare Quarterly*, XIII (1962), 287-97.
59. Holdsworth, I, 500.
60. Maitland, p. 147.
61. Maitland, p. 134. *Works of Francis Bacon,* ed. Spedding, Ellis and Heath (1861), XIV, 292.
62. Quoted by C. H. McIlwain, *The High Court of Parliament* (1910), p. 330.
63. McIlwain, p. 294.

In the native English conception, law is logically prior to equity, hence the maxim "Equity follows law". In Roman law, as we have seen, equity can be called the source or foundation of law: *lex est super aequitate fundata; ius simpliciter sumptum est aequitas.*[64] Without equity law has nothing to do with justice: *summa ius, summa iniuria.* In the England of Elizabeth there was a conflict between the common and the imperial interpretation, and Spenser favours the latter. The fount of imperial equity is the emperor; and the relation of *lex scripta* to his will is analogous to the relation of Scripture to the will of God.[65] On this view the object of a court of equity is to enable the emperor to *justify* the law (even when it proceeds like Star Chamber, to do so, by ear-lopping and other mutilation). The theological parallel is intimate. Like her father, Elizabeth, as head of Church and State, must have found comfort in the Roman law; she wielded the two swords, and was charged with all the powers of *imperium* and *sacerdotium.*

With all this in mind, let us look at the Church of Isis, Spenser's *Templum Iustitiae.* He begins with a conventional assertion of the pre-eminence of Justice over the other virtues, and approves the ancient custom of establishing temples to Justice *(Iustitiam namque colimus quasi Deam sanctissimam* says an old jurist, who cannot think of Justice as merely a virtue).[66] But what he then celebrates is not Justice but Equity—"that part of Iustice, which is Equity"; and in the end he will show it to be the better part. The choice of Plutarch's myth has all Spenser's subtlety of invention. Plutarch notices that at Hermopolis Isis was identified with Justice.[67] She is also associated with Astraea; with the moon, emblem of the *imperium;* and with matter.[68] He wants us to remember that Justice and Equity reflect a vast cosmic process; that Equity is like matter, and that Justice gives it mutable forms. But he also means that Osiris is the common law considered in isolation from the equity courts. The priests of Isis are Ulpian's learned civilians, servants of the imperial equity (their long hair distinguishing them from the tonsured canonists) and they practise in such prerogative courts as Chancery and Star Chamber. (Spenser apparently borrowed the detail of their long hair from an account of the priesthood of Rhea.)[69] Their slightly feminine appearance may also be appropriate to the service of an empress, and their asceticism to the intense virginity cult which attached to this inheritor of the titles *vicarius Iustitiae* (from the Empire) and *vicarius Christi* (from the British King Lucius). But chiefly their abstinence from wine, the blood of the rebellious Titans, alludes to their implacable opposition to innovation and recusancy (we recall the earlier association of the giant with Anabaptism). The foot set on the crocodile and the foot fast on the ground (vii) reflect the criminal equity of Star

64. Ullmann, p. 43.
65. Ullmann, p. 53.
66. Kantorowicz, *The King's Two Bodies,* p. 111, n. 70.
67. *De Iside et Osiride,* in *Moralia,* ed. Babbitt (1936), V,11.
68. See F. A. Yates, "The Religious Policy of Giordano Bruno", *Journal of the Warburg Institute,* III (1939-40), 183-4. The Egyptian goddess could conceivably also suggest the ancient Church of England, which Bruno called "Egyptian".
69. *Variorum,* V, 214-15.

Chamber; the wand, like the one in Delbene which signified the control of Justice by Equity, stands for the power of Chancery in civil cases. Why does the crocodile enwreath her waist with his tail? (For I assume we must emend vi. 9: "That with *his* wreathed tail . . .") In Plutârch the crocodile is Typhon, an evil force, destroyer of Osiris. Here the Plutarchan sense is present also; Plutarch speaks of Typhon as discord and heat. Crocodiles were engendered by the sun on the mud of the Nile, and were in consequence a product, like wine, of the earth, and so in Spenser's allegory associated with rebellion and injustice. Here the crocodile is purely human law: *summa ius, summa iniuria*. Its tail suggests an impotent enmity towards imperial Equity; but the foot of Isis controls it as firmly as, in the woodcuts, that of Elizabeth controls the papacy.

In her dream, Britomart becomes a priest, but is at once (xiv) transformed into an empress, robed in imperial purple and crowned with the sun symbol. In view of what we already know about her as progenitress of the Tudors, we see that Britomart is now, in a vision, the imperial power of the dynasty. The Typhonic tempest and fire that follow are rebellion against this power, as established by the settlement—rebellion both political and religious, and suppressed by the common laws of England, here represented by the crocodile.[70] The presumption of the crocodile after this can represent the impatience of the common lawyers with absolutist claims, and with the increased use of prerogative courts; and the strange union of Britomart and the crocodile is the full union of justice and equity in the imperial dispositions of the queen. Human law, according to medieval jurisprudence, can attain to natural law only in union with equity; and the source of equity is the empress. According to the priestly interpreter of the dream, the crocodile is Arthegall, who throughout the Book has stood for Justice considered independently of Equity; and from the union springs a lion, symbol of the natural law. Thus the empress, maintaining a proper relation between the common law and equity, is making proper use of her prerogative courts for the purpose of controlling the habitual and inevitable injustice of the law, and the forces tending to rebellion. Spenser, in short, has refashioned the traditional figures of Justice allegories in order to intervene in the current controversy between the courts of law and the courts of equity; and this in its turn implies a defence of the imperial claims of Elizabeth, which necessarily involve the Roman law.

We turn now to the Court of Mercilla. It is often said that Spenser's methods are not truly pictorial; but sometimes *The Faerie Queene* has the air of a great fresco, where one part should be seen in a simultaneous spatial relation with another, as in Lorenzetti's great allegories for the Palazzo Pubblico in Siena. So it is here. We remember that Britomart, fortified by her night in Isis Church, goes off to overthrow Radigund, the type of female tyranny. This is exactly echoed in Canto ix; for Mercilla is an aspect of Isis. They are related to one another much as are Iustitia

70. *Moralia*, V, 133.

and Buon Governo in Lorenzetti.[71] And in Mercilla's presence we are
once more in the prerogative courts of England. Overseen by Awe, regu-
lated by Order, the people seek the true justice denied them in the common law, a justice not perverted by "brybes, or threates" (xxiv). A poet
punished by the nailing of his tongue to a post has committed slander (he
accused the queen of "forged guile", which is a quotation from the Isis
Church canto [VII. vii. 3] and there associated with the rebellious Typhon-
crocodile). His offence and its punishment remind us of the jurisdiction
and also of the penalties of the Court of Star Chamber. The queen's throne,
with the lions and fleurs-de-lys of England and France, recall the obligatory presence of her State in that court. Above her is a cloud-like canopy
borne up by angels, perhaps a deliberate reminiscence of the *maestà*.[72]
She has two swords—the sceptre of peace and clemency and the rusted
sword of justice; the *imperium* demands clemency,[73] but equity is not
merely a matter of mercy, and the rusted sword is sometimes used. The
presence of two swords can, in addition, hardly fail to suggest the *potestates
distinctae* of medieval political theory; she embodies both the *imperium*
and the *sacerdotium*.[74]

She is surrounded by the daughters of Jove, the Litae, properly the
horai of Hesiod, whose function is equity. They are Dike (Justice, and
sometimes called Astraea), Eunomia, Ius, and Irene (Pax). With them
are Temperance and Reverence. These are imperial virtues. Long before
Elizabeth, the emperor has been enthroned with Dike and Eunomia; the
other virtues echo those represented in Lorenzetti's Sienese frescoes.
The lion at the feet of Mercilla—and reminding us of the statue at Nonsuch
of Henry VIII trampling a lion—again fulfils Britomart's dream, but is
the common law in bondage to equity.

The tone of this passage is that of a courtly version of the popular
Queen's Day celebrations, wherein Elizabeth was thanked for delivering
the realm from the evil power of the Pope, and for maintaining the peace
and security of the realm. Her Accession Day God had ordained as a Holy
Day "next to that of his sonne Christ",[75] and Spenser, though he thinks
of her as Astraea and as Isis, also thinks of her as the Blessed Virgin.
Being herself Justice incarnate as Equity, she proceeds, as Britomart
proceeded to the suppression of Radigund, to the trial of Duessa. Duessa
is frankly Mary Queen of Scots, the most distinguished victim of Elizabeth's prerogative courts; and the book moves on to an easy historical
allegory of the Netherlands campaign against the Spanish supporters of
antichrist. We are reminded of III. iii. 49, and the prophecy of a universal

71. See George Rowley, *Ambrogio Lorenzetti* (1958); N. Rubenstein, "Political Ideas in Sienese
Art", *Journal of the Warburg and Courtauld Institutes,* XXI (1958), 179 ff; E. Kantorowicz,
The King's Two Bodies, pp. 112-13. For Iustitia and the emperor represented as equally enthroned—as might be said of Isis and Mercilla—see the article of E. Kantorowicz cited in n. 3,
p. 141.
72. H. Kantorowicz compares Placentinus' Iustitia with a Renaissance *maestà* (*Glossators,*
p. 186); but E. Kantorowicz contests this (*The King's Two Bodies,* p. 112, n. 76). For elements of
Mariolatry in the Elizabeth cult see Yates, "Queen Elizabeth as Astraea", pp. 76 ff.
73. Yates, "Queen Elizabeth as Astraea", p. 62.
74. Ullmann, p. 170.
75. Strong, "Accession Day", p. 99.

peace under a royal virgin who "shall Stretch her white rod over the Belgicke shore"—the rod, we see, was the rod of Isis-Equity in the seventh canto of the Book of Justice.

It would seem, then, that the Fifth Book has, at its critical points, a most elaborate juristic-imperialist allegory. I have not explained it in full; for my immediate purposes I shall be satisfied if it appears that scholars are wrong to reduce the Isis Church episode to a "marriage debate", and explain the vision of the crocodile threatening Britomart as a recapitulation of the rape of Amoret. Even Woodhouse's elaborate and rather fine interpretation[76] makes it only a dream allegory of the future union of Britomart and Arthegall. I have tried to put the episode into a context of juristic allegory, and restore its links with Spenser's dominant heroic theme, the vision of Empire.

I have said enough, perhaps, in arguing for Protestant-imperialist ecclesiastical history in Book I, and for Protestant-imperialist equity in Book V, to show that I believe in a Spenser more rather than less histor-ical in his allegory, a Spenser more susceptible than it has lately been fashionable to believe, to historical analysis. In fact I do not think one can enter fully into his long dream without the kind of knowledge such analysis has provided, and should provide. Spenser followed the antique poets heroical in this: he excluded no learning that would subserve his national theme, and enable him to show knowledge and history as they are related to a vision of his country as the heir of Empire and of Eden.

76. *E.L.H.* (1949), p. 216, n. 42.

25

Varieties of Scholarly Interpretation: Expertise and Cruxes

Evert Sprinchorn

The Odds on Hamlet

When as a teen-ager I first read *Hamlet,* I was not especially troubled, as far as I can recall, by the hero's delay in carrying out his revenge, or by his antic disposition, or by the seeming inconsistencies in his character, or by any of those things that most Shakespearean critics write about. What made me raise my eyebrows and gnaw my thumb was the scene of the duel: not the swordplay itself, but the dialogue leading up to it — particularly, the toast proposed by the villainous King Claudius:

> Set me the stoups of wine upon that table.
> If Hamlet give the first or second hit,
> Or quit in answer of the third exchange,
> Let all the battlements their ordnance fire.
> The King shall drink to Hamlet's better breath,
> And in the cup an union shall he throw,
> Richer than that which four successive kings
> In Denmark's crown have worn.

When I found out that an union was a pearl of exceptional quality, I despaired of ever understanding these peculiar Elizabethans. Whenever in the ensuing years I came to that passage, I recalled my initial response; and though I had learned a great deal more about Elizabethan customs (I knew that Gresham, for instance, had once toasted Queen Elizabeth with a cup of wine in which a pearl had been dissolved; pearls do not dissolve in wine and Gresham undoubtedly got his pearl back — that's Gresham's law), I was still upset by the backhanded compliment of proposing such a magnificent toast to Hamlet for merely scoring a point or two in a match that might well continue for ten or more passes — like

This essay first appeared in The Columbia University *Forum,* Volume VIII, Number 4, pp. 41-45. Copyright © 1964 by Columbia University.

congratulating a boxer for surviving a round or two against a champion. What an insult to the noble Prince Hamlet! What a waste of pearls!

But recently, reading the play for clues to its staging in Shakespeare's time, I suddenly realized that the King's toast was most appropriate, a tribute to a truly worthy swordsman, and the duel scene was revealed in an entirely different and more dramatic light. The duel scene in *Hamlet* has always created problems in staging. It is the end of Shakespeare's longest play and the high point of its action, but however exciting a finish it may have furnished Elizabethan audiences, to the modern playgoer it often seems simply a contrived device for mass slaughter; indeed, the corpses pile up so fast that the greatest care must be taken to avoid the effects of farce. Yet I think now that Shakespeare had more in mind than ending with a flourish; indeed, much of our response to *Hamlet* depends on a proper understanding of the duel, and that, in turn, hinges on its conditions.

It is the court flunky Osric who first presents to Hamlet the terms of the proposed match with Laertes:

> The King, sir, hath laid, sir, that in a dozen passes between yourself and him, [Laertes] shall not exceed you three hits. He hath laid on twelve for nine.

The last sentence is the joker, of course, for what can be the relation between "twelve for nine" and the "dozen passes"? Dr. Johnson was at a loss to explain it. In the notes to his 1765 edition of Shakespeare, he said he could not comprehend "how in a dozen, there can be twelve to nine," and dismissed the passage as of "no importance." He assumed that "twelve for nine" refers to the passes rather than to the odds and that, by the terms of the duel, Laertes, the favorite, must score twelve hits before Hamlet scores nine. This is the construction that is usually placed on the passage when it is given any attention at all. In many productions of *Hamlet* the line is simply cut as needlessly confusing, for under such conditions the match might conceivably go on for 20 passes, which contradicts Osric's statement that the match is to consist of a dozen bouts.

J. Dover Wilson, one of the few critics who senses the importance of the passage, realizes that a large part of the Elizabethan audience would have followed the technicalities of the duel as intently as a modern audience follows a poker game in the movies. In his edition of *Hamlet (The Cambridge Shakespeare)*, he attempts to avoid the difficulty by making three assumptions, none of which is easy to accept. In "He hath laid on twelve for nine," Wilson assumes, first, that "he" refers to Laertes; second, that "laid on" means "laid down" conditions; and, third, that "twelve for nine" means twelve bouts instead of nine bouts. According to Wilson, the terms are that Laertes must score three more hits than Hamlet. And since a match of nine bouts (which Wilson assumes with very little evidence was the usual number in a friendly duel) would give him little elbow room, Laertes stipulates twelve. But this explanation runs against the basic sense of the passage. Furthermore, Laertes would scarcely have agreed to winning by "three up" before the number of bouts had been settled, any more than a runner would agree to beat an opponent by 50 yards before making certain the race was not a hundred-yard dash.

The 18th-century editor Edmond Malone argued that "twelve for nine" expressed a ratio "tantamount to four to three," and that Laertes must accordingly win four bouts to every three that Hamlet wins; that is, in a match of twelve, Laertes would have to win eight before Hamlet wins six. But if Shakespeare meant four to three, why did he not write four to three? And, moreover, if Laertes can win by scoring eight hits to Hamlet's six, what is the meaning of the stipulation that Laertes must exceed Hamlet by three hits? George Steevens, an editor contemporaneous with Malone, dismissed the passage as unimportant and referred it to the gamblers at the Jockey Club, "who on such matters may prove the most enlightened commentators, and most successfully bestir themselves in the cold unpoetic dabble of calculation."

I do not share Mr. Steevens' prejudice against calculation; indeed, I think a mathematical approach most promising. Two bits of information seem quite clear: the match is to consist of twelve hits; and the odds are twelve to nine in favor of Laertes, who is rated the better fencer. The obscurity arises from the King's wager that Laertes will not exceed Hamlet by three hits. This may be construed in two ways. To win, Laertes must either score three more hits than Hamlet does in twelve passes or he must get three successive hits before the match ends. In the first case the match might consist of as few as eight passes with Laertes winning them all, or even as few as five if Hamlet won them. In the second case the match might conceivably end in just three exchanges. Oddly enough, this second construction is not placed on the passage by Shakespearean editors and commentators, though it immediately occurred to one of the three game-players I asked to read the terms of the duel.

It may seem that I have only further confused the issue; however, we can test which of the two interpretations is mathematically closer to the stated odds of twelve for nine. To calculate the odds against Laertes in each case we may propose the following two problems:

I. Given a bout between equally able players, A and B, that is to continue either until A has won eight games or B has won five, what are the odds against A?

II. Given a bout between equally able players, A and B, that is to continue until one of the players has scored three hits in a row, and given further the condition that A must score three hits in a row within a total of twelve games in order to win, what are the odds against A?

In each case the odds against A represent the odds Laertes is accepting in the unequal match in which he is considered Hamlet's superior. The answer to the first question can be quickly worked out using binomial coefficients, and the probability of A's winning turns out to be 794/4096, or .194. Expressed in odds, this is approximately four to one against Laertes, shameful odds in a two-man sporting event, really too disgraceful for a prince such as Hamlet to accept—and not at all close to twelve to nine.

The answer to the second problem is a little more difficult; I give the main steps for those who, like myself, do not find probabilities "cold and unpoetic."

I. The number of all possible matches consisting of twelve bouts each is 2^{12}, or 4096.

II. To simplify matters, consider half of these, the 2048 matches in which A scores the first hit.

III. In how many of these 2048 matches does neither A nor B win three in a row? The answer can be expressed in combinatorial notation:

$$\binom{12}{0} + \binom{11}{1} + \binom{10}{2} + \binom{9}{3} + \binom{8}{4} + \binom{7}{5} + \binom{6}{6}$$
$$= 1 + 11 + 45 + 84 + 70 + 21 + 1$$
$$= 233.$$

IV. In all the remaining games, to wit, 4096 minus 2(233) or 3630, either A or B or both win three hits in a row.

V. And in one-half of these, or 1815, A would be the victor.

VI. Hence the probability of A's winning is 1815/4096, or .4431.

As one might have surmised, it is much easier in a match of twelve games to score three hits in succession than to win by a plurality of three. But how close is .4431 to the given odds of nine to twelve? Nine to twelve equals 9/21 equals .4286! The Shakespearean odds are only one and one-half per cent off the actual odds!*

The student of mathematical history might well object that Shakespeare's odds are altogether *too* accurate. For the fact of the matter is there was no science of probabilities in Shakespeare's time. Not until 1654, when Fermat and Pascal discussed in their correspondence certain gambling problems that had been brought to their attention, did there begin a serious investigation of probability. It is doubtful that mathematicians in general (let alone playwrights or gamblers) had any knowledge of the elementary principles of probability until at least a generation after that. But, as is generally acknowledged, gamblers gain from experience a pretty good notion of odds, even though they may not be able to calculate them mathematically. The gambler who brought his problems to Pascal knew that there was something wrong with the odds on a certain event, even though the odds were, as it turned out, less than 1 per cent off.

*NOTE TO GAMBLERS: Game-playing readers might wonder if the odds against Hamlet were equalized in the amount wagered rather than in the terms of the duel. The King puts up six Barbary horses, Laertes six handsome swords. Might not the swords be worth more than the horses in the ratio of twelve to nine? But such an inference is not supported by anything else in the play and is contradicted by the fact that Laertes accepts the three-hit handicap in the duel. We must assume that Claudius and Laertes regard the horses as equal to the swords in this gentlemen's wager. Others might put yet another construction on the terms of the duel in addition to the two I discussed. Could the winner be the one who at any point in the match is ahead in the total score by three points? I find this an unlikely kind of game. Furthermore, the game limit would be set at eleven, not twelve, since a score of 4 to 7 represents the greatest number of games necessary to determine a winner. Finally, the odds against the handicapped player would be about six to four (794/2048), not twelve to nine.

Now, the conditions of the challenge match can be clearly stated. The only way Laertes can win is to score three hits in succession within the twelve-hit limitation. Hamlet, on the other hand, need only keep Laertes from scoring three in a row. Or, of course, he can score three in a row himself. Once these conditions have been established, some of the dialogue and much of the action in the last part of the play can be seen in a new light.

Consider the duration of the duel. As a teen-ager I was disappointed to see how quickly it was all over. Under the assumption that Laertes must win by a plurality of three, the match would still require, as I have pointed out, an absolute minimum of five exchanges in the unlikely event that Hamlet won them all. In a movie version a montage or series of shots could synopsize the first exchanges and bring us quickly to the crucial last exchange, with tension being built up throughout. But on the Elizabethan stage, where the first passes could not be synopsized, the duel would tend to drag at the most unpropitious of times when the audience would be eagerly awaiting the outcome of the whole play. It may have been to avoid this fatal deceleration of the action that Shakespeare arranged the terms to make possible a bout of just three passes.

However, Shakespeare is doing much more than solving a problem of pace. At the end of five acts of equivocation, he must decisively increase the stature of his hero. The dialogue suggests to the audience that Hamlet, rated the underdog, is potentially capable of winning in three straight hits. To accomplish this Shakespeare himself does some clever fencing. In the second act, some time after Polonius had bidden farewell to Laertes, Hamlet confessed that he had "foregone all custom of exercise." Now in the fifth act, just prior to the duel, Hamlet informs us that since Laertes "went into France, I have been in continual practice."

By building up Hamlet's skill as a fencer immediately after Laertes has been established as the favorite, Shakespeare prepares the audience for the possibility of an upset, and simultaneously increases Hamlet's stature by making him an opponent dramatically worthy of the King. Indeed, Claudius knows all along that Hamlet is the better fencer! Consider the dialogue spoken as the weapons are being readied:

> *King.* ... You know the wager?
> *Hamlet.*   Very well, my lord.
>   Your grace has laid the odds o' th' weaker side.
> *King.* I do not fear it, I have seen you both —
>   But since he is bettered, we have therefore odds.

Laboring under the misapprehension that Hamlet is in fact the poorer fencer, commentators have been able to make no sense of this passage. But is it not now crystal clear? A modern paraphrase might run:

> *Hamlet.* ... Your grace has made a good wager: you've made the weaker man the odds-on favorite.
> *King.* I have no doubt; I've seen you both. But since Laertes is rated the better by the experts, they have to give us odds.

The poisoned cup of wine and the extravagant toast, too, are tributes to Hamlet's superior skill. If the bout continues for more than three exchanges, Laertes must by definition score a hit with his "unbated and envenomed" sword, poison Hamlet, and consummate the plot. But what if Hamlet should win in three straight hits? To guard against this possibility the King has decided to poison the wine and propose the toast. Under the assumption that the duel is to be won by a plurality of three hits, the King's proposal to toast Hamlet with a pearl is simply a meaningless bit of conspicuous consumption. But with the three-in-a-row stipulation, the toast is not only altogether appropriate in the event Hamlet scores a stunning victory over the favorite; it is also absolutely necessary from the King's point of view. Hamlet can escape Laertes' rapier by winning the first three hits — but if he does so, he will have to drink the wine. ("Quit" in the King's toast is usually taken to mean "to draw" or "to get even with"; now we see that it is used in the obsolete sense of "to carry through to completion," or as synonymous with "finish.")

Imagine now the expectations of the Elizabethan audience. They are eager to see Hamlet turn from soliloquy to physical action; not the action of the moody and ironic procrastinator who plays at charades, not the action of the rash and tormented son who reviles his mother and impulsively kills an eavesdropper, and not the action of the ranting but unfeeling lover who leaps into a grave to wrestle with the distraught Laertes, but the action of the accomplished and controlled Renaissance prince that Hamlet was before the play began. The audience dares to hope now that Hamlet may win the perilous bout without so much as a scratch. But even as this hope, implanted by the toast, mounts when Hamlet wins the first exchange, the audience sees the King drop the poison into the cup of wine under the pretext of dissolving a pearl. Hamlet is unaware of the trap he is in, but the audience knows its jaws are closing inexorably. The King remains master of the situation.

Having brought the drama to this point of balanced tension, Shakespeare now defeats the expectations he has raised. Queen Gertrude drinks the poison intended for her son, and Laertes virtually stabs Hamlet in the back. The careful student of *Hamlet* may object to my denigration of Laertes, but the dialogue makes it clear that Hamlet is infuriated by something that Laertes does. What can it be but some form of unfair play? And so it has been staged, according to A. C. Sprague (*Shakespeare and the Actors*), at least since Henry Irving's time. But the unfair play only opens up another question. Why does Laertes lunge at Hamlet when he is off guard? Laertes, a man almost pathologically concerned with honor, must know that such an act will expose him to public contempt. Once again, the trouble is with the terms of the duel, for if the match is to be won on the basis of three-up, as is generally assumed, Laertes would certainly bide his time for at least another round, especially since his real intention is not to win the match but merely to prick Hamlet just once. Circumventing this difficulty has usually resulted in a distortion of Laertes' character. In the recent production by Sir John Gielgud with Richard Burton, for example, Laertes is made to seem so eager to get at his foe that he simply cannot wait longer. But if the match is to be won on the basis of three in a row, then Laertes is in a desperate situation at the end of the second round. He had counted on dallying with Hamlet; now it is Hamlet who is dallying with him:

> Come, for the third, Laertes! You do but dally.
> I pray you pass with your best violence.
> I am afeared you make a wanton of me.

As Laertes and Hamlet begin the third bout, the audience recognizes Laertes' position. He must score now or fail to carry out his personal revenge. The fencers take their on-guard positions, lunge at each other, and they both miss! Then, as they are about to resume their positions, Laertes, without the customary "Come on" of warning, cries "Have at you now!" ("Take that!") and pricks Hamlet. Incensed, Hamlet scuffles with him, the envenomed sword changes hands, and Laertes, too, is mortally wounded.

In accordance with the King's speech, the toast should be drunk when Hamlet has won by scoring three hits in succession, but in fact the King drinks to Hamlet after the first hit. Here logic must give way to dramatic effectiveness and the need to kill off four persons in as many minutes. (Indeed, Shakespeare seems to hedge — note the equivocal use of "or" in the King's toast where "and" would be the logical conjunction.) To kill off Laertes with the others, Shakespeare must not allow the duel to reach its stated completion, and consequently the King must drink to the victor before the victory has actually been secured. Moreover, the drinking must come after the *first* hit both so that the King may poison the wine with the "pearl" and so that after the second hit the Queen may drink the cup intended for Hamlet. Immediately thereafter Hamlet and Laertes wound each other. Both wounds are, of course, fatal, and as they are inflicted, the Queen, too, falls. Only the King has so far escaped, but now, at last released, Hamlet acts. The dying Prince turns the double plot against its inventor, stabbing the King with the envenomed sword and forcing him to drink the poison.

Thus the duel becomes a single dramatic net in which Shakespeare catches his four victims in a manner appropriate to each. By using every trick of his trade, he makes it the most exciting scene in the play. More important, in allowing his Prince the final mastery, Shakespeare restores to Hamlet much of the Rennaissance *virtù* that had rubbed off him as he writhed in the coils of his complexes.

IV

NEWER DIRECTIONS

26

Linguistics and Literature

Samuel R. Levin

Suprasegmentals and the Performance of Poetry

One of the important side-benefits accruing from the isolation of the suprasegmental phonemes of stress, pitch, and juncture lies in their application to the analysis of poetry. Perhaps most interesting in this connection is their use in the study of rhythm, where literary critical notions of the "tension" set up between the meter and the ordinary language prosody have been put on a much more realistic basis by showing explicitly what the linguistic prosody actually is.[1] But the important role that the suprasegmental features play in the rhythmic dynamics seems to have led some linguists into an unwarranted assumption. Perhaps because of the fact which suprasegmental analysis has made more obvious, namely, that for purposes of linguistic analysis the spoken and not the written language must serve as the basis, they seem to assume, tacitly or explicitly, that the "performance" of a poem consists in reading it aloud. Thus, Seymour Chatman, in a reply to an article by Arnold Stein, in which the latter discussed Donne's line from *Elegy X,* "Makes me her Medal, and makes her love me," and suggested that there are three metrical possibilities for reading the last two words, says, "Nor can I agree with Mr. Stein that the metrical ambiguity of another [the above] line in the poem contributes metaphorically to the whole; I believe this ambiguity too demands a resolution in oral performance. It is a paper ambiguity only." Further, he says, "My major point is that this ambiguity, in terms of the sound the line will assume, is more apparent than real. The mind may persist, but the voice is required to make a choice between the alternatives by the very structure of the language." Finally, "The very act of perform-

From *Quarterly Journal of Speech,* XLVIII (1962), 366-372. Reprinted by permission of the Speech Association of America and Samuel R. Levin.
    1. See Archibald A. Hill, "An Analysis of *The Windhover:* An Experiment in Structural Method," *PMLA,* LXX (December 1955), 968-978; Seymour Chatman, "Robert Frost's 'Mowing': An Inquiry into Prosodic Structure," *Kenyon Review,* XVIII (Summer 1956), 421-438; Edmund L. Epstein and Terence Hawkes, *Linguistics and English Prosody (Studies in Linguistics: Occasional Papers 7,* 1959); Henry Lee Smith, Jr., "Toward Redefining English Prosody," *Studies in Linguistics,* XIV (Winter 1959), 68-76; George B. Pace, "The Two Domains: Meter and Rhythm," *PMLA,* LXXVI (September 1961), 413-419.

ance more often than not forces the reader to resolve ambiguities, to decide between alternatives; where performance *does* require a decision, we can only conclude that the ambiguity is mainly textual—that is, it inheres in the inadequacies of the English writing system in representing intonation patterns, and not in the structure of the poem as a sequence of English vocal signals. . . . Many textual ambiguities cannot be preserved in oral performances, simply because the stress-pitch-juncture system of English demands a resolution."[2]

It can be seen from the above quotations that the question of oral performance is bound up with the question of ambiguity in poetry. According to Chatman, one of the results of oral performance is the resolution of these ambiguities. This is freely granted; it remains precisely here, nevertheless, that one can take issue. One can argue that ambiguity is built into poetry, and that resolution of this ambiguity represents not a service to a poem, but a disservice. Now not all types of ambiguity are on a par with one another; especially pertinent in the present context is the fact that not all types are resolvable by the introduction of suprasegmental analysis. At this point, therefore, some discussion of ambiguity is necessary.

In critical discussions of poetry, "ambiguity" is used as a term to cover a variety of things: a character's relation to his environment or to other characters may be ambiguous; an action may be ambiguous; the poem's theme may be ambiguous. Or any of these may be ambivalent. In the present discussion, however, we are concerned only with those ambiguities that are occasioned immediately by a single, restricted stretch of language, not with those—however important and meaningful they may be for the full appreciation of the poem—which may be inferred by comparing different portions of the same poem or play. We are not concerned, that is, with the ambiguity of a character like Hamlet or the ambivalent attitudes frequently found in the poetry of Hopkins.

Eliminating from our concerns ambiguities that are built up in the body of a poem or play, and considering only those that may be apprehended immediately from a single, restricted stretch of language, we may yet distinguish two types of ambiguity in poetry—as in language generally. One type is occasioned by the use of individual words. On the one hand, we have homonymous words like *air* ("melody," "breeze," "manner"), *punch* ("blow of a fist," "kind of drink"), et cetera, which are ambiguous in reference, while on the other hand, we have the general polysemia of practically all words. Polysemia is usually held to be different from ambiguity but, unless we use historical criteria, it is generally very difficult to determine whether the semantic range of a given word comprises a real ambiguity (i.e., is really the range of two homonymous words) or is merely an instance of polysemia.[3] In the practice of literary criticism little effort is made to distinguish between these two linguistic phenomena; words with more than a single reference, whether they be homonyms or words like *faith, retire, ordinary,* et cetera, with polysemantic

2. Seymour Chatman, "Mr. Stein on Donne," *Kenyon Review,* XVIII (Summer 1956), 447 f. 449, 450. The last statement is quoted with approval by Smith, p. 74 f.

3. See Henry M. Hoenigswald, *Language Change and Linguistic Reconstruction* (Chicago, 1960), pp. 18 ff.

spectrums, are simply termed ambiguous and treated as such. But in any case, most discussions of ambiguity in poetry concern themselves chiefly with the semantic ranges of individual words, or with what we may call lexical ambiguity.

The second type of ambiguity, and the one which is more directly our concern here, is that occasioned by constructional homonymity, i.e., where two meanings are supported by the one construction. Here again there are two subtypes: cases of constructional homonymity which are ambiguous even when the suprasegmental features are taken into account, and cases which are rendered unambiguous when that is done. A construction like Chomsky's "They are flying planes," uttered as — ²Thèy are flying ³plánes¹ # — would answer equally well the question "What are they?" and "What are they doing?" On the other hand, Fries' well-known example, "Ship sails today," is ambiguous only when the suprasegmental features are left out of account. Chomsky's sentence would be arrived at by two different derivation and transformation procedures even if the suprasegmental features were incorporated into the derivations, whereas, with those features incorporated into the grammar, it would generate, instead of Fries' sentence, the two different sentences: ²Shìp ³sáils todày¹ # — and — ³Shíp ²sâils todày¹ # — and there would thus be no ambiguity. From the point of view of the present discussion, constructions which are ambiguous even when the suprasegmental features are included ("They are flying planes") occupy the same general position as do cases of lexical ambiguity, described above. They are of little interest, since no performance of a poem, whether oral or visual, would resolve their ambiguity. Cases of the other type of ambiguity, those cases, that is, where the ambiguity is resolved when the suprasegmental features are taken into account, are of considerable interest, however, in comparing the relative merits of oral and visual performance of poetry.

In oral delivery or performance, the voice dynamics can be said to communicate two different types of information: one of these types consists of information about the speaker; the other consists of information about the message.[4] The former type of information has recently been described, and the features communicating this type of information have, collectively, been given the name "paralanguage." The paralinguistic level includes properties of voice set, voice quality, and vocalizations — the latter comprising features like laughing, crying, whining, intensity, general pitch height, et cetera.[5] The other type of information is that provided by the suprasegmental phonemes of stress, pitch, and juncture, whose essential function is to mark constructions. This function is evident in comparing segmentally identical utterances, one of which is a compound, the other a phrase; or one of which is a statement, the other a question; or one of which is a restrictive, the other a non-restrictive clause. The suprasegmental phonemes function, however, to mark — and thus to distinguish — a great many more subtle relations between constructions. Some of these functions will be suggested when we come to analyze a poem in the following sections.

4. See Seymour Chatman, "Comparing Metrical Styles," in *Style in Language,* ed. Thomas A. Sebeok (New York, 1960), pp. 150 ff.

5. See George L. Trager, "Paralanguage: A First Approximation," *Studies in Linguistics,* XIII (Spring 1958), 1-12.

Since we are primarily interested in what is communicated about the poem, and not about the performer, it is the suprasegmental level of communication that concerns us. If we assume, as many critics do, that syntactic ambiguities, i.e., those deriving from constructional homonymity, are, like lexical ambiguities, a conscious part of a poem's complexity, then an oral performance renders a real disservice to the poem. For, unlike what is the case with lexical ambiguities, where performances – oral or visual – as a rule do nothing to resolve the ambiguity, in the realm of syntax an oral performance frequently does resolve the ambiguity – in favor of one or another syntactic interpretation. This is, of course, exactly the point made by linguists who favor the oral performance of poetry, and no argument is possible here. The argument arises when we consider the question of what kind of structure a poem is: is a poem like an ordinary language message, in which ambiguity is, as a rule, carefully avoided, or is a poem a structure in which ambiguity is a constitutive device? Depending on what our answer is to the preceding question, we will favor a performance which eliminates ambiguities or one which preserves them. Needless to say we are not interested in preserving, in any performance, ambiguities which lead to outlandish or bathetic results. Such ambiguities would have to be resolved whether the performance were oral or visual. The ambiguities that we are interested in preserving are those that contribute to a poem's complexity or richness.[6] My own answer to the question posed above is that ambiguity is composed into a poem. I therefore favor that type of performance which optimally sustains that ambiguity, and to my mind that is a visual performance, by which is meant a silent reading.

As was pointed out earlier, ambiguities involving the suprasegmental features are of two types: those in which the suprasegmental phonemes are also ambiguous or, put another way, those in which the phonemic phrases are ambiguous; and those in which only the phrases are ambiguous – where the inclusion of the suprasegmental features renders the phrase unambiguous. Strictly speaking, of course, only the former type of construction should be labeled ambiguous. The latter type is quasi-ambiguous: its analysis as ambiguous is achieved at the expense of abstracting the segmental sequence from the total linguistic utterance and is perhaps conditioned by the analytic conventions which separate the segmental and the suprasegmental levels of language. In any case, for reasons discussed earlier, it is the latter type of ambiguity with which we are concerned. Now in order for this type of construction to be ambiguous in a performance, the suprasegmental phonemes marking both possible constructions would have to be simultaneously present. This is patently impossible in an oral performance. Is it any more possible in a visual performance? Obviously, it would be impossible to *prove* the affirmative of this question. All that can be said is that a number of literary critics argue as if this balancing act – involving not only rival intonations, but competing meters as well – can be and is managed.[7] Beyond that, the answer lies with one's own experience.

---

6. See Francis Lee Utley, "Structural Linguistics and the Literary Critic," *Journal of Aesthetics and Art Criticism,* XVIII (March 1960), 324 f.

7. See Arnold Stein, "Donne's Prosody," *Kenyon Review,* XVIII (Summer 1956), 440, 442, and John Crowe Ransom, "The Strange Music of English Verse," in the same issue, p. 463.

In the remainder of this paper, we shall analyze a poem by Dylan Thomas. The analysis is by no means to be regarded as an attempt at a full-scale interpretation of the poem. Such features as imagery and metaphor, for example, are omitted from the discussion as not necessarily bearing on the point at issue. Also omitted are many other features that would be relevant in a full-scale discussion.

What we are principally concerned to demonstrate is that syntactic ambiguity is built into the poem, and that oral performance nullifies that ambiguity. In other words, given our assumption as to the nature of poetry, we shall try to show, using the same techniques of suprasegmental analysis employed by other linguists, that an oral performance does not optimally represent the poem. While this conclusion does not prove the superiority of visual performance, it at least indicates that the question of performance is not a closed issue. Thomas's poem follows:

1 O make me a mask and a wall to shut from your spies
2 Of the sharp, enamelled eyes and the spectacled claws
3 Rape and rebellion in the nurseries of my face,
4 Gag of a dumbstruck tree to block from bare enemies
5 The bayonet tongue in this undefended prayerpiece,
6 The present mouth, and the sweetly blown trumpet of lies,
7 Shaped in old armour and oak the countenance of a dunce
8 To shield the glistening brain and blunt the examiners,
9 And a tear-stained widower grief drooped from the lashes
10 To veil belladonna and let the dry eyes perceive
11 Others betray the lamenting lies of their losses
12 By the curve of the nude mouth or the laugh up the sleeve.

A fundamental ambiguity in the poem arises from the fact that it could be Thomas, the poet, making the plea that the poem represents, or the poem itself. We have to do, that is, with a poem or a metapoem. The poem is thus a plea for separation between the pryers/critics of the world and the poet/poem. The first word in the poem that figures in this ambiguity is the word *me* in line 1, which can refer either to Thomas or to the poem itself. Actually it is the construction *make me a mask* which is ambiguous; it represents the transform of both *make a mask for me* and *make a mask of me*. This construction is, also, one whose ambiguity is total; it is not resolved by the suprasegmental phonemes. Furthermore, the remainder of the poem does not resolve this ambiguity; it serves rather to hold *me's* reference in suspension between the poet and the poem itself. In the following analysis we shall treat *me* as referring to the poet; whatever is said from this point of view, however, would apply *mutatis mutandis* from the point of view of the poem.

We are primarily interested, as we have said, in those syntactic ambiguities which are resolved by the suprasegmental phonemes. We shall, therefore, now offer two syntactic parsings of the poem and then discuss the relations between each parsing and the particular suprasegmental prosody that accompanies it. One possible parsing of the poem runs as follows: Someone (God or mankind) is being asked to *make* for the poet a *mask and a wall* for the purpose of shutting out the *rape and rebellion* (present in the poet's face) from that someone's *spies (of the sharp, enamelled eyes and the spectacled claws)* [ll. 1-3]. *Gag of a dumbstruck tree* in line 4 is another object of *make*. The purpose of the *gag* is to *block* (keep away) *from bare enemies (spies) the bayonet tongue* and *the present mouth, and the sweetly blown trumpet of lies,* which are present in *this undefended prayerpiece* (the poet's face). *Shaped in old armour and oak the countenance of a dunce* [l. 7] modifies the whole complex of protection represented by *mask, wall,* and *gag*. The purpose of the complex, further, is to *shield the glistening brain* (of the poet) and *blunt the examiners (spies, enemies).* *And a tear-stained widower grief drooped from the lashes (to veil belladonna)* is another property of the complex of protection *(Shaped . . . the countenance of a dunce)*. The poem ends with the complementary plea to *let the dry eyes* (those of the poet) *perceive others betray . . . ,* where the *others* are the *spies, enemies, examiners.*

The notation of the poem given below indicates the way in which it might be performed aloud so as to convey the syntactic interpretation just given. The suprasegmental phonemes are analyzed essentially according to the Trager-Smith analysis:[8] four degrees of stress, from loudest to weakest, the symbols ´, ˆ, `, being used for the loudest, second loudest, third loudest, respectively, and absence of a stress mark on a syllable indicating weakest stress; four pitch heights, from highest to lowest, indicated by 4, 3, 2, 1, respectively. The terminal junctures are indicated by #, ‖, |, indicating terminal fall, terminal rise, and terminal sustention, respectively. Consideration of plus juncture is omitted here as not being particularly relevant to the analysis that follows:

1 ^{2}ò mâke mè a másk ^{1} | ^{2}ànd a ^{2}wáll^1 # ^{2}tò shût from yòur spíes^2 |

2 ^{2}of the shârp, enâmèlled éyes^2 | ^{2}ànd the spêctaclèd cláws^2 |

3 ^{2}râpe ànd rebêlliòn in the nûrserìes of mỳ ^{3}fáce^1, #

4 ^{2}gâg of a dûmbstrùck ^{3}trée^1 | ^{2}tò blôck from bâre énemìes^2 |

5 ^{2}the bâyonèt tôngue in this ûndefênded ^{3}práyerpìece^1, |

6 ^{2}the prêsent ^{3}móuth^1, | ^{2}ànd the swêetlỳ blôwn trûmpèt of ^{3}líes^1, #

7 ^{2}shâped in ôld ârmòur and óak^2 | ^{2}the côuntenànce of a ^{2}dúnce^1 |

8 ^{2}tò shîeld the glîstenìng ^{3}bráin^1 | ^{2}ànd blûnt the exâminèrs^1, #

9 ^{2}and a têar-stâined wîdowèr grîef drôoped from the láshes^2 |

10 ^{2}tò vêil bêlladónna^3^{1} # ^{2}ànd lêt the drỳ ^{3}éyes^2 | ^{2}pèrcêivè

11 ^{3}óthers^1 | ^{2}betrâỳ the lamêntìng lîes of thèir ^{2}lósses^1 |

12 ^{2}bỳ the cûrve of the nûde ^{3}móuth^1 | ^{2}òr the lâugh ùp the ^{3}sléeve^1! #

---

8. George L. Trager and Henry Lee Smith, Jr., *An Outline of English Structure (Studies in Linguistics: Occasional Papers 3,* 1951).

Following is, I believe, another consistent syntactic parsing of the poem, one which, taken by itself, leads to a somewhat different interpretation of the poem. (Our point is, of course, that no one of the possible syntactic interpretations need be taken by itself): Someone is being asked to *make* for the poet a *mask and a wall* for the purpose of shutting out from the poet's face the *rape and rebellion* which, in this reading, are those of the *spies (of the sharp . . .)* [ll. 1-3]. *Gag of a dumbstruck tree* is another object of *make*. It is asked for to *block* from the poet's face *(this undefended prayerpiece) the bayonet tongue, the present mouth,* and *the sweetly blown trumpet of lies,* which are those of the *bare enemies (spies).* Line 7 is the same as in the first reading. Line 8 emphasizes *blunt (the examiners),* thus making *blunt* parallel to *shut* and *block* of lines 1 and 4. Lines 9 and 10, to *belladonna,* are as in the first reading. The remainder of the poem is read, however, so as to make the *dry eyes* those of the outsiders (cf. l. 2), and makes the request to let them *perceive others betray . . . ,* where the others are people other than Thomas.

The notation below indicates this second syntactic interpretation in an oral performance:

1   ^{2}ò mâke mè a mâsk ^{2}| ^{2}ànd a ^{2}wáll^1#^{2}tò shút^2|^{2}from yòur spîes^2

2   ^{2}of the shârp, enâmèlled êyes and the spèctaclèd clâws^2|

3   ^{2}râpe and rèbéllìon^1| ^{2}in the nûrserìes of mỳ ^{2}fáce^1,#

4   ^{2}gâg of a dûmbstrùck ^{3}trèé^1| ^{2}to blóck|^{2}from bâre ênemìes^2

5   ^{2}the bâyonèt ^{3}tóngue^1| ^{2}in this ûndefénded ^{2}práyerpìece^1,|

6   ^{2}the prèsent ^{3}móuth, |^{2}and the swèetlỳ blôwn trùmpèt of ^{3}lìes^1, #

7   ^{2}shâped in ôld ârmòur and óak^2| ^{2}the côuntenànce of a ^{2}dúnce^1|

8   ^{2}tò shîeld the glîstenìng bráìn^2|^{2}and blúnt the ^{2}exâmìnèrs^1,#

9   ^{2}and a têar-stâined wîdowèr grîef dròoped from the láshes^2|

10   ^{2}tò vêil bèlladónnà^1#^{2}and lêt the drỳ êyes pèrcêive^2

11   ^{3}óthers^1| ^{2}betrây the lamèntìng lîes of thèir lósses^2|

12   ^{2}bỳ the cûrve of the nûde ^{2}móuth^1|^{2}òr the lâugh ùp the ^{2}sléeve^1.#

Still other, minor syntactic variations, conduced by different suprasegmental prosodies, and reflecting slightly differing interpretations of portions of the poem, could also be described, but the two analyses demonstrate our point.

Implicit in our discussion of the way in which a poem is performed has been the assumption that the performance, whether oral or visual, does not represent the first reading of a poem. Although we cannot specify how many prior readings are necessary before the reading should count as a "performance," some number of preliminary readings is always presupposed—again, whether the performance is oral or visual. More is built into a poem than can be apprehended at a first reading. The performances we are interested in are those made after the performer has succeeded in interpreting the poem. This involves a process in which various hunches are generated by examination of the poem, these hunches then being systematized into a general hypothesis which the poem is required to support. It is extremely doubtful whether such heuristic procedures admit of codification. But in any case, a performance, if it is oral, can only present a reading in which certain syntactic ambiguities have been resolved. An auditor, if he is aware of other syntactic possibilities, must either disagree with the performance or consider it inadequate. As we have said earlier, it is not possible to prove the contention that in a visual performance one can balance against each other the different syntactic possibilities which preliminary readings of the poem have yielded; perhaps we have shown that the assumption that oral performance of poetry is superior to visual performance need not go unchallenged.

27

The Use of Statistical Methods

Claude S. Brinegar

Mark Twain and the Quintus Curtius Snodgrass Letters:

A Statistical Test of Authorship

Introduction and Summary

Mark Twain's role in the Civil War has long been a subject of dispute — a dispute that has at times flared even beyond the realm of scholarly debate.[1] In 1940, for example, Twain was accused on the floor of the House of Representatives of being a Confederate deserter, and was defended, in turn, in the editorial pages of the *New York Times,* as a young man of mixed emotions and loyalties.[2]

Twain's own public comments on the matter were confined to a few humorous remarks 20 or so years after the fact and to the partly fictional, partly defensive "The Private History of a Campaign that Failed."[3] A. B. Paine likewise failed to contribute much in the way of solid fact in *Mark Twain, A Biography,*[4] for it is evident that Paine was strongly influenced by "The Private History" and by Twain's personal reminiscences from 1906 until his death in 1910. Although these reminiscences are enormously valuable as literary source material, they should not be mistaken for history. Twain was not unaware of this, for as he noted at one point: "When I was younger I could remember anything, whether it happened or not; but now I am getting old and soon I shall remember only the latter."[5]

Essentially all that we know for sure of Twain's Civil War experiences was recently stated in four sentences by Edward Wagenknecht:

From *Journal of the American Statistical Association,* LVIII (1963), 85-96. Reprinted by permission of the American Statistical Association and Claude S. Brinegar.

1. Good summaries can be found in Fred W. Lorch, "Mark Twain and the Campaign that Failed," *American Literature,* XII (January, 1941), 254-270, and John Gerber, "Mark Twain's 'Private Campaign,'" *Civil War History,* I (March, 1955), 37-60.

2. *Congressional Record,* Vol. 86, Part 1 (January 25, 1940), p. 698; *New York Times* (February 7, 1940), p. 20.

3. First published in *Century Magazine,* December, 1885; also included in *Merry Tales,* New York: Harper & Brothers, 1892, pp. 9-50.

4. A. B. Paine, *Mark Twain, A Biography,* New York: Harper & Brothers, 1912, 2 Volumes. See especially Volume I, Chapter XXX.

5. Mark Twain, *Autobiography,* New York: Harper & Brothers, 1924, p. xii of Paine's introduction.

Mark Twain's connection with the Civil War was both brief and loose. He may have had some military connection in New Orleans; if so, we know none of the details. Nor do we know a great deal more about his adventures with an informally organized Confederate group in Missouri, for "The Private History of a Campaign that Failed" mingles fact with fiction. Nevertheless the fact remains that Lieutenant Clemens shortly mustered himself out of Confederate service and went to Nevada with his brother Orion, a staunch Union man, whom President Lincoln had appointed Secretary of the Territory.[6]

This study is concerned only with the evidence regarding Twain's possible military connection in New Orleans. The evidence is drawn entirely from the content of 10 letters published in the *New Orleans Daily Crescent* in early 1861. In these letters, which have been widely credited to Twain, the writer described his military adventures while serving as a "High Old Private of Louisiana Guard." The letters were signed "Quintus Curtius Snodgrass." Based on the results of applying a statistical test of authorship both to the 10 Quintus Curtius Snodgrass letters and to known contemporary Twain writings, we conclude that Twain was *not* the author of the disputed letters. It follows, consequently, that the evidence supporting the claim that Twain served with a New Orleans Confederate garrison must likewise be discounted.

Quintus Curtius Snodgrass Letters

The Quintus Curtius Snodgrass (QCS) letters were first brought to light in 1934 by Miss Minnie M. Brashear, in *Mark Twain, Son of Missouri*.[7] She reprinted one letter and described three others, and then commented:

> None of the *Crescent* letters suggests the later Mark Twain as satisfactorily as one wishes they did. The peculiar type of exaggeration, anti-climax, and irony which gave flavor to his sentences is discoverable in the earlier Snodgrass letters,[8] but not here— though the satire at the expense of the military profession was often a theme during the earlier period of American humor. And yet, if it can be proved that they are authentic, they are immensely significant as a link in Mark Twain's development as a humorist.[9]

Miss Brashear then argues that they should be recognized as Twain's, and that the difference in style reflects the fledgling writer's efforts to achieve a more consciously literary manner.

6. Edward Wagenknecht, *Mark Twain: The Man and His Work*. Norman, Oklahoma: University of Oklahoma Press, New and Revised Edition, 1961, p. 11.

7. Minnie M. Brashear, *Mark Twain, Son of Missouri*. Chapel Hill, North Carolina: University of North Carolina Press, 1934.

8. This reference is to three letters Twain wrote in 1857 for the Keokuk (Iowa) *Saturday Post*, which he signed "Thomas Jefferson Snodgrass." This earlier use of "Snodgrass" is one of the main clues that led to attributing the Quintus Curtius Snodgrass letters to Twain. See Mark Twain, *The Adventures of Thomas Jefferson Snodgrass*, Chicago: Pascal Covici, Publisher, Inc., 1928, edited by Charles Honce.

9. Brashear, *op. cit.*, pp. 191-2.

The remaining six QCS letters were uncovered by Ernest E. Leisy and published together with the first four, in 1946.[10] Leisy's careful study of parallels provides the strongest case for admitting the QCS letters to the Mark Twain canon. Leisy also emphasized the literary significance of the discovery:

> I believe that scholars and collectors will rejoice to have these letters reprinted, because if they are by Mark Twain they throw new light on the young soldier and developing writer. . . .[11]

Biographers and literary researchers have reacted in various ways toward the QCS letters.

Lorch, in his 1941 study of "The Private History," relegated the possibility that Twain was the author to a questioning footnote.[12] De Lancey Ferguson, on the other hand, writing in 1943 concluded: "There is little reason to doubt that they [the QCS letters] were the work of Sam Clemens."[13] This belief was echoed by Gerber in 1955.[14] However, in 1961 Wagenknecht noted that Twain's proposed authorship was still only a "conjecture." [15]

It is clear that considerable doubt remains about Mark Twain's hypothesized authorship of the QCS letters.

Statistical Test of Authorship

A related problem, though one on a far grander scale, is the long time controversy about the authorship of Shakespeare's works.[16] In 1955 Calvin Hoffman, in *The Murder of the Man Who Was "Shakespeare,"*[17] called attention to two statistical studies of authorship by T. C. Mendenhall, published in 1887 and 1901,[18] that had apparently gone unnoticed by modern statisticians. Subsequent to Hoffman's discussion, Mendenhall's work was reviewed and several of his charts redrawn by C. B. Williams in *Biometrika*.[19] Mendenhall's method forms the basis of the statistical test we here apply to the QCS letters.

The method, although laborious, is simple in concept and application: By forming a frequency distribution of a great many words classified according to their length, it is possible to obtain a graphic representation

10. Mark Twain, *The Letters of Quintus Curtius Snodgrass*. Dallas, Texas: Southern Methodist University Press, 1946, edited by Ernest E. Leisy.

11. *Ibid.*, p. v.

12. Lorch, *op. cit.*, p. 462n.

13. De Lancey Ferguson, *Mark Twain: Man and Legend.* New York: The Bobbs-Merrill Company, 1943, p. 59.

14. Gerber, *op. cit.*, p. 37n.

15. Wagenknecht, *op. cit.*, p. 231.

16. In his late years Twain himself developed considerable interest in this controversy. See Mark Twain, *Is Shakespeare Dead?*. New York: Harper & Brothers, 1909.

17. Calvin Hoffman, *The Murder of the Man Who Was "Shakespeare,"* New York: Julian Messner, Inc., 1955. Reprinted in 1960 in paperback by Grosset and Dunlap. Hoffman's nominee for authorship is Christopher Marlowe.

18. T. C. Mendenhall, "The Characteristic Curve of Composition," *Science*, IX (March 11, 1887), 237-49; "A Mechanical Solution of a Literary Problem," *The Popular Science Monthly*, LX (December, 1901), 97-105.

19. C. B. Williams, "Studies in the History of Probability and Statistics," *Biometrika*, 43 (1956), 248-56. Figures 4 and 5, showing the "characteristic curve" for Shakespeare, contain separate plotting errors.

(called a "characteristic curve of composition" by Mendenhall) that would "become a means of identification, at least by exclusion."[20] The use of this method assumes that every author unconsciously uses words that, at least in the long run, could be considered as random drawings from a fixed frequency distribution of word lengths.[21] (This assumption stands up surprisingly well, as subsequently shown.) Although it is conceivable that every author's word frequency distribution is as unique as his finger-prints, it is (1) often difficult to obtain a large enough sample (Mendenhall suggested that at least 100,000 words would be needed—although this is probably far too large) and (2) even with such a large sample the statistical tests that can be used to distinguish between frequency distributions that closely resemble each other are far less sensitive than fingerprint tests. Probably a better analogy is to consider the test as similar to the blood test in a paternity case—a test that by itself can exonerate but cannot convict. If the large-sample word frequency distributions for two sets of writings differ greatly, this should be considered as strong evidence that the two sets were not written by the same person; if the distributions are quite similar, this supports but does not prove the hypothesis that they could have been the work of the same person.

Chart 1
WORD FREQUENCIES FOR TWO SAMPLES OF 1000 WORDS FROM "VANITY FAIR"

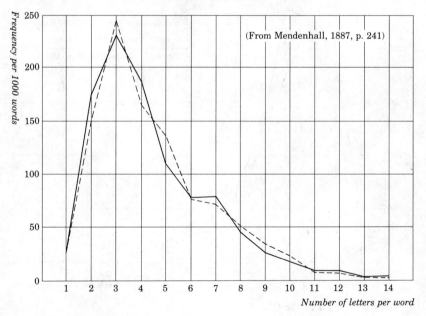

(From Mendenhall, 1887, p. 241)

Frequency per 1000 words

Number of letters per word

20. Mendenhall, *Popular Science Monthly,* p. 97.

21. This should be true at least for writings of a related type over a reasonable span of years. Consciously different styles (for example, fiction heavily laden with dialect conversation as contrasted with the description of a trip to Europe) might be expected to show statistically significant variation.

Chart 1, redrawn from Mendenhall (1887), illustrates the method by plotting the distributions for two small samples from Thackeray's *Vanity Fair*. Mendenhall's study contains numerous such examples. Near the end of the 1887 study he commented:

> Many interesting applications of the process will suggest themselves to every reader; the most notable, of course, being the attempt to solve questions of disputed authorship, such as exist in reference to the letters of Junius, the plays of Shakespeare, and other less widely known examples.[22]

Mendenhall's 1901 study was largely devoted to a report on the work in the intervening years, during which, thanks "to the liberality of Mr. Augustus Heminway, of Boston," a staff—two ladies from Worcester, Massachusetts—had been paid to "count and classify nearly two million words." Mr. Heminway was evidently seeking to resolve the Bacon-Shakespeare controversy once and for all. The results of counting 400,000 words from Shakespeare and 200,000 words from Bacon are shown in Chart 2. These two curves were not encouraging to the Baconians.

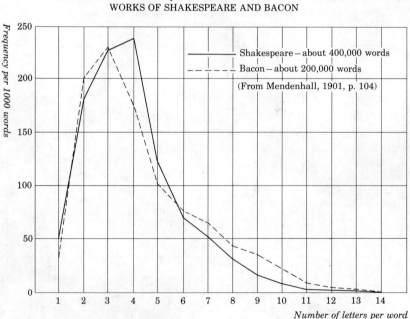

Chart 2

ESTIMATED WORD FREQUENCIES FOR LARGE SAMPLES FROM
WORKS OF SHAKESPEARE AND BACON

Shakespeare—about 400,000 words
Bacon—about 200,000 words
(From Mendenhall, 1901, p. 104)

Frequency per 1000 words

Number of letters per word

Application of Test to the QCS Letters

Applying Mendenhall's method to the QCS letters required that we initially determine Mark Twain's frequency distribution before and after 1861, and

22. Mendenhall, *Science,* p. 245.

also if it was consistent within itself. For this purpose the following word counts were made from writings that are indisputably his:

1. A letter, known as the "Sergeant Fathom" letter, published in the New Orleans *True Delta* in 1859, in which Twain burlesqued an old-time river pilot (Captain Isaiah Sellers); a letter to his brother Orion in early 1861 describing his visit to a New Orleans fortune-teller, known as Madame Caprell. These two letters total about 1,900 words.[23]

2. The first four letters in which he is known to have used the name "Mark Twain," published in 1863 in the *Territorial Enterprise*.[24] These letters total about 6,100 words.

3. The first letter to the *Alta California,* published in 1867, describing his adventures with the "Innocents Abroad."[25] This letter, covering the visit to the Azores, contains about 3,000 words.

These three items — coming before, during, and after the time of the QCS letters — form the control group for the test. Although 11,000 words falls far short of Mendenhall's standard, the consistency of the three suggests that a sample of this size can be satisfactory.

The counting was done by the tally method, with the count limited to text words. Arbitrarily, it was decided to omit headings, proper names, direct quotes, foreign words, abbreviations, and involved dialect spellings.[26] Hyphenated words were counted as separate words.

The three frequency distributions for the control group — expressed as frequency per 1,000 words — are shown in Chart 3. Considering that the samples are individually fairly small, the consistency of the pattern within the samples is encouraging.

As a check on the consistency over a long span of time, two additional samples of Twain's work were counted:

1. Four passages, selected randomly, from *Roughing It* (1872), totaling about 3,200 words.[27]

2. Three passages, selected randomly, from *Following the Equator* (1897), totaling about 2,700 words.[28]

These two samples, together with the 11,000 word composite of the first three samples, are shown in Chart 4. Based on the visual evidence of Charts 3 and 4, we conclude that the word frequency distribution for

23. Both are included in Paine, *Mark Twain, A Biography.*

24. Collected by Henry Nash Smith in *Mark Twain of the Enterprise.* Berkeley, California: University of California Press, 1957.

25. Collected by Daniel Morley McKeithan in *Traveling with the Innocents Abroad.* Norman, Oklahoma: University of Oklahoma Press, 1958. These letters were the raw material for Twain's first big success, *Innocents Abroad.*

26. This was done in an effort to eliminate any unusual characteristics of the subject matter. For example, after counting Dickens' *Christmas Carol* Mendenhall observed that there was an excess of seven-letter words, resulting from the repeated appearance of "Scrooge." See Mendenhall, p. 244.

27. Mark Twain, *Roughing It.* Hartford, Connecticut: American Publishing Company, 1872.

28. Mark Twain, *Following the Equator.* Hartford, Connecticut: American Publishing Company, 1897.

Chart 3

WORD FREQUENCIES FOR KNOWN MARK TWAIN WRITINGS,
1858-1867

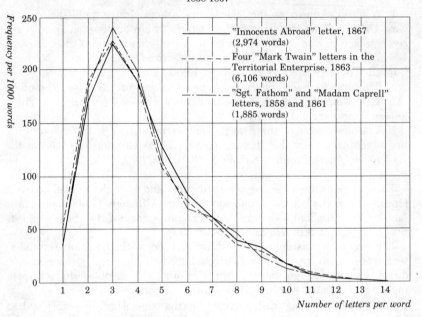

Number of letters per word

Chart 4

WORD FREQUENCIES FOR KNOWN MARK TWAIN WRITINGS,
1858-1867, 1872, 1897

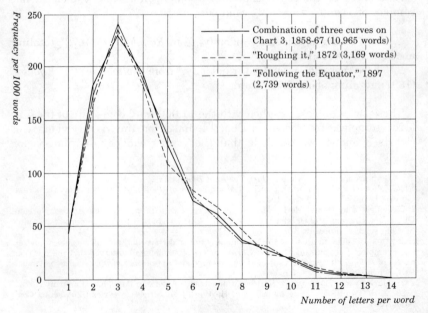

Number of letters per word

Twain's "travel letters" maintained a high degree of consistency over a span of 40 years.

The 10 QCS letters were counted in three groups:

1. Letters I, II, and III. About 5,000 words.
2. Letters IV, V, and VI. About 4,000 words.
3. Letters VII, VIII, IX, and X. About 4,000 words.

Chart 5 shows the frequency distribution for each of the three QCS segments. The two principal conclusions are (1) the samples are consistent within themselves and (2) the curves of the QCS letters are quite unlike those of Charts 3 and 4. These differences are shown more clearly in Chart 6, where the 11,000 words of the Twain control group are compared to the 13,000 words of the QCS letters. Particularly noticeable are the differences in frequencies in words of 1, 2, 3, and 4 letters, and in the tendency for Twain to use relatively fewer words of 7 or more letters.

From the standpoint of visual inspection of the results of this literary blood test, we conclude that Mark Twain could *not* have fathered the QCS letters.[29]

Chart 5

WORD FREQUENCIES FOR QUINTUS CURTIUS SNODGRASS LETTERS, 1861

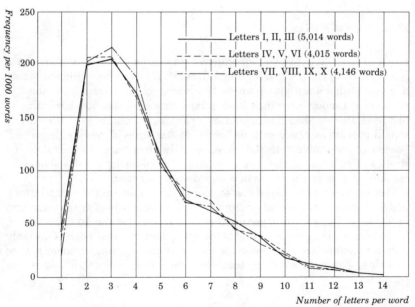

29. This does not mean, of course, that he could not have somehow offered suggestions to whoever did write them. Some of the unusual parallels cited by Leisy could have occurred in this way. For example, the name "Snodgrass" and the "Brown" to whom they were addressed, both of which are known to have been literary favorites of the young Twain, might have been suggested by him.

Chart 6
WORD FREQUENCIES FOR KNOWN MARK TWAIN WRITINGS
AND QUINTUS CURTIUS SNODGRASS LETTERS

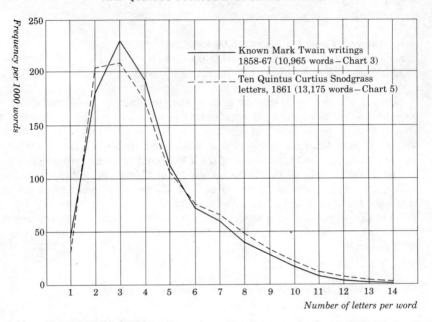

Number of letters per word

χ^2 *Goodness of Fit Test*

It is also possible to test the agreement of the various samples to the control group by using the χ^2 "goodness of fit" test.[30] Although we would not expect a given author's output of words to always conform strictly to the hypothesis of random drawings from a fixed frequency distribution,[31] the χ^2 test nevertheless should be useful as a ranking procedure (i.e., the results should provide evidence such as "probably the same," "possibly the same," "virtually impossible to be the same," etc.). In any case, until more detailed studies of this use of the test are made, the following results should be considered only in the terms of a tentative exploration.

The word counts for the three segments that make up the control group and for the two samples taken from Twain's later writings are summarized in Table 1. Table 2 summarizes the word counts for the 10 QCS letters. Since tallying is an obviously monotonous and error-prone job, it is unlikely that the counts are as precise as the numbers suggest. Random double checking, however, suggests that counting errors are small and unimportant.

30. See, for example, Wilfrid J. Dixon and Frank J. Massey, Jr., *Introduction to Statistical Analysis.* New York: McGraw-Hill Book Company, Inc., 1951, pp. 184 ff.

31. An analogy might be to a statistical quality control chart for variables that would show a few out-of-control points because of an occasional deliberate change in the production process. Similarly, an author could consciously change his normal style enough to produce segments that would result in large values of χ^2.

Table 1

WORD COUNTS FOR KNOWN MARK TWAIN WRITINGS

Word Length	Sergeant Fathom and Madame Caprell Letters (1858; 1861)	Four "Mark Twain" letters from Territorial Enterprise (1863)	First Innocents Abroad Letter (1867)	Sample from Roughing It (1872)	Sample from Following the Equator (1897)
1	74	312	116	138	122
2	349	1,146	496	532	466
3	456	1,394	673	741	653
4	374	1,177	565	591	517
5	212	661	381	357	343
6	127	442	249	258	207
7	107	367	185	215	152
8	84	231	125	150	103
9	45	181	94	83	92
10	27	109	51	55	45
11	13	50	23	30	18
12	8	24	8	10	12
13 and over	9	12	8	9	9
Total	1,885	6,106	2,974	3,169	2,739

The χ^2 test was carried out by comparing the frequency distribution of the Mark Twain control group to each of the two later Mark Twain samples and to the QCS letters. The results are summarized below.[32]

Control group compared to:	Value of χ^2	$P(\chi^2 > Value)$ — 12 d.f.
Sample from *Roughing It*	12.4	.41
Sample from *Following the Equator*	8.5	.73
QCS letters (in total)	127.2	Nil

Table 2

WORD COUNTS FOR QUINTUS CURTIUS SNODGRASS LETTERS

| Word Length | Letter Number | | | | | | | | | | Total |
	I	II	III	IV	V	VI	VII	VIII	IX	X	
1	100	71	45	27	33	57	25	20	21	25	424
2	492	208	297	266	230	335	168	239	242	208	2,685
3	504	247	275	266	254	308	196	250	235	217	2,752
4	423	205	228	201	212	256	158	188	193	238	2,302
5	266	139	160	125	150	145	84	134	113	115	1,431
6	162	96	108	113	112	101	60	86	75	79	992
7	152	81	85	91	107	95	63	77	81	64	896
8	114	60	84	62	64	57	41	59	48	49	638
9	93	43	50	57	44	49	27	27	29	46	465
10	43	25	28	22	26	46	29	15	16	26	276
11	32	16	15	16	11	22	11	14	10	5	152
12	17	10	15	11	11	8	6	12	4	7	101
13 and over	10	5	10	8	6	11	6	2	1	2	61
Total	2,408	1,206	1,400	1,265	1,260	1,490	874	1,123	1,068	1,081	13,175

32. The computation procedure is outlined in Dixon and Massey, *op. cit.*, p. 190.

Table 3

TWO SAMPLE *t* TESTS FOR FREQUENCIES OF
2, 3, AND 4 LETTER WORDS

Item	Proportion of Each Work		
	2-letter words	3-letter words	4-letter words
SAMPLE 1: Mark Twain Group			
Sergeant Fathom Letter	.214	.225	.187
Madame Caprell Letter	.152	.262	.212
Mark Twain Letters in *Territorial Enterprise*			
First Letter	.176	.217	.196
Second Letter	.196	.240	.179
Third Letter	.190	.230	.189
Fourth Letter	.190	.229	.208
First *Innocents Abroad* Letter			
First Half	.172	.235	.195
Second Half	.161	.217	.185
Average – Sample 1	.181	.232	.194
SAMPLE 2: QCS Letters			
I	.204	.209	.176
II	.172	.205	.170
III	.212	.196	.163
IV	.210	.210	.159
V	.183	.202	.168
VI	.225	.207	.172
VII	.192	.224	.181
VIII	.213	.223	.167
IX	.227	.220	.181
X	.192	.201	.220
Average – Sample 2	.203	.210	.176
Value of *t* (16 d. f.)	−2.43	+3.88	+2.57
Approx. $P(|t|>\text{value})$	.028	.002	.022

The small χ^2 values for the samples from *Roughing It* and *Following the Equator* confirm our conclusion about the consistency of Mark Twain's writings reached by visual inspection of Charts 3 and 4. The very large χ^2 for the QCS comparison confirms the conclusion drawn from Chart 6 that the QCS letters were not the work of Mark Twain.

Two-Sample t Test

The two-sample *t* test for testing the difference between sample means can also be used as a simple statistical technique for comparing the Mark Twain writings and the QCS letters. Whereas the χ^2 test provided a measure of agreement of an entire large-sample frequency distribution to a control distribution, this test considers independently the frequency of occurrence of individual words of specified lengths. That is, sample data on two-letter words make up one test; sample data on three-letter words another test; and so on. The sensitivity of this test is increased by dividing the data into a larger number of segments than used in the x^2 test.

The data used and the results of the calculations are summarized in Table 3. As shown there, the control group (making up sample 1) was divided into eight subsamples of roughly equal size and the 10 QCS letters (making up sample 2) were treated as 10 separate subsamples (giving a total of 16 degrees of freedom). The tests were limited to 2, 3, or 4 letter words (about 60 per cent of the total).

Based on the large *t* values (shown at the bottom of Table 3) we conclude that it is highly unlikely that the 2, 3, and 4 letter words in the QCS letters came from the same distribution[33] that produced the words of these lengths in the Mark Twain control group.[34] This conclusion agrees with the one reached above based upon use of the x^2 test and upon visual inspection of the frequency distribution.

Postscript

At the conclusion of the above research, the author wrote to Henry Nash Smith, literary editor of the Mark Twain Papers, asking his opinion about the QCS letters. No reference was made in the author's letter to any of the above work or conclusions. The following reply was received from Frederick Anderson, assistant to Professor Smith:

> Professor Henry Nash Smith has asked me to write to tell you that we are quite sure that Mark Twain did not write the Quintus Curtius Snodgrass letters. In addition to the fact that their prose style and attempts at humor are considerably more primitive than other writings by Clemens during this period, there is external evidence that he could not have been at some of the places mentioned in the letters at the time the writer of the letters was there. A graduate student [Allan Bates] at the University of Chicago is writing a dissertation on Mark Twain as a pilot and has established a chronological account of Clemens' movements during these years which supports this idea.[35]

Thus, there is independent corroborative evidence to support the conclusion reached in this study through Mendenhall's word frequency distribution test.

33. The null hypothesis has the implicit assumption of normality. When the data of Table 3 are plotted on normal probability paper, each set of subsample points falls reasonably well on a straight line.

34. I am indebted to the referee for suggesting this additional test procedure. The referee's further suggestion that the values be weighted was considered to be too great a refinement for these data, particularly since most of the sample sizes are of the same order of magnitude. (Of the 18 samples in Table 3, all but three contain between one and two thousand words.) The calculation procedure is outlined in Dixon and Massey, *op. cit.,* Second Edition, 1957, p. 121.

35. Personal letter, September 6, 1961.

28

Computer Studies

Ephim G. Fogel

Electronic Computers and Elizabethan Texts

Librarians, archivists, linguists, and students of literature are rapidly coming to realize that electronic computers, or, better, data-processing machines, can help to solve problems in fields ordinarily regarded as remote from the world of advanced technology.[1] Already there is a formidable bibliography of books and articles discussing automation in the library, automatic search, indexing, and abstracting of documents, automatic linguistic analysis, and automatic translation.[2] So far as I know, however, no papers have been published on the application of electronic aids to the solution of problems in Elizabethan scholarship. The chief purpose of the present essay is to stimulate wider discussion of such applications. I shall concentrate mainly on the possible uses of computer-prepared concordances to and magnetic tape files of Elizabethan texts.[3]

I

It has long been recognized that concordances are essential tools in the critical, historical, and philological analysis of literary texts. Until very recently, it was also apparent that anyone who agreed to compile a concordance had assumed an appalling task. "An exhaustive concordance to the Bible, such as that of James Strong," John W. Ellison estimates, "takes about a quarter of a century of careful, tedious work to guarantee accuracy."[4] When in February, 1911, Professor Lane Cooper of Cornell

From *Studies in Bibliography,* XV (1962), 15-31. Reprinted by permission of the author.

1. The present essay is a revised version of a paper written for the *Report* of M.L.A. Conference 20 (Opportunities for Research in Renaissance Drama) and delivered before the Conference on Dec. 28, 1960. I am indebted to my colleague Professor Stephen M. Parrish, who introduced me to the mysteries of computers and who has answered my queries with invariable kindness and lucidity.

2. See the classified bibliography in B. Quemada, "La Mécanisation dans les Recherches Lexicologiques," in the Univ. of Besançon *Cahiers de Lexicologie,* I (1959), 41-46. See also *Proceedings of the International Conference on Scientific Information,* 2 vols. (1959); Martha Boaz, ed., *Modern Trends in Documentation* (1959); M. E. Maron, "Handling of Non-Numerical Information," Chap. 11 in Vol. 2 of *Handbook of Automation, Computation, and Control,* ed. Eugene M. Grabbe *et al.* (1959); and for a non-technical discussion of information-retrieval systems, Francis Bello, "How to Cope with Information," *Fortune,* LII (Sept., 1960), 162-167, 180-192.

3. I use "Elizabethan" as a convenient term referring to the period from Wyatt to Milton.

4. Preface to *Nelson's Complete Concordance to the Revised Standard Version Bible* (1957).

University, with the aid of sixty-seven workers, saw the Wordsworth concordance through the press only two years and three months after excerpting of the Hutchinson edition had begun, his achievement was quite properly regarded as remarkable. After tens of thousands of man-hours had been spent in excerpting, alphabetizing, and checking, a concordance-editor was usually compelled to search far and wide for a publisher (the Wordsworth was delayed about nine months until a suitable one could be found) and, often, a handsome subvention. As printing costs soared, large concordances became more and more rare. The only conventionally-produced large concordance to an English or American poet which has appeared since the end of 1941 seems to be Professor Eby's concordance to Whitman's *Leaves of Grass* and selected prose. This work of 980 pages lists at $25.

That concordance-makers should turn to electro-mechanical and electronic aids was only to be expected. After World War II, there were efforts to compile indexes by the use of punched-card systems. But the limited capacity and sorting speeds of electro-mechanical equipment made the automatic production of very large concordances impractical. In the last few years, therefore, researchers have turned to large-scale electronic data-processing machines such as those marketed by Remington Rand and IBM.[5] The year 1957 witnessed three independent developments: Paul Tasman, with the collaboration of Rev. Roberto Busa, S.J., worked out a program for indexing the words in the Dead Sea Scrolls on the IBM 705;[6] John W. Ellison brought out *Nelson's Complete Concordance to the Revised Standard Version Bible,* automatically indexed by the Remington Rand Univac I; and Cornell University launched a program for a computer-produced series of concordances, with Stephen M. Parrish as General Editor.

In the same year, the University of California published the late Guy Montgomery's concordance to Dryden's poetry. Since this cumbersome oddity has given many of its users an erroneous impression of what a machine-prepared concordance looks like, it deserves some mention here. One must emphasize that it is not at all an electronically produced work and indeed only in small part an electro-mechanically produced one. When Professor Montgomery died in 1951, he left 240,000 *manually* indexed cards based on Noyes's edition of Dryden's complete poetical works. Out of the decision to use accounting machines to help in checking these cards grew the decision to print by offset from IBM sheets a list of index-words with abbreviated references to the places where they occurred, but without any context whatsoever. A sample entry from page

---

5. In "Literary Data Processing," *IBM Journal of Research and Development,* I (1957), 256, Paul Tasman gives comparative figures for compiling a lexicon file index and concordance to the *Summa Theologica* of St. Thomas Aquinas (a work of about 2,000 pages and almost 1,600,000 words): manual method—3 persons, 20,000 hours; punched-card method—3 persons, 1,000 hours; large-scale data-processing method—1 person, 60 hours, "exclusive of the presentation and programming time." ("Programming" means devising a sequence of operations so that a computer can perform a particular job of data-processing.) For discussions of techniques involving small-scale equipment, see n. 10, below.

6. See Tasman (n. 5, above), and Busa, "The Index of all Non-Biblical Dead Sea Scrolls Published up to December, 1957," *Revue de Qumran,* I (1958), 187-198.

1 of the resulting concordance will indicate the difficulties that confront the user:

ABIDE   HAP   1928

For each such entry under ABIDE, the reader must consult the prefatory list of full titles geared to the cryptic symbols. He will then learn that HAP stands for "The Hind and the Panther" and that the poem begins on page 218 of Noyes. He must next turn to that page and move forward until he locates line 1928, "No Martin there in winter shall abide," in column B of page 243. But his work is just beginning. In order to ascertain Dryden's various uses of ABIDE (eighteen instances), he must either write out each line as he locates it or else jot down all the page and line numbers of Noyes in which ABIDE occurs and riffle the pages back and forth as he tries to compare instances. One doesn't like to think of the agonies of a reader who wishes to locate and analyze occurrences of the fifty-seven words in "Dryden's major vocabulary" which, according to the preface, occur "from 400 to 1,100 times apiece."

Professor Parrish's *Concordance to the Poems of Matthew Arnold* (Ithaca, 1959) shows that a concordance compiled and printed by electronic data-processing machines (in this case the IBM 704) can give as complete a verse-context and an array of identifying data as the manually compiled type. The first three entries under ABIDE will indicate the advantages of the Arnold:

OTHERS ABIDE OUR QUESTION THOU ART FREE . . 2	SHAKESPEARE	1
HE ESCAPES THENCE BUT WE ABIDE 58	RESIGNATION	213
THE LAW IS PLANTED TO ABIDE 94	SICK KING BOKH	208

Here the concordance provides a full line of context for each instance of the index-word and prints the instances in the order of their occurrence in Tinker and Lowry's edition of Arnold's *Poetical Works*. The identifying information to the right gives the page of Tinker and Lowry on which the line appears, then the title of the poem in which it occurs, or a rather full and readily understood abbreviation, and lastly the line number. In most cases, the reader will probably be able to determine the different uses of the index-word from the entries themselves, but if he should wish to consult an even fuller context, he can immediately turn to the indicated page of Tinker and Lowry. An appendix gives a helpful index of words in order of their frequency in Arnold's text. The production of this volume of 965 pages required some two hundred hours of card-punching, tape-recording, data-processing, and listing.[7] The IBM sheets were then reproduced by offset and bound in an attractive volume which is priced at $10.

Cornell concordances to follow the Arnold will incorporate refinements as rapidly as they are developed. Special print-wheels will provide a

---

7. For a breakdown of the time, which is, again, exclusive of editorial work and of programming, see the preface to the Arnold, pp. vii-viii; for an account of the programming, see James A. Painter, "Computer Preparation of a Poetry Concordance," *Communications of the A [ssocia-tion for] C [omputing] M [achinery]*, III (1960), 91-95.

full array of punctuation marks and of characters such as the thorn and the ligatures (the Arnold has only the hyphen). Presently available techniques can instruct computers to discriminate between homographs and print them under separate headings, to cross-index hyphenated words, and, for earlier poets, to collect the old-spelling variants of a single word under their modern-spelling equivalent, as in Osgood's Spenser or Tatlock and Kennedy's Chaucer.

New possibilities in concordance-making and in other kinds of literary data-processing will doubtless emerge as computers rapidly become more and more complex, swift, and powerful. "The latest [computers]," writes Ritchie Calder, "are a thousand times faster than those of three years ago and a million times faster than those of ten years ago," and he reports that in June, 1959, in Paris, at an International Conference on Information Processing, scientists seriously discussed "machines which would memorize all the knowledge in the world."[8] One's mind reels and retreats to somewhat less staggering fantasies in which the C. W. Wallaces and Leslie Hotsons of the twenty-first century, working in American repositories, ask computers to search magnetic tapes of British archives for all occurrences of names with, say, the components Sh, k, sp, r or M, r, l. A daydream highly fantastical, perhaps; yet the photoduplication during World War II of a vast number of British documents, now available at the Library of Congress on microfilm, provides a notable precedent for the internationalization of archives.[9]

But consideration of what can be done now is likely to be more fruitful than heady speculations about the future. Literary scholars should give earnest thought to making use of the machines available to them on their campuses: much can be done even with small-scale computers or punchcard and perforated-tape equipment.[10] Efforts should be coordinated in order to determine important needs in different specialties, to prevent duplication of work at different universities, and to disseminate information about new developments in the processing of literary texts. In this connection I am authorized to state that the Department of English at Cornell University will be glad to share its experience in preparing concordances by computer, and its knowledge of work being done at other centers, with those who may be ready to embark on projects of their own.

II

The scholar is the key person in the development of specific programs to process literary data. It is he who must define goals for research and arrive at the most rational procedures for achieving these goals. His in-

8. *The Unesco Courier,* Jan., 1960, pp. 26-27.

9. See *British Manuscripts Project* (1955); this insufficiently known checklist of the microfilms, compiled by Lester K. Born, is sold by the Photoduplication Service of the Library of Congress.

10. See the extended discussion by Quemada, "La Mécanisation," pp. 9-33. Cf. also the useful mimeographed *Reports* of the Groth Institute, founded by Professor Ray Pepinsky at the Pennsylvania State University. With the aim of preparing a revised edition of Paul von Groth's encyclopedia of crystallography "in perhaps a hundred volumes," Professor Pepinsky and his co-workers have developed effective techniques of indexing and information-retrieval using inexpensive electro-mechanical equipment: see esp. *Reports* Nos. 40, 41, 44-48, 53.

dispensable colleague, the computer-engineer, cannot move forward until the scholar himself knows what he wants to do. On the other hand, the scholar must have some awareness of how a literary text is prepared for computer-processing. I shall limit myself here to a simplified, non-technical outline of the steps required to record a text on magnetic tape.

i. Having selected a base-text, the scholar edits it for punching.

ii. Working at a machine with a conventional typewriter keyboard, an operator punches the text on cards. Each card contains a line of poetry or a similar amount of prose; the punched text is automatically recorded in print at the top of the card.

iii. The cards are verified to insure accuracy of transcription. In this process, a second operator punches the same text on the already punched cards. A light flashes if there is any discrepancy between her punch and that of the first operator; she then pulls the card in question, checks the print for errors, and punches the line correctly.

iv. Identifying data (page of base-edition and line of poem) are automatically punched onto each card in the set; title cards separately punched for each poem are introduced into the set.

v. The information on each card is transferred seriatim onto a magnetic master-tape and can then be processed on a computer according to a previously designed program. When the computer-run is finished, the master-tape can be stored indefinitely, or processed again as required. Through the use of other tapes, the recorded data can be altered so that a fresh master-tape is produced.

It will be apparent that the master-tape is in many ways more important than any single list of analyzed data which can be automatically printed from it. The tape is a compact, permanent record. It gives the editor of a computer-prepared concordance, for example, much greater flexibility than the editor of a manually prepared work can enjoy. If he decides at the last moment to include five "common" words that he had originally planned not to print, he need only instruct the computer to add those words to its processing list. And long after his concordance is published, he can quickly retrieve from the tape any verbal data excluded from the book: "the [IBM 704] computer can locate all occurrences of even a high-frequency word in about 20 minutes."[11]

So far as data-processing equipment is concerned, then, the tasks of Elizabethan scholarship in the coming years may be defined as the recording on master-tapes of the widest possible array of literary works in their most authoritative and most usable textual form; the duplication and depositing of such tapes in key centers of scholarship; the searching of the tapes on request to provide individual scholars with information that will increase the comprehensiveness and validity of their conclusions; and the selective publishing of machine-prints made from these tapes (concordances, lexicons, frequency lists, textual collations, etc.) so as to serve the needs of the profession as a whole. It will of course be necessary for appropriate groups of scholars to rationalize and allocate these labors.

---

11. Parrish preface to the Arnold p. xiii, n. 1.

For the rest of this paper, I should like to suggest the kinds of aid that philology, textual criticism, concordance-making, enumerative bibliography, and canonical studies can expect from data-processing machines. I am obviously taking on more than can be handled by any man, unless there exists somewhere a Hercules who is both a computer-engineer and a master of the immense domain of Elizabethan scholarship. It will be understood, then, that the following remarks, whether they assume an imperative or interrogative form, are provisional. They are meant rather to raise questions for discussion than to try to supply definitive answers.

Philology

The philological and linguistic applications of computers have been much discussed. Various classes of documents from different historical periods and linguistic communities can be recorded on tapes which computers can then process to produce indexes of graphic and graphic-semantic forms, with accompanying context. As a result, philological studies can be more comprehensive and exact than in the past. Anyone who has come upon instances of a usage earlier than those recorded by the monumental *Oxford English Dictionary,* and upon other usages that are not recorded at all, can testify to the need for a complete and accurate dictionary of Elizabethan English. Computers could speed the publication of such a dictionary.

Textual Criticism

An editor preparing a critical old-spelling edition of an Elizabethan poet or dramatist must process an enormous amount of literary data. Collation of early printed editions can be facilitated by machines, as Professor Charlton J. K. Hinman has demonstrated in his collation of dozens of copies of the First Folio. Future editors will also wish to explore the possibilities of computer collation. The more complicated the textual tradition, the more the scholar will appreciate electronic aid in reconstructing a stemma.[12] Again, every editor has to analyze such matters as characteristic locutions and linguistic preferences through all of his author's extant writings, as well as the spelling of any surviving holographs, so that he can decide to what extent a base-text which is not a holograph, and perhaps was not transcribed or printed from a holograph, represents his author's idioms and orthography. In the past, an editor has had to depend upon his memory, at best an incomplete and unreliable guide, or to compile by hand a private concordance, as it were, an index of his author's graphic-semantic patterns. Computers can relieve him of this labor, which adds far too much to his already heavy burdens. Accurate and complete counts of an author's particular word-sequences can also help to detect contaminations. On the basis of such analyses, computers can automatically fill in lacunae or offer conjectural emendations of corrupt or suspect

12. John W. Ellison, for example, is planning to collate electronically 800 versions of the Greek text of the Bible.

passages;[13] these reconstructions may then serve as a check on the editor's conjectures, or they may stimulate further insights. It is not, of course, a question of a machine's replacing the judgments of a Greg or a Grierson, but of freeing future Gregs and Griersons from the mechanical drudgery that must precede final editorial judgment.

Since a concordance is valuable for textual criticism, we may expect that editors of Elizabethan dramatists and poets will also edit concordances to their authors. A preliminary tape that will help the editor to establish his text can be corrected to embody final editorial decisions and a concordance can then be published by offset from machine-prints.

Concordance-Making

Here I should like to pose a series of questions. Some of the answers given below have been worked out during preliminary preparations for a concordance to the poems of Ben Jonson, to be edited by Professor Parrish and myself. None of the answers, however, are necessarily final, and I should appreciate comments and suggestions.

1. What kind of base-text should one use? A concordance will have the greatest value for philologists, editors, and canonical scholars if it is based on a definitive edition, preferably in old spelling. The concordance can then refer to the page and line numbers of a readily available standard work and can include editorial emendations as well as authorial variants. If there is no definitive edition, it might be possible to compile a concordance from an early printed text, provided that an acceptable photoduplicate of that text has been published.[14] In that case, the concordance-maker can identify citations by referring to signature and line number of page or column, in the manner of Professor Hinman's references to lines in the Shakespeare First Folio. But reference to authorial variants in other early texts (one thinks of Daniel's and Drayton's frequent revisions) and to modern emendations will perhaps pose a problem.

If an acceptable photoduplicate or a definitive edition is unavailable, the concordance-maker should probably pass on to another author. To provide the general reader with references to a virtually inaccessible text is of little use, and to base a concordance on an inadequate edition is unwise. If there were a Jonson concordance based on the Gifford text, it would of course be helpful, but it would have to be redone now that the Herford and Simpson text is available, even as Bartlett's Shakespeare will probably have to be redone when a critical old-spelling edition appears.

2. To what extent should one normalize the text? It seems to serve no useful purpose and is in some cases impossible to retain scribal abbrevia-

---

13. Tasman, p. 256, mentions reconstructions of lacunae in the Dead Sea Scrolls. "Up to *five* consecutive words," he reports, "have been 're-written' by the data processing machine in experimental tests where the words were intentionally left out of the text and blank spots indicated."

14. I am indebted to Professor Fredson Bowers for this suggestion.

tions. On the other hand, to normalize *i-j* and *u-v* according to modern usage, if the base-edition has not done so, seems to require excessive intervention extending to many lines in every poem or passage of dialogue. The automatic collection of variant spellings under a single head-word will assure that such forms as IELOSIE and IOYND will be conveniently indexed under their modern equivalents.

3. What about textual variants and emendations? As has been indicated, one should include authorial variants. Both a textual crux and the emendation adopted by the editor of the base-text should be indexed. Variants and emendations should be labeled as such (in Professor Parrish's Arnold, a "V" for "variant" precedes the line number).

The concordance-maker is not the editor of a critical edition, but he should correct obvious misprints in his base-text and include variants unavailable to or perhaps overlooked by the editor. Sometimes he may have to display the courage of an editor's convictions. The Herford and Simpson text, for example, reproduces in square brackets "a letter or word wrongly inserted in the original." There is no point in indexing such a word; in our Jonson concordance, we have substituted the reading which Herford and Simpson indicate as correct.

4. Should stage directions be indexed? By all means. Stage directions are important elements in plays, masques, pageants, and entertainments. But Ariel's making the banquet vanish with a quaint device and Jack Cade's striking his staff on London stone cannot be located in Bartlett's concordance, which omits all stage directions, as do Crawford's Kyd and Marlowe. Lists of *dramatis personae* in the early prints should also be included; that such lists call Shakespeare's Lucio "a fantastique" and his Apemantus "a Churlish Philosopher" is surely worthy of alphabetized record. Whether one should include in the same index with the dialogue and the stage directions the copious marginalia which edify the reader of Jonson's masques seems rather more doubtful.

5. How comprehensive should the index be? This is one of the most difficult questions confronting the concordance-maker. Every concordance leaves out all or most of the instances of many common words such as prepositions, articles, pronouns, and auxiliary verbs. In general, computer-prepared concordances will have to follow suit: common words make up more than half of the individual words of any text; a decision to index all of them may push some computers beyond their capacity, will in any case materially increase the running time of a very busy and very expensive machine, and will swell the printed version of, say, a Shakespeare or Jonson or Bible concordance to grotesque proportions. According to John W. Ellison, 131 common words "account for approximately 59% of the text of the Bible," and the large Nelson Bible Concordance would have been "two and a half times its present size" if these words had been indexed (Preface).

Yet who is to say that even the commonest word is without poetic or dramatic significance? LIKE, THAN, AS, and SO can lead us directly to the poet's similes; I and related forms to his use of an autobiographical mask and his personifications ("I bring fresh showers for the thirsting flowers"); O and THOU to his apostrophes ("O wild West Wind, thou breath of Autumn's being"); ME, THEE, and HIM to striking inversions of word order ("Him the Almighty Power/ Hurled headlong flaming from th' ethereal sky"). Philological interests also press their claims. Tatlock and Kennedy index all instances of SHALL and WILL "owing to the importance of these words for the history of the future tense" (preface to the Chaucer, p. viii). The Elizabethan philologist may point out, further, that complete omission of the following common words will deprive him of an opportunity for rapid location of the special meanings indicated parenthetically: A (he), AN, AND (if), FROM (at variance with, alien to), ON (of), SHE (woman), WHETHER (which of the two). A canonical scholar may object that failure to list a dramatist's common contractions or his uses of YOU and YE will compel him to duplicate the arduous labors of Cyrus Hoy in compiling tables of linguistic preferences so as to discriminate between different authors in collaborate plays.[15]

All true enough. But a concordance to a prolific dramatist will nevertheless have to exclude some of these words and list others only in part. Consider the ubiquitous I. In the 17,500 lines of Arnold's poetry there are more than a thousand I's, and their listing takes up almost twelve pages. In the more than 100,000 lines of Shakespeare's plays, there are probably many times that number. Will the reproduction of all these instances yield advantages proportional to the space required? The concordance-maker will have to answer many such painful questions. At least he can assure fellow scholars that omitted index-words can be retrieved from the master-tape at some later time.

I should like to plead, however, for the routine printing in all drama concordances of such common words as ALL, ANY, NEVER, NONE. These terse counters can contribute greatly to dramatic magnitude and intensity. Moreover, in drama as in life, the extent to which a person makes categorical statements is an important clue to the quality of his mind. I have the impression, for example, that Hamlet makes more all-or-nothing assertions ("Thus conscience does make cowards of us all." "We are arrant knaves all; believe none of us.") than does any other Shakespearean character. But I cannot verify my impression in Bartlett, since it entirely omits ALL and gives only a partial listing of NONE.[16] It is doubtless a weakness on my part, but I have thus far been unwilling to make up the deficiencies in the available concordances by tracking all instances of these words through thirty-six plays.

6. *Should a writer's dramas and poems be indexed separately?* Bartlett's Shakespeare separates drama and poetry; Crawford's Marlowe combines

---

15. See Hoy's "The Shares of Fletcher and his Collaborators in the Beaumont and Fletcher Canon," *SB*, VIII (1956), 129-146, IX (1957), 143-162, XI (1958), 85-106, XII (1959), 91-116, and XIII (1960), 77-108.

16. Neither word is indexed in Mrs. Cowden Clarke's concordance; except for a few inadvertent omissions, all occurrences in *Hamlet* only are listed in the Appendix to Crawford's Kyd concordance.

them. Combination seems appropriate for a moderately productive writer. Separation seems desirable when a writer is prolific in one of the genres and almost inevitable when he is prolific in both (cf. Dryden). Separation facilitates study of the verbal artistry appropriate to each genre and enables the compiler to make separate decisions about comprehensiveness (e.g., to omit I from the drama but include it in the poetry concordance).

7. To what extent should disputes about authorship determine the design of the concordance? Crawford's Kyd and Marlowe concordances are both "designed to be helpful to students who wish to study" questions of authorship (Marlowe, p. vii). In the Kyd proper, Crawford includes *Arden of Feversham,* which he believes is Kyd's; in an appendix he indexes the first two quartos and the folio version of *Hamlet* in order to lighten "the labour of those who are interested in investigating the claim of Kyd to the *Ur-Hamlet.*" In the Marlowe proper, he includes the three parts of *Henry VI, Edward III, Selimus,* and *Locrine,* which last, he believes, is certainly not Marlowe's but has borrowed heavily from his work.

These procedures are indefensible. It is not the concordance-maker's office to argue for or against a disputed attribution. "That task," as Sister Eugenia Logan rightly observes in her Coleridge concordance (p. ix), "belongs in another field of scholarship." Where an attribution has in its favor evidence approaching certainty, the concordance-maker should include the attributed work. Where the evidence is weak, he should exclude the work. Where the evidence is highly probable but not certain, he should index the work and indicate its status, perhaps by an appropriate symbol. Apparently distinguishable portions of collaborate plays should be analyzed not in separate concordances, but in a single concordance bearing the names of the collaborators.[17] Anonymous plays and plays whose authorship is in serious dispute should be left for the last, and should be grouped in concordances of convenient size according to chronology of composition, as nearly as that can be determined.

Enumerative Bibliography

The concordance principle has been successfully applied to the production of fully analyzed enumerative bibliographies in the fields of chemistry and physics.[18] A new publication called *Chemical Titles* indexes the key words of titles of articles in 550 journals so that each key word appears in context in a concordance of key words. The bibliography in each issue consists of two parts: a list of articles alphabetized according to author, with full titles and publication data, and a concordance of key title-words in context, with an easily interpreted identifying code that provides a

17. Here as elsewhere, procedure will have to be flexible. It would probably be advisable to include all the plays in the "Beaumont and Fletcher" canon in one concordance. Again, if a successor to Bartlett believes that hands other than Shakespeare's are present in *Henry VIII* and *Pericles,* he should nevertheless include these two plays in his concordance and content himself with stating his views in the preface.

18. See "Chemical Literature Gets a Quicker Index," *Chemical and Engineering News,* XXXVIII (April 4, 1960), 27-28.

cross-reference to the first part. On the average, there are 5.3 concordance-entries per title. The indexing of key words is entirely automatic. As soon as the journals are received, the titles of articles are transcribed into machine-readable form by punch-card operators. When the file of punch-cards is complete, it is transferred to magnetic tape, which is then processed by an IBM 704. Omitting non-distinctive words such as OF, ON, AND, EFFECTS, ANALYSIS, CHEMISTRY by referring to a dictionary of excluded terms stored in its core memory, the computer edits the materials on the tape in 12 minutes; auxiliary equipment arranges and prints the bibliography in 18 to 20 hours; altogether no more than 21 days elapse between the time the journals are received and the time *Chemical Titles* is published.

Leading scholarly organizations should seriously consider the production of bibliographies by computer. Apart from the rapidity of its appearance in print and its comprehensiveness, a computer-produced bibliography in the field of English literature will satisfy the criterion of full analysis more completely than any of the presently available bibliographies. Each item will appear under various subject-headings, so that a scholar interested in a subject covered only in part in a given book, chapter, or article will find a reference to that source under the subject-heading of his interest. A title such as *"Hamlet, Antonio's Revenge, and the Ur-Hamlet"*[19] ought rightly to appear not only under "Shakespeare" but also under "Marston" and under the key word "Revenge," so that the article will be brought to the attention of anyone interested in the theme of revenge in Elizabethan literature. In the latest *PMLA* bibliography, the title seems to appear only under "Shakespeare."[20] I am not, of course, singling out the *PMLA* bibliographies for special criticism. Within the limits of their chosen form, they are admirably comprehensive, and they offer many cross-references; the instance just mentioned is doubtless atypical. My point, rather, is that all of the present bibliographies are subject to human error which can be much reduced by computer techniques and that none of them meet the criterion of full analysis, which computers can easily satisfy.

A certain amount of processing will probably be necessary before one can be certain that a reference will appear under all appropriate rubrics. If "Shakespeare" and "Marston" were inserted in square brackets in the title cited above, the article would be automatically indexed under those names. For purposes of subject-analysis, it would help if scholars curbed their metaphorical propensities and made their titles as nearly descriptive as possible. But even such titles as *The Unicorn and the Crocodile* can be made to yield their literal contents, sometimes by reference to the descriptive subtitle *(A Study of Allegorical Motifs in Medieval and Renaissance Painting and Literature),* sometimes by a little effort on the part of the scholars who will review the titles before passing them on to punch-card operators.

May one take this opportunity to plead for a coordinated effort to satisfy still another criterion of enumerative bibliography, the criterion of effi-

---

19. John Harrington Smith *et al., SQ,* IX (1958), 493-498.
20. LXXV, No. 2 (May, 1960), 203.

ciency or non-duplication? As printed materials in active fields of research increase exponentially, it becomes increasingly wasteful for independent groups of workers to prepare largely identical bibliographies. The devotion of scholars who spend long hours compiling indexes of current research is impressive, but it is disheartening to think of the extravagant repetition of routine tasks. Does it really serve the needs of our profession to produce half a dozen annual bibliographies of Shakespearean scholarship? Would not one bibliography – complete, fully analyzed, and swiftly produced by data-processing machines – suffice?

A bibliography becomes even more useful when it provides a brief summary of the contents of a work. Since the beginning of 1958, *English Abstracts* has been filling a serious gap in research resources. But this excellent publication may some day be confronted by grave problems. Its coverage has been growing constantly and gives every promise of continuing to do so. In January, 1958, the journal listed 32 abstractors on its cover; in December, 1960, it listed 122, an increase of almost 400 per cent. To be sure, the number of items abstracted did not increase by so large a factor. But it did increase very considerably. The first three issues of 1958 printed 426 abstracts on 79 pages; the last three issues of 1960 printed 678 abstracts on 144 pages – an increase, in less than three years, of about 35 per cent in the number of items and 80 per cent in the number of pages. In the not so distant future, *English Abstracts,* like its kindred services in scientific fields, may be forced to seek machine aid to avoid being engulfed by a tidal wave of publications. Should such a need arise, there is a good chance that data-processing machines will be able to meet it. H. P. Luhn, the IBM engineer whose research made possible the concordance-index of *Chemical Titles,* has already conducted successful experiments in automatic abstracting.[21] Before very many years pass, text-reading machines may be scanning printed articles, encoding them on magnetic tape, and producing a rapid succession of automatic abstracts – in translation, where necessary.

Studies in Attribution

Concordances and magnetic tape files will obviously facilitate the gathering of internal evidence for the solution of canonical problems. They will enable one to find parallels more rapidly and to make various special checks. Professor R. C. Bald, for example, observes that Hand D in *The Booke of Sir Thomas More* makes likely a "graphic confusion between *x* and *y*" and that such a confusion seems to have occurred in *Troilus and Cressida* v.i.16, where "the Quarto reads 'box' [and] the Folio corrects to 'boy' "[22] J. Dover Wilson has collected similar examples of misreadings which could easily have resulted if a good quarto was printed from copy

---

21. See Luhn's "Auto-Encoding of Documents for Information Retrieval Systems," in Boaz, *Trends in Documentation,* pp. 45-58.

22. "*The Booke of Sir Thomas More* and its Problems," *Shakespeare Survey,* II (1949), 58.

in a hand such as D's.[23] If all of the Shakespeare quartos and the First Folio were recorded on magnetic tape, one could ask a computer to sort out all words that ended in x and y and other easily confused characters. Or one could ask it to search tapes of other Elizabethan dramatists for complete lists of linguistic preferences such as Professor Hoy used to determine the shares of various collaborators in the Beaumont and Fletcher canon. Freed from the tedium of amassing examples, scholars could devote their higher energies to the interpretation of evidence retrieved and classified by machines.[24]

Again, the more concordances there are, the easier it will be to make negative checks — to show that a seemingly unusual parallel occurs in many writers and is not therefore probative of a particular author's claim to an anonymous work. One hopes that the use of parallels, whether for purposes of proof or disproof, will cease to be fragmentary and unsystematic. If we had reliable information about the average frequencies of certain locutions in the vocabularies of educated men using certain forms of discourse at a certain time, the coincidence of many above- or below-average occurrences of even common phrases might become probative of authorship. Perhaps the accumulation of linguistic frequencies by computers will encourage mathematicians with an interest in literature or literary scholars with a flair for mathematics to push onward in the directions indicated by G. Udny Yule's *The Statistical Study of Literary Vocabulary*.[25]

Unfortunately, however, electronic computers and their printed products will probably fail to discourage some scholars from playing the game of parallels badly. Those who in the past have been intent on parading insignificant agreements between two texts as strong arguments for common authorship have seldom taken the trouble to make negative checks in available concordances. Will a special pleader in a hurry pause to reflect merely because aids to reflection are more abundant? "It is the peculiar and perpetual error of the human intellect," Francis Bacon warns us (*Novum Organum,* I, xlvi), "to be more moved and excited by affirmatives than by negatives; whereas it ought properly to hold itself indifferently disposed towards both alike." "Indeed," he adds, "in the establishment of any true axiom, the negative instance is the more forcible of the two." Computers will not do away with the Idols of the Tribe; to guard against such illusions is the province of education in the spirit of scholarly and scientific argument. With the spread of that spirit, one may hope with

23. "Bibliographical Links Between the Three Pages and the Good Quartos," in A. W. Pollard *et al., Shakespeare's Hand in "Sir Thomas More"* (1923), pp. 113-141.

24. The kinds of evidence bearing on attribution are more various than can be discussed here. By counting distances between punctuation marks, a computer can gather statistics about sentence-length and sentence-segmentation. By collecting all words with certain medial or terminal letters, it can help one to establish authorial or compositorial spellings. By retrieving blank-verse lines with two- or three-letter final words, it can provide information about weak endings. The scholar armed with knowledge of a computer's capabilities will readily think of ways of exploiting them.

25. Since I wrote these remarks, I have learned that Professors Frederick Mosteller and David L. Wallace, using computers, have applied statistical methods to the determination of the authorship of the disputed *Federalist* papers. A report on their work will appear shortly in a book on the Harvard Computer Symposium.

Bacon (I, cxxx) "that the art of discovery may advance as discoveries advance."

Meanwhile, one trusts that more and more scholars will find ways to advance Elizabethan studies by enlisting the aid of electronic data-processing machines. The chief barrier to such an effort is likely to be a lingering suspicion that these machines are somehow baleful, that they somehow constitute a threat to the humanist's distinctive values. But such fears are groundless; they can only be damaging to the progress of Elizabethan and indeed of all humane studies. It is surely inhumane to scorn mechanical aids which by releasing from soul-killing drudgery that most remarkable of all instruments, the brain, free it for its proper function – the enlargement of man's intellectual and spiritual realms through the use of creative intelligence. It may be appropriate to conclude with a striking Elizabethan example of humanist initiative and persistence in making available a novel means for the achievement of a noble end.[26] On March 16, 1542/3, the musician John Marbeck, organist at St. George's Chapel, Windsor, was arrested for possessing heretical writings, among which were materials for a concordance to the English Bible. On July 26, 1544, Marbeck was found guilty of heresy and was sentenced to die at the stake the following day. Fortunately for music and scholarship, however, he was pardoned by Henry VIII and was released from prison. When the accession of Edward VI created a friendlier climate for innovation, Marbeck again took up his suppressed project. In July of 1550 he at long last published *A Concordāce, that is to saie a worke wherein by the ordre of the letters of the A. B. C. ye maie redely finde any word conteigned in the whole Bible, so often as it is there expressed or mencioned.* Elizabethan scholars may well take inspiration from this Elizabethan precedent.

---

26. I am indebted to Professor J. B. Bessinger, Jr., editor of the forthcoming Cornell Concordance to Old English poetry, for calling my attention to Marbeck's concordance. The biographical information that follows is taken from the *DNB*.

V

CAVEATS

29

The Unreliability of Texts

John W. Nichol

Melville's "Soiled" Fish of the Sea

In chapter xcii of *White-Jacket,* Melville describes his fall into the sea from the yardarm of the U. S. frigate *Neversink.* F. O. Matthiessen selects this passage to illustrate the manner in which Melville, the artist, worked.[1] His discussion is an excellent example of judicial and appreciative critical comment, but on one important point Mr. Matthiessen is the victim of a rather unlucky error. After setting forth the series of trancelike moods which Melville employs in describing his experience of falling, Matthiessen quotes, evidently from the Constable Standard Edition of Melville's *Works,* the following passage in which Melville relates his feelings while still under the water:

> I wondered whether I was yet dead or still dying. But of a sudden some fashionless form brushed my side — some inert, soiled fish of the sea; the thrill of being alive again tingled in my nerves, and the strong shunning of death shocked me through.[2]

Commenting on these lines, Matthiessen says:

> But then this second trance is shattered by a twist of imagery of the sort that was to become peculiarly Melville's. He is startled back into the sense of being alive by grazing an inert form; hardly anyone but Melville could have created the shudder that results from calling this frightening vagueness some "*soiled* fish of the sea." The *discordia concors,* the unexpected linking of the medium of cleanliness with filth, could only have sprung from an imagination

From *American Literature,* XXI (1949), 338-339. Reprinted by permission of Duke University Press and John W. Nichol.

1. *American Renaissance: Art and Expression in the Age of Emerson and Whitman* (London and New York [1941]), pp. 390-395.
2. *The Works of Herman Melville* (London, 1922-1924), VI, 497.

that had apprehended the terrors of the deep, of the immaterial deep as well as the physical.[3]

The unlucky error of all this lies in the fact that Melville in all probability used the adjective *coiled* rather than *soiled* in describing his "fish of the sea," and that it was some unknown typesetter, rather, who accounted for the "shudder" and the "*discordia concors*" of the "unexpected linking." If, as is probable, Constable made up the *Works* from first editions, then the word "soiled," which Matthiessen quotes correctly from his source, is really a misprint for Melville's "coiled," for both the American and English first editions of *White-Jacket* printed the latter word.[4] It is interesting to note that the change in this case does not invalidate the general critical position arrived at by Matthiessen; it merely weakens his specific example. However, such a textual slip could, in the proper context, have promulgated an entirely false conception.

3. *American Renaissance*, p. 392.
4. I am indebted to Dr. Howard P. Vincent for checking a copy of the English first edition.

30

The Limitations of Transcripts

Jack Stillinger

Keats's Grecian Urn and the Evidence of Transcripts

In "Keats's Ideal in the *Ode on a Grecian Urn*," *PMLA*, LXXII (March 1957), 118, Jacob D. Wigod writes: "That Keats meant the urn to speak the last 2 lines is clear from the transcripts made by Charles Brown and Richard Woodhouse (Houghton Library), and the transcripts of George Keats (British Museum) and Dilke (Hampstead House). Punctuation in all transcripts is basically as follows: 'Beauty is Truth,—Truth Beauty,— that is all / Ye know on earth, and all ye need to know' (Brown). See Alvin Whitley, 'The Message of the Grecian Urn,' *Keats-Shelley Memorial Bulletin*, No. 5, ed. Dorothy Hewlett (London, 1953), pp. 1-3." Each reader may decide for himself whether the division of these lines by dashes into three parts, even if Keats himself made the division, renders "clear" the intention that the urn is to "speak" both lines. Everybody, however, may on good grounds doubt whether the agreement of punctuation in the four transcripts necessarily shows that Keats ever punctuated the lines in the same way. (There is no extant version in Keats's handwriting, though some critics persist in quoting one.)

The validity of citing four transcripts as evidence depends on the knowledge (1) that each transcriber made his copy directly from a Keats holograph; (2) that any transcript made from a Keats holograph faithfully reproduced its punctuation; (3) that no different version strongly contests the transcripts' reading for authority (i.e., that a holograph copied represents Keats's intention better than any other version that he may have been responsible for). No such knowledge can be established. Woodhouse copied Brown's version, not Keats's, as he indicated by adding "from C. B." at the end of his transcript. George Keats made his copy when he returned briefly to England in January 1820, some eight months after the poem was written. The first page of the notebook containing his transcript bears the inscription "George Keats. 1820," and on 15 January 1820 Keats wrote that "George is busy this morning in making copies of my

From *PMLA*, LXXIII (September 1958), 447-448. Reprinted by permission of the Modern Language Association.

verses" (*Letters,* ed. M. B. Forman, Oxford Univ. Press, 1952, p. 451). It cannot be shown that George copied Keats's manuscript rather than, say, Brown's presumably more readable transcript. Nothing is known of the circumstances behind the transcript made by Dilke, who moved away from Hampstead before the poem was written. It *is* likely that Brown copied directly from Keats's manuscript (and did so before the poem was printed), but the possibility that his was the only firsthand transcript is just as strong as the possibility that there was a plurality of such copies. The agreement of the four transcripts is, then, not very significant, considering the lack of facts about them.

No one has reported on the abilities and peculiarities of the transcribers in question. The most scholarly of them, Richard Woodhouse, is disqualified here because he did not follow Keats's manuscript directly. As the one most likely to have copied Keats, Brown especially should be tested, but which extant Brown transcripts were made from which extant Keats holographs has never been determined. One available example, though not a very satisfactory one, is Keats's letter of 30 (dated 28) September 1820, in which, many years later when he copied it into his manuscript "Life of John Keats," Brown made forty-seven additions and changes in punctuation (see *Letters,* pp. 521-523, and *The Keats Circle,* ed. H. E. Rollins, Cambridge, Mass., 1948, ii, 80-82). Keats's holograph and Brown's transcript of "Lines on the Mermaid Tavern" in the Harvard Keats Collection may briefly illustrate the general problem of the reliability of transcripts, regardless of whether the holograph is the original draft or whether it is the one that Brown copied. A comparison of the two shows seventeen additions and variants in punctuation in Brown's transcript. If one assumes (for the sake of argument) that the holograph uniquely represents Keats's approved form of the poem—it is the same kind of assumption that citing four transcripts of "Ode on a Grecian Urn" makes—then, if the holograph had been lost, we would be clearly wrong in attributing to Keats every mark of punctuation in Brown's transcript. Reliance on Brown's copy of "Ode on a Grecian Urn" is liable to the possibility of similar error.

Against the transcripts' three-part division of the lines stand the two original printed versions, which set off "Beauty is truth, truth beauty" as a unit by itself. The first appeared in James Elmes' *Annals of the Fine Arts, for* MDCCCXIX (ca. January 1820): "Beauty is Truth, Truth Beauty.—That is all / Ye know on Earth, and all ye need to know." Its authority is sometimes discounted on the ground that Haydon, as he recalled in 1845, "begged a copy [of the nightingale and Grecian urn odes] for the Annals . . . and there they appeared at my request before the[y] came out in a Volume" (*Keats Circle,* ii, 142). Haydon's words can hardly be taken to mean that *he* transcribed the version for Elmes. As a matter of fact, in June 1819 Keats himself copied and sent to Elmes some "verses" (*Letters,* pp. 348, 351)—presumably the "Ode to a Nightingale," which appeared in the *Annals* in July 1819—and it is likely that Elmes' text of "Ode on a Grecian Urn" came directly from Keats in the same way, perhaps even at the same time.

The other early printing is in the *Lamia* volume, published around 1 July 1820: " 'Beauty is truth, truth beauty,'—that is all / Ye know on earth, and all ye need to know." This text is often denied authority on the ground that Keats was too ill to supervise publication, and the idea gains some support from Woodhouse's draft of an "Advertisement" to *Lamia*, in which he says "the Author's health is not at pres^t such as to enable him to make any corrections" (*Keats Circle*, I, 116), and from Keats's disavowal (which he inscribed in Davenport's copy, now at Harvard) of the "Advertisement" that was finally printed: "This is none of my doing—I w[as] ill at the time." The fact is, however, that Keats *did* proofread. He made corrections in the incomplete set of proof sheets of *Lamia* owned by Harvard, and early in June (perhaps on the eleventh) he read and corrected proof of "The Eve of St. Agnes" after visiting his publisher Taylor (*Letters,* pp. 491 f.). From 11 June to 22 June, when he suffered an attack of blood-spitting, nothing is known about his life, except that on one day (ca. 18 June) he saw Haydon, visited the British Institution, and met Thomas Monkhouse. In ten days he *could* have proofread the *Lamia* volume several times over, and his and Woodhouse's remarks about his health *could* apply to the days after the hemorrhage of 22 June.

None of the readings in the transcripts, the *Annals,* or *Lamia* can be offered as conclusive proof of Keats's own reading. With the evidence at hand it would seem that the two-part division of the printed versions deserves authority over the three-part division of the transcripts; even if a transcript did reproduce Keats's manuscript accurately one could always argue that Keats sanctioned the later change—perhaps for clarity. The *Lamia* reading should be used in modern editions, because it is probably the latest one that Keats approved. The point is that textual scholarship alone cannot interpret the meaning of the last two lines, nor even pronounce confidently on how much of them the urn is supposed to say to man. It can, by weighing the facts and probabilities, provide the best text for the critic to interpret, and it can, as here, correct the misuse of evidence.

31

Criticism and Scholarship Once Again

Martin C. Battestin

John Crowe Ransom and *Lycidas:* A Reappraisal

Since its initial publication in *The American Review* for 1933, John Crowe Ransom's surprising essay, "A Poem Nearly Anonymous," has been considered as perhaps the outstanding modern evaluation of Milton's *Lycidas,* and it continues to find favor in places likely to perpetuate its popularity. James Thorpe's highly selective anthology of Milton criticism, for example, includes Mr. Ransom's paper among sixteen essays of "permanent significance." Similarly, Cleanth Brooks and John Edward Hardy, recent editors of the minor poems, find it "among the most intelligent and suggestive, most solidly critical works in the field thus far in the century." And perhaps the most important and influential recommendation of all is that by James Holly Hanford, dean of Milton scholarship in America, who interrupts his discussion of the poem in *A Milton Handbook* to direct readers to Mr. Ransom's "admirable" essay in appreciation.

Incidental objections to Mr. Ransom's extraordinary commentary have, of course, appeared — notably in articles by Miss Winifred Lynskey *(CE,* 5, 1944, 242-243) and Professor Ants Oras *(MP,* 52, 1954, 22); but, despite its disturbing prominence, the essay has too long remained without serious and substantial challenge. In reality, "A Poem Nearly Anonymous" contributes nothing of value to an understanding of *Lycidas.* Rather, Mr. Ransom's undisciplined impressionism — his fragile hypothesizing on the nature of the creative psychology behind the poem's irregularities — tends toward a depreciation of Milton's justly famous monody by questioning the artistic integrity of its author. Although there is neither the space nor the need at this time to undertake a fully detailed refutation of the essay, I believe it can be demonstrated that Mr. Ransom's principal speculations about Milton and *Lycidas* are unsupported either by the autograph text of the poem or by the literary tradition from which it evolves.

From *College English,* XVII (January 1956), 223-228. Reprinted with the permission of the National Council of Teachers of English and Martin C. Battestin.

In an attempt to support the perfectly defensible theory that in poetry a fundamental tension may exist between the prescribed and impersonal art form and the spontaneous expression of personal feeling, Mr. Ransom turns to *Lycidas,* whose prosodic irregularities have long been recognized. Disclaiming the possibility of any significant precedent for a poem admittedly unique in its structural pattern, he asks why Milton, entirely capable of technical conformity, should have permitted himself so much freedom in composition. Three formal irregularities particularly disturb him: (1) the eleven unequal stanzas; (2) the ten unrhymed lines scattered throughout; and (3) the character of the digressions (especially that on Fame), which interrupt the logical structure of the poem.

Proceeding from the form-versus-feeling thesis and apparently without any prior corroborative examination of the Trinity College Manuscript, Mr. Ransom insists that the unusual prosody of *Lycidas* results from a deliberate, *ex post facto* roughening of an originally smooth and perfectly conventional composition. To explain this remarkable allegation, he offers alternative propositions. First, as "kinsman to some tortured modern artists," Milton felt that a too regular formalism would operate unfortunately by masking the sincerity of sentiment which the poem intended to convey. Mr. Ransom argues as follows:

> In the irregular stanzas and the rhymeless lines is registered the ravage of his modernity.... And we imagine him thinking to himself, precisely like some modern poets we know, that he could not longer endure the look of perfect regimentation which sat upon the poor ideas objectified before him upon the page of poetry, as if that carried with it a reflection upon their sincerity. I will go further. It is not merely easy for the technician to write in smooth metres; it is perhaps easier than to write in rough ones, after he has once started; but when he has written smoothly, and contemplates his work, he is capable actually, if he is a modern poet, of going over it laboriously and roughening it. I venture to think that just such a practice, speaking very broadly, obtained in the composition of *Lycidas;* that it was written smooth and re-written rough; which was treason.

Or, should we find unacceptable Mr. Ransom's speculation that Milton attempted to inject spurious vitality into his verse by conscious deformation, a second, even less palatable, proposition is offered. Here, Mr. Ransom suggests, the hypothetical roughening stems from Milton's irrepressible egoism, his wish to posture before his public. Too perfect an art might make the poem appear as cold and lifeless as its subject, Edward King. "So he read the formal poem he had written, and deformed it," consciously counterfeiting the illusion of a restless, imposing individuality behind the work of art, an individuality so powerful as to be unconfinable within the traditional discipline of the pastoral. By a curious kind of spiritualism, Mr. Ransom even discloses to us the processes of Milton's psychology as he composed his monody:

"The formalism," he was thinking, "if unrelieved, will dull the perceptions of the reader, and unprepare him for my surprises, and my tireless fertility. Therefore let him sense an exciting combat between the artist and the man, and let the man interrupt with his prose (or comparative prose) the pretty passages of the artist." In that case [comments Mr. Ransom] the artist was only pretending to give way to the man, calculating with the cunning of a psychologist, perhaps of a dramatist, and violating the law of his art entirely for its public effect; a Jesuit of an artist.

If we admit Mr. Ransom's assertions, we must credit his conclusion, that "*Lycidas,* for the most part a work of great art, is sometimes artful and tricky," guilefully "counterfeited" in its affected tension between form and feeling, "properly an illusion." The result of such irresponsible theorizing can only be to cheapen the reader's estimate of the greatness of *Lycidas* and of its author's integrity.

A close and disciplined consideration of both text and tradition, how-ever, invalidates Mr. Ransom's position. The entire structure of his imaginings with regard to Milton's creative psychology—a species of critical telepathy in itself fruitless—must rest upon the remarkable "roughening" hypothesis, for the unusual prosody of *Lycidas* has long been recognized and more satisfactorily explained as Milton's free han-dling of the Italian *canzone,* an adequate knowledge of which Mr. Ransom frankly disclaims. It would be difficult, for instance, to improve upon F. T. Prince's brilliant and exhaustive analysis of this aspect of the poem in his recent book, *The Italian Element in Milton's Verse* (1954), a study which is the culmination of several prior, but tentative, investigations and which serves to discredit any claim that Milton's technical liberties were unprecedented or that they constitute "the gesture of his rebellion against the formalism of his art."[1] Mr. Prince's findings, further rein-forced and extended by Professor Oras' independent studies, do not require detailed recapitulation here; but it is worthwhile noting that, while sensibly offering no precise early parallel to the form of *Lycidas,* his examination cogently establishes the poem as an outgrowth of Milton's familiarity with the kind of experimentation apparent in Italian verse of the sixteenth century. In particular, the efforts of Tasso and Guarini toward a liberation of lyric poetry from strict *canzone* patterns—their use of irregular, partially rhymed stanzas and their over-all submergence of rhyme in favor of diction as an element of structure—have apparently influenced the technique of Milton's monody. For the rhymeless lines which are made to carry so much of the burden of Mr. Ransom's argument,

---

1. Although Mr. Ransom obviously cannot be criticized for ignorance of Mr. Prince's work, his failure to heed such scholarship as was available to him before postulating a theory of Milton's "surliness" and "insubordination" in formal matters is indicative of his general un-regulated, *a priori* approach. Suggestions toward an establishment of Milton's debt to Italian forms could have been derived from various sources: for example, C. S. Jerram, ed. *The Lycidas and Epitaphium Damonis of Milton* (1874), pp. 43-44; H. F. Hamilton, *SR,* 17 (1909), 235-240; James Holly Hanford, *PMLA,* 25 (1910), 438; and W. P. Ker, *Form and Style in Poetry* (1928), p. 165.

authoritative precedent may furthermore be found as early as Dante.[2]
In view of Mr. Prince's analysis, then, it would seem unnecessary to
propose prior English analogues to the kind of formal effect toward which
Milton strove in *Lycidas;* yet such exist not only in Spenser's *Epithalamion,*
which Mr. Ransom discusses, but more especially in Lodowick Bryskett's
The Mourning Muse of Thestylis and *A Pastorall Aeglogue upon the Death
of Sir Phillip Sidney, Knight,* &c., both of which display unconventional
rhyme schemes clearly derivable from Italian techniques. Such evidence
does not, of course, establish any one previous model for *Lycidas,* but
rather indicates that certain formal experiments had already occurred
which defined the direction toward which Milton moved in composing his
elegy. If, therefore, it can be demonstrated that Mr. Ransom's "roughening" hypothesis is untenable, his injudicious and disparaging commentary
will appear as a considerable misrepresentation of the motives which
determined the pattern of Milton's monody.

Incredibly enough, in postulating a deliberate deformation of *Lycidas*
in revision, Mr. Ransom has apparently neglected to investigate what
ought to have been his primary consideration, the evidence of the Trinity
College Manuscript. Whether or not the manuscript constitutes the
original draft or simply a transcription is, of course, impossible to determine, and there can be no dogmatizing in this regard. Yet despite the
relative cleanness of the copy and the strong skepticism of Professor John
S. Diekhoff (in *PMLA,* 52, 1937, 705-727; 54, 1939, 177-178), to whom any
textual study of *Lycidas* must be indebted, I am inclined to agree with
earlier students in judging the manuscript a first draft. Milton's well
known habit of composition in sweeps of thirty and forty lines, his holding entire paragraphs in mind until they assumed the desired shape and
then committing them to paper for final revision, would readily account
for the comparatively clean condition of the manuscript. Furthermore,
the existence of the "false start" on the page preceding the full autograph
version of the poem, with the refashioned Orpheus and flower passages
occurring just below, suggests that an earlier draft used for scratch purposes did not exist. However that may be, we have here the only known
revised manuscript of the poem, and it is safe to agree with Professor
H. J. C. Grierson, who in his preface to *The Poems* (1925) asserts that
"in the case of 'Lycidas' we can almost see Milton at work."

A careful examination of the manuscript will definitely discredit Mr.
Ransom's "roughening" hypothesis. Since Milton's revisions of *Lycidas*
have been discussed at some length by Professor Diekhoff (*PMLA,* 54,
1939, 177-183; 55, 1940, 748-772), my analysis will be brief and directed
only toward the principal objective of this paper, the reappraisal of Mr.
Ransom. Initially, although her early study of the corrections has been
much elaborated by Professor Diekhoff, it would be difficult to better Miss
Laura E. Lockwood's generalization that Milton's intention in revising

---

2. Although Dante's *canzones* are customarily regular, exceptions do occur, of which *canzone*
XVI (*"Lo doloroso amor che mi conduce"*) is most notable; this is a poem of fifty lines, of which
nine are unrhymed. In *canzones* XII, XIII, XVI, and XXI as well, the line introducing the
commiato is left rhymeless.

his poems was to render the thought clear, logical, and vivid (*MLN,* 25, 1910, 203). This practice, together with the visible effort to improve upon the ring and richness of particular lines and, in two instances, to effect a submerged Italianate rhyme pattern, may be seen to operate in the case of *Lycidas*. If the aim of the great majority of the revisions were to be briefly stated, it would be to polish and perfect, rather than to roughen, the poem.

In all fairness, however, attention should be called at the start to two exceptional verses which might possibly be construed in support of Mr. Ransom's thesis. These are the extrametrical lines—"who would not sing for Lycidas he well knew" and "Oh Fountaine Arethuse and thou honour'd flood"—in which Milton seems deliberately to have made each verse hendecasyllabic. In the former instance unevenness results from the insertion of *not* into the "false start" version and its retention in the fresh draft. In the second example, Milton substituted *honour'd* for the more metrically acceptable *smooth* and *fam'd*, his original choices; however, here there is the possibility—admittedly awkward—of eliding the words *thou honour'd*. These changes gain greater precision of meaning for the lines, of course, but it is hard to believe that Milton could not have smoothed them out had he wished. No one, however, would care to question Milton's art and integrity solely on the basis of these two lines. In fact, ironically, Mr. Ransom has not even noticed them, for he comments as follows on Milton's "loving exactitude" of line structure: "He counts his syllables, he takes no liberties there."

Significantly, of the ten rhymeless lines upon which Mr. Ransom bases so much of his case, *not one* results from revision. Rather, they are there from the start and reasonably explainable as part of Milton's Italianate development of the verse paragraph toward the disciplined freedom of blank verse. Milton, in fact, principally reworked his poem at only three stages in composition, none of which can fairly be interpreted as "roughening" the original. For example, the first and false rendering of the introduction read as follows:

> yet once more O ye laurells and once more
> ye myrtl's browne wth Ivie never sere
> I come to pluck yor berries harsh and crude
> before the mellowing yeare
> and crop yor young. . . .

Here Milton happily deleted the extremely awkward phrasing of lines 4 and 5, and substituted the much improved form by which we now know them. The new reading—"and wth forc't fingers rude/shatter yor leaves before ye mellowing yeare"—has perfected the meter in line 4 by achieving six, instead of seven, syllables, in accord with the *canzone* adaptation here employed. In addition, although the rhyme pattern has been altered, the rhymes themselves have not been tampered with.

A more extensive revision occurs in the perfecting of the well known Orpheus passage. This had originally read as follows:

> what could the golden hayrd Calliope
> for her inchaunting son
> when shee beheld (the gods farre sighted bee)
> his goarie scalpe rowle downe the Thracian lee

After an equally unsatisfactory intermediate attempt to render the passage, Milton chose this much more fortunate version:

> what could the muse her selfe that Orpheus bore
> the muse her selfe for her inchanting son
> whome universal nature did lament
> when by the rout that made the hideous roare
> his goarie visage downe the streame was sent
> downe the swift Hebrus to yᵉ Lesbian shoare.

The improvement here is obvious and consists first of all in the elimination of the halting, parenthetical interruption which is inessential to the sense of the passage and confuses the normal syntactical flow. Secondly, by repeating the phrase "the muse her selfe," Milton places a more logical stress upon the central idea of the lines, that is, the tragic helplessness even of Calliope, whose son's death is intended to bear a functional analogy to the drowning of Edward King. Also, the trimeter line, "for her inchaunting son," has been filled out to regularize the metrical pattern. Furthermore, although a more appropriate sonority has been achieved with the substitution of the *-ore* rhyme for the harsh tonal effect of a terminal *-ee*, and though a new rhyme has been added in the expanded rendering, there has been no such "roughening" of line endings as Mr. Ransom suggests. We do notice, however, that the resultant enlarged pattern involves a somewhat wider separation of like rhymes; thus, if the line immediately preceding the passage in question be included, a scheme of *abacbcb* replaces the earlier *ababb*. This slight irregularity, comparable in effect to the revised flower passage, tends to reduce the rhyming to a subordinate position — a practice generally in evidence throughout the poem.

The flower passage itself, apparently an afterthought, is the last of the major revisions. Although a full account of the emendations here would require too much space, a glance at the manuscript will reveal in the corrected verses a noticeable improvement in compression and felicity of phrasing. More pertinent to our discussion is the alteration of the rhyme scheme in the tightened version so as to submerge the lyric effect of the original three consecutive couplets. Thus, if we omit the initial line, which rhymes outside the passage, the new arrangement consists of a pair of dissimilar quatrains rhyming *abba cdcd,* where the last two lines of the final quatrain have been intentionally transposed to alter the more regular prior scheme of *cddc.* Again, this modification simply contributes in a minor way to the general liberation of the poem from any unnatural dependence on rhyme. The prosody of *Lycidas* is most readily understandable in the light of F. T. Prince's examination of previous Italian experiments. The irregularities of the poem result from a similar controlled improvisation of rhyme and stanzaic patterns, tending — appropriately enough for one whose greatest successes were to be made with the blank verse paragraph — toward a reconciliation of form and freedom. The remaining manuscript corrections are minor, involving, for instance, changes in alliterative patterns or toward the improved suggestiveness or clarity of certain lines; they can in no significant way be interpreted as contributing to Mr. Ransom's position.

Finally, Mr. Ransom's post-Coleridgean principles are further outraged by what he judges to be several breaks in the poem's logic of composition, lapses so flagrant, it seems, as to denote, "in another work, an amateurism below the level of publication." Phoebus's reply, in particular, is an "incredible interpolation" turning a poem which began as a dramatic monologue into a clumsy *mélange* of dialogue and narrative, and violating the modern critical shibboleth of organic unity. For a classicist such as Milton, however, authority for shifts in tense and form could be found in the eclogues of Virgil, one of which (the sixth) contains lines clearly echoed in the Phoebus passage. Virgil, for example, prefaces Phoebus's admonition to him against untimely ambition with the words, *"Cynthius aurem / vellit et admonuit,"* the apparent inspiration for Milton's, "But not the praise / Phoebus repli'd, and touch't my trembling eares." Although Virgil's quotation of Phoebus occurs as part of the narrative introduction to his poem and does not, therefore, constitute a marked interruption such as we find in Milton, his practice throughout is to shift his tenses at will from the narrative past to the historical present, and vice versa, a familiar Latin grammatical usage with which Milton would be well acquainted. Most noticeable of the shifts from present to past occurs at line 47, where Virgil begins his digressive apostrophe to Pasiphaë. An even more striking analogy is the form of the interpolated cry of the Fates in *Eclogue IV* — *"'Talia saecla' suis dixerunt 'currite' fusis / concordes stabili fatorum numine Parcae"* — which interrupts the poet's direct address to the infant Pollio. Milton could not know twentieth-century theories on structural logic, but he did understand the practice of the Latin poets. Furthermore, if we accept the conclusions of H. V. S. Ogden's well-documented study, "The Principles of Variety and Contrast in Seventeenth Century Aesthetics, and Milton's Poetry" (*JHI*, 10, 1949, 159-182), Mr. Ransom's consternation over such an interruption of logical continuity will be seen to proceed from the misapplication of modern criteria to a work fashioned under a different aesthetic. Viewing *Lycidas* in relation to the seventeenth-century principles of variety and contrast, Mr. Ogden believes the poem's startling transitions and abrupt turns in new directions to be wholly in accord with contemporary critical theory.

Contributory to these final efforts of Mr. Ransom to establish Milton as a rebellious innovator in form is a minor argument of rather strict inaccuracy. Remarking that Milton's concluding stanza is not rendered typographically distinct from the body of the poem, he says that, though a pastoral elegy might traditionally have a prologue and epilogue, these should be "so denominated in the text, and printed in italics, or in a body separate from the elegy proper." The inference to be drawn, of course, is that Milton carried his break with precedent even to matters of format, again anticipating his "kinsmen," the modern *vers librists,* in the exploitation of typography for purposes of showmanship. Both the generalization and its implications, however, may be adequately discredited by a glance at the form of any of several early pastorals: for example, the fourth eclogue of William Browne's *The Shepherd's Pipe,* the first in Francis Davison's *Poetical Rhapsody,* Spenser's *January* and *December,* or William Drummond's *A Pastorall Elegie on the Death of S. A[ntonye] A [lexander].*

Mr. Ransom's essay exemplifies an approach to literature too nearly autonomous, too little governed by sound historical inference and too much dependent on intuition. The New Criticism has made frequent contributions to the better understanding and appreciation of poetry, of modern poetry in particular, but it can (and here, I am afraid, Mr. Ransom does) approach very near to an anarchy of impressionism. Mr. Ransom customarily strives for objectivity in his judgments, but in this instance his method of propounding theory from assumption without factual substantiation has gone too long uncorrected. Perhaps unintentionally, "A Poem Nearly Anonymous" is in effect simply one more document, especially damaging because of its ill-found popularity, in the modern denigration of Milton. Mr. Ransom's view of *Lycidas* as the meretricious creation of a crafty artist contributes nothing to an understanding of poem or poet. Happily, it is without foundation.